Becoming Visible

—Becoming Visible—
Women in European History

SECOND EDITION

edited by

Renate Bridenthal
Brooklyn College

Claudia Koonz
College of the Holy Cross

Susan Stuard
Haverford College

Houghton Mifflin Company   Boston
Dallas   Geneva, Illinois
Lawrenceville, New Jersey   Palo Alto

To the memory of Joan Kelly

Cover painting by Sofonisba Anguissola (1535/40–1625), "Three of the Artist's Sisters Playing Chess," 1555. National Museum, Poznan, Poland. A member of a noble family of Cremona, Italy, the artist was educated and trained as a painter; she was invited to the court of Philip II of Spain, and remained there about twenty years.

Printed in the U.S.A.

Library of Congress Catalog Card Number 86-81542

ISBN: 0-395-41950-6

IJ-MP-998765

Contents

Preface

In the first edition of *Becoming Visible: Women in European History*, we directed our questions about women in the historical context toward the origins of inequality, the sources of women's awareness of injustice, and the prospects for a better future. Ten years later, as we survey this new and completely revised edition, we find many of the themes inspired by these questions interwoven among the essays. The contents of these essays reflect the intensive scholarly output about women during the past decade—books that have filled the shelves of libraries and bookstores, new journals that have published specialized studies on women, and international conferences that have facilitated discussion among feminist scholars.

In this edition, as in the first, the periods covered conform to standard surveys of European history: the dawn of civilization; the Greco-Roman world; medieval Europe; the Early Modern Period; and nineteenth- and twentieth-century industrial society. Such surveys reveal, of course, that major cataclysms like wars and plagues profoundly disrupt life for all members of society, male and female, and that long-term developments like industrialization, political change, and improved standards of living transform everyone's lives. But our special focus shows that women have experienced these massive changes in ways distinct from the experiences of men. Besides the focus on women as historical actors, an important thematic development unifies the twenty essays in this collection: an analysis of the social construction of gender over time and across cultures.

The essays in this volume illuminate previously unknown areas of the past and simultaneously place women in a broader social context. The contributors, who have conducted archival research in specialized areas, have expanded their horizons for this text and written for nonspecialists about long-term trends in many nations. Aware of the ambiguity of the early historical record and the complexity of women's participation in shaping earlier societies, the authors examine how individual women manipulated prevailing cultural norms to maximize what power they had, and how they came to challenge oppressive norms. Because women operated within such diverse public frameworks, they fashioned not one but many feminisms. The authors also address the questions raised by women who used their ingenuity to enhance their own situation but at the same time to deepen the oppression of other women.

In this volume, we have again collected essays that present the results of the latest research on five thousand years of women's history. Of the twenty chapters, fourteen are new and five have been revised. The chapter by the late Joan Kelly-Gadol remains as it appeared in the first edition except for the updated bibliographical material at the end. In the process of writing and revising, the authors have exchanged drafts in order to highlight the major themes that run through all of women's history. The editors thank them for the collaborative spirit that produced this set of integrated essays. Although their essays interlock, the contributors have brought their own individual approaches, viewpoints, methods, and styles to this volume, so the reader can apprehend the diversity in the rapidly expanding and exciting field of women's history.

We want to thank the editorial staff at Houghton Mifflin Company for their dedication and helpfulness. Thanks, too, to Charlotte Sheedy who offered her advice in the early stages of this edition. We extend our special gratitude to the following individuals who offered valuable suggestions on several essays: Clara Hempsted, Lynne Beretoni, Deborah Fehervary, Katherine A. Healy, Mary Grace McClain, Lisa Norling, Pamela Walker, Tracey Weis, Susan Whitney, Torun Willits, and Julie Wilson. We are grateful for the support of Martin Fleisher, Joan Kelly's husband, and for the expert help from Margaret King in updating Joan Kelly's bibliography (Chapter 7). We also thank Danila Spielman for her careful proofreading of the first ten chapters.

We are especially grateful to the reviewers of this edition, whose comments helped polish the final draft.

Susan D. Amussen
Connecticut College

Shirley J. Black
Texas A&M University

Laura Frader
Northeastern University

Janelle Greenberg
University of Pittsburgh

Christine Holden
University of Southern Maine

Ronald K. Huch
University of Minnesota, Duluth

Patricia S. Kruppa
University of Texas, Austin

Patricia A. O'Brien
University of California, Irvine

Leila J. Rupp
Ohio State University

Deborah Symonds
Bucknell University

Sara W. Tucker
Washburn University of Topeka

RENATE BRIDENTHAL
CLAUDIA KOONZ
SUSAN STUARD

Introduction

When we embarked on this second edition, several people wondered whether *Becoming Visible* was still an appropriate title. After all, they asked, hasn't women's history become a field of its own and made dramatic contributions to the study of all areas of history? A decade of research has produced hundreds of books, monographs, articles, and dissertations and women's history has become a subdiscipline within the field. Does that not mean women have "become visible?" After briefly considering *No Longer Invisible*, we decided to keep the original title, first because it has won recognition in the field and secondly because in this edition the contributors make a new set of questions visible.

Writing history is itself a process. When we began the first edition in the early 1970s, we hoped to strip away myths about womanhood and restore real women to history. Then, as now, we concluded that a vision of human nature that alienates men from women is neither natural nor neutral, but exploitative and unjust. Ten years ago we discarded prejudices about women in order to explore the reality behind those prejudices. Now, a decade later, the contributors to this edition turn back to those myths in order to analyze their relationship to the social context that produced them. By analyzing man-made systems we question inherited moral and political assumptions. We explore the effect of such century-old assumptions as the belief that human potential is bound by "masculine" and "feminine" attributes. One of the original contributors, Joan Kelly, has noted elsewhere, "In thought and practice, neat distinctions we once made between class and sex, family and society, reproduction and production, even between women and men seem not to fit the social reality with which we are coping."[1] The essays in this volume try not only to make women visible as historical actors, but to examine the socially constructed and historically changing gender systems that divide masculine from feminine roles. As a result of a decade of research and theory, this edition reflects a proliferation of new discoveries and more theoretical complexity.

Two main trends have shaped women's history. One is an accelerating rate of economic and bureaucratic differentiation, that is, a breakdown of tasks and responsibilities into more and simpler ones coordinated by central-ized authority. As societies become more complex, power flows to the top and generally into the hands of a few men; most women remain at the bottom. The second historical trend is the attempt to justify women's loss of power and authority by simplifying gender difference into a system of appositions labeled male and female. "Feminine" qualities are counterposed to "masculine": women are labeled passive, men active; women are defined as emotional, men described as intellectual; women are assumed to be "naturally" nurturant, men "naturally" ambitious.

In societies where the division of labor became more refined, gender categories (and eventually notions about race and ethnicity) served to assign the less desirable and remunerative tasks to people stigmatized as "inferior." By contrast, earlier, less differentiated societies, such as those at the dawn of civilization or in the early medieval period (fifth to tenth centuries, A.D.), demanded flexibility in task assignment and valued the ability of people to replace one another easily in case of need. In those eras, survival depended on recognizing women's and men's likeness to each other.

Much of the analysis of economic differentiation and gender polarization in this edition is based on this long-term perspective. Five thousand years of women's documented history is chronicled in these pages. The essays in this volume fit into generally accepted historical periods: the emergence of civilization; the rise and decline of empires; the emergence of a new Christian religion; the agricultural, commercial, industrial, and scientific revolutions in Europe; the wave of social and political revolutions; the world wars. Has the system of gender polarization separated women's experience from men's in these diverse historical eras? How do the contours of women's history correspond to the course men's history has taken? This volume addresses these and related questions.

Such a sweep of time frequently tempts historians and their audiences to read the course of history as progress, but women's historical experience will not fit neatly into that mold. To the extent that women share the same history as men, progress may benefit both equally. For example, women may gain as men do from improved agricultural cultivation, paved roads, and the discovery of penicillin. However, when the system of gender separates women's experience from men's, benefits do not necessarily accrue to women. For example, as centralized monarchies replaced feudal courts, noblewomen lost access to direct political power. Vastly improved opportunities for men to control their environment did not automatically benefit women. The general level of nutrition among European working people, for example, declined from the thirteenth century onward, that is, during the centuries of dynamic change that we associate with capitalism and the Industrial Revolution. The loss of essential nutrients however, was greater in the diet of working women than in the diet of working men.[2] On the other hand, in eras traditionally considered periods of decline, it appears that the status of women did not decline relative to men's. In so-called progressive eras, benefits were distributed unequally by class and gender. Finding women's experience so out of phase with that of men means that the old divisions of history into periods must be reinterpreted.

In the five thousand years, from prehistory to the 1980s, chronicled in this volume, we have ample opportunity to observe gender relations in highly developed premodern societies as well as in industrial settings. Often it seems that in simpler times societies depended upon looser definitions of masculine and feminine, which were themselves not always consistent or authoritative. The few surviving texts from those eras provide rare glimpses of dramatically different worlds. Fuller understanding of the differences depends on a sophisticated reading of scarce sources. As political scientists and anthropologists engage in heated debates about the emergence of tyrannical states, feminist scholars also speculate about the sources of patriarchy.

There is a noticeable tendency among some contributors to this book to look back nostalgically—not exactly to a golden age, but to earlier periods during which the asymmetry in the gender system seemed less pronounced. Authors of the later essays, however, seem less taken by backward glances and present a more optimistic, future-oriented view. This tendency results in part from the much shorter chronological span of the later articles. More importantly, women's lives during the last century generally showed areas of improvement when compared to earlier generations. So, even though the women of more recent generations may have experienced losses relative to the men of their age, their lives reflected the benefits of improved material conditions. This amelioration came at a price. With the industrialization of the last two centuries, much of the social cost of progress has been exported to the Third World.

Eleanor Leacock indicates that women and men shared roughly equal opportunities before the emergence of civilized institutions. By analogy to more recent stateless societies, she suggests that in prehistoric times women and men readily exchanged tasks and duties and participated in a wide range of productive and administrative roles in religious, political, and economic life. Leacock critically examines historical evidence recorded by male visitors to a stateless society in the context of her own anthropological research and feminist insights into the ways in which prehistoric communities developed methods to regulate aggressive instincts without creating a strong patriarchy. Barbara Lesko demonstrates that a rough parity between the sexes lasted long into the first millennia of civilized life in the Nile and Tigris-Euphrates river valleys. By the end of the Bronze Age, that parity had disappeared. Lesko explains how competition for scarce resources, warfare, and the increasing importance of private property in trade made conditions worse for women. She notes as well that Egypt and Sumer, acting against new trends, preserved women's status for centuries on end.

Marilyn Arthur charts women's status over the course of the Classical era in Greece and Rome. A rigid system of gender (in which men saw women as "naturally" opposite) characterized *polis* life in Greece and represented part of its legacy to Rome and to subsequent European intellectual and cultural life. So totally did the tradition of an earlier parity disappear that the Greek historian Herodotus called Egyptian customs "contrary to nature." Arthur reminds us, however, that this brief era of extreme prejudice in Greece was followed by the longer Hellenistic period (323–19 B.C.) in which women assumed a greatly expanded role in cultural and social life.

Christianity and other late antique mystery cults offered women a new empowering sense of self and either directly or obliquely denied the inherited Classical gender system, the legacy from fifth-century Greece. "In Christ there is no male or female," only the radical equality of all souls before God—or so early Christian women believed when they espoused the new faith. Previously closed out of public life by the polarities popular with the ancient Greeks, women, according to Jo Ann McNamara, opted for a new faith that ignored gender oppositions. Thus, the late Classical world (first through the fifth centuries, A.D.), far from having been one long era of unrelieved decline as historians often depict it, provided important opportunities for women. Improved rights in Roman law and women's central role in the mystery cults inspires us to rethink our basic assumptions about the age. From this perspective, the late antique world represents a new beginning rather than a decline into decadence.

Women made some of their most consequential and lasting contributions to European culture in the early medieval centuries. Christianity and a decentralized economic and political system provided a less gender-dominated world than either the Classical age that preceded it or the modern age that followed. Suzanne Wemple depicts women and men cooperating in the challenging work of creating a new society. To them, their universal, shared human capacities as children of God seemed more consequential than differences between male and female. However, these fluid assumptions about gender gave way in the High Middle Ages (between the twelfth and thirteenth centuries) to a rigid system of gender that revived Classical Greek notions of polarity. Susan Stuard points out that this revival occurred at the very time when economic systems became increasingly complex and centralized bureaucracies more powerful.

The revived system of gender featured in the Scholastic thought of the thirteenth century, with its polarities of female to male, became part of the mental equipment of Europeans and has remained so until relatively recent times. When Joan Kelly asks if women had a Renaissance and answers that they did, but not, on balance, as men did, she calls into question the rigid system of gender that characterized humanist culture. Although a powerful new idea of man emerged in the Renaissance, no comparable rigorous and logical rethinking produced new concepts about the "Renaissance Woman." Assumptions about women remained bound by prejudices and unexamined notions based on inherited classical texts. As William Monter shows, Classical notions about women were not re-examined in the Reformation era by either the Protestant or Catholic parties. On the contrary, the polarized notions of human nature lay behind the wave of witch-hunts that swept across Reformation Europe. Men were defined as perfectible and created in the image of God, women as weak and prone to the Devil's temptations. With these polar definitions, witch-hunters overwhelmingly identified women as the possessed in the sixteenth and seventeenth centuries. The polarities ruled thought and action in almost all aspects of life. During festivals, however, especially in Catholic regions, when ribald humor turned the world upside down in carnival (or mardi gras), men and women could cross-dress. At least temporarily, revelers could express forbidden feelings and play with the roles that constrained them in the real world.

Simplifying the system of gender had unquestionable advantages for those men whose control of economic resources placed them in positions of power. Women remained highly productive members of families and communities throughout the early modern era but a rigid gender system denied them positions of authority and, as often as not, the fruits of their labor. Merry Wiesner shows how the new stratification affected women's work in the early modern economy and undervalued much of the work done by women. The most enduring polarity in the West has been the belief in woman's incapacity and imperfectibility in contrast to man's capacity and perfectibility. Wages, which came more and more to define the value of work, fell more "naturally" to those found capable and perfectible. These same assumptions eliminated women from positions of authority.

Polar notions of gender also influenced thinking and attitudes toward sexuality. Both ancient and early medieval writers allotted to women an active role in sexual reproduction. But once the Greek polarity of man's capacity and women's incapacity became fashionable in the High Middle Ages, authors began depicting woman as a mere vessel for sexual reproduction. According to this system, an infertile woman was responsible for her failure to produce offspring; but a mother could take no credit for success in childbearing. In the same way, in terms of sexuality, late Classical authorities had recognized women's orgasmic response in sexual intercourse and associated it with the clitoris. This was confirmed by other authorities until the vogue of polarities came to dominate Western thought in the High Middle Ages. Then writers on sexuality defined man as active, therefore orgasmic, and woman as passive, capable of arousing men's desire but not of experiencing pleasure themselves. Furthermore, men were thought to be diminished by the sex act, to suffer a "little death." Even the belief in insatiable sexual needs of sixteenth-century witches fit this system since the witch's insatiability was believed to arise not from her desire for pleasure but from a diabolic urge to be filled to compensate for her deprived and passive nature. Over the centuries, European thinkers went so far as to downplay women's role in child-bearing, defining them as merely the carriers of the fetuses created by men.

By the time of the Enlightenment, as Elizabeth Fox-Genovese points out, the middle-class woman had become defined as an unattainable object of men's erotic desires. Leisured young women participated in what was almost a cult of virginity, enhancing their suitors' passions by inaccessibility. After marriage—a woman's only respectable option—women were to become maternal, without having ever experienced sexual pleasure. Victorian writers later transformed these simplistic notions into complex codes of behavior for the "proper lady," and biologists developed sophisticated theories about women's innate intellectual inferiority. By the nineteenth century, the message was clear. The bourgeois "lady" was too pure for sexual pleasure and too inferior for emancipation. Meanwhile, poverty drove thousands of poor women into brothels that made a mockery of bourgeois men's pious attempts to keep womanhood on the proverbial pedestal. Male lust, become prurient through the frustration built into Victorian ideology, found an outlet among prostitutes, who were drawn from the ranks of violated domestics and other destitute women.

The most important economic event of the late eighteenth and early nineteenth centuries was the Industrial Revolution, an accelerated change in the production of commodities which was centralized in factories and fueled by investment in new sources of energy and new forms of technology. In the process of capital accumulation, increasing numbers of people became dependent wage laborers, while a few moved upward into highly diversified middle strata in the services, professions, and clerical work. In this new and more highly differentiated social structure, Laura Frader shows, most women fell toward the bottom as new divisions of labor continued to widen the gender gap. Although most women continued to work in the countryside, increasing numbers of young girls came into towns and cities to work in the new factories.

Ultimately, the overwhelming majority of women employed in industry and services married, and often these working-class women had to continue working for a wage, usually in their own homes for even lower rates. The development of industrial capitalism brought an expansion of subcontracted work done at home, for example making artificial flowers, sewing lingerie, rolling cigars, and producing other luxury items for the increasingly wealthy bourgeoisie. By the end of the nineteenth century, the pattern of men working outside the home and women remaining in the home, although not universal, was well established as a model for working class as well as middle class people. Since economic dependency contributes to powerlessness in personal relations as well, the myth of women's weakness came to be grounded in hard economic fact. Nevertheless, family survival often depended upon women's ability to "pinch hit" or "make ends meet" in the unstable economic environment of industrializing Europe.

By the twentieth century, as Renate Bridenthal shows, industrialization had assumed the features we recognize today. Especially during World War I, more young women entered industry, among them many former domestic servants. After that war, the level of women's employment in industry stabilized, although it shot up sharply in the service sector when World War II broke out. The gradual acceptance of birth control freed most women from the exhausting cycle of continuous pregnancy, although not from major responsibility for homemaking, which now became more demanding because of new standards of hygiene and psychology.

However, it would be misleading to conclude that all women remained meekly in their homes. As essays on the premodern period show, women as artisans' or merchants' wives and daughters, as nuns, and as noblewomen had a long tradition of public activity. Several of the essays on the nineteenth and twentieth centuries explore the ways in which women forged new public identities and struggled for equal rights in industrialized societies. Among the diversity of organizations and personalities, three sources of women's newfound sense of entitlement emerge. One source was women's traditional identification with their family responsibilities. A second source was the result of women claiming the "natural" rights extolled by Enlightenment thinkers. The third source was the socialists' more comprehensive analysis that showed both oppression and the hope of emancipation to be vitally connected to economic change.

Elizabeth Fox-Genovese points out that noblewomen of the eighteenth century still played a strong public role, often advancing their families' and husbands' interests in cultural or economic activities and occasionally acting as intellectual facilitators in salons and other gatherings where progressive ideas were formed. After the onset of the Industrial Revolution women of all classes were active in public life as a part of their family responsibilities. During the French Revolution, as Darlene Levy and Harriet Applewhite show, women demonstrated, petitioned, and participated in political discussions. In the course of acting on their ancient rights as family provisioners, women protested against food shortages in peremptory demonstrations that escalated to demands for popular sovereignty and in some cases led to successful revolutions. Temma Kaplan argues that "female consciousness" has often taken women out of their homes and into the public arena during times of political instability or economic disaster. When food is scarce, prices high, and politics chaotic, women depart from the normally accepted domestic models and violently demand their due.

At times, too, women have exercised a decisive impact on the course of modern revolutions. Richard Stites suggests that under the extreme repression of Tsarist Russia women played a vital role in terrorist, revolutionary organizations. Thus, in dire circumstances, received notions about masculine and feminine responsibilities may be reinterpreted by women as justification for entering into the "masculine" public arena. However, only long-term, sustained, concerted organization produced legal and economic gains for women.

Among the more leisured middle classes, the women Karen Offen calls "relational feminists" demanded expansion of their narrow "feminine" roles.

Accepting the family or the private world as the appropriate sphere for women, they enlarged traditional definitions of femininity to include participation in corresponding areas of public life. For example, they argued that, as mothers, women could demand better formal education so they could raise their children to become good citizens; as nationalists or pacifists, women could argue that their familial responsibilities entitled them to speak out on war and peace, and perhaps even to vote. In liberal England, many women's energies went into imperial conquest. Margaret Strobel describes how a class of privileged women, acting in the name of Victorian womanhood, upheld the interests of white rule and their identity as mothers and wives. Some forged new careers for themselves in missionary work, anthropology, and social reform. Women operating in authoritarian or bureaucratized institutions (like the Catholic church or the British Empire) faced formidable opposition. Demanding a special status within the masculine order, they hoped to share the glory of the larger enterprise—and enhance their own influence. Rather than demanding equal rights as citizens, these women asked to share equal burdens as subjects.

In the twentieth century, women in Mussolini's Italy and Hitler's Germany continued that strategy. Claudia Koonz points to the paradox that while no modern governments have so explicitly relegated women to inferiority, none have as energetically recruited women into national organizations. Fascist societies, structured on rigid racial and gender divisions, offered ambitious and nationalistic women the chance to organize their separate sphere for "racially acceptable" women. These powerful dictatorships harnessed women's energies rather than overtly repressing them with either a "back to the home" agenda or a "feminine mystique."

The women who used their claims to uniquely feminine traits as a wedge into public life discovered limits on their aspirations because the priorities of male-dominated institutions invariably took precedence over women's needs. However, contemporary feminist movements have a wider heritage. Two other powerful ideologies, liberalism and socialism, inspired women to act on their own behalf in the nineteenth and twentieth centuries. These women framed their claim to rights not only "in relation" to men and children, but in universal terms.

Over the centuries a few educated women and men, in the tradition of Christine de Pisan, had defended women against misogynist attacks. Philosophically, in praising women's inherent worth, they laid the basis for modern feminism. Only after industrialization restructured society, however, could masses of women turn to the state with demands for equality. During the nineteenth and twentieth centuries, an historically unique movement brought hundreds of thousands of women together in all European nations in the quest for equal rights.

Especially in industrializing Protestant nations, the heritage of the

Enlightenment inspired women's claim to equality. Although the reformers reinforced marriage and the patriarchal family by removing convent life as an option, their theology offered an emancipatory potential for women. The elimination of the clergy as a special caste, together with the mandate that every Protestant should read and interpret his or her own Bible, laid down the potential for seeing all human beings as equal in God's eyes. However, as William Monter points out, because in practice literacy among Protestants did not increase rapidly, this potential was only realized in the nineteenth and twentieth centuries.

Enlightenment theories of individualism, although not applied to women at the time, further advanced the notion that human potential should be fulfilled. Applewhite and Levy describe the few educated women who moved beyond the sporadic protests of wives and market women to lay claim to their natural rights as woman and citizen. In the short term, they met resounding defeat. But even as the Napoleonic Code made French women's situation in some ways worse than before 1789, Mary Wollstonecraft's *Vindication of the Rights of Women* affirmed the double heritage of women in the French Revolution with its insistence on women's special status as mothers and its demands for women's equal rights as citizens.

Sharing with the Liberals the conviction that the elimination of unjust laws would usher in an era of liberty, English feminists began to win major reforms in divorce and property law and, in many localities, achieved the right to hold local office by the middle of the nineteenth century. In response to laws regulating prostitution in seaport cities and requiring state inspection of prostitutes, Josephine Butler launched a successful crusade to repeal the hated legislation. Feminists in Germany and Russia launched similar antivice campaigns, but met with less success.

Bourgeois women mobilized to share in the power and privileges held by the men of their class. Such women, enjoying more leisure for political activism than working-class women, organized around a growing sense of gender-based injustice, an early form of feminism. Ironically, suffragists' campaigns made little headway in Europe until after World War I, when many nations granted women the vote more as a reward for patriotic service than as recognition of women's fundamental human equality.

"Success" nearly killed middle-class feminism. However, as Bridenthal notes, the gender gap in income, political power, and family responsibility remained wide. World War II intensified pressure on women for the double duty of producing armaments and reproducing the population, reduced by 50,000,000 people during the war. After the war the myth of women's place in the home was restored, though it corresponded even less to reality than it had before.

The achievement of political equality marked the highwater mark of liberal feminism. But throughout the nineteenth century, working-class women struggled for a very different concept of emancipation. Socialist feminists located the source of their exploitation in the economic system, capitalism, instead of in the legal system. From their broader vision, they developed strategies distinct from those of liberal feminists. Urbanization, new economic ties to employers and husbands, demographic changes, and increasing literacy made new forms of collective action both possible and necessary. By the twentieth century, labor union efforts had reduced the wage gap between women and men and won maternity provisions and protective laws. However, the worldwide Depression of the 1930s crippled all union efforts. Competition for scarce jobs revived male hostility to women workers and many governments curtailed women's access to jobs and welfare benefits. World War II temporarily engaged more women in unionized manufacturing jobs, but after the war the steady relocation of female workers into traditionally nonunionized white-collar jobs set back labor organization among women until very recently.

Moving beyond immediate work-related reforms, socialists aimed to eliminate capitalism. Socialist leaders, as Charles Sowerwine demonstrates, varied widely in their reactions to women's claim to equality, but women themselves forged their own organizations under the larger rubric of International Socialism. Women succeeded within the predominately male socialist parties when they formed semi-autonomous associations, published their own periodicals, and held separate congresses, even as they joined with their male comrades in the struggle against capitalism. Marxists provided powerful new analyses of women's oppression. They argued that it was reinforced by capitalism, which made women dependent on and therefore subservient to male wage earners. This allowed employers to pay women a "supplementary," that is, much lower, wage when they did enter the labor force. The logical political corollary was that women should join men in fighting capitalism. Nevertheless, because male-dominated socialist parties did not always welcome women's full participation, it took militant women to compel their parties' attention. Although international feminist socialist solidarity never recovered from the divisive impact of World War I, in every European nation socialist parties have led in demanding not only suffrage and equal legal status, but maternity benefits, access to abortion and birth control, family subsidies, divorce reform, and improved pay for women workers.

A totally different course was followed in the Soviet Union after the Russian Revolution of 1917. Richard Stites shows how here, for the first time in history, across-the-board legislation proclaimed equality between the sexes in voting, education, marriage, property rights, and birth control. This program proved to be too radical for most people, and too costly for a government facing civil war and staggering economic crises. Finally, Stalin's emphasis on rapid and forced industrialization in the 1930s, while consciously advancing some women professionally, nevertheless reimposed a traditional family structure. With the approach of World War II, natalist policies encouraged women to fulfill their patriotic duty by bearing more children and taking up strategically vital jobs in defense industries.

Jane Jenson's essay underscores the complexity of the woman question in the contemporary welfare state. Comparing the role of their respective governments in supporting families and liberating women, Jenson explains how French and British feminists have evolved two different agendas for emancipation. French feminists tend to regard the state as a potential ally while British feminists view it as the inevitable source of patriarchal power. Looking back over the centuries, we see that both viewpoints had their roots in concrete situations and in the social construction of gender.

A continual tension arises from women's double identity. On the one hand, women in most ages have had less access to public power and economic status than men; on the other hand, women have evolved distinctive values within male-dominated societies that in crucial ways diminished their status. How, generations of women have asked, can one integrate claims to full equality with a sense of women's special identity? In the history of women's consciousness we see a steadily expanding vision. The diversity of strategies for women's rights and the rich array of futuristic visions attest to the vitality of feminism.

As historians, we depict dramatically shifting realities and visions across the centuries. The reality of women's lives will not fit into static models, nor will feminist historians easily agree on the origins and meaning of all these transformations. In editing this volume, we have not endeavored to impose a single set of values, or even a uniform definition of feminism. Rather, we have encouraged variations in contributors' methods, assumptions, and interpretations in order to illustrate the diversity of our concerns in the quest for a usable past. Perhaps the most striking change in our own times has been the addition of the goal of personal fulfillment to the political and economic goals of women's movements throughout Europe. Until the interwar era most crusaders for women's rights accepted the double standard and distrusted sexuality. Since then, the dream of political equality and economic security has been gradually enriched by the quest for sexual fulfillment. Taking up Freud's suggestion that all human beings begin life with undifferentiated sexual desires that are shaped later by social constraints, feminists have explored alternatives to the double standard, to male dominance, and to what Adrienne Rich termed "compulsory heterosexuality."[3] A polarized gender ideology that has for centuries alienated women and men from their human potential is giving way to an acknowledgement of greater likeness and more freedom. Recent history also makes it clear that gender justice is linked to the end of oppression based on class and race.

We, the "new women," are searching for a new identity with freer attitudes toward work, sexuality, family relationships, individual development and sisterhood. We are trying to create a new social matrix that will allow, even nurture, realization of this identity. In this quest, we need to understand what brought us to this place. This book helps us realize that goal.

NOTES

1. Joan Kelly, *Women, History and Theory* (Chicago: University of Chicago Press, 1984), p. 56.
2. H. J. Teuteberg, "The General Relation Between Diet and Industrialization," in Elborg and Robert Forster, eds., *European Diet from Pre-industrial to Modern Times* (New York: Harper, 1975), pp. 61–109.
3. Adrienne Rich, "Compulsory Heterosexuality and Lesbian Existence," in Ann Snitow, Christine Stansell, and Sharon Thompson, eds., *Powers of Desire: The Politics of Sexuality* (New York: Monthly Review Press, 1983).

figures des montaignais

This detail from Samuel de Champlain's engraved map of New France (1613) depicts a Montagnais woman and man. Engraving by David Pelletier. (Library of Congress)

chapter 1

Women in Egalitarian Societies

Eleanor Leacock

The present inequality between the sexes has necessarily been the starting point of any investigation of its origins. That is, one asks whether or not inequality has always existed and to what degree. We can never have full knowledge of the earliest social relations, but the outlines may be partially reconstructed with archeological and anthropological data. Eleanor Leacock here attempts such a reconstruction through comparative examination of European archeological evidence and anthropological studies of American Indians. The material suggests that these early societies practiced a primitive form of communism, marked by egalitarian economic and social organization. In spite of sexual division of labor, the entire group shared decision making and responsibility for children. The transformation into unequal and stratified societies occurred through a social process in which sharing developed into barter, barter developed into trade and specialization of labor, and these in turn led to individually held wealth and power. This materially and culturally enriching process had the unforeseen result of changing the structure of human relations from egalitarian to hierarchical and exploitative. The communal kin group was undercut by conflicting economic and political ties. It was replaced by social strata composed of individual family units having parental responsibility for children. Women's role was relegated to private service. The first and most important·step in the process that created social inequality between the sexes had taken place. The process itself set the outlines of a pattern that recurred, in more complex form, in later times.

Popular images of the relations between women and men in primeval society are epitomized by the club-carrying "cave man" of the *New Yorker* cartoon who drags off his woman by the hair of her head. At a higher, supposedly scientific, level, the writings of Robert Ardrey, Desmond Morris, and the sociobiologist David Barash reinforce this image.[1] Behind the laughter at the cartoon, or behind whatever picture is being woven from bits and pieces of ethnographic data pulled out of context, the message remains basically the same: humans have always been aggressive and competitive, and men, being more so than women, have always been "dominant." The theme repeats, with variations, that our "primitive" or "animal nature" reflects the "law of the jungle," whereby might makes right. Our social problems arise because a fundamentally brutish human nature—so the argument runs—lies beneath the superficial gloss of "civilization," with its Golden Rule of "do unto others as you would have them do unto you," and the value our culture claims to place on human life and human individuality.

When, however, we weigh the data of social and physical anthropology, archeology, and primatology in their entirety, rather than selecting from them arbitrarily, they tell a different story. Sociality, curiosity, and playfulness, not assertive competitiveness and aggressiveness, made it possible for a fairly small and defenseless creature to evolve into the human being that created many different ways of life around the world. Sociality, that is, an abounding desire to be close to others of the same species and an overriding interest in them, characterizes our primate relatives. Fighting and scrapping occur as subsidiary, not primary, motives. Humanity did not evolve from an innately competitive forebear as postulated by Thomas Hobbes. By hindsight it is clear that it *could* not have done so. The basis for the successful evolution of human beings was the group life that both required and made possible cooperative patterns. In turn, cooperation led to and became dependent upon the development of refined tools and utensils, and the elaboration of language.[2]

Much has been written about the fact that our primate ancestors turned to hunting for meat as a supplement to foraging for vegetable foods. One reads that the killing of animals at an early stage in human history led to deeply embedded aggressive drives. The argument has been persuasive, especially since it can be used to rationalize the dominance drives of ambitious politicians and the powerful financiers who back them, by blaming their actions on *our* human nature. People forget that, among animals, to kill other species does not lead to killing their own kind, but that to kill one's own species is specifically *human*. One must ask, what significance does killing animals actually have for people who depend on hunting to live?

A few peoples, beyond the reaches of industrialization, until recently sustained themselves largely by gathering wild vegetable foods and hunting. They paid great attention to hunting skills, but aggression as we know it in our society was played down. Hunting was usually hard work—certainly at times an exciting challenge, but also drudgery. The feeling for the animals killed, especially for large animals, did not resemble our egoistic pride in conquest; it revealed instead attitudes of gratitude and respect. Animal gods were commonly honored, and in stories humans and animals interacted closely; they intermarried, gave birth to one another, taught one another, and entered into compacts sealing their relations. Such peoples cooperated in the obtaining of meat and shared the animals procured. From the San gatherers and hunters of the Kalahari Desert in southwest Africa to the Eskimo sea mammal hunters of the Arctic, the social arrangements of foraging peoples were similar. Societies that lived by gathering and hunting (and fishing) were cooperative. People shared food, and thought of greed and selfishness much as we might think of aberrant or criminal behavior. People made and valued fine possessions, but as much to give away as to keep.[3]

People did not follow a single leader but participated in the making of decisions important to them. Social codes stressed the importance of muting animosities and of restraining jealousy and anger. Sometimes personal enmity was ritualized, as in the Eskimo drum duel, where two opponents hurled insults back and forth at one another in song. People criticized each other through banter and teasing, which usually led to outbursts of laughter in which even the person being criticized joined. When serious fights led to a person hurting or killing another, atonement, not punishment, was sought. Warfare was rare or unknown. When it occurred, it took the form of short-lived raids, not organized conflict for lands, slaves, or tribute. Colin Turnbull has written about two hunting peoples—the gentle and cheerful Mbuti of Zaire, and the unfriendly and grimly competitive Ik of Kenya.[4] It is the Mbuti, until recently living their own free life, who give us the better approximation of our gathering and hunting forebears, for the Ik have been removed from their hunting lands and, totally demoralized, they seem bent on collective suicide.

Private property, social stratification, political subjugation, and institutionalized warfare with standing armies are all social inventions that evolved through the course of human history. They do not automatically express some innate human nature. Otherwise the vast majority of us today would not seek so hard to work out some minimally satisfying, secure, and friendly way of living but would wholeheartedly revel in the competition, aggression, and violence allowed and encouraged by our social structure.

The institutionalized inequalities so familiar to us, the dominance hierarchies and the constant concern with large-scale warfare, first arose in the fourth millennium B.C., during what has been called the *urban revolution*. In the long course of human history, various egalitarian gathering and hunting, and later, horticultural (or hoe agricultural) societies elaborated ritually on various forms of social and ceremonial rank, but still maintained, as far as can be determined, the equal right of all to basic sources of livelihood. Then, as a result of human ingenuity and inventiveness, specialization of work gradually developed and removed part of the population from basic food production. Barter became transformed into commerce and traders into merchant intermediaries. Priest-chiefs increasingly manipulated the goods that were stored with them for redistribution, and what had been ritual rank was transformed into exploitative elitism. Equal access to land became restricted as free lands were turned into privately controlled, terraced, irrigated, fertilized, or otherwise worked fields. In short, class systems were created, although not quickly or without resistance and attempts to preserve cooperative mores. Fully stratified societies emerged first in southwest Asia and northeast Africa, in Mesopotamia, Egypt, Jerusalem, and Persia. In the Western hemisphere, urban, stratified societies evolved independently among the precursors of the Incas, Mayas, and Aztecs. In subsequent millennia, mercantile urban centers with stratified, competitive social and political forms repeatedly developed from societies that had been organized around egalitarian clans, as reconstructions of early history in Africa, Asia, Europe, and Central and South America indicate.

Nearly five thousand years after cities arose in Asia and Africa, the next major social transformation, the Industrial Revolution, took shape. Inextricably bound up with European colonial and imperial expansion, the Industrial Revolution brought to a close the relative autonomy of the earth's myriad cultural traditions. Gradually, the peoples of all continents became enmeshed in a single world system of militarily, politically, and economically exploitative relations. A constant theme recurs in careful ethnohistorical reconstructions of the many lifeways developed by different peoples. Archeological data, accounts by early explorers, missionaries, and traders, as well as later ethnographic material, reveal that systematized cooperativeness has repeatedly been undercut by systematized competitiveness.[5] Fortunately, increasing numbers of the world's people are now seeking to create new forms of cooperation. It is urgent indeed that we succeed, lest we render our planet unfit for life.

WOMEN IN CLASSLESS SOCIETIES

Where does this leave us in relation to the social status and role of women in classless societies? What insights do anthropological data offer us in the effort to understand the basis for women's present low status and to identify the sources for change?

The dictum most commonly expressed in anthropological writings is blunt: the general egalitarianism of nonstratified societies did not fully apply to women. Anthropologists agree that women in such societies were by no means oppressed in the ways that developed in the classic patriarchal societies of the Mediterranean world and the Orient. Nonetheless, in the view of most anthropologists who write on the subject, women have always been to some extent subordinate to men. Hence, one may read such statements as: "It is a common sociological truth that in all societies authority is held by men, not women"; "Men tend regularly to dominate women"; "Subordination of females happens to occur with remarkable persistence in a great variety of cultures"; "Men have always been politically and economically dominant over women"; and "Regardless of the form of social structure, men are always in the ascendency."[6] It is admitted that the widespread institution of matrilineality—the reckoning of descent through women—enhanced women's status, but, it is argued, matrilineality merely substituted the authority of maternal uncles and elder brothers for that of fathers and husbands. A rough and ready equality of the sexes is generally seen as existing among foragers, but men are still said to have slightly higher status. "Men's occupations are always the focus of greater cultural interest and prestige. . . . Women can exert influence outside the family only indirectly through their influence on their kinsmen. Therefore, however important the woman's work may be to the domestic economy, it does not elicit the public esteem accorded the work of men." Women's role is always "private," men's "public," most anthropologists have asserted.

> Women's work is . . . bounded by the domestic framework, concerned with the familial, private sectors of society. Roles within the public sphere are the province of men, and the public sphere is the locus of power and prestige. . . . In effect, whatever the nature of women's work, or its economic value, it is never invested with glamour, excitement, or prestige.[7]

Contemporary studies of women and men in other, earlier societies are beginning to revise such views. The thesis that a stage of egalitarian economic and social organization—primitive communism—preceded the emergence of stratification in human history has only recently become widely accepted by anthropologists; not long ago such a notion was laughed at as nineteenth-century naiveté. Careful analysis reveals the influence women held in such societies and the great measure of autonomy with which they functioned. The stereotyped characterization of women's roles in terms of the cliché of male dominance is fast being discredited.[8]

Four main distortions perpetuate confusion about women in classless societies. First, societies that are not part of the specific historical traditions of either Europe or the Orient are commonly lumped in a single category, designated "primitive." Yet stratified and urban societies had emerged or were emerging in many parts of the world at the time of European expansion. Only a few of the societies called "primitive" retained fully egalitarian institutions at that time. Therefore, general statements about women's status in "primitive" society reflect the wide variations that existed around the world and deflect attention from the analysis of their status in truly egalitarian societies.

Second, the cultures that anthropologists describe are for the most part, not autonomous but exist in the context of a colonial world. Too commonly, anthropologists have drawn generalizations about tribal cultures from twentieth-century ethnographies without taking account of colonialism and imperialism and their worldwide effects. Neither do the societies that American Indian elders described to early anthropologists represent aboriginal life in unchanged form. Trade with Europeans, conquest and resistance, work and in some cases enslavement, intermarriage, and missionizing, all created problems with which native Americans have been dealing for the last 400 years or more. In Africa, for two, three, or four hundred years (depending upon the region) peoples were willy-nilly involved, directly or indirectly, in the development of capitalist Europe and an imperialist world order. They traded and politicked; went to work on plantations and in mines to pay newly imposed taxes; were missionized or themselves became missionaries; were conquered, enslaved, or otherwise subjugated; and resisted and fought for political independence.[9]

Patriarchal practices and attitudes brought by the Europeans who imposed imperialist control accelerated the decline in the status of women in several ways. Public positions of prestige and influence were relegated to men, first informally by European emissaries and traders, later formally by colonial administrators. Women's rights to land were eroded or abolished altogether. Reciprocal economic ties within clans and lineages were undermined, and women and children became dependent on individual, wage-earning, male family heads. Finally, missionaries extolled European ideals and exhorted women to obey and be sexually faithful for life to a single man.[10]

The third impediment to an objective cross-cultural analysis of women's roles is male bias. Anthropologists have on the whole been men who interview other men and assume that the data collected thereby are sufficient for understanding a society. Women anthropologists have generally gone along, and only recently has the emergence of a self-conscious feminist scholarship led a goodly number of women, along with some men, to examine the distortions flowing from male bias.

The fourth difficulty in arriving at a clear picture of sex roles and functions in preclass societies results from an ethnocentric approach to social organization. Two pervasive and misleading assumptions are: 1) that male-female dyads exist as the core of basic social-economic units in all types of societies and function with respect to dependent children much as they do in Western society; and 2) that social action is everywhere divided into a public, formal, and politically crucial male sphere, and a private, familial, and informal female sphere, much as it is in Western society. Where data are thin, the ethnographer can always dispatch the discussion of women's activities with a paragraph or two about producing and preparing food and caring for children and home. In monograph after monograph such allusions recur with a lack of rigor or explicitness, although the restriction of women to these activities may be belied by a close reading between the lines of the monograph itself.

Given these problems, is it possible to define with any certainty what the role of women was in egalitarian societies? The answer is yes; the foundation for an adequate cross-cultural definition of women's roles is now being laid as anthropologists (mostly but not exclusively women) collect new data on women's participation in different kinds of societies and reexamine allusions to women scattered through old data. The picture that emerges falls, in my estimation, within the broad outlines proposed by Frederick Engels in his much debated *Origin of the Family, Private Property and the State:* the initial egalitarianism of human society included women, and their status relative to men declined as they lost their economic autonomy. Women's work was initially public, in the context of band or village collectives. It was transformed into private service within the confines of the individual family as part of the process whereby, through the specialization of work and increase of trade, both women and men lost direct control of the food and other goods they produced and economic classes emerged. The process was slow, and one that women apparently banded together to resist in various ways, judging from what we know of West African women's organizations and of patterned hostility between the sexes in Melanesia and other areas.[11]

In Europe, no enclaves of foraging or horticultural peoples were left as direct representatives of egalitarian lifeways by the urban and industrial revolutions. For such cultures we have only archeological evidence. Written historical records, however, indicate two broadly differing streams in the later social history of Europe: 1) that of the Mediterranean world, where the classic patriarchy of the ancient Middle East finally succeeded in submerging what had been the formal public participation of women in social, political, and religious matters; and 2) that of the northern European periphery described by Tacitus, where women, though far from equal to men, nonetheless retained a relatively higher status than in Mediterranean cultures—a status that persisted long enough to have its effect on early medieval society. Tacitus noted that the "Britons make no distinction of sex in their appointment of commanders," and his assessment of the "reverence" felt for women leaders among the Germans is interesting. He referred to it as "untainted by servile flattery or any pretence of turning women into goddesses," which suggests a real respect, rather than the self-serving pattern of placing women on a pedestal as evidence of upper-class status.[12]

Mediterranean patriarchal traditions and northern traditions that suggested earlier, more egalitarian mores were both late, of course, in terms of human history as a whole. Archeological remains indicate that they were preceded by egalitarian horticultural societies, that were in turn preceded by societies based on some combination of fishing, hunting, and gathering of wild vegetable foods. In order to make educated guesses about women's changing roles among these past European peoples, it is necessary to describe societies in parts of the world where egalitarian forms were not transformed as early.

In the Western hemisphere, urbanization and stratification developed in Mexico and the Andes, but by the time of Columbus's voyages had not engulfed the far-flung peoples of what are now the northern United States and Canada. Therefore, we can look to these groups for an understanding of how egalitarian societies functioned. As an example of a hunting people who lived in a forested area quite similar to north central Europe, I shall take the Innu hunters of the Labrador Peninsula in eastern Canada (known to anthropologists as the Montagnais-Naskapi), and describe their social relations as they were at the time Champlain first voyaged up the St. Lawrence River. Although the details of their culture—their homes, clothes, tools, art, religious ideas, and so on—had their own special features, the Innu shared with many other gathering and hunting peoples their ways of handling interpersonal relations and making group decisions. Moreover these are well documented, for in the winter of 1633–1634 a Jesuit missionary, Paul le Jeune, lived with an Innu band and wrote a detailed account of his experiences in his mission report to his superiors in Paris. Le Jeune's letters afford an invaluable record of the mores and ethics of an egalitarian people, and he made explicit references to the prestige and autonomy of all individuals, women as well as men.

THE INNU (MONTAGNAIS–NASKAPI), NATIVE AMERICANS

The Innu lived almost entirely on fish and game. The collecting of roots and berries was minimal. People moved camp many times during the winter, but during the short summer fairly large numbers came and stayed together at lake and river shores, to visit and court, and to prepare snowshoes, canoes, and clothing for the next winter. Some fifteen or twenty people, several nuclear families, lived together in a large skin- or bark-covered lodge. In the winter two or three lodge groups traveled and camped together or somewhat near each other. They would join with others from time to time for short periods of feasting if hunting was good or would turn to one another for help if the hunt was poor.

All adults participated in the procuring of food and manufacture of equipment necessary for life in the north. In general, women worked leather and bark, while men worked wood, with each making the tools they needed. For instance, women cut strips of leather and wove them onto the snowshoe frames that were made by men, and women covered with birch bark the canoe frames the men made. Women skinned game animals and cured the hides for clothing, moccasins, and lodge coverings. Everyone joined in putting up lodges; the women went into the forest to chop down lodge poles, while men cleared the snow from the ground where a lodge was to be erected.

All able-bodied members of the camp, women, men, and older children, participated in collective hunts, when migrating caribou were driven into compounds or across rivers to be speared from canoes. Men in twos and threes hunted solitary game in the forests. Women hunted occasionally when they wanted meat and the men were away, or if they wished to join their husbands on a hunting trip. Both sexes procured small game around camp, setting traps and snares. Cooking also involved the cooperation of both sexes. Large animals were roasted in pits with hot stones placed on top, cut in chunks to be skewered on stakes held over the fire, or boiled in bark dishes into which heated stones were placed. With the advent of the copper pot, a valued trade item from the sixteenth century on, meat could be simmered over an open fire without requiring much labor or attention. Everyday cooking fell to the women, although men helped prepare food for feasts or cooked for themselves when on a hunt.

Virtually everyone married, although divorce was easy and could be obtained at the desire of either partner. An inept or lazy person might have trouble keeping a spouse, and a man might be ridiculed for doing work usually done by women as evidence that he could not keep a wife. Some men had more than one wife, a practice that the seventeenth-century missionaries deplored. Le Jeune wrote, "Since I have been preaching among them that a man should have only one wife, I have not been well received by the women; for, since they are more numerous than the men, if a man can only marry one of them, the others will have to suffer."[13]

Children observed almost the entire gamut of work, recreation, and religious life that went on around them; their training was therefore largely informal as they played, helped, listened, and watched. Although the care of infants devolved mainly on their mothers, fathers were not inept or impatient with small children. Le Jeune wrote of a man soothing a sick baby with what he considered "the love of a mother" as well as "the firmness of a father."[14] Over three centuries later, I observed the unquestioning patience with which an Innu man sat cradling his sick and fretful infant in his arms, crooning over it for hours, while his wife occupied herself at the long and demanding task of smoking a deerskin.

Le Jeune wrote of the "patience" shown in daily life, and of how well people agreed. "You do not see any disputes, quarrels, enmities, or reproaches among them," he stated, as people went about their work without "meddling" with one another.[15] During the summers of 1950 and 1951, I myself witnessed an ease in the course of daily interaction that persisted even though the economic basis for Indian autonomy was fast being whittled away and there were growing reasons for new anxieties. Not that everyone was at peace: a woman in one camp had a reputation for always scolding; a man in another became drunk whenever he could procure molasses or sugar for making beer. But it was beautiful to see the sense of group responsibility for children that still obtained, and the sense of easy autonomy in relationships unburdened by centuries of training in deferential behavior by sex and status.

Not surprisingly, however, there was an evident feeling of constraint when whites were around. In an earlier period, this had not been the case. Le Jeune described the banter and joking, the love of sharp talking and voracious eating that characterized relaxed periods in the daily life of the Innu in the early seventeenth century. "They have neither gentleness nor courtesy in their utterance," he wrote, "and a Frenchman could not assume the accent, the tone, and the sharpness of their voices without becoming angry, yet they do not."[15] To his dismay, both sexes indulged freely in bawdy language that had to him "the foul odor of the sewers,"[17] and in the ribald teasing that to his surprise was usually taken with great good humor by the victims themselves. Today we understand ridicule as an important means of reinforcing group mores in a society devoid of formal controls. As the missionary saw it, however,

> Their slanders and derision do not come from malicious hearts or from infected mouths, but from a mind which says what it thinks in order to give itself free scope, and which seeks gratification from everything, even from slander and mockery.[18]

Some observers said of Innu women, as they said of other Native American women, that they were virtual slaves. Their hard work and the lack of ritualized formalities surrounding them contrasted sharply with ideals of courtesy for women in the French and British bourgeois family and were taken as evidence of low social status. Those who knew the Indians well reported otherwise. "The women have great power here," le Jeune wrote, and he exhorted the men to assert themselves. "I told him then that he was the master, and that in France women do not rule their husbands."[19] Another Jesuit father stated, "The choice of plans, of undertakings, of journeys, of winterings, lies in nearly every instance in the hands of the housewife."[20]

It is important to recognize that these decisions about movements were not private family affairs but were community decisions about the main business of the group. There were no formal chiefs or superordinate economic or political bodies to which people had to defer, either with or without direct orders being given. In fact, the Jesuits bemoaned the independence of Indian life. Le Jeune complained, "Alas, if someone would stop the wanderings of the Savages, and give authority to one of them to rule the others, we could see them converted and civilized in a short time."[21] Recurrent themes in the seventeenth-century letters and reports of the *Jesuit*

Relations were the attempts to establish the authority of elected chiefs over their bands and of husbands over their wives.

Spokespeople for a group vis-à-vis outsiders were those respected for their rhetorical abilities. Their influence was personal only. They would be ridiculed if they tried to exert any power in their group. Le Jeune wrote that the Indians "cannot endure in the least those who seem desirous of assuming superiority over the others; they place all virtue in a certain gentleness or apathy."[22] Knowledgeable people would come forth to lead the hunting groups, but their responsibilities as temporary chiefs would terminate with the end of a hunting trip. Shamans, religious practitioners who communicated with the various gods, held no formal power, but merely personal influence, and women as well as men became shamans. One Jesuit father tried to stop a powerful female shaman who was rallying her people to fight against the Iroquois. She drew a knife and threatened to kill him if he did not stop interfering.[23]

A lack of formalized authority was possible since the small groups that lived together and depended upon each other shared common interests in group survival and well-being. Also, people could easily leave one group and join another if they wished, a flexibility that enabled those who felt animosities toward others to move away before too great discomfort or disruption occurred. Anger might burst out in violence or even lead to murder, but it could be handled by separation. At worst, then, personal animosities functioned at a distance. Illness was sometimes attributed to the manipulation of supernatural forces by a personal enemy.

The kind of power over others familiar to our society did not govern egalitarian societies. Since we find it difficult, however, to interpret how such societies did in fact function, we commonly project the terms of our own social order upon them, an error especially common with respect to the status of women. As noted before, by failing to collect adequate data on women or to interpret data from the vantage point of women, anthropologists may all too casually distort the true state of affairs. The kind of statement le Jeune has made available remains rare; most of the time one must read between the lines of ethnographic accounts for indications of women's actual roles. When one does, assumptions about brutal men asserting domination over women among hunting peoples become revealed for what they are—contemporary mythology.

EARLY HUNTING PEOPLES OF EUROPE

In Europe, the few hints left about the life of the Neanderthals, the ancestors of modern humans who lived until 40 or 50,000 years ago, confirm the essentially social nature of human evolution. Several families shared single large dwellings in the community sites that have been found, and the infirm were cared for, as shown, for example, by a skeleton of a relatively old arthritic cripple in one site, and in another, one of an older man whose right arm had been amputated when young. Writing of an unusually rich find in Iraq, where one Neanderthal was buried with flowers and six others were found, the archaeologist Ralph Solecki makes a comment that applies as readily to Neanderthal sites in eastern Europe:

> The picture of the lone stalker cannot be ruled out in the case of the Neander-thal but, since these people lived in a communal setting, it would be more natural for them to have engaged in communal hunting. And the fact that their lame and disabled . . . had been cared for . . . is excellent testimony for commu-nal living and cooperation.[24]

It has been argued that cannibalism was practiced, but, if so, ceremonial group burials suggest it was highly ritualized. Ritual cannibalism in later times has been practiced in many parts of the world, sometimes on respected enemies, sometimes as part of the funeral service of beloved relatives.[25]

The cave paintings executed by early modern humans, the Cro-Magnon successors of the Neanderthals, tell us more. They reveal a respect for the animals that were hunted and an appreciation of their beauty that concurs with what we know to be felt by recent hunters like the Innu. Some contemporary theorists stress the ritualization of the hunt and the impor-tance of male hunters, to the detriment of women, among our early ancestors. However, cave paintings suggest a ceremonial life in which both women and men participated. Numerous female figurines, ranging from very fat to almost sticklike but always very stylized, indicate the ritual importance of women. No comparable male figurines were made, though paintings of men were. It could well be argued that female figurines need not imply women's high status; ubiquitous representations of the Virgin Mary in Catholic countries do not, nor do the endless representations of the female form in our own media. However, the link between ideology and behavior is neces-sarily far more direct among egalitarian peoples than in hierarchical societies, where the glossing over of inequality and exploitation with ambiguous and contradictory ritual and rhetoric is elaborately institutionalized. All told, we have every reason to assume that autonomy and prestige for women obtained among early European hunters as they formerly did among other hunting and gathering peoples. Tacitus said of the Stones, one of the peoples east of the Germans, that among them "woman is the ruling sex," and of the Fenni in what is now Lithuania, that women hunted alongside the men and "insist in taking their share in bringing down the game."[26]

Generally, foraging and hunting as ways of life eventually gave ground to agricultural and/or pastoral economies. In the Middle East, the domesti-cation of plants was developed some 13,000 years ago, presumably by women who gathered and processed wild seeds. Horticulture as a way of life spread northward into Europe, as evidenced by village remains of grain-growing peoples. These societies retained their earlier egalitarianism; the class distinctions revealed by differences in dwellings and burials took time to develop.

What kind of life did early European villagers lead? What roles did women play? The individual histories of different peoples and their cultures vary widely, yet certain broad similarities in social structure characterize known egalitarian horticultural societies. For an ethnological insight into such a society, we turn to a group whose history and culture is better documented than that of most horticultural peoples—the Iroquois, native Americans of New York State.

THE HO–DE–NO–SAU–NEE, OR PEOPLE OF THE LONG HOUSE

The People of the Long House, known as the Iroquois, included from west to east in New York State the Nun-da-wa-o-no, or Great Hill People (Seneca), the Gwe-u-gweh-o-no, or People at the Mucky Land (Cayuga), the O-non-da-ga-o-no, or People on the Hills (Onondaga), the O-na-yote-ka-o-no, or Granite People (Oneida), and the Ga-ne-a-go-o-no, or People Possessors of the Flint (Mohawk), as well as later, to the south of the Oneida, the Dus-ga-o-weh-o-no, or Shirt-Wearing People (Tuscarora). Recently, a group of Mohawks, along with members of other Indian nations, moved back onto a piece of former Mohawk land in northeastern New York State. They wish to return, in their words, "to the cooperative system of our ancestors," and to re-create "a people's government" with broad community participation in decision making. These contemporary pioneers come from urban as well as rural areas, but they differ from other cooperative movements in their sense of their history and former traditions.

At the time of European intrusion in the sixteenth century, the Iroquois lived in villages of 2,000 people and more, and worked as gardeners and hunters. The women farmed, using digging sticks and hoes with deer scapula blades. They planted some fifteen varieties of maize, as many as sixty different kinds of beans, and eight types of squash. They also collected wild fruits and nuts, roots, and edible or medicinal leaves. The men hunted deer, bear, and small game, and fished and took birds, using a variety of snares, traps, and nets, as well as bows and arrows. Both sexes worked together to build the fairly permanent large, bark-shingled frame houses that were shared by up to twenty-five families. These longhouses had anterooms at either end for storage and a row of fireplaces down the center. Families that lived across from each other used the same fireplace, and back from the fireplaces, family sleeping quarters were set off from each other by partitions.

During the course of the sixteenth and seventeenth centuries, the Iroquois became heavily involved in the fur trade, and when they exhausted the beaver in their homelands, they either acted as intermediaries in the trade with outlying peoples or fought with them to extend their own sphere of operation. They became the enemies of the Innu, and in the competition between the French and English for control of American lands that came to a head during the eighteenth century, the Iroquois allied with the English and the Innu with the French.

By the nineteenth century, when the anthropologist Lewis Henry Morgan wrote *League of the Ho-De-No-Sau-Nee or Iroquois*, published in 1851, longhouse life was a distant memory, although the longhouse remained a strong symbol of the still functioning Council of the Confederacy. Fundamental changes had been taking place in Iroquois society since the sixteenth century, resulting from the fur trade and the warfare engendered by competing colonial powers and by the loss of Indian lands to them. The confederacy of the six tribes acted as a powerful unifying force, and the formal powers of the council increased in order that it might deal effectively with the political and economic rivalries and pressures of the Dutch, French, and British. At the same time, however, the fur trade enabled economically independent entrepreneurs to detach themselves from responsibilities toward their people. The effect was eventually to undermine the previously unchallenged communism practiced by the families sharing a longhouse, a process aided both by missionary teaching and governmental policies. Descriptions of Iroquois society, therefore, and especially of women's position, abound in contradictions, as people with different viewpoints and sources of information make judgments at different points in time.

That women at one time held a relatively high status in Iroquois society, however, no one questions. The Iroquois counted descent matrilineally, a common practice among horticultural peoples, and rights to use clan lands passed down from mother to daughter. A man usually moved into his wife's household when he married and could be sent home if he displeased her. The matrons of a longhouse controlled the distribution of the food and other stores that made up the wealth of the group; they nominated and could depose the sachems or chiefs that represented each tribe in the Council of the Confederacy; and they "had a voice upon all questions" brought before the clan councils.[27] Women and men held in equal numbers the important positions of Keepers of the Faith, influential people who admonished others for moral infractions and sometimes reported them to the council for public exposure. Compensation to her kinfolk for a murdered woman was twice that for a murdered man. An early eighteenth-century missionary, Lafitau, writing either of women among the Iroquois or the similar Huron, or both, stated that "All real authority is vested in them. . . . They are the souls of the Councils, the arbiters of peace and of war."[28] Well over a century later, Reverend Wright, a missionary to the Seneca, wrote:

The women were the great power among the clans, as everywhere else. They did not hesitate, when occasion required, "to knock off the horns," as it was technically called, from the head of a chief, and send him back to the ranks of the warriors.[29]

In his book *The Inevitability of Patriarchy*, however, sociologist Steven Goldberg three times makes reference to the statement made by Lewis Henry Morgan that "the Indian regarded women as the inferior, the dependent, and the servant of man, and from nurture and habit, she actually considered herself to be so."[30] Morgan also wrote that women's influence

> did not reach outward to the affairs of the gens [clan], phratry [grouping of clans], or tribe, but seems to have commenced and ended with the household. This view is quite consistent with the life of patient drudgery and of general subordination to the husband which the Iroquois wife cheerfully accepted as the portion of her sex.[31]

How do these statements square with the previous account of women's high status among the Iroquois?

Part of the answer lies in the changes that took place as women's control of the longhouse became replaced by their dependence on wage-earning husbands in the context of the individual nuclear family. Such institutions as the dormitories where adolescent girls had lived and courted their lovers, alluded to disapprovingly in sixteenth- and early seventeenth-century accounts, were not even a memory by Morgan's time. By the mid-nineteenth century, when Morgan was writing about the Iroquois, chastity had been enjoined for unmarried women, along with the double standard and the public whipping of women for adultery.

Part of the discrepancy in evaluations of Iroquois women's status also lies in the failure to understand their control over the household in its full significance. In modern times, to speak of women's high position in the household and of their prestige and influence in male councils would imply no more than the usual power behind the throne, whereby women manipulate their families to gain some measure of control over their lives in a fundamentally patriarchal society. In the Iroquois case, however, the fact that the households constituted the communities meant that women's decision-making power over the production and distribution of food and other goods gave them a large measure of control over the group economy itself. Such decisions did not have the private character they have in our society, where production and distribution of any importance are carried on by corporate business, and power lies with complex and formidable institutions far beyond the community.

Council decisions were not backed up with the kind of power held by a modern state, but rather expressed group consensus in relation to intervillage affairs and policies toward outside groups. In a paper on women's position among the Iroquois, Judith Brown gives an example of the practical power inhering in their economic role: they could choose to support or to restrain a proposed war party by agreeing to furnish, or by withholding, necessary supplies. Were societies like the Iroquois, then, matriarchal? The answer is yes if the term means that women held public authority in major areas of group life. The answer is no if the term alludes to a mirror image of Judeo-Christian and Oriental patriarchy, where power in the hands of men (or an occasional woman) at the top of hierarchical structures is reflected in the petty power men exercise over their wives in individual households.[32]

In precolonial Iroquois society, it was necessary to regularize the production and distribution of food by and among hundreds of villagers who lived together. This must have lessened somewhat the kind of personal autonomy that characterized Innu life. Nonetheless, Iroquois society remained basically communal and egalitarian. The artistic, ritual, and other cultural elaborations that a settled life made possible were participated in by everyone according to interest. People of personal prestige and influence lived, worked, and ate along with everyone else. At worst, prisoners of war who were adopted into a clan might have to do the more tiresome chores for a while, but they partook of the same food and housing as the others and could with time win a respected place in the group. In his classic work *Ancient Society*, Morgan wrote:

> All the members of an Iroquois gens were personally free and they were bound to defend each other's freedom; they were equal in privileges and in personal rights, the sachems and chiefs claiming no superiority. . . . [This] serves to explain that sense of independence and personal dignity universally an attribute of Indian character.[33]

HORTICULTURAL SOCIETY IN EUROPE

The archaeological remains of the European horticultural societies that preceded what is known from written history look much like the remains of Iroquois-type villages. The peoples of the early third millennium B.C. in central Europe were horticulturalists who used stone tools, and, in the words of the eminent prehistorian V. Gordon Childe, lived in "commodious and substantial rectangular houses from 10 to 40 m in length and 6 to 7.5 m wide." Childe stated that "the 'household' must have been more like a clan than a pairing family," and he described the culture as "peaceful" and "democratic." There were few weapons, and no hint of chiefs concentrating the communities' wealth." Some of the early northern European peoples, such as those of Denmark in the first part of the second millennium B.C., also dwelt in large frame houses. Others lived in clusters of small one-room houses. In both instances, remains indicate egalitarian societies.[34]

Successors of egalitarian villagers, however, began to show evidences of stratification, with chiefly dwellings and burials much more elaborate than those of the common folk. Metal tools became important and were traded from the south, and warfare increased. Childe wrote of the central European peoples of about 2000 B.C.:

> Settlements were often planted on hilltops as well as in the valleys, and were frequently fortified. Competition for land assumed a bellicose character, and weapons such as battle-axes became specialized for warfare. The consequent preponderance of the male members in the communities may account for the general disappearance of female figurines. Part of the new surplus population may have sought an outlet in industry and trade; imported substances such as Baltic amber, Galician flint and copper began to be distributed more regularly than heretofore. Warriors would appreciate more readily than cultivators the superiority of metal, and chiefs may already have been concentrating surplus wealth to make the demand for metal effective.[35]

The accounts by Tacitus of central and northern European societies described women's position as higher than in the classic patriarchies of the Mediterranean world, though below that of men, a decline that presumably developed slowly over the some two millennia following the period Childe studied. In connection with certain sites around 2000 B.C., Childe stated that the female figurines, so common in earlier levels, "are no more in evidence." He continued, "The old ideology has been changed. That may reflect a change from a matrilineal to a patrilineal organization of society."[36] In Europe, then, as in so much of the world, women's position was transformed from early autonomy and equality to one of lesser status and, subsequently, of oppression. What was responsible for this transition?

The theme that innate human drives toward dominance, and especially the aggressiveness of males, have determined human history threads through most answers given to this question. Precise formulations vary, but in general, arguments run along the following lines: Human populations recurrently grow to the limits of their different environments, given the technical skills at their disposal. This leads to competition for resources, and to warfare. As the technological means for producing food and other necessities improve, populations grow, and so does the competition for land. Warfare increases, which enables the more ambitious and aggressive men to acquire surplus wealth and assert dominant status over others in their group and over women, as well as over other groups. From the viewpoint of recent history, the assumption seems reasonable enough. From the perspective of cultural history as a whole, however, the argument turns out to be over-simplified to the point of serious distortion; it does not really work.

THE TRANSFORMATION OF EGALITARIAN SOCIETY

As mentioned earlier, everything known about foraging life indicates that human hunters and gatherers were not engaged in an unremitting struggle with each other for survival as they wrested food from a stingy world and faced the problem of population always growing to the very limit of its resources. Human society evolved through the application of ingenuity and the expression of sociality, not merely some drive to dominate. With skills and knowledge, early humans were able to use an extremely wide variety of plants and animals, and they moved into new environments as they learned how to handle new resources. Fighting was apparently disliked and avoided by foraging societies, and such societies persisted far longer than have the warring societies that succeeded them. All indications are that there was abundant leisure for the sheer fun of talking, joking, and storytelling in foraging/hunting societies, and for artistic and ritual pursuits. Le Jeune complained of the Innu that "their life is passed in eating, laughing, and making sport of each other, and of all the people they know."[37]

Furthermore, group size and ratio of children to adults were apparently maintained at a level well within the limits of environmental resources. All evidence points to conscious population limitation in egalitarian societies. A variety of means was employed, some more, some less effective: periods of abstinence, prolonged lactation, herbs for birth control or abortion, mechanical attempts at abortion, and, as a last resort, infanticide. Infants who followed siblings so closely as to overburden the mother, and hence the group, were not allowed to live. The Jesuits commented on the seventeenth-century Innu families with two, three, and rarely more than four children, by contrast with the large families of the French.[38]

The transformation from egalitarian society to societies built on inequality and stratification was not due to a psychobiological combination of dominance drives and population pressures. Instead, a profoundly *social* process—sharing—sparked the change, for sharing developed into barter, which in turn developed into the systematic trade and specialization of labor that eventually led to the innovation of individually held wealth and power. The exchange of resources from different areas is as old as human society itself. In ancient sites, seashells occur many miles from ocean shores. Flint, obsidian, and other desirable stones have wandered far from their original locations. Such rarities as fascinatingly beautiful amber have been passed from hand to hand great distances from their sources. In the course of human history, the increasingly stable village life made possible either by agriculture or by unusually dependable seasonal supplies of wild foods (such as the salmon runs that supported the coastal villagers of British Columbia) called for more and more regularized exchange both within and among groups. In turn, specialization became common in the production of goods to be traded for luxury items and special tools and foods. The process enriched life and promoted skill. As an unforeseen result, it ultimately transformed the entire structure of human relations from the equality of communal groups to the exploitativeness of economically divided societies.

Networks of exchange relations were originally egalitarian in form, for profit was not involved. However, the production and holding of goods for future exchange created new positions and new vested interests that began to divide the commitments of some individuals from those of the group as a whole. The role of economic intermediary developed and separated the process of exchange from the reciprocal relations that had bound groups together. Concomitantly, the holders of religious and chiefly statuses, traditionally guardians of produce that was redistributed as needed, acquired novel powers from the manipulation of stores of locally unavailable and particularly desirable merchandise. As Engels outlined in his *Origin of the Family, Private Property and the State*, the seeds of class difference were sown when people began to lose direct control over the distribution and consumption of the goods they had produced. Simultaneously, the basis for the oppression of women was laid as the communal kin group became undercut by conflicting economic and political ties. In its place, individual family units emerged, in which the responsibility for raising future generations was placed on the shoulders of individual parents, and through which women's public role (and consequent public recognition) was transmuted into private service (and loss of public esteem).[39]

Recent analyses of the structural components of women's social status indicate the critical role played by their degree of control over goods and resources. In an article comparing twelve societies with respect to women's position, Peggy Sanday wrote that for this sample "the antecedent of female political authority is some degree of economic power, i.e., ownership or control of strategic resources."[40] The importance of control over resources is illustrated by Judith Brown's comparison of early Iroquois society with the nineteenth-century Bemba of Zambia. Among the latter, women no longer controlled their produce and they held relatively lower status. Among the Iroquois, Brown wrote, the hospitality of women in the dispensing of food redounded to their own prestige; among the Bemba, it reflected the prestige and power of the male household heads. In Bemba society, inequality and individual family units had replaced communal groups, and a man's right to his labor was "subject to the superior claims of certain older relatives and ultimately to that of the chief himself."[41] Chiefs held and distributed food to reinforce their own economic and political power.

Karen Sacks compared four African societies, the hunting/gathering Mbuti of Zaïre, the horticultural Lovedu and pastoral/agricultural Pondo of South Africa, and the stratified Ganda of Uganda. She showed the relative decline in women's status as the societies moved from "collective social production by women, as against that by men: equal in Mbuti and Lovedu, unequal in Pondo, and absent in Ganda."[42] These differences persisted in spite of the effects, both direct and indirect, of colonialism.

Where women were traders and marketers, as in many West African societies, they retained greater economic autonomy and resultant status than when trading was carried on by men. The Ibo of Nigeria afford an unusually well-documented example of women marketers. When their status became threatened by the external economic ties—negotiated by men— that expanded rapidly following World War I, women protested publically, rioting and demonstrating, first in 1919, then again in 1925 and 1929. Accordingly, women's organizations among the Ibo were studied in detail, while elsewhere we have only hints of their existence. Women sat together in public meetings and through their organizations made their "own laws for the women of the town irrespective of the men," regulated the markets, protected women's interests, and negotiated legal cases where women and men were both implicated. The issues women raised in their protests reveal the close relation between their economic position and their personal rights vis à vis men. A major issue that sparked women's demonstrations was the possibility that a new market tax might be imposed by the British. As another issue women asserted their traditional right to have sexual relations with men other than their husbands, a right that was being threatened by missionary teachings and the influence of British family law.[43]

With regard to Europe, cross-cultural studies such as the above that reveal the relationship between, on the one hand, trade, marketing, and the warfare that accompanied competition over trade routes, and, on the other hand, social inequalities within and between the sexes, jibe with such archeological and ethnohistorical data as are available. By contrast with the egalitarian village sites described by Childe for the Neolithic period, Bronze and early Iron Age sites show evidence of long-distance luxury trade networks, inequalities in wealth, and increasing fortification, while historical data throw light on later phases in the rise of hierarchical societies based on the patron-client tie in place of kin-based societies.[44] In an ethnohistorical study of gender relationships, Viana Muller finds evidence for the concomitant development of female dependency and male control in the individual family among the Anglo-Saxons and Franks, and, with some variations, the Welsh.[45] These developments in northern Europe were initially of course influenced by Roman conquest and trade. In turn, Roman development had been influenced by the earlier emergence of class-based, politically organized, hierarchical states in the Ancient East. These dimensions of European culture history, however, are the subjects of the following chapters.

NOTES

1. Robert Ardrey, *African Genesis: A Personal Investigation into the Animal Origins and Nature of Man*, Atheneum, New York, 1961, and *The Social Contract*, Atheneum, New York, 1970; Desmond Morris, *The Naked Ape*,

Dell, New York, 1966. David Barash, *The Whisperings Within: Evolution and the Origin of Human Nature*, Penguin Books, New York, 1981. For a critique of these writings, see Marian Lowe and Ruth Hubbard eds., *Woman's Nature, Rationalizations of Inequality*, Pergamon Press, Elmsford, N.Y., 1983.

2. For an account of human evolution, written from the viewpoint of the part played by women, see Nancy Makepeace Tanner, *On Becoming Human*, Cambridge University Press, London, 1981. Were humanity by nature that disposed to fighting, we would all be fully involved in the contemporary melee with great enjoyment. Instead, despite our competitive socialization, most of us try to find some reasonably peaceful niche in which to gain some pleasure from life.

3. For a summary of gathering/hunting society, see Eleanor Leacock and Richard Lee, Introduction, in their *Politics and History in Band Societies*, Cambridge University Press, London, 1982.

4. Colin Turnbull, *The Forest People*, Doubleday, Garden City, N.Y., 1965; *The Mountain People*, Simon & Schuster, New York, 1972.

5. Eric R. Wolf, *Europe and the People Without History*, University of California Press, Berkeley, Calif., 1982.

6. T. O. Beidelman, *The Kaguru: A Matrilineal People of East Africa*, Holt, Rinehart & Winston, New York, 1971, p. 43; Walter Goldschmidt, *Man's Way: A Preface to the Understanding of Human Society*, Holt, Rinehart & Winston, New York, 1959, p. 164; Marvin Harris, "Women's Fib," *Natural History* (Spring 1972), and *Culture, Man, and Nature: An Introduction to General Anthropology*, Crowell, New York, 1971, p. 328; E. E. Evans-Pritchard, *The Position of Women in Primitive Societies and Other Essays in Social Anthropology*, Faber & Faber, London, 1965, p. 54.

7. Dorothy Hammond and Alta Jablow, *Women: Their Economic Role in Traditional Societies*, Addison-Wesley Module in Anthropology, No. 35, Reading, Mass., 1973, pp. 3, 8, 26, 27.

8. For new accounts of women's autonomy in gathering/hunting societies, see Diane Bell, *Daughters of the Dreaming*, McPhee & Gribble/Allen & Unwin, Melbourne/Sydney, 1983 (Aborigines of Australia); Agnes Estioko-Griffen and P. Bion Griffin, "Woman the Hunter: The Agta," and Colin M. Turnbull, "Mbuti Womanhood," both in Frances Dahlberg, ed., *Woman the Gatherer*, Yale University Press, New Haven, Conn., 1971; Eleanor Leacock, "Montagnais Women and the Jesuit Program for Colonization," in Mona Etienne and Eleanor Leacock, eds., *Women and Colonization: Anthropological Perspectives*, Praeger, New York, 1980: and Polly Wiessner, "Risk, Reciprocity, and Social Influences on Kung San Economics," in Eleanor Leacock and Richard Lee, eds. op. cit. For accounts of women's autonomy in egalitarian farming societies, see Robert Steven Grumet, "Sunksquaws, Shamans, and Tradeswomen: Middle Atlantic Coastal Algonkian Women During the 17th and 18th Centuries," in Mona Etienne and Eleanor Leacock, eds. op. cit.; John Phillip Reid, *A Law of Blood: The Primitive Law of the Cherokee Nation*, New York University Press, New York, 1970; and Alice Schlegel's chapter on the Hopi in her book, *Sexual Stratification: A Cross-Cultural View*, Columbia University Press, New York, 1977. Among the many recent analyses of women's publically recognized and independent spheres of action and responsibility in "ranking" societies, the best

known is Annette B. Weiner, *Women of Value, Men of Renown: New Perspectives on Trobriand Exchange*, University of Texas Press, Austin, 1976.

9. Eric R. Wolf, *op. cit.*

10. Eleanor Leacock, "Montagnais Women and the Jesuit Program for Colonization," in Mona Etienne and Eleanor Leacock, eds., op. cit.

11. Eleanor Leacock, "Women, Power and Authority," in Leela Dube, Eleanor Leacock, and Shirley Ardener, eds., *Visibility and Power, Essays on Women in Society and Development*, Oxford University Press, New Delhi, Forthcoming.

12. Tacitus, *Agricula and the Germania*, Penguin, New York, 1971, pp. 66, 108. The decline in women's status is discussed by Viana Muller in "The Formation of the State and the Oppression of Women: A Case Study in England and Wales and some Theoretical Considerations," *Review of Radical Political Economics*, Vol. 9, No. 3 (Fall 1978), pp. 7–21.

13. R. G. Thwaites, ed., *The Jesuit Relations and Allied Documents*, Burrows Brothers, Cleveland, 1906, vol. 12, p. 165.

14. Ibid., vol. 11, p. 105.

15. Ibid., vol. 6, p. 233.

16. Ibid., vol. 6, p. 235.

17. Ibid., vol. 6, p. 253.

18. Ibid., vol. 6, p. 247.

19. Ibid., vol. 5, p. 181; vol. 6, p. 255.

20. Ibid., vol. 68, p. 93.

21. Ibid., vol. 12, p. 169.

22. Ibid., vol. 16, p. 165.

23. Ibid., vol. 9, pp. 113–117.

24. Ralph S. Solecki, "Neanderthal Is Not an Epithet but a Worthy Ancestor," *Anthropology, Contemporary Perspectives*, eds. David E. Hunter and Phillip Whitten, Little, Brown, Boston, 1975. With respect to the *New Yorker* cartoon image of the cave man dragging his woman off by the hair, it is interesting to note that in fact Neanderthal women were as big and as heavily muscled as Neanderthal men (Erik Trinkaus, "Hard Times Among the Neanderthals," *Natural History*, Vol. 87, 1978). Presumably both sexes were doing the same heavy work.

25. It is important to note that despite a great deal of rumor and hearsay, there are no authenticated records of eating human meat as a regular practice. Cannibalism occurs as either a highly patterned ritual, or as an act of desperation from starvation or famine.

26. Tacitus, *op. cit.*, pp. 140–41.

27. For a summary statement of the position of Iroquois women, see Judith K. Brown, "Iroquois Women: An Ethnohistoric Note," *Toward an Anthropology of Women*, ed. Rayna R. Reiter, Monthly Review Press, New York, 1975.

28. Ibid., p. 238.

29. Lewis Henry Morgan, *Ancient Society*, ed. Eleanor Leacock, Peter Smith, Gloucester, Mass., 1974 [1877], p. 464.

30. Lewis Henry Morgan, *League of the Ho-De-No-Sau-Nee or Iroquois*, vol. 1, Human Relations Area Files, New Haven, 1954, p. 315; Steven Goldberg, *The Inevitability of Patriarchy*, Wm. Morrow, New York, 1973 [1851], pp. 40, 58, 241.

31. Lewis Henry Morgan, *Houses and House-Life of the American Aborigines*, University of Chicago Press, Chicago, 1965 [1881], p. 128.

32. In her recent book, *The Creation of Patriarchy* (Oxford University Press, New York, 1986, p. 30), Gerder Lerner misrepresents this passage. In this and her footnote reference (fn. 43, p. 249) to my supposed "assertion of the existence of matriarchy," Lerner attributes to me a reification of the concept that I have assidously avoided in my analysis of egalitarian gender relation (Eleanor Leacock, *Myths of Male Dominance*, Monthly Review, New York, 1981). More importantly, however, Lerner misses the main point of this entire section on Iroquois gender and the structure of decision making in an egalitarian society with which it is dealing. In such societies there is (or at least was) no formal political power as such above and beyond the kin communities that inhabit large communal households (or, among gatherer/hunters, camps). Decisions are made by consensus and people are not bound by decisions they have not participated in making. It is important to realize that among the Iroquois the sachems were not "chiefs" or "political leaders" in the Western sense. They were spokesmen only. No decision making power was attached to their status, and they were appointed by the matrons who could depose anyone felt not to be carrying out his responsibilities properly.

33. Morgan, *Ancient Society*, pp. 85–86.

34. V. Gordon Childe, *The Dawn of European Civilization*, Random House, New York, 1964, pp. 106–107, 109, 182–183.

35. Ibid., p. 119.

36. Ibid., p. 123.

37. Thwaites, vol. 6, p. 243.

38. Ibid., vol. 52, p. 49.

39. Gerda Lerner (*op. cit.*, p. 52) unfortunately ignores data on women as exchangers of goods, and, influenced by Lévi-Strauss, Meillassoux, and others on women as objects exchanged, argues that the "first appropriation of private property consists of the appropriation of the labor of women as *reproducers*" (her italics). I have elsewhere (Leacock, *op. cit.* 1981) criticized such an approach, arguing that failure to deal with the way in which exchange itself and production for trade rather than for direct use and sharing, undercut the structure of egalitarian relations, makes it difficult to understand why the exchange of women develops in societies where stratification is beginning to emerge. The appropriation of women's labor—like that of men—is not possible until women—like men—begin to lose control over the distribution and consumption of what they produce. It is through the increasing importance of trade and its control by a budding elite that this occurs. Control of women's sexuality was part and parcel of the development of exploitation generally; one does not have to resort to the vagaries of "ecological conditions and irregularities in biological reproduction" (Lerner, *op. cit.*, p. 52) to explain it.

40. Peggy R. Sanday, "Female Status in the Public Domain," *Woman, Culture, and Society*, eds. Michelle Zimbalist Rosaldo and Louise Lamphere, Stanford University Press, Stanford, 1974, p. 193.

41. Quoted by Brown from Audrey I. Richards, *Land, Labour and Diet in Northern Rhodesia*, Oxford University Press, London, 1939; pp. 188–189.

42. Karen Sacks, "Engels Revisited: Women, the Organization of Production, and Private Property," Rosaldo and Lamphere, *Woman, Culture, and Society*, p. 215.

43. G. T. Basden, *Among the Ibos of Nigeria*, Barnes & Noble, New York, 1966, p. 95. See also G. T. Basden, *Niger Ibos*, Seeley and Service, London, 1938, and C. K. Meek, *Law and Authority in a Nigerian Tribe*, Oxford University Press, London, 1937.

SUGGESTIONS FOR FURTHER READING

Etienne, Mona and Eleanor Leacock, eds.: *Women and Colonization, Anthropological Perspectives*. Praeger, New York, 1980.

Engels, Frederick. *The Origin of the Family, Private Property and the State*. Edited and Introduction by Eleanor Leacock. International Publishers, New York, 1972.

Leacock, Eleanor. *Myths of Male Dominance*. Monthly Review, New York, 1981.

Leacock, Eleanor, and Helen Safa, eds. *Women's Work, Development and the Division of Labor by Gender*. Bergin and Garvey, South Hadley, Mass., 1986.

Lebeuf, Annie M. D. "The Role of Women in the Political Organization of African Societies." *Women of Tropical Africa*, ed. Denise Paulme. University of California Press, Berkeley, 1971.

Liebowitz, Lila. Females, Males, Families: A Biosocial Approach. Duxbury Press, North Scituate, Mass., 1978.

Martin, M. Kay, and Barbara Voorhies. *Female of the Species*. Columbia University Press, New York, 1975.

Reid, John Phillip. *A Law of Blood: The Primitive Law of the Cherokee Nation*. New York University Press, New York, 1970.

Reiter, Rayna, R. *Toward an Anthropology of Women*. Monthly Review Press, New York, 1975.

Rohrlich-Leavitt, Ruby, ed. *Women Cross-Culturally: Change and Challenge*. Mouton, The Hague, 1975.

Sacks, Karen, *Sisters and Wives, The Past and Future of Sexual Equality*. Greenwood Press, Westport, Conn., 1979.

Schlegel, Alice, ed. *Sexual Stratification: A Cross-Cultural View*. Columbia University Press, New York, 1977.

Hatshepsut, the greatest of the female pharaohs of Egypt, governed a united and prosperous kingdom for twenty years during the brilliant Eighteenth Dynasty. (The Metropolitan Museum of Art, Rogers Fund, 1929)

chapter 2

Women of Egypt and the Ancient Near East

Barbara S. Lesko

The earliest cities emerged in the Near East five thousand years ago. Civiliza-
tion multiplied the disadvantages women faced, but as the following essay
by Barbara Lesko argues, those disadvantages were not immediately apparent.
The earliest agrarian kingdoms in the river valleys of the Nile and the
Tigris-Euphrates come down to us in brief glimpses of supremely confident
patriarchies. These societies gave women access to institutions, important
religious and political offices, and opportunities to work and profit individu-
ally from their own labor. Restriction and exclusion occurred over a vast
stretch of time as rivalries over scarce resources, ecological degradation,
militarism, and the clash of elites eroded women's status and limited their
rights. Civilization's early promises and the very gradual subordination of
women reveals a process, one which sheds light on that compelling question
we frequently ask: why did women allow rights and opportunities to be
taken away from them? Here we see the first historically traceable system-
atic subordination of women as a result of material conditions, in a pattern
that recurs in the classical world and again in Europe during the Middle
Ages.

Where did woman stand in the beginning of civilization: as an equal of man or his property? Did an age ever exist in which woman was foremost? Was God originally a woman? Many ask such questions and many theories appear in print, but for facts we must turn to the historical record—the written document (unfortunately the earliest history of woman must remain speculative). Those who assume that total male dominance was the rule in antiquity—doubtless due to Biblical accounts—say that existence of Patriarchy in the Hebrew Bible negates all our questions. The Biblical texts however, date to the first millennium B.C., and civilizations flourished long before that in the Near East. We shall examine these early societies to reconstruct the social status of their women and to determine what legal and marriage rights and opportunities women possessed. We shall attempt to discover the truth about the existence of patriarchy: the system under which men ruled in the family as well as in the larger social unit; only male children inherited from the paternal estate; and women were not legal adults. This is the system under which, when a young woman married, she entered her husband's family home where she might become a secondary wife, due to the practice of polygyny.

The first written records that tell us about the status of women in antiquity date back nearly five thousand years and are from Egypt, which flourished in the valley of the Nile in North Africa, and from Sumer, in the fertile basin between the Tigris and Euphrates rivers, in what is now southern Iraq. Of these two civilizations, Egypt's lasted by far the longest (3000 years), but Sumer passed on aspects of her culture, such as the writing system (cuneiform) and artistic and literary themes and some religious beliefs, to the Semitic peoples who gradually replaced the Sumerians on their own soil and whose city-states grew into empires further to the north in Mesopotamia. Other records come from these later states of Babylonia and Assyria, which flourished in the second and third millennia, and from early Israel, probably the most familiar to us of all the ancient Near Eastern nations.

Despite the distance in time from us, there is a wealth of written documents of all sorts surviving from the ruins of the towns, cities and cemeteries of these lands. Fortunately, the Sumerians wrote on clay tablets that when fired like pottery became almost indestructible. Many documents of daily life in ancient Egypt survive on potsherds, flakes of limestone or broken pottery pieces, which served wider use than more expensive and more fragile papyrus paper. Advances in decipherment and translations of thousands of ancient documents bring these peoples back to life and reveal surprising facts at odds with long-held theories.

For instance, women in Egypt (and apparently Sumer as well) enjoyed legal rights equal to men. Considered as fully adult and responsible for their own acts, they inherited and disposed of property as free agents, just as they gave testimony in court or entered into business contracts on their own with no male cosignatory needed. Not all walks of life were open to the Egyptian woman, however, and in Western Asia the freedoms enjoyed by Sumerian women gradually diminished for their Babylonian heiresses and became totally lost to the Assyrian and Israelite women, who truly dwelt under patriarchal tyranny.

Why did this sad turn of events occur? We can make some suggestions based on evidence. The growth of private wealth and the rise in importance of commerce seems to have affected women's freedom, particularly their sexual freedom, as women became, in time at least in western Asia, a commodity of exchange through marriages arranged by male heads of families. The continual warfare which raged in Mesopotamia for centuries led to the rise of standing armies and professional militarism, which also deleteriously affected women's status. The insecurity bred from the threat of continual invasion and the rise in importance of the armed defenders of the State (surpassing the food producers' importance) denied women a useful role and equal status in society.[1] Furthermore, it seems logical, judging from the contemporary scene, that insecure and impoverished men are most likely to vent frustrations upon the women in their lives and most likely to try to control them, and that the same should be true collectively for groups of men who feel threatened and insecure.

Although some roles in the clergy and state bureaucracy were increasingly closed to women in ancient Egypt, particularly during the second millennium, women's social and legal status were not significantly affected. Egypt fought most of her battles outside of the country's boundaries and only sporadically had need of a standing army. Furthermore, the state had a virtual monopoly on commerce, with private wealth consisting mainly of land and foreign slaves. The social and political convulsions of the ancient Near East touched Egypt only lightly, and her people were far enough removed and for the most part well enough looked after by what they saw as their divine ruler to feel optimistic and secure through most of their history.[2]

As will be seen, speculation about women's status in ancient Sumer relies mainly on anachronistic texts that suggest an early period of peace and prosperity followed by population growth and more frequent disputes between expanding city-states that gradually called for permanent strongman leadership and professional armies and led to a weakening of status and freedoms for the female population.

Because there appear to have been similarities in the status and roles of women in ancient Egypt and earliest Sumer, we shall first examine those ancient cultures to discover what else they shared in common that would have influenced social developments and then move on, through time, to subsequent cultures in western Asia to demonstrate the downward trend in women's rights and responsibilities.

Several problems, however, confront the student of the ancient history of women: the nature of the source material, its availability, and distortions caused by the personal interests of modern researchers. Source material for the earliest historical period in Egypt and the ancient Near East consists mainly of written texts ranging from economic accounts to very brief tomb markers and personal seals. Later, lengthier texts appear on the monuments, but these usually reflect the deeds of gods or kings and throw little light on the concerns or careers of common women. Archeologists have tended to concentrate more on excavating palaces, temples, and royal tombs than on town sites which could yield more valuable testimony to the lives of ordinary people in antiquity. Philologists who translate texts often give first priority to resolving lexicographical and grammatical problems and seldom analyze the content of texts as thoroughly as one might wish to aid in furthering understanding of social history. These factors combined with the fragile nature of the written document itself has meant that much data from the past has not survived or is currently unavailable.

Fortunately, law codes survive from Sumer, Babylonia and Assyria and these reveal much about these societies' attitudes toward women as well as the extent of women's rights. Unfortunately, no law codes survive from ancient Egypt, so tax rolls, business and personal correspondence, wills and contracts as well as records of court testimony must be sifted for details about women's legal and social status. From all the areas, names with titles help draw a picture of women's involvement in religious, economic and social life.

Not only her legal status, but the visibility of the ancient woman interests us. Surely these are linked. A woman restricted by law and custom to her home and child care is often regarded as a legal minor with no control over property, no ability to earn wages, and seldom participates in the religious and social life of the nation to any great extent. Work outside the home, full obligations of citizenship, the right to marry and divorce as she wished, the ability to attain positions of authority over others—these reflect a liberal society where the dominance of men is limited. Such conditions prevailed in ancient Egypt and earliest Sumer.

EGYPT

Royal Women

The Egyptian woman's legal status equaled that of the men of her own social class, and starting at the highest level, in the royal family, women enjoyed positions of great prestige and power. While not always practiced consistently, in theory the right to succeed to the throne passed through the women of the royal family. Thus the king (considered an incarnation of the sky-god Horus) had to marry a princess of the royal blood known as the *Daughter of the God* because of her kingly father's acknowledged divinity. Often in the royal family brother married sister to keep the throne within the family. The king, however, could have more than one secondary wife and several concubines. The idea that the familial line of descent passed through the women of the family (matriliny) shows up frequently among African tribes and survived in the royal family because theology and tradition governed much of their life. One Fifth Dynasty list of kings records the names of mothers of the first kings of Egypt because of their role in succession.

Splendid tombs provide evidence of the high respect kings', mothers enjoyed. The golden furniture buried with Queen Hetepheres from her tomb alongside the great pyramid of her son Khufu of the Fourth Dynasty (ca. 2590 B.C.) demonstrates this queen's importance in the realm. Thousands of years later, chronicles in the Roman period identified Nitokerty, who reigned as female pharaoh at the end of the Old Kingdom (2686–2181 B.C.), as being the most beautiful and bravest woman of her age. Another queen, at the end of the Fifth Dynasty, seems to have owned a very large pyramid complex. This now-nameless queen had also probably attempted to reign alone after the death of her husband Djedkare-Isesi. Royal women did not dwell secluded in harems but took an active role in court life, assuming the duties of regents if their husbands died before the heir apparent came of age.

In the Old Kingdom the administration of Egypt was mainly in the hands of the ruler, so the entire royal family—including the wife, mother, and daughters of the king—occupied administrative positions. The women had religious functions and officiated as priestesses in the cults of major deities like Thoth and Hathor. A number of goddesses ranked high in the pantheon, among these the embodiment of the two regions of Egypt, the embodiment of the heavens, of the throne, and of justice. Indeed, the queen was the living image of the goddess Hathor and the goddess, the embodiment of the royal house, provided legitimacy for the ruler. Other high-born ladies called *possessors of reverence* held positions as priestesses in cults of the goddesses Hathor, Nut, and Neith.

At times queens became involved in political intrigue. A conspiracy against the crown implicating the queen took place in the reign of Pepi I (ca. 2300 B.C.). Once discovered, the King's Wife and Great of Scepter, Intes, was privately investigated by a judge and one other official. This plot against Pepi came to nothing, but Amenemhet I, founder of the Twelfth Dynasty (1991–1786 B.C.) did apparently die, in 1962 B.C., in an assassination plot hatched in his harem. His son later claimed that "women had marshalled the ranks" against him.

TABLE 2-1
Comparative Chronologies for the Ancient Near East

EGYPT	SUMER	AKKAD	BABYLON	ASSYRIA	ISRAEL
First dynasty 3100–2890 B.C.	Proto-historic period 3100–2700 B.C.				
Second dynasty 2890–2686					
Old Kingdom	**Early Dynastic Period**				
Third dynasty 2686–2613	First dynasty of Kish ca. 2700 B.C.				
Fourth dynasty 2613–2498	Third dynasty of Kish ca. 2450 B.C.				
Fifth dynasty 2494–2345					
Sixth dynasty 2345–2181	Urukagina of Lagash ca. 2378	Sargon 2378–2316			
First Intermediate Period 2181–2030	Third Dynasty of Ur. ca. 2100–2000 B.C.				
Middle Kingdom 2030–1786	**Isin-Larsa Period** ca. 2000–1800	Amorites in Syria-Palestine	**Old Babylonia** Hammurabi 1792–1750	Trading colonies Shamshi-Ada ca. 1800	
Second Intermediate period 1786–1567				**Mari** Zimri-Lin ca. 1780	

TABLE 2-1 (continued)

EGYPT	SUMER	AKKAD	BABYLON	ASSYRIA	ISRAEL
New Kingdom					
Eighteenth dynasty 1567–1320				**Middle Assyria**	
Nineteenth dynasty 1320–1200			Kadeshman-Enil II 1279–1265 B.C.	Shalmaneser I 1274–1245	Exodus ca. 1250
Twentieth dynasty 1200–1085					Judges ca. 1200
Third Intermediate Period 1085–664					David 1000–960
					Solomon 960–930
Saite Period			**Neo Babylonia**		
Twenty-sixth dynasty 664–610			Nebuchadrezzar II ca. 630 B.C.		
Alexander's conquest 323 B.C.					
Ptolemaic rule 305–30 B.C.					

SOURCE: After The Cambridge Ancient History, Third Edition, Volumes 1:2–3:1 (Cambridge: Cambridge University Press, 1971–1982). Reprinted by permission of the publishers.

Common Women

Women among the commoners assumed roles outside the home. Tomb murals of the Old Kingdom portray unveiled women selling products and food in the marketplace. Women appear in harvest scenes working beside men and forming long lines of laden basket carriers. Egyptians apparently did not characterize women as the "weaker sex," so women could be called up by the state for labor service, apparently as part of the tax program. Women not only gathered but also winnowed wheat and handpicked flax, spun it into thread, and wove it into linen cloth used for everything from ship's sails to bedlinens and clothing. The servant statues from the Old Kingdom tombs show women at kitchen tasks—brewing beer and grinding wheat for flour. Household accounts of an Egyptian farm in 2000 B.C. reveal that *all* members of one family received wages for the work they performed, adult men *and* women receiving *equal* amounts, youths less.[3] We note respect for the intelligence of women, even those of humble birth. A didactic text attributed to Ptahhotep, a Fifth Dynasty vizier (prime minister) observed that "eloquence is rarer than malachite, yet may be found in the mouths of maidservants at the grindstone."[4]

It appears that the equality between men and women, including husband and wife, expressed in the portraiture of the age existed as well on the practical level of inheritance, wages, and employment. As early as the Third Dynasty we have a legal text showing that a mother who possessed considerable property willed it to both her sons and daughters and needed no male cosigner of the document to make it legal.[5] A daughter could succeed to her father's position in certain lines of work. For instance, a mortuary priest, who earned his living from the endowments left by deceased persons for the maintenance of their tombs, passed on his position to sons and daughters alike.

Political and Social Changes

The Egyptians depended upon their divine ruler to uphold *ma^cat:* the essence of justice and right order in the kingdom and in nature itself. With the belief that their king could magically ensure the desired annual flood of the Nile and rich harvests, the Egyptians felt themselves a secure and elect people, indeed the only true human beings on earth. Fearing little, they accomplished much. Yet the energetic and self-confident society of the Old Kingdom, which had flourished under the divine kings for several centuries, suffered a collapse, caused in part by climatic changes in Africa in the third millennium. Calamities discredited the god-king and his magical powers to control the Nile and ensure plenty. The centralized government broke down and near anarchy reigned for a time; the nation splintered into several feudal states from 2181 to 2040 B.C. If we can believe the contemporary observer,

Ipuwer, this precipitated many social changes to the disadvantage of the old aristocracy, including the redistribution of land to landless farmers. Actually, political power had already broadened in the late Fifth Dynasty when an expanding civil service required leaders from outside the ranks of the king's family.

Egypt survived this First Intermediate Period, with its breakdown of law and order and the loss of fortunes, but the Middle Kingdom that followed was a changed society. The provincial governors had power and wealth and built fine tombs in their home towns and commissioned life-sized statues for themselves and their wives in the style of royalty. Even lower-class women and men could acquire the proper religious books and coffins to share in the afterlife, once the prerogative of royalty. The provincial governors also imitated royalty by tracing the inheritance of their local rule through the women of their family line.

Women in the Workforce

During this period there are more records of women in professional positions. On the grand private estates of the Middle Kingdom, women held such positions of responsibility as major domo and treasurer. Although, in general fewer administrative titles appear in the documentary records of Middle Kingdom than those of the large central government of the Old Kingdom, several titles are recorded that were held in common by both sexes: one such was that of "scribe", suggesting that some women were literate; "reciter" also numbers among the positions for women in wealthy households. The title *Nb.t Pr,* "mistress of the house," appears as the title for housewives, and a title translated as citizen, *ᶜankh n niw.t,* is believed to designate a freewoman. Actually slavery was so far quite limited in Egypt and slaves were generally foreigners captured by or sold to Egyptians. Women could contend in court (the sage Ptahhotep warns against contending with one's wife in court) and one Middle Kingdom woman even sued her own father.

More women held actual priestly titles in the Middle Kingdom than at any other time. Their titles include those of "prophet" and "purified-one," shared with male clerics. Similar to the royal family, priestly families of the Middle Kingdom reserved important administrative posts for their own womenfolk. The sisters of a High Priest of Ptah bore the titles of directors of works and held positions of real authority. Women continued to serve as funerary priests, conserving and expending endowments set up for the maintenance of tombs.[6]

Common women, along with men, were subject to the temporary enforced labor service for the state and sometimes they rebelled. One document from the Middle Kingdom (ca. 2000 B.C.) records the case of a daughter of a scribe (certainly not a peasant) liable for this enforced labor who ran away from her duties and became a fugitive. The unpopularity of the annually demanded stint of labor caused the ancient Egyptians to try to prevent its imposition at least in the next life beyond the grave (a life they hoped would be better than their life on earth) by having servant statues and later small mummiform figurines called "answerers" to substitute for them on any required labor service.[7]

Although it may have been distasteful to some women, public labor for the state would have been the strongest determining factor in the status of the Egyptian woman, for it assured her role as an equally productive member of society. Recognized by her state as a full adult, with the same obligations as a man, the Egyptian woman did not become subordinated to her menfolk or restricted to life in the private domicile. Kin were seized by the state when either a man or woman ran away from this *corvée*. The practice of taking hostages indicates official recognition of the close-knit character of the Egyptian family, evidenced in a happier way by the numerous tomb art scenes of whole families hunting, fishing, playing, and feasting together.

Although the government was intrusive, in many ways, it did not provide welfare services, or so it might be inferred from the boasts by local governors and men of high standing of charitable deeds towards widows and orphans. We do know that during this period the kings of the Twelfth Dynasty gradually seized more power and became masters of a tightly organized state once again and diminished the power and wealth of the great provincial families. Commoners did not lose gains in the religious sphere, however.

Royal Women in the Middle and New Kingdoms

The Great Royal Wife continued to be regarded as the great heiress and, in theological terms, the embodiment of the goddess Hathor. Amenemhet III's queen was entombed in a pyramid that rivaled her husband's in size and Sobekneferu, a queen of the Thirteenth Dynasty, ruled alone as king at the end of that period (1789–1786 B.C.).

In the New Kingdom (1567–1085 B.C.), queens achieved an apogee of power and possessed great wealth in the form of extensive estates and their own palaces. The Great Royal Wife often lived apart from her husband and some of the most prominent men of the kingdom served her as stewards, tutors, and advisors. Pharaoh would have had to travel to his consort's palace if he wished her company. As one male scholar has commented: "Here was matriliny and matrilocal residence with a vengeance!"[8]

Political life was closed to common women, but royal women played a particularly important role in the Eighteenth Dynasty, the beginning of the New Kingdom. The founder of this dynasty, King Ahmose (1554–1529 B.C.) left a monumental inscription honoring his grandmother and exhorting his subjects to render gratitude to his mother, Queen Ahhotep, for her vital leadership role in the war of liberation against the Hyksos (foreign invaders who for a time had ruled Egypt). Apparently Aḥḥotep had rallied the Egyptian soldiers to keep up their fight after her first son Kamose fell in battle. Queen Aḥḥotep was buried with ceremonial weapons and military medals. Her daughter-in-law, Aḥmose-Nefertari, received great honors and bore the title Female Chieftain of Upper and Lower Egypt. She probably ruled as regent for her son, but we no longer can assess the extent of her power. Queen Aḥḥotep was the first queen to bear the important religious title "God's Wife." The title made the queen a full-fledged priestess in the cult of the King of the Gods, Amun–Re, at the great temple at Karnak, which would be adorned and added to by subsequent rulers for the next 1000 years. She participated in temple ritual alongside the male priests and took an interest in building projects. She may have functioned as the king's representative on the scene and for this she received an endowment in land and other property. Queen Aḥmose-Nefertari who inherited the God's Wife title had a temple dedicated to her and received worship as a goddess for generations at a village of workers on the royal tombs located across the river from Karnak. She and her son were considered as the founders of the community.

A great ruler in the spirit of Nefertari emerged in the person of Hatshepsut. Hatshepsut was the sole surviving child of the great warrior-king Thutmose I and his Great Royal Wife Aḥmose. She had reasons for feeling a stronger right to rule than her husband, Thutmose II, who possessed a less illustrious lineage on his mother's side. Upon his death Hatshepsut shared the throne as Regent for the young Thutmose III, but after she obtained wide support from the powerful men of her father's reign and from her own ministers and servants, she assumed the full regalia and power of king.

Increasing Power for Royal Women

Hatshepsut vigorously continued the policies of her father to strengthen Egypt's defenses and bolstered its economy through trading expeditions to foreign lands. Contemporary texts tell of her leading Egyptian armies south into Nubia to secure that southern flank (and ensure the flow of Africa's tribute into Egypt). Her brilliant reign saw the improvement of Egypt's landscape by many splendid building projects including her impressive terraced temple, Deir el Bahri, the greatest surviving monument from antiquity to a woman. Hatshepsut originally intended that her only child and daughter Neferure succeed her as king, but when the girl died Hatshepsut bowed to political expediency and accepted Thutmose III as her heir. She allowed him control of the army, which did not disturb their cooperative arrangement. Years after his stepmother's death, however, Thutmose attempted to destroy the memory of the woman who had kept him so long in the shadows by chiseling her figure from the wall reliefs which decorate her temples.

Four generations later the title of God's Wife had fallen into disuse, but another outstanding female personality appeared in the palace. Tiy, the daughter of commoners, became the Chief Royal Wife of Amenhotep III. The apparently love-smitten king had his wife portrayed with him in equally colossal statuary groups; Tiy's sculpted image became an object of its own cult in a temple constructed by him. Significant state documents reveal that Tiy was involved in the conduct of foreign affairs and matters of state, corresponding with foreign rulers among Egypt's allies.

Then into Egypt's history stepped Tiy's daughter-in-law, the famous and beautiful Nefertiti, wife of the so-called heretic king Akhenaten. Akhenaten went further than any other pharaoh in publicizing the close and loving relationship between himself and his family and in demonstrating support for his wife's new role in the political and religious innovations of this reign. The pharaoh, his queen and their six daughters were depicted at worship, on the reviewing stand, and even in scenes of private life. Intimate scenes of family life and affection became standard fare for the royal artists. Early in the reign Nefertiti appeared on temple walls in monarchical style officiating at altars either with the king or alone, suggesting co-rule. Later Nefertiti appears portrayed in traditional kingly regalia, brandishing a scimitar over a cowering foreign captive or driving alone in her chariot. Not only buildings but boats plying the Nile carried such scenes for all the populace to see that king and queen shared the stewardship of Egypt. Increasingly the evidence suggests Nefertiti served, not as a queen consort, but a queen regnant, and finally as successor to her husband as Pharaoh Smenkhkare.

Such political power for queens was destined to be short-lived, however, and a backlash occurred, precipitated by Nefertiti's third daughter. Widowed by Pharaoh Tutankhamun, she tried to stay in command of Egypt by means of an unprecedented political and personal alliance with a prince of the far-off powerful kingdom of the Hittites, Egypt's chief rival in the Near East. The discovery of this plot before it succeeded had unhappy consequences for the ambitious queen, diminishing the glory of the formidably feminine Eighteenth Dynasty. As if in response, some Nineteenth Dynasty literati wrote satirical pieces which reflect badly on the character of highly placed women. Still, Ramses II (1304–1237 B.C.) honored his queen Nefertari with a lovely temple at Abu Simbel, adorned by colossal images of the royal couple, and at the end of that dynasty another queen, Tausert, reigned as pharaoh.[9]

Women in Politics

Denied actual positions in the State's bureaucracy, New Kingdom women had to resort to plots and rebellions to make a political impact. In the Twentieth Dynasty palace women retained their ambitions and their influence with others. A harem conspiracy ended the life and the thirty-year reign of Ramses III. Three papyri documents tell of this plot and the investigation into it. They tell of highly placed men who conspired with a secondary queen named Tiy and other women of the harem who remained unnamed. An Overseer of the Treasury and Chief of the Chamber, both men, apparently carried messages for the women of the harem to their mothers and brothers urging them to gather and incite groups of people to rebellion. One woman seems to have written to her brother, a troop commander in Nubia, asking him to return to Egypt and attempt a military insurrection. After the plot's discovery, some or all of the harem women must have escaped detention because members of the official board of inquiry tracked them down and then caroused with them (literally: "made a beer hall with them") bringing severe penalties upon themselves after discovery.[10]

The last years of Ramses III's reign had been wracked with internal problems and occasional breakdowns in central authority. Records show that ordinary women participated in the first labor strike in recorded history against this government on behalf of their civil servant husbands. From about the same time comes a record of a highly placed woman in religious circles plotting with a general in the murder of two troublesome policemen.

Women in Religious Life

There seem to have been fewer women in high clerical positions during the New Kingdom. Growing specializations in many walks of life mark this period of the Egyptian empire and would have effected male employment patterns as well. However, many ordinary women did take an active role in religious activities, many proudly recording their comparatively low ranking positions in the temple hierarchies. One concludes that almost every Egyptian woman participated in a temple cult. Egyptian life focused on religion at all class levels and women obtained ritual importance without apparent regard for their social status. Unmarried women and the wives of the humblest craftsmen performed as musician priestesses who entertained the deities and provided accompaniment for the religious rituals.

At more elevated ranks, the wives of the temple priests at the major shrines had some ritual functions and administrative responsibilities. The wife of the First Prophet of the "King of the Gods" at Karnak bore the title "Chief Concubine of Amon Re." The more common title of "Songstress of Amon" fell to the wives of lesser-ranking prophets in the same temple. Eventually the top hierarchy expanded and a few exalted ladies simultaneously held the rank of Chief Concubine, and a superior held the new title of "First

Chief Concubine." The position of god's concubine involved no actual sexual responsibilities. Only respectable married women held the position, which carried administrative responsibilities for the temple and its vast estates. Some records show these women clerics acting authoritatively in the greater community too. For instance, one tells of a Chief Concubine acting on behalf of those civil servants in the royal necropolis who had not received their government pay regularly and who went on strike to protest the fact. "Knowing women," diviners, played some community role too, and civil disputes in the Egyptian community may occasionally have been settled by appeals to them.[11]

Women in Economic Life

We find plentiful documentation of secular activities for the common woman in the New Kingdom period. Tomb scenes show women traders in the market place in increasing numbers. Women still labored in the fields and labor service for the state still existed. Larger textile workshops now thrived, producing some of the finest cambric ever woven. Women not only staffed but supervised these workshops, which were often located on the estates of the queens. Only agriculture surpassed the textile industry's importance in Egypt's economy. The fine cloth produced was used as temple offerings to the gods and diplomatic gifts by the crown. Women labored in the perfume manufacturing industry, some as supervisors, and filled jobs in the wig workshops as well. Besides jobs in industry, women supervised dining halls, performed as dancers and musicians in music halls and at private parties, and hired out as professional mourners at the elaborate funerals Egyptians loved. Many scenes of festive banquets adorn Eighteenth Dynasty tomb walls, and show both men and women guests in attendance.

Education

The vigorous imperialistic foreign policy of the New Kingdom pharaohs brought numbers of war captives into Egypt where they worked as slaves, not only on the royal and temple estates, but also in private households. This contributed to an increase in leisure time for men and women, which probably fostered the growth of literacy. Schools began teaching the colloquial language that is known to us as Late Egyptian. This placed reading within the grasp of more people, and it has been recently pointed out that tomb scenes portray wealthy ladies of the period with writing equipment near their chairs as if to emphasize their literacy.[12]

Sex and Marriage

Literature, such as the love poetry which appeared for the first time, now reflected women in a different light. Many of the love songs express women's own very frank words suggesting a free mingling of the sexes outside of, or prior to, marriage. A class of wealthy and literate knights developed in the Eighteenth Dynasty, some of whom composed courtly love poetry with a lady as object of veneration. Adoration and respect for high-ranking women may also be seen in a letter written by an officer to his deceased wife. In this he recalls to her how his young charioteers used to come and prostrate themselves before her and bring her many pretty gifts. The husband also tells his wife that, in proof of his devotion to her memory, he has abstained from sexual relations for three years after her death.[13]

Tomb scenes of naked serving girls and entertainers at banquets, erotic papyri and some documents of daily life seem to indicate that the Egyptians of the New Kingdom tolerated, even encouraged, free sexual expression. Yet homosexuality was condemned and the death penalty threatened both participants in adultery. Still, documents show that divorce more often than prosecution followed adultery.

How free were Egyptians to marry whom they pleased? The love lyrics recording the sentiments of women run the whole spectrum of emotions—bold and sensual, confused and wistful. These women's songs suggest a free mingling of young men and women prior to marriage: love affairs with the boy next door and secret trysts in a garden or field. Virginity mattered little in arranging marriage. Couples were brought together by the "Golden One of Women," the goddess Hathor, patroness of love and joy. Love songs contain prayers and entreaties that the boy who won the heart might be given the hand as well, with the proviso that one's mother concur. Men's prayers beseached the goddess for a pretty wife.

In New Kingdom times, the sage Any went beyond traditional sentiments about wives' importance as a source of heirs by pointing out that women also have skills and feelings which must be respected:

> Do not control your wife in her house
> When you know that she is excellent
> Do not say to her "where is it? Bring (it)!"
> When (she) has put it in the best place
> Behold her proficiency![14]

Here a prominent moulder of public opinion is upholding a long-established official view of the equal worth of male and female Egyptians. He further urged generous support for mothers, noting their devotion to their children's physical and mental development. Census lists of women and men generally included the names of both parents, but sometimes only the mother's name. Marriage among commoners was monogamous.

As early as the New Kingdom there were two kinds of marriage in Egypt—formal, with a marriage document, and common law, involving only cohabitation. Copies of marriage contracts survive from only the late New Kingdom and on, but it seems certain that the property settlements documented in these marriages resemble features from earlier times. Sometimes a deed of marriage dated from years after a couple had lived together and brought children into the world; such a document could serve as important proof of a settlement on behalf of the wife and her children. Thus the rights of those children would be protected after their mother's death against the claims of any other progeny of their father. A grandmother's marriage document might serve years later as proof of a family's rightful claim to property. Two documents, each concerning settlement of a wife's property, survive from the Twentieth Dynasty. In the first, a husband makes a settlement of his own property on his wife at the time of their marriage. In case of his death or their divorce, his wife will be able to keep this property. The second document concerns the case of a father who has settled two-thirds of his estate upon his daughter on the occasion of her marriage. She and her husband shared this property but later divorced, and the woman retained half of the settlement, although her father feels she should have received more.

A woman generally brought to a marriage some property (land or movable goods) and she, or her parents, received a "bundle" brought by the groom that may have played the role of a traditional male dowry. The woman then moved into a new house with her husband. Sages exhorted young men not to marry until they could afford a home of their own, so young married couples would not reside within the husband's parental home. The wife shared everything acquired by the husband and inherited one-third of the estate upon his death with children receiving two-thirds. If no children survived, a husband could "adopt" his wife legally to make her his sole heir and recipient of his entire estate.

Up until the Twenty-sixth Dynasty (ca. 660 B.C.) parents, at least technically, arranged their daughters' marriages, but thereafter bride and groom entered into the bond themselves. Sometimes, the bride received a gift from the groom and sometimes she went to the groom with presents from her family. In still another, presumably later, arrangement, the bride herself presented her intended with "money to become a wife." The most advantageous arrangement for the bride developed around 563 B.C. with the s^{c}nh deed, which obligated the husband to provide a regular income for his wife. She gave him a substantial sum, repayable on demand, and as security the husband pledged his entire wealth. Such a marriage could not terminate without the wife's agreement. This may have been the policy which horrified a Greek traveler in Egypt in the first century B.C., Diodorus Siculus, who shook a disapproving head over the state of marriage among the Egyptians when he told his readers "the wife lords it over the husband, as in the deed about the dower, the men agree to obey the wife in everything." (Diod. 1,27,2)

Either the man or woman could initiate divorce. If the wife initiated it, she could still receive support from the husband even though she left his house. If the husband repudiated his wife, except in cases of adultery, the law compelled him to grant her that part of his wealth that had been pledged upon marriage to her.

Legal Rights and Social Status

Women enjoyed equal rights with men throughout Egyptian history: a married woman maintained her status as a completely independent legal personality and did not render up her rights to her husband upon marriage. She did not need a male cosignatory when she witnessed documents, executed her own last testament, inherited, bought, administered or sold property, freed slaves, adopted children, or sued. She also testified in court, even in the highest courts of the land. The practice of sons and daughters sharing equally in an inheritance continued, but a mother could leave out any children who did not look after her in old age.

In addition to her interest in her husband's estate, a married woman could own property and have an income (inherited from her parents or previous husband or earned as the result of her own labors or investments) and she had the right to administer or dispose of it. Surviving documents tell of a widow selling her house, another pledging her house as security for a loan, still another leasing out her property. Women might loan money, buy or sell slaves or land and all managed without the need for any male cosignatory.

After the conquest of Egypt by Alexander the Great in 323 B.C., two parallel legal systems functioned in the country—the original Egyptian and the imported Greek. One crucial difference between the two was that under the Egyptian system a woman held the same position as the Egyptian man while under the Greek system a woman required a guardian in order to perform many legal acts. Whether in the market place, at labor service, on the picket line, or at social events, the Egyptian woman, throughout her history, took her place beside her menfolk. Herodotus, the so-called father of history, who traveled to Egypt in the mid-fifth century B.C., was so struck by the oddity of seeing women in public that he scoffed:

The Egyptians themselves, in their manners and customs, seem to have reversed the ordinary practices of mankind. For instance, women attend market and are employed in trade, while men stay at home and do the weaving.

HERODOTUS, HISTORIES II, 35

It is clear that the Egyptian woman continued to enjoy a basic equality with men regardless of differences in work or occupation.

Yet such equality *should* have changed, if we are to believe the materialistic theory of Friedrich Engels which directly links women's status to the economic organization of a society and traces decline in woman's status to the rise in the importance of significant private property such as herds and land. Women's status did *not* change markedly over the millennia in Egypt even though private property became more widely distributed. Several factors seem to have contributed to the Egyptian woman's equal status including the basic optimistic and secure outlook of that people; preservation and respect for age-old traditions; and the state's official view that women could be depended upon to perform useful work for the greater society outside the home.

Conclusion

In retrospect, the ancient Egyptian woman stands out as the first documented example of relative liberation. Although not totally equal, these ancient women provide important precedents for today's goals: they achieved equal pay for equal work; independent and equal legal status; and equal opportunity in many kinds of work, including opportunities for leadership positions with authority over others.

On the other hand, one finds disappointing evidence that when women gained control of the supreme power in the land, resentment arose, manifested in attempts to erase the memory of that female rule. The Fifth Dynasty's ruined pyramid complex of an unknown queen; the defacement of Hatshepsut's monuments; the official eradication of Nefertiti's memory — these demonstrate the threat men felt when women took power in the political arena and strove to fill roles traditionally played by men. These Egyptian women ruled during relatively secure times, while other women pharaohs were allowed to take command in times of crisis, perhaps when no man wished for responsibilities in what seemed impossible economic or political situations. It is gratifying to find women at the helm in the Egyptian state, but one must recall that ancient Egypt's history is 3000 years long, and the female examples of pharaonic rule remain in the minority.

Egypt endured as a practical and successful civilization for so long that the amount of source material for it far exceeds that from the shorter-lived civilizations of Sumer, Old Babylonia, or Assyria. With the possible exception of the people of the Old Testament, far more attention has been paid by scholars to reconstructing Egypt's society than to the others. Sumerologists and Assyriologists have extensive archives of texts preserved on indestructable clay tablets, but very few of these texts have been published with an eye to analysis of social issues. Thus neither a clear nor total picture of women's status has yet emerged.

SUMER

Introduction

The scarcity of records and the personal predilections of researchers plague those who would attempt to reconstruct ancient Sumerian society. Although scholars have already translated thousands of more than a half million surviving tablets from Sumer and the later civilizations of western Asia, very few Sumerologists and Assyriologists have, until recently, begun to analyze this material for what it can reveal about social conditions and traditions, particularly as these pertained to women, and still fewer have published on these topics. The British scholar P.R.S. Moorey explains in a reappraisal of the rich tombs discovered by Sir Leonard Wooley at Ur that "we still know too little of family relationships within the Early Dynastic Sumerian ruling families, of the nature of their marriages, of their lines of inheritance, of the distribution of ranks, titles and religious offices, and their precise contemporary terminology, confidently to analyse the sociology of the royal tombs."[16] Theories have been put forth on the basis of scant evidence or imperfectly understood material. The reconstruction of the status of women in earliest Sumerian society presented here is thus tentative.

The aboriginal inhabitants had already developed agriculture, weaving, pottery, and metallurgy when the Sumerians, speaking a different language (somewhat similar to Ural-Altaic languages) migrated into the valleys of the lower Tigris and Euphrates from some point near the Caspian Sea. Semitic-speaking people were also present quite early, perhaps dominating the trade that already thrived between the towns and the outside world. The earliest word for "trader" in Sumerian documents is Semitic. Once the Sumerians arrived in the second half of the fourth millennium B.C., a "fruitful fusion" with the native peoples brought about the essential creative spark which ignited one of the world's two earliest civilizations, bringing into being monumental architecture, economic and political organization, and a system of writing.

Economic/Political/Religious Organization

As did Egypt, Sumer had an agrarian economy and both sexes probably worked at farming, fishing and birdcatching. Individual city-states developed out of the early villages founded even before the Sumerians migrated into the fertile plain.

Life in the individual city-states originally centered on the temple of the local deity with its large establishment of offices, workshops, storerooms, and kitchens near to the shrines and residence of the god. Women worked alongside men in serving their divine patron. Kingship did not exist in early Sumer; instead leaders, when needed in times of crisis, were elected for the duration of the crisis by a bicameral congress of free men (nobles and commoners). Continuous moral leadership fell to the priests and priestesses of the god or goddess of the city-state.

Women in Religious Life

Female priestesses served male deities and vice-versa. A monumental vase from Uruk, dating to the Early Dynastic Period (2900–2500 B.C.), shows a long line of male tribute bearers before an exalted lady; probably the attendants on that city's goddess Inanna. Nothing comparable in Sumerian art honors a male figure. At Ur the richest of the so-called royal graves, which feature the remains of numerous male and female retainers slain to accompany their deceased mistress, probably belong to the priestesses who served Ur's moon god Nanna. While human sacrifice may have been peculiar to this cult at Ur, the need to prepare the dead for an effective existence after life may also be seen in the objects left in the "chariot graves" at Kish, another early city-state in Sumer.

The elaborate graves of these ranking women at Ur clearly show their predominance in that early state where cult and daily life were tightly intermeshed. From an Early Dynastic temple in the Diyala region comes an assemblage of statues of worshipful people, both women and men, showing that ordinary women mingled with men in the temple worship. The wide-eyed, intent statues of these devout worshippers represent well a people still believing earnestly in the justice and saving power of their gods.

Women in the Economy

Many people in the city-state, both men and women, worked for the temple and its resident deity, and the temple in its turn supported the skilled artisans and craftspeople. Women worked in the kitchens and flour mills, breweries and textile workshops and participated in the cult of the deity as musicians and singers.

Not everyone worked for the temple however. That private property emerged early on is clear from deeds of sale of both fields and houses. Private land holdings appeared among all classes of society; even the humblest owned houses and gardens, although land belonging to ordinary citizens actually belonged to the larger family unit rather than to any individual member. Large family clans held and administered their own property. They often chose a single representative of the family (not necessarily its head) to look after their interests in the property holdings.[17]

Marriage

Once property became an issue, marriage became an economic concern for the clan or family and a bethrothal, arranged by parents, was often consumated officially by a contract inscribed on a tablet. However, a Sumerian proverb speaks of a young girl having the right to choose her own spouse, and love songs suggest freedom of association between young men and women, as in Egypt. Other texts reveal that an older woman, as a legal adult, could marry the man of her own choice. A poem illustrates the Sumerian marriage ceremony, in which a young woman opens the door of her parental house to the groom accompanied by his best man. She receives a gift of jewelry from the groom and a dowry from her parents. The Gilgamesh Epic describes a feast with cakes to celebrate a marriage. A woman could be divorced on very slim grounds, however, and, if she did not bear children her husband was allowed to take a second wife.[18]

In other respects, a woman in Sumer had certain legal rights equivalent to the men of her society. She might own property, engage in business, and act as a witness for legal documents. As private property increased, however, so did debts. The temple, a source of financing, made loans at high interest, and many people went too deeply into debt. To pay off those debts, parents often resorted to selling their children into slavery to the temple for up to three years of labor. Daughters were more often liable to be so sold, because a son was expected to train for and inherit his father's trade and was therefore more essential to the family's future.

Women in Political Life

As changes in the economy seriously effected women's freedom, so did changes in political life. War became increasingly common among the Sumerian city-states as population increased, which resulted in increases in disputes over water and boundary rights. Increasing crises brought about a demand for a permanent and strong leadership, and kingship as a permanent institution soon appeared in Kish, then in Uruk and Ur. Once monarchy appeared, royal women helped legitimate the king's succession to the throne. Lists of rulers compiled later remain the only historical records of the earliest reigns, but in some of the oldest cities the highest office holders were listed, along with their fathers *and* their wives. A ruler of Umma claimed that city by virtue of his marriage to the daughter of a previous ruler. Two successive queens of Lagash held their own court and had their own ministers and attendants. They dated documents by the year of their own reigns (as kings did), and one of these queens kept up a diplomatic exchange with the king's wife of another city-state. Each had her own official seals, as did the queens of Ur. Each managed her own estates and took part in public and religious events.[19]

The first woman ruler known in history—Ku-baba—ruled the city of Kish in its Third Dynasty (ca. 2450 B.C.). That she began her career as a tavern keeper or "ale-wife" indicates, not only the existence of private enterprise for women but also the height to which an ordinary woman could rise within her community.

Political Changes

The emergence of permanent kingship in response to continuing crises in time changed ordinary women's status in Sumer. First, the largest proportion of the land came to belong to the nobility of princes and palace administrators and priests. Eventually temple holdings and the property of priests was bought up by the royal dynasties until the houses and fields of the king, the royal harem and the palace nursery "crowded each other side to side." Royalty grew in wealth and abused its tax-gathering privileges. Originally a permanent kingship presented the best solution to the security problems of the city-state. Before long, however, the citizens' militia gave way to a standing army loyal to the king, supplied with a heavily armed chariotry, and supported by a regular system of tax collecting. Next private property became more heavily taxed and the crown appropriated temple lands to support the king and his expensive policies. Although acceded to with little reluctance in time of war, this heavy taxation grew unpopular as it became permanent. The redistribution of wealth which ensued led to sharp social stratification and ultimately to a class struggle. The class of commoners were reduced to the status of clients of the palace or a nobleman's estate, and some free citizens were reduced to debt slavery. The king and queen now supervised the administration of the local temple and managed the estates of its deity.

Fortunately, a good ruler, in the person of Urukagina of Lagash, arose. He determined to re-establish "divine law" or a just way of conducting the affairs of his kingdom. He removed tax collectors and unjust administrators and gave the temples back their old lands. Under his reforms, citizens imprisoned for debts went free and the desperate plight of orphans and widows received the king's attention. Among his reform statements there is an enigmatic reference to women having once had two husbands at a time, a practice he now prohibits. This reference conjures up visions of unusual sexual freedoms permitted to women in earlier Sumerian society, but this same king also passed a severe penalty against women saying certain evil words to men.[20]

Fall of the Goddesses

Growing restrictions upon women in Sumerian society correspond to the loss of prestige for the originally powerful and important female deities. In the beginning She had created the gods and the universe, She being the goddess Nammu. So deity in Sumer had never been all-male. However, once lists of deities were drawn up She no longer received first ranking, and theologians turned her originally vast powers as goddess of the sea over to her son Enki. Nammu's daughter Ki, the "Mother Earth," also underwent a gradual decline in rank, losing top billing altogether and slipping to third place in the pantheon and finally down to fourth place. Fortunately, myths survive in which Mother Earth dominates and shows herself to be a stronger personality than her nearest male rival. Although their importance was downplayed by chauvinistic theologians, Nammu and Ki retained their people's loyalty and continued to be worshipped. Other goddesses also survived in the popular worship, such as Nidaba, patroness of learning, and Bau, goddess of medicine and healing. Bau, who originally held a higher rank than her divine spouse, matched other goddesses such as Nanshe of the city state of Lagash, who was the judge of all mankind at the start of every new year. None rivalled the great goddess Inanna (later identified with the more warlike Semitic goddess Ishtar) the "queen of Heaven" about whom many myths, epics, and hymns were woven. This goddess was a superwoman—by turns brave, crafty, and tempestuous; then loving, desirable, and gracious. It was Inanna, the personification of female sexuality, whom the ruler would embrace at the annual sacred marriage rite that ensured the ongoing fertility of nature and the continuance of the human race.[21]

Why, one must ask, when goddesses were ascribed such a vital role in creation and in the continuance of the race, were they accorded less importance by the scribes and theologians—the intelligentsia of the time? The answer lies in the changing value system of the society. As the strong-armed male warrior replaced the benign and devout farmer in society's estimation of its most vital citizens, esteem for women slipped too. Women may enjoy equality of purpose and importance in an agricultural society, but Sumer was fast becoming an urban and militaristic society in which trade and private property were the major concerns of most of the population. Woman could not bear arms, but in times of crisis needed to stay at home tending the children, the sick, and the wounded. They could not defend the city or defend their family's private property. Thus women's status slipped to that of dependents, to be protected along with property by a professional military elite.

Women of Akkad

The reformer Urukagina in time fell victim to the imperialistic ambitions of the ruler of the state of Umma, and this strongman was in turn conquered by the first true empire-builder in world history—Sargon of the Semitic city of Akkad to the north of Sumer. He ushered in a number of social, religious, and artistic changes that had lasting significance in the ancient Near East. We know little about this Sargon or how he accomplished his successes, although he seems to have had a high regard for women and goddesses, at least Ishtar, whom he credited for his rise to power. He showed an enlightened attitude toward his daughter, Enheduanna, whom he appointed as chief priestess of the gods at Ur and at Uruk. Sargon entrusted her not only with high religious responsibilities but also with representing his authority in conquered territory and thus sealing the cultural and political union of the Akkadians and Sumerians.[22]

An intelligent woman who took her position seriously, the princess became proficient in the Sumerian language. She may have written at least two great cycles of Sumerian hymns and started a collection of Babylonian hymns dedicated to her father's patron goddess Ishtar. One Sumerologist called her "the first systematic theologian." As demanded by her office, the priestess-princess remained celibate, but the practice of kings sharing responsibility with these royal princesses continued for many years in Sumer and Akkad. Priestesses outlasted some rulers and proved to be a force for continuity and unity in the realm by confirming the legitimacy of new rulers. Thirteen royal priestesses followed Enheduanna over the next 500 years. Each held the office for life.

Women in Late Sumerian Society

Sargon's Akkadian empire did not long outlast him, but eventually Sumer enjoyed a renaissance of power with its Third Dynasty of Ur where absolute kings soon styled themselves as divine and had chapels built to their cults. The Crown now owned the temple lands and self-government faded to a minimum. Numerous war captives, including women, labored on great construction projects and received only meagre rations. At the same time, the Third Dynasty kings affirmed, as did Urukagina before them, their responsibility for protecting widows and orphans and the poor. One wonders whether these often-expressed good intentions ever delivered, and why, in a culture of the extended and clanlike family, were widows and orphans in such need of state aid? The problems of civilized life were clearly apparent, although queens still played a significant role in the economy of this last Sumerian dynasty and royal women and priestesses probably knew how to read and write. Indeed, the Sumerian temple, the dispensor of education in ancient Sumer, reveals the names of professional female scribes from the 3rd millennium.

The earliest extant list of female professions from Sumer (ca. 2400 B.C.) names prostitutes along with scribes, doctors and cooks—there is no apparent stigma attached. In the beginning, the prostitutes may have been exclusively cultic, that is, employed by the temples, where sexual revels by the entire populace accompanied the celebrations of the annual sacred marriage rite. Sumerians continued to view sexuality and procreation as mystical and even divine acts and the sexual embracing of the high priestess by the ruler of the city-state was a vital civic duty to ensure bounteous harvests and prosperity for all. The Epic of Gilgamesh attributes a civilizing effect to a harlot who cohabits with the barbarian "wild man" Enkiddu. She humanized him and instilled wisdom in him so much so that the wild beasts, formerly his friends, were now afraid of him. In time, however, attitudes about prostitution changed, possibly with its increasing commercialization and its spread, which was one result of the desperate indebtedness that befell many families after the rise of kingship and its severe taxation policies. Society's first attempts to regulate women's sexual life appear in the reform text of Urukagina and continue with intensity in the law code of Hammurabi, the Babylonian ruler.

From the end of the history of the Sumerians comes the extensive legal text comprised of the judgments of the last king of the city-state of Isin.[23] Lipit-Ishtar speaks of seeking to establish justice for the daughters and sons of the cities of the realm. This judicial code ranks as the first full surviving text pertaining to family law. Old Sumerian practices continued: a daughter inherited and lived in her father's house if she remained unmarried; children inherited equally; a mother's dowry passed to her children; and a childless wife could not be set aside in favor of another. Neither childless wives nor divorced wives could be forced out; they were owed support from the former husbands, even if the husbands remarried.

In the code of Eshnunna, another Sumerian city-state of this period, the law also protected women against unjust husbands.[24] If a man divorced a wife by whom he had children, the law stated: "he shall be driven from his house and from whatever he owns." In this law code, a man convicted of the rape of a betrothed girl or a married woman was sentenced to death, as was a wife caught in adultery or a husband found in a homosexual relationship. A raped slave girl won recompense of a payment in silver. A prostitute who bore a child to an otherwise childless man would get his support—food and clothing—but would not be allowed to share the domicile with his legal wife. Generally fines formed the punishments in these codes, but the king decided the punishment in capital offences. It appears that this society divided along class lines. Men and women of the same class had similar rights and opportunities, but people of different classes did not. If a class system is very much in evidence here, so is the state's intrusion into private matters in order to protect and regulate private lives.

THE AMORITE KINGDOMS OF BABYLONIA AND ASSYRIA

Introduction

Sumerians as a cultural group disappeared from history early in the second millennium after a combination of catastrophes including famine and invasion from Persia. Fierce Amorite (western Semitic) sheikhs came from the steppes to conquer the old city-states of Sumer and Akkad and establish dynasties. Originally pastoral nomads, Amorites were largely dependent for their wealth on animal husbandry and trading in livestock—activities usually associated with males. Texts from this period illustrate new developments in the status of women and document the re-emergence of private property as a powerful force. A middle class based on trade arose in the towns and survived independently of temple or palace and eventually controlled the economic and social life of the entire Mesopotamian region. Independent merchants carrying on long-distance trade increased in numbers, but family farms, inns, and small businesses of various types flourished. Private fortunes increased.

Economic Implications for Women

To conserve their newfound wealth, the families of the newly propertied classes came up with an ingenious solution. Under a social system that sent their daughters to other men's households equipped with a sizeable dowry, fathers had often lost a good part of their fortunes. A mother's dowry property passed to her children, so the marriage of several daughters seriously depleted their father's holdings. To avoid this, prominent families dedicated one or more daughters to be "brides of the god" of their city. Young women inducted into cloisters under the supervision of clergy lived chaste, celibate lives until death. To be sure, they received dowries, as in any marriage arrangement, but these *naditu* women died without issue and their dowry did not pass into the temple's treasury but reverted back to their own families. These women pursued business themselves, leasing land and loaning out their money at good interest, and this income added to the original dowry and eventually enlarged the family fortune. Clearly the daughters of the capitalist and royal families were subordinated to the commercial interests of those families. Freed from the burdens of childrearing, however, *naditu* women could participate more fully in economic activities and often enjoyed longer-than-average life spans. Many had time to learn to read and write, as is evidenced by the correspondence of women who served as scribes in the cloister at the great commercial city of Sippar.[25] Among the celibate priestesses, the daughter of the king of Uruk wrote a long letter which became a classic text for use in schools. Women filled some secular positions too, a woman doctor practiced at the palace at Larsa and at Mari a female administrative assistant served the king.

The site of Mari on the Middle Euphrates yields significant information about Amorite women in public life, especially from the letters of the royal family from 1779 to 1745 B.C. Included are letters from female relatives and acquaintances of the king many with honors and influence in the kingdom. Such status, however, depended upon the goodwill of the king, who maintained a patriarchal rule that reflected his tribal heritage. Generally, male functionaries had charge of the administration of the land, with all actual authority in the hands of the king. Male correspondence predominates in the Mari archive, often peppered with disparaging remarks about the weak and unheroic character of women. Nevertheless, two powerful administrators at Mari were the king's chief wife, Sabitu, and the intelligent and capable official Addudirri, a woman with who may have had no relation to the royal family. The queen appears to have been designated by her husband as a substitute for him during his prolonged absences and, as such, she played a significant role as quasi-official head of state, active in palace, religious, and governmental affairs. Secondary wives administered at lesser palaces, overseeing the concubines of their royal husband. At Mari domestic concerns were largely left to highly placed women in the royal household while the king and his men fought many an armed and diplomatic battle.[26]

Legal Changes Affecting Women

The political predominance of the Semitic people in Mesopotamia brought about cultural changes with far-reaching outcomes. The widespread notion of a hopeless hereafter, not only meant that grave goods—food, weapons, jewelry buried with the dead—disappeared, but may well account for harsher penalties in the law code. The Akkadian elaboration upon the Sumerian Gilgamesh Epic stresses the finality of death, holding out no hope of eternal life for mankind (tablet 10). The Semitic-speaking people's lack of faith in a final judgment with good rewarded and evil punished may help explain why their law codes stand out as so much harsher than the Sumerians', and why monetary fines were replaced by corporal punishment.

The most famous collection of legal pronouncements from the ancient Near East is that of Hammurabi of Babylon, successor to a family line established by an Amorite chieftain who had come to power in the region of old Ur around 1894 B.C. Hammurabi (1792–1750 B.C.) exerted his control over a number of city states and by his thirtieth year of reign claimed sovereignty over all of ancient Sumer and Akkad. His legal text of 280 judgments attributed to the sun god dealt with both civil and criminal law and sought to protect the weak from the strong. It differs markedly from earlier codes of the Sumerian tradition by introducing the principle of *lex talionis* (eye for an eye; tooth for a tooth) from the more conservative law of the desert.

With the code, Hammurabi tried to establish fair dealing among the people of his kingdom and to protect the rights of women to their property (forbidding its use by a husband or father to pay his debts). The code acknowledged a wife or daughter's right to receive an inheritance from a male relative if he willed it to her. A mother's dowry automatically descended to her children. As with the Sumerians, a marriage was legally solemnized and recorded with a deed, and the bride received a dowry from her father and gifts from her intended. The code affirmed her right to keep property even in cases of divorce, and this might well befall her if she could not bear children. Some couples, however, adopted children when faced with childlessness.

In their rights to inherit and own property and to testify in court, the Old Babylonian women seem to enjoy the same advantages of men. The code reveals a definite class system, however; for instance, the wife of a wealthy free man was protected, not only from the disrespectfulness of his concubine, but even from the maliciousness of the town gossip, but the wives of poor men could be sold into slavery for up to three years to pay off a husband's debts. Still, a woman who could demonstrate to the authorities just cause for leaving a husband had hope of a legal separation supported by the return of the dowry, but a widow who wished to remarry, if she had young children, had to gain the consent of judges who first investigated the late husband's estate and then formally granted it. This was to protect the children of the first marriage and ensure their rights of inheritance, but the children of a poor debtor could be sold into slavery. The code reveals definite class structure as well as a deep ambivalence toward woman's capacities and her societal role.

Apparently face-saving was very important for husbands; if a wife embarrassed him she could be divorced. If the husband proved his wife had been adulterous, she could be killed; if she had been a spendthrift, she could be divorced and given no settlement. If she wished to engage in business on her own, this too was deemed a humiliation to her husband, and the wife had to leave him and obtained no settlement. It is possible that those women who still engaged in business were widows who no longer had to fear a husband's or society's disapproval. Later Neo-Babylonian texts reveal that women generally married as teenagers, men about ten years older, and that the average lifespan was, in the first millennium, about 55 years. Thus, if a woman was widowed around the age of 45, she still had a good ten years in which to handle her estate on her own.[27] A wife accused by another of adultery, even though known to be innocent, had to throw herself into the river "for the sake of her husband" (for his good name?), but if accused only by her husband she need take only an oath of innocence, unless he could prove otherwise. Respectability was being legislated for the upper classes and women maintained their respectability at the cost of self-expression and freedom. A definite double standard of sexual behavior had emerged.[28]

On the whole, the judgments of Hammurabi startle the modern reader by their severity. For instance, if a pregnant woman died after being struck by a man, that man's daughter could be put to death, just as could the son of a builder if his building collapsed and killed another's son. The principle of an eye for an eye, and a tooth for a tooth extended to families, not just individuals immediately involved with the guilt.

Assyria

Hammurabi's ideas of justice appear harsh and primitive compared to the Sumerians', but they seem enlightened when compared to the cruel intolerance and misogyny of the Assyrians, another people of western Semitic stock who dominated northern Syria from their capital Assur on the northern Tigris river. A vigorous mercantile people, the Assyrians had a trading colony in Anatolia as early as the nineteenth century B.C., and during the second half of the second millennium often went to war in order to open up or protect trade routes. In the first millennium they founded an empire which reached briefly, at its furthest extent, to Egypt. Their kingdom was vulnerable to invasion on three fronts, and its survival depended on ceaseless military vigilance. Their brutality in war was proverbial and brought vilification in the Old Testament. Even their art had a remarkable brute strength: its forms are heavy and muscular and the themes of warfare and lion hunts predominate. Assyrians expressed little, if any, faith in a future life beyond the grave. The best source for knowledge about women's status stems from a Middle Assyrian law code surviving on tablets from the twelfth century B.C., but believed to have been composed as early as the fifteenth century.[29]

Here we find the position of women far poorer than it had been in earlier times. Many lengthy, bitter wars consumed Assyria's energies and in such insecure times, women stayed close to the hearth and willingly put themselves under the protection of their menfolk. Certainly Middle Assyrian laws benefited males far more than females and strove for the preservation of patriarchal power and wealth.

Economics and Women's Rights

The importance of commerce in this society colored the official attitude, which regarded women as the property of men. Girls did not inherit from their parents, but parents received payment for the daughters they gave in marriage. Marriages resembled business alliances between two families with the virginity of the daughter gaining her father a handsome price. Among the Assyrians the levirate marriage prevailed, whereby a woman if widowed was obliged to marry a close male relative of her deceased spouse even if that relative already had a wife, and a girl bethrothed to a man who died had to marry his father or brother, even if this meant she became a secondary wife.

Assyrian women could not own property. Even goods brought into a marriage could be taken away by the husband and given to whomever he pleased. If a woman's husband divorced her, she had to leave everything behind, including her children. A wife could be held responsible for her husband's debts, and a daughter could be enslaved with no time limit for her father's debts. A wife left abandoned because of her husband's disappearance had to wait five years before remarrying.

When a woman was the victim of crime, she still suffered at the hands of justice—or so it seems to us. An unmarried woman who had been raped could be given to her tormenter in marriage, presumably because her monetary value to her family was now diminished through loss of her virginity. The rapist of a virgin was punished by his own wife being ravished by his victim's father, while the rapist of a married woman was put to death. Casual romantic attention paid by a man to another's wife could mean his disfigurement by the state as punishment, while adultery meant death to both parties.

Regulation of Female Sexuality

In a society where women were not entrusted with wealth, Assyrian women were totally dependent upon their menfolk, and the state concerned itself with regulating women's sexuality as well as their status. There were laws against abortion that carried the penalty of impalement on a stake with no burial after death and a law mandating the veiling of all respectable women. Respectable women were those under the protection of a man—wives, daughters, concubines and even the maids of married ladies. The veil became an enforced badge of respectability and social standing. Women not under a man's protection went unveiled in public places and, as slave women and professional prostitutes, were fair game for all comers. Men attempting to protect these "nonrespectable" women by veiling them while accompanying them in public were severely and publicly punished. Thus the State tried to discourage anything but the most casual of encounters with such women, possibly as a way to make marriage essential for all women and would-be respectable men. Such at least would appear to be the motivation in a society where fathers received great rewards by arranging marriages for their virgin daughters.

Even the queens were secluded, in harems with the king's concubines. They were guarded by eunuchs, under threat of death if they stepped out of line. The obsession with regulating women's lives is best seen in the Middle Assyrian law code where the first 16 laws deal specifically with women as the perpetrators of crimes (not people in general). Surviving Assyrian anti-witchcraft literature shows that they considered women to be far more prone to witchcraft than men. The average Assyrian woman's social role was so circumscribed that any activity outside familial controls was suspect.[30]

Assyrian society, like ancient Greece exclusively obsessed with male importance, even had corps of male prostitutes. This is revealing, not only of Assyrian male's sexual preferences, but of the complete absence of women from all types of social life outside the home and of the dehumanizing effect of the arranged marriage system, in which personal choice may not have figured even for the prospective grooms. It seems likely that meaningful relationships of all types could only be built between members of the same sex in such a segregated society.[31]

Never before had a civilization commanded so narrow a role for its average free woman, rendering her completely dependent on the males of her family. Where the pathology—a repressive, patriarchal double standard in which women had almost no civil rights—is so extreme, the causes are correspondingly evident: the vital importance of trade and wealth enhanced conservative patriarchic attitudes inherited from the nomadic past, and a highly sophisticated military organization made possible such a strictly regulated society.

ISRAEL OF THE OLD TESTAMENT

In studying ancient Israel, social historians have as source material bountiful writings by the "People of the Book" which are well known and which shed much light on life in that ancient society. The texts of the Old Testament include several literary genres—proverbs and hymns, sermons and instructions, law and history, and these span almost one thousand years. Not surprisingly they reveal some diversity in attitudes about women.

The Israelites by the late thirteenth century B.C. inhabited the hill country on both sides of the Jordan river, as settlers in small villages or nomads. They supported themselves by farming and pasturing. Warfare with other peoples in the region and along the coastal plain dominated their history. Poor agricultural land contributed to the frail economic state of the nation, which remained on the defensive or dependent upon a more powerful neighbor and at the mercy of the armies of the conquerors who crossed the region over the centuries. Assyria conquered the northern tribes in 722 B.C. and Babylon the southern tribes in 587 B.C.

Even periods of strong centralized rule, as under King David, who founded the capital, created a standing army, and forced the quarrelsome tribes into a united kingdom, were marked by political coups. Solomon came to power by means of a harem conspiracy. Poor land and geographical and political fragmentation constantly plagued the Israelites. Weak leadership by authorities meant prophets did not hesitate to berate kings. Religious law handed down to Moses was the basis of this society. Old Testament

Israel had a patriarchal family structure featuring patrilineal descent and patrilocal residence. Over the years, however, a trend towards increased urbanization diminished the authority of the tribes, although the leading elders of the city were just as influenced by religious law.

Membership in the greater society, whether in the sociopolitical or religious realms outside the home, fell exclusively to men. Only men were deemed responsible individuals, and, as such, were considered responsible for the acts of their dependents. Women had dependent and inferior status. When the "people" were exorted, as when Moses warned them not to approach a woman lest they be defiled before a religious act, only males were addressed. Home provided the only environment in which the woman of the Old Testament functioned. Only there, once married and the mother of children, did she exercise her authority over other people. In her role as mother the Hebrew woman gained status and honor equivalent to a man's, but she remained always subject to the authority of some male relative. While theologians disdained the old fertility cults, this society gave reverence to the reproductive role of its mortal women.[32]

The law of ancient Israel "excused" women from many religious and civic obligations expected of men, while women gained honor and protection through motherhood. The Old Testament (Prov. 31:10) describes the "good wife" as industrious, prudent, wise, and gracious. She taught her children, planted and maintained a vineyard, produced the food and clothing for her family, helped the poor and, through her virtue, enhanced her husband's reputation. Regarded as a natural and god-ordained helpmate, the good wife was called the "crown of her master." Children owed mothers honor, love, and respect and the same burial rites accorded to their fathers. However, a woman's status, as reflected in the Old Testament, remained inferior to that of men. The interests of the family were commonly identified with those of the male head.

Sex, for women, belonged to the marriage bed and even a girl who had been raped had to become, or be treated as, the wife of her attacker (Exod. 21:7-11; Deut. 21:10-14). A bride found to be not a virgin could be stoned to death by the elders of the town. Death was also the ordained punishment for the adulterous wife, whereas infidelity by the husband with harlots won toleration (although not encouragement) and polygamy gained acceptance (although not enthusiastically). A woman could never divorce her husband, but divorce lay within the husband's rights, and texts say nothing about any obligation of the husband toward the wife he set aside. The arranged and levirate marriage predominated in the early period (Gen. 38). The male commanded higher value than the female: the votive offering of the male in the temple had a higher monetary value in the eyes of the priests (Lev. 27) and some laws treated women as the property of men (Exod. 20:17; Deut. 5:21). For instance, a man might sell his daughter in order to pay his debts for a period up to six years. (Exod. 21:2; 21:7). Only a few women (those without brothers) might inherit property since sons, if there were any, inherited everything from their parents. The woman who did inherit still had to marry within her tribe, so the inheritance fell to her husband (Num. 36: 1–9).

Although society subordinated the woman economically and socially to the man (the word for husband was "master"), wives were not legally chattels. Husbands could not sell their wives, nor could they divorce them without substantial cause (Deut. 22:15 ff.) and nowhere does the Old Testament state that a wife must obey her husband.

Men dominated sociopolitically in early Israel, and they also controlled the religious life of the community; the initiation rite of male circumcision was of central importance. Purity laws, which deemed a woman impure for seven days each month (Lev. 12:1; 15:18–33), made the priesthood a male profession (Exod. 23:17; 28:1), as did the especially long and complex postparturient purification which followed each pregnancy. A woman who gave birth to a female child required twice as long a time for purification (Lev. 12:1–5). Although mothers taught their children the Torah, within the family the father represented the religious authority for his wife and children in the sacrificial rites. Only men of the community were bidden to come before the Lord (Exod. 23:17 & 34:23 and Deut. 16:16). References appear to "wise women" or diviners who may have practiced the occult, and prophetesses like Miriam, Deborah, and Huldah spoke for Yahveh and received honor for this. However, unlike earlier priestesses in Babylon or Egypt, these prophetesses cannot be considered cultic authorities or connected with the sanctuary and officiating in the ritual. For this reason, perhaps, foreign cults from Babylon attracted the veneration of some women in ancient Israel (Jer. 7:8; 44:15–19; and Is. 17:10).

Despite the strong patriarchal bent to this society, Old Testament history does include stories of women who save their people or their cities from catastrophe through leadership and acts of courage. Abigail, Esther, Judith, and Jael all play this strong female role. In times of crisis women found identity and inspiration independent of gender roles. Normally, however, when the Old Testament woman became visible, it was "as a dependent and usually an inferior in a male-centered and male-dominated society."[33]

Male strength, vigilance, and domination doubtlessly appeared necessary for the security of the state throughout a tumultuous history. Israel suffered again and again assaults and humiliations from the super powers of the world of the first millennium. Constant preparation for war left little space for creative self-development within the general female population whose singular contribution as replenisher of the race was deemed most essential. Women would produce the citizens who would man the ramparts. Individual women might give advice, might rally the people, but women, as a group, were the least effective members of this often poor and war-torn society.

There is surely a special irony in regard to ancient Israel: the main object of the state was to secure justice and to respect the worth of the human spirit, yet the spirit of its women was strictly kept in check. The prophets did not challenge the inferior status of women any more than they railed against the institution of slavery.[34]

CONCLUSION

What was the real cause of the rise of patriarchy, which became increasingly oppressive to women in the Near East after Sumerian civilization waned? Several reasons suggest themselves. The first is militarism. In an early agrarian society like Egypt where internal disputes were effectively handled by the strong, centralized government, where wars usually took place beyond the borders, where no standing army existed during the first 1500 years of recorded history, and where invasion seldom affected the country, women continually shared the burdens, full rights, and obligations of citizens. However, in the newer societies, founded by the sons of ever-vigilant and suspicious desert nomads, where warfare between cities was frequent and invasion by outside hostile forces familiar, militarism developed, excluding women and rendering her a dependent. Second, where commercialism held sway at the same time—as in Assyria—the worst examples of patriarchy were found. Commerce based on private initiative first appears on a well developed scale in the Old Babylonian period where the first concerted effort by men to control women for financial gain is also documented. This is seen not only in the laws of Hammurabi but in institutions like that of the cloistered *Naditu* women. Coupled with virulent militarism, as in Assyria, the rise of commercialism had a devastating effect on women's rights. In Egypt large scale commerce long remained a virtual monopoly of the state, so its impact on society remained less significant.

We might further point out that, even during the somewhat militaristic Egyptian empire of the New Kingdom, women's status and freedoms did not diminish significantly. This introduces a third factor: confidence. A supremely confident nation can afford tolerance. Egypt had confidence in its gods, in the eternity of life, and in the bounty of its land. Sumer, in its early formative years, shared these advantages too. Not so the subsequent societies. It is the threatened male and the threatened society—like Assyria, surrounded on three sides by deadly enemies, and weak impoverished Israel—which created such a restricted role for their women.

NOTES

1. Many theorize that in the beginning women were preeminent in tribal life as the acknowledged source of life itself and were valued as food producers as well—involved with fishing and bird trapping (as still seen in historical records). The

first garden cultivators were likely women, and they relinquished this major task only when the development of the heavy plow pulled by oxen replaced the pickax and hoe in broad scale farming.

2. John A. Wilson, *The Culture of Ancient Egypt*, University of Chicago Press, Chicago, 1951, Chapters IV and V.

3. T. G. H. James, *The Hekanakhte Papers and Other Early Middle Kingdom Documents*, Metropolitan Museum of Art, New York, 1962, p. 34.

4. William Kelly Simpson, ed., *The Literature of Ancient Egypt*, Yale University Press, New Haven, 1973, p. 161.

5. James Henry Breasted, *Ancient Records of Egypt*, Russell and Russell, New York, 1906, p. 79.

6. William A. Ward, *Index of Egyptian Administrative and Religious Titles of the Middle Kingdom*, American University of Beirut, Beirut, 1982, pp. 83 and 113; and Henry G. Fischer, *Egyptian Studies I Varia*, Metropolitan Museum of Art, New York, 1976, pp. 79–89.

7. William C. Hayes, *A Papyrus of the Late Middle Kingdom in the Brooklyn Museum* (Wilbour Monographs V), The Brooklyn Museum, Brooklyn, 1955, pp. 64–65.

8. Donald B. Redford, *History and Chronology of the Eighteenth Dynasty of Egypt: Seven Studies*, University of Toronto Press, Toronto, 1967, p. 72.

9. Barbara S. Lesko, *The Remarkable Women of Ancient Egypt*, B.C. Scribe Publications, Berkeley, 1978, pp. 4–10; and Julia Sampson, *Nefertiti and Cleopatra*, Rubicon Press, London, 1985, pp. 22–26, 96–97; Leonard H. Lesko, "Three Late Egyptian Stories Reconsidered," *Egyptological Studies in Honor of Richard A. Parker*, ed. Leonard H. Lesko, University Press of New England, Hanover, N.H., 1986, pp. 98–103.

10. John A. Wilson, "Results of a Trial for Conspiracy," *Ancient Near Eastern Texts Relating to the Old Testament*, ed. James B. Pritchard, 2nd ed., Princeton University Press, Princeton, 1955, pp. 214–16; and Hans Goedicke, "Was Magic Used in the Harem Conspiracy Against Rameses III?," *Journal of Egyptian Archaeology*, 49 (1973), pp. 71–92.

11. Lesko, *op. cit.*, pp. 19–21.

12. Betsy M. Bryan, "Evidence for Female Literacy from Theban Tombs of the New Kingdom," *Bulletin of the Egyptological Seminar*, 6 (1984), pp. 17–32.

13. Barbara S. Lesko, "True Art in Ancient Egypt," *Egyptological Studies in Honor of Richard A. Parker*, ed. Leonard H. Lesko, University Press of New England, Hanover, N.H., 1986, pp. 85–97; and Alan H. Gardiner and Kurt Sethe, *Egyptian Letters to the Dead*, The Egypt Exploration Society, London, 1928, pp. 8–9.

14. My translation. For larger excerpt see Miriam Lichtheim, *Ancient Egyptian Literature*, Vol. II, University of California Press, Berkeley, 1978, p. 141.

15. T. G. H. James, *Pharaoh's People*, The Bodley Head, London, 1985, p. 97; G.A. Gaballa, *The Memphite Tomb-Chapel of Mose*, Aris and Phillips, Warminster, 1977, pp. 22 ff.; J. Černý and T. Eric Peet, "A Marriage Settlement of the Twentieth Dynasty," *Journal of Egyptian Archaeology*, 13 (1927), pp. 30–39; Alan H. Gardiner, "Adoption Extraordinary," *Journal of Egyptian Archaeology*, 26 (1941), pp. 23–29; and P.W. Pestman, *Marriage and Matrimonial Property in Ancient Egypt* (Papyrologica Lugduno-Batava, IX), Leiden, 1961.

16. P. R. S. Moorey, "What Do We Know About the People Buried in the Royal Cemetery?" *Expedition*, Vol. 20, No. 1 (1977), 40.

17. Samuel Noah Kramer, *The Sumerians, Their History, Culture, and Character.* University of Chicago Press, Chicago, 1963, pp. 75–77.

18. *Ibid.*, p. 78.

19. William W. Hallo, in *The Legacy of Sumer*, ed. Denise Schmandt Besserat, (Bibliotheca Mesopotamica, 4) Undena Press, Malibu, 1979, p. 27.

20. However, see S. N. Kramer in *Legacy of Sumer*, page 12, where he points out that Urukagina's wife, Queen Shagshag "was the mistress of vast estates and ran her affairs every bit her husband's equal" and, further, that Urukagina made an attempt to equalize wages between men and women in one known instance, so that he should not be regarded as anti-women (pp. 12–13).

21. Kramer, *op. cit.* pages 13–16 and Kramer, *The Sacred Marriage Rite*, University of Indiana Press, Bloomington, 1969, pp. 49–84.

22. Hallo in *Legacy of Sumer*, page 29 and William W. Hallo and J. J. A. Van Dyk, *The Exaltation of Inanna*, Yale University Press, New Haven, 1968, pp. 1–11.

23. S. N. Kramer, "Lipit-Ishtar Lawcode," in Pritchard, *Ancient Near Eastern Texts*, pp. [159]–61.

24. Albrecht Goetze, "The Laws of Eshnunna," in Pritchard, *Ancient Near Eastern Texts*, pp. 161–63.

25. Rivkah Harris, *Ancient Sippar: A Demographic Study of an Old-Babylonian City*, Nederlands Historisch-Archaeologisch Instituut, Istanbul, 1975, pp. 142–269.

26. Bernard Frank Batto, *Studies of Women at Mari*, Johns Hopkins University Press, Baltimore, 1974, pp. 8–36, 64–73.

27. Theophile Meek, "The Code of Hammurabi," in Pritchard, *Ancient Near Eastern Texts*, pp. 161–80; and Elizabeth Mary Macdonald, *The Position of Women as Reflected in Semitic Codes of Law*, University of Toronto Press, Toronto, 1931, pp. 11–32.

28. Martha T. Roth, "Age at First Marriage and the Neo-Babylonian Family," paper read at the American Oriental Society, One Hundred and Ninety-Sixth Meeting, New Haven, Conn., March 9, 1986.

29. Theophile Meek, "The Middle Assyrian Laws," in Pritchard, *Ancient Near Eastern Texts*, pp. 180–88.

30. Gerda Lerner, *The Creation of Patriarchy*, Oxford University Press, New York & London, 1986, pp. 134–137; Sue Rollin, "Women and Witchcraft in Ancient Assyria," *Images of Women in Antiquity*, Wayne State University Press, Detroit, 1983, pp. 65–78.

31. Jean Bottero, "La femme dans l'Asia Occidentale Ancienne: Mesoptamie et Israel," *Histoire Mondiale de la femme*, ed. P. Grimal, Nouvelle Librarie de France, Paris, 1957, p. 176.

32. Phyllis Bird, "Images of Women in the Old Testament," in *Religion and Sexism*, ed. Rosemary Radford Reuther, Simon and Schuster, New York 1974; and P. Trible, "Women in the Old Testament," *Interpreter's Dictionary of the Bible*, supplementary volume, K. Crim general editor, Abingdon Press, Nashville, 1976, pp. 963–66; and Carol Meyers, "The Roots of Restriction: Women in Early Israel," *Biblical Archaeologist*, Vol. 41, no. 1 (1978), pp. 91–103.

33. Bird, *op. cit.*, p. 56.

34. Herbert J. Muller, *Freedom in the Ancient World*, Harper, New York, 1961, p. 135.

SUGGESTIONS FOR FURTHER READING

The most reliable source for reconstructing the social history of ancient peoples is surely their own writings. Fortunately, published anthologies of texts are available in English to the student, the most comprehensive of these being *Ancient Near Eastern Texts relating to the Old Testament* containing literary and nonliterary works from the Egyptian, Sumerian, Babylonian, Hittite and Assyrian cultures. Now in its third edition and accompanied by a volume of plates illustrating monuments from these civilizations, *Ancient Near Eastern Texts* was edited by James B. Pritchard, contributed to by an impressive roster of leading orientalists, and published by Princeton University Press. A large collection of mostly literary texts from ancient Egypt has been brought out in three volumes as *Ancient Egyptian Literature* by Miriam Lichtheim for the University of California Press (1973–1980).

Probably the leading historical work encompassing the entire ancient world is the third edition of *The Cambridge Ancient History* (Cambridge 1971–1975), again with contributions from several leading scholars of that decade.

The awakened interest in women's history is reflected by among others, *Histoire Mondiale de la Femme: Préhistoire et Antiquité*, a large volume edited by Pierre Grimal for Nouvelle Librairie de France, Paris, 1957; *When God was a Woman* by Merlin Stone, Dial Press of New York, 1976; and more recently *Images of Women in Antiquity*, edited by Averil Cameron and Amelie Kuhrt for Wayne State University, Detroit, 1983; and *Reflections of Women in Antiquity* another collection of essays edited by Helene P. Foley for Gordon and Breach Science Publishers of New York.

More specifically focused studies are Barbara S. Lesko's *The Remarkable Women of Ancient Egypt*, B. C. Scribe Publications, Berkeley, 1978, with a second edition due in 1987; and Ilse Seibert's *Women in the Ancient Near East*, Schram, New York, 1974; and Bernard F. Batto's *Studies on Women at Mari* for The Johns Hopkins University Press, Baltimore, 1974. Most recently, historian Gerda Lerner has produced the controversial *The Creation of Patriarchy*, Oxford University Press, 1986, which, for a good part, focuses on the cultures of Mesopotamia and ancient Israel.

Left: Perseus slaying Medusa, vase early fifth century B.C. *Right:* Mask of Medusa, sixth century B.C. The myth of Perseus and the Medusa illustrates the familiar Greek theme of male triumph over female monstrosity. The monster Medusa ("ruler" in the feminine gender), who turned men to stone by her glance, was slain by Perseus with the help of the goddess Athena. Athena's ambivalent allegiance to both male hero and female monster was shown by her use of the mask of the Medusa on her armor. Here Medusa's potential survived, but in a form that subordinated it to the control of the patriarchal state. (Vase from the Metropolitan Museum of Art, Rogers Fund, 1906. Mask from the Metropolitan Museum of Art, Fletcher Fund, 1931.)

—————————— chapter 3 ——————————

From Medusa to Cleopatra: Women in the Ancient World

Marylin Arthur

Classical Greece and Rome continued in the direction of social and political differentiation with a corresponding reduction in women's role. Culture also became more sophisticated in its rationalization of these trends. Literature and art can be decoded to give us insights not only into the daily reality of the ancients, but also into their psychic lives. The classical Greek polis justified its patriarchal social structure in myths that civilization had been a hard-won victory over nature, with male moral authority triumphing over female irrationality. This misogynistic sentiment arose during the transition from an aristocratic to a more broadly based society.

In the period when a new class of commercial entrepreneurs came into being, the nuclear family assumed a more important role in creating and transmitting wealth. The oikos (household) was the basis for citizenship, so women's role as mother and wife assumed legal and moral dimensions: their main function was to ensure the legitimacy of heirs. They remained, however, in the legal custody of the male heads of their households. Thus, the democratic freedom of the classical polis entailed the legal and cultural subordination of women.

In the later Hellenistic period, large, bureaucratically organized empires overwhelmed small city-states. Households no longer functioned as socio-economic nuclei of the state, and women gained in independence in proportion with the decline of the oikos and the polis. As the gap between public and private life widened, the latter emerged as the principal arena of self-definition; women's sexuality, previously feared as threatening to civilization and rationality, now appeared as a model for human enjoyment and individual satisfaction. Women's position improved in law, life, and literature. Misogyny as a cultural expression declined in popularity.

The passage in Rome from republic to empire evidences certain similarities with the transition in Greece from aristocracy to democratic polis. As in Greece, leaders in the later, more broadly based form of the state found it necessary to design and implement a series of regulations affecting women's sexual, economic, and cultural lives. The ideological accompaniment of this transformation was the development of a particularly Roman form of misogyny organized around social issues, and highly ambivalent in its call for female subordination.

> *As a general proposition: Social advances and changes of periods are brought about by virtue of the progress of women towards liberty and the decadences of the social order are brought about by virtue of the decrease of liberty of women. . . . The extension of privileges to women is the general principle of all social progress.*[1]
>
> CHARLES FOURIER

This chapter will treat one historical stage that, in our view, has peculiar and important ramifications for women: the transition from the aristocratic to a more egalitarian form of the state. This transition is a recurrent one in history; it appears later most notably as the passage from feudalism to capitalism, and occurs in antiquity in the course of the development of the Greek and Roman states. In outlining the general historical forces that brought about this transition in both Greece and Rome, and in correlating in some detail the concomitant change in the status and cultural evaluation of women, we expect to show, as Fourier put it, "the progress of women towards liberty" as a measure of both the general character of human relations and of the relationship between human beings and the natural world.

We shall proceed by first discussing the correlation between the ideological evaluation of women in ancient Greece and their social position; second, we shall present the transformation that both the attitude toward women and women themselves underwent in the Hellenistic period, when the social and political organization of the state was transformed; third, we shall examine the Roman situation and the dynamics behind the alteration in women's status and in the attitude toward them in the course of the transition from republic to empire.

APHRODITE DENIED: CLASSICAL GREECE

In his epic poem *Theogony*, Hesiod explains the origins of the cosmos through myths describing the births of the gods. His narrative centers on a series of succession myths that conform to a single pattern: the youngest son enters into an alliance with his mother to overthrow his father. In the first stage the female goddess Earth (Gaia) generates Heaven (Ouranos) and together they produce the Titans (gigantic monsters). Ouranos attempts to prevent the birth of his children by holding them in Gaia's womb, and she retaliates by arming her youngest son Kronos with a sickle and setting him in ambush against his father. Kronos castrates Ouranos and thereby establishes himself as ruler of the gods. In the second stage of the succession myth Kronos and Rhea generate the Olympian gods. Kronos, afraid of losing his supremacy to his son, swallows his children as Rhea brings them forth. But she, upon the advice of Gaia and Ouranos, deceives her husband by giving him a rock wrapped in swaddling clothes instead of her youngest son, Zeus. When Zeus grows to maturity he and Gaia trick Kronos into vomiting up all of the children. Zeus establishes his supremacy over the universe by defeating the Titans in battle and escapes from the succession cycle by swallowing his wife Metis (Intelligence). He thus gains control over her powers of reproduction. His first child is the goddess Athena, who in Greek religion remains affiliated with her father and symbolizes male dominance of the universe. Zeus's wives bear his other children, but these represent no threat, since the birth of Athena establishes the principle of male dominion and female subordination. These children (Justice, Good Order, Peace, etc.) betoken Zeus's sponsorship of a moral order associated with civilized life. In addition, since they are all female, they signify the beneficence of the female principle when subjected to regulation by patriarchal authority.

The Greek Polis and Male Dominance (Seventh to Fourth Centuries B.C.)

Hesiod's model for the evolution of the cosmos and the birth of civilization thus involves a progression from a world dominated by the generative powers of the female to one overseen by the moral authority of the male. Associated with the early era of female dominance is the primacy of nature in her most uncontrolled, spontaneous, and violent form: Gaia sends forth both rampant vegetation and monstrous, semihuman creatures. The triumph of the male deity signifies the subjugation of the procreative power of nature to some form of control that renders it useful to civilization and the restraint of her more violent, chaotic, and destructive aspects.

The struggle Hesiod portrays is a pervasive theme in Greek thought. In the "Homeric Hymn to Delphian Apollo," for example, Apollo has to contend with the schemes and monsters bred by the indigenous female deity before he can establish the famous oracle at Delphi. The sculptural ornamentations on many classical Greek temples, including the Parthenon, depict the battles of the Olympian gods against the Titans and of the Athenians against the Amazons. Both the Olympian gods and the Athenian state stand for the forces of order, control, and harmony; the Amazons and the Titan giants symbolize chaotic monstrosity and hostility to political and social order.

This mythological scheme applies also to the conflict underlying the foundation of the Greek city-state (polis). The Oresteia of Aeschylus celebrates the birth of civil society and the triumph of the rule of law over the more primitive forms of tribal justice and represents this victory as a divine vindication of Orestes's murder of his mother Clytemnestra. She had killed her husband Agamemnon when he returned victorious from the Trojan war, bringing with him the Trojan priestess Cassandra as his concubine. In the trial with which the trilogy culminates, the Olympian divinity Apollo, son of Zeus, takes Orestes' side and the Furies, foul, animalistic creatures who pursue and torture Orestes, defend Clytemnestra's rights. The characters themselves present the confrontation as the struggle between two systems, one old and one new, one associated with mother-right, the other with the authority of the father. Apollo, in pleading on Orestes' behalf, affirms the superiority of the father by disparaging the female's part in generation:

> The mother is no parent of that which is called
> her child, but only nurse of the new-planted seed

that grows. The parent is he who mounts. A stranger she
preserves a stranger's seed, if no god interfere.[2]

Athena, who settles the dispute by casting her vote for Orestes, proclaims
herself partisan to the male for the following reasons:

There is no mother anywhere who gave me birth,
and, but for marriage, I am always for the male
with all my heart, and strongly on my father's side.[3]

The moral and legal underpinnings of the Greek polis are thus represented
as the result of an evolution from mother-right to father-right. Further, the
patriarchal form of society is proclaimed as the necessary correlate to a
higher form of civilized life. The goddess Athena is the ideal symbol for the
new state, for as a female she embodies the dynamic principle of growth and
generation, but her subordination to her father means that her potential
finds expression in a socially useful form. She is a masculinized deity, for
what is essentially female about her (the power of generation) never achieves
expression: she remains a virgin goddess. And through Athena, Perseus'
triumph over Medusa is both ratified and negated. For the goddess wears the
Gorgoneion (head of the Gorgon Medusa) as part of her protective armoring,
or else she carries it on her shield and thus she is identified with the
fearsome, monstrous aspect of the female which is at the same time rendered
harmless through decapitation. Athena is the major deity of ancient Greece.
None of the other goddesses achieves Athena's preeminence in the art and
literature of classical antiquity. When Aphrodite finally displaces her in the
Hellenistic period there is a correlative change in both the status of and
attitude toward women.

The threat women presented to the Greek mind emerges with particular
clarity when the struggle is transferred to the arena of the individual human
psyche. Euripides' *Hippolytus* is a drama played out between the inner
and outer forces that compete for domination of the souls of the protagonists, Hippolytus and Phaedra. Aphrodite and Artemis symbolize the two
extremes—one, the goddess of the passion that disrupts life and conflicts
with social values; the other, a virgin goddess who stands for denial and
control of instinctual urges. Aphrodite inspires in Phaedra not merely passion but an overwhelming and illegitimate desire for her stepson Hippolytus.
Artemis, whom Hippolytus adopts as his patron, supports his hatred for the
female sex and total rejection of sexuality. Phaedra, the character who in the
play represents the sexuality Hippolytus has denied in himself, acts as the
instrument of his destruction. The excess of Hippolytus's attack upon the
female sex leads Phaedra to retaliate by accusing him of rape; the false
accusation results in Hippolytus's death.

Euripides does not suggest a resolution of competing claims in the
manner of Hesiod or Aeschylus. The action in the play moves between two

irreconcilable opposites. The polarity is thus represented as an opposition between two autonomous goddesses: there is no longer a male deity to symbolize the possibility of transcendence. There remain only the alternatives of sterile repression, symbolized by Artemis, and the free reign of the instincts for which Aphrodite stands. The action of the play demonstrates that these instincts are by their nature uncontrollable, irresistible, and totally without regard for the limits of social custom and moral law. Insofar as they are exclusively associated with women in Greek thought, women themselves come to represent all that is opposed to civilized life, the whole world of the instincts and passions that must submit to restraint and modification in order for civilization to survive.

From Hesiod to Euripides and beyond, Greek thought contains a consistent and systematic association of the world of nature (including human nature) with female potency both expressed (as by Aphrodite) and denied (as by Artemis or Athena). Misogynistic sentiment, therefore, generally expresses a feeling of being at war with nature. We often encounter these two themes together. The most famous example of misogyny in Greek literature, for example, is the long diatribe against the female sex by Semonides of Amorgos that associates the various types of women with different animals. Characteristically, in the only other long fragment of this author that survives, Semonides portrays man as a helpless victim of divine caprice and the unpredictability of the natural world.

In Sophocles's tragedy *Antigone* this theme is even more explicit. The famous hymn to mankind takes the form of a catalogue of the ways in which man, by his ingenuity and will, has bent nature to his needs. Of particular interest to us is the praise of man's subjugation of the female earth:

> And she, the greatest of gods, the earth—
> ageless she is, and unwearied—he wears her away
> as the ploughs go up and down from year to year
> and his mules turn up the soil.[4]

This celebration of man as tamer of nature reveals the extent to which man, in his most human aspect, was conceived by the Greeks as something alien to and opposed to nature. He therefore asserted himself most fully as man and as human through the control he exercised over the natural world. Insofar as woman was identified with this world she was conceived of as hostile to man; if the Greeks thought of civilization as a triumph of man over nature, it was a triumph of man over woman no less.

A remarkable and peculiarly Greek manifestation of this notion of woman's fundamentally antisocial disposition was the theory and practice of Dionysiac religion. Dionysus (who became Bacchus in the Roman pantheon) was a fertility god associated with the growth of the vine, and hence with wine. "The Greeks," as Plutarch explained it, "think that Dionysos presides, not only over the wine, but over the whole realm of the wet element." The latter included plant sap, life blood, and semen. But more important, Dionysus was a wild and potentially destructive god, worshiped especially by women. His savage nature was revealed in the practice of the *omophagia* ("eating raw," usually animals and sometimes children) associated with his worship. His followers, the maenads, celebrated their devotion to Dionysus in a state of ecstatic possession. The worship took the form of frenzied dancing that could lead to violent acts of brutality like the *sparagmos* ("tearing apart") of animals or children.

The worship of Dionysus was a regular part of Greek social life and did not ordinarily involve savagery. But the poetry, drama, and art of the classical period kept alive the wild potentiality of the cult and its worshipers. In vases dealing with religious themes there is hardly a motif so common as the maenad, alone or with the god or his attendant satyrs. She rushes forward barefoot, her hair and clothing disheveled; snakes swirl about her head and arms, animal skins hang from her shoulders, and her neck strains backward into the curve of ecstasy. In her hand she wields the tree branch that was a symbol of the cult. The maenad was thus a constant reminder of women's close association with the natural world of rampant vegetative growth and wild animal drives.

How can we account for such ideas as women's fundamental hostility to civilized life? The answer, we suggest, is that such ideas represent a configuration of themes that ordinarily arise at a particular moment in history: that of the transition from an aristocratic or feudal to a more egalitarian type of society in which the nuclear family, for reasons we shall explain, assumes sudden and overwhelming importance.

Transition from Aristocracy to Democracy: The Oikos and Restrictions on Women

Aristocratic or feudal society is usually dominated by a landholding nobility defined by birth whose social relationships preserve many of the features of tribal society. In such societies every social relationship finds concrete expression in an exchange of objects, including women. Aristocratic solidarity is maintained by these ties among men; women, as the medium of exchange, remain outside the principal social grouping.

In the midst of this society a class of commercial entrepreneurs arises. They derive from all social and economic groups: wealthy landowners interested in trade, younger or illegitimate sons of the nobility involved in maritime ventures, craftsmen and other specialists, and wealthy, independent peasants. In archaic Greece the rise of this class was associated with the discovery of iron, whose ready availability made possible small-scale cultivation of land and thus transformed the method of production. The artisans worked the new metals, the merchants traded in it, and agriculture was intensified through its use. This new middle class was thus still strongly tied to the land (the economic base of society was agricultural throughout all of antiquity), but it was a larger and more diverse group than the landowning aristocracy. At this point in history the small household emerged as the productive unit of society, and any head of a household (who was simultaneously a landowner) automatically became a citizen or member of the state. Conversely, the state itself, the polis, was defined as the sum of all individual households.

The more inclusive and more egalitarian state that resulted from these shifts in political and economic strength in the eighth and seventh centuries B.C. was thus bound up with the increasing importance of the *oikos*, or household, which was a small corporation composed of its male head, his wife, their children, and the slaves who served it and worked the land that was its economic base. The legal rights over this property were vested in the male head and transferred to his son to assure the continuity of the individual oikoi. The whole of the productive output of this small corporation was appropriated by its male head as the basis for his claim to participate in the state.

The transformations that occurred in Greece in the political, economic, and social arenas were internally consistent and marked the beginning of a new and important phase of human development. For the transition from aristocracy to democracy was not merely one in a series of historical advances but a stage in which the character of society was altered. Property holding in the form of household units was the first advance over tribal ownership; the corresponding legal system that came into being at this time was the first step in the dissociation of the state from civil society; finally, the myth of a struggle between male and female gods culminating in the establishment of a patriarchal reign was the first articulation of an ideological pattern that, ever since, has accompanied such transformations. We shall see, for example, that in Rome a conceptual scheme like that of the Greeks, which implies women's basic hostility to civilized life, did not arise until historical conditions paralleled those under which it arose in Greece.

The new importance of the oikos in the Greek democracy had important ramifications for the position of women. For the woman was a necessary part of the oikos: she produced the sons who kept it together, and she supervised its day-to-day activities. The nuclear family, which in tribal and aristocratic society had existed only as a biological and social unit, now became a political and economic reality. The functions of wife and mother that women had always performed were now construed as a necessity and a duty, and the failure to perform them had legal and moral consequences.

The laws of the new democratic state therefore imposed restrictions on women's freedom designed to insure their subservience to the needs of the state. The patriarchal orientation of Greek society is nowhere more clearly demonstrated than by the legal system, which prohibited women from ever achieving the status of fully autonomous beings. Throughout her life a woman remained the legal ward of the head of her oikos, who was called her *kyrios* (or lord) and who might be her father, husband, or male child. His consent and supervision was necessary for any legal action undertaken on her behalf. Women could not engage in transactions involving property valued at over one *medimnos* (bushel), about three days' wages for a skilled laborer; this restriction allowed women to trade and barter on a small scale but prevented them from transferring any landed property and therefore from interfering in the political and economic operation of the oikos. A woman could not inherit family property outright (with one exception discussed below). Her share consisted instead of her dowry, a sum provided by her father to insure her maintenance. When she married it was added to the oikos of her husband, and the wife herself could not ever dispose of it. It remained a legally separate piece of property, however, and her husband was liable for its repayment to the oikos of his wife's father in the event of divorce.

The word for marriage in ancient Greece betrays its function and character. It was called *ekdosis*, loan, and so marriage was a transaction whereby a woman's father lent her out to the head of another oikos so that she might perform for the latter the functions of wife and mother. The children of the marriage belonged to the oikos of the husband. The marriage itself was quite ordinarily contracted with a near relative (an uncle or cousin on the father's side). Divorce was a simple procedure for either the husband or the wife and returned the wife to the oikos of her father.

Behind all of these laws and restrictions there lay one primary principle: the inviolability of the individual oikos unit. A woman's procreative function was a duty owed ultimately to the oikos of her birth, should it ever be in danger of passing out of existence for want of an heir. A woman who was the only child in an oikos was in a special situation and was called an *epikleros*, "heiress." She "inherited" the oikos property but was legally obligated to contract a marriage with the next of kin on her father's side. Strictly speaking, then, she inherited only the right to transfer ownership of the property, and the laws required that it be transferred to a male member of the same family to whom it had already belonged (usually to her father's brother). The unbreakable bond between a woman and the oikos of her birth thus insured against the disappearance of that oikos.

This contrasts with earlier aristocratic practice, which allowed women to transfer ownership of property they might inherit to their husbands regardless of family affiliation. For marriage in aristocratic society entailed the forging of a powerful political, economic, and social bond between two houses. The upwardly mobile lower classes in aristocratic society therefore commonly regarded the right of intermarriage with women of the upper classes as an important privilege. In the democratic polis, too, marriage might lead to the political and economic advancement of the husband, since he gained an affiliation with the woman's family and the right to manage her dowry, which could involve a considerable amount of property. But there were some crucial restrictions: he could not dispose of the dowry; and if by marriage he acquired rights over the property of the woman's oikos (i.e., if she were an epikleros), he forfeited his rights to inheritance within his own family line. Further, he was not registered as kyrios of the newly acquired oikos until he had produced a son to inherit it. The state thus limited individual freedom to dispose of property to prevent the exercise of that right from conflicting with the higher principle of the inviolability of each oikos. This primary principle, in turn, derived its force from the Greek idea that, as Aristotle put it, "The best form of political society is one where power is vested in the middle class." And it was essential to the definition of this group that "its members should possess a moderate and adequate property" (i.e., neither the large estates of the aristocratic class nor the impoverished farms of the peasants).

The centrality of the oikos to the polis caused a revaluation of the crime of adultery. Since adultery threatened the integrity of the oikos, it became a crime against society rather than a personal transgression. The state, therefore, regulated the sexual lives of citizen women. Adultery of a free Athenian woman made her liable to exclusion from participation in religious ceremonies and festivals, and her husband had to divorce her. Adultery was punished more severely than rape or seduction because that crime threatened the preservation of the household by casting doubts on the legitimacy of its heir. Such a penalty was tantamount to loss of citizenship for a woman, since religion and marriage were the only two areas where the citizen woman was privileged. The male adulterer could be killed with impunity. Men who raped or seduced unmarried free women were punished with a fine; an unmarried daughter caught with a man could be sold into slavery. The schedule of penalties shows that in this area of Greek life, too, the sanctity of the oikos dictated law.

Although men suffered heavy penalties for committing adultery with citizen women, their sexual lives were in other respects far less circumscribed than those of their wives. Prostitutes and courtesans were available in addition to homosexual partners. A famous statement by the orator Demosthenes distinguishes three kinds of women: "We have hetairai [courtesans] for the sake of pleasure, prostitutes for the daily care of the body, but wives to bear us legitimate children and to be the trusted guardians of our households." Demosthenes's description of the wife's function summarized her importance to the state and demonstrated that this importance was conceived of in terms of her role in the oikos. This subordination of women to their husbands in the interests of the oikos whose prosperity benefited them both was a unique feature of middle-class democracy. And so the relationship between man and woman in ancient Greece became the model for the relationship between citizen and state. For the polis required the subordination of man's individual and private self to its interests, and it was even proposed that the proper relation of the citizen to the state was that of a "lover": "I want you to feed your eyes upon Athens every day, and become filled with passion for her . . . " said Pericles in his Funeral Oration.

Women's Role in the Polis

Regardless of her subordination to her husband, the married woman was held in high regard in ancient Greece. The association she formed with her husband was a kind of partnership; each party made a contribution to the oikos that was their mutual concern. The woman's job, aside from bearing children, was to supervise the household. She lived almost entirely in the private sphere and did not ordinarily participate in her husband's social activities. In the everyday life of the polis, however, the contributions of women were recognized by the important role they played in the celebration of religious festivals. For example, in the Parthenon frieze that depicts the Panathenaic procession in honor of Athene, young girls carry the sacrificial vessels and the more mature women of the city, both married and unmarried, bear to the goddess the robe they had woven for her. The presentation of this robe climaxed the procession. The women's prominent role in this important celebration reveals that their contributions to the state were recognized and honored, even though women were not granted commensurate legal and economic privileges.

Noncitizen women lived a very different kind of life in ancient Greece. For example, the hetaira whom Demosthenes mentioned was a professional. She might be free or a slave, but she was only infrequently a citizen woman. Prostitutes, by contrast, were invariably slave women. The hetaira's job was to entertain at male drinking parties (*symposia*); this is the "pleasure" to which Demosthenes refers. The hetaira was educated in poetry and music with an eye to the enjoyment her presence could provide for the men at their symposia; she was thus more cultivated than cultured, although this fact has often led to the misrepresentation of courtesans as a highly educated, almost scholarly elite. Some, like Aspasia, the mistress of Pericles, formed liaisons with the leading poets, philosophers, orators, and statesmen of the day, but ordinarily a free woman resorted to courtesanship only out of financial necessity.

Other professions lower-class free women and slaves practiced were those of wool working (spinning and weaving), nursing, midwifery, retail selling of such wares as the garlands used in religious sacrifice, cobbling, and vase painting. Household slaves mainly spun yarn and wove cloth and performed other menial tasks. Even in households that could not afford male slaves, there would always be a few female slaves.

The Greeks themselves realized that women's lot was not an enviable one. The theme of the incapacities under which women must labor recurs throughout classical literature. Medea, for example, in Euripides's play of the same name, complains:

> We women are the most unfortunate creatures.
> Firstly with an excess of wealth it is required
> For us to buy a husband and take for our bodies
> A master; for not to take one is even worse.
> And now the question is serious whether we take
> A good or bad one; for there is no easy escape
> For a woman, nor can she say no to her marriage.
> She arrives among new modes of behavior and manners,
> And needs prophetic power, unless she has learned at home,
> How best to manage him who shares the bed with her.
> And if we work out all this well and carefully,
> And the husband lives with us and lightly bears his yoke,
> Then life is enviable. If not, I'd rather die.
> A man, when he's tired of the company in his home,
> Goes out of the house and puts an end to his boredom
> And turns to a friend or companion of his own age.
> But we are forced to keep our eyes on one alone.
> What they say of us is that we have a peaceful time
> Living at home, while they do the fighting in war.
> How wrong they are! I would very much rather stand
> Three times in the front of battle than bear one child.[5]

In what remains to us of the lyric poetry written by women, laments over lost virginity are a frequent theme. Several of the most beautiful fragments of Sappho treat this idea:

> FIRST   Virginity O
> VOICE   my virginity!
>   Where will you
>   go when I lose
>   you?
>
> SECOND   I'm off to
> VOICE   a place I shall
>   never come back
>   from
>   Dear Bride!
>   I shall never
>   come back to you
>   Never![6]

Erinna addressed a hexameter poem to her childhood friend Baucis, who died shortly after marriage, and whom the poet gently chides for having transferred her affections to her new husband:

O Baucis!
the delights of a husband's bed,
the magic of white sheets
rustling
charmed your heart
into forgetfulness of childish
pleasures
Aphrodite
has stolen you away
into death.[7]

Such poetry, clearly, refers less to some supposed sexual trauma than to the jolt to their emotional and personal lives the sudden transition to the married state brought for women. This is the message of the lament of Procne in Sophocles's drama *Tereus*, who bewails her marriage to a barbarian Thracian king:

Now I'm nothing—and all alone. . . . But I've given some thought to this life we women lead and what nothings we are. I think we're happiest as young children in our fathers' homes, where we lead the lives of human beings, and our nurses are carefree joys. But once we're grown to youth and reason—then we're thrown out of our family and country. Some of us go off to strangers, some to barbarians, some to be treated gently, some to be abused. And once one night has yoked us to this lot, we're obliged to commend it and think it fine![8]

Aware though they may have been of the shortcomings of women's social role in the polis, the Greeks clearly regarded it as a necessary concomitant to the city-state. And so, whenever a modification of that role was proposed, it was always as part of a plan for a wholesale transformation of the state. Plato's *Republic* is the famous example, and his advocacy of equality between the men and women of the upper, or guardian, class is often cited as an example of liberated thinking. But the Greeks never advanced such ideas for the sake of their intrinsic merit; they always saw a change in family relations as a necessary but secondary issue. Plato, for example, proposed a return to an earlier era: the luxurious or aristocratic state was to be purified of those features that led to its transformation into the democratic polis. *The Republic* displays great similarities to the state of Sparta, which was peculiar in the Greek world precisely because it stopped developing in the seventh century. Its aristocratic form was preserved by a set of laws that maintained it as a military aristocracy instead of leading it toward a democracy.

The equality between the sexes Plato proposed really entailed the very different idea of "holding wives and children in common," as in the aristocratic state. Women, as the exchange objects, were to be held in common by the men of the class as a whole. The proverb with which Plato introduced this idea, "Friends' possessions are held in common," refers to a system of free exchange within a restricted group. This ideal is a poor alternative indeed to counterpose against the Greek ideal of married life as exemplified in the relationship between Odysseus and Penelope in the *Odyssey* of Homer:

> It's a great strength and a fine thing
> when a man and a wife share their household
> as they share their thoughts:
> enemies gnash their teeth, friends are happy —
> and the two of them know it.[9]

This praise of women in the marriage relationship does not invalidate the idea that the fundamental attitude of the Greeks toward women remained misogynistic. As social beings, women in the polis entered into a partnership with men that fostered civilization, and only in this relationship did women gain favor. As we have seen, the misogyny of the Greeks originally sprang from the association of women with the world of instincts and passions, which was hostile to civilized life. Unlike man, the woman of the polis was regarded as a hybrid creature, a domesticated animal who could be adapted to the needs of society but whose fundamental instincts were antagonistic to it. Woman, says Euripides in an unidentified fragment, is a more terrible thing than the violence of the raging sea, than the force of torrents, than the sweeping breath of fire. Thus, her very existence was a testimony to the gods' hatred of mankind. This is the Greek view of women; this is the way in which women's ties with nature manifest themselves; this, finally, is the supreme articulation of man's alienation from the sources of his own essence as a natural being.

THE TRIUMPH OF APHRODITE: THE HELLENISTIC ERA

On the east frieze of the Parthenon the twelve Olympian gods watch the solemn Panathenaic procession. Of all the gods in this pantheon, the only two who survived as important deities into the Hellenistic period (323–19 B.C.) were Aphrodite and Dionysus, just those two gods who sat most uneasily in the solemn assembly. For both deities shared an eastern origin that, in the context of classical Greece, always caused them to appear as intruders, outsiders, usurpers. In order to assimilate them into the Olympic pantheon their barbaric heritage had to be suppressed or overcome through some kind of ritual of adoption or rebirth. In the Hellenistic period this eastern origin reasserted itself, as the interests of the time turned in the direction of mystery religions and fertility cults. Aphrodite became one of the most important subjects of artistic representation as the ideal form of the female, now seen nude for the first time. Unlike her classical predecessor she does not stand cool and detached, but more usually bends or crouches to display more fully the elaborate curvature of her body. Dionysus became in this period the most important Greek god outside of Greece. He was the patron of artistic guilds, and he supplanted other deities in established religions such as that of the Orphics; one of the Ptolemies planned to make him the chief god of the empire.

The cultural transformations of the Hellenistic period, of which the increased importance of Aphrodite and Dionysus was only one sign, brought a change also in the attitude toward the relation between men and women. Here, as in the case of the classical Greek world, man's evaluation of nature and of his relation to it correlated with his attitude toward women. Let us therefore examine first the political and social organization of the Hellenistic world, then some of the very concrete ways in which women's position improved during this period, and finally the relation between the human and natural worlds.

The Hellenistic World (323 B.C. to 19 B.C.)

After the death of Alexander the Great in 323 B.C., his vast kingdom was divided up into four distinct empires, each of which was still huge. The Ptolemaic empire was the most important. It included upper Egypt, extended over to the area along the Gaza strip, and took in the island of Cyprus. The kingdom contained a diverse population, but the government was highly centralized. Although ultimately the king controlled everything, the vast bureaucracy included a complex system of checks and counterchecks. The main business was agriculture, and the state monopolized oil and grain production. The native population, a pool of forced labor, performed all of the manual work. Their overseers were mostly Greeks or other foreigners, but the native Egyptian aristocracy maintained its position of social influence and power.

Alexandria, its capital, exemplified the characteristics of the empire as a whole. It was a conglomeration of individual settlements: there was an Egyptian village, a Jewish *politeuma* (corporation), a Greek polis modeled on the classical type and inhabited by Greeks, and a settlement of foreign soldiers. The Greek polis was the most important subunit and it, like the others, kept its own constitution but was overseen by a royal official who worked closely with the magistrates of the polis. Ethnic affiliation thus replaced national identity, and by the second century B.C. Greeks no longer identified themselves by the name of their polis (e.g., as Athenians) but called themselves simply "Hellenes," Greeks. In such an atmosphere clubs and associations of all sorts grew up. Many of the philosophical schools of this period were more like exclusive clubs than the schools of the late classical period, the great Academy of Plato and the Lyceum of Aristotle.

Individualism and the Improved Position of Women

Under this centralized pluralism a new kind of individualism found expression. In the Hellenistic city citizenship no longer depended upon membership in a family, and the laws therefore ceased to concern themselves so exclusively with women as childbearers. The household as a social unit did not pass out of existence, however. Quite the contrary, it began to serve more truly the partnership ideal. And so, in the Hellenistic period, the marriage contract reflected both the new humanistic bias that treated each person as an autonomous unit and an emphasis on marriage as a compact between two persons, each with separate duties and responsibilities. One such contract from the Ptolemaic period (92 B.C.) runs as follows:

> Let Apollonia be the wife of Philiscus, having been persuaded by him that it is fitting for her to be his wife, and let her have mastery in common with him over all their possessions. And let Philiscus provide for Apollonia all the things that she needs and her clothing and all the rest that it is suitable for a married woman to have provided for her—and let him do this wherever they live, according as their means allow. And let him take no other wife but Apollonia, and no concubine, and let him have no boyfriends or beget children from any other woman so long as Apollonia is living nor inhabit any other household than the one over which Apollonia rules; nor let him repudiate her or do violence to her or treat her badly or alienate any of their property in a manner which is unfair to Apollonia. If he is caught doing any of these things . . . then let him pay back immediately to Apollonia her dowry of two talents and four thousand drachmas of bronze. By the same token, let Apollonia not be permitted to spend the day or the night away from the house of Philiscus without his knowledge, nor may she sleep with another man, nor may she squander their common household property, nor may she disgrace Philiscus in the ways in which men get disgraced. But if Apollonia willingly does any of these things, let her be sent away from Philiscus, and let him repay to her the dowry simply within ten days of her departure.[10]

This contract represents to a very significant degree the fulfillment of that ideal of mutuality the classical Greeks had originated, but failed to translate into reality. However, the double standard persists, and common threats to the relationship are indicated by the proscriptions.

With the breakdown of the link between citizenship and property ownership, women were not only freed from the restrictions imposed by their function as legitimizers of the heirs of family property but became property owners themselves. Other evidence for women's improved position are the scattered references to women who performed duties or held offices previously restricted to men. Women were granted citizenship as a reward for outstanding service of one kind or another; a first century B.C. inscription from Asia Minor indicates that a woman named Phyle held the highest state office there and constructed a reservoir and aqueducts for her city. Another inscription describes a woman who served as *archon* (high magistrate) of her city, Histria. And an inscription from Delphi cites the honors, including the right to own land, conferred upon Polygnota, a female harpist, and her nephew, as a reward for her services to the temple. Hipparchia, wife of Crates, the cynic philosopher, exemplifies the women of this age. She was a woman of high birth who threatened her parents with suicide if they would not betroth her to Crates, to whose philosophy she was attracted. She married Crates and defended herself to a critic of both her style of life and her presence at symposia as follows: "Do I seem to you to have been advised poorly about myself if I have devoted my time to my education instead of wasting it at the loom?"[11]

Women figure in this period as the subject matter of poetry, as they had in the classical era. But women no longer appear as the antithesis to the cultural ideal, because the focus has shifted to the private realm with which women are traditionally associated. This is nowhere more clearly shown than in the literary mime, a form popular with cultured Alexandrian poets. The poet Theocritus illustrates the genre in his fifteenth idyll:

GORGO: Is Praxinoa in?

PRAXINOA: Gorgo dear! it's about time—yes, I'm in. It's a wonder that you're here now. Get her a chair, Eunoa, and put a cushion on it.

GORGO: It's just fine.

PRAXINOA: Do sit down.

GORGO: What a foolish thing I am—I barely saved my soul getting here, Praxinoa, what with the huge crowd, the huge number of chariots, boots everywhere, everywhere men in soldiers' cloaks. And the road was unending. You certainly live far out.

PRAXINOA: It's because of that husband of mine; he comes to the ends of the earth and buys a pig-sty, not a house, so that we can't be neighbors, whether out of bitterness or evil jealousy—he's always the same.

GORGO: Don't talk that way about your husband Dinon, my dear, when the little one's around; see, woman, how he's staring at you. It's all right, Zopyrion, sweet child; she's not talking about daddy.

PRAXINOA: The baby understands, by the goddess!

GORGO: Daddy's nice!*

The sixth mime of Herodas illustrates a new attitude of acceptance and freedom toward women's sexuality. In this piece two women discuss the fine qualities of one cobbler's wares:

We're alone, so let me tell you about these dildoes:
harder than men, softer than sleep and laced with wool.
Now there's a cobbler who likes women![12]

*From *The Idylls of Theokritos*, a verse translation by Barriss Mills, © 1963 Purdue University Press by Purdue Research Foundation, West Lafayette, Indiana 47904. Reprinted with permission.

Women and the Natural World

The mystery religions and ecstatic cults that in the late classical period especially had attracted women now dominated religious life as a whole. The goddess Isis was the most important deity of the period, and she gradually assimilated the functions of every major divinity. In a catalogue of her divine prerogatives, Isis includes among her functions a wide range of activities:

> I gave and ordained laws for men which no one is able to change.
> I am she that is called goddess by women.
> I divided the earth from the heaven.
> I brought together women and men.
> I ordained that parents be loved by children.
> I revealed mysteries unto men.
> I caused women to be loved by men.
> I made an end to murders.
> I am in the rays of the Sun.
> I am the Queen of War.
> I am the Lord of Rainstorms.[13]

From this selection it is clear that Isis's realm included the whole of the human and natural worlds, and she herself came to symbolize their essential unity. The natural world was no longer viewed as the antithesis of the human sphere, and consequently women were seen in a more positive light. The realms with which they had traditionally been associated—marriage, sexual love, family life, the natural world—had become the common cultural concern.

In the mystery religions nature was the arena of the great cycle of birth and death, of the coming-into-being and passing away in which all existence shared. The common humanity that the mystery religions affirmed had as its basis the universal participation in the condition of mortality and the shared expectation of immortality in a life after death.

This same spirit and these same ideas also found expression in the philosophical schools of the Hellenistic period. The two most important philosophies were Stoicism and Epicureanism. Although opposed in other respects, both schools regarded nature as not only the biological but moral source of man's being. In the philosophy of the Stoics, for example, nature was the realm in which the ultimate rationality of the world was expressed, and it was animated by a divine being who was the quintessence of reason. A rational and moral life, therefore, was a life lived in conformity with nature.

Within the life of the individual, natural instincts, such as the sexual urge, no longer appeared as malign forces. Both the love experience and its deities were evaluated positively. The love deity was either Eros or Aphrodite, depending on whether the poet wished to focus on the playful, even devilish, aspects of the experience or on its pleasurable and beautiful quality. The following two epigrams, one by a male, the other by a female, poet, will illustrate the difference:

> Wanted: Eros, mischievous child—just now
> At dawn, he fluttered away from my bed.
> Description: fast, fearless, cute when he laughs,
> Gentle when he cries; on his back: wings and a quiver.[14]
>
>   —MELEAGER

> "Nothing's sweeter or lovelier than love—everything else
> Takes second place; even honey: I spit it out."
> Nossis has this to say: the woman whom Aphrodite never loves
> Never discovers the rose among the summer flowers![15]
>
>   —NOSSIS

The theme of hostility between male and female as a model of the cosmic struggle has disappeared from literature. And in the sphere of politics and social relations women's range of activity was far greater than in the classical polis. But the productive system of this period rested upon the backs of the enslaved masses who performed the agricultural tasks; the more liberated, individualized mode of life in this world brought in its train a lowering in the standard of living that was ultimately fatal to it. As Nietzsche noted, this sunny world harbored a dark secret:

> Let us mark this well: Alexandrian culture, to be able to exist permanently, requires a slave class, but with its optimistic view of life it denies the necessity of such a class, and consequently, when its beautifully seductive and tranquilizing utterances about the "dignity of man" and the "dignity of labor" are no longer effective, it drifts toward a dreadful destruction.[16]

Our evaluation of the position of women in this world must ultimately be informed by the same cynicism. Women were free to own property, but property ownership no longer led to citizenship; women were citizens and officials of the polis, but the polis was no longer the dominant political form; women were no longer a testimony to the gods' hatred of mankind, but it was the gods who ceased to hate men, not men who ceased to hate women.

VENUS ENTHRONED: THE ROMAN PERIOD

The political organization of the Roman state and in particular the principle of *patriapotestas* ("right of the father") guaranteed the Roman female citizen even fewer citizen rights than the Athenian matron. But because the Roman state was at all times a remarkable blend of indigenous with imported elements, of archaic with sophisticated features, women were actually freer in some ways than their Greek and Hellenistic predecessors. In this section we shall explore this paradox and, in particular, its different application in the republican and imperial periods. For in the area of women's position, as in every other sphere, the transition from republic to empire is the great dividing line.

Women in the Republic: Under Guardianship for Life (Third to First Centuries B.C.)

Ennius, in his epic poem *The Annals*, written in the third century B.C., celebrated the history and rise of the Roman state. Ilia, the mother of Rome's founders, Romulus and Remus, was a fully developed character. She was not the passive recipient of the god's seed but an active participant in her own destiny. At one point she relates to her sister a dream that prophesies her destiny. It is interpreted to mean that she, like the traditional hero, will undergo a period of trial and suffering, but eventually her fortunes will be restored and she will be hailed as a founder of the race. Another reminiscence of early times occurred in a speech of Cicero, in which he reproached a contemporary noblewoman for failing to live up to her illustrious female ancestors. He describes the "womanly glory" of one who had achieved fame by pulling free the image of a goddess grounded at the mouth of the Tiber River. Another had defended her father against an attack by the Roman populace. These examples, common in Roman history, demonstrate that women's fulfillment of their traditional duties could be consistent with action in the political and social spheres.

The Romans, unlike the Greeks, did not see women as intrinsically hostile to the aims of civilized political life. On the contrary, within their limited sphere of action, they were as apt as men to serve the state and were honored and glorified for their contributions. Certainly, the tradition of individualism and humanism inherited from the Hellenistic era was responsible for some of this. Far more important, however, was the fact that the women of whom we hear all belonged to the aristocratic class and were all acting in defense of their class or family interests. Thus, the woman who defended her father was saving him from attack in a popular uprising against aristocratic oppression. The possibility of greater participation in society and politics for the Roman matron was, therefore, tied directly to the class structure of the Roman Republic.

The Roman Republic was an aristocracy, and so it shared certain features with the archaic Greek state. But it was a vital and adaptable form of the aristocratic state, so the history of the republic was not one of steady undermining of aristocratic domination and progress toward democracy, as in Greece. Rather, the aristocratic class in Rome adapted itself to new economic conditions and gradually absorbed the wealthiest and most prestigious plebeian (lower-class) families through intermarriage.

Family law and marriage regulations retained their aristocratic character throughout this period. The most striking feature of the legal system was patriapotestas, which gave to the legal head of the household absolute power, including the right of life and death and the right to sell into slavery, over all the members of his family: wife, children, slaves. A Roman woman, like her Greek counterpart, remained under guardianship for life, her father's or husband's if she was in patria potestate ("under the legal authority of the father") or in manu ("under [his] hand", that is, physical authority), that of a male specifically appointed for the purpose if she was not. However, unlike Athenian women, Roman citizen women could inherit and acquire real property and could dispose of it with the consent of their guardians. This privilege is characteristically associated with the aristocratic form of society, and its purpose is to maintain the strength of the class through the formation of powerful bonds between the families that make it up. Marriage in aristocratic society is a form of exchange between the male heads of families, and therefore entails the complete severance of the woman's ties with her original family. In Rome the oldest forms of marriage were of this kind. A woman was married either by confarreatio (a religious ceremony performed by a priest), or by coemptio (purchase), where the father "sold" (rather than "leased," as in Greece) his daughter to the prospective husband, or by usus (what we would today call "common-law" marriage). In all three cases the woman abandoned legal and religious ties with her original family and was virtually incorporated into her husband's family. Such a marriage delivered her into her husband's manus (power and legal authority), an authority equivalent to patriapotestas. As her guardian, her husband had absolute power over her, including the power of life and death. A woman who was an Athenian citizen, by contrast, was in such a position only as an unmarried daughter caught having intercourse with a man; otherwise, the laws of the state guarded her life and her well-being.

The continued aristocratic character of the state made appropriate the preservation of this archaic, crude, and even inhuman legal system. Yet, the sophistication of the Roman state and the heritage of Hellenistic moral philosophy caused a modification of some of the effects of the legal code. Guardianship, for example, originally restricted a woman's right to the free disposal of her property, but eventually became the means to insure this right. For a woman gradually acquired the legal right to dismiss her guardian if he refused to obey her will. Roman marriage practices provide another example of the ways in which the modification of restrictions benefited women. The institution of the trinoctium allowed a woman not to pass under the manus of her husband. If she absented herself from his home for three successive nights in any one year she retained her ties with her original family. This institution was probably an attempt to prevent a patrician woman's loss of her class standing in the event that she married a plebeian. But it quickly became women's principal means for acquiring freedom from the legal domination of either husband or father, for the woman could put herself under a guardianship she could more easily control.

The art and literature of the republican period demonstrate that the same principles that determined women's social and legal position informed their cultural evaluation as well. Republican literature does not employ the paradigm of a deep-seated opposition between man and woman to articulate a view of man's place in the world. In the poetry of the late republican period both sexuality in general and the sexual relations between men and women are evaluated positively. For example, Lucretius's philosophical poem *On the Nature of the Universe* gives a scientific explanation of the forces governing the cosmos. It opens with an address to Venus, "mother of the Roman race, delight of men and gods, dear goddess." Lucretius subsequently characterizes her as "the guiding power of the universe" and hence an apt inspirational deity for his poem. Venus was a socialized, but not masculinized, deity: her erotic and sexual aspects were not suppressed but transformed into her characterization as nurturing, sustaining mother. Such an adaptation would have been inconceivable for the Greek goddess Aphrodite, whose threatening aspect caused her instead to be relegated to the fringes of the Olympian pantheon. The Roman view of love, as of the world of nature in general, was far more tolerant. In the Roman mind man was not tragically but fortunately a natural being. His natural side was not, as it was for the Greeks, the opposite of his existence as a political creature. The Roman Venus was a benign goddess, and her world was a sunlit, joyous, and life-giving realm. She was the mother of the Romans as well, and therefore sanctioned their natural and divinely given right to rule.

In the love poetry of this period the women emerge as strong and lively, if secondary, characters. And the affair itself was typically evaluated in terms of traditional Roman moral standards; it became the arena in which to fulfill, rather than threaten, the conventional code. Catullus, for example, described his feelings for his beloved Lesbia as follows: "I loved you once not as men love women, but as a father cherishes his children and family." In a moment of cautious optimism about Lesbia, whose habitual unfaithfulness constantly troubled him, Catullus prayed to the gods that they might "link their lives together in an eternal treaty of sacred friendship." Propertius, a poet of later date but writing in the same tradition, expressed his love for Cynthia using a military metaphor: he has, he says, enrolled himself as a soldier in the service of love's army. Elsewhere he described the relationship as if it were a complete and traditional Roman family: "You, Cynthia, alone are for me a home, and you alone are parents for me."

This poetry manifested a more generalized notion of late republican thinking, which held that only in the private sphere of life could one find genuine happiness. In this context, the world of the passions acquires a new interest, as it did in the Hellenistic world under the influence of a new attitude toward nature. Within the love relationship all human emotions and intense feelings can be given full play and express their true range. This contrasts with the Greek view of passionate love, which construed its essential irrational character as dangerous. The chorus of Euripides' *Hippolytus* prays that it might never feel the "wild and measureless rhythms of love" that are the prelude to destruction. The Romans, by contrast, felt the pain and torture of love, but welcomed it as the means of communication with the emotional wellsprings of their beings. Women, in both cases, were associated with passion but were judged differently, according to the prevailing cultural view of natural instincts.

The Empire and the Shifting Social View of Women (19 B.C.–First Century A.D.)

There were dramatic changes on all levels of society when Augustus acceded to power in 19 B.C. as the emperor of Rome. In form Rome remained a republic governed by an aristocracy; in fact it evolved into an empire ruled by one man. Augustus's base of support was the newly developed bourgeoisie, local and provincial notables whose status derived in large part from their achievements in business or the military. Under Augustus's rule the power and influence of the old Roman aristocracy, which controlled the Senate, was considerably weakened.

The transition from republic to empire in Rome, therefore, involved the rise to prominence of the same class that in Greece had supplanted the aristocracy with the polis. Although in Rome the transformation was more gradual and did not feature the adoption of a new constitution, many parallel changes occurred. For instance, Augustus attempted to revive the official state cult, which had been neglected and undermined by ecstatic cults and philosophical speculation; similarly, the Athenian tyrant Pisistratus had inaugurated the Panathenaic festival. Augustus embarked upon an ambitious building program, also like the tyrants of the early Greek city-states. The system of property ownership was not altered, but the laws having to do with debt were, as in Solon's reforms in Greece. For example, laws allowing the sale of family property and its transfer to creditors were introduced. The Roman legal system was already highly developed by the time of the late republic, but under the empire some reforms occurred that strengthened the state's interest over that of private individuals. Crimes that had previously been civil offenses now became breaches of criminal, or public, law. Jury courts were set up to try offenders. One such crime was adultery, and Augustus himself introduced the use of jury courts to deal with this offense. This was part of a whole legislative program designed to promote the growth of the nuclear family and to undermine the authority of and allegiances among the few remaining aristocratic families.

The propaganda of the time hailed these laws as a kind of moral rearmament program for the dwindling aristocracy, but it seems clear from what we can gauge about the effects of these laws that the interest behind them was not the old but the new Roman state. The two most famous of these laws were the lex Julia of 18 B.C. and the lex Papia Poppaea of A.D. 9. These laws made marriage virtually compulsory; parents of three children received special rewards: the mother acquired a grant of independence in the management of her property. Some provisions restricted movement across class lines; this preserved the prestige of the old nobility while at the same time it made more freedwomen available as marriage partners for freedmen or poor freeborn men. Adultery now became a criminal offense, and normally the two offenders were banished to different islands for life. Until the time of Constantine, three centuries later, a wife could not prosecute her husband for this crime. As in Greece, husbands were required to divorce adulterous wives, and in addition the wife was penalized by the loss of one-sixth of her dowry and one-third of her property (the adulterer lost half of his property). The lex Papia Poppaea relaxed some of these restrictions, especially those having to do with property inheritance, and this mitigation of the law's severity is usually interpreted as a response to widespread protest by the wealthier groups of landowning Romans.

We found in Greece that a change in the cultural attitude toward women accompanied the emergence of the polis out of aristocratic society. A similar transformation occurs in the literature of the early empire, where for the first time in Roman culture the idea appears that woman is hostile to civilization. Virgil expresses this idea most notably in the *Aeneid,* his epic of imperial destiny that embodied the ideals of Augustus's regime. One of its main themes is that women, or the female force as manifested by certain men, impede Aeneas from the fulfillment of his destiny. In Book II he risks his life and mission by returning for his wife Creusa, whom he discovers has perished in the assault on Troy. Aeneas leaves the ruined city with his aged father and young son. The famous trio symbolizes the salvation from Troy of the masculine element, the family and future conceived in exclusively patrilineal terms.

Aeneas's sojourn in Carthage and his affair with its queen Dido is the most famous instance of the female character of the obstacles he must confront. However, Aeneas must escape not women per se, but love affairs that are pursued for their own sake. So the new ideal of the Roman citizen repudiates the ideal of the Latin love poets. Dido herself was a thoroughly competent ruler of her city until she succumbed to passion; under its influence she destroyed herself and her city and nearly dragged Aeneas down with her.

When Aeneas finally arrives in Italy, he forms bonds of friendship with a rustic people whose royal house conveniently lacks women. His main opponents are the Latins stirred against him by the queen mother, who rejects Aeneas as a suitor for her daughter and objects to the use of Lavinia for a political alliance with the newcomers. The two are finally married, and the mother of all future Romans is the only woman in the book who has not uttered a word. On the three occasions when she appears in the narrative, she casts her eyes down modestly, blushes with maidenly shyness, or leads the women in lamentation over a dead hero. We are very far at this point from Ilia and other early Roman heroines who served their class or country in an active way.

The historians of the period express similar attitudes. Livy was the first Roman to glorify the housewife who, according to the traditional formula, "watched over the household and spun the wool." The good wife had been admired before, but her admirable qualities were tied to her nobility of character. Most often this included devotion to the ideals of the state, political acumen, and even visibility on the political scene. In the Augustan period, however, a contrast developed that reminds us very strongly of themes we encountered in the poetry of ancient Greece. The assertive woman became identified as an immoral virago; the ideal wife increasingly assumed the attributes of silence, obedience, and submissiveness to her husband.

This pattern was developed most completely in the history of the empire as related by the historian Tacitus. He attributed the degeneracy of the empire and its rulers to the power of women in the royal households. The emperor Claudius, according to Tacitus's narrative, was merely simple, even naive. But his third wife Messalina was devious, immoral, and murderous. She had her female rivals prosecuted and compelled young men to be her lovers, even if this meant divorcing their wives. She was eventually executed, justly, as Tacitus thought, but with lamentable consequences, for Claudius was then open to the influence and control of all the women competing for the position of empress. The successful candidate, Agrippina the Younger, was also the mother of Nero, whose succession to the throne Agrippina plotted and achieved. In the narrative of Nero's reign Tacitus suggests that all of the famous outrages connected with that emperor's name were directly or indirectly the result of the female influence in his life.

From this period too comes our only surviving Roman diatribe against women: the sixth satire of the poet Juvenal. Juvenal, like his Greek counterpart Semonides, catalogued women's vices in a long poem, drawing his examples from contemporary life. Like Tacitus, he found corruption under the empire best demonstrated by its women. In the opening lines of his poem Juvenal invokes Cynthia and Lesbia, the lovers of Propertius and Catullus, to illustrate the decline in moral standards; and like Semonides he reproaches women most severely for their sexual appetites.

CONCLUSION

Virgil, Livy, Tacitus, and Juvenal provide evidence that there occurred in Rome, as in Greece, a revaluation of the attitude toward women at a particular moment in history. In both cases the shift in outlook can be correlated with political and social developments. The forces that brought into being the middle-class state, whether it be the Greek polis or the Roman Empire of the first century B.C., produced a focus of attention on the nuclear family and hence on women's social role. Cultural perceptions of the limitations on women's lives cast them as the symbol of social malaise. The form of the symbolic process depends on the particular society: in Greece they epitomized all that was untamed, irrational, and imperfectly assimilated to civilized life. In contrast, the absence of systematized misogyny from the cultural life of the Hellenistic world must be connected with a form of government that made the nuclear family politically meaningless. And in Rome, as the nuclear family became more important to the state, misogyny reappeared. But the Romans' tendency to see things in specifically social rather than metaphysical terms meant that women represented to them a more specific social threat. They typified the immorality of the age and were used as an index of degeneration. And the fact that the final stage of Augustus's victory was his defeat of Cleopatra invited the use of a model of the empire as the triumph of male over female forces. This same fact, however, enabled a sympathetic portrayal of the queen to stand for a noble and valuable aspect of life whose expression the demands of empire precluded. Horace makes the point most strongly in his "Cleopatra Ode," ostensibly a poem celebrating the triumph of Augustus:

> She sought a nobler death: no woman's fear
> turned her trembling from the sword, no coward's
> spirit winged her swift ships to secret shores.
>
> No—she could stand the sight of her realm's collapse.
> Cooly and firmly she grasped the bitter serpents,
> and fed her body full on their black poison.
>
> So fierce was she in her deliberate death!
>
> Stripped bare of her army's strength, she scorned the role
> of star in the Roman triumph's haughty parade.
> Cleopatra was no woman meant to crawl![17]

NOTES

1. *Design for Utopia: Selected Writings of Charles Fourier*, tr. Julia Franklin, Schocken Books, New York, 1971, p. 77.
2. Aeschylus, *Eumenides*, tr. Richard Lattimore, *Aeschylus I: Oresteia, The Complete Greek Tragedies*, eds. D. Grene and R. Lattimore, University of Chicago Press, Chicago and London, 1953, p. 158 (lines 658–661). Copyright © University of Chicago.
3. Ibid., p. 161 (lines 736–738).
4. Sophocles, *Antigone*, tr. Elizabeth Wyckoff, *Sophocles I: The Complete Greek Tragedies*, eds. D. Grene and R. Lattimore, University of Chicago Press, Chicago and London, 1954, p. 170 (lines 338–341). Copyright © University of Chicago.
5. From *Media* from *Three Great Plays of Euripides*, translated by Rex Warner. Copyright © 1958, 1986 by Rex Warner. Reprinted by arrangement with New American Library, Inc., New York, N.Y. Also from *The Medea of Euripides* translated by Rex Warner, published by The Bodley Head.
6. Sappho, *Songs*, tr. Mary Barnard, University of California Press, Berkeley and Los Angeles, 1958, no. 32. Copyright © 1958 by The Regents of the University of California; reprinted by permission of the University of California Press.
7. Author's translation.
8. Author's translation.
9. Author's translation.
10. Author's translation.
11. Diogenes Laertius, *Lives of Famous Philosophers*, VI, 98 (translated by Marylin Arthur).
12. Author's translation.
13. Adapted with permission of Macmillan Publishing Company from *Hellenistic Religions: The Age of Syncretism*, edited and translated by Frederick C. Grant. Copyright 1953 by Macmillan Publishing Company, renewed 1981 by Estate of Frederick C. Grant.
14. Author's translation.
15. Author's translation.
16. Friedrich Nietzsche, *The Birth of Tragedy and the Case of Wagner*, tr. Walter Kaufmann, Vintage Books, a Division of Random House, Inc., New York, 1967, p. 111. © 1967, Random House.
17. Author's translation.

SUGGESTIONS FOR FURTHER READING

Note: For this section I have selected both those books that have influenced my own point of view and those that are nontechnical enough to be of use to the general reader. Many of the sources are reprints of much older works, but all are cited in their latest available editions.

Arethusa, 6, no. 1 (Spring, 1973). Special issue on Women in Antiquity.

Arethusa, 10, nos. 1, 2 (Spring & Fall, 1978). Special issue on Women in the Ancient World.

Balsdon, J. P. V. D. *Roman Women. Their History and Habits.* London: The Bodley Head, 1962. A dated but still useful survey.

Cameron, Averil, and Amelie Kuhrt, eds. *Images of Women in Antiquity.* Detroit: Wayne State University Press, 1983. An edited collection of essays.

duBois, Page. *Centaurs and Amazons. Women and the Pre-History of the Great Chain of Being.* Ann Arbor: University of Michigan Press, 1982.

Foley, Helene, ed. *Women's Studies*, 8, nos. 1, 2 (1981). Special issue on Women in Antiquity.

——, ed. *Reflections of Women in Antiquity.* New York and London: Gordon and Breach Science Publishers, 1981. A slightly expanded version of the preceding.

Gardner, Jane F. *Women in Roman Law and Society.* Bloomington and Indianapolis: Indiana University Press, 1986.

Hallett, Judith P. *Fathers and Daughters in Roman Society. Women and the Elite Family.* Princeton, N.J.: Princeton University Press, 1984.

Humphries, S. C. *The Family, Women and Death. Comparative Studies.* London and Boston: Routledge & Kegan Paul, 1983.

Lacey, W. K. *The Family in Classical Greece.* Ithaca, N.Y.: Cornell University Press, 1968.

Lefkowitz, Mary R. *Heroines and Hysterics.* New York: St. Martin's Press, 1981.

——, and Maureen B. Fant. *Women in Greece and Rome.* Toronto: Samuel Stevens, 1977.

——, and Maureen B. Fant. *Women's Life in Greece and Rome. A Source Book in Translation.* Baltimore: The Johns Hopkins University Press, 1982.

Peradotto, John, and J. P. Sullivan, eds. *Women in the Ancient World: The Arethusa Papers.* Albany, N.Y.: SUNY Press, 1984. A selection from the earlier volumes listed above, with updated bibliography.

Pomeroy, Sarah B. *Goddesses, Whores, Wives, and Slaves. Women in Classical Antiquity.* New York: Schocken Books, 1975.

——. *Women in Hellenistic Egypt: From Alexander to Cleopatra.* New York: Schocken Books, 1984.

Rawson, Beryl, ed. *The Family in Ancient Rome: New Perspectives.* Ithaca, N.Y.: Cornell University Press, 1986.

Schaps, David M. *Economic Rights of Women in Ancient Greece.* Edinburgh: Edinburgh University Press, 1979.

Tyrrell, William Blake. *Amazons. A Study in Athenian Mythmaking.* Baltimore and London: The Johns Hopkins University Press, 1984. Includes a general survey of women in Greek thought.

Orant with group of women are shown on a relief from a sarcophagus now in Rome's Museo Laterano. (From Andre Grabar, *Early Christian Art* [New York: Odyssey Press, 1968], plate 145. Reprinted with permission.)

chapter 4

Matres Patriae/ Matres Ecclesiae: Women of the Roman Empire

Jo Ann McNamara

Women were the agents of change in the Mediterranean societies amalgamated under the Roman Empire. Roman empresses created new public roles following the precedents of Hellenistic queens like Cleopatra. Roman law evolved along lines dictated by a new individualism that helped transform the old gender system that rigidly segregated women and men in political life, economic enterprise, and even private power. The Roman patriarchy crumbled as its representatives were subordinated to the power of the emperors, and women found their way into positions of political influence, gained limited control of money and increased independence from paternal power. During the first through the third centuries A.D., women showed themselves to be true mothers of the country (a title conferred on empresses) as well as mothers of the Church, contributing far more than we normally recognize to the shape of Christianity as they used it as the vehicle for their own aspirations.

By the fourth century, some of Rome's most distinguished women had converted to the new Christian faith, paving the way for its acceptance as a state religion. This essay discusses the significance of women's role in the cultural changes and religious innovations of the age. In the context of a new belief system, women ceased to define themselves within the limits of the antique gender system which classified them only in relation to men, as daughters, wives, and mothers. They discovered a new sense of individual selfhood and common sisterhood.

The Roman Republic was a patriarchy in the strictest sense of the word. Private life rested upon *patria potestas*, paternal power over the subordinate women, children, slaves, and clients who formed the Roman *familia*. The Roman matron was highly respected within limits established by a strong gender system that defined her role as the supporter of the patriarch's power. Public life was conducted in the name of the Senate and People of Rome, institutionally defined as exclusively male. In the last days of the Republic, the power of these institutions was destroyed by civil war at the same time that the army, led by its emperors (originally only a military title), carried the standards of Rome to victory over the many civilizations of the Mediterranean world and ultimately took power over the city of Rome itself.

Under the Empire, the boundaries between public and private lives became porous and women began to use their familial roles as instruments of public power. Religion, in particular, offered women a bridge across class and gender differences, from private to public life. Roman women experimented widely with a variety of pagan cults, but increasingly Christianity attracted women with a vision of a community where in Christ "There is neither Jew nor Greek, . . . neither bond nor free, . . . neither male nor female." (Galatians 3:28)

Christianity was founded at about the same time as the Roman Empire was established, and for the next three centuries the imperial government and the Christian religion developed on separate but converging tracks. As an outlawed sect, the new religion was peculiarly susceptible to the influence of wealthy and noble women. Their participation was so energetic and prominent that critics often labeled Christianity a religion of women and slaves. In the fourth and fifth centuries, when the Empire had become Christian, it consolidated new political and religious hierarchies which reinforced one another. The synthesis was basically a restructured patriarchy with Christian men firmly in control of both government and church. But Roman Law and Roman Christianity contained a wider range of choices for women regarding marriage and property which passed into the hands of Rome's European successors.

THE PAGAN EMPIRE

Augustan Renovation (First Century A.D.)

Half-sincere and half-fraudulent, Augustus founded the Empire as a de facto monarchy dominated by the twin institutions of the bureaucracy and the military, while officially proclaiming the restoration of the Republic. This rhetoric of restoration had a powerful appeal to him and his successors. They designed laws and institutions to impose an ancient Roman vision of the right order of society upon an Empire exhausted by war and civil strife. They enlisted poets to construct a mythological past that glorified old-fashioned paternal power and patriotism. If they could, the emperors would have sent men back to the plough and women to the nursery. While recognizing that the provincial constitution of the Republic could not encompass the multiethnic Mediterranean world Rome had conquered, its rulers hoped that Republican virtues could give the Empire stability. Among the chief agents of disorder, the emperors counted women who had slipped out of paternal control into sexual license and political intrigue. The early emperors decreed that the restoration of order and propriety required the reinforcement of the Roman family.

Believing that the failure of Roman fathers to do their duty threatened the stability of the state, Augustus used his imperial powers as an all-encompassing *patria potestas*, bringing women under the scrutiny of public law. He penalized persistent bachelors with loss of offices and status and with restrictions on inheritances and the right to make wills. He offered women who bore three children recognition as legal persons in their own right—adults capable of controlling their own lives and property without a legal guardian. Freedwomen, who had been emancipated from slavery but not promoted into the full rights of freeborn women, could achieve the same status after bearing four children. Augustus ordered married men to shoulder their responsibilities as guardians of their wives and daughters and to enforce marital chastity. The *Lex Julia de Adulteriis* in 18 B.C. transferred jurisdiction from the family to the state and established a permanent court to hear cases against married women and their lovers. The wronged husband could be punished as his wife's accomplice if he failed to prosecute her adultery. Other laws forbade upper-class women to register as prostitutes in order to consort freely with men and threatened to prosecute men who consorted with women not registered as prostitutes. Over the next three centuries, emperors reissued and strengthened these laws. They attempted vainly to force marriage upon an increasingly reluctant population and to stem the high divorce rate by transferring some of a father's power over women to their husbands.[1]

But Augustus' attempts to shore up the old Roman civic morality were hopelessly out of date. The emperor's own private life exemplified the ambiguity and contradictions in his public policies. He formally released his wife Livia from *patria potestas* and granted her the Right of Three Children in 9 B.C. (although she had but one child, Tiberius, her first husband's son). As a result, no one could interfere with her administration of her vast personal wealth or subject her to the laws restricting women's inheritance. Livia's private power became part of the imperial structure although it was hidden by the empty facade of Republican institutions. She routinely rewarded service on her personal staff with promotion in the imperial administration. Livia herself was never allowed to enter the Senate, the sanctuary of the antique patriarchy. In his will, Augustus adopted her into the imperial family, and she became high priestess of his cult, which entitled her to the insignia of public office. His successor, Tiberius, fearing to enhance his mother's power, vetoed the Senate's resolution to award her the title, *Mater Patriae*, Mother of the Country. In time, however, Emperor Claudius proclaimed his grandmother a goddess.

The unbridled use of personal power by women and men alike still casts a baleful glitter over the early Roman Empire. The imperial office and the government that supported it were essentially undefined, and their limits untested. With no constitutional sanction, the privatization of power inherent in the monarchical principle favored the ambitions of women in the imperial family. Agrippina the Elder, for example, strengthened her son Caligula's imperial claims by cultivating his popularity among the soldiers.

If we are to believe scandal-mongering second-century chroniclers, the politics of the bedchamber and the poison cup replaced the politics of the Forum and the battlefield. Without constitutional restrictions, emperors pursued their caprices until assassination ended their course. Both lust and fear made them vulnerable to private pressures and persuasions. Emperors no longer listened to the Senate or its officials but took the advice of their wives and mothers. Fearful of enhancing the power of their rivals, emperors entrusted unprecedented governmental powers to their slaves.

This was not necessarily an evil course. From Tacitus and Suetonius in the second century to modern times, historians have attributed the multiple deaths of Augustus' immediate heirs to Livia's ambitions for her son Tiberius. They have accused Claudius' wife, Messalina, of every sexual excess and sadistic cruelty imaginable and have blamed Nero's mother, the younger Agrippina, for producing his psychotic symptoms by manipulating him with both sexual and maternal wiles. But, in fact, there is no particular reason to suppose that the influence of these and other women was inherently malevolent. Certainly, the Julio-Claudian empresses used both charm and intelligence to achieve their ambitions. They were often ruthless and, like their husbands, often needed every resource to stay alive and prosper once they had entered the dangerous imperial sphere. In their turn, they inspired fear in others.

We must beware the historian's cliché. Whenever women succeed in manipulating their private positions to gain a share of public power, nervous chroniclers blame the lustful weaknesses of men or the unnatural powers of feminine sorcery. Livia the poisoner, Messalina the sexual athlete, and Agrippina the devouring mother are the creations of such chroniclers. Madness stalked the Julio-Claudian emperors, and most of their women died violently. But they were indeed the mothers and fathers of their country. They laid the foundations for a government that lasted for many centuries and brought long periods of peace and prosperity to millions.

Christian Innovation (First Century A.D.)

Lower on the social scale, the people of the fledgling empire suffered the ravages of family breakdown, urbanization, religious failure, and social alienation in the aftermath of war. Rome's armies subjected peoples of diverse cultures to a single imperial government, but it was a harder task to consolidate a homogeneous citizenry. The cities of the Empire mixed people together mercilessly, but provided no remedy for the consequent culture shock. Challenged by religious and cultural novelties, tribal and family authority decayed. Inevitably city life fostered individualism, while the loss of family networks and old local gods isolated many people from the socializing influences that normally contribute to a secure personal identity. Despite legal and social pressures, men failed to marry. Women pushed into the marketplace to support themselves in a variety of ways. Slaves became freedwomen, and free women became concubines. In the wake of the wars, every city was full of soldiers too restless to farm and widows too poor and friendless to maintain themselves. In a public expression of *patria potestas*, the emperors treated their male *proles* (children) to an increasingly generous dole. Women with no male provider were given no share in this public charity, but were forced to fend for themselves.

These are the women who appear and reappear fitfully in the New Testament. Urban women, slipping out of familial control, tested the dangers and hopes of an uncharted social wilderness. Alone and unprotected, many sank into the desperate masses of the Roman state's unwanted children. But for women of wealth and prestige, the opportunity to influence the shape of society was unprecedented. Very often they used religion as the vehicle of their hopes.

Many cults competed for worshipers, and many of them offered women prestige and public activity. The cults of the Egyptian goddess Isis and other goddesses were noteworthy in this regard, but even in so patriarchal a religion as Judaism, there is evidence that women widened their devotional roles and enjoyed positions of influence that we do not today associate with the synagogue. Other cults, called *mysteries* because they subjected new candidates to secret initiation rites, were more radical. The mysteries were individualistic by nature. They stressed secret knowledge and personal salvation, thus posing a subversive challenge to both family and state authority. Satirists like Juvenal noted that women were peculiarly susceptible to the influence of unsavory champions of orgiastic sex, subverters of the rites of conjugal procreativity. He saw women as the unguarded gates through which the destroyers gained entrance to the upper reaches of Roman society.[2] The shocked men of the Empire faced a nightmare world where women ran loose, their most destructive powers unshackled; they threatened the future of the Roman race, the ruling class itself, by their refusal on the one side to bear children and on the other to abide by a sexual code that would certify the paternity of the children they did bear. In A.D. 83, after the Empire had suffered several military reverses, three of the six Vestal Virgins, the only Roman women recognized as free of paternal or conjugal authority, were executed for behaving unchastely.

Fearing that the political system as well as the gender system was under attack, the emperors often responded with persecution. In A.D. 19, according to the historian Josephus, a matron was accused of having allowed herself to be seduced in Isis' temple by a lecher masquerading as the god Anubis. As a result, Tiberius had the priests of Isis crucified and their worshipers—four thousand in number—exiled to Sardinia, to kill the brigands there or be killed by them. Along with the worshipers of Isis, he banished a number of Jews, who were accused of cheating a matron by pocketing alms she had given for the community in Jerusalem.[3] In A.D. 57, Nero tried the wife of the Roman general in Britain for "addiction to a foreign cult." A few years later, Nero accused the Christians of setting fire to the city of Rome, possibly to divert suspicion from himself. He used the burning bodies of Christians for torches in his gardens and forced some Christian women to play the leading roles in violent pornographic spectacles.[4] This imperial savagery was not without purpose. The public cults of Rome, culminating in the worship of the emperor himself, focused the loyalty and devotion of his subjects. The personal religions of the new age diverted their devotees from Caesar and his concerns.

In the reign of Tiberius, the female followers of an itinerant preacher from Galilee, whom Roman soldiers had executed in Judaea, announced that their teacher had risen from the dead. All but one of his male followers had run away, fearing that they too might be executed. But as they heard of the women's claims, they took heart and rejoined them in Jerusalem. Women and men together experienced a fierce religious awakening whose force scattered them as missionaries throughout the Mediterranean world.

The men among Jesus' followers were generally described as humble folk and even slaves. The women, however, spanned the entire social range. Rich or poor, what the female disciples shared was a general sense of isolation from the safe centers of society. The women mentioned in the Gospels lacked the only badge of respectability antique society conferred on women: the matronal guardianship of a patriarchal household. Humble as Jesus' immediate family in Nazareth appears to have been, his mother was related to the wealthy Joseph of Arimathea. Her marriage to the poor carpenter Joseph was an apparent misalliance that critics of Christianity explained by ascribing Mary's pregnancy to an agency other than the Holy Spirit.

Several wealthy women roamed about the country with Jesus, providing money for the group's sustenance. Jesus cured three of these of demonic possession: Joanna, wife of King Herod's steward; Mary of Magdala; and Susanna. These three stayed with him to the end. The "woman who loved much" and anointed Jesus with costly ointment before his death was dismissed by the Evangelist as an anonymous sinner. So was the Samaritan woman to whom Jesus first revealed his divine claims. No wonder these women embraced his message that the last shall be first and propagated it with such enthusiasm. No wonder they showed themselves so ready to leave home and family and follow after him. Critics of the new religion consistently despised it (as they despised most of the mysteries) for its appeal to women and lower-class men, who were considered to be emotionally unstable. The heart of the Christian message—of individual worth separate from worldly social status—was well calculated to speak to these alienated people.

By the end of the apostolic generation, between A.D. 70 and A.D. 100, there were Christian churches in Egypt, Syria, Asia Minor, Greece, and Italy. Subsequent sources register their appearance across the Roman world from Britain to Mesopotamia and even beyond into India. Such a vast reach could have been accomplished only by an equally vast multitude of agents. Yet only one record survives in the canonical Gospel, centering on the work and teaching of Paul. The passionate discussions and experiments that engaged scores of women and men in other communities are all but forgotten. Fictional sources and obscure legendary traditions of the second century indicate that many of the early missionaries were women. In addition to the women who prophesied and presided over house churches in the New Testament, many women heard the message of wandering Christians and rooted it within their household and among their friends. When the preacher had gone on, sometimes only women kept the faith and practiced their religion unassisted by priest or teacher. One first-century letter warned male missionaries, for fear of scandal, not to take shelter in communities where the only Christians were women.[5]

Women Under Roman Law (Second Century A.D.)

In the second century, a long period of peace and the increasing homogenization of the provinces fostered rapid communication of new ideas given concrete shape by developing Roman law and the spread of eastern philosophy and religions. Most of the emperors of the age came from outside Italy and spent most of their time in the provinces. The benefits of Roman citizenship gradually spread to all the free people of the Empire. The ruling class slowly yielded to a humanitarian perspective that encouraged the emancipation or partial emancipation of the unfree. A growing class of freedwomen and freedmen occupied an intermediate place in the social scale between the freeborn and the slave.

The trend of legislation, however, remained traditionalist. The new emperors remained committed to the old family system, periodically reinforcing the Augustan laws on marriage and adultery. These rulers sought to impose monogamy on everyone, although they did not prohibit divorce.

They encouraged childbearing, but did not prohibit fathers from exposing unwanted children to death or any other fate that might await them in the public streets.[6] The new laws put more emphasis on the element of consent in marriage (although this was probably intended to encourage men to marry, not to free women from male control).

Christian morality often simply extended many of the aims of Roman law. It strengthened monogamy by prohibiting divorce, limiting men's freedom to abandon their wives. Christians wrote treatises in the late second century praising the virtues of conjugal love and parental affection for children. Christians opposed the exposure of unwanted children, mostly girls, to death or prostitution.

Roman law also sought to protect the class structure of the Empire and viewed cross-class marriage as a deadly threat. Men who wanted relationships with women of a lower social status could take them as concubines. (Although not considered wives, concubines and their children enjoyed legal recognition.) However, women who wished to enter unions with men lower in the social scale were seen as the instruments of class degradation. In A.D. 52, Claudius sponsored a law reducing to slavery any freeborn woman who lived in concubinage with a slave if she had acted without the knowledge of the man's master. If the master had known about this, she would be degraded to freedwoman status and her children would be slaves. Later, Emperor Hadrian modified this law so that the child would be free if the mother remained free. In the early third century, Emperor Septimius Severus decreed that a Roman woman could not free a slave in order to marry him.

These prohibitions aimed to control both women and men in the name of the public-spirited morality of Roman paganism. But they fell hardest on women who lacked freedom either to choose or to reject sexual experience or childbearing. At the end of the first century, the Emperor Domitian exiled his kinswoman, Flavia Domitilla, for unknown crimes. Later Christian tradition held that after two of her slaves converted her to Christianity, she defied her family and refused to marry. From that time forward, the annals of martyrdom consistently claim that Christian women who refused to sacrifice their virginity to the population needs of the Empire often suffered frightful tortures and death.

Roman lawyers of the second century took an increasingly liberal view of the capacities of women to own and manage property, freely bestowing the Right of Three Children on growing numbers of applicants. Christian women used their wealth and freedom to establish house churches where they and their slaves and the poorer members of the Christian congregation could practice their religious feasts. The Book of Acts remarks that the apostles were fortunate in converting "leading women" in many cities, and second-century sources confirm that this continued to be the case. By a decree of A.D. 212, Emperor Caracalla extended the economic and social privileges of citizenship to all free men and free women in the Empire.

Henceforward, women would enjoy legal protection of their inheritance rights and personal liberty, but not, of course, the privileges reserved for men. Women's marriages would have the full security of Roman law and, eventually, the relations of Roman soldiers with their provincial concubines would be transformed into legal marriages and the children of such marriages would be recognized as legitimate. Again, Christian attitudes complemented the progress of Roman society. The Roman dole was restricted to men and their families; Christian charity aimed at widows and orphans in the community. The Roman tradition upheld the virtues associated with male virility; the developing Christian tradition consciously urged the feminine virtues of compassion and humility on both women and men.

The Female Imperium (Second and Third Centuries A.D.)

Throughout the history of the Roman Empire, each successful dynasty sought to obscure the brutal truth that its power rested upon its soldiers' arms by emphasizing the familial quality of monarchy. This encouraged second- and third-century empresses to create a public presence that reinforced their husbands' military offices. The five "good emperors" (Nerva, Trajan, Hadrian, Antoninus Pius, and Marcus Aurelius), whose reigns spanned most of the second century, were all adopted at the peak of their military careers by their childless predecessors, a policy which, by co-opting the most threatening rival, secured the Pax Romana for nearly a century.

Much of this happy period in the Empire's history was dominated by Trajan's wife, Plotina, with his sister and aunt, Marciana and Matidia. It was Plotina who acted in her own name, within an hour of her husband's death, to sign Hadrian's adoption decree that secured him the imperial throne. In exchange, he married Matidia's daughter, Sabina, whom he kept with him through all his travels although they did not like each other very much. These empresses were not chosen for sexual allure. Some of the "good emperors" were simply not sexually attracted to women. They married women with strong political connections and skills. Power had moved steadily upward, centralizing in the emperor's hands. Only the empress, as his divine alter ego, shared his prestige. She was formally installed in the imperial title "Augusta" and, like her husband, became a goddess at death.

The seat of the Empire gradually moved away from Italy, and few of the second- and third-century emperors came from the old Roman families. Their constant travels became a sort of nonmilitary version of the triumphs that had once expressed the warlike capacities of Republican emperors. The empress and her entourage became central figures in these elaborate public ceremonials, with which the Empire focused the loyalty of its subjects. In A.D. 100, Pliny the Younger delivered a panegyric for Plotina, calling her a fit partner for the emperor. Hadrian himself delivered Matidia's funeral oration, a rite which underlined her central position in the web of Roman imperial family politics. Faustina, the wife of Marcus Aurelius, shared the imperial prerogative of having a town named after her. She was commemorated with a coin issue and the endowment of a maintenance allowance for poor girls, which suggests that she was seen in a special way as a patron of poor women, as the emperor was the patron of poor men through the administration of the dole.

The third century began with renewed conflict over the succession. A provincial military leader, Septimius Severus, emerged triumphant with the formidable assistance of his wife, Julia Domna, who was from a Syrian family accomplished in the arts of Hellenistic queenship and eastern religion. The four Severan women — Domna, her sister Maesa, and Maesa's daughters, Soemias and Mamaea — grasped the office of empress firmly and extended it broadly through the next generations. Julia Domna's name appears widely on inscriptions and coins, and she was publicly acclaimed as Mother of the Army (*Mater Castrorum*). She was swift to destroy the men who challenged her influence over the emperor, and had one son killed to secure the throne for another son Caracalla, who was more susceptible to her influence. After Septimius' death in A.D. 211, she held the reins of government while her son distracted himself with gambling. In 214–215, while he was with the army in the East, Domna answered petitions and other official correspondence and sent dispatches to the Senate under both their names.

Domna's sister Maesa was equally decisive. After Caracalla's death, she seized command of the army in the name of her daughter Soemias' son, Elagabalus. She and Soemias stemmed a rout by leaping from their chariots to make an appeal that turned the tide of battle. Soemias won the honors for which Livia and Agrippina had striven: a seat beside the consuls in the Senate with power to join them in signing decrees. As ruthless as Domna before her, Maesa did not hesitate to put her daughter and grandson to death when she saw that Elagabalus could not maintain the power she had won for him. She successfully conspired with Mamaea, her second daughter, to promote Mamaea's son, Alexander Severus. Maesa died four years later and Mamaea, after fending off a bid for independence by her son, took charge. She presided over a Senate of Women, intended as a complementary body to the Senate of Men, which established a complicated code of etiquette for the women of Rome. Although the Senate of Women was dissolved on Alexander's death, it was revived by Aurelian and possibly other emperors on various occasions.

As they gained in political and economic power, women extended their intellectual interests, making a strong impact on the creative thinking of the age. Plotina took an active part in religious and philosophical speculation; she was particularly influenced by Epicureanism, a school of philosophy that explored the possibilities of gender equality. In moments of insecurity and political danger, Domna turned to philosophy for support, establishing a following of learned people who called her Julia the Philosopher.

Clement of Alexandria, one of the principal formulators of Christian theology, boasted of Christian women who taught their religion to prospective converts. In writings addressed to pagan outsiders, he maintained that women were defined as a separate gender only by their reproductive capacities but could not be distinguished from men in their spiritual abilities.[7] Origen, his successor in the Alexandrian school, castrated himself so that, as the fourth-century historian of early Christianity, Eusebius, believed, no fear of scandal would prevent the admission of women to his school.

According to a plausible Christian tradition, Julia Maesa toyed with the possibilities of utilizing Christianity to enhance her status by giving some of her indispensible patronage to Origen. Mamaea invited him to preach at the palace, and the empress Olalitia Severa, with her husband Philip the Arabian, carried on a joint correspondence with Origen. The Severan women made several experiments with religion as an instrument of political unification. They originated with a family of Syrian priests serving the cult of Elagabalus, for whom Soemias' son was named. Believing himself to be the god, Elagabalus married Aquilia, a Vestal Virgin, whose sacrosanct chastity was supposed to be the guarantee of Rome's fortunes. He dispensed her from her vows in order to unite their two religions, but it is highly probable that the union remained symbolic. While the empresses of his family moved aggressively into spheres formerly reserved for men, Elagabalus is said to have displayed feminine attributes, such as working with wool, wearing a hair-net, and painting his eyes with feminine cosmetics. He held a special festival to mark the day he shaved his beard and afterward he had the hairs plucked out, so as to look more like a woman. The former Vestal Virgin whom he married has been tentatively identified as the "Severina" to whom the Christian writer Hippolytus dedicated a treatise. Perhaps she had a special sympathy with Christian values and the contemporary ideal that some of their women drew from the Clementine analysis that virginity was a "manly" condition that transcended gender. In any case, we know that Roman women acted as conduits for the ascent of Christianity from the lower levels of society to its upper reaches.

Female Christianity (Second and Third Centuries A.D.)

For a long time, many Christian communities were isolated and autonomous. Even in established centers of Christianity like Alexandria, the schools were not yet subordinated to the authority of bishops, and women felt free to cultivate a wide range of religious experience. Clement of Alexandria said that the women of the city spent their days running from church to church to meet their friends. Alternatively, they entertained wandering preachers and religious visionaries in their homes, a practice which Clement feared would lead to trouble. He urged that women and men attend church together and worship as family units.[8]

Some women threatened to destroy gender barriers by rejecting the traditional sexual and procreative roles that defined women solely by their relationships with men. The pre-Christian world did not provide recognition, validation, or regularized economic support to women who failed to enter the married state or fell out of it through widowhood. Even the Vestal Virgins were really paternal offerings sacrificed as hostages for the good fortune of the state, automatically doomed to death if their closely guarded virginity was lost. Pagan writers occasionally urged men to show compassion to the widow and the orphan, but those same writers gave women no institutional recognition. Christian women, however, took the initiative in using the new religion to redefine themselves by rejecting traditional relationships with men in favor of a network of women.

These communities of widows and virgins appear wherever Christians are visible to us. Associated with these communities are a series of historical novels known as the Apocryphal Gospels, whose heroines treated conversion to Christianity as synonymous with a vow of strict chastity. These books gave examples of valorous and intelligent women defying menacing husbands, parents, and imperial troops, and provided role models for a spreading culture of women, married and single, in revolt against their traditional matronal roles.

The Apocrypha also expressed rejection of a class system that separated women from one another. One of the most popular story lines involves the joint conversion of noble women with their slaves and the subsequent union of these converts against husbands, fathers, and public authorities. The story ends either in martyrdom for all concerned or in the successful conversion of the male persecutors to Christianity and asexuality, but from the author's point of view, either resolution was a happy ending.

An eyewitness account of the sufferings of a group of second-century Gallic martyrs confirms that the apocryphal fictions reflected a grim reality. A slave girl, Blandina, had been arrested with her mistress. Both women suffered bravely, but the witness concentrated on the inspiration of Blandina who overcame her deficiencies of class and gender to fulfill the Christian message that the last shall come first.[9]

About twenty-five years later, at the beginning of the third century, the prison diary of the martyred Perpetua provides direct insight into the mind of such a woman.[10] Perpetua, an aristocratic matron and a recent mother, was arrested with a group that included the pregnant slave Felicity, who gave birth during their imprisonment. Perpetua turned a deaf ear to the pleas of her respectable pagan family that she recant her faith and save her life. Estranged from her husband, she surrendered her baby to her parents and turned instead to her companion Felicity, who was sentenced to die with her.

Perpetua and Felicity formed a revolutionary union, attacking the patriarchal Roman family from both ends of a social scale that had formerly obscured their mutual interests as women. Perpetua's diary stresses the additional pain that she and her companion suffered in childbearing and thwarted motherhood before their final ordeal. At the end, Perpetua overcame this anguish and broke through the barriers of her gender. She dreamed that she entered the arena of combat, where she was transformed into a man. Perpetua's dream expressed a revolution in female consciousness.

The women of the second century who preached Christianity, nurtured it in their homes and villages, and showed themselves willing to die for it had taken up the religion as an instrument of their own liberation from the constraints of pagan tradition and pagan sensibility. As prophets and deaconesses entrusted with the instruction and baptism of women, they found a new role to absorb their energies and creative imaginations. As the directors of *house churches*, where communal meals were organized, charity dispensed, and hospitality given to itinerant preachers, they could put themselves at the center of a new social grouping. As virgins or chaste widows, they could set themselves outside of the gender system. If they were wealthy, they could use their power to bring their former slaves out of the class system.

As women, they found two things in the religion that they found nowhere else. First, they found their own selfhood. Second, they found one another. The Apocryphal Gospels and the testimony of martyrs consistently reveal a community of women—widows, virgins, and rebellious matrons— who renounced their marital condition and who turned away from the society of men to cooperate with one another in establishing a new vision of life here and in the world to come.

By the end of the second century, male Christian writers were increasingly attentive to this female challenge and began to take steps to repair a gender system that had deteriorated too much for their comfort. Irenaeus of Lyon and other orthodox writers began to criticize sects in which women prophesied and led the ceremonies. Clerical writers became increasingly articulate and increasingly exclusive in defining the doctrines of their religion. Such writers tried ruthlessly to brand persons of variant opinions as heretics and to remove from the flock prophets of both genders whose preaching was guided by their inner mystic vision.

From apostolic times, while many Christians were pursuing alternative visions of community, the Church had been perfecting a male hierarchy which mirrored the Roman bureaucracy. Bishops, priests, and deacons were gradually being separated from the laity and monopolizing the developing sacramental system. Women were excluded from all clerical orders except that of deaconess, which was responsible for charitable and instructional services to women. Gradually, deaconesses lost their single sacramental function of conferring baptism upon women when a modest sprinkling with water replaced immersion. The clergy took steps to prevent the privatization of their order into a conjugal partnership on the imperial model. Their wives were excluded from the female diaconate. Only widows (who had long enjoyed special status in Christian communities) and virgins of suitable maturity could be consecrated.

Yet women continued to number significantly among the volunteers for martyrdom. In spite of Christianity's growing institutionalization into a church that excluded them from intellectual, administrative, and liturgical leadership, women still clung to it fiercely. Women immersed in the charitable and instructional aspects of the diaconate may have underestimated the seriousness of the limitations imposed on them. Other women may have been too engrossed in preaching Christ's message of equality to give their attention to the practical inequalities that were multiplying under clerical leadership. Women's radical attacks on the gender system may have slowed and become muted in the face of outside persecution, while martyrdom enhanced their claims, however elusive, to transcend the gender system altogether by gaining first place in another world.

In the end, the last force of pagan Rome, was pitted against a religion that boasted that it was strong in its women. The Great Persecution, launched at the beginning of the fourth century by Emperor Diocletian, finally snapped the long tension between the Augustan ideal of renovation and the hopes of the alienated for Christian innovation. The all-conquering Empire and its soldier ruler faced a company of virgins, widows, and slaves who made their own suffering the implement of victory for a God who offered a kingdom in which there would be neither bond nor free, neither male nor female, neither marrying nor giving in marriage.

THE CHRISTIAN EMPIRE

The Conversion of the Empire (Fourth Century A.D.)

The victory of Constantine over his rivals for the throne ended the Great Persecution. His mother, Helena, had been the Christian concubine of Maximian, Diocletian's partner in the Empire. Under the laws of the pagan Empire, neither Helena nor Constantine were of the upper rank. A concubine could not aspire to the office of empress, so when the throne came within his grasp, Constantine's father had repudiated Helena to take a legitimate wife. But Christianity, anxious to discourage all sexual relationships outside of permanent and indissoluble marriage, urged cross-class marriage if it guaranteed harmony of religion and sexual virtue. Early Christianity declared women free to refuse marriage if they chose to live independently and freed them from the constraints of class if they chose to marry a man of lower status. Constantine, whose first official act was to decree tolerance for Christianity, revised Roman Law to express these attitudes. He did not, however, convert to his mother's religion until he was on his deathbed.

Few men had the impact on the Church that contemporaries attributed to Helena. She used her great wealth to establish churches containing inscriptions in her honor. She contributed heavily to the building of Constantinople, her son's new Christian capital in the East, and the city blossomed with statues of her. Helena even deposed the bishop of Antioch, whom she regarded as a dangerous theologian.

Previous emperors based their authority on military power and their claim to divinity. Constantine translated the imperial cult into patronage of the Christian Church. Helena, building on the religious roles that enhanced the public positions of earlier empresses, transformed the office by promoting popular devotions outside of the sacerdotal sphere, particularly pilgrimage and the associated cult of relics. When she traveled to Jerusalem in search of the holy places, she enjoyed the hospitality of the community of virgins, showing her respect for their calling by waiting on them at table. She built churches in Bethlehem and on the Mount of Olives to mark the holy sites for later pilgrims.

The Virgin Mary had long been a central figure in the female communities for whom the apocryphal Gospels were written. But there was no Marian shrine until Helena built one in Nazareth to commemorate her pilgrimage in 325. Thereafter, the cult spread rapidly. In 350, the church of Santa Maria Maggiore, whose site was reputedly chosen by Mary herself in a miraculous vision, was built in Rome. Ever since, the shrine has stood as a pilgrim site to rival St. Peter's, the great bastion of the male hierarchy.

Throughout the fourth century, many people followed Helena's example in visiting the holy places. Women in particular sought to change their lives by physical departure from their accustomed environment. Wealthy widows deserted the unsympathetic milieu of aristocratic Rome to travel in the Holy Land and ultimately settle there. A woman from Spain or Gaul named Egeria or Etheria (manuscripts differ) made a systematic tour of the places mentioned in both the Old and New Testaments and wrote a record of the devotions she practiced there for her sisters in religion at home.[11]

Helena also assisted the growth of the cult of relics. Claiming to be guided by a vision, she demolished a temple to Venus that covered the site that is honored today as the Holy Sepulchre. There she found a cross and nails that she brought to Constantinople. Under imperial patronage, the fragments were ultimately dispersed to hundreds of shrines.

Meanwhile, throughout the fourth century, men of the senatorial ruling class routinely continued to conduct pagan rituals while organizing the games, taking omens, or simply doing obeisance to the god-emperor in the ceremonies of public life. Soldiers worshiped their standards and senatorial notables tended the altars of their forefathers. While these men clung to their satisfying old ways, women explored the possibilities of the new religion. Christianity still kept its distance from the state, offering a separate sphere of power in which the wealth and rank of aristocratic women might be deployed to advantage. By the middle of the fourth century, the conversion of an obstinate pagan man by a pious wife or persistent mother was a common story.[12]

Documents written by men, often of a critical nature, reveal a metropolitan world in which women daily congregated at the churches—sometimes traveling in litters from one church to another—to pray, to meet with their friends, to dispense charity, and to refresh themselves with picnics in the midst of their devotions. Excluded from the clergy, women often turned to the cult of saints to satisfy their religious ambitions, collecting relics and establishing shrines at the tombs of martyrs. A heroic literature developed, with biographies of Macrina, Melania the Elder and her granddaughter of the same name, Paula and Eustochium, Olympias and Gorgonia, and a host of others whose admirers sought to hold them up as rivals to the fighting heroes of antiquity.[13]

The history of Christian men in the fourth century tends to be a history of the developing hierarchy and its relationship to the imperial state and of the creation of orthodox doctrine. The women of the imperial family and of the great aristocratic houses involved themselves in these theological quarrels and the politics that attended their progress with fanatical enthusiasm by lobbying, supplying money, and demonstrating in the streets. They were as ideologically involved in the politics of orthodoxy as the clergy themselves. But they must also have enjoyed the opportunity to use their political and intellectual skills. The clergy, for all its claims to superiority, flattered and courted women who had political power and economic resources. These women controlled appointments to church offices, construction of church buildings, and patronage for scholars and preachers. Though excluded from the ecclesiastical orders, these women deployed other sources of power to back their own candidates and their own opinions.

The Cult of Virginity (Fourth and Fifth Centuries A.D.)

Late in the third century, groups of women and men began to move out of the cities into the deserts of Egypt and Syria to live in colonies devoted to the rejection of all worldly ties and interests. Some were hermits like the semi-legendary Mary of Egypt, who roamed the wilderness like an animal, far from humanity, seeking God without benefit of priests or sacraments. Others entered formal communities like those established by Pachomius and his sister Mary in the Egyptian deserts near Thebes. The men lived on one side of the river and the women on the other. The women were strictly secluded from all other men, dependent on the monks to provide for their subsistence from donations solicited from admirers and the sale of their handiwork. As we have seen, women had practiced some aspects of asceticism since apostolic times. It is not clear from the sources, however, whether the sisters in the desert chose their cloistered way of life or whether the brothers (who were probably their relatives) imposed it upon them.[14] Sources equally difficult to interpret claim that where fear of temptation caused men to exclude women altogether from monastic communities, women infiltrated them in male disguise. The legends of these "transvestite saints" demonstrate the confidence of contemporaries that chastity empowered women to compete equally with men for the laurels of self-imposed martyrdom.[15]

In general, however, women tended toward a less organized form of ascetic experience and remained closer to the centers of civilization. From Asia Minor to Gaul, fourth-century women formed small communities in their own homes devoted to the practice of the ascetic life and the study of its philosophical aspects. Saint Basil, generally credited with the foundation of Greek monasticism, was converted to the ascetic ideal by his sister Macrina who headed an establishment with her mother, brother, former servants, and an unknown number of other women and men, at least one of whom was a wealthy aristocratic widow. Melania the Younger also clearly institutionalized the cross-class aspect of female Christianity by claiming to be the equal of her former slaves in her new community. Paula's monastery in Bethlehem included women of every class, although she retained her superiority over the whole community. Marcella organized a circle of Roman aristocratic women who studied the ascetic life together. In Gaul and Spain there was a wide circle of ascetic women living in their own homes. All these communities and networks still shine through the correspondence of men whose letters future generations regarded as worthy of preservation. The letters written by the women have been lost.

Mothers and widows often helped their daughters to evade marriage and motherhood, and then joined them in the monastic life. Melania the Elder helped to rescue her granddaughter from the dynastic ambitions of her family. Paula took her daughter, Eustochium with her to Bethlehem, abandoning her son and other relatives. Often they were wealthy enough to turn their large estates into communities of women under their own direction. Everywhere we look among women of the last century of the Roman Empire in the West, we see mothers and daughters and mistresses and slaves united to resist the last pressures of the old classical *familia*. Jerome rejoiced that Eustochium's virginity brought one of Rome's most ancient houses to an end. The Roman world was falling and its patriarchal structure, the failed design of Augustus, was being buried beneath the rubble.

Many women of the fourth century found a new relationship with men. Pious women, most of them chaste widows and a few consecrated virgins, made firm and lasting alliances with bishops and other leading ecclesiastical figures. These relationships usually involved the contribution of money and political connections by the women to doctrinal or political causes espoused by the men. The men in turn brought their female friends into the inner councils of the Church. Real affection marked many of these relationships, as can be seen in the surviving letters and biographies written by the men.

Classical writers argued that heterosexual friendship was impossible because equality forms a necessary foundation for all friendship. But in the individualistic world of the celibate Christians, at least in this adventurous time when the wealth and prestige of Roman women balanced the hierarchical pre-eminence of Christian clergymen, a new vision of partnership was possible. Some women, among them Melania the Younger and Therasia, wife of Paulinus of Nola, could not preserve their virginity but eventually persuaded their husbands to forego their conjugal rights. A whole circle of such self-denying couples corresponded with one another and exchanged insights into the novelties opened up by their radical way of life.[16]

Outside the framework of marriage, the age delighted in stories of beautiful courtesans like Thaïs, who was converted to religious life by the desert monk who saw the soul within her well-tended body and risked the temptations of her beauty in order to wrest her from the devil. On the other hand, young virgins without great wealth and independence apparently sought to join forces with clergymen, living chastely in joint households. Despite the condemnation of gossiping neighbors and scolding bishops, these women and their male friends were trying valiantly to make reality conform to the ancient Christian formula, "In Christ there is neither male nor female." Chrysostom, the tempestuous bishop of Constantinople, though sympathetic and supportive of the religious life established by his friend Olympias, was horrified by mixed-sex households and denounced them for the scandal they provoked even if they maintained their purity. By the end of the fourth century, the women who led such daring lives and the men who abetted them suffered a stinging backlash. Christianity was becoming respectable and no longer smiled sympathetically upon its radicals. Thus Jerome says that even in Bethlehem critics hounded Paula and threatened to confine her as insane.

Christian Queenship (Fifth and Sixth Centuries A.D.)

At the end of the fourth century, the Emperor Theodosius declared Catholic Christianity to be the only recognized religion of the Empire. Fifth-century empresses of the Theodosian house systematically built upon Helena's revision of the imperial office for women. They created special imperial liturgies, and used pilgrimage, charity, political patronage, and asceticism to develop a distinct political clientele.

One princess, Pulcheria, used her virginity and the legal freedom it gave her to take control of the Empire. In youth, she consecrated herself and her sisters to a life of holy virginity and thus escaped subordination to the powers of a husband. She promoted feasts and celebrations honoring virgins, putting herself at the center of the ceremonies. She patronized churches and controlled bishops as she dominated her brother Theodosius. When her brother died, she seized control of the government and married a soldier to fulfill the military requirements of the imperial office. In return, he vowed publicly to devote himself to guarding his wife's virginity. Like later Byzantine emperors, Pulcheria put herself at the head of the ecclesiastical hierarchy. She was an enthusiastic promoter of the cult of the Virgin Mary and influenced the council of Chalcedon to condemn the Nestorian heresy, which would have relegated Mary to a mere vessel who bore only a human baby and not the Godhead.

The freedom to experiment with the ascetic life and the wealth and power to intervene in both secular and ecclesiastical politics depended finally on the security and prosperity of the Roman Empire. Increasingly through the fifth century, women and men alike suffered from growing violence as barbarian armies began to pillage the cities of the Empire. Marcella died in the sack of Rome in 410, and the imperial princess Galla Placidia Augusta was carried away as a hostage to marry the Visigothic prince Ataulf. The virgin empress Pulcheria was obliged to marry a soldier who could sustain the military obligations of the Empire. The days of pilgrimage and retreat were ending.

In the sixth century, Justinian, the last emperor to rule in Italy and the last emperor to use Latin as his official language, presided over the exhaustive codification of the Roman law which was destined to dominate the legal tradition of the West.[17] There, he enshrined many of the rights won by Roman women during the five centuries of the Empire. The law guaranteed their right to control their own property after the age of twenty-five and to leave it where they liked when they died. Justinian extended Constantine's recognition of virginity as a way of life by granting consecrated women the Right of the Three Children. He clarified the ambiguity of classical jurists concerning marriage and ratified the Christian view of marriage as a contract between consenting individuals.

In his government, as in his private life, Justinian was inseparable from his wife Theodora, whose image faces his in the commemorative mosaics at Ravenna, the seat of the sixth-century western Empire. Theodora came from the underworld of entertainers and prostitutes. To enable her to marry his heir, Emperor Justin, Justinian's uncle, was obliged to revise the laws forbidding a senator to marry a harlot. Once they were married, her power was institutionalized. As joint ruler of the Empire, she fulfilled Livia's dream of participating in all the imperial functions. In church affairs, she encouraged Justinian's preference for theological positions that ultimately contributed decisively to the growing rift between East and West.

In the tradition established at the beginning of the Empire, the historian Procopius attributed Theodora's influence to her unreserved sexual prowess.[18] He sneered at her efforts to utilize the monastic system as a refuge for women who started life, as she had done, with no alternative but prostitution.

He claimed that the prostitutes whom she placed in monasteries were so unhappy that they flung themselves into the sea rather than submit to her virtuous regime. But friends and enemies alike had to bow in awe to her greatness when she stood before a rebellious mob in the city, refusing to let the emperor flee and forsake his power by reminding him that "purple makes the best shroud."

CONCLUSION

From Livia to Theodora, from Mary of Nazareth to Mary of Egypt, the first five hundred years of our era was an age of heroines. They wove their way through a loosened social fabric to form dramatic patterns of life in which women could exercise power through manipulation of their matronal positions and invent new liturgies and new relationships on earth and with heaven. It was an age of women who wielded enormous power and women who voluntarily suffered torture for the sake of the kingdom to come. Their world ended in darkness and violence, but they left a lasting legacy. They triumphantly achieved the ideal of the autonomous woman, released from the confinement of the antique family system. The economic and legal rights they gained marked the most influential law code the world has ever produced. To a very large extent, many of Christianity's social ideas and the vitally important concept of asceticism were the creations of women. Roman law and Roman Christianity would unite the dying world of the Empire with the emerging West. In the new world, to be sure, men would still be dominant and most women would still be defined in terms of their relationship with men; but during the long centuries of the imperial age, that dominance had been greatly curtailed and those definitions broadened to include women with a bright new vision of themselves and of one another.

NOTES

1. The problem of reconstructing these laws and a summary of their history can be traced in Leo F. Raditsa, "Augustus' Legislation Concerning Marriage, Procreation, Love Affairs and Adultery," *Aufstiege und Niedergang der Römische Welt*, 2, No. 13 (1980), 278–339.
2. Juvenal, *Satires*, 6: 525–530.
3. Josephus, *Jewish Antiquities*, 18:81–84.
4. Tacitus, *Annales*, 15, 43.
5. Pseudo-Clement of Rome, *On Virginity*, 2, 1.
6. Justin Martyr, *Apologia*, 1, 29, said that most exposed children were picked up by people anxious to exploit them as slaves or prostitutes.
7. Clement of Alexandria, *Paedagogus*, 1.4.

8. *Ibid.*, 3.12.

9. Eusebius, *Historia Ecclesiastica*, 5, 1, 7.

10. *The Martyrdom of Saints Perpetua and Felicitas* in *Acts of the Christian Martyrs*, ed. and trans. H. Musurillo, 106–131. (Oxford: at the Clarendon Press, 1972).

11. *Egeria's Travels*, ed. and trans. John Wilkinson (Jerusalem: Ariel; Warminster: Aris & Phillips, 1981).

12. For extended examples see Peter Brown, "Aspects of the Christianization of the Roman Aristocracy," in *Religion and Society in the Age of Augustine*, (London: Faber and Faber, 1972), pp. 161–182.

13. "The Life of Macrina," by her brother Gregory of Nyssa can be found in his *Ascetical Works*, tr. V. W. Callahan (Washington, D.C.: Catholic University of America, 1966). Melania the Elder is treated at length in Palladius' *Lausiac History* (Westminster, MD: Ancient Christian Writers, 34 n.d.) and Melania the Younger's life by Gerontius is translated into French in *Sources Chrétiennes*, 90. (Paris: Editions du cerf, 1972) Paula and Eustochium appear frequently in the letters of Saint Jerome, whose Letter no. 108 is a lengthy autobiographical eulogy of the latter. "The Life of Olympias" may be found in Elizabeth A. Clark, *Jerome, Chrysostom and Friends* (New York: Edwin Mellen Press, 1979), pp. 107–157.

14. See Palladius, *Lausiac History, passim* and the Biographies, and *Rule of Pachomius*, trans. Armaud Veilleux, *Pachomian Koinonia* (Kalamazoo, Mich.: Cistercian Publications, 1980).

15. Though often popularized in later literature, these lives have not been translated. Most of them are available in Latin in Migne's *Patrologia Latina*, vol. 73.

16. The letters of Paulinus of Nola form a particularly rich source for these relationships, *Epistolae* CSEL 29–30 (Turnholt: Brepols, n.d.).

17. A new translation and edition of Justinian's *Code* has just been issued by the University of Pennsylvania Press, Philadelphia, 1985.

18. Procopius, *The Secret History* (Baltimore: Penguin Classics, 1966)

SUGGESTIONS FOR FURTHER READING

Scholars of these five centuries have been generous in furnishing translations for the use of readers who do not command Latin or Greek. Most of the major classical works of the period are obtainable in several editions. The *Loeb Classical Library* is the most comprehensive series.

Similarly, the works of early Christian writers have been translated often. One easily accessible collection is the *Ante-Nicene Christian Library* and the *Nicene and Post-Nicene Fathers*, while individual pieces have been collected in *The Fathers of the Church* and *Ancient Christian Writers* series. In general I have drawn upon the letters of Jerome, Ambrose, Augustine, Basil, Paulinus of Nola, and Sulpicius Severus, as well as the works specifically referred to in the footnotes.

Available in separate editions are:

Egeria, *Travels to the Holy Land.* Ed. and trans. John Wilkinson. Jerusalem: Ariel Publications, 1981.

Hennecke, Edgar, and Wilhelm Schneemelcher. *New Testament Apocrypha.* Philadelphia: Westminster Press, 1963–1965.

James, Montague R. *The Apocryphal New Testament.* Oxford: Clarendon Press, 1972.

Feminist scholarship in all the areas covered by this chapter has burgeoned over the last decade or so to almost unmanageable dimensions. Among books covering the pagan women of the Roman Empire, the first path breaker was J. P. V. D Balsdon, *Roman Women* (New York: John Day Co., 1963). Sarah B. Pomeroy's, *Goddesses, Whores, Wives and Slaves* (New York: Schocken, 1975) has become the acknowledged leader in the field, supplemented by many subsequent articles by the same author and her most recent book, *Women in Hellenistic Egypt* (New York: Schocken, 1985).

A small selection of the other recent works on specific topics that I have used for specific areas of the subject are:

Beard, Mary. "The Sexual Status of Vestal Virgins." *Journal of Roman Studies,* 70 (1980), 12–27.

Cohen, Shaye J. D. "Women in the Synagogues of Antiquity." *Conservative Judaism,* 34, No. 2 (1980), 23–29.

Hallett, Judith P. *Fathers and Daughters in Roman Society.* Princeton University Press, 1984.

Raditsa, Leo F. "Augustus' Legislation Concerning Marriage, Procreation, Love Affairs and Adultery." *Aufstiege und Niedergang der Römische Welt,* 2, No. 13 (1980), 278–339.

The period of the New Testament continues to attract scholars of high caliber, and a feminist dimension has added electricity to their work in recent years. I have myself used many of these works and included them in an extensive bibliography in my book, *A New Song: Celibate Women in the First Three Christian Centuries* (New York: Haworth Press, 1983) and in two subsequent articles dealing with the fourth and fifth centuries:

McNamara, Jo Ann. "Muffled Voices: The Lives of Consecrated Women in the Fourth Century." In *Distant Echoes: Medieval Religious Women.* Ed. John A. Nichols and Lilian Thomas Shank. Kalamazoo, Mich.: Cistercian Publications, 1984.

McNamara, Jo Ann. "Cornelia's Daughters: Paula and Eustochium." *Women's Studies,* 11 (1984) 9–27.

The works I have drawn upon most heavily for this chapter are:

Brown, Peter. *The Cult of the Saints.* Chicago: University of Chicago Press, 1981.

Brown, Peter. *Religion and Society in the Age of Saint Augustine.* London: Faber and Faber, 1972.

Clark, Elizabeth A. *Jerome, Chrysostom and Friends.* New York: Edwin Mellen Press, 1979.

Davies, Stevan. *The Revolt of the Widows: The Social World of the Apochryphal Acts.* Carbondale: Southern Illinois University Press, 1980.

Fiorenza, Elizabeth S. *In Memory of Her: A Feminist Theological Reconstruction of Christian Origins.* New York: Crossroad, 1983.

Holum, Kenneth. *Theodosian Empresses.* Berkeley, University of California Press, 1980.

Meeks, Wayne A. *The First Urban Christians: The Social World of the Apostle Paul.* New Haven: Yale University Press, 1983.

Pagels, Elaine. *The Gnostic Gospels.* New York: Random House, 1979.

Abbess Hitda offering her Gospel Book to the cloister's patron, Saint Walburga, *c.* 1020. (Hessische Landes und Hochschulbibliothek, Darmstadt)

chapter 5

Sanctity and Power: The Dual Pursuit of Early Medieval Women

Suzanne F. Wemple

Did the status of women in the ancient world shape medieval conceptions of women? Or did the additional dimension of Christianity determine early medieval women's role? Suzanne Wemple discusses the duality of the Christian tradition regarding women: negative perceptions of female nature mandated their subordinate role in ritual, yet theology proclaimed spiritual equality of all believers.

The egalitarian strand predominated during the Christians' early struggle for survival and later, when they expanded the frontier into northern and eastern Europe. We know most about aristocratic and religious women in this sparsely documented age. Feudal relations, based on kinship, allowed aristocratic women a relatively wide scope for activity. During the early medieval period, women had access to positions of considerable responsibility and power as abbesses. But by the later phases of feudalism, the status of nuns had declined sharply, as they came increasingly under the control of male monastic orders. Still the age speaks to us of what women can accomplish if their age affords them the opportunity.

From the fifth to the eleventh centuries, the frontier age of western Europe, women played a vital and expanding role in laying the foundations of our modern society. In the era following the end of the Roman Empire in the West, invading Germanic tribes intermarried freely with the conquered Romans, thus forming families that united their different cultures. Recognized marriage alliances eased the difficult process of social integration in this early age, and women's familial roles expedited the consequential process of assimilation. Also, the practical need for the talents of women, not merely as wives and mothers but as administrators, educators, and religious leaders, largely determined the attitudes toward them. This was more sharply pronounced in the changing laws and institutions of the time than in theological attitudes, which remained fairly constant.*

Christian attitudes, however, were also equivocal in many areas. The early Christians aspired to create a spiritual revolution rather than a series of social changes. While they preached the spiritual equality of all, including women, they did not wish to scandalize their contemporaries by according women a position equal to men in the practical direction of the new religion. The idea that the weaker sex required restriction and support was not altogether absent from the writings of the Christian fathers, and this attitude provided ammunition for those who sought to cloister women in home or convent.

Until the ninth century, significant instances exist where status and wealth overcame the prejudice against women in establishing authority in the social order. Women like Roman Empress Theodora in the sixth century sometimes rose from humble backgrounds to positions of prominence and carried out their offices masterfully, particularly when they made brilliant marriage alliances. In the ninth century, the place of the wife was made quite secure in Carolingian families, and such breathtaking exercises of ambition diminished. Wives content with church-sanctioned marriages gained the protection of stricter laws. Christianity, with its decisive influence over marriage laws, deserves credit for terminating the mobility so much enjoyed by some women. However, in the two following centuries, the impact of the Church's influence weakened and once again some of the old practices—out-of-wedlock liaisons and divorce, which the opportunistic could exploit—cropped up in western Europe. But social distinctions hardened over the long term, and social mobility on the upper levels of society diminished substantially. Kings and princes no longer could practice polygyny (marriages to several women at the same time) nor raise a favored mistress to high position. Women who formed sexual liaisons outside of marriage had the low status of concubines.

Sanctity became a route to authority. Noble birth allowed women to

*The chapter was originally composed by Jo Ann McNamara and Suzanne F. Wemple for the first edition of *Becoming Visible.*

exercise spiritual leadership, especially when they showed generosity in endowing churches and monasteries. Caring for the poor required wealth. Occasionally, through charismatic personality and force of character, women of humbler background gained a position of authority in the convent and sometimes also in sainthood. Women found opportunities to demonstrate their talents in religious houses, large and small; in some, only women resided, while in others, both men and women. Later in Germany, particularly in Saxony, female monasteries—usually restricted to the nobility—flourished. These powerful new institutions devoted to women's holy purposes and directed by women themselves partially offset their loss of opportunities that fluid conditions formerly provided.

CHRISTIANITY AND THE GERMANIC KINGDOMS: 500–750

Missionaries and monks converted newly settled people in areas not yet penetrated by Christian culture. The Church expected much of Christian women and encountered new requests in return. Pope Gregory I (590–604), whose voluminous correspondence has survived, wrote to Bertha, Catholic wife of King Aethelbert of Kent in England. In the letter, the pope admonished her because she had not yet converted her heathen husband to the Catholic faith. Daughter of the King of Paris, high expectations had been placed on her missionary work. Eventually her husband did become Christian. By the seventh century, the Church could already claim a series of successful conversions of kingdoms through the work of Christian queens.

Gregory also responded to women's questions conveyed by the missionaries he sent to preach to the heathen English. "May an expectant mother be baptized? How soon after childbirth may she enter the church? . . . And may a woman properly enter church at certain periods? And may she receive Communion at these times?" He answered, "Why should not an expectant mother be baptized?—it is no offense in the sight of Almighty God to bear children." Speaking of the woman suffering from an issue of blood who touched the hem of Christ's robe he stated, "A woman, therefore, should not be forbidden to receive the mystery of Communion at these times. . . . The monthly courses of woman are no fault, because nature causes them."[1] His answer was received favorably by women who converted to the new faith in large numbers, and promoted Christianity to their families.

In the chaotic age that followed the collapse of the Roman Empire in the West, monasticism proved singularly suited to women's needs. Sixth and seventh century, monks and nuns became the principal agents in the civilizing of tribes who occupied the former Roman lands. In contrast to the ascetics of the late Roman Empire, who rejected the secular world with its decadent institutions, the monks and nuns of the early

Germanic kingdoms enthusiastically began to convert the world to Christianity. Although nuns, unlike monks, could not aspire to episcopal appointments, they made equal contributions in the establishment of monasteries in the wilderness. Monks and nuns alike preserved learning and counseled newly converted rulers. The lands abbesses controlled and the people they governed gave them a practical power equal to that of abbots and sometimes even bishops. Among secular women, only queens exercised comparable power.

Germanic Law and Social Structure

The social structure of Germanic tribes before their appearance within the Roman Empire and their conversion to Christianity is shrouded in the darkness of their own illiteracy. The occasional comments of Roman observers and the retrospective writings of the early medieval chroniclers provide a gloss to the mute evidence of archaeology. In the later first century, Tacitus glorified the purity of Germanic family life in order to rebuke Roman immorality. He admitted, however, that the royal families were polygynous and that wife purchase was a common practice, although he interpreted it to be a measure of the esteem in which the Germans held their women. Tacitus also testified to the high place of women as priestesses and seeresses among the tribes of his period. He noted the Germanic practice of bringing wives to the battlefield. At a later period, Ammianus Marcellinus maintained that Germanic wives took an active part in the fighting itself. The Lombard ("longbearded") people, according to their eighth-century chronicler, believed that their name derived from a time when their women went into battle with their hair tied under their chins to delude the enemy.

Apart from these tantalizing glimpses of the early society of the Germanic tribes, information can be gleaned about the life of women from law codes. By the time of their compilation, however, contact with Rome and conversion to Christianity were already beginning to change the basic nature of Germanic society. On the whole, these early codes reflect a society that regarded women primarily as property belonging to their families. The highest bidder received a marriageable girl, although those codes that were influenced by Christian and Roman customs divided the bride price paid by the new husband between his wife and her nearest relatives. Unmarried women who allowed themselves to be abducted were severely punished. Germanic laws thus conflicted with Christian tenets; in questions of marriage, Christianity placed the individual's choice over that of the family. Moreover, the Germanic codes put the highest cash penalties on the injury of a woman of childbearing age, demonstrating that they did not share the Church's view that virgins and widows were vastly superior to wives and mothers. This opposition was never to be fully resolved and, at least until the ninth century, secular society and its values predominated.

The surviving Germanic law codes, which provide our best evidence of secular values, did specifically protect the virtue and modesty of women. Any men who vexed or harassed women received heavy punishments. For example, according to the Pact of the Salic Code, if a man pressed the hand of a woman, he paid a fine of fifteen solidi; if he put his hand above her elbow, thirty-five solidi. In the Code of the Alemanni it cost a man six solidi if he pulled the headdress of a young girl out walking, and increasingly heavy fines were given for more serious transgressions of propriety and a woman's right to frequent public places. The Code of the Alemanni went so far as to punish a man who falsely accused a woman of witchcraft or poisoning; he paid a fine of eighty solidi if she was a freewoman, and fifteen solidi if a maidservant. In 546, when the Ostrogoths had captured Rome, the leader Totila had forbidden his followers to rape the Roman women, much to the wonder of the city dwellers.[2] Protecting traditional values while encountering unusual conditions of war and settlement clearly required harsh penalties.

Christian chroniclers of the sixth and seventh centuries were reluctant to depict pagan marriage customs or the protection afforded women, but they clearly describe the role played by women in the Christianization of the new kingdom of the Franks. In the late fifth century, Clothilde, the wife of the Frankish king Clovis, persisted in her efforts to convert her husband despite his anger over the death of her first son—immediately following his baptism. Through her efforts the Franks became the first tribe to embrace orthodox Christianity. Moreover, she continued to nourish the Church with practical assistance. Many Frankish monastic foundations and churches owed their existence to her generous and ready goodwill. In the following century Bertha, the Frankish queen of Kent in England, did succeed in converting her husband and prepared the way for Augustine of Canterbury to convert that land. A succession of princesses went out from Kent in the succeeding generations to marry other Saxon kings and to help convert their new people.[3]

Formal conversion to Christianity, however, did not change the everyday lives of these peoples for many generations. The sixth-century Franks described by Gregory of Tours were still very pagan in their practices. Although, to our knowledge, none of the Frankish sovereigns relapsed so far as to pay active homage to pagan gods (as did some of the English), their customs bore little resemblance to the Christian life preached by the Church fathers. Polygyny and incest characterized their marriages. The heavy compensation legally demanded for the abduction or injury of the daughters and wives of the Franks did not deter violence and rape. Widows, seized on the very field where their dead and defeated husbands lay, had to marry the victors. Daughters were dragged to the beds of their fathers' murderers. Such was the fate of the sixth-century Frankish queen Radegond, who was captured and forced to marry Chlotar I, the murderer of several of her relatives. Luckier than many of her contemporaries, she succeeded, after several attempts to escape from her polygynous mate, in gaining release from her marriage. She lived out her life in a convent she established at Poitiers, where she acted as a counselor to Frankish kings and spiritual companion of the poet Fortunatus.

A few Frankish women in those violent and unsettled times bent their circumstances to improve their status. Some slave and peasant women used their beauty and seductiveness to advance themselves on the social ladder. The slave Fredegonda, for whose sake King Chilperic murdered his Visigoth wife, became a queen and proved herself capable of holding her position after her husband's death. Her savage rivalry with her sister-in-law, Queen Brunhilda, dominates the history of the late sixth century. There is evidence that these socially mobile women sometimes remembered the less fortunate people from whom they came. Another slave who became a queen in the seventh century was Balthilda, wife of Clovis II. As regent for her sons, she actively opposed and alleviated the evils of the slave trade.

Women and the Monastic Life

The wives of Anglo-Saxon, Lombard, and Frankish kings favored retirement to religious institutions when they were widowed. For example, Gregory of Tours wrote that Queen Clothilda, after the death of King Clovis, passed the rest of her days in the Basilica of St. Martin. Balthilda had to retire as a widow to Chelles, the monastery she founded. The Lombards' Queen Ansa, according to some sources, joined her daughter in the monastery of St. Salvatore at Brescia when the Franks dethroned her husband and forced him to go to France. Other noblewomen followed suit, and female monasteries everywhere in Christian Europe held the daughters and widows of powerful men. The very nature of the wifely role in the aristocratic family, replete with its movable wealth of jewels, foodstuffs, articles of clothing, and medicines, gave the opportunity to cement alliances with bishops and abbots. These women easily gravitated toward the approved task of founding religious houses.

In the work of the English chronicler Bede, histories of violent queens and the wars they waged are succeeded by lives of saintly virgins and widows and the great convents they established. The most popular type of establishment for women in the seventh century, both in the English and Frankish kingdoms, was the double monastery in which religious men and women observed a common rule and obeyed a common superior—usually an abbess. Monks attached to a convent provided heavy labor, performance of priestly functions, and, in those troubled times, some degree of protection. The Christian doctrine that men and women are spiritually equal countenanced the subjection of men to the rule of a woman. The Mozarabic *Liber Ordinum* of the fifth century instructed bishops to declare at the installation of abbesses that before God there could be no discrimination of sex and no disparity between the souls of the saints because men and women received equal calls to participate in the spiritual battle. In addition, the position of women in most of the double monasteries of this age no doubt owed much to the fact that they came from royal lineage.

By Bede's time, double monasteries had become so fashionable in England that he complained of nobles who built such institutions on their own estates, one for themselves and one for their wives, without any intention of observing continence. This type of establishment, however, was exceptional. Most of the convents that spread over seventh-century England were true religious centers. Bede suggests that a whole generation of women from the royal families of Anglo-Saxon England preferred the celibate life of the convent to marriage. Women fled from the world to the cloister before and after marriage and, in many cases, while their husbands still lived.

The convent provided shelter from an unwelcome union, but it also offered liberty and scope for the ambitious. The nuns of this period did not necessarily practice strict enclosure. Many of them, filled with the spirit of adventure, left the convent and undertook arduous pilgrimages to far-flung centers of worship. When Abbess Bugga of Minster proposed to go to Rome in the eighth century, Boniface warned her that brothels staffed by English nuns lined the roads of Italy, but that did not deter her. Abbesses ruled establishments that sometimes included thousands of men and women and vast territories. And abbesses exercised influence commensurate with their functions. For example, Hilda of Whitby founded several monastic institutions, acted as a consultant to her royal relatives, and gave shelter to the great Synod of Whitby in 664, which submitted the English church to Rome. Five bishops received their training in her convent at Whitby.

The correspondence of the great eighth-century English missionary Boniface with the nuns of Wimbourne shows the important role played by these women in the expansion of Christian civilization. Responding to repeated requests, the English sisters supplied him with books, money, and altar cloths. Most impressive was the copy of St. Peter's epistle, done in gold lettering by the abbess of Thanet, Eadburga. As soon as he had gained a foothold in pagan lands, Boniface requested that Tetta, Abbess of Wimbourne, send him a mission of women to establish nunneries for his new converts. Heeding his call, the learned Leoba followed him into the wilderness to establish the first convent in German lands at Bischofsheim. In later years, when Boniface and Leoba engaged in the reform of the Frankish church, Leoba became the friend and confidante of Charlemagne's empress Hildegard.

The church hierarchy kept an eye on the activities of convents. In 816 a Frankish bishop exhorted the abbesses within his episcopal jurisdiction to take care that the nuns were never idle. In addition to doing routine housekeeping, the bishop had noticed that nuns were distinguishing themselves by the production of fine cloth and needlework. Fearing the temptations to vanity inherent in too much attention to spinning, weaving, and embroidery, the bishop recommended reading as a preferable activity. Similarly, the Council of Cloveshove in England declared that nuns ought to occupy themselves with reading and singing the Psalter.

During these centuries of upheaval and brutality, neither men nor women produced a very large body of original literary or artistic work. Education for both sexes rarely expanded beyond a sturdy knowledge of the Bible and some acquaintance with the writings of the Church fathers. Yet in every Christianized area of early medieval Europe, learned nuns played a vital part in culture and learning. Radegond, in the sixth century, was widely admired for her familiarity with the writings of the Christian fathers. A century later, Hilda of Whitby helped to lay the foundations of the English poetic tradition by inspiring and instructing the herdsman Caedmon, the "father of English poetry." The eighth-century Belgian canonesses Herlinda and Renilda of Eika received their contemporaries' praises for their mastery of the techniques of copying and miniature painting. Manuscripts produced by the nuns of Chelles number among the finest of the age. The nun Baudonivia wrote the life of Radegond; Dominica, a canoness of Nivelles, produced the biography of the convent's founder, Gertrude; and Bertha of Vilich wrote the life of Adelheid. About 760 a nun at the convent of Heidenheim composed a narrative of Wunibald's pilgrimage to the Holy Land. Leoba, one of several nuns who turned her hand to the composition of religious poetry, produced her writing during respites from her active religious life of prayer.

THE CAROLINGIAN AGE: EIGHTH AND NINTH CENTURIES

Saint Paul's injunction that it was improper for women to teach men was ignored through the eighth century because of the demands of the frontier situation in most of Europe. Convents and monasteries monopolized education and instructed children of both sexes, whether or not they intended to enter the monastic life. Only in the late eighth and ninth centuries did an effort to introduce segregation of sexes in monastic education succeed. Simultaneously, the position of secular women was secured by social legislation that eliminated unilateral divorce by men. The Carolingians enhanced the importance of wives by conferring official recognition upon their administrative and economic rights and duties. Thus, ninth-century women amassed property and secured their position in the secular world through their status as wives with legal rights, not through freewheeling behavior.

Prohibition of Women as Teachers

In the mid-eighth century, Pepin the Short, the ruler of the Franks, invited Saint Boniface to reconstitute the decaying church in his kingdom. The reform was continued into the ninth century by his son, Charlemagne. Churchmen in Charlemagne's entourage reintroduced the principle that "the weakness of her sex and the instability of her mind forbid that [women] should hold the leadership over men in teaching and preaching." In his effort to restore the monastic system to its pristine purity, Charlemagne invoked ancient prejudices against women that his predecessors had ignored. He legislated against too close an association of the sexes in monasteries. Nuns and canonesses had to be strictly cloistered. No longer could they assist priests in the celebration of the mass and the administration of the sacraments. Abbesses were placed under the control of bishops. Bishops could even interfere with decisions about life in the convent and the admission of new members. Indeed, bishops alone could consecrate new applicants—a right formerly exercised by abbesses.

The emperor prohibited nuns and canonesses from educating boys in their convents. This reform tended to be more detrimental for laymen than for laywomen because it became increasingly rare for the sons of the nobility to be educated in convents. This meant that laymen frequently received no literary education at all while noble ladies continued to be raised and educated in convents until they reached a marriageable age. For several centuries thereafter, it was not uncommon that a representative of the sex whose "instability" of mind made her unfit to teach boys might find herself wed to an illiterate husband.

Emperor Charlemagne himself never ceased to regret his own illiteracy and strove to master writing even as an adult. The emperor's biographer, Einhard, notes that Charlemagne insisted that his daughters be educated with his sons at the palace school. His sister, Gisela, Abbess of Chelles, was a learned lady who corresponded with the master of the palace schools. Very often in the two centuries that followed, the scant efforts to establish secular centers of culture were promoted by educated women. For example, the founder of the Saxon dynasty of German emperors, Henry I, was illiterate, while his wife Mathilda, educated at Hereford, patronized learning and founded one of the chief literary and scholastic centers of the West at Quedlinburg. This singular disparity of education between men and women may even in part explain why the knightly class described the learned monk as "womanish."

Hroswitha: Nun and Writer

Within the monasteries, the level of learning rose through Carolingian educational reform, which introduced a curriculum based on the seven liberal arts. The tenth-century nun Hroswitha of Gandersheim displayed great familiarity with the products of classical learning. She wrote a series of original dramas of her own, making her the only European dramatist in nearly five centuries. In addition, she produced two histories (one of the German imperial house and one of her own convent of Gandersheim) and short stories based on the apocryphal Gospel of Mary and various lives of the saints, which formed the bulk of the legacy on early Christian womanhood. The preface to Hroswitha's first volume of poetry paid homage to the nuns among whom she lived and especially to Abbess Gerberga. Hroswitha's description of her writing, her first efforts and laborious revisions, gives the modern reader an astonishing picture of a true artist at work within the conventual atmosphere. As her confidence in her own talents grew secure, she portrayed women of courage and resourcefulness. One of her female characters, Sapientia, on the very brink of martyrdom, instructs her male persecutors in the finer points of philosophy, mocking their efforts to turn her from her faith. However, even Hroswitha occasionally succumbed to stereotypes. Thus in one of her prefaces she referred deprecatingly to the "imbecility" of her own sex. Still, this authentic voice of a medieval nun expressed the ideals and aspirations of her less gifted sisters across the centuries:

> There are many Catholics, and we cannot entirely acquit ourselves of the charge, who, attracted by the polished elegance of the style of pagan writers, prefer their works to the holy scriptures. There are others, who, although they are deeply attached to the sacred writings and have no liking for most pagan productions, make an exception in favor of the works of Terence, and, fascinated by the charm of the manner, risk being corrupted by the wickedness of the matter. Wherefore, I, the strong voice of Gandersheim, have not hesitated to imitate in my writings a poet [Terence] whose works are so widely read, my object being to glorify the limits of my poor talents, the laudable chastity of Christian virgins in that self-same form of composition which has been used to describe the shameless acts of licentious women.[4]

Commanding a dramatic style ranging from melodrama to slapstick comedy, Hroswitha pursued the subject of chastity, its defense, its loss, and its restoration. Her heroines sometimes display the standard courage of the virgin martyr faced with death and dishonor. Sometimes they meet death with mockery and impudent humor—other times with resolution and self-sacrifice. In other plays, the heroines' resourcefulness and sense of diplomatic strategy bring about a happy outcome. They are self-reliant and never hesitate to assert themselves against any lustful or bloodthirsty men who persecute them. Hroswitha's dramas should not be regarded simply as heroic fantasies based on the events of times long gone by. Although she preferred a traditional historic setting for her work, contemporary examples of steadfast heroism were not lacking had she chosen to use them.

In addition to meeting the everyday demands of suitors and the hazards of warfare among Christians, women faced a new wave of pagan invasions that broke through Europe in the ninth and tenth centuries. The flourishing monastic culture of Ireland, England, and wide areas of Frankland fell before the Vikings. Convents, with their wealth, their women, and their lack of protection, were favorite targets for these savage marauders. Vikings, unlike their Ostrogothic predecessors who sacked Rome in the sixth century, favored the more brutal practices of warfare, including rape. Women were dragged through the streets by the hair, raped, and tortured. A new generation of martyrs was in the making. Particularly dramatic is the story of the death of Saint Ebba and all the nuns of her convent. In 870, an army of Danes landed in Scotland and proceeded south, spreading terror, ruin, and rapine. The convent at Ely was burned, and the army headed for the nunnery at Coldingham. Seeing no hope of flight, Ebba took heroic measures to defend the honor of her sisters. As the Danes approached, the nuns gathered together and, following Ebba's example, slashed off their noses and upper lips to confront their would-be rapists with a line of ghastly, bleeding virgins. The horrified Danes burned the convent, and the sisters victoriously achieved the status of martyrs. The barbarian Magyars and rampaging Saracens similarly raped women and ransacked monasteries.

Secular Women and Property

Women who found martyrdom or fulfillment in the convent were, of course, only a small proportion of the female population. In the early Middle Ages, as in most ages of human history, the majority of women lived in the secular world, married, and bore children. By the ninth century a complex series of social measures had produced a change for the individual woman vis-à-vis the family interests. Women now ensured their independence within the limits of whatever social sphere they occupied by their control of some property. The Germanic custom of bride purchase practically disappeared. Instead of giving a purchase price to the bride's family, the groom endowed her directly with the bride gift, usually a piece of landed property over which she had full rights. To this, he frequently added the morning gift following the consummation of the marriage. In addition to the economic independence derived through marriage, the women of the ninth century enjoyed an increased capacity to share in the inheritance of property. Women had always been eligible to receive certain movable goods from either their own relatives or from their husbands, but now law and practice allowed women to inherit immovables. A reason for this trend may be discerned from a deed from the eighth century in which a loving father left equal shares of his property to his sons and daughters. He justified his act by explaining that discrimination between the sexes was an "impious custom" that ran contrary to God's law and to the love he felt for all of his children.

Women's ability to inherit property had far-reaching social effects, which modern demographers are still investigating. Although a young woman still could not marry a man against her family's will, her independence after marriage increased when she possessed her own property. After their father's death, Charlemagne's daughters withdrew from the court of their brother and led independent lives because Charlemagne had endowed them with substantial property. As widows, too, women acquired increased status when they controlled their sons' and their deceased husbands' property. The most dramatic example of this permanently affected the political future of England. The daughter of Alfred the Great, Ethelflaeda, widow of the king of Mercia, devoted her long reign to cooperation with her brother in the pursuit of their father's policy of containing the Norse invaders. Together they established a strong, centralized kingdom centered on Wessex. After a life of campaigning against Danish, Irish, and Norwegian enemies, she succeeded in willing the kingdom away from her own daughter, the rightful heiress, and leaving it to her brother. This act destroyed the independence of Mercia with its rival claims to Anglo-Saxon supremacy and assured that the English kingdom would be dominated by Wessex and the line of Alfred. Ironically, Ethelflaeda's indisputable contribution to the future of England deprived another woman of her right to rule.

Women Under the Carolingian Government

On the Continent, the Carolingian house imposed a relatively stable peace for over a century. This was an age not only of religious but also of social reform aimed at reconstituting a political order that had vanished with the Roman state. Inspired by the vision of Augustine centuries earlier, Charlemagne endeavored to devise an imperial system that would give expression to the City of God. To this end, he redefined the duties of the great officials and created some new positions. These reforms, however, did not favor the advancement of women. The government of his empire was vested in counts, bishops, and other local officials under the supervision of the king's traveling agents, the *missi dominici*. The counts received some assistance from their wives, but it never occurred to the emperor or any of his advisers to appoint a woman.

The establishment of the Carolingian system of government barred women from the power they sometimes wielded under the earlier Frankish kings and possessed again in the first feudal age, which began in the late ninth century. The legitimate rights of women as wives, in contrast, received formal recognition in the imperial period. To support their own rather dubious claims to the crown, the Carolingians had introduced the custom of anointment and solemn coronation with its overtones of divine sanction for the monarchy. From Pepin forward, their queens shared in this ritual: once crowned in their own right, their names appeared in the royal liturgies. As head of the royal household the queen had power to affect the economic administration of the kingdom.

In the ninth century no one distinguished between an office and the person who held it or between private and public authority. The ministers of state had the titles of palace servants; indeed the ancient concept of the state was but a dim memory. The whole realm was regarded as the ruler's property. His finances and real power rested on the vast estates he owned directly. All the ninth-century sources agree that the queen had the duty of running the royal estates—that is, the finances and domestic affairs of the realm—in order to leave the king free for what he considered more important duties. In the *Capitulare de villis*, Charlemagne specifically endowed his queen with such power: "We wish that everything ordered by us or by the queen to one of our judges, or anything ordered to the ministers, seneschals or cupbearers . . . be carried out to the last word."

In the creation of royal prerogative, the Carolingians authorized one powerful office for women, that is, reigning queen or queen consort. Specific responsibilities were assigned to the queen, chiefly the administration of crown lands and resources. In imitation of the powerful Carolingians, other kingdoms adopted this office, along with the ceremony of coronation and anointment that sanctioned it. In Wessex in England, *queen* replaced *king's wife*. Later the royal Saxon dynasty in Germany, the Capetian royal family in France, as well as ruling families of the Iberian peninsula and the British Isles took up the practice. The Carolingians first gave official recognition to what became the practice in the West: crowned women actively participating in royal rule. The challenge of establishing authority absorbed the energies of entire dynasties. Frequently subjects associated the queen consort and other women in royal families with the prosperity and welfare of the realm.

The same pattern repeats itself through the ranks of the aristocracy, where competent and trained wives were expected to administer the affairs of thousands of dependents in their extended "household." Occasionally, too, the lady entrusted with such responsibilities might not be working simply as her husband's supporter. We have one extraordinary example of a "professional" in the life of Saint Liutberga. Raised in a convent, Liutberga's intelligence and good disposition recommended her as a companion to Gisela, a wealthy widow who had inherited the broad lands of her father, Count Hessi of Saxony. Liutberga proved an apt pupil of her patron, who spent most of her time traveling to supervise her lands. On her deathbed, Gisela advised her son and heir, Bernard, to entrust the administration of the estates to Liutberga. He did so and under her management his family prospered. As she advanced in age, however, Liutberga became increasingly devout and possibly also increasingly weary of being exploited by this wealthy family. In any case, she withdrew from them and established herself as a recluse near the convent of Wendhausen. Here the great men and women of the area frequently visited her and looked to her for counsel and elevating discourse. Due to her popularity, the convent attracted the attention of leading bishops and gained rich endowments. It soon figured as one of the leading centers of education for young women.

The position of Carolingian women as wives gained further support from the introduction into secular legislation of the principle of marital indissolubility. The general position of the early church found a wife's barrenness or illness insufficient cause for her repudiation. Her husband might find her repulsive but he could not put her away for a wife that suited him better. Only if she committed adultery could she be repudiated. But these principles lacked the power of enforcement in early times. The Carolingians, who depended heavily on church support to secure their own power, worked steadily to bring their own laws into conformity with canon law. Charlemagne, who in youth had repudiated at least one wife, adopted a guise of marital decorum once he had issued his prohibitions against divorce. Despite the urging of his counselors, he refused to repudiate his unpopular queen Fastrada. After the death of a subsequent wife, Liutgard, he did not again submit himself to the legal bonds of marriage.

The new laws met several dramatic tests under Charlemagne's successors, but they were finally upheld. Louis the Pious, Charlemagne's son, succeeded in retaining his unpopular wife, Judith of Bavaria, by relying on synodal legislation, which entitled the accused woman to a trial in defense of her honor and position. An alliance of prelates and nobles, grouped behind the sons of the emperor's first marriage, had sought to drive Judith from her place with charges of adultery and even sorcery. They had succeeded in forcibly separating the royal couple and placing them in monasteries for repentance. When, however, Louis could reassemble his forces, he was able to force an ecclesiastical court to hear the case and accept the queen's successful purgation. The final test came later in the ninth century when Louis's grandson, King Lothar II of Lotharingia, attempted to repudiate his wife, Tetberga, and marry his mistress, Waldrada. Through a champion, the queen underwent the ordeal of boiling water and successfully negated his charges of adultery and incest. Ignoring the verdict, Lothar then dragged her before a series of ecclesiastical tribunals, one of which, manned by bishops he had appointed, found in his favor. This, however, drew upon the king the wrath of the leading Frankish prelate, Hincmar of Rheims, and finally of Pope Nicholas I. Even though the queen, exhausted and frightened, begged to retire into a convent, the pope insisted that Lothar take her back. The inviolability of marriage triumphed; whether this constituted a genuine gain for women poses another question entirely.

The church proclaimed that even adultery did not excuse divorce. To insure the utmost legal recognition for the wife, Hincmar advised a formal contract, parental consent, and personal vows with a blessing by the clergy. These formalities, however, could be avoided. Through the five centuries that followed, the Church steadily expanded its jurisdiction over marital problems. A body of legislation accrued aimed at applying the principle of indissolubility to common-law marriages; betrothals, especially where the couple had consummated their relationship; and even to promises made by seducers to their victims.

Although little information about the lives of ordinary people in this period survives, it seems clear that they (like their royal and noble rulers) regarded themselves primarily as parts of family units. The new rules prohibiting divorce, for example, tightened family ties for them as well as for the elite. It must be remembered that for men and women of the Carolingian age, obtaining the necessities of life was a never-ending pre-occupation. In the peasant class, burdened with the support of the entire society, the labor of each member of the family was indispensable for survival itself. Even without legal and spiritual compulsions, the most pressing necessities served to strengthen the marital bond. Moreover, what these women did, who they married, how they disposed of what small income came to them concerned the lord who ruled them. The records of the great abbeys and other manorial documents specifically list the status of each man and woman on the estate with the exact obligations each individual owed in labor and in provisions. The manorial rolls reflect a respect for women despite the fact that peasant women were bound to their husbands and to the land. As laborers, peasant women produced wealth. Each person who could work mattered, and no ideas about the "inherent weakness" of women excluded them from their place in a world of productive people.

Charlemagne paid attention to the importance of peasant women in the *Capitulare de villis* that laid out the authority of the queen. In addition to their general duties in their own family circles, the women of the royal domain, like their husbands, owed certain services to the lord. On the Carolingian estate, as in the manufacturing establishments of the later Middle Ages, women's exclusive province was the making of cloth. To supply the emperor with the household linens and clothes he and his retainers needed, the women of his estates worked at set periods in the great hall of a manor, providing "linen, wool, woad, vermillion, madder, wool-combs, teasels, soap, grease, vessels and other objects." In addition, they performed duties related to the provision of food in the hall itself and probably participated in the preparation of the foodstuffs owed by the family to the lord: "lard, smoked meat, salt meat, partially salted meat, wine, butter, malt, beef, mead, honey, wax, flour."

Carolingian men and women wore clothes produced in the same workshops. Women worked individually or in teams on linen and wool; they sheared sheep, washed fleece, carded wool with thistles, combed it, spun it, and wove it. Peasants harvested flax almost everywhere and delivered it to workshops regularly. It was then steeped, washed, beaten, and woven into linen. Women subsequently dyed the bolts of cloth with woad, madder, and vermillion (natural dyes).[5] When he received a fine chess set and an elephant from the great Caliph Harun Al-Rashid, Charlemagne returned the compliment with a vermillion-dyed Frankish cape of fine wool, the best his realm had to offer in the way of rich gifts.

Carolingian Families, Classes, and the Church

Outside of royal workshops the family was the essential unit of production. If we judge by the scattered surviving demographic evidence of the age, peasant and artisan families weighed their resources and productivity against their reproductive capacities. The fertility rate in Carolingian society cannot be estimated, but these early medieval centuries did show a reverse in the trend toward decline so evident in the society of late antiquity. The idea of birth control appears in capitularies, concilar canons, and penitentials of the Carolingian age.[6] Women and men so effectively "fooled nature" that they seldom had large families. To be more precise, families in the upper, affluent levels of society were often large, but among the lower classes families tended to be small. Despite church legislation against birth control, those of limited means attempted to bring family size in line with resources. This effort to adjust births to resources bears responsibility for population stability with only a slight increase.

Still the church allowed sexual relations only for the purpose of procreation and forbade all types of contraception. Theodulf, a churchman, in "On Fornication Against Reason" wrote, "They call it pollution, or the abominable sin—the deed of not lying with a woman in the normal fashion."[7] Women usually found themselves accused of using potions: "A woman who kills her [unborn] child by magical practice, by drink or by any art, will do seven years penance. If she did it from poverty, the penance will be reduced to three years."[7] The clergy who adamantly prohibited birth control made some concession for poor women.

The aspirations of all medieval men and women were limited by their class. Within those bounds, peasants, like their noble masters, pursued their own ambitions. The most important social fact of this age is the practical disappearance of ancient forms of slavery. Many factors combined to achieve this elevation of the lowest ranks among the agricultural workers. Since the peasants derived their legal status through their mothers, it has recently been suggested that by marrying free women dependent men achieved the freedom of their offspring.

The short-lived effort of Charlemagne and his descendants to achieve a structured society tended to deprive women of some of the powers they had exercised in the sixth and seventh centuries. In this sense the Carolingian period foreshadowed twelfth-century developments. As the control of church and state came increasingly to be vested in the hands of men, women's activities narrowed to the home and the cloister. Yet, the Carolingian age strengthened the rights of women within the family. By enforcing the principle of marital indissolubility, the Church protected women from the caprices of their husbands. Women's contributions to the well-being of society earned some recognition. Their right to share in their patrimonial inheritances and to enjoy the rewards of their own labor found protection under the law.

THE FIRST FEUDAL AGE: TENTH AND ELEVENTH CENTURIES

Endowed with their own property and rights of inheritance, secure in their marital status, women were equipped to act with power and decision in the fluid society of the first feudal age, which followed the collapse of the Carolingian empire in the late ninth century. The institutions of Charlemagne proved incapable of sustaining themselves under the dual assault of new invasions and the claims of blood that caused the emperors themselves to divide their dominions among their sons. Land, power, and title passed from one to another of their warring successors. Out of the ruins of the Carolingian state, the family emerged as the most stable and effective element in a troubled world. Profiting from the almost unlimited power of their families, women for two centuries were able to play a central political role. Since land had become the only source of power, by exercising their property rights, secured in the Carolingian period, a growing number of women appear in the tenth and eleventh centuries as chatelaines, mistresses of landed property and castles with attendant rights of justice and military command, proprietors of churches, and participants in both secular and ecclesiastical assemblies.

By the middle of the tenth century, the most stable and secure power in Europe, the German kingdom of Otto I, changed the fate of Germany forever. With imperial ambitions, Otto contracted a marriage to Adelaide of Burgundy, who had come into possession of large estates in the kingdom of Lombardy after the death of her first husband. Control of these lands laid the base for a possible renewal of the Roman imperial title. Competitors literally besieged the widow in order to win her hand and all that went with it. With Adelaide's marriage to Otto began the connection between Italy and Germany that lasted until the nineteenth century. In recognition of his wife's political power and prestige, the emperor issued diplomas with their joint signatures and minted coins with her portrait on them.

With most of Europe beset by violence and political disintegration, tenth- and eleventh-century Germany represented an oasis of culture and security. The great convents continued to flourish there as centers of learning. Under the rule of the Salian and Saxon emperors and the regencies of their wives, widows, and sisters, Germany prospered. Among the women who helped to rule this empire, one of the most interesting was the sister of Otto II, Matilda, Abbess of Quedlinburg. When her brother was occupied with his government in Italy, she ruled in his name and even presided over church councils. Even when acting only in her own name, she exercised the enormous political and economic power vested by Otto I and his successors in the great offices of the Church. Her biographer used the word *metropolitana* (overseer of bishops) to describe her authority.

Outside Germany, western Europe broke up into a collection of small principalities or seigniories; the authority of each extended as far as its lord, with his limited resources, could enforce his will. The bonds of lineage represented the principal source of strength for the men and women of this anarchic age. With their dowries and their family connections, women could make a vital contribution to the advancement of their families. For example, in the tenth century, Hugh Capet defended his claim to the throne of France against his rival, Charles of Lorraine, with the argument that Charles had married beneath his station, the daughter of one of Hugh's own vassals, a mere knight. Hugh's wife, by contrast, was the daughter of Empress Adelaide by her first marriage.

Wherever one looks during this period there seem to be no effective barriers to the exercise of power by women. They appear as military leaders, judges, chatelaines, and controllers of property. In tenth-century Italy the independent and powerful women shocked and appalled their monkish chronicler, Liutprand of Cremona. His world appeared to be in the grip of this horrible "pornocracy," government by prostitutes. Liutprand was utterly incapable of explaining the source of this power. Rather than attribute it to the possibilities of inheritance or to personal competence, he repeatedly suggested that when such a woman beckoned from her perfumed couch, no man could help but do her bidding. For example, he noted that the daughter of the Marquess of Tuscany and widow of the Marquess of Ivrea Ermengarde "held the chief authority in all Italy." But his only explanation was that "the cause of her power, shameful though it be even to mention it, was that she carried on carnal commerce with everyone, prince and commoner alike. . . . Ermengarde's beauty, in this corruptible flesh, roused the fiercest jealousies among men: for she would give to some the favours she refused to others."[8]

The holders of sovereign rights in the tenth century claimed control of the Church as well. Regarding churches as their own property, they held it their right to appoint church officials—bishops, abbots, and even parish priests. In Rome itself, the great proprietary rights of the family of Theophylactus and the political influence attached to them passed into the hands of Lady Theodora and then to her daughter Marozia. The papacy itself lay under their control. Mistress to one pope, mother of another, Marozia, through her marriage to the king of northern Italy, nearly succeeded in uniting the whole peninsula under her influence until she was thwarted by the violent intervention of one of her sons. Not all chroniclers viewed this feminine influence as uniformly evil. Many a bishop, interested in reform and good government, relied on the influence of the ladies who controlled appointments to local churches and sought their assistance in restoring order to disturbed parishes and monasteries.

The ecclesiastical reformers of the late eleventh and twelfth centuries have often interpreted the events of this earlier and less institutionalized age to the detriment of its forceful women. Wielding influence through the family, women often initiated reforms on a local scale that later reforming popes built upon. Time and again in the first feudal age, lay patronage meant a woman with the resources and interest to begin the process of reform in her local parish.

CONCLUSION

Women in the undeveloped frontier stages of medieval society took advantage of the broad opportunities available to elevate themselves to positions of wealth and power. An unstructured society afforded ambitious women substantial range for their capabilities, and class lines had yet to harden and thus to fetter women and men alike. The most significant conclusion that emerges from the study of early medieval women is that women showed they were capable of carrying responsibilities equal to those of men. The participation of women from the fifth through the seventh centuries in spreading Christianity and building a new society led to the legal recognition of their economic and marital rights in the Carolingian period. Whether the inheritance and family rights women won then outweighed the loss of opportunity to better their station in life is another question, but women certainly gained through the exclusive control of the ecclesiastical institutions placed under their authority. After the breakup of the Carolingian empire, noble women of the tenth and eleventh centuries had an unprecedented opportunity to use their talents. The inheritance and property rights won in Carolingian times remained in force by custom and practice. The age valued its women, who participated vigorously in the endeavors of the day, secure in the knowledge that they were crucial to feudal governance, to society, and to economic life.

Affording women ample opportunities, providing them customary rights of inheritance and property, and giving women control of powerful institutions helped set Europe on a successful course.

NOTES

1. Venerable Bede, *History of the English Church and People*, trans. Leo Sherley-Price (Baltimore: Penguin, 1955), pp. 76–77.
2. Thomas A. Walker, *A History of the Law of Nations* (Cambridge, England: Cambridge University Press, 1899), I, 65.
3. The details of this process may be found in Jo Ann McNamara, "Living Sermons," in *Peaceweavers: Medieval Religious Women*, eds. J. Nicols and L. T. Shank (Kalamazoo, Mich.: Medieval Institute, 1986), II.
4. *Hroswitha Plays*, trans. Christopher St. John (New York: Benjamin Press, 1966), p. xxvi, and also by Katharina M. Wilson (Saskatchewan, Canada, 1985).
5. Pierre Riché, *Daily Life in the World of Charlemagne*, trans. Jo Ann McNamara (Philadelphia: University of Pennsylvania Press, 1978), p. 163.
6. Capitularies were edicts issued by the ruler of the kingdom. When bishops met in church councils, the proceedings included settlements on ecclesiastical law called concilar canons. The penitentials were issued by the Church as models for clergy to use in assigning penances for confessed sins. On the surviving documents from the early Middle Ages, see Suzanne Wemple, *Women in Frankish Society* (Philadelphia: University of Pennsylvania Press, 1981), bibliography.
7. Theodulf, *Statuta*, ed. J. de Clerq, in *La législation religieuse franque* (Louvain: Bureau de Recueil, Bibliothèque de l'Université, 1936–1958), I, 338.
8. Regino, *De synodalibus*, II: 82, "*Paupercula pro difficultate nutriendi*," see J. T. Noonan, *Contraception*, (Cambridge: Belknap Press, 1966), p. 193.
9. Liutprand of Cremona, *Antatapodasis*, Book 3, Chapter 8, *The Works of Liutprand of Cremona*, trans. F. A. Wright (New York, E. P. Dutton, 1930), p. 113.

SUGGESTIONS FOR FURTHER READING

Perhaps the only aspect of the history of women in the Middle Ages that has been adequately studied is the legal rights of women. Such studies, however, were written mainly in French and German and are not available in English translation. Most important among these are Louis-Maurice-André Cornuey, *Le régime de la "dos" aux époques mérovingienne et carolingienne* (Ph.D. dissertation, Université d'Alger, 1929), which traces the transformation of the dowry into the dower, and Aimée Ermolaef, *Die Sonderstellung der Frau im französischen Lehnrecht* (dissertation, University of Bern, 1930), which analyzes the extensive powers women held under French feudal law. See also Doris Stenton's *The English Woman in History* (London: George Allen & Unwin, 1950). In her analysis of the power of Anglo-Saxon women, the author has heavily drawn upon Frank Stenton's study of place names, "The Place of Women in Anglo-Saxon Society," *Transactions of the Royal Historical Society*, 14th Ser., vol. 25 (1943), 1–113. See also Suzanne Wemple, *Women in Frankish Society* (Philadelphia: University of Pennsylvania Press, 1981) and Pierre Riché, *Daily Life in the World of Charlemagne*, trans. Jo Ann McNamara (Philadelphia: University of Pennsylvania Press, 1978).

Local histories, in which the French excel, usually contain material on women. The overall conclusions of the grand master of this type of historical inquiry, Georges Duby, have been integrated into his general survey, *Rural Economy and Country Life in the Medieval West*, trans. Cynthia Postman (Columbia, S.C.: University of South Carolina Press, 1968). A fine example of American scholarship is Archibald Lewis, *Development of Southern French and Catalan Society* (Austin: University of Texas, 1956).

A modern approach to social history is through demographic study, which also yields information of importance for the history of women. Especially useful for our period are David Herlihy's "Land, Family and Women," *Traditio*, 18 (1962), 89–113, and Emily Coleman's "Medieval Marriage Characteristics: A Neglected Factor in the History of Medieval Serfdom," *Journal of Interdisciplinary History*, 2 (1971), 205–219.

For the history of medieval convents we still have to rely on two nineteenth century works: Lina Eckenstein, *Woman under Monasticism* (Cambridge: Cambridge University Press, 1896), and Mary Bateson, "Origin and Early History of Double Monasteries," *Transactions of the Royal Historical Society*, 13 (1899), 137–198. These may be supplemented by Eileen Power, *Medieval English Nunneries* (Cambridge: Cambridge University Press, 1922), and M. P. Heinrich, *The Canonesses and Education in the Early Middle Ages* (Ph.D. dissertation, Catholic University of America, 1924). There are also histories of individual convents.

Because biographies of medieval women are of varying quality, we would rather recommend the reading of collective biographies, such as Eileen Power, *Medieval People* (London and New York: University Paperbacks, 1966, new rev. ed.). An analysis of the role of queens is provided by Marion F. Facinger, "A Study of Medieval Queenship: Capetian France," *Studies in Medieval Renaissance History*, 5 (1968). For an understanding of developments in the later Middle Ages, the most essential study is Eileen Power, "The Position of Women," *The Legacy of the Middle Ages*, ed. G. C. Crump and E. F. Jacob (Oxford: Clarendon Press, 1926), pp. 401–434.

An Italian woman selling leeks, *c.* 1385, as pictured in *Tacuinum sanitatis.*
(Österreichische Nationalbibliothek)

chapter 6

The Dominion of Gender: Women's Fortunes in the High Middle Ages

Susan Stuard

We know that stereotyping affects women's lives but we seldom have a chance to see how and why new stereotypes arise and to follow their course as they gain acceptance. The years from the eleventh to the fourteenth century afford the opportunity to view that process at a time when Europe was coming of age as a separate and distinct civilization. Changed attitudes toward women, which employed notions of polarity juxtaposing woman's nature to man's, accompanied and supported significant changes in the economy and society. Out of this process a systematic program of gender emerged.

At the beginning of the age women contributed leadership and creative skills to the major movements promoting growth in European communities. As wealth concentrated into fewer, typically male, hands, women saw their social and legal rights, their access to institutions, and their opportunities erode. The newly systematic gender system affected royal women and the exercise of political power. Soon gender changed the lives of women in towns and in rural areas. Notions of gender, however, were not applied in a wholly consistent manner. Where women's work was still deemed essential, notions of gender might not be employed or even mentioned.

Using the Song of Solomon as authority, young clerks at the cathedral school in Beauvais, France, praised woman in the early twelfth-century *Play of Daniel.* "Woman's value is like that of a strong man come from afar. . . . for the eloquence of her words overcomes the wisdom of the learned."[1] The clerks' thoughts on gender, the system of relations between women and men, favored likeness, not difference, to link the sexes. In the course of the next two centuries, theologians reconstructed gender on the authority of Aristotle, not Solomon, featuring polar oppositions of woman to man, not likenesses. This profound change in thinking helped set women's history on a separate trajectory from men's in the West, with implications down to the present day. The new thinking on gender accompanied and strengthened fundamental changes in western society to which women's experience bears earlier and clearer witness than does the experience of men. When the popular *Play of Daniel* was first performed, women still contributed to all the major movements that spelled success for an emerging European civilization. In the next two centuries, women were successively closed out of opportunities to profit from Europe's increasingly complex institutions, although their contributions remained essential to society's well-being.

The new thinking about women consisted of notions of polarity rather than rigorously argued ideas and arrived in the twelfth and thirteenth centuries embedded in classical arguments devoted to entirely different questions. Theologians employed notions of polarity between woman and man as part of a greater apparatus of thought that purported to explain God's rational plan of a dual human creation, that is, one both female and male. The notions served as a cog in an abstract system that the holy scholars used to explain to themselves why the creation of man alone was not enough in God's benevolent scheme. But Scholastic theologians taught as well as wrote; their students—the priests, lawyers, and doctors prepared at universities—served later in powerful positions where they employed the new notions on woman's nature to justify new practices and the elimination of some traditional ones. How learned opinions carried over into generally accepted commonplaces, that is, moved from the scholar's page to conventional wisdom uttered in the streets, forms a complex story. This essay addresses the question of how and why that transference took place.

TENTH– AND ELEVENTH–CENTURY OPPORTUNITIES FOR WOMEN

Before that transference occurred, women inhabited a different world. After the breakup of the Carolingian Empire, when Europeans entered the tenth century, an age so filled with war it has often been called "the age of iron," women had actually encountered opportunities to act with power and decision. They were equipped with property and inheritance rights and sustained by gender assumptions based on similarities between women and men. Institutions painstakingly constructed by Charlemagne and his successors had disappeared. The new, more fluid conditions favored forceful persons who possessed strong family backing. Women fit these qualifications as well as men, and in the contest for land, power, and title sometimes achieved impressive gains. A growing number of women appeared in the tenth and eleventh centuries as chatelaines, that is, mistresses of landed property and castles with attendant rights of justice and military command; as proprietors of churches; and as participants in both secular and ecclesiastical assemblies. Feudal institutions intended for the conduct of war adapted to women's participation, while religious orders produced an impressive line of women administrators and learned authorities. But women's most consequential long-term contribution in this era lay in the anonymous work of peasant agriculture. This age produced two breakthroughs in technology that turned the seasonal lands of Europe to surplus production: the three-field system (crop rotation) and the use of nonhuman sources of energy — the horse and the mule, the water mill, and then the windmill. Europe's peasant women as well as its peasant men produced Europe's agricultural revolution.

Women and men worked closely together in peasant households, so that tracing the anonymous achievements of women peasants and separating their accomplishments from those of men proves nearly impossible. Still, some tantalizing shreds of evidence remain from these early times. On the ninth-century manor of St. Germain-des-Près, women headed farm households in settled and developed areas; in fact, large farms included proportionally more adult women than men. Because peasants constantly expanded arable holdings, men left to gain new lands, often leaving women at home to produce the agricultural surplus that provided families their livelihood. Men dominated on new farms where assarting (slashing and burning to clear fields) increased the arable land by opening formerly wooded lands for planting. Brides traditionally received farm implements and tools for cloth production as wedding gifts. Wives and their kin, often referred to as the distaff side of the family, practiced cultivation and crafts. The distaff used in spinning symbolized production. A husband and his kin were referred to as the sword side of the family, recalling men's roles in warfare. This division of labor gave women responsibilities in agricultural administration as well. The treasurer of the Carolingian court answered to the queen about taxes on agricultural produce. The king was likely to be off in seasonal campaigns when taxes came due, and few kings showed much interest in agricultural development.

Chronic warfare postponed the aggregate effects of this sexual division of labor except where feudal powers provided a measure of peace. As the previous chapter noted, Germany and northern Italy, united under the Saxon dynasty in the tenth century, succeeded first. We have often allotted too much credit to the sword side of that dynasty and overlooked the productive roles played by its royal women. Not so the contemporaries of Empress Adelaide, wife of Otto I, whose coins bore her portrait. Adelaide's daughter, Matilda, saw women's dynastic power institutionalized in the vast endowments assigned her monastic house at Quedlinburg. While her brother fought on in northern Italy, Matilda brought peace to Germany and earned the title *metropolitana* (overseer of bishops) from her biographer. Quedlinburg and its sister convent at Gandersheim lay at the heart of the Ottonian system of the use of church office to provide secular rule and pacify the land. A traditional division of labor that associated women with the productive arts expedited Saxon policies, and earlier advances in agriculture began to yield identifiable surpluses.

Ottonian Germany prospered under Matilda's guidance, but even greater benefits lay in store for northern Italian lands after she and her brother died. Responsibility for the Empire's welfare fell to their surviving mother, Adelaide, and her daughter-in-law, the Byzantine Princess Theophano. They established a joint regency to sustain the election to the throne of the three-year-old heir of the family, Otto III. Proud, mutually jealous, quarrelsome, and as overbearing as other members of the dynasty, Adelaide and Theophano nonetheless put aside their personal animosities and worked for a lasting peace. Together they achieved two critical decades of stability in northern Italy that permitted commerce and industry to establish a foothold in the region. Towns flourished, and the pace of development quickened.

This growth provided opportunity to a people still lightly taxed by their feudal overlords, who had yet to learn how to wring the most out of their urban subjects. Flexible work patterns within urban artisan families, in which an imprecise line between women's and men's work accommodated uneven labor demands, drove the economy. Those patterns warrant a place alongside other and more frequently acknowledged factors: agricultural surplus, trade over the Mediterranean Sea, and a fortunate geographical setting. Through these decades, women in towns seized the opportunity to work and became shopkeepers, artisans, and craftswomen. Families staffed the earliest commercial enterprises and workshops, much as they had formed the essential working unit upon manors and farms. While husbands peddled goods, wives watched over stores and purchased or produced supplies, or women sold wares in markets or at fairs while their husbands produced goods in home workshops. Enterprising women followed lucrative crafts— such as wool-working, textiles, felt-making, and hat manufacture—which became mainstays of the export trade.

These informal and home-based initiatives yielded some remarkable results. Anonymous but important technical innovations in manufactures came out of home workshops: mechanical fulling of cloth and mills for tanning or laundering, for crushing anything from olives to ore, for polishing, or for reducing pigments to paints or pulp to paper.[2] These innovations should be credited to artisan women as well as to men. In Genoa, brides from laboring families listed stock and tools comparable to those of their husbands when entering marriages. Their marriages sound as much like business partnerships as pacts to establish a household and family. Family workshops in emerging towns throughout Europe produced a whole range of trade-worthy products. Women worked as brewers, glassmakers, and textile workers; or in sales as fishwives; or as associates of their husbands in the heavier industries of coopering, smithing, tanning, and salt-panning.[3] Flexible division of labor between women and men populated towns with industrious inhabitants who accommodated their skills and labor to tasks in a highly supple and elastic fashion.

Although the most dramatic results of economic growth appeared in northern Italy in the cities within the Saxon dynasty's authority, Spain, France, England, and the Low Countries saw changes as well. Ruling families throughout feudal Europe made little or no distinction between public and private authority. With rights to lands and resources went sovereign rights of military impressment, justice, minting, taxation, and other responsibilities of rule. Abbesses sent their knights to war. Noble ladies sat in judgment of their vassals and peasants, and held the castles when lords fought in the field. Some made laws. The Countess Almodis of Barcelona coauthored the *Usages of Barcelona*, one of the earliest written law codes of the age.

The Bayeux Tapestry, among the finest works of art of the age, records William of Normandy's conquest of England. It owes its importance not only to superb design and workmanship but also to its accurate depiction of the technology of the eleventh century. Women designed and worked this historic document that witnesses to their acute awareness of their age and of consequential changes in their own lifetimes.

Not all feudal women stayed home to administer lands. In the eleventh century, when the Normans entered the Mediterranean area and carved out a kingdom in Sicily and southern Italy, women fought along with men. Gaita, a Norman and Robert Guiscard's wife, accompanied her husband on campaign, on horseback, helmeted and armored. Gaita fought "like another Pallas, if not a second Athena," commented Anna Comnena, the historian of Constantinople.[4] If any of her Norman knights proved timorous, Gaita rallied them back into the line of battle.

By the middle years of the eleventh century in most of Europe, the results of efforts at peacekeeping had produced quite a settled world. Population increased steadily, assarting and improved cultivation continued to produce marketable surpluses, and commerce and towns expanded. World historian L. S. Stavrianos, comparing the late, swift rise of the West to the earlier rise of other civilizations, said, "The root of [the] fateful difference is to be found in the unique characteristics of the new Western Civilization — pluralistic, adaptable, and free of the shackles of tradition."[5] This includes, on the practical level, a fluid rather than a static sexual division of labor that enabled both women and men to contribute their capacities.

Contemporaries associated feudal women with the administration and defense of land resources, and their husbands with acquiring new lands; however, no absolute rules governed this division of responsibility. In the eleventh century, Agnes of Burgundy did not hesitate to ride into battle — with her second husband when their political goals were compatible and against the kin of her first husband. Peasant women tied their efforts and fortunes to cultivation, and peasant men tied theirs to assarting; again, no clear-cut line mandated this division, and the labor-intensive but still sparsely populated manors of Europe profited from this elasticity. In towns, women often produced cloth rather than iron tools, but because families formed small workshops, even this distinction could be ignored when a widow wished to keep the family business for her heirs. In convents, women prayed as devoutly in expectation of God's blessing as did men in monasteries.

Several considerations, namely a fortunate birth, a calling to the spiritual life, a recognized skill, wealth, or a particularly forceful personality, overrode habitual or even new assumptions about women's proper roles. In fact, the combination of high birth, an affiliation with an endowed institution such as a royal convent, a penchant for book-learning, and a spiritual calling offered the age's best opportunities for self-cultivation. No wonder some wellborn monastic women issued learned opinions that carried authority in the day. Often revered as closer to God because of the sanctity assigned to female virginity, these women had also siphoned off a most potent mix of worldly advantages, which they directed toward their own cherished goals without hesitation.

HOW THE GREGORIAN REVOLUTION AFFECTED WOMEN

The eleventh century brought other profound changes to Europe that affected women. In England the date of the Norman Conquest, 1066, constitutes a watershed, not only in regard to the opportunities women and men encountered, but also in regard to opinions offered on what women could accomplish. In Saxon and early Norman times English chroniclers, who wrote in their capacity as monks and priests, had seen nothing at all remarkable about women in authoritative positions. However, by the twelfth century, new attitudes began to take over, and histories labeled such behavior as "manly" and exceptional.[6] Clearly churchmen responded to some new notions about sex roles and the differing capacities of women and of men. In Europe at large, the Church with its corps of literate clerks, priests, and monks took the lead in establishing a new tone. With its increased bureaucracy and new assumptions about women, the Church ultimately tended to restrict the wide variety of roles women had played in the tenth and eleventh centuries.

The campaign against clerical marriage and the rights of priests' wives drew the attention of the popes first. Pope Gregory VII (1073–1085) and the reforming popes who preceded and succeeded him vowed to enforce clerical celibacy. This was no new issue in the Church; critics had long mounted attacks on the traditional practice of clerical marriage for parish priests. The tenth-century Bishop Atro of Vercelli had criticized wives of parish priests for diverting revenues to their personal and their heirs' use, taking church land into private hands, distracting husbands from pastoral duties, and involving priests in lawsuits that ended in trials before civil rather than ecclesiastical courts. These women's inheritances and their labor contributed to parish welfare, but critics chose to ignore that fact. In the eleventh century, voices like Atro's, which had drawn little attention in an earlier day, found an audience among the higher clergy fortified now by stronger notions of gender difference.

Popes zealously eliminated lay influence in the bestowal of church offices that culminated in the drive to establish a hierarchical church under the absolute control of the papacy. Aristocratic women of an earlier age had shared with the men of their class in the disposition and protection of ecclesiastical positions. In fact, the active participation of laywomen who provided interested and energetic patronage allowed the Church to initiate its reforming measures. Then with the destruction of this lay patronage, women lost that influence. The success of the papal reform movement depended heavily upon the financial and military support of two women, Beatrice of Tuscany and her daughter Matilda. Their castle at Canossa provided the meeting place for the momentous confrontation in 1077 of Emperor Henry IV and Pope Gregory VII over the right to invest, that is, place, churchmen in office. Ultimately Matilda left all her lands to the papacy, providing the substantial base of the pope's landed power.

Papal reforms removed control from the hands of secular leaders and deprived other devout women like Matilda of their former influence. At the same time, the importance of convents in the leadership of society began to decline, although learned and powerful nuns still flourished in the late eleventh and twelfth centuries. After the eleventh-century Gregorian reform, the papacy ordered the dissolution of double monasteries (inhabited by both nuns and monks) in western Europe. Since women led these establishments, their dissolution sharply curtailed women's access to the church hierarchy. In Slavic Catholic lands less touched by reform, double monasteries remained, and women played important roles in the management of ecclesiastical affairs. In the West, nuns continued to study within convents and to educate girls. But like the monks of the twelfth and thirteenth centuries, nuns tended to turn toward mysticism. Women like Hroswitha of Gandersheim, Elizabeth of Schongau, Herrad, Gertrude, and Hildegarde of Bingen, who in their intellectual curiosity contributed substantially to all fields of human knowledge and never doubted their right to do so, disappeared. The last nonmystical literary composition attributed to a nun in the Middle Ages is the "Hortus Deliciarum," written in prose and poetry in part by Herrad of Landsberg between 1160 and 1170.

Reforming clergy of the twelfth century seldom considered how to provide institutions devoted to women's religious enthusiasm, despite the fact that their own reforms depended in no small measure on devout women's patronage and charity. A few of the reform movements, such as Fontevrault, a new popular order in France, gave women access to the religious life and channeled women's energies into reforming activities. But most church leaders responded only to men's reforming impulses and demands, with increasingly complex and well-endowed ecclesiastical institutions. In any event, monasteries no longer remained the center of intellectual ferment after the Gregorian reform. The focus had shifted to endowed cathedral schools and universities, which trained clerks for the priesthood and therefore excluded women. The great age of monastic learning came to a close, and the papacy restricted women's access to new religious institutions. In subsequent decades of the twelfth century, secular institutions swiftly followed the lead of the Church in this matter.

CHANGES IN TWELFTH-CENTURY DOWRY AND MARRIAGE

At first glance, however, women shared in the flowering of the Middle Ages that occurred in the twelfth century. From all walks of life come scattered examples of women valued for their daring or their learning. Early in the twelfth century, the nun Hildegarde of Bingen, albeit piously protesting her unworthiness, still gave political advice to prelates of the Church, kings, and even the pope. In fables of the day, the wily peasant woman outwitted the monk or the great lord to the audience's great satisfaction. Eleanor of Aquitaine and her daughters and granddaughters became the objects of adoration in the new cult of courtly love. The famous romance of Eloise and Abelard occurred in this century, and Marie de France wrote her popular lays in which forthright women took the initiative in solving problems of the heart and of society. In everyday life, women matched their participation in agriculture with roles in new industries and trade that contributed substantially to the economic growth of the era. They counted themselves members of guilds and dominated some guilds such as that of the silk workers, although they were increasingly excluded from others. Women's wills of the time demonstrate that they shared fairly in proceeds from work and joint business enterprises. They increased their personal fortunes from the fruits of their labor. Women continued to own property in their own right, and they still received wedding gifts from their husbands, now often in cash; they could buy and sell property and designate their own heirs in conformance with both law and practice.

Important if quiet changes occurred in commercial towns as well as among that handful of high clergy and powerful feudal families who dominated the emerging institutions of medieval Europe. The family (understood as a chain of generations reflecting a set of inherited values) underwent some of the earliest reactions in response to new conditions. In the towns near the Mediterranean where urban growth accelerated swiftly and economic success arrived early, the way townspeople arranged their personal lives as well as their commercial networks may be reconstructed from surviving notarial charters or "documents of practice." Business people relied on the same notarial instruments (legal papers) that their families had traditionally used to arrange personal affairs: the *fraterna* (pact among brothers) and *societas* (partnership that tied family members together), the will, and the dowry or *dos*, which distributed wealth. In this enterprising manner, families appropriated what they had on hand to use as the building blocks for a commercial economy. The original personal needs that a will or a dowry met expanded to meet the needs of business alliances, to channel capital, and to underwrite new ventures. These practices promoted economic growth and figured among the more clever ploys devised by resourceful individuals, but only at some cost to family relations.

Awards of marriage gifts or dowries in Italy after 1140 provide a good example of how purposes other than those originally intended could affect the dowry itself, and through it marriage, family relations, and women's lives. The most dramatic changes occurred among affluent urban families because, of course, they had accumulated the capital to award handsome gifts to their offspring at marriage. Germanic practice had designated a morning gift from husband to wife—a true dowry that transferred goods, land, or money from the groom to the bride. In prosperous towns, new civil statutes passed in the 1140s instituted Roman dowry (a gift to the groom from the wife's family) and restricted or outlawed other gifts. As in classical times, gifts of linens, jewels, and clothes, which a wife's family also supplied to the new couple, accompanied the cash gift. Legally, the dowry belonged to the wife but in practice she could only control it if her husband died or if she wished in turn to endow her own offspring.

Since women had owned and disposed of their morning gifts and other marriage portions in earlier times, Roman dowry, although increasingly large, implied a loss of positive legal rights for wives. Over the decades, more and more capital transferred from one family to another through the dowry until it became less a guarantee of a woman's status in her marriage than a system for distributing capital within a developing and vastly more complex commercial economy. A woman's wishes in her choice of marriage partner mattered little because so much rode on this transfer of funds. Still, husbands never legally possessed dowry either. They invested it safely for their wives as their elders dictated. If patriarchy drew strength from Roman dowry, and it most assuredly did, fathers more than husbands increased their authority over women's lives. By the 1180s, when Pope Alexander III issued directives on marriage, churchmen had begun to regard this new development with alarm. Pope Alexander made consent of the partners the sole valid ground for marriage, intending by this measure to preserve the marriage sacrament. He did not, apparently, institute the change to protect marriageable daughters from their family's manipulations.

In the course of the next two centuries, as dowry awards scaled up so did a husband's age at marriage, while the age at marriage of a wife dropped. By the economic hard times of the late fourteenth century, plague-depleted families awarded even higher dowries, a practice that lessened the chance to marry for those with small dowries or none at all. The gap in the ages of bride and groom meant fewer affectionate matches were likely. Less effort was devoted to taking suitability into account when matchmaking. Families inculcated passivity and obedience in daughters in preparation for the delicate negotiations for the proper bridegroom. Wives pleased their husband's kin if they restricted their attention to the domestic household. So dowry, once a gift to the bride that she controlled, became a gift to the groom hedged by restrictions. Over time, fewer marriages occurred, since not all could now afford marriage, and this continued the decline in urban populations that the plague had begun.

The changes in the practice of dowrying transformed the less affluent levels of urban society as well. Affluent families dowred not only daughters but the female servants who found favor with them. Even marriage among artisans soon required a dowry from the bride. Dick Whittington of *Mother Goose* fame, who ran away to London town with his cat and became in the end Lord Mayor, illustrates the ideal of medieval social mobility, but his parable does not apply to the female experience. The very real Draga, enslaved in the Balkan highlands, serving in a Dalmatian town until freed, dowred, and wed, followed a less attractive path into town life.[7] Preachers inveighed against poor urban parents prostituting some daughters as a way to gain a dowry. Still, urban prostitution was lucrative and therefore attracted some to choose this course to earn their dowries. Guiraude of Béziers and Elys of Le Puy, setting up as prostitutes in Montpellier, had money enough from that profession to plead cause for a recognized place to carry on their businesses in town in 1285.[8] Thus they were able to afford to retire by marrying and did not end their careers, like other prostitutes, with the Repentant Sisters of Saint Mary Magdalene.

In the later medieval centuries in Florence, *fantine* (girls as young as eight) worked for affluent households. The master owed them only some clothes and sheets to sleep on besides their daily food, because he contracted to provide them a small dowry at sixteen. There was even a sly carnival song about *fantine*'s availability to men of the household:

This one, who is a girl to be married
You keep for your chamber maid,
And a dowry in five years you will give her;
But above all we want to beg of you
That she not have to go
To husband before the proper time,
As is done to all of them today.[9]

North of the Alps, Roman dowry took centuries to take hold as it had in the south, but the twelfth and thirteenth centuries saw the common law, following its own rhythm, change on the marriage portion (*maritagium*) in England. Feudal custom traditionally disadvantaged the married woman, employing guardianship to deprive her of rights she had held when single; therefore, losses of control over the marriage portion reduced already circumscribed legal rights. With state-building a primary concern, royal women's experiences with inherited property set the scene for changes for women in less exalted stations. Queens who brought into marriage great portions and titles underwent a loss of authority over their own inheritances. In earlier times they had typically continued to rule their possessions by their own right, but in the twelfth century their inheritances were integrated into the crown's resources and fell under the administration of the ruling monarch's clerks. In the process, the office of queen consort, significant since Carolingian times, changed beyond recognition or, in the case of France, disappeared except in name. Eleanor of Aquitaine fought long and hard during her second husband's lifetime for the right of one of her younger sons to rule her inherited possessions in France at her death. Her husband (the English King, Henry II) insisted on keeping her inheritance as part of his crown lands, to pass through primogeniture to his eldest son and heir.

In the aftermath of this change a queen might still influence a husband or son, and his bureaucracy, or as the surviving parent, she might be trusted with the power of regent during the minority of her son. But neither her office itself nor her inheritance rights and marriage portion sustained her position. Royal women, except those who could claim the right of primogeniture in the event that they had no brothers, lost authority. If they exerted any power at all, they derived it from their intimacy with and access to the reigning king. A royal mistress had the same opportunity to influence monarchical policy as the royal queen.

Dismantling institutions such as double monasteries, eliminating rights that had given women an initial foothold in the complex structures of an emerging European civilization, and appropriating family devices like dowry to serve as conduits for an emerging cash economy directed women into more private roles. In the new private domestic sphere, acquiescence brought more approval than the skilled labor and control of property that had previously brought women honor. Changes began among the powerful and affluent, but in time the new priorities affected poorer townspeople, villagers, and even the rural peasantry. In this changed environment, notions that would have been irrelevant or practically unthinkable in an earlier age suddenly had an appeal. They gained a certain cachet that allowed them to be brought forward and offered in justification for action taken. Since changes in women's actual condition corresponded with the general awakening of interest in theology, philosophical inquiry, and classicism, authorities used classical notions, such as those defining "woman," to sway public opinion. Carrying the authority of theology and ancient learning, these notions generally prevailed.

Old axioms about the nature of woman possessed a long history in Western culture. In one guise or another they had appeared in Christian theology, in the treatises on medicine circulated under the name of the second century physician, Galen, and in the inherited Roman civil law code. Most ancient pagan authorities had employed polarities that juxtaposed woman's to man's nature in their writings. This system of assigning qualities by sex, with women usually assigned the more negative traits, had not enjoyed much popularity in the early Middle Ages, however, nor had it been politic when abbesses, queens, and other powerful women distributed so much patronage. But when the legal scholar Gratian offered polar notions assigning such qualities once again in his *Decretals* published in the 1140s, they struck a responsive chord. Gratian provided Italian towns legal precedents for introducing Roman dowry and outlawing other marriage gifts to women; in fact, he stated: no dowry, no marriage (*sine dote nullum conjugium facit*).[10] Gratian taught at the University of Bologna and trained the lawyers who practiced in towns throughout Italy. When towns decided to outlaw all but Roman dowry, they had Gratian's great study that incorporated the classical Greek Aristotelian notion that women were passive and men were active to explain why dowry passed through a woman to her husband but not to her.

Notions about men's and women's natures as polar opposites played into other metaphors. In fact, toying with these polarities grew into a rather fashionable intellectual pastime. The twelfth-century Parisian scholar Abelard employed the metaphor that man was the sun and woman the moon, and as the light of the moon shone paler than the sun, woman's frailer nature made her virtue more worthy in God's eyes.[11] Authorities cleverly reversed gender associations to make theological points. Cistercian monks of the twelfth century spoke of Christ as mother; God was defined as *sapientia*, the feminine noun for wisdom. Even Pope Gregory VII had referred to his benefactor, Beatrice of Tuscany, as "dux," masculine leader and warrior for Christendom. Women writers of the age showed a fondness for employing polarities when they spoke of women's nature. The *De passionibus mulieris*— an eleventh-century Salernitan treatise on women's diseases known as *Trotula Major* —claimed that women possessed cool natures and men hot ones. The woman physician who wrote it saw this as a sign of women's superior physiology. The twelfth-century Hildegarde of Bingen agreed with Abelard that women had frailer natures than men, but found this of no advantage to them in finding favor with God.

When polarities became fashionable in the twelfth century, they stimulated imaginations and provided apt images for theological debate. By no means consistently pejorative to women, these images did depend on a polar construct that first assigned a trait to man, then the opposite trait to woman; thus, the construct itself tended powerfully toward misogyny. When opportunity came to the Church to enforce strict enclosure on women's religious orders, or to justify women's exclusion from educational institutions, or to eliminate women from some of the attractive new reform orders, those polar arguments could be brought out. They served now as part of the mental equipment of learned authorities.

GENDER TRIUMPHS IN THE LATE MIDDLE AGES

Concepts with little circulation and consequence in one age have a way of becoming more authoritative over time when they provide a rationale for new actualities. Where twelfth-century thinkers experimented with polar schemes, the thirteenth-century thinker Thomas Aquinas firmly advanced them, on the authority of Aristotle, as essential to natural order. Aquinas placed Aristotle's polar arguments on woman's nature into the first book of his *Summa Theologica*. There *Question 92* defined woman after and in juxtaposition to man, to whom Aquinas gave a place in the universe halfway between the beasts and the angels. Aristotle had developed a systematic polarity in which an arranged set of qualities associated with male—limit, odd, one, right, square, at rest, straight, light, and good—were opposed to a parallel alignment of traits associated with female—unlimited, even, plurality, left, oblong, moving, curved, darkness, evil. Adapting Aristotle to Christian dogma, Aquinas defined man in the image of God as active, formative, and tending toward perfection, unlike woman, whom he defined as opposite, or passive, material, and deprived of the tendency toward perfection. The very simplicity of the scheme recommended it. Nothing could be less taxing than finding an opposite quality to man's and assigning it to woman.

The axiomatical quality of this thinking eased application to everyday life. Laypeople, even the illiterate, could grasp polarities and employ them as unquestioned assumptions, sanctioned by theologians; that is, they could rely on notions rather than on more difficult, rigorously developed ideas. Medieval theologians did not themselves subject such notions to the same rigorous logical review they routinely applied to ideas in their philosophical discourse. This new definition of woman passed on an inherited system of notions that remained largely unexamined, in which the polar construct remained constant while any particular comparison (men are at rest, women are moving) could be constructed to fit new circumstances.[12]

Gender, which first appeared in Western thought as a notion, slipped into the intellectual baggage of later generations. Expositions of this notion on women may have begun as little more than dry sophistry among male scholars whose very isolation at cathedral schools and universities meant a separation from society at large, where women might have objected to the exercise. In earlier centuries, women had participated in intellectual discourse. They now found themselves cut off from that opportunity and thus could not comment effectively on this newly popular system of gender. A notion practically unthinkable in earlier centuries went largely unchallenged in the thirteenth century.

The schools and universities that revived these classical notions also taught students, and institutions capable of propagating orthodox theology were staffed by these former students in due course. Professionalization of the disciplines or fields of knowledge had come a long way by the turn into the fourteenth century. The developing fields of medicine, law, ethics, and theology all relied to some extent or another upon graduates of the universities and upon the same scholastic corpus of thought in which the notion of gender figured. Priests, increasingly trained at schools, offered their parishioners expository sermons and writings. They could give their parish congregations the theologians' opinion on woman's nature if they felt the need to do so. In the years after the Black Plague (1348–1350), cities recruited university-trained physicians to care for the sick and the poor. Physicians could prescribe cures according to their own notion of man's and woman's polar natures. The increased complexity and bureaucracy in church, state, and commerce demanded lawyers. In their hands, causal notions became legal precedents. Gratian's *Decretals* on woman's incapacity, for example, was offered against women's exercise of positive legal rights. Authorities in many fields of knowledge used notions of gender to simplify schemes of thought. They provided rationales for expedient acts using the opposition of female to male as justification. Europeans began to speak and think of "woman" as a category rather than of women as they knew them. This tendency became an overriding consideration in justifying women's roles, responsibilities, rights, and their place in Christian society.

In the early twentieth century, Alice Clark, an economic historian, looked back on the role of women in late medieval towns and guilds and found the late Middle Ages a "golden age" of opportunity for women in contrast with early modern times.[13] But we must travel back far beyond the well-documented thirteenth century to find those better times for women. Recent research indicates that thirteenth-century guilds often allowed only the participation of women as wives of masters, and the few women who became guild members in their own right did so as widows who had inherited that status from their husbands. In fact, biographies of women who succeeded and grew wealthy in their occupations turn out to be, in most cases, the biographies of widows who by accident of death and inheritance rights carved out for themselves roles unavailable to other women. Although women still remained active in agricultural and industrial production, their society no longer saw a "natural" role for them in the administrative hierarchy. These roles, for the most part, were reassigned to men. With the new notion of gender ascendant, women were more likely to find themselves being directed, rather than directing activities as they had done in the past.

The economic downturn of the fourteenth century played a crucial part in hardening the roles we have associated with gender expectations until recently. After more than three centuries of almost uninterrupted economic growth, Europe experienced a disastrous shrinkage in the middle years of the fourteenth century. Many factors caused this, women's lessened opportunity to play active, problem-solving roles numbering among them. Also, the series of famine years from 1317 onward, the closing of the silk route to the Orient, the banking crisis of 1343–1345, the Black Death (bubonic plague), which in its first visitation to Europe in 1348 may have taken the lives of one-third to one-half of the inhabitants, all contributed to the crisis. By the second half of the century, cities had lost substantial population, and the economy slowed. Europe entered a period of protracted and costly wars, the plague returned every decade or so, and the population did not recover its late thirteenth-century peak for at least a century and a half.

If dowry inflation had existed in cities before, it grew to monumental proportions in these decades. Affluent Italian families who could afford dowries sometimes chose one daughter who could make a brilliant marriage and endowed her at the expense of her sisters. This meant fewer marriages and the number of unmarried women increased, so that they became a substantial group for the first time in Europe. Since poor families' opportunities also became fewer, and the poor lacked this alternative of the more affluent, they were more likely to contract their daughters into domestic service that promised a dowry. Urban families, if moderately wealthy, could place their unmarried daughters in convents, which also required dowries, although smaller ones. Convents seldom possessed adequate endowments to handle the increased new demand and still perform their traditional roles of prayer, industry, education, and service. The presence of inmates without a true vocation for the spiritual life diluted a convent's sense of spiritual calling.

Among the poorer classes, women postponed marriage and sometimes did not marry at all. In time the new tendency to associate *maids* (unmarried girls) with *domestic servants* made the two terms all but indistinguishable. Some women who did not marry because they lacked a dowry joined informal religious groups like the Beguines and Beghards (religious bands working together, dedicated to reform society). The Church offered only perfunctory supervision and resources to these new groups. Women joined these groups for the opportunity this afforded them to set their own priorities, but they soon encountered problems. A newly alerted and soon alarmed Church hierarchy deemed that strict enclosure on all women in religious life was the only answer for channeling single women's religious practices. Enclosure eased the Church's task of supervising women's religious life, but these new groups resented enclosure. They often survived as a group because of strong bonds among members, and desired to remain "in the world" and to follow their own concept of an active Christian life.

In a world where the Church responded slowly, if at all, to women's religious enthusiasm and propagated negative views of their nature among the clergy, some heretical groups offered greater participation and equality to women. Religious responses to a series of issues that had underlying economic and social causes opened up the monumental problem of popular heresies for authorities in the Church. Albigensians made many converts among women, and Lollardry in England attracted a following of women; in Bohemia the Hussites numbered women among their most dedicated followers and noblewomen among their patrons.[14] Beatrice de Planissoles of Montaillou, twice widowed by 1300 and imprisoned as a heretic in 1322, does not appear remarkable for any religious beliefs she held, but still her behavior disturbed her inquisitors. She claimed varied sexual liaisons in her village, admitted to having her four well-loved daughters tutored so they could learn to read and write, and formed close bonds with the peasant women in her community regardless of her noble name and status.[15]

Women crusaders finally won the right to wear the sign of the cross (*crucesignata*) on their own in the later Middle Ages. Mystics like Julian of Norwich still inspired the faithful, and a few extraordinary women still led, at least in moments of severe crisis and demoralization. Joan of Arc, the Maid of Orleans, claimed heavenly voices had sent her to lead the French troops in the war against the English king and bring the Dauphin Charles VII to Rheims to be anointed and crowned. Charles believed Joan and, donning armor, she led the troops to victory. But when her leadership no longer benefited the new king and the army, the Burgundians who had captured Joan handed her over to the English. Among other issues, her failure to conform to gender expectations (at her trial she was accused of wearing men's clothes) brought the charge of acting "against nature." She was charged with demonic possession and burned.

Gender expectations now figured as critical categories of thought and organizing principles for society. "Womanly" conduct appeared to be ordained by God and sanctioned by earthly institutions. Because gender seemed a component of the natural order of things, it could not easily be challenged. The world of fantasy, play, and humor reveals this tellingly. During carnival preceding Lent—or "the world turned upside down"—women dressed in men's clothes and walked boldly in the streets. This was a ritual enactment of the unseemliness and absurdity of women failing to uphold their ordained roles — even while women mocked their roles. The system of gender had become conventional wisdom and came to be policed even by the people themselves.

In this period of heightened tension and bewilderment because of economic hard times, chronic warfare, and continual concern over periodic plague epidemics, people sought answers from authorities. In this way Scholastic notions about gender and about women gained wider acceptance. Yet a deep ambivalence still marked the application of the classical gender system, which may be seen where women's work mattered in the economy. Etienne Boileau, a medieval provost of Paris, in his *Livre des métiers* noted about glass cutters: "No master's widow who keeps working at this craft after her husband's death may take on apprentices, for the men of the craft do not believe that a woman can master it well enough to teach a child to master it, for the craft is a very delicate one." Boileau saw men as "right" or dexterous in the lucrative trade of glass cutting, and women as "left" or clumsy. This belief provided justification for eliminating them from positions of authority within the guild.[16] He disregarded the fact that women practiced the even more dexterous work of lace-making. Even the most exquisite, expensive, and fiercely difficult lace-making could be fitted in around household tasks and child-rearing, so the notion of women's clumsiness did not need to be trotted out. The "traditional" division of labor recognized today had emerged, and notions of gender served wherever they sustained that system.

With a notion of gender in reserve to call upon, Europeans fell into a division of labor between women and men that continued to underlie economic development until the Industrial Revolution. Women accomplished essential work although they were denied access to positions of power. Marriage practices made further accommodations to working habits, and a more rigid set of expectations for men's and women's work affected the sharing out of tasks both within the home and in the working place. However, women's contributions remained essential to all kinds of economic endeavors, and women continued to have access to workshops and markets in some, usually subordinate, activities.

Prevailing views of women deserve no credit for this continued productivity. Peering out from behind negative societal opinions stood more affirming assumptions about inherent worth that women assimilated in their natal families and applied to their roles in adult life. Among peasants and artisans, in particular, a marriage pattern that historians have labeled "western European" emerged by the late Middle Ages.[17] Women's choices essentially defined that pattern: women of the popular classes married relatively late, that is, late enough to have put aside savings to provide a stake or dowry. They chose husbands near them in age, if not younger. Women did not necessarily marry when they became sexually active, but when they had accumulated savings. Some never married at all. The obligations women assumed by viewing marriage as an economic pact to which they were active, lifelong contributors assured women's productivity to the economy. Working women, that is, all women but a tiny leisured minority, saw themselves as indispensable. Against pejorative views of their nature, this sense of indispensability helped sustain women in the essential work they performed for society.

CONCLUSION

The course of women's history diverged from men's during the centuries from the eleventh to the fourteenth when gender became an important category for organizing thoughts about society. This should make us pause and think a moment about transitions in history. The Renaissance has often been presented as an important transition for Europe because revived classical humanism and secular individualism together yielded an empowering new ideal of mankind. The Reformation, too, has been understood as a dividing point in the history of European civilization. The Middle Ages that preceded both eras are seldom understood as such an age for men; rather this period is represented as a time of steady development in which many of the institutions essential to European civilization took shape. But, in fact, the loss of rights accompanying the triumph of gender constituted an important transition for women, and it forced a substantial change in their lives. Certainly for women this era represented as great a change as the Renaissance represented for men later. Women lost ground in the increasingly complex institutions that could enforce the code of gender and in the commercial centers where authority over resources concentrated into fewer, largely male, hands. Perhaps this critical watershed in the course of Western history has been overlooked not only because it requires focusing attention on women. Perhaps it has been ignored because our histories seldom count the costs of development and infrequently acknowledge that progress comes with a price.

NOTES

1. *The Play of Daniel*, ed. Noah Greenberg (New York: Oxford University Press, 1959), pp. 50–53.
2. Lynn White, *Medieval Technology and Social Change* (Oxford: Clarendon Press, 1962), pp. 83, 89.
3. On women as glass makers, see Meredith Parsons Lillich, "Gothic Glaziers: Monks, Jews, Taxpayers, Bretons, Women," *Journal of Glass Studies*, 27 (1985), 72–92.
4. *The Alexiad of Anna Comnena*, trans. E. H. A. Sewter (Hammondsworth, England: Penguin, 1909), p. 66.

5. L. S. Stavrianos, *The World to 1500*, 2nd ed. (Englewood Cliffs, N.J.: Prentice Hall, 1975), p. 324.

6. Betty Bandel, "The English Chroniclers' Attitude Towards Women," *Journal of the History of Ideas*, 16 (1955), 113–118.

7. Susan Mosher Stuard, "Domestic Slavery in Medieval Ragusa," *Journal of Medieval History*, 9 (1983), 155–171.

8. Leah Lydia Otis, *Prostitution in Medieval Society* (Chicago: University of Chicago Press, 1984), p. 65.

9. Christiane Klapisch-Zuber, *Women, Family and Ritual in Renaissance Florence*, trans. Lydia Cochrane (Chicago: University of Chicago Press, 1985), p. 107. Copyright © University of Chicago. "Goes to husband" means an arranged marriage.

10. Gratianus, *Decretum*, II, Causa 31, Questio V, cap. VI (Rome: In aedibus populi Romani, 1584).

11. Peter Abelard, *Epistolae 7*, ed. J. -P. Migne, *Patrologiae cursus completus: scriptores latini* (Paris: Garnier, 1885), 178:245a. "*Naturaliter femineus sexus est infirmior, eo virtute est acceptabilior et honore dignior.*"

12. Ian MacLean, *The Renaissance Notion of Woman* (Cambridge: Cambridge University Press, 1980).

13. Alice Clark, *The Working Life of Women in the Seventeenth Century* (London: Routledge and Son, 1919).

14. Albigensians were thirteenth-century Christians following practices unacceptable to the Church in southern France. Lollards in England followed John Wycliffe, who believed in translating the Bible into English and interpreting Scripture for oneself. The Hussites followed John Huss in Bohemia. Women in this religious sect were famous for their exploits in battle.

15. Emmanuel LeRoy Ladurie, *Montaillou, The Promised Land of Error*, trans. Barbara Bray (New York: George Braziller, 1978).

16. Etienne Boileau, *Livre des métiers*, ed. G. B. Depping (Paris: René de Lespinasse et François Bonnardot, 1837), p. 79.

17. J. Hajnal, "European Marriage Patterns in Perspective," in *Population in History: Essays in Historical Demography*, ed. D. V. Glass and D. E. C. Eversley (Chicago: Aldine, 1965), pp. 101–143.

SUGGESTIONS FOR FURTHER READING

Among general studies, Eileen Power, *Medieval Women*, ed. M. M. Postan (Cambridge: Cambridge University Press, 1979); Derek Baker, *Medieval Women* (Oxford: Basil Blackwell, 1978); Susan Mosher Stuard, ed., *Women in Medieval Society* (Philadelphia: University of Pennsylvania Press, 1976); and Barbara Hanawalt, ed., *Women and Work in Pre-industrial Europe* (Bloomington: Indiana University Press, 1986) are valuable.

On dowry, Diane Owen Hughes, "From Brideprice to Dowry in Mediterranean Europe," *Journal of Family History*, 3 (1978), 385–411, and Christiane Klapisch-Zuber, *Women, Family and Inheritance in Renaissance Florence*, trans. Lydia Cochrane (Chicago: University of Chicago Press, 1985), provide information on the early and the later period, respectively.

For readings on the depiction of women in literature, see the suggested readings following Chapter 7. Ian MacLean, *The Renaissance Notion of Woman* (Cambridge: Cambridge University Press, 1980), provides a useful introduction to scholastic notions on women. On changes in perceptions of women, see Betty Bandel, "The English Chroniclers' Attitude Toward Women," *Journal of the History of Ideas*, 16 (1955), 113–118. See also Peter Dronke, *Women Writers of the Middle Ages* (Cambridge: Cambridge University Press, 1984).

A number of books have appeared recently on medieval women: Carolyn Bynum, *Jesus as Mother* (Berkeley: University of California Press, 1982); Heath Dillard, *Women of the Reconquest, Town Women in Castile, 1100–1300* (Cambridge and New York: Cambridge University Press, 1984); Leah Lydia Otis, *Prostitution in Medieval Society* (Chicago: University of Chicago Press, 1984); and Penny Schine Gold, *The Virgin and The Lady* (Chicago: University of Chicago Press, 1985); *Women of the Medieval World: Essays in Honor of John H. Mundy*, ed. Julius Kirshner and Suzanne Wemple (New York and London: Basil Blackwell, 1985).

Agnolo Bronzino's *Portrait of Laura Battiferri*, c. 1555. The poet Laura Battiferri
was the platonic love of Bronzino, with whom she exchanged Petrarchan verses.
Bronzino painted her with a volume of Petrarch's sonnets in her hand, and portrayed
her very much as he described her in one of his sonnets—"all iron within and ice
outside." (Alinari/Art Resource)

chapter 7

Did Women
Have a Renaissance?

Joan Kelly-Gadol

In this essay, Joan Kelly-Gadol challenges traditional periodization in her very title—thus emphasizing, yet again, that women's historical experience often differs substantially from that of men. We note the reappearing interrelationship between changing property relations, forms of institutional control, and ideology. The author demonstrates that an emerging class created new forms of political and social organization that tended to reduce options for women. She examines how literature rationalized and perpetuated class interests and how it reflected political and sexual relations. She traces major changes in the courtly love tradition. Courtly love is first attributed to powerful feudal women, who made it responsive to their sexual and emotional needs, which harmonized with the needs of their class as a whole. In its Renaissance form, courtly love is attributed to powerful male princes and their courtiers, who had an interest in creating dependency in women. In this period, female chastity and passivity better suited the needs of the expanding bourgeoisie and the declining nobility. The modern relation of the sexes, with its subordination of women, makes its appearance. Like Marylin Arthur, Joan Kelly-Gadol uses literature as an index to the interaction of class needs, state forms, sexual and family relations, and ideology.

One of the tasks of women's history is to call into question accepted schemes of periodization. To take the emancipation of women as a vantage point is to discover that events that further the historical development of men, liberating them from natural, social, or ideological constraints, have quite different, even opposite, effects upon women. The Renaissance is a good case in point. Italy was well in advance of the rest of Europe from roughly 1350 to 1530 because of its early consolidation of genuine states, the mercantile and manufacturing economy that supported them, and its working out of postfeudal and even postguild social relations. These developments reorganized Italian society along modern lines and opened the possibilities for the social and cultural expression for which the age is known. Yet precisely these developments affected women adversely, so much so that there was no renaissance for women—at least, not during the Renaissance. The state, early capitalism, and the social relations formed by them impinged on the lives of Renaissance women in different ways according to their different positions in society. But the startling fact is that women as a group, especially among the classes that dominated Italian urban life, experienced a contraction of social and personal options that men of their classes either did not, as was the case with the bourgeoisie, or did not experience as markedly, as was the case with the nobility.

Before demonstrating this point, which contradicts the widely held notion of the equality of Renaissance women with men,[1] we need to consider how to establish, let alone measure, loss or gain with respect to the liberty of women. I found the following criteria most useful for gauging the relative contraction (or expansion) of the powers of Renaissance women and for determining the quality of their historical experience: 1) the regulation of *female sexuality* as compared with male sexuality; 2) women's *economic* and *political roles*, that is, the kind of work they performed as compared with men, and their access to property, political power, and the education or training necessary for work, property, and power; 3) the *cultural roles* of women in shaping the outlook of their society, and access to the education and/or institutions necessary for this; 4) *ideology* about women, in particular the sex-role system displayed or advocated in the symbolic products of the society, its art, literature, and philosophy. Two points should be made about this ideological index. One is its rich inferential value. The literature, art, and philosophy of a society, which give us direct knowledge of the attitudes of the dominant sector of that society toward women, also yield indirect knowledge about our other criteria: namely, the sexual, economic, political, and cultural activities of women. Insofar as images of women relate to what really goes on, we can infer from them something about that social reality. But, second, the relations between the ideology of sex roles and the reality

"Did Women Have a Renaissance?" by Joan Kelly-Gadol is reprinted with the permission of Martin Fleisher, Executor of the Joan Kelly Estate.

we want to get at are complex and difficult to establish. Such views may be prescriptive rather than descriptive; they may describe a situation that no longer prevails; or they may use the relation of the sexes symbolically and not refer primarily to women and sex roles at all. Hence, to assess the historical significance of changes in sex-role conception, we must bring such changes into connection with all we know about general developments in the society at large.

This essay examines changes in sex-role conception, particularly with respect to sexuality, for what they tell us about Renaissance society and women's place in it. At first glance, Renaissance thought presents a problem in this regard because it cannot be simply categorized. Ideas about the relation of the sexes range from a relatively complementary sense of sex roles in literature dealing with courtly manners, love, and education, to patriarchal conceptions in writings on marriage and the family, to a fairly equal presentation of sex roles in early Utopian social theory. Such diversity need not baffle the attempt to reconstruct a history of sex-role conceptions, however, and to relate its course to the actual situation of women. Toward this end, one needs to sort out this material in terms of the social groups to which it responds: to courtly society in the first case, the nobility of the petty despotic states of Italy; to the patrician bourgeoisie in the second, particularly of republics such as Florence. In the third case, the relatively equal position accorded women in Utopian thought (and in those lower-class movements of the radical Reformation analogous to it) results from a larger critique of early modern society and all the relations of domination that flow from private ownership and control of property. Once distinguished, each of these groups of sources tells the same story. Each discloses in its own way certain new constraints suffered by Renaissance women as the family and political life were restructured in the great transition from medieval feudal society to the early modern state. The sources that represent the interests of the nobility and the bourgeoisie point to this fact by a telling, double index. Almost all such works—with certain notable exceptions, such as Boccaccio and Ariosto—establish chastity as the female norm and restructure the relation of the sexes to one of female dependency and male domination.

The bourgeois writings on education, domestic life, and society constitute the extreme in this denial of women's independence. Suffice it to say that they sharply distinguish an inferior domestic realm of women from the superior public realm of men, achieving a veritable "renaissance" of the outlook and practices of classical Athens, with its domestic imprisonment of citizen wives.[2] The courtly Renaissance literature we will consider was more gracious. But even here, by analyzing a few of the representative works of this genre, we find a new repression of the noblewoman's affective experience, in contrast to the latitude afforded her by medieval literature, and some of the social and cultural reasons for it. Dante and Castiglione, who continued

a literary tradition that began with the courtly love literature of eleventh-
and twelfth-century Provence, transformed medieval conceptions of love
and nobility. In the love ideal they formed, we can discern the inferior
position the Renaissance noblewoman held in the relation of the sexes by
comparison with her male counterpart and with her medieval predecessor as
well.

LOVE AND THE MEDIEVAL LADY

Medieval courtly love, closely bound to the dominant values of feudalism
and the Church, allowed in a special way for the expression of sexual love
by women. Of course, only aristocratic women gained their sexual and
affective rights thereby. If a knight wanted a peasant girl, the twelfth-
century theorist of *The Art of Courtly Love*, Andreas Capellanus, encouraged him "not [to] hesitate to take what you seek and to embrace her by
force."[3] Toward the lady, however, "a true lover considers nothing good
except what he thinks will please his beloved"; for if courtly love were to
define itself as a noble phenomenon, it had to attribute an essential freedom
to the relation between lovers. Hence, it metaphorically extended the social
relation of vassalage to the love relationship, a "conceit" that Maurice
Valency rightly called "the shaping principle of the whole design" of courtly
love.[4]

Of the two dominant sets of dependent social relations formed by
feudalism—*les liens de dépendence*, as Marc Bloch called them—vassalage,
the military relation of knight to lord, distinguished itself (in its early days)
by being freely entered into. At a time when everyone was somebody's
"man," the right to freely enter a relation of service characterized aristocratic bonds, whereas hereditability marked the servile work relation of serf
to lord. Thus, in medieval romances, a parley typically followed a declaration of love until love freely proffered was freely returned. A kiss (like the
kiss of homage) sealed the pledge, rings were exchanged, and the knight
entered the love service of his lady. Representing love along the lines of
vassalage had several liberating implications for aristocratic women. Most
fundamental, ideas of homage and mutuality entered the notion of heterosexual relations along with the idea of freedom. As symbolized on shields
and other illustrations that place the knight in the ritual attitude of
commendation, kneeling before his lady with his hands folded between hers,
homage signified male service, not domination or subordination of the lady,
and it signified fidelity, constancy in that service. "A lady must honor her
lover as a friend, not as a master," wrote Marie de Ventadour, a female
troubadour or *trobairitz*.[5] At the same time, homage entailed a reciprocity
of rights and obligations, a service on the lady's part as well. In one of Marie
de France's romances, a knight is about to be judged by the barons of King

Arthur's court when his lady rides to the castle to give him "succor" and pleads successfully for him, as any overlord might.[6] Mutuality, or complementarity, marks the relation the lady entered into with her *ami* (the favored name for "lover" and, significantly, a synonym for "vassal").

This relation between knight and lady was very much at variance with the patriarchal family relations obtaining in that same level of society. Aware of its incompatibility with prevailing family and marital relations, the celebrants of courtly love kept love detached from marriage. "We dare not oppose the opinion of the Countess of Champagne who rules that love can exert no power between husband and wife," Andreas Capellanus wrote (p. 175). But in opting for a free and reciprocal heterosexual relation outside marriage, the poets and theorists of courtly love ignored the almost universal demand of patriarchal society for female chastity, in the sense of the woman's strict bondage to the marital bed. The reasons why they did so, and even the fact that they did so, have long been disputed, but the ideas and values that justify this kind of adulterous love are plain. Marriage, as a relation arranged by others, carried the taint of social necessity for the aristocracy. And if the feudality denigrated marriage by disdaining obligatory service, the Church did so by regarding it not as a "religious" state, but an inferior one that responded to natural necessity. Moreover, Christianity positively fostered the ideal of courtly love at a deep level of feeling. The courtly relation between lovers took vassalage as its structural model, but its passion was nourished by Christianity's exaltation of love.

Christianity had accomplished its elevation of love by purging it of sexuality, and in this respect, by recombining the two, courtly love clearly departed from Christian teaching. The toleration of adultery it fostered thereby was in itself not so grievous. The feudality disregarded any number of church rulings that affected their interests, such as prohibitions of tournaments and repudiation of spouses (divorce) and remarriage. Moreover, adultery hardly needed the sanction of courtly love, which, if anything, acted rather as a restraining force by binding sexuality (except in marriage) to love. Lancelot, in Chrétien de Troyes's twelfth-century romance, lies in bed with a lovely woman because of a promise he has made, but "not once does he look at her, nor show her any courtesy. Why not? Because his heart does not go out to her. . . . The knight has only one heart, and this one is no longer really his, but has been entrusted to someone else, so that he cannot bestow it elsewhere."[7] Actually, Lancelot's chastity represented more of a threat to Christian doctrine than the fact that his passion (for Guinevere) was adulterous, because his attitudes justified sexual love. Sexuality could only be "mere sexuality" for the medieval Church, to be consecrated and directed toward procreation by Christian marriage. Love, on the other hand, defined as passion for the good, perfects the individual; hence love, according to Thomas Aquinas, properly directs itself toward God.[8] Like the churchman, Lancelot spurned mere sexuality—but for the sake of sexual love. He defied Christian *teaching* by reattaching love to sex; and experiencing his love as a devout vocation, as a passion, he found himself in utter accord with Christian *feeling*. His love, as Chrétien's story makes clear, is sacramental as well as sexual:

> ... then he comes to the bed of the Queen, whom he adores and before whom he kneels, holding her more dear than the relic of any saint. And the Queen extends her arms to him and, embracing him, presses him tightly against her bosom, drawing him into the bed beside her and showing him every possible satisfaction. . . . Now Lancelot possesses all he wants. . . . It cost him such pain to leave her that he suffered a real martyr's agony. . . . When he leaves the room, he bows and acts precisely as if he were before a shrine. (p. 329)

It is difficult to assess Christianity's role in this acceptance of feeling and this attentiveness to inner states that characterize medieval lyric and romance, although the weeping and wringing of hands, the inner troubles and turmoil of the love genre, were to disappear with the restoration of classical attitudes of restraint in the Renaissance. What certainly bound courtly love to Christianity, however, aside from its positive attitude toward feeling, was the cultivation of decidedly "romantic" states of feeling. In Christian Europe, *passion* acquired a positive, spiritual meaning that classical ethics and classical erotic feeling alike denied it. Religious love and courtly love were both suffered as a destiny, were both submitted to and not denied. Converted by a passion that henceforth directed and dominated them and for which all manner of suffering could be borne, the courtly lovers, like the religious, sought a higher emotional state than ordinary life provided. They sought ecstasy; and this required of them a heroic discipline, an ascetic fortitude, and single-mindedness. Love and its ordeals alike removed them from the daily, the customary, the routine, setting them apart as an elite superior to the conventions of marriage and society.

Religious feeling and feudal values thus both fed into a conception of passionate love that, because of its mutuality, required that women, too, partake of that passion, of that adulterous sexual love. The lady of medieval romance also suffered. She suffered "more pain for love than ever a woman suffered" in another of Marie de France's romances. As the jealously guarded wife of an old man, ravished by the beauty of her knight when she first saw him, she could not rest for love of him, and *"franc et noble"* (that is, free) as she was, she granted him her kiss and her love upon the declaration of his—"and many other caresses which lovers know well" during the time she hid him in her castle.[9] So common is this sexual mutuality to the literature of courtly love that one cannot take seriously the view of it as a form of Madonna worship in which a remote and virginal lady spurns consummation. That stage came later, as courtly love underwent its late medieval and Renaissance transformation. But for the twelfth century, typical concerns of Provençal *iocs-partitz*, those poetic "questions" on love posed at court (and

reflecting the social reality of mock courts of love played out as a diversion)
were: "Must a lady do for her lover as much as he for her?"; or, "A husband
learns that his wife has a lover. The wife and the lover perceive it—which of
the three is in the greatest strait?"[10] In the same vein, Andreas Capellanus
perceived differences between so-called "pure" and "mixed" love as accidental,
not substantial. Both came from the same feeling of the heart and one could
readily turn into the other, as circumstances dictated. Adultery, after all,
required certain precautions; but that did not alter the essentially erotic
nature even of "pure" love, which went "as far as the kiss and the embrace
and the modest contact with the nude lover, omitting the final solace"
(p. 122).

The sexual nature of courtly love, considered together with its voluntary character and the nonpatriarchal structure of its relations, makes us
question what it signifies for the actual condition of feudal women. For
clearly it represents an ideological liberation of their sexual and affective
powers that must have some social reference. This is not to raise the fruitless
question of whether such love relationships actually existed or if they were
mere literary conventions. The real issue regarding ideology is, rather, what
kind of society could posit *as a social ideal* a love relation outside of
marriage, one that women freely entered and that, despite its reciprocity,
made women the gift givers while men did the service. What were the social
conditions that fostered these particular conventions rather than the more
common ones of female chastity and/or dependence?

No one doubts that courtly love spread widely as a convention. All
ranks and both sexes of the aristocracy wrote troubadour poetry and
courtly romances and heard them sung and recited in courtly gatherings
throughout most of medieval Europe. But this could happen only if such
ideas supported the male-dominated social order rather than subverted it.
The love motif could, and with Gottfried of Strasbourg's *Tristan* (c. 1210)
did, stand as an ideal radically opposed to the institutions of the Church and
emerging feudal kingship. But in its beginnings, and generally, courtly love
no more threatened Christian feeling or feudalism than did chivalry, which
brought a certain "sacramental" moral value and restraint to the profession
of warfare. While courtly love celebrated sexuality, it enriched and deepened
it by means of the Christian notion of passion. While the knight often
betrayed his lord to serve his lord's lady, he transferred to that relationship
the feudal ideal of freely committed, mutual service. And while passionate
love led to adultery, by that very fact it reinforced, as its necessary premise,
the practice of political marriage. The literature of courtly love suppressed
rather than exaggerated tensions between it and other social values, and the
reason for this lies deeper than literature. It lies at the institutional level, where
there was real agreement, or at least no contradiction, between the sexual
and affective needs of women and the interests of the aristocratic family, which
the feudality and Church alike regarded as fundamental to the social order.

The factors to consider here are property and power on the one hand, and illegitimacy on the other. Feudalism, as a system of private jurisdictions, bound power to landed property; and it permitted both inheritance and administration of feudal property by women.[11] Inheritance by women often suited the needs of the great landholding families, as their unremitting efforts to secure such rights for their female members attest. The authority of feudal women owes little to any gallantry on the part of feudal society. But the fact that women could hold both ordinary fiefs and vast collections of counties—and exercise in their own right the seigniorial powers that went with them—certainly fostered a gallant attitude. Eleanor of Aquitaine's adultery as wife of the king of France could have had dire consequences in another place at another time, say in the England of Henry VIII. In her case, she moved on to a new marriage with the future Henry II of England or, to be more exact, a new alliance connecting his Plantagenet interests with her vast domains centering on Provence. Women also exercised power during the absence of warrior husbands. The lady presided over the court at such times, administered the estates, took charge of the vassal services due the lord. She *was* the lord—albeit in his name rather than her own—unless widowed and without male children. In the religious realm, abbesses exercised analogous temporal as well as spiritual jurisdiction over great territories, and always in their own right, in virtue of their office.

This social reality accounts for the retention of matronymics in medieval society, that is, a common use of the maternal name, which reflects the position of women as landowners and managers of great estates, particularly during the crusading period.[12] It also accounts for the husband's toleration of his wife's diversions, if discreetly pursued. His primary aim to get and maintain a fief required her support, perhaps even her inheritance. As Emily James Putnam put it, "It would, perhaps, be paradoxical to say that a baron would prefer to be sure that his tenure was secure than that his son was legitimate, but it is certain that the relative value of the two things had shifted."[13] Courtly literature, indeed, reveals a marked lack of concern about illegitimacy. Although the ladies of the romances are almost all married, they seldom appear with children, let alone appear to have their lives and loves complicated by them. Much as the tenet that love thrives only in adultery reflected and reinforced the stability of arranged marriage, so the political role of women, and the indivisibility of the fief, probably underlies this indifference to illegitimacy. Especially as forms of inheritance favoring the eldest son took hold in the course of the twelfth century to preserve the great houses, the claims of younger sons and daughters posed no threat to family estates. Moreover, the expansive, exploitative aristocratic families of the eleventh and twelfth centuries could well afford illegitimate members. For the feudality, they were no drain as kin but rather a source of strength in marital alliances and as warriors.

For these reasons, feudal Christian society could promote the ideal of courtly love. We could probably maintain of any ideology that tolerates sexual parity that: 1) it can threaten no major institution of the patriarchal society from which it emerges; and 2) men, the rulers within the ruling order, must benefit by it. Courtly love surely fit these requirements. That such an ideology did actually develop, however, is due to another feature of medieval society, namely, the cultural activity of feudal women. For responsive as courtly love might seem to men of the feudality whose erotic needs it objectified and refined, as well as objectifying their consciousness of the social self (as noble), it did this and more for women. It gave women lovers, peers rather than masters; and it gave them a justifying ideology for adultery which, as the more customary double standard indicates, men in patriarchal society seldom require. Hence, we should expect what we indeed find: women actively shaping these ideas and values that corresponded so well to their particular interests.

In the first place, women participated in creating the literature of courtly love, a major literature of their era. This role they had not been able to assume in the culture of classical Greece or Rome. The notable exception of Sappho only proves the point: it took women to give poetic voice and status to female sexual love, and only medieval Europe accepted that voice as integral to its cultural expression. The twenty or more known Provençal trobairitz, of whom the Countess Beatrice of Die is the most renowned, celebrated as fully and freely as any man the love of the troubadour tradition:

> Handsome friend, charming and kind,
> when shall I have you in my power?
> If only I could lie beside you for an hour
> and embrace you lovingly —
> know this, that I'd give almost anything
> to see you in my husband's place,
> but only under the condition
> that you swear to do my bidding.[14]

Marie de France voiced similar erotic sentiments in her *lais*. Her short tales of romance, often adulterous and always sexual, have caused her to be ranked by Friedrich Heer as one of the "three poets of genius" (along with Chrétien de Troyes and Gautier d'Arras) who created the *roman courtois* of the twelfth century.[15] These two genres, the romance and the lyric, to which women made such significant contributions, make up the corpus of courtly love literature.

In addition to direct literary expression, women promoted the ideas of courtly love by way of patronage and the diversions of their courts. They supported and/or participated in the recitation and singing of poems and romances, and they played out those mock suits, usually presided over by "queens," that settled questions of love. This holds for lesser aristocratic women as well as the great. But great noblewomen, such as Eleanor of Aquitaine and Marie of Champagne, Eleanor's daughter by her first marriage to Louis VII of France, could make their courts major cultural and social centers and play thereby a dominant role in forming the outlook and mores of their class. Eleanor, herself granddaughter of William of Aquitaine, known as the first troubadour, supported the poets and sentiments of Provence at her court in Anjou. When she became Henry II's queen, she brought the literature and manners of courtly love to England. When living apart from Henry at her court in Poitiers, she and her daughter, Marie, taught the arts of courtesy to a number of young women and men who later dispersed to various parts of France, England, Sicily, and Spain, where they constituted the ruling nobility. Some of the most notable authors of the literature of courtly love belonged to these circles. Bernard of Ventadour, one of the outstanding troubadours, sang his poems to none other than the lady Eleanor. Marie de France had connections with the English court of Eleanor and Henry II. Eleanor's daughter, Marie of Champagne, was patron both of Andreas Capellanus, her chaplain, and Chrétien de Troyes, and she may well be responsible for much of the adulterous, frankly sexual behavior the ladies enjoy in the famous works of both. Chrétien claimed he owed to his "lady of Champagne" both "the material and treatment" of Lancelot, which differs considerably in precisely this regard from his earlier and later romances. And Andreas's *De remedio*, the baffling final section of his work that repudiates sexual love and women, may represent not merely a rhetorical tribute to Ovid but a reaction to the pressure of Marie's patronage.[16]

At their courts as in their literature, it would seem that feudal women consciously exerted pressure in shaping the courtly love ideal and making it prevail. But they could do so only because they had actual power to exert. The women who assumed cultural roles as artists and patrons of courtly love had already been assigned political roles that assured them some measure of independence and power. They could and did exercise authority, not merely over the subject laboring population of their lands, but over their own and/or their husbands' vassals. Courtly love, which flourished outside the institution of patriarchal marriage, owed its possibility as well as its model to the dominant political institution of feudal Europe that permitted actual vassal homage to be paid to women.

THE RENAISSANCE LADY: POLITICS AND CULTURE

The kind of economic and political power that supported the cultural activity of feudal noblewomen in the eleventh and twelfth centuries had no counterpart in Renaissance Italy. By the fourteenth century, the political units of Italy were mostly sovereign states, that, regardless of legal claims, recognized no overlords and supported no feudatories. Their nobility held property but not seigniorial power, estates but not jurisdiction. Indeed, in northern and central Italy, a nobility in the European sense hardly existed at all. Down to the coronation of Charles V as Holy Roman Emperor in 1530, there was no Italian king to safeguard the interests of (and thereby limit and control) a "legitimate" nobility that maintained by inheritance traditional prerogatives. Hence, where the urban bourgeoisie did not overthrow the claims of nobility, a despot did, usually in the name of nobility but always for himself. These *signorie*, unlike the bourgeois republics, continued to maintain a landed, military "class" with noble pretensions, but its members increasingly became merely the warriors and ornaments of a court. Hence, the Renaissance aristocrat, who enjoyed neither the independent political powers of feudal jurisdiction nor legally guaranteed status in the ruling estate, either served a despot or became one.

In this sociopolitical context, the exercise of political power by women was far more rare than under feudalism or even under the traditional kind of monarchical state that developed out of feudalism. The two Giovannas of Naples, both queens in their own right, exemplify this latter type of rule. The first, who began her reign in 1343 over Naples and Provence, became in 1356 queen of Sicily as well. Her grandfather, King Robert of Naples—of the same house of Anjou and Provence that hearkens back to Eleanor and to Henry Plantagenet—could and did designate Giovanna as his heir. Similarly, in 1414, Giovanna II became queen of Naples upon the death of her brother. In Naples, in short, women of the ruling house could assume power, not because of their abilities alone, but because the principle of legitimacy continued in force along with the feudal tradition of inheritance by women.

In northern Italy, by contrast, Caterina Sforza ruled her petty principality in typical Renaissance fashion, supported only by the Machiavellian principles of *fortuna* and *virtù* (historical situation and will). Her career, like that of her family, follows the Renaissance pattern of personal and political illegitimacy. Born in 1462, she was an illegitimate daughter of Galeazzo Maria Sforza, heir to the Duchy of Milan. The ducal power of the Sforzas was very recent, dating only from 1450, when Francesco Sforza, illegitimate son of a condottiere and a great condottiere himself, assumed control of the duchy. When his son and heir, Caterina's father, was assassinated after ten years of tyrannous rule, another son, Lodovico, took control of the duchy, first as regent for his nephew (Caterina's half brother), then as outright usurper. Lodovico promoted Caterina's interests for the sake of his own. He married her off at fifteen to a nephew of Pope Sixtus IV, thereby strengthening the alliance between the Sforzas and the Riario family, who now controlled the papacy. The pope carved a state out of papal domains for Caterina's husband, making him Count of Forlì as well as the Lord of Imola, which Caterina brought to the marriage. But the pope died in 1484, her husband died by assassination four years later—and Caterina made the choice to defy the peculiar obstacles posed by Renaissance Italy to a woman's assumption of power.

Once before, with her husband seriously ill at Imola, she had ridden hard to Forlì to quell an incipient coup a day before giving birth. Now at twenty-six, after the assassination of her husband, she and a loyal castellan held the citadel at Forlì against her enemies until Lodovico sent her aid from Milan. Caterina won; she faced down her opponents, who held her six children hostage, then took command as regent for her young son. But her title to rule as regent was inconsequential. Caterina ruled because she mustered superior force and exercised it personally, and to the end she had to exert repeatedly the skill, forcefulness, and ruthless ambition that brought her to power. However, even her martial spirit did not suffice. In the despotisms of Renaissance Italy, where assassinations, coups, and invasions were the order of the day, power stayed closely bound to military force. In 1500, deprived of Milan's support by her uncle Lodovico's deposition, Caterina succumbed to the overwhelming forces of Cesare Borgia and was divested of power after a heroic defense of Forlì.

Because of this political situation, at once statist and unstable, the daughters of the Este, Gonzaga, and Montefeltro families represent women of their class much more than Caterina Sforza did. Their access to power was indirect and provisional, and was expected to be so. In his handbook for the nobility, Baldassare Castiglione's description of the lady of the court makes this difference in sex roles quite clear. On the one hand, the Renaissance lady appears as the equivalent of the courtier. She has the same virtues of mind as he, and her education is symmetrical with his. She learns everything—well, almost everything—he does: "knowledge of letters, of music, of painting, and . . . how to dance and how to be festive."[17] Culture is an accomplishment for noblewoman and man alike, used to charm others as much as to develop the self. But for the woman, charm had become the primary occupation and aim. Whereas the courtier's chief task is defined as the profession of arms, "in a Lady who lives at court a certain pleasing affability is becoming above all else, whereby she will be able to entertain graciously every kind of man" (p. 207).

One notable consequence of the Renaissance lady's need to charm is that Castiglione called upon her to give up certain "unbecoming" physical activities such as riding and handling weapons. Granted, he concerned himself with the court lady, as he says, not a queen who may be called upon to rule. But his aestheticizing of the lady's role, his conception of her femaleness as centered in charm, meant that activities such as riding and skill in weaponry would seem unbecoming to women of the ruling families, too. Elisabetta Gonzaga, the idealized duchess of Castiglione's *Courtier*, came close in real life to his normative portrayal of her type. Riding and skill in weaponry had, in fact, no significance for her. The heir to her Duchy of Urbino was decided upon during the lifetime of her husband, and it was this adoptive heir—not the widow of thirty-seven with no children to compete for her care and attention—who assumed power in 1508. Removed from any direct exercise of power, Elisabetta also disregarded the pursuits and pleasures associated with it. Her letters express none of the sense of freedom and daring Caterina Sforza and Beatrice d'Este experienced in riding and the hunt.[18] Altogether, she lacks spirit. Her correspondence shows her to be as docile in adulthood as her early teachers trained her to be. She met adversity, marital and political, with fortitude but never opposed it. She placated father, brother, and husband, and even in Castiglione's depiction of her court, she complied with rather than shaped its conventions.

The differences between Elisabetta Gonzaga and Caterina Sforza are great, yet both personalities were responding to the Renaissance situation of emerging statehood and social mobility. Elisabetta, neither personally illegitimate nor springing from a freebooting condottiere family, was schooled, as Castiglione would have it, away from the martial attitudes and skills requisite for despotic rule. She would not be a prince, she would marry one. Hence, her education, like that of most of the daughters of the ruling families, directed her toward the cultural and social functions of the court. The lady who married a Renaissance prince became a patron. She commissioned works of art and gave gifts for literary works dedicated to her; she drew to her artists and literati. But the court they came to ornament was her husband's, and the culture they represented magnified his princely being, especially when his origins could not. Thus, the Renaissance lady may play an aesthetically significant role in Castiglione's idealized Court of Urbino of 1508, but even he clearly removed her from that equal, to say nothing of superior, position in social discourse that medieval courtly literature had granted her. To the fifteen or so male members of the court whose names he carefully listed, Castiglione admitted only four women to the evening conversations that were the second major occupation at court (the profession of arms, from which he completely excluded women, being the first). Of the four, he distinguished only two women as participants. The Duchess Elisabetta and her companion, Emilia Pia, at least speak, whereas the other two only do a dance. Yet they speak in order to moderate and "direct" discussion by proposing questions and games. They do not themselves contribute to the discussions, and at one point Castiglione relieves them even of their negligible role:

> When signor Gasparo had spoken thus, signora Emilia made a sign to madam Costanza Fregosa, as she sat next in order, that she should speak; and she was making ready to do so, when suddenly the Duchess said: "Since signora Emilia does not choose to go to the trouble of devising a game, it would be quite right for the other ladies to share in this ease, and thus be exempt from such a burden this evening, especially since there are so many men here that we risk no lack of games." (pp. 19–20)

The men, in short, do all the talking; and the ensuing dialogue on manners and love, as we might expect, is not only developed by men but directed toward their interests.

The contradiction between the professed parity of noblewomen and men in *The Courtier* and the merely decorative role Castiglione unwittingly assigned the lady proclaims an important educational and cultural change as well as a political one. Not only did a male ruler preside over the courts of Renaissance Italy, but the court no longer served as the exclusive school of the nobility, and the lady no longer served as arbiter of the cultural functions it did retain. Although restricted to a cultural and social role, she lost dominance in that role as secular education came to require special skills which were claimed as the prerogative of a class of professional teachers. The sons of the Renaissance nobility still pursued their military and diplomatic training in the service of some great lord, but as youths, they transferred their nonmilitary training from the lady to the humanistic tutor or boarding school. In a sense, humanism represented an advance for women as well as for the culture at large. It brought Latin literacy and classical learning to daughters as well as sons of the nobility. But this very development, usually taken as an index of the equality of Renaissance (noble) women with men,[19] spelled a further decline in the lady's influence over courtly society. It placed her as well as her brothers under male cultural authority. The girl of the medieval aristocracy, although unschooled, was brought up at the court of some great lady. Now her brothers' tutors shaped her outlook, male educators who, as humanists, suppressed romance and chivalry to further classical culture, with all its patriarchal and misogynous bias.

The humanistic education of the Renaissance noblewoman helps explain why she cannot compare with her medieval predecessors in shaping a culture responsive to her own interests. In accordance with the new cultural values, the patronage of the Este, Sforza, Gonzaga, and Montefeltro women extended far beyond the literature and art of love and manners, but the works they commissioned, bought, or had dedicated to them do not show any consistent correspondence to their concerns as women. They did not even give noticeable support to women's education, with the single important exception of Battista da Montefeltro, to whom one of the few treatises advocating a humanistic education for women was dedicated. Adopting the universalistic outlook of their humanist teachers, the noblewomen of Renaissance Italy seem to have lost all consciousness of their particular interests as women, while male authors such as Castiglione, who articulated the mores of the Renaissance aristocracy, wrote their works for men. Cultural and political dependency thus combined in Italy to reverse the roles of women and men in developing the new noble code. Medieval courtesy, as set forth in the earliest etiquette books, romances, and rules of love, shaped the man primarily to please the lady. In the thirteenth and fourteenth centuries, rules for women, and strongly patriarchal ones at that, entered French and Italian etiquette books, but not until the Renaissance reformulation of courtly manners and love is it evident how the ways of the lady came to be determined by men in the context of the early modern state. The relation of the sexes here assumed its modern form, and nowhere is this made more visible than in the love relation.

THE RENAISSANCE OF CHASTITY

As soon as the literature and values of courtly love made their way into Italy, they were modified in the direction of asexuality. Dante typifies this initial reception of courtly love. His *Vita Nuova*, written in the "sweet new style" (*dolce stil nuovo*) of late-thirteenth-century Tuscany, still celebrates love and the noble heart: *"Amore e 'l cor gentil sono una cosa."* Love still appears as homage, and the lady as someone else's wife. But the lover of Dante's poems is curiously arrested. He frustrates his own desire by rejecting even the aim of union with his beloved. "What is the point of your love for your lady since you are unable to endure her presence?" a lady asks of Dante. "Tell us, for surely the aim of such love must be unique [*novissimo*]!"[20] And novel it is, for Dante confesses that the joy he once took in his beloved's greeting he shall henceforth seek in himself, "in words which praise my lady." Even this understates the case, since Dante's words neither conjure up Beatrice nor seek to melt her. She remains shadowy and remote, for the focus of his poetry has shifted entirely to the subjective pole of love. It is the inner life, *his* inner life, that Dante objectifies. His love poems present a spiritual contest, which he will soon ontologize in the *Divine Comedy*, among competing states of the lover poet's soul.

This dream-world quality expresses in its way a general change that came over the literature of love as its social foundations crumbled. In the north, as the *Romance of the Rose* reminds us, the tradition began to run dry in the late thirteenth-century period of feudal disintegration—or transformation by the bourgeois economy of the towns and the emergence of the state. And in Provence, after the Albigensian Crusade and the subjection of the Midi to church and crown, Guiraut Riquier significantly called himself the last troubadour. Complaining that "no craft is less esteemed at court than the beautiful mastery of song," he renounced sexual for celestial love and claimed to enter the service of the Virgin Mary.[21] The reception and reworking of the troubadour tradition in Florence of the late 1200s consequently appears somewhat archaic. A conservative, aristocratic nostalgia clings to Dante's love poetry as it does to his political ideas. But if the new social life of the bourgeois commune found little positive representation in his poetry, Florence did drain from his poems the social content of feudal experience. The lover as knight or trobairitz thus gave way to a poet scholar. The experience of a wandering, questing life gave way to scholastic interests, to distinguishing and classifying states of feeling. And the courtly celebration of romance, modeled upon vassalage and enjoyed in secret meetings, became a private circulation of poems analyzing the spiritual effects of unrequited love.

The actual disappearance of the social world of the court and its presiding lady underlies the disappearance of sex and the physical evaporation of the woman in these poems. The ladies of the romances and troubadour poetry may be stereotypically blond, candid, and fair, but their authors meant them to be taken as physically and socially "real." In the love poetry of Dante, and of Petrarch and Vittoria Colonna, who continue his tradition, the beloved may just as well be dead—and, indeed, all three authors made them so. They have no meaningful, objective existence, and not merely because their affective experience lacks a voice. This would hold for troubadour poetry too, since the lyric, unlike the romance, articulates only the feelings of the lover. The unreality of the Renaissance beloved has rather to do with the *quality* of the Renaissance lover's feelings. As former social relations that sustained mutuality and interaction among lovers vanished, the lover fell back on a narcissistic experience. The Dantesque beloved merely inspires feelings that have no outer, physical aim; or, they have a transcendent aim that the beloved merely mediates. In either case, love casts off sexuality. Indeed, the role of the beloved as mediator is asexual in a double sense, as the *Divine Comedy* shows. Not only does the beloved never respond sexually to the lover, but the feelings she arouses in him turn into a spiritual love that makes of their entire relationship a mere symbol or allegory.

Interest even in this shadowy kind of romance dropped off markedly as the work of Dante, Petrarch, and Boccaccio led into the fifteenth-century renaissance of Graeco-Roman art and letters. The Florentine humanists in particular appropriated only the classical side of their predecessors' thought, the side that served public concerns. They rejected the dominance of love in human life, along with the inwardness and seclusion of the religious, the scholar, and the lovesick poet. Dante, for example, figured primarily as a citizen to his biographer, Lionardo Bruni, who, as humanist chancellor of Florence, made him out as a modern Socrates, at once a political figure, a family man, and a rhetor: an exemplar for the new polis.[22] Only in relation to the institution of the family did Florentine civic humanism take up questions of love and sexuality. In this context, they developed the bourgeois sex-role system, placing man in the public sphere and the patrician woman in the home, requiring social virtues from him and chastity and motherhood from her. In bourgeois Florence, the humanists would have nothing to do with the old aristocratic tradition of relative social and sexual parity. In the petty Italian despotisms, however, and even in Florence under the princely Lorenzo de' Medici late in the fifteenth century, the traditions and culture of the nobility remained meaningful.[23] Castiglione's *Courtier*, and the corpus of Renaissance works it heads, took up the themes of love and courtesy for this courtly society, adapting them to contemporary social and cultural needs. Yet in this milieu, too, within the very tradition of courtly literature, new constraints upon female sexuality emerged. Castiglione, the single most important spokesman of Renaissance love and manners, retained in his love theory Dante's two basic features: the detachment of love from sexuality and the allegorization of the love theme. Moreover, he introduced into the aristocratic conception of sex roles some of the patriarchal notions of women's confinement to the family that bourgeois humanists had been restoring.

Overtly, as we saw, Castiglione and his class supported a complementary conception of sex roles, in part because a nobility that did no work at all gave little thought to a sexual division of labor. He could thus take up the late medieval *querelle des femmes* set off by the *Romance of the Rose* and debate the question of women's dignity much to their favor. Castiglione places Aristotle's (and Aquinas's) notion of woman as a defective man in the mouth of an aggrieved misogynist, Gasparo; he criticizes Plato's low regard for women, even though he did permit them to govern in *The Republic*; he rejects Ovid's theory of love as not "gentle" enough. Most significantly, he opposes Gasparo's bourgeois notion of women's exclusively domestic role. Yet for all this, Castiglione established in *The Courtier* a fateful bond between love and marriage. One index of a heightened patriarchal outlook among the Renaissance nobility is that love in the usual emotional and sexual sense must lead to marriage and be confined to it—for women, that is.

The issue gets couched, like all others in the book, in the form of a debate. There are pros and cons; but the prevailing view is unmistakable. If the ideal court lady loves, she should love someone whom she can marry. If married, and the mishap befalls her "that her husband's hate or another's love should bring her to love, I would have her give her lover a spiritual love only; nor must she ever give him any sure sign of her love, either by word or gesture or by other means that can make him certain of it" (p. 263). *The Courtier* thus takes a strange, transitional position on the relations among love, sex, and marriage, which bourgeois Europe would later fuse into one familial whole. Responding to a situation of general female dependency among the nobility, and to the restoration of patriarchal family values, at once classical and bourgeois, Castiglione, like Renaissance love theorists in general, connected love and marriage. But facing the same realities of political marriage and clerical celibacy that beset the medieval aristocracy, he still focused upon the love that takes place outside it. On this point, too, however, he broke with the courtly love tradition. He proposed on the one hand a Neo-Platonic notion of spiritual love, and on the other, the double standard.[24]

Castiglione's image of the lover is interesting in this regard. Did he think his suppression of female sexual love would be more justifiable if he had a churchman, Pietro Bembo (elevated to cardinal in 1539), enunciate the new theory and had him discourse upon the love of an aging courtier rather than that of a young knight? In any case, adopting the Platonic definition of love as desire to enjoy beauty, Bembo located this lover in a metaphysical and physical hierarchy between sense ("below") and intellect ("above"). As reason mediates between the physical and the spiritual, so man, aroused by the visible beauty of his beloved, may direct his desire beyond her to the true, intelligible source of her beauty. He may, however, also turn toward sense. Young men fall into this error, and we should expect it of them, Bembo explains in the Neo-Platonic language of the Florentine philosopher Marsilio Ficino. "For finding itself deep in an earthly prison, and deprived of spiritual contemplation in exercising its office of governing the body, the soul of itself cannot clearly perceive the truth; wherefore, in order to have knowledge, it is obliged to turn to the senses . . . and so it believes them . . . and lets itself be guided by them, especially when they have so much vigor that they almost force it" (pp. 338–339). A misdirection of the soul leads to sexual union (though obviously not with the court lady). The preferred kind of union, achieved by way of ascent, uses love of the lady as a step toward love of universal beauty. The lover here ascends from awareness of his own human spirit, which responds to beauty, to awareness of that universal intellect that comprehends universal beauty. Then, "transformed into an angel," his soul finds supreme happiness in divine love. Love may hereby soar to an ontologically noble end, and the beauty of the woman who inspires such ascent may acquire metaphysical status and dignity. But Love, Beauty, Woman, aestheticized as Botticelli's Venus and given cosmic import, were in effect denatured, robbed of body, sex, and passion by this elevation. The simple kiss of love-service became a rarefied kiss of the soul: "A man delights in joining his mouth to that of his beloved in a kiss, not in order to bring himself to any unseemly desire, but because he feels that that bond is the opening of mutual access to their souls" (pp. 349–350). And instead of initiating love, the kiss now terminated physical contact, at least for the churchman and/or aging courtier who sought an ennobling experience—and for the woman obliged to play her role as lady.

Responsive as he still was to medieval views of love, Castiglione at least debated the issue of the double standard. His spokesmen point out that men make the rules permitting themselves and not women sexual freedom, and that concern for legitimacy does not justify this inequality. Since these same men claim to be more virtuous than women, they could more easily restrain themselves. In that case, "there would be neither more nor less certainty about offspring, for even if women were unchaste, they could in no way bear children of themselves . . . provided men were continent and did not take part in the unchastity of women" (pp. 240–241). But for all this, the book supplies an excess of hortatory tales about female chastity, and in the section of the dialogue granting young men indulgence in sensual love, no one speaks for young women, who ought to be doubly "prone," as youths and as women, according to the views of the time.

This is theory, of course. But one thinks of the examples: Eleanor of Aquitaine changing bedmates in the midst of a crusade; Elisabetta Gonzaga, so constrained by the conventions of her own court that she would not take a lover even though her husband was impotent. She, needless to say, figures as Castiglione's prime exemplar: "Our Duchess who has lived with her husband for fifteen years like a widow" (p. 253). Bembo, on the other hand, in the years before he became cardinal, lived with and had three children by Donna Morosina. But however they actually lived, in the new ideology a spiritualized noble love *supplemented* the experience of men while it *defined* extramarital experience for the lady. For women, chastity had become the convention of the Renaissance courts, signaling the twofold fact that the dominant institutions of sixteenth-century Italian society would not support the adulterous sexuality of courtly love, and that women, suffering a relative loss of power within these institutions, could not at first make them responsive to their needs. Legitimacy is a significant factor here. Even courtly love had paid some deference to it (and to the desire of women to avoid conception) by restraining intercourse while promoting romantic and sexual play. But now, with cultural and political power held almost entirely by men, the norm of female chastity came to express the concerns of Renaissance noblemen as they moved into a new situation as a hereditary, dependent class.

This changed situation of the aristocracy accounts both for Castiglione's widespread appeal and for his telling transformation of the love relation. Because *The Courtier* created a mannered way of life that could give to a dependent nobility a sense of self-sufficiency, of inner power and control, which they had lost in a real economic and political sense, the book's popularity spread from Italy through Europe at large in the sixteenth and seventeenth centuries. Although set in the Urbino court of 1508, it was actually begun some ten years after that and published in 1528—after the sack of Rome, and at a time when the princely states of Italy and Europe were coming to resemble each other more closely than they had in the fourteenth and fifteenth centuries. The monarchs of Europe, consolidating and centralizing their states, were at once protecting the privileges of their nobility and suppressing feudal power.[25] Likewise in Italy, as the entire country fell under the hegemony of Charles V, the nobility began to be stabilized. Throughout sixteenth-century Italy, new laws began to limit and regulate membership in a hereditary aristocratic class, prompting a new concern with legitimacy and purity of the blood. Castiglione's demand for female chastity in part responds to this particular concern. His theory of love as a whole responds to the general situation of the Renaissance nobility.

In the discourse on love for which he made Bembo the spokesman, he brought to the love relation the same psychic attitudes with which he confronted the political situation. Indeed, he used the love relation as a symbol to convey his sense of political relations.

The changed times to which Castiglione refers in his introduction he experienced as a condition of servitude. The dominant problem of the sixteenth-century Italian nobility, like that of the English nobility under the Tudors, had become one of obedience. As one of Castiglione's courtiers expressed it, God had better grant them "good masters, for, once we have them, we have to endure them as they are" (p. 116). It is this transformation of aristocratic service to statism, which gave rise to Castiglione's leading idea of nobility as courtiers, that shaped his theory of love as well. Bembo's aging courtier, passionless in his rational love, sums up the theme of the entire book: how to maintain by detachment the sense of self now threatened by the loss of independent power. The soul in its earthly prison, the courtier in his social one, renounce the power of self-determination that has in fact been denied them. They renounce *wanting* such power; "If the flame is extinguished, the danger is also extinguished" (p. 347). In love, as in service, the courtier preserves independence by avoiding desire for real love, real power. He does not touch or allow himself to be touched by either. "To enjoy beauty without suffering, the Courtier, aided by reason, must turn his desire entirely away from the body and to beauty alone, [to] contemplate it in its simple and pure self" (p. 351). He may gaze at the object of his love-service, he may listen, but there he reaches the limits of the actual physical relation and transforms her beauty, or the prince's power, into a pure idea. "Spared the bitterness and calamities" of thwarted passion thereby, he loves and serves an image only. The courtier gives obeisance, but only to a reality of his own making: "for he will always carry his precious treasure with him, shut up in his heart, and will also, by the force of his own imagination, make her beauty [or the prince's power] much more beautiful than in reality it is" (p. 352).

Thus, the courtier can serve and not serve, love and not love. He can even attain the relief of surrender by making use of this inner love-service "as a step" to mount to a more sublime sense of service. Contemplation of the Idea the courtier has discovered within his own soul excites a purified desire to love, to serve, to unite with intellectual beauty (or power). Just as love guided his soul from the particular beauty of his beloved to the universal concept, love of that intelligible beauty (or power) glimpsed within transports the soul from the self, the particular intellect, to the universal intellect. Aflame with an utterly spiritual love (or a spiritualized sense of service), the soul then "understands all things intelligible, and without any veil or cloud views the wide sea of pure divine beauty, and receives it into itself, enjoying that supreme happiness of which the senses are incapable" (p. 354). What does this semimystical discourse teach but that by "true" service, the courtier may break out of his citadel of independence, his inner aloofness, to rise and surrender to the pure idea of Power? What does his service become but a freely chosen Obedience, which he can construe as the supreme virtue? In both its sublimated acceptance or resignation and its inner detachment from the actual, Bembo's discourse on love exemplifies the relation between subject and state, obedience and power, that runs through the entire book. Indeed, Castiglione regarded the monarch's power exactly as he had Bembo present the lady's beauty, as symbolic of God: "As in the heavens the sun and the moon and the other stars exhibit to the world a certain likeness of God, so on earth a much liker image of God is seen in . . . princes." Clearly, if "men have been put by God under princes" (p. 307), if they have been placed under princes as under His image, what end can be higher than service in virtue, than the purified experience of Service?

The likeness of the lady to the prince in this theory, her elevation to the pedestal of Neo-Platonic love, both masks and expresses the new dependency of the Renaissance noblewoman. In a structured hierarchy of superior and inferior, she seems to be served by the courtier. But this love theory really made her serve—and stand as a symbol of how the relation of domination may be reversed, so that the prince could be made to serve the interests of the courtier. The Renaissance lady is not desired, not loved for herself. Rendered passive and chaste, she merely mediates the courtier's safe transcendence of an otherwise demeaning necessity. On the plane of symbolism, Castiglione thus had the courtier dominate both her and the prince; and on the plane of reality, he indirectly acknowledged the courtier's actual domination of the lady by having him adopt "woman's ways" in his relations to the prince. Castiglione had to defend against effeminacy in the courtier, both the charge of it (p. 92) and the actuality of faces "soft and feminine as many attempt to have who not only curl their hair and pluck their eyebrows, but preen themselves . . . and appear so tender and languid . . . and utter their words so limply" (p. 36). Yet the close-fitting costume of the Renaissance nobleman displayed the courtier exactly as Castiglione would have him, "well built and shapely of limb" (p. 36). His clothes set off his grace, as did his nonchalant ease, the new manner of those "who seem in words, laughter, in posture not to care" (p. 44). To be attractive, accomplished, and seem not to care; to charm and do so coolly—how concerned with impression, how masked the true self. And how manipulative: petitioning his lord, the courtier knows to be "discreet in choosing the occasion, and will ask things that are proper and reasonable; and he will so frame his request, omitting those parts that he knows can cause displeasure, and will skillfully make easy the difficult points so that his lord will always grant it" (p. 111). In short, how like a woman—or a dependent, for that is the root of the simile.

The accommodation of the sixteenth- and seventeenth-century courtier to the ways and dress of women in no way bespeaks a greater parity between them. It reflects, rather, that general restructuring of social relations that entailed for the Renaissance noblewoman a greater dependency upon men as feudal independence and reciprocity yielded to the state. In this new situation, the entire nobility suffered a loss. Hence, the courtier's posture of dependency, his concern with the pleasing impression, his resolve "to perceive what his prince likes, and . . . to bend himself to this" (pp. 110–111). But as the state overrode aristocratic power, the lady suffered a double loss. Deprived of the possibility of independent power that the combined interests of kinship and feudalism guaranteed some women in the Middle Ages, and that the states of early modern Europe would preserve in part, the Italian noblewoman in particular entered a relation of almost universal dependence upon her family and her husband. And she experienced this dependency at the same time as she lost her commanding position with respect to the secular culture of her society.

Hence, the love theory of the Italian courts developed in ways as indifferent to the interests of women as the courtier, in his self-sufficiency, was indifferent as a lover. It accepted, as medieval courtly love did not, the double standard. It bound the lady to chastity, to the merely procreative sex of political marriage, just as her weighty and costly costume came to conceal and constrain her body while it displayed her husband's noble rank. Indeed, the person of the woman became so inconsequential to this love relation that one doubted whether she could love at all. The question that emerges at the end of *The Courtier* as to "whether or not women are as capable of divine love as men" (p. 350) belongs to a love theory structured by mediation rather than mutuality. Woman's beauty inspired love but the lover, the agent, was man. And the question stands unresolved at the end of *The Courtier* —because at heart the spokesmen for Renaissance love were not really concerned about women or love at all.

Where courtly love had used the social relation of vassalage to work out a genuine concern with sexual love, Castiglione's thought moved in exactly the opposite direction. He allegorized love as fully as Dante did, using the relation of the sexes to symbolize the new political order. In this, his love theory reflects the social realities of the Renaissance. The denial of the right and power of women to love, the transformation of women into passive "others" who serve, fits the self-image of the courtier, the one Castiglione sought to remedy. The symbolic relation of the sexes thus mirrors the new social relations of the state, much as courtly love displayed the feudal relations of reciprocal personal dependence. But Renaissance love reflects, as well, the actual condition of dependency suffered by noblewomen as the state arose. If the courtier who charms the prince bears the same relation to him as the lady bears to the courtier, it is because Castiglione understood the relation of the sexes in the same terms that he used to describe the political relation: that is, as a relation between servant and lord.

The nobleman suffered this relation in the public domain only. The lady, denied access to a freely chosen, mutually satisfying love relation, suffered it in the personal domain as well. Moreover, Castiglione's theory, unlike the courtly love it superseded, subordinated love itself to the public concerns of the Renaissance nobleman. He set forth the relation of the sexes as one of dependency and domination, but he did so in order to express and deal with the political relation and its problems. The personal values of love, which the entire feudality once prized, were henceforth increasingly left to the lady. The courtier formed his primary bond with the modern prince.

In sum, a new division between personal and public life made itself felt as the state came to organize Renaissance society, and with that division the modern relation of the sexes made its appearance,[26] even among the Renaissance nobility. Noblewomen, too, were increasingly removed from public concerns—economic, political, and cultural—and although they did not disappear into a private realm of family and domestic concerns as fully as their sisters in the patrician bourgeoisie, their loss of public power made itself felt in new constraints placed upon their personal as well as their social lives. Renaissance ideas on love and manners, more classical than medieval, and almost exclusively a male product, expressed this new subordination of women to the interests of husbands and male-dominated kin groups and served to justify the removal of women from an "unladylike" position of power and erotic independence. All the advances of Renaissance Italy, its protocapitalist economy, its states, and its humanistic culture, worked to mold the noblewoman into an aesthetic object: decorous, chaste, and doubly dependent—on her husband as well as the prince.

NOTES

I first worked out these ideas in 1972–1973 in a course at Sarah Lawrence College entitled "Women: Myth and Reality" and am very much indebted to students in that course and my colleagues Eva Kollisch, Gerda Lerner, and Sherry Ortner. I thank Eve Fleisher, Martin Fleisher, Renate Bridenthal, and Claudia Koonz for their valuable criticism of an earlier version of this paper.

1. The traditional view of the equality of Renaissance women with men goes back to Jacob Burckhardt's classic, *The Civilization of the Renaissance in Italy* (1860). It has found its way into most general histories of women, such as Mary Beard's *Women as Force in History* (1946), Simone de Beauvoir's *The Second Sex* (1949), and Emily James Putnam's *The Lady* (1910), although the last is a sensitive and sophisticated treatment. It also dominates most histories of Renaissance women, the best of which is E. Rodocanachi, *La femme italienne avant, pendant et après la Renaissance* (Paris: Hachette, 1922). A notable exception is Ruth Kelso, *Doctrine for the Lady of the Renaissance* (Urbana: University of Illinois Press, 1956), who discovered there was no such parity.

2. See the essay by Marylin Arthur. The major Renaissance statement of the bourgeois domestication of women was made by Leon Battista Alberti in Book 3 of *Della Famiglia* (c. 1435), which is a free adaptation of the Athenian situation described by Xenophon in the *Oeconomicus*.

3. Andreas Capellanus, *The Art of Courtly Love*, trans. John J. Parry (New York: Columbia University Press, 1941), pp. 150–151.

4. Maurice Valency, *In Praise of Love: An Introduction to the Love-Poetry of the Renaissance* (New York: Macmillan, 1961), p. 146.

5. "E il dompna deu a son drut far honor/Cum ad amic, mas non cum a seignor." Ibid., p. 64.

6. Lanval (Sir Launfal), *Les lais de Marie de France*, ed. Paul Tuffrau (Paris: L'Edition d'Art H. Piazza, n.d.), p. 41. English ed., *Lays of Marie de France* (London and New York: J. M. Dent and E. P. Dutton, 1911).

7. Excellent trans. and ed. by W. W. Comfort, *Arthurian Romances* (London and New York: Dent and Dutton, Everyman's Library, 1970), p. 286.

8. Thomas Aquinas, *Summa Theologiae*, pt. 1–2, q. 28, art. 5.

9. Lanval, *Les lais*, p. 10.

10. Thomas Frederick Crane, *Italian Social Customs of the Sixteenth Century*, (New Haven: Yale University Press, 1920), pp. 10–11.

11. As Marc Bloch pointed out, the great French principalities that no longer required personal military service on the part of their holders were among the first to be passed on to women when male heirs were wanting. *Feudal Society*, trans. L. A. Manyon (Chicago: University of Chicago Press, 1964), p. 201. See also, in this volume, the essay by Suzanne Wemple.

12. David Herlihy, "Land, Family and Women in Continental Europe, 701–1200," *Traditio*, 18 (1962), 89–120. Also, "Women in Medieval Society," *The Smith History Lecture*, University of St. Thomas, Texas, 1971. For a fine new work on abbesses, see Joan Morris, *The Lady Was a Bishop* (New York and London: Collier and Macmillan, 1973). Marie de France may have been an abbess of Shaftesbury.

13. Emily James Putnam, *The Lady* (Chicago and London: University of Chicago Press, 1970), p. 118. See also the chapter on the abbess in the same book.

14. From *The Women Troubadours*, trans. and ed. Meg Bogin (New York/London: Paddington Press, 1976). Reprinted by permission of Meg Bogin.

15. Friedrich Heer, *The Medieval World: Europe 1100–1350* (New York: Mentor Books, 1963), pp. 167, 178–179.

16. This was Amy Kelly's surmise in "Eleanor of Aquitaine and Her Courts of Love," *Speculum*, 12 (January 1937), 3–19.

17. From *The Book of the Courtier*, by Baldassare Castiglione, a new translation by Charles S. Singleton (New York: Doubleday, 1959), p. 20. Copyright © 1959 by Charles S. Singleton and Edgar de N. Mayhew. This and other quotations throughout the chapter are reprinted by permission of Doubleday & Co., Inc.

18. Selections from the correspondence of Renaissance noblewomen can be found in the biographies listed in the bibliography.

19. An interesting exception is W. Ong's "Latin Language Study as a Renaissance Puberty Rite," *Studies in Philology*, 56 (1959), 103–124; also Margaret Leah King's "The Religious Retreat of Isotta Nogarola (1418–1466)," *Signs*, Winter 1977.

20. Dante Alighieri, *La Vita Nuova*, trans. Barbara Reynolds (Middlesex, England and Baltimore: Penguin Books, 1971), poem 18.

21. Frederick Goldin, trans., *Lyrics of the Troubadours and Trouvères* (New York: Doubleday, 1973), p. 325.

22. David Thompson and Alan F. Nagel, eds. and trans., *The Three Crowns of Florence: Humanist Assessments of Dante, Petrarca, and Boccaccio* (New York: Harper & Row, 1972).

23. For Renaissance humanistic and courtly literature, Vittorio Rossi, *Il quattrocento* (Milan: F. Vallardi, 1933); Ruth Kelso, *Doctrine for the Lady of the Renaissance* (Urbana: University of Illinois Press, 1956). On erotic life, interesting remarks by David Herlihy, "Some Psychological and Social Roots of Violence in the Tuscan Cities," in *Violence and Civil Disorder in Italian Cities, 1200–1500,* ed. Lauro Martines (Berkeley: University of California Press, 1972), pp. 129–154.

24. For historical context, Keith Thomas, "The Double Standard," *Journal of the History of Ideas,* 20 (1959), 195–216; N. J. Perella, *The Kiss Sacred and Profane: An Interpretive History of Kiss Symbolism* (Berkeley: University of California Press, 1969); Morton Hunt, *The Natural History of Love* (New York: Funk & Wagnalls, 1967).

25. Fernand Braudel, *The Mediterranean World* (London: Routledge & Kegan Paul, 1973); A. Ventura, *Nobiltà e popolo nella società Veneta* (Bari: Laterza, 1964); Lawrence Stone, *The Crisis of the Aristocracy, 1558–1641* (Oxford: Clarendon Press, 1965).

26. The status of women as related to the distinction of public and private spheres of activity in various societies is a key idea in most of the anthropological studies in *Women, Culture, and Society,* ed. Michelle Zimbalist Rosaldo and Louise Lamphere (Stanford: Stanford University Press, 1974).

SUGGESTIONS FOR FURTHER READING

On Renaissance women: Stanley Chojnacki, "Patrician Women in Early Renaissance Venice," *Studies in the Renaissance,* 21 (1974), 176–203; Susan Goag Bell, "Christine de Pizan," *Feminist Studies,* 3 (Spring/Summer 1976), 173–184; Joan Kelly-Gadol, "Notes on Women in the Renaissance," *Conceptual Frameworks in Women's History* (Bronxville, N.Y.: Sarah Lawrence Publications, 1976); Margaret Leah King, "The Religious Retreat of Isotta Nogarola," *Signs,* Winter 1977; Kathleen Casey, "Reconstructing the Experience of Medieval Woman," *Liberating Women's History,* ed. Berenice Carroll (Urbana: University of Illinois Press, 1976), pp. 224–249. With the exception of Ruth Kelso, *Doctrine for the Lady of the Renaissance* (Urbana: University of Illinois Press, 1956), and Ernst Breisach, *Caterina Sforza: A Renaissance Virago* (Chicago: University of Chicago Press, 1967), all other serious studies stem from the first wave of the feminist movement. They form a necessary basis, although they concern themselves almost exclusively with "exceptional" women and are not sensitive to socioeconomic factors. Among them, Marian Andrews (pseud. Christopher Hare), *The Most Illustrious Ladies of the Italian Renaissance* (New York: Scribner's, 1904); Julia Cartwright (Mrs. Ady), *Isabella d'Este,* 2 vols. (New York: Dutton,

1903) and *Beatrice d'Este* (1899); Ferdinand Gregorovius, *Lucrezia Borgia* (Blom, 1968 reprint of 1903 ed.); E. Rodocanachi, *La femme italienne avant, pendant et après la Renaissance* (Paris: Hachette, 1922); T. A. Trollope, *A Decade of Italian Women*, 2 vols. (London: Chapman & Hall, 1859).

The most significant studies in demographic and social history bearing upon Renaissance women are those of David Herlihy, among whose several articles are "Mapping Households in Medieval Italy," *The Catholic Historical Review*, 58 (April 1972), 1–24; "Vieillir à Florence au Quattrocento," *Annales*, 24 (November–December 1969), 1338–1352; "The Tuscan Town in the Quattrocento," *Medievalia et Humanistica*, I (1970), 81–110; also, a forthcoming book on the Tuscan family [see Addendum]. Two demographic studies on infanticide and foundlings in Florence by Richard C. Trexler are in *History of Childhood Quarterly*, 1, nos. 1 and 2 (1973); Gene Brucker has excellent selections from wills, marriage contracts, government minutes, legal judgments, etc., in *The Society of Renaissance Florence: A Documentary Study* (New York: Harper, 1971).

Histories of family life and child-rearing among the courtly aristocracy of early modern France supplement very nicely Castiglione's portrayal of the courtier and court lady. Among them, Philippe Ariès, *Centuries of Childhood: A Social History of Family Life* (New York: Knopf, 1965), and David Hunt, *Parents and Children in History* (New York: Harper, 1972). Although he does not deal with Renaissance Italy, Lawrence Stone's *The Crisis of the Aristocracy, 1558–1641* (Oxford: Clarendon Press, 1965) is indispensable reading for information about aristocratic social life.

Primary sources on medieval and Renaissance love used in the text in English translation are: Andreas Capellanus, *The Art of Courtly Love*, trans. John J. Parry (New York: Columbia University Press, 1941); *Lays of Marie de France* (London and New York: J. M. Dent and E. P. Dutton, 1911); Chrétien de Troyes's Lancelot from *Arthurian Romances*, trans. and ed. W. W. Comfort (London and New York: Dent and Dutton, Everyman's Library, 1970); Baldassare Castiglione, *The Book of the Courtier*, trans. Charles S. Singleton (New York: Doubleday, 1959); Dante Alighieri, *La Vita Nuova*, trans. Barbara Reynolds (Middlesex, England and Baltimore: Penguin Books, 1971). In addition to sources given in the footnotes and by E. William Monter in his essay in this volume, see F. X. Newman, *The Meaning of Courtly Love* (Albany: The State University of New York Press, 1967) for contemporary opinion and a good bibliography. The soundest and most sensitive study is still Maurice Valency's *In Praise of Love* (New York: Macmillan, 1961). Two fine articles on the literature of love, sex, and marriage in early modern Europe are by William Haller, "Hail Wedded Love," *A Journal of English Literary History*, 13 (June 1946), 79–97, and Paul Siegel, "The Petrarchan Sonneteers and Neo-Platonic Love," *Studies in Philology*, 42 (1945), 164–182.

ADDENDUM

We now possess a major historiography of women in the Renaissance. Many of the works published since 1976 acknowledge a specific debt to Joan Kelly's innovative essay first published in *Becoming Visible* in 1976 and republished unchanged in the 1987 edition.

The works cited below suggest the directions in which Renaissance women's history has moved in the past ten years. They should be addressed in evaluating Kelly's now classic study.

For entry into the literature on the problem of women and learning see Patricia H. LaBalme, *Beyond Their Sex: Learned Women of the European Past* (New York: New York University Press, 1980), and the sources published in Margaret King and Albert Rabil, *Her Immaculate Hand*, Medieval Texts and Series, 20 (Binghamton, N.Y.: SUNY Press, 1983). Christine de Pizan's *A City of Ladies* has been translated by E. R. Jeffries (New York: Persea Books, 1983). See on Christine de Pizan the study by Charity Cannon Willard, *Christine de Pizan: Her Life and Works* (New York: Persea Books, 1984). See also Hanna Fenichel Pitkin, *Fortune is a Woman: Gender and Politics in the Thought of Niccolo Machiavelli* (Berkeley: University of California Press, 1984), and Margaret Tomalin, *The Fortunes of the Warrior Heroine in Italian Literature: An Index of Emancipation* (Ravenna: Longo Editore, 1982). These as well as Ian MacLean's study cited in the notes of Chapter six will acquaint readers with the place of women in Italian Renaissance literature.

For Renaissance women in England, see Retha M. Warnike, *Women of the English Renaissance and Reformation* (Westport, Conn.: Greenwood Press, 1983), and Linda Woodbridge, *Women and The English Renaissance: Literature and the Nature of Womankind* (Urbana and Chicago: University of Illinois Press, 1984); on women in English literature, see Suzanne W. Hull, *Chaste, Silent, and Obedient: English Books for Women, 1475–1640* (San Marino, Calif.: The Huntington Library, 1982), and Constance Jordan, "Feminism and the Humanists: The Case of Sir Thomas Elyot's Defence of Good Women," *Renaissance Quarterly*, 36 (1983), 181–201.

For women in social and economic life, see David Herlihy and Christiane Klapisch-Zuber, *Tuscans and Their Families* (New Haven: Yale University Press, 1985), and David Herlihy, *Medieval Households* (Cambridge, Mass.: Harvard University Press, 1985). Christiane Klapisch-Zuber's collected articles appear in *Women, Family and Ritual in Renaissance Florence*, trans. Lydia Cochrane (Chicago: University of Chicago Press, 1985). See also Diane Owen Hughes, "Sumptuary Law and Social Relations in Renaissance Italy" in *Disputes and Settlements: Law and Human Relations in the West*, ed. John Bossy (Cambridge: Cambridge University Press, 1983), pp. 66–99, and Judith C. Brown, *Immodest Acts: The Life of a Lesbian Nun in Renaissance Italy* (Oxford and New York: Oxford University Press, 1985).

G. L. Bernini's *Ecstasy of Saint Teresa* (1644–1647), inspired by a passage from her autobiography about the "exquisite joy caused by this incomparable pain," illustrates the continuity of the medieval tradition of the visionary nun during the Catholic Counter-Reformation. (Alinari/Art Resource)

chapter 8

Protestant Wives, Catholic Saints, and the Devil's Handmaid: Women in the Age of Reformations

William Monter

In the sixteenth century Europe experienced two reformations, not one, and both Protestants and Catholics persecuted witches. The powerfully misogynistic mood that encouraged witch-hunting marks a nadir for women in European history. New ideas alone cannot explain this phenomenon; in fact, neither the Protestant Reformation nor the Catholic Counter-Reformation introduced any significant new theories about the nature or role of women. During this period, however, the states of early modern Europe increased patriarchal authority in both religious and secular life.

In this essay William Monter examines the gains women made and the opportunities they lost. On balance, the increased validation of women's domestic roles by both Catholics and Protestants probably did not improve women's status. The only substantial gain—some new roles for women in teaching and preaching—occurred in the seventeenth century, when the witch hunt in Europe finally began to abate.

Along with the Renaissance, the Protestant Reformation has traditionally been considered one of the great watersheds in European civilization and a major foundation of modern history. But such periods of so-called progressive change reveal a fairly regular pattern of diminished public opportunities for women, so we can rephrase Joan Kelly-Gadol's question from the previous chapter and ask, "Was there a Reformation for women?" For several reasons, this question is difficult to answer.

The sixteenth century saw not one but two reformations within Christendom. The Church of Rome did not speedily wither away, as Martin Luther had hoped; instead it undertook a Counter-Reformation, which enabled it to check the expansion of Protestantism after 1570. Therefore, beyond the problem of whether or not Protestantism offered any benefits to European women, the existence of this second movement provokes other questions: Did the Catholic Reformation mean reform for women? How did opportunities differ for Protestant and Catholic women?

Moreover, other major issues, connected with the development of modern Europe, affected women during the sixteenth and seventeenth centuries, but intersected only partially with the history of these reformations. Some of the most important developments of concern to early modern European women occurred independently of either the Protestant or the Catholic Reformation. Both movements occurred in a swiftly changing world where, for example, the increased power of monarchies and the reinforcement of patriarchal ideology affected women profoundly.

Gender definitions, solidified by centuries of custom and now reinforced by the Renaissance revival of classical precedents, strengthened the grip of patriarchal ideology after 1500. Renaissance education, neoclassical in orientation and normally confined to boys, persisted until the nineteenth century and probably did more than religious instruction to influence official male opinion about women. Given such conditions, patriarchal "reforms" often took directions clearly disadvantageous for women. Tragic consequences resulted from zealous enforcement of laws against witchcraft and infanticide. The resultant deaths of tens of thousands of women across Europe owed much to the patriarchal pressures of this age, but they cannot be causally linked to either Reformation; both persecutions would probably have occurred even if no Reformations had taken place.

To help determine whether there was a Reformation for women, we will examine how the various confessional churches of Reformation-era Europe offered specifically "sectarian" policies affecting women; then see where both Protestant and Catholic tradition provided substantially similar answers to other issues concerning women's place in Christian society; and finally, discuss those contemporaneous developments only peripherally affected by competing religious ideologies but bringing women face to face with a restrictive and often misogynous world view.

WOMEN AND PROTESTANTISM

Martin Luther's successful defiance of papal authority ultimately led to a permanent schism within Christendom and created at least one significant change in women's roles. Luther vehemently attacked clerical celibacy and the traditional Christian assumption that virginity was the ideal condition for both sexes. Instead he promoted marriage for the clergy, and eventually followed his own advice; Luther's important pamphlet *On Christian Marriage* (1522) preceded his own wedding by three years. His wife, Katherine von Bora, had escaped from a convent in 1523. Aware that canon law defined his marriage as doubly sacrilegious, Luther undertook it partly to "defy the devils and the Pope." It nonetheless worked out very well. He and Katherine had six children; his letters and conversation testify to the reciprocal love and trust that permeated their union until his death more than twenty years later. Nevertheless, this successful pioneer of clerical marriage maintained his ambivalence about the legitimacy of sexual intercourse. Although he criticized the Church Fathers for denigrating marriage in favor of "unclean celibacy," Luther still believed that marital sex, no matter how "chaste," remained to some degree sinful.

Protestants saw marriage as a responsibility for both sexes. The first Protestant wedding service (Nuremberg, 1526) included reading the story of Adam and Eve, humankind's fall from grace. Each new couple assumed the suffering consequent to the Fall, with the husband "toiling" for his family's well-being and his wife "laboring" in childbirth. Luther and his fellow Protestant leaders wished to promote the dignity and importance of marriage, but not to infringe male supremacy. As a Puritan manual emphasized, "we would that the man when he loveth should remember his superiority." At best Protestantism offered a "differentiated equality" between the sexes, as when Calvin simultaneously stressed women's Biblical subordination to men and the reciprocal obligations of both sexes. God's design, he said, demanded neither male tyranny nor female autonomy, but mutual cooperation— under male leadership.

Other Protestant reforms attempted, though with less success, to treat men and women symmetrically. For example, Protestants accepted the possibility of complete divorce, with permission for the innocent party to remarry, whereas Catholicism allowed only "separation from bed and board" to remedy failed marriages. However, Protestants granted very few divorces; Calvinist Geneva, whose court complained in 1600 that "we have the reputation of rupturing marriages easily," averaged fewer than one divorce a year until well after 1750. Moreover, although Protestants claimed to base their divorce policy on the Bible, a careful study of their practice in the city of Strasbourg shows that they quickly adopted the rules of canon law governing separations. In one major Protestant country, England, divorce with permission to remarry began more than a century after the Reformation had been introduced. Nuremberg, the last important Lutheran city in Germany to permit full divorce, shut down its public brothel (the last in Lutheran Germany) in the same year.

Only rarely did Protestant reformers directly attack the double standard; husbands, but not wives, obtained divorces for adultery. Calvinist Geneva ("the most perfect school of Christ seen on earth since the days of the apostles," according to the great Scottish reformer John Knox, and a "paradise for women," according to a peasant in 1610) had passed edicts in 1566 requiring equal punishments for men and women for sexual misconduct: prison terms with a diet of bread and water for fornication; banishment for adultery with an unmarried person; and death for adultery between two married people. Only women, however, were ever executed for adultery. Male citizens managed to avoid banishment for adulteries committed with their servants. Repeal of these edicts in 1610 was "greatly regretted by the zealous supporters of justice, since it opened the door to an infinity of fornications." No other European government even dared attempt this particular reform, because patriarchal attitudes generally precluded such utopianism in both Catholic and Protestant Europe.

Frau Luther, Katherine von Bora, became the prototype of the minister's wife, after having served as the prototype of the renegade nun. Her marriage became exemplary among Protestant leaders; although no major Protestant group formally required a man to marry before serving as minister, virtually all Protestant clergy married, partly in order to distinguish themselves from Catholics. But few nuns followed her example; the role of minister's wife offered only an uncertain compensation for definite losses. Although many girls still entered convents unwillingly during the Reformation era, women voluntarily left their cloisters far less frequently than men. Protestant governments abolished nunneries wherever they could, but usually against the strong wishes of their inhabitants. Sometimes, as in Lutheran Sweden, pressures from local families forced Protestant governments to maintain the convents for their current residents, while forbidding new entrants. Elsewhere, Calvinist Geneva simply expelled all its nuns to the nearest Catholic territory. Occasionally, as in England, nuns received pensions and returned to their families. Protestantism had no special place for an ex-nun and, perhaps more importantly, it offered no socially prestigious communities of unmarried women to replace the convents of Catholic Europe.

Other Protestant reforms affected European women indirectly. For example, Luther's denial of papal authority led to Protestant reliance on Holy Scripture alone and to its famous (though divisive) principle of the "priesthood of all believers." Protestant leaders believed that women as well as men should read the Bible and participate in this priesthood, although they did not systematically teach girls to read. However, other Protestant innovations posed significant drawbacks for women beyond the assault on their communal life in convents. For example, Protestantism abolished traditional festivities in which women had played an active role; it destroyed the worship of female as well as male saints; and most significantly, it dethroned the Virgin Mary from her position as the Mother of God and protector of women in childbirth, and deprived her of her nearly equal rank with the Trinity. (Luther had a difficult time breaking his wife of saying the *Ave Maria.*)

Individual women rarely converted to Protestantism during the sixteenth century; they usually joined Protestant groups in the company of male kin. Wherever Protestantism depended on family-based congregations, women provided about a third of the recorded sixteenth-century membership, as with the 420 Anabaptist martyrs in the major Flemish cities of Antwerp, Ghent and Bruges before 1592. But female converts without male Protestant relatives proved extremely rare, especially in places where prosecution made conversion to Protestantism highly dangerous. Only 28 women appear among the 795 "Lutherans" investigated by the Venetian Inquisition. The same low ratio of 4 percent women reappears among the 184 accused Protestants of Sicily from 1540 to 1572; in sharp contrast, about half of the 95 accused Jews tried by the same tribunal during the same years were women. Women could obtain Bibles and other Protestant literature both in Venice and in the Flemish cities, and many urban women could read. Only the absence of family groups among Mediterranean Protestants satisfactorily explains such disparities between north and south. Many women's response to the Protestant Reformation depended upon the commitment of their fathers or husbands—understandably, in an age which has been characterized as the zenith of the patriarchal nuclear family.[1]

However, "patriarchal" families imply paternal control over children at least as much as husbands' control over wives; both attitudes permeated Reformation Europe. Luther had published a pamphlet in 1524 entitled *Parents Should Neither Compel Nor Hinder the Marriage of Their Children, and Children Should Not Become Engaged without the Consent of Their Parents,* but only the second problem preoccupied Protestant leaders.[2] They encouraged their governments to create new civil courts for marital cases, especially in order to punish "clandestine" marriages made without parental consent. Protestant theologians demanded two adult witnesses as preconditions for a valid betrothal, and required a church ceremony for a fully valid marriage. Imitation is the sincerest form of flattery: Catholic theologians subsequently accepted both reforms and Catholic governments implemented them. A French edict of 1556 allowed parents to disinherit children who married without their consent, and established the minimum legal age for marriage without such consent at 30 for men and 25 for women. The assault on "clandestine" marriages provided an important legal safeguard for patriarchy in Reformation Europe, together with systems like the *entails* of Protestant England or the *mayorazgos* of Catholic Spain, which protected both essential patrimonial property and the paternal name across several generations.

In Protestant Europe, home of the minister's wife and of timidly "reformed" divorce laws, the most interesting innovations always occurred among its many sectarian communities. In some radical Protestant groups of the early sixteenth century, marital experimentation took forms appropriate to an age of reinforced patriarchy: arranged marriages among the German Hutterites, for example, or the famous polygamous phase of the "New Jerusalem" proclaimed by male Dutch Anabaptists at Münster in 1534. The second wave of Protestant sectarianism, however, centered in seventeenth-century England, produced some very different ideas about women's roles within the church.

The most important new development, the woman preacher, began among these British sects. She represented a step beyond the prophetess, a figure well known to St. Paul and tolerated at several points in Christian history. Even the ordinarily silent Anabaptist women of the Rhineland produced an occasional sixteenth-century prophetess like Ursula Jost. Like many other sectarians, English separatist churches included sizable numbers of women among their early congregations; but only when these congregations separated physically as well as religiously from the Church of England did they begin to acquire women as lay preachers. The first famous female speaker was Anne Hutchinson, leader of the Antinomians in Massachusetts in 1636. In London, a woman preached regularly at the General Baptist Church after the outbreak of the English Civil War in 1640, while other women spoke in different parts of the realm. Anglican pamphleteers hysterically lamented *A Discoverie of six women preachers* in 1641, and complained about *A Spirit moving in the women preachers* five years later.

The apogee of women's role within Protestant sectarianism came later in the English Civil War after the founding of the Quakers, or Society of Friends, in 1648. Women provided the first Quaker sermons in London, in British universities, in Ireland, and in North America; women began the first Quaker mission in the Ottoman Empire. The best-known early woman Quaker, Margaret Fell, organized a Women's Petition in 1659, and eight years later published a work on *Women's speaking justified*. Like most prominent Quakers of both sexes, she spent long periods in prison. By 1671, Quakers held regular Women's Meetings on a monthly or a quarterly basis. This "separate sphere" provided care for Quaker servants, distributed charity, and examined future spouses; it did not directly threaten the patriarchal family. Sects such as the Baptists or the Quakers, through intermarriage, eventually created households almost as patriarchal as those of the German Anabaptists, but by 1700 they had also accommodated the prototypes for the female Protestant church official into their institutional hierarchies.

WOMEN AND THE CATHOLIC REFORMATION

The most significant innovation for Catholic women in early modern Europe developed erratically, and against vehement opposition. Rome only grudgingly learned to tolerate the socially useful nun, actively engaged in education or nursing. By the thirteenth century, male monasticism had successfully combined communal life and prayer with public service, particularly in education. Female monasticism, however, was hampered in its attempts to do so by repeated demands from Rome for strict enclosure, and achieved only limited and partial successes by 1700.

The Catholic Counter-Reformation had little immediate positive effect on women. As one would expect from a group of "Church Fathers" in a highly patriarchal age, the Council of Trent (1545–1563) copied the Protestants' campaign against "clandestine" marriages made without parental consent. Catholics after Trent tried to popularize the earthly father figure of St. Joseph, long the forgotten parent of the Holy Family. The Council also reaffirmed clerical celibacy, multiplying its attacks on concubines (still found among 20 percent of the parish clergy in Luxemburg as late as 1580).

The Council of Trent had no program of reform for female monasticism other than reaffirming thirteenth-century rules of rigid enclosure. A Catholic historian recently suggested that "the attempt to make of female convents less a part of lay society and more a part of the hierarchical and professional church, with clerical male control, was not a success—arguably the least successful campaign of the Counter-Reformation."[3] Despite reforming bishops, many convents continued to serve as dumping-grounds for surplus daughters of Catholic aristocrats. The consequences could be seen in the bouts of collective frenzy, diagnosed as demonic possession, in some seventeenth-century convents in France and Spain, or in the laxity of the eighteenth-century convents where Casanova spent so much time. At best, the nuns of post-Tridentine Europe continued the medieval traditions of the learned abbess and visionary mystic, characteristics attractively combined in the person of St. Teresa of Avila (see page 202). But such exceptions produced no significant innovations in the purposes of female monasticism.

A genuine Catholic reformation in female religious life began with the foundation of the Ursulines by Angela Merici in 1535. Her Institute, which included a hundred members by the time she died in 1540, marked the first attempt in Europe to gather women together in a formal organization devoted to teaching girls. Like the Society of Jesus, founded at almost the same time by St. Ignatius Loyola, this innovative group quickly won papal approval, but soon became embroiled in controversies. However, the Ursulines faced even greater obstacles than the Jesuits, because after the Council of Trent they lacked the physical mobility needed by successful teachers. By 1566 it had become papal policy to suppress all female congregations that did not practice enclosure; so the Ursulines, who until then had adopted no such rule or special clothing, began to wear habits and live in cloisters. Thus "reformed" by St. Charles Borromeo, they continued their mission of teaching girls, spreading from Italy into France (1576) and the Low Countries (1611). By the mid-seventeenth century the Ursulines had produced a saint in distant Quebec and a demonically-possessed niece of Cardinal Richelieu in France; they became a regular order of cloistered nuns in 1667. The Ursulines accommodated to the constricting rules of the Counter-Reformation, but remained an order of nuns devoted to teaching.

Angela Merici's original vision of an uncloistered group of religious women devoted to educating other women reappeared almost a century later. However, its new apostle, Mary Ward, soon faced stiff opposition from the Jesuits and the papacy, almost at the same time that they jointly humbled Galileo. Her fledgling Institute of the Blessed Virgin Mary, which had spread rapidly from Belgium and the Rhineland into southern Germany, Italy, and Hungary, officially disbanded in 1629, and Mary Ward retired to her native England. Her organization went underground, eventually resurfacing in eighteenth-century Germany and winning full papal approval of its Jesuit-style constitution only in 1840.

Other would-be innovators in seventeenth-century female religious life, mostly French teams of a male cleric and a female disciple, eventually stumbled against the requirement of strict enclosure. The Order of the Visitation, created by St. Francis de Sales and Jeanne de Chantal, survived at the cost of exchanging its original charitable duties for the role of a contemplative order. The Canonesses of St. Augustine, begun by St. Peter Fourier and Alix le Clercq, similarly accepted enclosure in order to survive.

In 1634 began the most original and most successful of all such innovative orders: the Daughters of Charity, founded by St. Vincent de Paul and Mlle. le Gras. Unlike his saintly peers, St. Vincent practiced a form of "holy cunning" in order to avoid the perils of canon law. Names mattered, so his Institute, or "company," led by a "Sister servant," had members called not nuns but "daughters of the parish." As he explained, "whoever says 'religious' says 'enclosed,' but the Daughters of Charity must go everywhere." Its key members took perpetual vows, but wore the gray gowns and headdresses of ordinary countrywomen (an ironic reversal of the practice adopted by nurses in early French municipal hospitals, who deliberately dressed to look like nuns). St. Vincent's system won papal approval and grew to three dozen houses by 1660. His casuistry protected the first female order devoted to nursing and works of practical charity.

By 1700 the Protestant and Catholic reformations had largely run their course, so far as their effects on women are concerned. A few modern features began to emerge. Women held increased public roles in some newer Protestant sects, and a few had proved to be successful preachers. Catholics had created some innovative forms of female monasticism—even though the Ursulines had to accept enclosure in order to continue teaching, and the

Daughters of Charity had to avoid looking like nuns in order to carry out their mission in the secular world. Because Catholicism after the Council of Trent retained its celibate clergy and strengthened its hierarchical principles, only the fragmented and married Protestant clergy proved ultimately permeable to women—but in the Europe of 1700 the outlines of the female Protestant minister seem almost as dim as those of the social-activist nun.

"ECUMENICAL" EXPERIENCES OF EARLY MODERN EUROPEAN WOMEN

We have seen that Protestants and Catholics alike reinforced parental controls over their children's marriages in the age of Reformation and Counter-Reformation; several other developments affecting women's history during these centuries also spanned confessional differences. For instance, historians of popular culture like Peter Burke have stressed the importance of the "Triumph of Lent"—an attempt to control the free-spirited frivolity and sexual license traditionally associated with Carnival—in sixteenth-century Europe. This reform movement, supported by Protestants and Catholics alike, affected women most obviously in the drive to close public brothels in important cities, which began in Lutheran Germany between 1530 and 1560. In Catholic Europe, brothels disappeared last in the Mediterranean region; the walled prostitutes' quarter of Valencia, often described as the best-run place of its kind in Europe, survived until 1635. Catholics tolerated their brothels much longer than Protestants, but they also created special foundations for repentant prostitutes. In Spain, the first such refuge opened in 1587. Protestants devised no special institutions for former prostitutes, a fact that reveals the same lack of concern shown to former nuns.

In Reformation Europe, the state implemented religious changes and increasingly interfered in domestic affairs as well; most states were run by hereditary monarchs whose subjects genuinely believed in the divine right of kings—or of queens. Because only France and the Holy Roman Empire formally prohibited women from ruling, several women sovereigns governed early modern European states. A leading Protestant theologian, John Knox, published an angry protest in 1558 against the principle of women rulers, who to him represented the ultimate denial of Biblical authority and natural law. He intended to attack the ruling queen of England, Mary Tudor, a zealous Catholic. However, she died before his book appeared, leaving a Protestant woman successor (her half-sister Elizabeth I) who loathed Knox because of it. Nevertheless, Elizabeth helped drive another woman ruler, Mary Queen of Scots, from the throne of Knox's native land. Elizabeth I was not the only ruling queen to establish Protestantism; Jeanne d'Albret and her daughter Catherine de Bourbon built and maintained the only Protestant principality within France in Béarn between 1560 and 1620. On the other hand, the inability to make public her conversion to Catholicism, or to convince her Lutheran subjects to follow her, led Christina of Sweden to abdicate voluntarily in 1654, at age 28. When gender ideology intersected with divine-right monarchy and confessional politics, the results were unpredictable.

A French Catholic historian, Jean Delumeau, emphasizes the close similarities between Protestant and Catholic modes of religious instruction through catechisms and argues that both sixteenth-century reformations, Protestant and Catholic, abruptly ended a millenium of Christian attempts to assimilate paganism, replacing them with a massive attack on "idolatry" and "superstition."[4] Girls and boys were catechized together, primarily through oral instruction. The need to teach Christian doctrine, pioneered by Luther but quickly copied by Catholics, led to some extension of primary education in Reformation Europe. But whether consequence or coincidence, the same generations of Protestant and Catholic children who learned their catechisms became the adults who carried out the most massive witch-hunts in European history.

WITCH–HUNTS

Fear permeated sixteenth-century society and helped turn the ecumenical attack on "superstitions" into an assault on witches. Most reformers, Protestant and Catholic alike, saw the remnants of paganism as diabolical. They created a pedagogy of fear, specifically fear of the Devil. From the presses of Germany, the center both of European publishing and of witch-hunting in this age, came an amazing number of *teufelbücher*, or works about the Devil. In the widely used catechisms of Martin Luther and the Jesuit St. Peter Canisius, the Devil was mentioned more often than Jesus Christ.

Protestants and Catholics alike provided theological justifications and moral imperatives for the two most remarkable phenomena affecting sixteenth-century European women: the great witch hunts and the sudden rise in infanticide trials. Men of the educated and propertied classes, regardless of creed, projected their considerable fears of the Devil's power onto the "superstitious" magical activities of thousands of old women scattered across every part of Europe. At the same time, the governments of Protestant and Catholic Europe implemented a crusade against unwed mothers charged with infanticide.

The groups of defendants were totally unlike. Accused witches often resembled the wrinkled crones of legend, while infanticide defendants were young; one group lived in rural villages, the other mostly in towns. Together they included almost every type of lower-class woman. Most importantly, the parallel prosecutions of witchcraft and infanticide gave this age the sad distinction of executing remarkably large numbers of women; the various legal systems of Protestant and Catholic Europe carried out misogynistic campaigns of unique savagery. Those who waged these campaigns justified them not only by Christian beliefs about the powers of the Devil, but also by Renaissance attitudes about gender roles and very ancient assumptions about women's nature.

The doctrine of Satanic witchcraft, that evil spells or *maleficia* could only be carried out through a pact with the Devil, long preceded the Reformation. The various ideas stirred together in the cauldron of witch-beliefs during the sixteenth century can be traced back to antiquity and to European folklore. Although a few poor people had been executed for witchcraft centuries before the Reformation, some of the crucial developments linking witchcraft to women occurred only during the fifteenth century. The first illustration of a female witch riding on a broomstick (ca. 1440) appeared in a manuscript of a poem that ridiculed the belief in witchcraft, Martin le Franc's *Champion des Dames* ("Defender of Women").

The *Malleus Maleficarum*, a handbook published in 1486 by two German Dominicans, proved more influential. Unlike most other early commentators on the subject, these inquisitors had actually tried almost fifty people for witchcraft, all but two of them women; significantly, they made "witch" a feminine noun in the book's title.

The *Malleus* includes a lengthy discussion of why women were especially prone to witchcraft. Women, the authors claimed, are more credulous than men and therefore become more impressionable; moreover, "they have slippery tongues, and cannot conceal from other women anything they have learned by evil arts." Drawing on the traditional belief in women's greater sexual appetite, the *Malleus* argues that women's insatiable lust leads them to accept even the Devil as a lover. Because "a wicked woman is by her nature quicker to waver in the faith," women will more easily turn to Satan, "which is the root of witchcraft." The authors conclude that because of women's "defect of inordinate affections and passions, they search for, brood over, and inflict various vengeances, either by witchcraft or by some other means," and they offer a self-congratulatory postscript: "blessed be the Most High who has so far preserved the male sex from so great a crime."[5] Pre-Reformation gender ideology had created a lethal formula to apply to dangerous women, who must be coerced if their impulses could not be controlled.

It was only in the sixteenth century, however, that large numbers of women were put to death for this quasi-religious crime, in virtually every corner of Europe. We shall never know the exact number of witches executed throughout Christendom during the peak of the craze, which lasted in most places from approximately 1560 to 1670. Germany clearly provided the center of witch-hunting: the largest collection of information (assembled by the Nazi S.S.) records almost 30,000 such trials in the Holy Roman Empire during this period. Surviving evidence lists about 3,500 deaths for witchcraft in the southwestern corner of Germany (Baden-Württemberg); Switzerland probably had as many, with Austria not far behind. Allowing for the incompleteness of surviving legal sources, somewhere close to 100,000 people probably went on trial for this crime in Europe between 1500 and 1750. Perhaps a third of them died. Even within the Holy Roman Empire, many people tried for witchcraft escaped death; while in most other parts of western Europe (France, Great Britain, and Scandinavia) fewer than one-fourth of witch trials ended in death sentences.

Although rates of trials and executions varied across Europe, everywhere women formed the vast majority of victims (see Table 8.1).

Not all women were equally liable to be identified as witches. Certain personality types predominated, especially the quarrelsome scolds whom the Scots claimed possessed *smeddum* (a specifically female type of feistiness). Older women, especially widows, predominated among accused witches. Occasionally widows formed the majority of women tried for witchcraft; in several places they comprised about one-fourth to one-third of accused women witches. We know little about the ages of accused women witches, but most widows had probably passed childbearing age. In New England, where widows comprised only 10 percent of accused female witches, more than 75 percent of the principal women suspects were older than 45.

Most witches lived in small villages, surrounded by suspicious neighbors. For example, Jeanette Clerc, the wife of a peasant in a hamlet near Geneva, was arrested in 1539 because her neighbor's cow died suddenly after Jeanette had fed it some herbs. Other accusations followed: a horse went mad after she bit it; two oxen refused to work after she had quarrelled with their

TABLE 8.1
Witch Trials in Selected Regions

Place (Dates)	Women Tried	Men Tried	% Women
Baden-Württemberg (1560–1680)	1,050	238	82
Canton of Vaud (1580–1620)	624	325	66
Duchy of Luxemburg (1550–1680)	417	130	76
County of Namur (1510–1650)	337	29	92
County of Essex (1560–1675)	267	23	92
Scotland (1590–1680)	2,153	369	85
Friuli Inquisition (1595–1670)	96	14	87

SOURCES: E. W. Monter, *Witchcraft in France and Switzerland* (Ithaca: Cornell University Press, 1976), pp. 119–120; Christina Larner, *Enemies of God* (Baltimore: Johns Hopkins University Press, 1981), p. 91; Marie-Sylvie Dupont-Bouchat, "La répression de la sorcellerie dans le duché de Luxembourg aux XVIe et XVIIe siècles," in *Prophètes et sorciers dans les Pays-bas, XVIe–XVIIIe siècles* (Paris: Hachette, 1978), p. 127; Peter Kamber, "La chasse aux sorciers et aux sorcières dans le Pays de Vaud," in *Revue historique vaudoise* (1982), p. 33; and E. W. Monter, *Ritual, Myth and Magic in Early Modern Europe* (Brighton: Harvester Press, 1983), p. 68. Vaud, Essex and Scotland were Protestant governments; Namur, Friuli and Luxemburg were Catholic; and Baden-Württemberg figures include both Protestants and Catholics.

owner; she gave an apple to a girl who got sick afterwards; and she fed a meal to a neighbor who vomited things "as black as ink" afterwards. Most serious of all, she had supposedly killed one of her husband's relatives several years before by throwing some diabolical powder in his face.

Jeanette Clerc's trial, like those of most witches, was rapid. After four interrogations during two weeks, her judges had assembled a final and complete confession. In it, she explained that she had become a witch in a fit of rage after losing a new pair of shoes. She confessed all the *maleficia* with which her neighbors charged her, and gave a full account of her activities at the diabolical assemblies (called *synagogues*) that she attended. She had been recruited by a large black devil with a raucous voice, named Simon; he had promised her all the money she wanted, and gave her some coins that turned into oak leaves the next day. Later she rode to the synagogue on Simon's back. There she made love to her devil ("in the rear, like animals"); his semen felt ice-cold. She did homage by kissing him on his cold left arm; he then marked her by biting the right side of her face. She renounced God "in a loud voice, as she remembers well, as if she had done it today," and also the Virgin. In other ways the synagogue seemed pleasant, with singing and dancing to tambourine music; the food (apples, white bread, and wine) tasted good, except for the undercooked meat. When it ended, Simon gave her a small white stick and a box of grease in order to attend more synagogues: she rubbed the grease on the stick and repeated the magic formula, "White stick, black stick, carry me where you should; go, in the Devil's name, go!" The Republic of Geneva beheaded Jeanette Clerc and confiscated her property.

Witch-hunting persisted almost everywhere throughout Europe for more than a century after Jeanette Clerc's execution, during the zenith of both the Protestant and Catholic reformations. But confessional preference did not determine witch-hunting zeal. Both Protestants and Catholics helped to make Germany the center of the craze. The two nations that share the honor of ending their witch-trials soonest stood at opposite ends of the European spectrum in terms of both religion and society. The remarkably tolerant Calvinist government of Europe's first bourgeois state, the Dutch Republic, fought an eighty-year religious war against the remarkably intolerant Catholics of feudal Spain. Yet both states stopped their witch trials during the middle of this war, about a half-century sooner than such major cultural leaders as England and France. The Netherlands executed its last witch in 1597 and held no witch trials after 1610. The much-maligned Spanish Inquisition tried thousands of women for witchcraft and related forms of illicit magic, but gave only very mild punishments after executing eleven people for it at an *auto-de-fé* in 1610. The Spanish Inquisition refused to believe the German inquisitors who composed the *Malleus*, even if they "wrote about it as something they have seen and investigated themselves, for the cases are of such a nature that they may have been mistaken, as others have been." Extremely intolerant religious attitudes have not always led to zealous witch-hunting.

INFANTICIDE

In addition to witches, the governments of early modern Europe executed a second large group of women for the crime of infanticide. Prosecutors had a difficult time proving either charge by ordinary rules of evidence. Witchcraft was by definition occult, and, until relatively recent times, physicians could not distinguish a stillbirth from murder of a newborn child. For that very reason, extremely few women had been prosecuted for infanticide before the sixteenth century. France decreed new laws in 1556, and England in 1624, placing the burden of proof in cases of death of a newborn on the defendants, who were mostly mothers of illegitimate children. Because stillbirths among married women were not recorded, no control group exists to help determine how often defendants might actually have been guilty. But conviction rates were remarkably high; trials and executions for infanticide multiplied in the late sixteenth and seventeenth centuries, exactly when witch-hunting peaked in many parts of Europe.

Courts tried many fewer women for infanticide than for witchcraft, since relatively few early modern Europeans lived in towns, where most infanticide cases originated. But accusations of infanticide, unlike charges of witchcraft, were almost entirely confined to women defendants; it seems pertinent that the minority of male witches were accused of nearly all the same *maleficia* as women, except for magical murders of babies. Moreover, the women accused of infanticide stood a greater proportionate risk of execution than did the larger group of women accused of witchcraft. For instance, courts in the rural English county of Essex executed two-thirds of the 51 women accused of bastard infanticide between 1575 and 1650, but hanged only one-fourth of the 267 women accused of witchcraft from 1560 to 1670.

Major differences separated the women accused of infanticide from those charged with witchcraft. Accused witches were usually past menopause; infanticide defendants were not. Most accused witches had been married, whereas very few infanticide defendants had husbands. Apart from gender and relative poverty, women accused of infanticide and those charged with witchcraft had little in common. The general significance of both phenomena for the history of European women lies in the huge number of young and old women convicted and executed for these unprovable crimes during the centuries most heavily marked by the Protestant and Catholic reformations. Misogyny has taken many forms throughout history, but it has seldom provided legal rationales for taking the lives of so many thousands of women.

Three key developments combined and interacted to shape the male hysteria about witchcraft and infanticide in Reformation Europe. First and foremost, public institutions—state and church alike—were increasingly interfering in daily life. Throughout Protestant and Catholic Europe, the state enforced attendance at church; church officials preached obedience to the state; and both increasingly tried to regulate everyone's behavior. Ecclesiastical courts such as Catholic inquisitions or Calvinist consistories depended heavily on state enforcement of their policies; states like England or France relied on clergymen to provide records of baptisms or to proclaim government edicts from the pulpit.

Secondly, these increasingly active public authorities inhabited a fear-ridden world. Most Protestant and Catholic Europeans still peered at their neighbors from walled towns and fortified castles; Luther's greatest hymn begins, "A Mighty Fortress is our God." We cannot find many material reasons for such pervasive fears at this time; bubonic plague, the great killer of pre-industrial Europe, did most of its damage either before or after the age of reformations. The reformers of Protestant and Catholic Europe, determined to attack all forms of "superstition" (including, of course, witchcraft), reduced the influence of benevolent magic, like exorcisms or special prayers, but provided nothing to replace them. Modern science did not yet exist; official medicine often had no explanations (and worse, no effective remedies) for many illnesses. Under such conditions, Protestant and Catholic reformers imposed the "Triumph of Lent" on unwed mothers of stillborns, and made old women with deviant dreams into scapegoats for sixteenth-century Christianity's obsession with the Devil.

Finally, the patriarchal theories of late-Renaissance Europe played an important role in determining which groups of women became victims of these obsessions. Accused witches were disproportionately widows, while infanticide defendants were single women; both groups lived outside direct male supervision in this age of reinforced patriarchal nuclear families. Their "unnatural" position aroused suspicion and sometimes fear; neighborhood enmities did the rest.

Explanations of why witch-hunting and infanticide prosecutions flourished during the age of the Reformations seem easier to find than reasons for their gradual decline. One useful approach emphasizes the extent of violence in early modern Europe, in contrast to the "gentler" eighteenth and nineteenth centuries. During the age of reformation and afterwards, women, unlike men, rarely employed direct physical violence. Renaissance society believed that whenever female anger and need for revenge boiled over, women would resort to the *magical* violence of spells to harm the bodies or property of their enemies—particularly if they lacked male kin to wreak violence on their behalf.

However, among European men the level of physical violence declined during the seventeenth century, as many criminal-court records attest. The threat of magical violence from witchcraft diminished together with the reduced danger of physical aggression. Under both forms of violence lay a climate of fear; and men's fears of the Devil, the witch's famous partner, similarly declined during the later seventeenth century. Prosecutions for infanticide, unrelated to adult interpersonal violence and rarely influenced by fears of the Devil, abated somewhat later than prosecutions for witchcraft.

CONCLUSION

On balance, the factors which influenced women's history most decisively during the age of reformations, like the persistence of Renaissance gender ideology or the growth of state controls, were largely independent of religious differences. The powerful sectarian enthusiasms generated by the Protestant and Catholic reformations, working against such a background, produced short-term explosive results. But over the long term—balancing intentions against results, fears against hopes, the handmaidens of God against the slaves of the Devil—did they constitute a Reformation for women?

NOTES

1. The phrase is taken from Lawrence Stone's influential book, *The Family, Sex and Marriage in England, 1500–1800* (New York: Harper & Row, 1977).
2. Fullest discussion in Steven Ozment, *When Fathers Ruled: Family Life in Reformation Europe* (Cambridge, Mass.: Harvard University Press, 1983).
3. A. D. Wright, *The Counter-Reformation* (New York: St. Martin's Press, 1982), p. 47.
4. Jean Delumeau, *Catholicism between Luther and Voltaire* (London: Burns & Oates, 1977).
5. J. Sprenger and H. Kramer, *Malleus Maleficarum*, trans. M. Summers (London: Pushkin Press, 1928), Bk. I, Question 6 (pp. 41–47).

SUGGESTIONS FOR FURTHER READING

The largest easily available work, R. H. Bainton, *Women of the Reformation*, 3 vols. (Minneapolis, 1971–73), consists entirely of biographical sketches. A more valuable source collection is Joyce Irwin, ed., *Women in Radical Protestantism, 1525–1675* (New York, 1979). The best discussion of Protestantism's positive and negative features for women is Natalie Z. Davis, "City Women and Religious Change," in her *Society and Culture in Early Modern France* (Stanford, 1975), pp. 65–95. Valuable articles of narrower scope include Keith Thomas, "Women and the Civil War Sects," in *Past and Present*, 13 (1958); William Monter, "Women in Calvinist Geneva, 1550–1800," in *Signs*, 6 (1980), and "Women and the Italian Inquisitions," in M. B.

Rose, ed., *Changing Perspectives on Medieval and Renaissance Women* (Syracuse University Press, 1985).

A useful discussion of reinforced sixteenth-century patriarchy is Lawrence Stone, *The Family, Sex and Marriage in England, 1500–1800* (New York, 1977), as is Steven Ozment, *When Fathers Ruled: Family Life in Reformation Europe* (Cambridge, Mass., 1983). On divorce, see T. M. Safley, *Let No Man Put Asunder: The Control of Marriage in the German Southwest, 1550–1600* (Kirksville, Mo., 1984). On witchcraft, a much-studied topic, see Keith Thomas, *Religion and the Decline of Magic* (London, 1971); Christina Larner, *Enemies of God* (Baltimore, 1981); H. C. E. Midelfort, *Witch-Hunting in Southwestern Germany 1562–1684* (Stanford, 1972); E. W. Monter, *Witchcraft in France and Switzerland* (Ithaca, 1976); and Gustav Henningsen, *The Witches' Advocate: Basque Witchcraft and the Spanish Inquisition* (Reno, 1980). On infanticide, the best available study is N. E. H. Hull and Peter Hoffer, *Murdering Mothers: Infanticide in England and New England 1558–1803* (New York, 1981).

A general survey of the effects of the Catholic Reformation on women is badly needed. By far the best available book is Sister Mary Monica, *Angela Merici and Her Teaching Idea (1474–1540)* (New York, 1927); still useful is M. C. E. Chambers, *Life of Mary Ward*, 2 vols. (London, 1882). See also Pierre Coste, *Life and Works of St. Vincent de Paul*, 3 vols. (London, 1934–35), I, pp. 177–468.

A fifteenth-century woodcut shows a mother and daughter spinning. The father is probably working on his account book, as he is using counting stones, and his son is reading. Note that the mother is also rocking an infant in a cradle while she spins, thus teaching her daughter more than spinning. This title illustration from an instruction book for parents appeared in Bartholomaeus Metlinger's *Regiment der jungen Kinder* (Augsburg, Germany: Günther Zainer, 1473).

chapter 9

Spinning Out Capital: Women's Work in the Early Modern Economy

Merry E. Wiesner

We now recognize that industrialization did not suddenly replace traditional handicrafts pursued in the home. A prolonged period of development anticipated the Industrial Revolution. Whole new industries, more complex means of trade, and new definitions of work emerged. All these affected women's lives; particularly serious .effects stemmed from a definition of work which recognized wage as sole criterion. While many women worked for wages, all did unrewarded and increasingly unrecognized household labor. Whole sectors of the economy—domestic service, or spinning, or marketing second-hand goods—depended on a stratified sexual division of labor.

Merry Wiesner reveals the irony of women's marginality as workers given the essential services they performed for society in early modern times.

All societies draw distinctions between men's work and women's work. Cultural norms and prevailing values, as well as popular beliefs, all play a part in drawing those distinctions. Anthropologists have long recognized this, but historians have only recently turned to the study of the way the boundaries between women's work and men's change over time. The definition of women's work, what women did or did not do at a particular time, was affected not only by economic trends and technological development, but changes in values, ideologies and political structures. These economic and cultural factors have at times shifted or blurred the lines between men's and women's work; they have also determined what sorts of activities will be defined as 'work' and how that work will be valued. This essay explores women's work from about 1500 to 1700, a time when the European economy and prevailing ideologies were both changing rapidly.

WORK IN THE MIDDLE AGES

In the medieval economy, the household had been the basic unit of production. Peasant families in rural areas raised crops and animals for their own and their landlords' use, and traded their surpluses in a nearby village or city for the items they could not produce themselves. They also made simple items such as brooms and wooden implements and agricultural products like butter and cheese for sale at local markets. Urban households often included several servants, journeymen, and apprentices who worked and lived with a husband and wife and their children. All stages of production, from the purchase of raw materials and tools to the sale of the finished product, were carried out by members of the household. The goods produced were traded within the household's particular city or region. Tasks were not sharply divided by gender or status among members of the household, and both domestic and manufacturing tasks contributed to the success of the family enterprise. Even members of the household who were not family members, the servants, apprentices, and journeymen, stood to benefit from successful production and sales, for this generally brought more and better food and clothing, which formed the major part (if not all) of their wages.

During the thirteenth and fourteenth centuries, craft guilds were established in many cities to organize and regulate production, setting quality levels, terms of apprenticeship, and prices for goods which required a high degree of skill and training to produce. The guilds set standards for the finished product and limited competition between household workshops, but did not regulate what went on within a household.

There were some individuals in both the countryside and cities who worked for wages in the medieval economy, but they were often hired by a household and so were still part of an essentially family-based economy. Employed as servants, agricultural laborers, and pieceworkers, they were generally the poorest people in any community, and if they maintained an independent household, all family members had to work to assure survival.

THE GROWTH OF CAPITALISM

During the later Middle Ages, a new form of economic organization appeared in Western Europe—capitalism. There is great debate among economic historians as to exactly when, where, and why capitalism started, but there is general agreement that it began among merchants, who traded luxury goods like spices and silk in an international market and often made enormous profits. Their businesses often began as family firms, but the opportunity for profit attracted nonfamily investors, and the firms gradually grew larger and more complex. As they grew, more and more of the actual labor was carried out by individuals who were paid wages rather than being rewarded with a share of the profits. This division between capital and labor is a hallmark of capitalism, and this initial stage is generally termed "mercantile capitalism" because it involved merchants and their enterprises in commerce, banking, and trade.

Prosperous merchants throughout Europe gradually sought to expand their investments beyond commerce, and began to purchase raw materials, tools, and machinery, hiring workers to produce goods. They then sold these manufactured goods along with their other articles of trade in an international market, using the trading networks, systems of agents, and offices they had already developed. Merchants invested in manufacturing in some parts of Europe as early as the thirteenth century, particularly in cloth production in Florence and Flanders. They hired entire households to carry out one stage of production, such as spinning or weaving, sending out raw materials and often lending out the necessary tools; this is called the putting-out system or domestic industry. This putting-out system often employed rural households, and directly challenged traditional urban methods of production. The household thus remained the production unit, but it was paid wages solely for the labor of its members and had no share in the profits from production.

Some investors began to concentrate their capital in production, moving out of commerce. This is often viewed as a second stage of capitalism. It is generally termed "protoindustrialization" because workers remained in their own homes or in very small workshops; only much later, in the eighteenth and nineteenth centuries, would industrial capitalism bring workers together into large factories.

Along with the putting-out system, the growth of capitalism brought additional changes to the rural economy. As cities grew, people in the rural areas surrounding them often turned to market gardening, producing fruits, vegetables, and other crops for urban consumers. Because of this development, such a region no longer produced grain, relying instead on imported grain from eastern Europe, where the landed nobility were enserfing the peasants to secure a steady supply of labor for their vast estates. The growth of agricultural capitalism thus had the opposite effect in western and eastern Europe; it brought the decline of serfdom in the west and the simultaneous rise of serfdom in the east. Because of these differences in the rural economies, rural women's work varied throughout Europe, and included both agricultural and protoindustrial production.

The early modern period was thus transitional in economic terms, with traditional domestic production existing side by side with both mercantile and protoindustrial capitalism. The household was still the basic unit of production, but increasing numbers of households depended on wages to survive, wages which were determined by international market conditions along with local demand for a product. There were great regional differences in the level of economic development, however, and some isolated areas remained largely bound to traditional patterns of production and trade.

The rise of capitalism brought ideological as well as economic change. During the Middle Ages, work was defined as an activity performed to support and sustain one's self and one's family. Domestic and productive tasks were both considered work, and all women, except perhaps those from very wealthy noble families, could be called working women. With the development of capitalism, work was increasingly defined as an activity for which one was paid, which meant that domestic tasks and childrearing were not considered work unless they were done for wages. Women's unpaid domestic labor freed men for full-time wage labor but was no longer regarded as work. As a result the proportion of women who considered themselves working women and were considered as such by authorities shrank during the period as the definition of work changed, though women's actual activities changed very little.

There were other major ideological and political changes during the sixteenth and seventeenth centuries as well. This was the period of the Protestant and Catholic Reformations, which brought with them not only new ideas about theology and religion, but also different attitudes toward marriage and the family, public and private morality, and the value of certain occupations. It was the time of the rise of the nation state, when the rulers of western Europe began to depend on a professional army and bureaucracy instead of on feudal and kin ties and allegiances. Governments at all levels expanded the scope of their activities. City, state, and national governments took over many of the institutions and services that the Church or private charity had maintained and provided in the Middle Ages, such as orphanages, hospitals, infirmaries, and poor relief. As governments secularized these services, they often created a centralized system so that they could more easily control who was receiving care and charity. The administration of these services and other government functions became increasingly professionalized, as did certain private occupations such as physicians, apothecaries, lawyers, and appraisers.

Economic change affected the lives of women very differently than the lives of men of their same social and economic class. It did not affect all women equally, however. Women's experiences varied according to social class, economic status, and geographic region, factors which have traditionally been taken into account when examining men's history. It also varied according to age, marital status, family size, and life span, factors which have rarely been noticed until very recently in standard histories.

Economic change affected the kinds of work women performed, but there was also continuity. The majority of women and men in early modern Europe continued to work in agriculture; at least three-quarters of the population remained in the countryside. Even in the cities, most of the economy was still "precapitalist" and continued to operate in the same way it had for centuries. Some occupations, such as domestic service and selling at the public market, changed very little during the period.

It is especially important to emphasize continuity when looking at women's work, for even dramatic changes in the structure and organization of institutions and industries may not have been evident to the women working in them, who were often clustered in the lowest-skilled jobs. Whether an industry was organized capitalistically or by guilds, or whether a hospital was run by the church or the city, made little difference to the woman who spun wool or washed bedding. Women remained in these low-status positions because they often fit their work around the life-cycle of their families, moving in and out of various jobs as children were born and grew up, or as their husbands died and they remarried.

To analyze both change and continuity, I have chosen in this study to focus on women in the cities, principally because urban sources are clearer and begin earlier than rural ones. In many parts of Europe city governments began to keep records centuries before villages or states did.[1] A focus on the urban economy takes in the activities of many rural women, who were often the ones to sell agricultural products in the cities. Though urban residents travelled out into the countryside for the harvest, in general the cities offered a wider variety of occupations for both men and women.

DEMOGRAPHIC PATTERNS AND THE
LEGAL STATUS OF WOMEN

Another reason for a focus on cities in terms of women's history is that it appears women outnumbered men in the cities. This has been noted for late medieval and early modern cities by a number of authors, who have discovered that there were between 110 and 120 women for every 100 men in many cities.[2] Various explanations have been offered for this—men dying in the frequent wars and skirmishes, the large number of men in monasteries (who would not show up on city records), women living longer in cities as they did not have to perform physically taxing agricultural work, women moving into cities in search of opportunities for both employment and charity. These last two factors suggest that men would outnumber women in the rural areas, but this is difficult to document as there are almost no rural population counts which might indicate a preponderance of males in the countryside. Whatever the reasons, this skewed population balance continued into the early modern period, so there were a large number of urban women who could not make marriage their "career," even if they had wished.

Because of this preponderance of women in the cities, there were a large number of women who lived alone or in households headed by women. Many of these were widows, but a significant share were young women who had not yet married. On the average, both men and women in western Europe during this period married in their mid-twenties—at least in the urban areas for which we have records.[3] In many cultures men wait until this age to marry, and then generally marry women who are much younger, often in their early teens. Late marriage for women is quite unusual, and there are several possible reasons for this peculiar marriage pattern. Married couples generally set up their own households, rather than moving in with the parents of one spouse, which meant that the husband had to be finan- cially secure and the wife able to run a household, rather than relying on her mother or mother-in-law. Many guilds forbade apprentices and journeymen to marry, because they were supposed to live with the master-craftsman; on the other hand, the guilds required masters to be married, because two people were necessary to run a shop properly. Because the master's wife fed and clothed this large household, craftsmen often preferred to marry an adult women rather than an inexperienced teenager. The preponderance of women in the cities meant that middle- and upper-class women were expected to provide dowries to their husbands, and delaying marriage gave a family and the woman herself an opportunity to save that dowry. Even a poor woman was expected to bring something as dower to her marriage—linens, dishes, and bedding, for example—which she could afford to purchase only after many years as a maid or pieceworker. In an era before effective contraception, delaying the marriage of women was one way to keep family size smaller. For poorer families, fewer children meant fewer mouths to feed, and for wealthier families, fewer dowries for daughters or training and education for sons.

Whatever the reasons for this unusual western European marriage pattern, it resulted in a large number of unmarried women living in cities. Households comprised of widows and unmarried women often made up between one-quarter and one-third of all households in many cities; such were generally the poorest households, often too poor to pay any taxes.[4] Their "household" was not an entire house, but rather a rented room, cellar or attic that no one else wanted.

During the medieval period, city and religious authorities had seen the large number of poor women living independently as an economic problem, because they recognized that these women would have to support themselves or would require assistance. Grudgingly, authorities allowed such women to make or sell various simple items, and left some low-skilled occupations such as laundering open to them. As tax records indicate, women living independently rarely earned more than enough to survive. Widows were generally better off than nonwidows, because inheritance laws allowed a widow to keep at least her dowry and any property she had brought into the marriage, as well as a proportion of the property or assets acquired since the marriage. Despite this, the household income of a widow was generally much less than it had been when her husband was alive.

In the sixteenth century, civic and religious authorities began to regard women living independently in terms of morality as well as economics. Both Protestant and Catholic authorities became increasingly concerned with public order, propriety, decorum, and morality. In what is termed "The Triumph of Lent," the authorities of cities throughout Europe expanded sumptuary laws, which attempted to regulate morality by limiting expenditure on dress, restricting public dances and carnivals, and prohibiting gambling and prostitution. In this new mood, governments toughened laws against vagrants, because of what was perceived as an increase in "masterless" persons—wandering journeymen, servants between positions, mercenary soldiers and their campfollowers, "sturdy beggars," itinerant actors and musicians. Whether economic changes were actually causing an increase in people moving from town to town or from household to household is difficult to say, but the perception of an increase on the part of civic and church authorities was very strong.

Migrants were suspect not only because they might engage in criminal activity or become a drain on community charitable endowments, but also simply because they were not part of a household. In a world that appeared to them to becoming increasingly disorderly, authorities viewed the household as an institution of social control. Moreover, they felt that men as the heads of households were more effective than women at exerting that control. As these attitudes developed, authorities began to consider women who lived alone as "masterless," lumping them in with other suspect groups. In Germany and France, laws were passed that forbade unmarried women to move into cities, required widows to move in with one of their male children, and obliged unmarried women to move in with a male relative or employer.[5] In Protestant areas, as convents were closed the nuns were encouraged to marry or move back to their families, and in Catholic areas, unmarried women not living under strict cloister were increasingly suspect.

This hostility to unmarried women was further exacerbated by the Protestant emphasis on marriage as a woman's only "natural" vocation, the Catholic church's increased concern (in response to Luther and other critics) with immorality among clergy and laity, and the increased currency of certain popular and scholarly notions about women's nature and proper role. The "debate about women" that had begun in the late Middle Ages among churchmen and scholars, in which women's nature and character, virtues and vices were discussed and debated, had begun to make educated men increasingly view women as a distinct group.[6] Sweeping generalities about women's nature were made not only by moralists and preachers, but also by humanists and writers of popular satire. Many of these expressed or reinforced the notion that women suffered from uncontrollable sexuality and lacked the ability to reason. Women's sexual drive was thought to increase with age, so that older unmarried women were viewed as potential seductresses, willing to do anything to satisfy their sexual urges. This explained, in the eyes of authorities, their readiness to become witches, for the devil promised sexual satisfaction. It was also one of the reasons all unmarried women were viewed with such suspicion and hostility.

Despite all their attempts, the authorities never reduced the number of female-headed households; but the idea that women should be married or somehow under the control of a man had a profound and negative effect on women's work. Although it was recognized that some women would have to work for wages, authorities always viewed that work as a stopgap or temporary measure, until the women could attain, or return to, their "natural," married state. Thus the authorities were reluctant to establish policies that allowed women to practice any highly skilled occupation, and were suspicious when a woman made more than subsistence wages. A woman could work if she needed to support herself and her family, but she had no absolute right to work.

Although widows and unmarried women suffered from widespread suspicion, they did have distinct legal advantages over their married sisters. Women differed from men in their legal capacity to be witnesses, make wills, act as guardians for their own children, make contracts, and own, buy, and sell property. In addition, the legal status of an adult woman depended on whether she was unmarried, married, or widowed, whereas adult males were generally treated as a single legal category. The kinds of work each woman could do was thus determined to some degree by her marital status, although this varied from area to area depending on which city, state, or national law code applied.

Generally, in the early sixteenth century, an unmarried woman or widow had the right to dispose of her own property as she saw fit, using the assistance of a legal guardian only if she chose. When a woman married, she theoretically lost the right to make any contract without the agreement of her husband; she became, in French and English legal parlance, a *femme couverte*. However, married women who wanted to conduct business on a regular basis could appeal to the appropriate governing body for a lifting of this restriction. This was granted fairly easily, and the woman was allowed to act independently of her husband; such a woman was termed a *femme sole* in England and France, and a *Marktfrau* in Germany. City and state laws did not note that a husband's approval was necessary for a woman to become a *femme sole*, and often spelled out in great detail just which occupations were appropriate for women; a Nuremberg ordinance mentions "female tailors, shop-keepers, money-changers, inn-keepers, wine-handlers, and market women."[7] In addition to those women who received formal legal approval, urban records indicate that many other married women were carrying out business independently, although the law still allowed anyone to deny a loan or refuse to make a contract with a married woman.

Throughout the sixteenth and seventeenth centuries, because of the increasing emphasis on the household as an instrument of social control, and the rise in the belief that the proper household was headed by a man, the power of (male) guardians over widows and unmarried women in many areas increased. City councils often appointed these guardians, who then appeared in court on the woman's behalf, although, previously, women had often represented themselves in inheritance disputes and other cases. In a number of cities, the guardians decided whether a woman should retain control of her children if she remarried. Adult women were not yet the legal minors they would become by the Victorian period, but the laws grew decidedly more restrictive. Women's actual legal and economic activities, however, did not decrease proportionately—another example of the discrepancy between law codes and reality.

With this demographic and legal backdrop in mind, we can now examine women's work itself. In order to analyze the change or lack of change in various occupations, it will be useful to organize them by their function in the economy. Economists generally divide occupations into three basic types—production, sales, and service. This division derives from the organization of male labor in the modern economy, and is somewhat misleading for the early modern period, when, for example, individuals engaged in production often sold their own products. It is also somewhat artificial as a way of looking at women's work in any period, because women often participated in more than one type of occupation simultaneously and combined their productive and reproductive work. As long as we keep these limitations in mind, however, these occupational categories can still be useful, for the pattern of women's work in each of them differed significantly. In addition, the cultural values and economic reality which determined women's work operated somewhat differently in these three sectors.

PRODUCTION

In the early sixteenth century, craft guilds controlled most production in many parts of Europe. In some cities, each craft had a separate guild, and as many as 150 or 200 different guilds might exist in a single city; in others, many crafts joined together in a few large guilds. In some cities, crafts guilds had won representation on the city council by revolution or peaceful negotiation; in others, the city councils, made up of wealthy merchants and bankers, had blocked all such attempts. Whatever the guild structure or level of political participation, however, all guilds treated women with remarkable similarity.

Craft guilds were, with the exception of a few female guilds in Cologne, Paris, and Basel, male organizations, organized according to the male life cycle. A boy studied for a set number of years as an apprentice, became a journeyman and usually worked under a number of different masters to perfect his skills, then finally made a "masterpiece." If it was judged acceptable by the current masters (and if they felt there was enough business to allow another shop to open) the young man settled down and opened a shop. Because guild members recognized that a master could not run a shop on his own—there were journeymen and apprentices to feed and clothe, raw materials and tools to buy, and merchandise to sell in the shop or at the public market—many guilds required that masters be married. Enterprising journeymen also recognized that the easiest way to acquire a shop complete with tools and customers was to marry a master's widow.

Though men dominated the guild structure, a large number of women could be found working in most guild shops. Besides the master's wife, his daughters and maids often worked alongside his journeymen and apprentices. Most workshops were small and attached to the master craftsman's house, so that women could easily divide their time between domestic duties and work in the shop. Early modern households were not self-sufficient; it was often more economical to purchase bread or finished clothing so that the women of the household could spend their time in production. The clothing and furnishings in all but the wealthiest houses in this period were few, simple, and rarely cleaned, so that there was relatively little of what we consider housework. This changed during the early modern period, as the sheer amount of consumer goods increased and the use of table linens, bed linens, and more elaborate clothing spread to the households of master craftsmen. By the late seventeenth century, a master's wife spent more of her time at domestic tasks because there were more things to take care of, and community social standards required fancier dress and more elaborate meals and table settings.

A woman's work in the craft guilds depended not on her own skill or level of training, but on her relation to a guildmaster and her marital status. A guild master was free to employ his daughter however he wished in the workshop, and she could learn the trade alongside his apprentices. She did not receive any formal apprenticeship certificate, but her skills could make her a more attractive marriage partner. Some women even continued working in their fathers' shops after they married, if the other masters did not object. If the master did not have enough daughters, he might hire additional women as maids or pieceworkers, particularly for the preparation of raw material or for simple tasks such as polishing or wrapping.

The most important woman in any workshop was the master's wife. Wives were often responsible for selling the merchandise which their husbands made, collecting debts, and keeping the books. Wives, as well as husbands, were held responsible for the payment of fees and taxes and for the quality of the product. The wife also distributed salaries and food to the journeymen, which occasionally brought her into conflict with them, for they complained of being shortchanged and underfed. Wives continued to operate the shop in the absence of their husbands when they were away, whether at war, purchasing raw materials, or selling finished products.

After the master-craftsman died, his widow confronted restrictions on what she could do which increased over time. The earliest guild ordinances (thirteenth century) made no mention of widows at all, who seem to have had unrestricted rights to carry on the shop, at least as long as they remained unmarried. Even in the heaviest industries, like iron-making and roofing, master's widows ran the shop for as much as fifteen or twenty years after the deaths of their husbands. Although the widows could not take part in the guild's political functions or represent the guild in negotiations, they paid all guild fees, took part in festivities, and provided soldiers for the city's defense. Workshops run by widows often made up as much as 10 to 15 percent of those in a particular craft.[8]

Beginning in the mid-fifteenth century, however, the length of time during which a widow could continue operating the shop was limited. In some cases widows could only finish work which they had already begun; often they could take charge of the business only if there was a son who could inherit the shop. By the midsixteenth century, widows in most crafts could hire no new apprentices, journeymen or pieceworkers, and in some cases could not keep the ones they had. This often meant that a widow's workshop became so small that she could not produce enough to live on. Tax records from many cities indicate that over two-thirds of widows were in the poorest income category.[9]

One can easily understand why widows were allowed to carry on a business—the tools, equipment, and organization were already there, contracts had been made, the household still needed to be supported, and the widow was usually skilled enough to carry on the work. Why, then, would widows' work be restricted? Generally the guilds and city councils gave no explicit reasons, but occasionally records do give us a glimpse of both the official, publicly stated justifications and the underlying reasons.

For example, in Frankfurt in 1624 a stonemason's widow asked to be allowed to continue working, as she had a large amount of stone left which her husband had purchased just before his death. The stonemasons refused her request, giving a number of justifications. First, other widows would want the same rights. Second, her husband had been the most successful stonemason in town, and the others felt bitter that he had taken business away from them. If his widow continued the shop, there would be many disputes between her and the other masters. Third, her husband had vigorously opposed allowing widows to work, so why should they go against his wishes in the case of his own wife? Fourth, she could not oversee the shop well enough and work might not be done properly, "which would bring shame to her and to the whole guild." Fifth, she could not control the journeymen, who might marry and have children, and later abandon their families with no means of support, making them a drain on the public treasury. Sixth, because she could not control the journeymen, they would want to work in her shop and not for other masters.[10]

In the stonemasons' answer, we can perceive a number of factors emerging: petty jealousy toward the most successful mason, suspicion between masters and journeymen, feigned or real concern about the guild's quality standards, and flagrant attempts to win over the city council with the spectre of more public welfare charges. Some of the reasons are economic, motivated by the desire to limit the number of stonemasons competing for customers. Some of the reasons are moral or ideological, motivated by the feeling that a woman could not or should not have authority over men or final responsibility for production processes. These kinds of considerations undoubtedly figured in other decisions to limit widows' rights in many crafts.

Widows often objected to these limitations, and city records are full of requests that they be allowed to continue working. They rarely argued that they, as widows, had an absolute right to work, but stressed factors they felt would be effective with authorities: their poverty, old age, infirmity, and number of dependents; the authorities' Christian charity; the limited scope of their business. The widows who were successful were usually those who could make the most pitiful case. Although this accomplished what they wanted in the short run, in the long run it was harmful, because it reinforced the idea that woman's work was temporary, small-scale, no threat to the larger producers, and essentially something to keep one from needing public charity. By the seventeenth century, fewer and fewer requests were being granted, and widows tended to sell the shop immediately after the death of their husbands.

This restriction of widows' rights was tied in with several larger trends in production. In many cities, the craft guilds themselves were declining in power and wealth—in Central Europe with the general economic decline of the sixteenth century and in Western Europe with the rise of capitalist production. Investors hired rural households to establish a putting-out system, thus avoiding the controls established by urban guilds and producing cheaper products. Guild masters often felt threatened, and sharply limited the number of workshops by restricting widows or allowing a journeyman to become a master only if he could inherit an existing shop.

As the opportunities for journeymen to become masters decreased, most became permanent wage workers rather than masters-in-training and formed separate journeymen's guilds. These journeymen's guilds demanded the right to determine who would work in a shop and refused to work alongside those who did not have their approval. At first, this meant men who were born out of wedlock, but it gradually came to include women. Journeymen demanded that the masters' maids be excluded from all production-related tasks, and then that his wife and daughters be excluded as well. They thus assured themselves of more workplaces, and preserved a shred of their former dignity by sharply differentiating their work from "women's work." They also achieved a symbolic victory over the master. The master may have determined their hours and wages, but the journeymen kept his female dependents out of the shop. In addition, the journeymen made sure they would never have to take orders or receive their wages from a woman.

As journeymen fought against female labor in the shops, they also demanded the right to marry, for they often no longer lived in the master's household. Their disapproval of women working in a craft shop extended even to their own wives and daughters, and they never requested that their wives be allowed to join them in their trade. Because a journeyman's low wages could not support a family, his wife and daughters also had to work but were relegated to lower-paying domestic service, sales, or unskilled labor. Thus the journeymen's sentiment that working next to any woman was somehow dishonorable worked against their own economic interests, but was still fervently proclaimed.

As the guilds restricted opportunities for female employment, women turned to crafts which the guilds had never regulated or to employment in the new capitalist industries. They produced cheap and simple items such as soap, candles, thimbles, brooms, brushes, needles and pins, combs, and wooden bowls and spoons. They often made them as a secondary occupation, after working in the fields near the city or as laundresses or porters, or during winter when there was less agricultural or domestic work available. Because such products required little training, produced a meager income, and could be made by one woman acting alone, guilds and city authorities rarely objected. In fact, city officials often viewed such labor as a preferable alternative to poor relief, and encouraged women to work rather than relying on public or private charity. This is evident in the official attitude toward seamstressing, for city councils often set up small endowments to provide poor girls with training in seamstressing. City orphanages had a seamstresses as part of the staff, responsible for teaching as well as sewing.

Domestic industry, particularly cloth production, provided a more significant source of employment for both rural and urban women. In some cities, craft guilds controlled cloth production and gradually excluded women from most weavers', drapers', tailors', and cloth-cutters' guilds. The guilds generally allowed women to continue producing cheaper cloth made specifically for women's clothing, such as veils. Guilds in a few cities allowed only married women or widows to weave veils as they attempted to prevent unmarried women from living independently. In cities such as Florence, where weavers were not an independent guild but were hired by capitalist investors, women as well as men wove, because weaving did not bring high status or financial prosperity.[11] In the cloth industry, organizational rather than technological factors determined the sexual division of labor. Women carried out the stages of production that could be carried out in the home, required little or no assistance, and did not have a public or political function attached to them. In some cities, this included weaving; in those, such as Hamburg, that had a strong weaver's guild, this did not. The weaving industry presents another instance in which the political power of a guild affected women's labor.

The initial stages of cloth production, carding the wool (to produce straight fibers) and spinning, provided ever-increasing employment for women. Early modern techniques of production necessitated at least twenty carders and spinners per weaver, whether he or she was an independent guild master or hired by a merchant investor. Each weaver got his or her thread from a variety of spinners. Some of it was spun by female servants who lived in the employer's household; some of it by pieceworkers who worked but did not live in the weaver's house; some of it by pieceworkers spinning in their own homes, using wool provided by the weaver or investor; and some was purchased at the public market from urban or rural spinners who bought their own wool.

Authorities regarded spinning as the perfect female occupation because it required little capital investment or training and could be easily worked around family responsibilities—taken up and put down frequently with no harm done to the work. City councils expected women to keep spinning when in jail for various crimes, after the rest of their household had been sold to pay off debts, or, if they were prostitutes, between customers. Even wealthy or highly educated women were expected to spin; when a young woman who could speak and write Latin, Greek, and Hebrew was presented to James I of England his first question was "But can she spin?"[12] In Norwich, an eighty-year old widow, "a lame woman of one hand," still spun with her good hand, while in Memmingen a suicidal woman was to be chained in her hospital bed "in a way that she can still spin."[13] The Strasbourg city council was offered the prospect of a young woman "with no hands and only one foot, but who can still do all sorts of handwork, like spinning"; the man who found her wanted to show her to the public, and the council agreed, allowing him to charge a penny an onlooker.[14]

As more and more women turned to spinning, wages were held down because the field was overcrowded, a phenomenon economists have discovered in many female occupations in the twentieth century. Spinners could not support a family on their wages, or in some cases even support themselves; as a woman in Frankfurt said, "What little I make at spinning will not provide enough even for my bread."[15] The growth of the putting-out system offered urban and rural women more jobs, but jobs with low pay, little security, and low status.

In production, therefore, the period saw a gradual proletarianization of women's work. In the early sixteenth century though men had hegemony over the public activities of the guilds, many women fulfilled essential functions in household workshops. The status of such women was recognized by the community, as was their authority over journeymen and apprentices as well as maids and children. Because this authority was not politically institutionalized, however, economic changes, combined with the rise of the sentiment that it was inappropriate for women to give orders to men, eroded women's position. By the late seventeenth century, many masters' wives and widows no longer took an active role in production, but concentrated their energies on domestic tasks. The wives of merchant capitalists rarely assisted their husbands in business, spending their time instead directing larger household staffs. The women who worked did so as wage laborers with much lower wages than men, and no supervisory authority. Of course, this proletarianization was also happening to most male workers, as we have seen in the case of the journeymen, but at least a few men had opportunities to increase their wealth, power, and prestige through business and investments, opportunities not available to any woman.

SALES

The market place stood at the center of economic life within any early modern city. Whether goods came from far away or close to home, they were usually bought, sold, or traded at the market, often a large open square in front of the cathedral or major church. Women conducted most of the business that went on at this market; they handled almost all retail distribution of food, used clothing, household articles, and liquor—things which made up the major share of most family budgets. In addition, the market place served as a gathering place for women, who were the majority of customers as well as vendors; men exchanged news, information and opinions in taverns, while women did this at the market place, at church, and at neighborhood wells.

The sales sector of the early modern economy ranged across a wide spectrum in terms of wealth and prestige, from itinerant vendors and hawkers at the low end to major merchants with international trading networks at the top. Few women could amass the capital necessary for long-distance trade, or be absent from household and family for the time required, so women predominated on the lower end of the spectrum and men on the upper. Cities began to use merchants as ambassadors, envoys, and representatives, roles considered inappropriate for women.[16] As business procedures became more complex, major merchants relied more on formally trained accountants and bookkeepers with experience in double-entry bookkeeping, preparing contracts, and drawing up insurance agreements. Because women were excluded from such training, the wives and daughters of major traders retreated from an active role in the business.

In many ways, this was no different from the situation in the Middle Ages, however; although there were a few women who travelled and traded all over Europe, the important merchants' guilds and trading companies had always been male organizations. Most women in sales, whether in 1300, 1500, or 1700, were retail distributors who sold from a basket they carried, a small stand at the marketplace, or a small shop bordering the market. City officials paid a great deal of attention to these women and what they sold, as they recognized the importance to their citizens of pure products, fair weights and measures, just prices and business practices, and legitimately obtained goods.

The poorest women were those who sold small items they had made or gathered, such as pretzels, nuts, wooden implements, cookies, candles, herbs, lace, and firewood. City councils often gave poor widows or other needy women special permission to sell such things so they would not need public charity; officials clearly saw this as an alternative to poor relief.

Women who had permanent stands might be slightly better off. Many of them sold fruits and vegetables, occasionally the products of their own gardens, but more often purchased from local farmers. Female peasants often brought their own produce into the city, and sold it along with eggs, cheese, and butter. City governments regulated prices, hours, and the variety of produce each woman could offer. They allowed each women only one stand, because they wanted to prevent monopolies and keep a large number of women off charity. In the late sixteenth century, some cities also tried to limit stands to widows, to prevent "young female persons who could easily do some other kind of work, like being a maid" from selling.[17] This is yet another example of the authorities' dislike of young women working—and thus perhaps living—independent of the household.

Female vendors continually broke restrictions and ignored regulations. They raised prices, withheld produce from the market in order to force up the price, and forced customers to buy less desirable merchandise before they could buy what they wanted. They sold house to house rather than at the market, a practice authorities disliked because it was hard to control and provided a good opportunity for selling stolen merchandise.

One such vendor, a woman named Anna Weyland, appeared before the Strasbourg city council many times over a thirty-year period. She was first charged in 1573 with illegally selling herring, but used an ongoing dispute between the city council and the fishers' guild to obtain the council's permission to continue selling. A short time later the fishers' guild complained that she refused to sell herring to people unless they also bought dried cod from her; they also complained that she bought her herring outside the city instead of at the public fish market, then sold it below the established price. She got into the candle business the same year, and was immediately charged with selling candles for less than the official price and with a number of other infractions of the candle ordinance. She answered she "would not obey any ordinance, no matter what in God's name the council made for an ordinance." At that the council ordered her to follow the ordinance and especially not to use children to sell candles illegally. If she spoke like that again the council threatened that she would be "pinched with glowing tongs and if she works (illegally) she will be thrown in the water."

Those threats apparently worked for a while, for she did not come before the council again for six years. At that point, she was charged with having candles that were underweight, but when the city inspectors checked them they were found to be all right. The council did not trust her, however, and decided "that the inspectors should watch her and send unknown people to her to buy candles, to see if we can catch her hand in the sack (so to speak)." This was done, and the candles were found to be too light. Attempting to anticipate all possible excuses, the council next ordered all her scales and weights to be checked secretly, and candles bought again "so that she can be caught in the act." Her scales and weights were found to be accurate, and the candles too light again.

Both she and her husband were ordered to appear before the council, but she pleaded some kind of illness, and he appeared alone. Despite his pleading, the council ordered him to shut the shop, after selling the things he had on hand already. His wife was to do nothing, "neither buying or selling, changing money or anything else that has to do with the business" and was not even to let herself be found in the shop. He promised "by the grace of God" never to do anything wrong again.

This time the promise lasted two years. In 1582 Anna Weyland was selling Dutch cheese illegally (she simply switched products whenever she was forbidden to sell something). This time the council sent out a representative to order her to stop or she would be banished—she had never yet come before the council to answer any of the charges against her. This was effective, for she never sold anything again, although she did ask for permission to do so in 1605, twenty-three years later. Still she was forbidden "to sell anything at the public market." Nearly a quarter century of good behavior was not enough to make the council forget all the trouble she had caused.[18]

Wives and husbands often shared in food sales. Butchers, bakers, fishmongers, game handlers, and poultry dealers generally had strong guilds, but, unlike the manufacturing guilds, they did not feel the competition of capitalist production or pressure by journeymen. Masters' wives therefore remained important in the distribution of products, particularly as their husbands needed to be out of the city fishing or hunting—or in the case of bakers, busy at their ovens—and so could not do any selling. Masters' wives, widows, and other women also made sausage, prepared tripe, pickled meat, smoked game, and salted fish—all domestic processes.

Women produced and distributed all types of alcoholic beverages. In both cities and villages, female brewers made beer and ran small taverns to distribute their beverage. Apparently, brewers were also in the money-lending business to a small degree, for they incurred debts not only for beer, but for loans of money. Female brewers in Munich also took care of women in childbed, nursing them during the delivery with plenty of beer (this was felt to increase a mother's milk supply and help her quickly regain her strength). Women made and sold mead and hard cider, and when the process of distilling was discovered in the midsixteenth century, distilled and sold brandy. They received licenses to operate taverns and inns and ran small sleeping houses to accommodate poor people and students who could not pay normal inn prices.

The wealthiest and most powerful saleswomen were those who sold used merchandise of all types along with other small items such as dishes and pots. They received their merchandise from citizens who needed money, thus serving as pawnbrokers. During the sixteenth century, such women also served as appraisers, and sold the merchandise they had appraised if there were no heirs or cash was needed to pay back creditors. City councils required them to put up a certain amount of money as security, and investigated an applicant's reputation before giving her a license, because market women were often suspected of being receivers of stolen merchandise.

These market women appeared frequently in court in disputes with various craft guilds, who accused them of selling new merchandise or fixing prices. In these conflicts the women used a wide variety of arguments and tactics to win their cases. They exploited rivalries and jealousies between guilds, often selling a commodity or product that two different guilds felt they had the sole right to, then turning the two guilds against each other when the case came up. The market women used conflicts between the city council and the craft guilds, turning to the council for protection from overzealous guild masters. These saleswomen used geographical conflicts within the city, for instance, selling from a place where selling was not allowed while knowing that the residents in that area would not complain—or would even defend them—because the residents wanted a market in that part of the city. As a last resort, they pleaded helplessness and incompetence, arguing that they could do nothing else and that their business was so small they couldn't possibly be hurting anyone by it, which may have been accurate, but promoted negative ideas about the nature and value of women's work.

Their businesses may have been small, but these women were far from helpless or reticent. Not only did they quickly bring anyone to court whom they felt was intruding on their territory, but they were also very frequently involved in slander and defamation cases. They called other women and men names—asshole, whore, and thief were the most common—and then refused to apologize until the case had gone all the way to the city's highest court. Even then, the woman's husband often came in first, pleading that she was "only an irrational woman, who lets talk flow so freely and unguardedly out of her mouth without thinking about it": not until a fine was set did the woman herself come in, and then simply to ask that the fine be reduced.[19] In one case in Strasbourg, only after three weeks in prison on bread and water did the woman apologize, and agree to mutter the formulaic "I know nothing but good and honor about this person."[20]

As did the midwives, these market women developed a strong work identity and described themselves first as "market women" rather than wives or widows; they often played a significant role in urban disturbances from the iconoclastic riots associated with the Protestant Reformation to the French Revolution.

SERVICES

The broad range of occupations which may be termed 'services' provided the most employment for women in the early modern period, as they do today. Part of the explanation for women's relative ease in finding employment in this area, whether in the sixteenth century or the twentieth, is that many of these occupations are considered stereotypically female or "natural" for women. They were and are often viewed as extensions of a woman's function and work in the home—cooking, cleaning, childcare, nursing the sick, and care for the elderly. Such occupations often required little or no specialized training, so women could start and stop frequently, work only when financially pressed, or work part-time if they had a family to care for. Because of this flexibility and fluidity, women working in the service sector were (and are) often underpaid and rarely organized or protested to get higher wages or salaries.

A large number of women worked in health care, both in institutions, such as hospitals, pest-houses, infirmaries, and orphanages, and as independent practitioners, such as midwives, wetnurses, and healers. During the early modern period, the administrations of most cities, both Protestant and Catholic, took over the operation of hospitals, infirmaries, and orphanages from the church or established new institutions for care of the sick, elderly, and infirm. As the authorities secularized these institutions, they often centralized them, setting up one major hospital to replace a number of smaller care centers. The city councils or officials appointed by them hired the staff and set forth the responsibilities and duties of each person.

These new institutions employed women in a variety of occupations, from administrative and medical to cooking and janitorial. The hospital mistress, or keeper, as she was occasionally called, was responsible for the physical needs of the hospital and patients. She made all purchases, occasionally including land for the hospital's endowments, and kept records of all income and expenditures. She oversaw the kitchen, ordered special diets for those too ill to eat regular food, and distributed excess food to the poor. Along with administrative functions, the hospital mistress—or mistresses, as in large institutions this job was divided among several women—also fulfilled medical and religious functions. She examined incoming patients and then visited them on a weekly basis, making sure they were ill enough to warrant being in the hospital. She led the patients in prayer and prayed for those who were dying.

Like male employees, female hospital personnel, no matter what their position, had to swear an oath of loyalty and agree to follow all directives laid out for the day-to-day operation of the institution. The city councils envisioned the hospital as a family, led by the hospital mistress who was to treat the patients "as a mother would her children" and do everything "that is appropriate for women to do." The women who assisted her, nurses, cooks, laundresses and children's maids, were to treat each other as "true and loving sisters."[21] This family imagery meant that such women, even though they had a wide range of responsibilities, were not considered professionals, and were therefore poorly paid, often receiving little more than board and room.

The hospitals were for the chronically ill, the elderly, expectant mothers, the handicapped, foundling children, and mentally retarded or psychologically disturbed children and adults. Those with contagious diseases, such as the plague, leprosy, or smallpox, were consigned to small pest-houses outside the city. The pest-houses and plague hospitals also employed women, usually on a short-term basis when an epidemic swept through an area. Very little could be done for such patients except to keep them fed and clean; we can get an idea of the low level of early modern medical knowledge from the instructions given to women to simply air out the sheets and clothing of patients who had died, so that they could be used as bandages for those coming in.

The city orphanages were modelled after the family as well, with a married couple in charge. The "orphan mother" taught the girls to spin, cook, and care for laundry; purchased food and clothing; oversaw servants; and took care of illnesses. She was responsible for the children's spiritual, as well as material, well-being, and instructed them in prayer. The orphanage did not admit very young children, who were given to wet nurses living in the city or in the surrounding villages. Wet-nursing provided employment for women whose own infants made other occupation difficult, and evoked no negative comments during the period, though it would come under increasing attack in the eighteenth century.

Midwifery was the most important occupation open to women. Until the eighteenth century, very few male doctors or accoucheurs worked in obstetrics and gynecology; midwives handled all births, from those of the very poor to those of the nobility. City councils recognized the importance of midwives, and paid them an annual salary to take care of poor women, granted them allotments of grain or wood, and encouraged trained midwives to move into the city. Individuals who could afford it also paid the midwife for her services, her fees varying with the social class of the mother. In the fifteenth century, city councils established organized systems of midwives, appointing upper-class women to oversee the midwives, and, in conjunction with city doctors, to examine and license prospective midwives. Midwifery is the one field in which there was an organized hierarchy of women similar to that of men in the craft guilds or the city government. This hierarchy was not called a guild, and was less independent of city authorities than the craft guilds, who wrote their own ordinances and set limits on their own membership; in many ways however, the hierarchy operated as a guild, particularly in the training and disciplining of midwives.

Midwives learned their skill through apprenticeship. They accompanied experienced midwives to births for a period of years, then took an examination with questions ranging from how to handle a breech birth to proper diets for newborns. After passing the examination, the midwife took an oath and received a midwife's license. These oaths illustrate a wide variety of functions. Besides delivering babies, the midwife was to instruct new mothers in child care, perform emergency baptisms if she felt the child might die, and report all illegitimate children and try to discover the identity of the father "during the pains of birth."[22] She swore not to perform abortions, use implements to speed the birth, or repeat superstitions. In the eighteenth century, male accoucheurs and "man-midwives" slandered female midwives as bungling, slovenly, superstitious, and inept, but earlier, in the sixteenth and seventeenth centuries, authorities held them in high regard. City councils often called upon midwives to give opinions in legal cases of infanticide and abortion and examine women charged with fornication or female prisoners who claimed to be pregnant in the hope of delaying their corporal punishment or execution. The midwives participated in the municipal welfare system, handing out food and clothing to needy women and serving as medical assistants during epidemics. More than women in any other occupation, they defended their rights against outsiders. Their testimony in court shows a strong sense of work identity, for they always proudly note that they are midwives when appearing in court, making an appeal, or acting in any other legal or public capacity.

Women, then, faced no opposition when working in hospitals or similar "domestic" institutions. No tracts declared them unfit or too delicate to care for even the most horribly afflicted patients. There was opposition to women in medicine during the period, but this centered around their treatment of people who were not in hospitals. Physicians, barber-surgeons, and apothecaries claimed this was their province alone.

Until the late fifteenth century, women as well as men had been listed as physicians on the citizens' lists of many communities. From that time on, however, that title was increasingly given only to men who had received theoretical medical training at a university, a path which was closed to women. As physicians became more clearly "professional," barber-surgeons and apothecaries who had completed formal apprenticeship attempted to identify themselves as also somehow professional. They drew increasingly sharp lines between those who had received formal training and those who simply practiced on their own. Gradually, as these men convinced city and state governments to forbid "women and other untrained people" to practice medicine, female physicians and barber-surgeons disappeared from official records.[23] Some women received permission to handle minor external problems, like eye infections, skin diseases, and boils, if they promised to charge only small fees and not to advertise. Even this was too much for some barber-surgeons, who complained that the status of their profession was irreparably damaged if any women could perform the same operations they did. Some men hinted that the women's skills must be diabolical in origin, for God would certainly never bestow medical talents on a woman.[24]

Professionalization also affected other occupations. Women had long served as appraisers, for many communities required an inventory when a spouse died or an estate was being divided. Appraisers listed the value of everything from fields and vineyards down to the last dishtowel, a procedure which required extensive knowledge of merchandise and prices. During the sixteenth century, however, cities began to require more formal legal language, which made it difficult for women with little formal education to write out an acceptable inventory. The testimony of a male appraiser was increasingly viewed as more credible because female appraisers were held to be more likely to take bribes. During the late sixteenth century, the appraisers were made elected city officials, which ended the chances for women in the field.

In most cities women could be found in several other service occupations —running small primary schools, overseeing charities, inspecting milk, grain, or vegetables, serving as gatekeepers and toll-collectors. Such positions were poorly paid, and city governments often rewarded needy widows with them to keep the women from depending on charity, much as they allowed poor women to bake pretzels or sew. Women worked alongside men as day laborers in construction and other types of heavy labor, often traveling to rural areas during harvest time, where their wages for harvesting, picking grapes or gleaning were set at one-half those of adult males.[25]

In the early sixteenth century, all major cities had public baths, with women serving as bath attendants, washing the customers' hair and bodies, trimming nails, and beating them with branches to improve circulation. Such women were often specifically designated as "rubbers," "scratchers," or "beaters." During the sixteenth century, public baths went out of style, and respectable people no longer celebrated weddings, christenings, and business agreements with a group bath as they had in the Middle Ages. During the same period, much of Europe was deforested to provide wood for ships and military equipment, leading to a dramatic increase in the price of firewood and making baths too expensive for journeymen and wage laborers. The increasing concern with public morality and decorum led city councils to prohibit mixed-sex bathing, which combined with higher prices to force most public baths to close.

This same concern for public morality also led to a closing of municipal brothels in the sixteenth century. During the Middle Ages, most large cities and many smaller ones had opened one or more municipal brothels, hiring a brothel manager and prostitutes, and passing regulations concerning the women and their customers. Municipal authorities protected the women from violence and overexploitation, and regarded prostitution as simply a necessary service for journeymen and out-of-town visitors. Such attitudes changed in the sixteenth century, and officials increasingly required prostitutes to wear distinctive clothing and prohibited them from appearing in public.[26] Eventually the municipal brothels were closed. Concern for "public decency" and the spread of syphilis were given as the reason for this action. Illicit prostitution continued, but the women involved were prosecuted rather than protected.

Domestic service was the longest single employer of women. About 15 to 20 percent of the population of most cities was made up of domestic servants; the larger commercial and manufacturing centers had a higher percentage of servants than the smaller cities whose economies were more dependent upon agriculture.[27] During the Middle Ages, many servants had been employed in noble households, and men as well as women cooked, served at the table and did other domestic tasks; these were simply part of their duties as household retainers, regardless of gender. Gradually, servants' duties were increasingly specialized and divided by gender, with men and boys becoming responsible for the stables and grounds and women and girls for the kitchen and interior household. By the beginning of the early modern period, bourgeois urban households employed the majority of servants in urban areas; since such employers rarely had extensive grounds or stables, they hired more women than men for the indoor domestic tasks that had come to be seen as female. Both women and men continued to be hired as agricultural servants in rural areas, but their duties were also increasingly defined by gender, with women taking care of the household and animals, and men performing more, though not all, of the field work.[28]

Service offered young women a chance to earn small dowries that enabled them to marry. In fact, many maids were not paid at all until the end of a set period of service, with the understanding that their wages were specifically to provide a dowry. For other women, service became a career. These women might work their way up in large households from goose-girl to children's maid to serving maid to cook. More typically, they remained with a family as its single servant for twenty, thirty, or forty years. Their wages were low, and inventories taken at the deaths of maids indicate they usually owned no more than the clothes in which they were buried. For many women, however, service was the only type of employment possible until they were married, or after the death of a husband left them penniless.

Because of the large numbers of people involved, some cities, such as Nuremberg and Munich, organized the hiring of servants through a system of licensed employment agents who found jobs for a girl (or boy) from the countryside. The agents were paid both by the servant and the employer and followed certain rules: they could not take gifts or bribes, let servants change positions more than twice a year, house any servants themselves, or store any servants' trunks (which might contain stolen goods). Most of the employment agents were the wives or widows of craftsmen or minor officials, and operated from a small stand at the marketplace or out of their own homes, with a sign hung out in front just like any other occupation.

City officials also tried to regulate the conduct, salaries, and social activities of servants once they were hired. This meant admonishing servants not to leave positions without just cause, stay in public inns or live independently between positions. Like unmarried women, both male and female servants were subjected to the hostility toward "masterless" persons. Those who married and tried to set up their own households could be banished, as could those who tried to live on their own as day laborers. They were to remain dependents, under the control of a preferably male head of a household. Wages were strictly limited, because servants in some areas were charged with causing the general inflation; the authorities in Stuttgart were horrified that "these servants now demand a salary along with room and board."[29]

In the late sixteenth and seventeenth century, regulations became harsher and more hostile to servants, and reflect a growing distrust between employer and servant. Servants who spoke against their masters or pretended to be ill were to be strictly punished, as were those who exhibited general "disobedience and pride." Sumptuary laws established clear class distinctions, with servants prohibited from wearing fancy clothing or jewelry even if this was a gift from an employer.

These ordinances paint a rather grim picture, but private household journals and accounts give a more peaceful view of employer/employee relations. Wet nurses and maids were made special guardians for children, and sometimes received substantial sums at the death of a master or mistress. Wealthy people often set up funds to provide small dowries or hope chests for maids who left their service to get married. Former servants often married late, had more freedom in choosing their own spouses, and played a more active role in courtship and marriage.

As opportunities for women to work in other occupations decreased, those in domestic service remained the same or increased as domestic tasks became feminized, larger household staffs became more fashionable, and maids were used for industrial tasks such as spinning. Men were more free to move in search of employment and opportunities, including those to be found in Europe's new overseas empires, while women had to look closer to home. By the seventeenth century, a greater percentage of the women who worked outside their own homes worked as a servant in someone else's.

CONCLUSION

In all three areas of the economy there was sharper differentiation in the early modern period between women's work and men's work. Occupations which required university education or formal training were closed to women, as they could not attend universities or humanist academies, or participate in most apprenticeship programs. Women rarely controlled enough financial resources to enter occupations which required large initial capital outlay, and social norms kept them from occupations with political functions. Family responsibilities prevented them from entering occupations which required extensive travelling. Unfortunately, it was exactly the occupations with formal education, political functions, capital investment, or international connections, such as physicians, merchants, bankers, lawyers, government officials, and overseas traders, that were gaining in wealth, power, and prestige.

This increasing separation of men's and women's work was an outgrowth of several major economic and political changes: from household production organized by guilds to capitalist domestic industry; from a definition of work based on use to one based on monetary exchange; from loose training requirements to rigid professionalization; from political power based on feudal family ties to centralized states. It was also a product of the increased concern for public order, propriety, and decorum and the emphasis on male-headed households as instruments of social control. City authorities kept women out of occupations in which they would supervise men, work extensively out in public, or live independently. For ideological reasons, domestic service became the perfect female employment, though the economy still required women's labor in production and sales.

Increasingly, women worked at jobs which required few tools, minimal formal training, and no supervisory responsibilities—in short, jobs which were poorly paid and could be done part-time. Women changed occupations much more frequently than men, and moved in and out of the labor force as their individual and family needs changed, fitting their work around the life cycle of their families. As they were restricted to fewer occupations, competition among them for workplaces increased and wages were held down.

Many men also worked in similar low-skill, low-paid occupations, but they increasingly felt a need to differentiate their work from "women's work." They increased training or investment requirements, and in some cases prohibited women from performing certain tasks. Men excluded women entirely from a shop or drew an artificial line between men's work and women's work down the middle of a workshop, leaving to women the tasks that were more domestic and reserving the productive tasks to themselves. As a result domestic tasks were devalued not only because they were not rewarded financially, but also because they were associated with women.

Women themselves often devalued their own work when appealing to authorities for the right to produce or sell. Recognizing that such arguments would be successful, they stressed that their work was temporary, small-scale, a stopgap, no threat to anyone, and essentially a substitute for poor relief. Unfortunately, authorities began to regard these qualities as intrinsic to all women's work, making it inherently inferior to men's work.

The line between men's and women's work gradually grew into a gulf, and eventually affected the definition of work itself. According to the German industrial code of 1869, women who spun, washed, ironed or knitted in their own homes were not considered workers (and thus not eligible for pensions), even though they worked for wages, while male shoemakers or tailors who worked in their own homes were.[30] The devaluation of women's work begun in the early modern period was complete; nothing a woman did, or at least nothing she did within her own home, was truly work.

NOTES

Many of the direct quotations in this article are from unprinted sources located in archives in Germany and France. Specific references to these may be found in my book, *Working Women in Renaissance Germany*, on the pages given in the following notes. I would like to thank the American Council of Learned Societies and the Deutsche Akademischeaustauschdienst for their support in the research for this article.

1. This is not true in England, and recent studies of English peasants have used rural sources to explore women's labor in the countryside as early as the medieval period. See Barbara Hanawalt, *The Ties that Bound: Peasant Families in Medieval England* (New York: Oxford University Press, 1986), pp. 141–155; Judith Bennett, "The Village Ale Wife: Women and Brewing in Fourteenth Century England," in *Women and Work in Preindustrial Europe*, ed. Barbara Hanawalt (Bloomington: Indiana University Press, 1986), pp. 20–36.

2. Friedrich Bothe, *Beiträge zur Wirtschafts–und Sozialgeschichte in der Reichsstadt Frankfurt* (Leipzig: Duncker and Humbolt, 1906); Karl Bücher, *Die Frauenfrage im Mittelalter* (Tübingen: H. Laupp, 1910); Gerd Wunder, *Die Stuttgarter Steuerliste von 1545* (Stuttgart: Klett, 1974).

3. Peter Laslett, *The World We Have Lost* (New York: Scribners, 1965), pp. 81–91; J. Hajnal, "European Marriage Patterns in Perspective," in D. Glass and D. E. C. Eversley, eds., *Population in History* (London: Edward Arnold, 1965); E. A. Wrigley and R. S. Schofield, *The Population History of England, 1541–1871* (Cambridge, Mass.: Harvard University Press, 1981).

4. Erich Maschke, *Gesellschaftliche Unterschichten in den südwestdeutschen Städten* (Stuttgart: Kohlhammer, 1967), p. 27; Christiane Klapisch, "Household and Family in Tuscany, 1427," in Peter Laslett, ed., *Household and Family in Past Time* (Cambridge: Cambridge University Press, 1972), p. 273; Barbara Diefendorf, "Widowhood and Remarriage in Sixteenth-century Paris," *Journal of Family History* 9.2 (Winter 1982): 380; Grethe Jacobsen, "Women's Work and Women's Role: Ideology and Reality in Danish Urban Society, 1300–1550," *Scandinavian Economic History Review* 31, no. 1 (1983): 15; Diane Willen, "Guildswomen in the City of York, 1560–1700," *The Historian* 46.2 (February 1984), 206; Mary Prior, "Women and the Urban Economy: Oxford 1500–1800," in her *Women in English Society* (London and New York: Methuen, 1985), p. 105.

5. Merry E. Wiesner, *Working Women in Renaissance Germany* (New Brunswick, N.J.: Rutgers University Press, 1986), p. 6.

6. Joan Kelly, "Early Feminist Theory and the Querelle des Femmes 1400–1789," *Signs* 8, no. 1 (1982): pp. 4–28.

7. Joseph Baader, ed., *Nürnberger Polizeiordnungen aus dem 13. bis 15. Jahrhundert.* Bibliothek des Litterarische Verein Stuttgart, vol. 63 (Stuttgart: Litterarische Verein, 1861), pp. 29–30.

8. Rainer Stahlschmidt, *Die Geschichte des eisenverarbeitende Gewerbes in Nurnberg von den ersten Nachrichten im 12.–13. Jahrhunderts bis 1630.* Schriftenreihe des Stadtarchivs Nurnberg, 4 (Nuremberg: Stadtarchiv, 1971), pp. 186–187.

9. Same references as note 4 above.

10. Wiesner, pp. 160–161.

11. Judith Brown and Jordan Goodman, "Women and Industry in Florence," *Journal of Economic History* 40 (1980): 73–80.

12. Quoted in Patricia Crawford, "Women's Published Writings, 1600–1700" in Mary Prior, ed., *Women in English Society*, p. 215.

13. Unpublished article by Diane Willen, "Women and Poor Relief in Pre-industrial Norwich and York"; Wiesner, p. 182.

14. Wiesner, p. 182.

15. Ibid., p. 184; Alice Clark, *Working Life of Women in the Seventeenth Century* (London: Routledge and Kegan Paul, 1919), p. 9; Donald Woodward, "Wage Rates and Living Standards in Pre-Industrial England," *Past and Present* 91 (May 1981): 39.

16. Martha C. Howell, "Women, the Family Economy and the Structures of Market Production in the Cities of Northern Europe during the Late Middle Ages," in Hanawalt, ed., *Women and Work*, pp. 198–222. Jewish women may have been somewhat of an exception to this. As the memoirs of Glückel of Hameln indicate, she continued to assist her husband and sons in all aspects of their trade in luxury goods into the eighteenth century, occasionally even travelling to fairs or distant cities to buy and sell gold, pearls, and precious stones. This may in part be due to the fact that male Jewish merchants were never used by Christian political authorities as ambassadors and envoys, so women would not automatically be excluded because they could not perform a political role. [*The Memoirs of Glückel of Hameln*, tr. Marvin Loewenthal (New York: Schocken, 1977)].

17. Wiesner, p. 123.

18. Ibid., pp. 124–126.

19. Ibid., p. 142.

20. Ibid.

21. Ibid., pp. 40–41.

22. Ibid., p. 63.

23. Ibid., p. 50.

24. Ibid., p. 52.

25. Ibid., pp. 92–93; Michael Roberts, "Sickles and Scythes: Women's Work and Men's Work at Harvest Time," *History Workshop* 7 (Spring 1979): 3–29.

26. Lyndal Roper, "Discipline and Respectability: Prostitution and the Reformation in Augsburg," *History Workshop* 19 (Spring 1985): 3–28.

27. Maschke, *Unterschichten*, p. 29; Rudolph Endres, "Zur Einwohnerzahl und Bevölkerungsstatistik Nürnbergs im 15./16. Jahrhunderts," *Mitteilungen des Verein für Geschichte der Stadt Nürnberg* 57 (1970): 249; J. Jean Hecht, *The Domestic Servant Class in Eighteenth-century England* (London: Routledge and Kegan Paul, 1956), pp. 33, 34; Judith Brown, "A Woman's Place Was in the Home: Women's Work in Renaissance Tuscany," in *Rewriting the Renaissance: The Discourses of Sexual Difference in Early Modern Europe*, ed. Margaret Ferguson, Maureen Quilligan, and Nancy Vickers (Chicago: University of Chicago Press, 1986).

28. Ann Kussmaul, *Servants in Husbandry in Early Modern England* (Cambridge: Cambridge University Press, 1981).

29. Wiesner, p. 88.

30. Jean H. Quataert, "The Shaping of Women's Work in Manufacturing: Guilds, Households, and the State in Central Europe, 1648–1870," *American Historical Review* 90, no. 5 (December 1985); 1146.

SUGGESTIONS FOR FURTHER READING

In addition to the works cited in the notes, the following books and articles are available in English which elaborate on the information given in the article.

Davis, Natalie Zemon. "Women in the Crafts in Sixteenth-century Lyon," *Feminist Studies* 8 (Spring 1982): 46–80.

Eccles, Audrey. *Obstetrics and Gynecology in Tudor and Stuart England*. Kent, Ohio: Kent State University Press, 1982.

Fairchilds, Cissie. *Servants and their Masters in Old Regime France*. Baltimore: Johns Hopkins University Press, 1984.

Fraser, Antonia. *The Weaker Vessel: Woman's Lot in Seventeenth-century England*. London: Weidenfeld and Nicolson, 1984.

Hanawalt, Barbara, ed. *Women and Work in Preindustrial Europe*. Bloomington: Indiana University Press, 1982.

McLaren, Dorothy. "Marital Fertility and Lactation 1570–1720," in Mary Prior, ed., *Women in English Society 1500–1800* (New York and London: Methuen, 1985), pp. 22–53.

Monter, E. William, "Women in Calvinist Geneva," *Signs* 6.2 (1980): 189–209.

This painting of Madame Geoffrin's salon in Paris in the 1740s depicts women's roles as mediators of enlightened thought—even as it reveals men's preponderance at the salon. (Giraudon/Art Resource)

chapter 10

Women and the Enlightenment

Elizabeth Fox-Genovese

The Enlightenment, with its focus on individualism and social criticism, affected women in contradictory ways. On the one hand, by challenging received authority, including the supposed inferiority of women, male thinkers re-opened the debate about women's worth and resolved it favorably. On the other hand, by that resolution they exalted women above the political world of men and relegated them to a "higher" sphere of morality, establishing the next century's ideology that put women on a pedestal. The Enlightenment's profession of faith in the individual and in the equality of all individuals was its main legacy to later movements for women's emancipation, but because Enlightenment thought on women remained tied to oppositions, women would have to appropriate that legacy for themselves; it was not given them by eighteenth-century male thinkers. Few women in this period promoted full equality between the sexes, but a number of socially prominent women sponsored the new discourse by establishing the literary salons in which it was shaped.

The Enlightenment revolutionized western intellectual life by establishing the (male) individual as the source and purpose of knowledge. The disparate group of Enlightenment thinkers, commonly referred to as *philosophes*, warred against superstition in all forms; pioneered in the systematic criticism of received authority; extended the principles of the scientific revolution to the study of society (social science); and paved the way for the revolutionary doctrines of "the rights of man and the citizen." They did not systematically extend their probing criticisms of dependence, inequality, and tradition to the relations between men and women or even to women's capacities as individuals. Yet from the perspective of women's history, the Enlightenment may also qualify as a revolution. Not a revolution primarily effected by women themselves, nor even a revolution that obviously reduced women's subordination to men, yet a great conceptual shift, the first perhaps since antiquity, certainly since the consolidation of western Christianity.[1]

Traditionally, the Enlightenment, like the Renaissance, has been viewed primarily as an intellectual movement, a watershed in the history of ideas. In this sense, most historians consider it to have begun in the late seventeenth century with a growth in skepticism among segments of the educated elite. The growth of rationalism, the dissemination of the principles of the scientific revolution, and the growing interest in religious toleration following the English Civil War (1642–1646) are widely recognized as formative influences on Enlightenment thought. Normally also, the Enlightenment is taken to have ended with the beginning of the French Revolution in 1789.

The Enlightenment, then, was a phenomenon of the eighteenth century, which was also an age of momentous economic, social, and political change—an age of the decisive expansion of capitalism, of the beginnings of industrialization, of the growing power of the bourgeoisie, and, not least, of the great American and French Revolutions. Many scholars resist any close linking of the ideas of the Enlightenment to the origins of the French Revolution in particular, and to social and economic change in general. Furthermore, scholars continue to debate whether eighteenth-century men of letters actually shared common goals, values, methods, or even questions, for the Enlightenment encompassed diverse contributions to literature, political thought, social theory, economics, and philosophy. Such debates exceed the scope of this essay; nonetheless, it remains difficult to deny some relation between Enlightenment ideas and social, economic, and political change, just as it remains difficult to deny some strong interrelations among the ideas themselves.

Through the extraordinary diversity of Enlightened ideas runs a common thread that might be called systematic individualism. Presumably, individual consciousness is as old as human history; but only during the

---

I dedicate this essay with affection and respect to Franklin L. Ford for his generous and patient contributions to one woman's enlightenment.

eighteenth century did individual consciousness emerge as the foundation and justification for knowledge and social organization. The thinkers of the Enlightenment pioneered a "science of man" that tacitly assumed that (male) human beings were simultaneously the subjects and the objects of thought. In this respect, they substituted the human mind for the mind of God. Men could discover the laws of nature and society by rational inquiry, which neither revealed religion nor traditional political institutions should be allowed to impede. In this very general sense, the thought of the Enlightenment contributed in various ways to the development of the modern social sciences and to modern, bourgeois political theories. In the same general sense, it decisively shaped bourgeois notions of women's and men's gender roles and gender relations. Taken together, these currents of thought provided the norms for and analyses of the capitalist society that was emerging during the eighteenth century. The point is not whether the ideas caused the social changes or the social changes caused the ideas, but that ideas and social change developed in a discernible, if problematic, relation to each other.

Significantly, Enlightenment thought reached its highest development in eighteenth-century France, where the contradictions between old social structures and new social and economic currents appeared most visible. Thus France has from the beginning of the movement been considered the home of the Enlightenment. Yet many of the ideas that the philosophes would develop originated in England, and British thinkers—notably Scottish philosophers, moralists, and political economists—continued to produce an important body of thought throughout the eighteenth century. These thinkers, known as the Scottish Historical School, included David Hume and Adam Smith as well as their colleagues Adam Ferguson, Francis Hutcheson, and David Millar. Recently, scholars have emphasized their contribution to the development of Enlightenment thought in the North American colonies. The ideas of the Enlightenment were broadly disseminated, at least through a segment of the elite, in the small states of Germany and Italy, as well as in Spain, Portugal, Sweden, Poland, and even the Russian and Austrian empires.

Standard discussions of the Enlightenment normally dwell on the writings of the men who have long been viewed as the leaders of the movement: first, the undisputed giants, Voltaire, Montesquieu, Diderot, and Rousseau, all of whom wrote in a variety of genres on general topics for a diverse elite; and, second, the more specialized social theorists, some of whom were accomplished scientists and many of whom espoused a more or less rigorous materialism—most notably d'Alembert, Condorcet, Helvétius, d'Holbach, and de la Mettrie. Yet the development of these thinkers' intellectual agenda remained closely linked to social changes, including a rising tide of professionalization for intellectuals and government officials. Although many of the best known philosophes were of the nobility and financially independent, others were not. Diderot and Rousseau, in particular, earned their living by their pens, and many of the important contributors to the Scottish Historical School were university professors.

Although thinkers throughout Europe contributed to the Enlightenment, its core, like its dominant style, bore the clear imprint of its quintessentially French setting and French contributors. In this chapter, therefore, we shall focus primarily on women's complex relations to the mainstream of Enlightenment thought in France, with some attention to the related developments in England. To speak of the Enlightenment even in the restricted, inherited sense of a stage in the grand history of ideas is to ask, following Joan Kelly: "Did women have an Enlightenment?" And to accept the question on those terms is, inescapably, to answer: No. But a simple negative is not enough. If the Enlightenment is to be understood as an important stage in the development (if not the very dawn), of modern thought, then it is essential to understand the ways in which that thought affected the many Europeans, women as well as men, who did not directly participate in its forging and dissemination. For the Enlightenment, even in the narrow sense of history of ideas, was both the product of broad historical change and a decisive influence on the modern world.

The Enlightenment inaugurated that systematic individualism in various spheres of thought which would simultaneously, in the short run, rigorously exclude women and, in the long run, offer them a model for their own equal participation as individuals and as members of a gender in society, in the polity, and in the republic of letters. But even these developments affected different groups of women differently. The heyday of the Enlightenment might almost be viewed as the swan song of aristocratic women in the special roles that a corporate society of estates permitted privileged women. In this respect, the intellectual movement that would decisively revise the concept of woman and the possible ways in which women might conceive of themselves developed with scant contribution from the bourgeois women whom it would most affect. In fact, the most significant changes in the concept of woman developed with little direct contribution from any women at all. The women who most visibly contributed to the development of the Enlightenment did so by mediating and nurturing men's ideas in those Parisian *salons*, or drawing rooms, to which they invited men to talk to each other. Other women made important contributions to the new ideal of womanhood that would constitute the most significant immediate consequence of the Enlightenment for women, but their contributions came more in the realm of domestic fiction and occasional treatises on women's education—that is, of women's personal perceptions and needs—than of general social analysis. Only during the political upheaval of the French Revolution did women turn to the direct defense of women's rights. And only after it did they begin systematically to map women's special sphere and responsibilities in treatises on domestic economy, early childhood education, and manners. Women prepared themselves and other women to identify with, if not to embrace, the new model of womanhood that resulted from the combined impact of the Enlightenment, Romanticism, and the French Revolution. But, in so doing, they drew, even more heavily than they knew, on the thought and methods of the male Enlightenment.[3]

Women's relation to the Enlightenment thus can be considered under three separate headings: women who participated, however indirectly, in its development; the view of women that emerged from the thought of the philosophes; and the agenda that women drew up for themselves as they slowly assimilated the implications of the Enlightenment, especially under the impetus of the social changes of the French Revolution.

WOMEN OF THE ENLIGHTENMENT

With one notable exception, women have not figured prominently in discussions of the Enlightenment. The exception concerns the role of specific women either as hostesses of influential salons or as mistresses of influential men. Julie de Lespinasse, Mme. d'Épinay, Mme. Geoffrin, Mme. Helvétius, Mme. Condorcet, and others have earned some recognition in the conventional histories of men and ideas. They have not yet received sustained attention from contemporary women's historians, who have tended to view them, like other worthies, as unrepresentative of the experience of most women. Among the galaxy of women whose names are most closely associated with the Enlightenment, only Émilie du Châtelet earned an independent intellectual reputation by her internationally respected contribution to mathematics and her treatise on happiness.[4]

Eighteenth-century France did not produce many female intellectuals of the first rank, but it did produce an impressive collection of famous, notorious, and accomplished women who left a strong imprint on French culture. The royal mistresses, notably Mme. de Pompadour and Mme. du Barry, patronized the arts, the theatre, and fashion, and Mme. de Pompadour actively participated in politics. For many, the art of Watteau, Fragonard, and Boucher, like the delicate porcelains of Sevres and the furniture that is known as Louis Quinze, all betray a preponderant female influence. Since the influential work of Edmond and Jules de Goncourt, male commentators have repeatedly called attention to women's "empire" during the eighteenth century.[5] They mean that elite women enjoyed unprecedented opportunities to influence taste. But in a society in which patronage remained an important source of artists' and writers' incomes and reputations, these female patrons ranked as amateurs who operated on the margins of the established institutions of church and state. Their marginality did not preclude, and may even have enhanced, their ingenious and growing talent for bridging the gap between the cultures of court and town, of the nobility and the bourgeoisie. The growing importance of salons (or showings) of paintings during the century perhaps reflected this growing importance of female taste.[6] It also reflected the transition from a patronage system to a market system in the dissemination of culture. In this context, women may be seen as the original voices of "popular opinion" in the world of high culture.

This emphasis on women's influence on style highlights the paradox of the simultaneous dominion and subordination of elite women, who might "rule" men in matters of taste in dress or furnishings or decorative arts, but who were ruled by men in matters such as choice of marriage partner, place of abode, access to property, and all political affairs. The taste that women favored included the extensive use of pastels, the depiction of ornate interiors, a sentimental portrayal of people and their relations, an emphasis on romantic love complete with cupids and bows, and a comparably sentimental and pastoral view of nature. The tendency may have reached its peak in Marie Antoinette's famous version of life as theater: the court playing at being shepherds and shepherdesses at the royal "dairy cottage" in the grounds of Versailles. This female influence in style would, eventually feed into the new ideals of womanhood, motherhood, and domesticity that were developing apace, albeit in separate streams, throughout the century and throughout Europe.

The female influence on eighteenth-century culture developed in tandem with the emergence of polite society, notably the attempt to civilize a military aristocracy.[7] This civilizing project had been simultaneously, although not jointly, undertaken by some aristocratic women, by wealthy bourgeois men and women, and by an emerging group of urban writers and artists all of whom, for discrete reasons, were developing the notion of an urbane civility. Their various attempts to construct a polite, urbane society, distinct from the royal court, complemented the attempts of Louis XIV and his successors to transform nobles from quasi-independent warriors into dependent courtiers. Elite women of the seventeenth and eighteenth centuries used the salons to establish a place for themselves in society and in intellectual life. From the original salon of Catherine d'Angennes, Marquise de Rambouillet, through those of the Duchesse de Maine, Mme. de Tencin, Mme. Geoffrin, Mme. du Deffand, Mlle. de Lespinasse, and on to Mme. de Marchais, Mme. Necker, Mme. Condorcet, and Mme. Roland, the salons seem to have provided informal "schools" in which women introduced other women into the combined virtues of social and intellectual life and helped to integrate them into the main currents of advanced thought. All of the great salon hostesses relied upon the assistance and companionship of daughters or female friends. All seem to have shared their skills with younger women. Thus Mme. du Deffand trained Julie de Lespinasse as if she had been her own daughter; their initial bond is highlighted by the acrimonious break that occured when de Lespinasse began to outshine her mentor.[8]

Women and the Salons

Beginning in the seventeenth century, women had played an important role in the development of salons that rivaled the court as meeting places for members of polite society. From the start, the salons had been closely associated with cultural activity and intellectual life—witness Molière's *Les Femmes Savantes*. But they also served as principal agents in a "civilizing process" that was attempting to promote general cultural standards, beginning with basic rules about how to eat at table—with knife and fork—and how to behave in the presence of ladies—with courtesy. The salons also helped to consolidate an emerging alliance between the nobility and the upper bourgeoisie by providing a venue in which to introduce eligible and well-dowried bourgeois women to well-titled and impoverished noble men.[9] Women made paramount contributions to both of these functions. The salons, as the literal translation of their name ("rooms") implies, constituted above all spaces in which women and men could meet and converse. The women who organized the meetings and presided over the rooms increasingly used them as a way of imposing their own standards of civilization on men. Their tactic proved especially effective with aspiring intellectuals who frequently came from modest backgrounds and craved the social legitimation that the salons could provide.

Women's roles as hostesses, as mediators and facilitators of an expanding secular culture, not only shaped the society outside the court, but offered women themselves new social and cultural opportunities, both in relation to men and in relation to other women. Not least, women, by their own general lack of advanced formal education, constituted a powerful force in favor of the popularization or, at least, simplification of elite culture. If the newest ideas were to be introduced in and initially disseminated through the salons, they must be comprehensible to the general cultural elite represented by women. In this respect, women's roles in the salons influenced the development of an elite secular culture and promoted a lay intelligentsia. Significantly, the Enlightenment completed the transition from Latin to French, or the other vernaculars, for serious intellectual works. Although in France university theses continued to be written in Latin, even doctors took up writing in French in order to reach a general public that included women.[10]

The salons, in special ways, made manifest the relations between social processes and cultural developments. The emergence of the male intelligentsia that constituted such an important feature of the Enlightenment cannot be divorced from the changing notions of polite society, which were so influenced by women, as hostesses and arbiters of cultural taste.

During the long history of the salons, various hostesses experimented with formats for entertaining, including restricted or open guest lists; with the kinds of meals served; and even with the styles of dress for the hostess.

Pierre Samuel DuPont de Nemours reported in some detail on his first visit to the salon of Mme. de Fourqueux, the wife of an important government official, and her daughters, at which a new kind of light meal called a "café" was served and at which the hostess and her daughters wore aprons over their dresses and served their guests themselves.[11]

The salons marvelously captured the ambiguities of women's position vis-à-vis the Enlightenment. The women who presided over salons probably drew as much upon the ideal of the patron as upon the ideal of dutiful wife in their creation of their own place in the Parisian intellectual scene. Although specific hostesses may have come from the upper bourgeoisie, these women as a group built upon traditions and nourished aspirations that were more aristocratic than bourgeois. It would be stretching all credulity to call these women feminist, yet they contributed to bringing at least some women into intellectual company and, especially, contributed to making intellectual discourse a matter for women as members of polite society. Their histories perfectly expose the contradictions between opportunity and subordination that characterized the lives of so many women of the elite during the eighteenth century. Yet even the most accomplished salon hostesses remained primarily objects of personal attachment and inspiration for the male intellectuals who were contributing to reformulating the culture's discourse on gender and sexuality.

Women and the Novel

As in the real world of the salons, in the imagined world of the novel women assumed important roles within the domestic sphere, which was at this time achieving its own importance. The novel, however, increasingly emphasized women's own perceptions of personal relations, instead of reinforcing male perceptions, as happened in the salons. Nonetheless, at least initially, men dominated the development of the novel, which essentially presented men's views of women's emotions and experiences. From the start the growing sophistication of the novel, first in England, but rapidly thereafter in France, Germany, and the rest of Europe, reflected the growing coherence of bourgeois culture. After the Revolution, that emerging bourgeois culture linked women tightly with the domestic sphere and increasingly with a set of values that criticized capitalism and bourgeois individualism even as they reinforced bourgeois cultural and political dominance. This was because novels were wonderfully suited for the representation of those domestic relations and interiors that bourgeois culture would champion. Furthermore, to the extent that bourgeois culture emphasized the distinction between the private (female) and the public (male) sphere, the novel took shape as the testimony to the female values associated with private family life.

Even before the Revolution, the novel had come to be especially associated with domestic and female concerns. In England, Samuel Richardson led the way in producing new kinds of fiction for a predominantly female audience. His novel *Pamela* (1740), for example, depicted a servant girl's successful defense of her virtue against the ingenious assaults of her noble master. The conclusion, as the subtitle, *Virtue Rewarded*, had promised, rewarded Pamela's determination with marriage to that same master and promotion to the status of mistress of the house. Along the way, its explicit sexualization of women had also offered its readers prurient thrills even as it invited their moral condemnation.

In successive novels, *Clarissa* (1748) and *Sir Charles Grandison* (1753), Richardson further developed his critique of the aristocratic values that threatened female virtue and his celebration of the bourgeois values that nurtured it. In his eyes, the aristocracy trifled with female virtue by forcing young women into loveless marriages, by exposing them to the dangers of public masked balls, and by tolerating, if not countenancing, marital infidelity. The bourgeoisie, on the contrary, valued love as the personal motivation for chastity and marital fidelity.

The three novels consisted of letters exchanged among the protagonists. The epistolary format served Richardson's purposes doubly: it permitted his readers to identify directly with his characters' point of view and it instructed his intended middle-class readers in the art of letter writing. While writing the novels, Richardson conducted tireless research among his female acquaintance in order to make sure that he was properly expressing female sentiments. Richardson's influence on French intellectuals was profound.[12] The personal emotions evoked in domestic fiction apparently offered men, as well as women, a welcome relief from the artificial standards of high, "classical" culture. Jean Jacques Rousseau clearly betrayed his debt to Richardson in his own immensely popular, quasi-confessional novel, *Julie, ou La Nouvelle Héloise* (1761).

THE PHILOSOPHES' VIEW OF WOMEN

During the early part of the eighteenth century a variety of men of letters, among whom Voltaire and Montesquieu rank high, began to apply the methods and questions of Isaac Newton's science, John Locke's psychology, and the political theory of the English Revolution to investigating nature and society, including French political and religious institutions. Their efforts, resulted in a growing belief in the rationality of nature and the desirability of a rational society. Neither entirely antireligious nor entirely egalitarian, Voltaire, Montesquieu, and others tended to see the universe as the equivalent of a great clock that God, the clockmaker, had set going and left to tick with mechanical regularity. They believed that the human mind could identify and understand the laws of nature, society, and polity. They strongly favored religious toleration and an appreciation of different cultures. Finally, they helped to popularize Locke's view that, at birth, the human mind was a *tabula rasa*, or blank slate. All of these ideas taken together implied a far-reaching criticism of all received ideas, including the belief in innate differences between women and men.

In practice, neither Voltaire nor Montesquieu pushed those views to their logical conclusions. Even as they advocated cultural relativism and religious toleration, they remained committed to the monarchy as the best form of government; to the system of estates, notably the existence of a nobility as the monarchy's necessary foundation; to the manifest inferiority of servants; and to women's special nature. Although they were not levelers, both reached a high pitch of irony and occasionally of outright bitterness in their recurring criticisms of bigotry, of the arbitrary abuse of power, and of flagrant injustice. They did not see women as victims of those abuses, however, except in other societies. (Later, Diderot would suggest in his novel, *La Religieuse* (1796), that French women might be so victimized— but at the hands of other women, in convents.[13]) In their separate ways, each envisioned a reformed and purified monarchical society, which they also considered the most favorable environment for women. From the perspective of church and crown, their views, especially those of Voltaire, who suffered imprisonment for them, constituted dangerous threats. From the perspective of women's history, they seem entirely to deny the implications of their nascent liberalism to women.

From women's perspective, Lockean psychology constituted a specially important strand in Enlightenment thought. The idea that society played the decisive role in shaping human intelligence and personality plainly suggested that whatever innate differences nature might have given women and men should not affect the opportunities allotted to the members of each sex to develop their talents. Many authors of treatises on education, of which Rousseau's *Émile* (1762) was merely the most famous, regularly called attention to the need to provide better education for women. Both female and male educators, however, retained conservative views of women's roles and educational needs. What was radical was the proposition that women be educated at all.[14] British women, more than French women, seem to have recognized the implications of Locke's psychology for their gender. Sophia, A Person of Quality, put it most directly when she insisted that in the soul "there is *no sex* at all."[15] Yet even Mary Wollstonecraft would argue for women's education on the basis of their special roles as mothers, as well as their rights as individuals. Throughout the age of Enlightenment and beyond, women's roles as mothers remained the primary justification for their education. The lesson that most writers on the subject drew from Locke was not that girls should be educated equally with boys, but that mothers would be responsible for children during those early, impressionable years in which their minds would be shaped. The thinkers of the Enlightenment hoped to prepare women to meet those responsibilities. And women themselves, notably Mme. de Genlis, the governor of the children of the Duc d'Orléans, and Mme. Le Prince de Beaumont, who had worked as a governess in England, began to meet the responsibilities by writing books specifically designed for early childhood education.[16]

The sustained campaign for improved education for women was but one element in a general determination to improve education for all as a way of improving a variety of social ills. Many of the literate members of French society came increasingly to accept the criticisms leveled by the *philosophes* at existing institutions as valid, if extreme. Social and cultural historians have demonstrated that on all levels of society people were reacting more and more sharply to what they perceived as serious abuses by the monarchy, the church, and even the nobility. Everything from the breakdown of the system of supplying grain to the poor to the excessive luxury and sexual display of the upper classes came under attack. To be sure, many demanded a return to "the ways of our fathers," but the precise character of those ways seemed less and less clear and, perhaps, less likely to cure the perceived contemporary ills. The inherited ways of seeing, thinking, believing, and behaving no longer meshed precisely with daily experience — no longer seemed to apply at all.

L'Encyclopédie

In 1751 Denis Diderot and Jean Le Rond d'Alembert launched the publication of *L'Encyclopédie*, a "rational dictionary of the sciences, arts, and crafts, by a society of people of letters." After an interruption by the royal censors, the seventeenth and final volume appeared in 1765. Eleven volumes of plates that accompanied the text were published between 1762 and 1772. The nature and impact of the dissemination of the work has remained debatable, but inexpensive, pirated editions, as Robert Darnton has demonstrated, were probably circulating among educated people during the final decades of the ancien régime. At the time of initial publication, as the skirmishing with the censors suggests, the authorities viewed the work with suspicion. Yet the separate articles were usually not frontal attacks. The authors worked, in the mode pioneered brilliantly by Montesquieu, by satire and indirection. But the authorities were not wrong. Although *L'Encyclopédie* was no revolutionary manifesto and surely was not read by the peasants or even the urban workers, it did subtly challenge established authorities and probably helped to encourage disaffection among the literate elite. Nonetheless, *L'Encyclopédie* as a whole did not represent a coherent "line." Individual authors mocked and criticized established institutions, manners, and preconceptions according to their own personal views. For example, the various articles that touched upon women differed significantly about women's nature, roles, and rights.[17]

Women who read *L'Encyclopédie* for themselves — and the evidence suggests that at least a number of elite women did—found widely diverging views about the "sex," as their gender was called. Altogether, *L'Encyclopédie* included four different articles, by four different authors, under the heading "Woman" and another twenty-seven articles whose titles began with "Woman." In the article "Woman (Natural law)," the author, Jaucourt, defended woman's equality with man in marriage and deplored the ways in which custom and law had undercut that natural equality in practice. In the article "Woman (Morality)," the author, Desmahis, stridently attacked women as weak, timid, shrewd, false, and less capable than men of paying attention to anything. The best Desmahis could say about women was to admit that their poor character derived at least in part from the corruption of society and faulty education. In the article "Woman (Anthropology)," the author, Barthez, waffled between appreciation and censoriousness, describing woman by turn as a failed man and as man's equal. He, too, emphasized the importance of education. Finally, in the article "Woman (Jurisprudence)," the author, Boucher d'Argis, offered a compendium of woman's actual status at law and suggested that the fragility of the female sex accounted for women's being excluded from certain offices. Both Barthez and Boucher d'Argis acknowledged the accomplishments of particular women whom they mentioned by name, thus confirming both the persistence of a tradition of learned women and men's awareness of it. But passing acknowledgement of such women did not amount to a serious rethinking of women's nature and rights on the part of these authors.[18]

The most radical and potentially most dangerous aspect of *L'Encyclopédie* lay in the theoretical implications of its format: It subordinated all knowledge and experience to the alphabet and thus implicitly undercut all established hierarchies. *L'Encyclopédie* offered a fresh look at the world—at its inhabitants and their customs and values. Thousands of entries held isolated aspects of experience, from the most mundane to the most exalted, up for scrutiny. In sum, *L'Encyclopédie* implicitly suggested that its readers look anew at all the component parts of experience and knowledge. It inaugurated a revolutionary attempt to reconsider each name or sign of experience in order to recombine them in a new view of society that derived from empirical examination of its component parts.

Of the many contributors to *L'Encyclopédie* only two are known to have been women, one, Mme. Delusse, the wife or sister of an engraver who worked on the plates, the other anonymous. Yet, taken as a whole, *L'Encyclopédie* made a small contribution to the broader reworking of the view of women. The volumes of plates depicted women in various aspects of life and, especially, production.[19] The plates did not correspond to the various articles devoted to women; they simply depicted women's presence in society. The disjuncture between text and image can be taken as that between discourse and experience; it reveals the gap between women's activities and the ways in which women were evoked in texts. With respect to women, as with respect to so many social questions, *L'Encyclopédie* implicitly invited its readers to substitute empirical observation for outmoded systems of thought.

L'Encyclopédie offers a useful paradigm for the thought of the Enlightenment as a whole. In effect, the philosophes undertook a joint operation of deck-clearing and recombination. Although many of them differed radically on any number of questions, the combined impact of their efforts constituted the rudiments of a "social science" grounded in the rights of the individual, including the primacy of individual perception as against revealed truth and established authority.

Women and the Idea of Equality

The Enlightenment's repudiation of arbitrary authority and shackles on the human mind, which amounted to a massive and systematic assault on the legacy of scholasticism and patriarchalism, would have portentous consequences for women. From Montesquieu on, the men of the Enlightenment, like their colleagues of the Scottish Historical School, insisted that the position of women in society constituted the litmus test of the level of civilization and decency. In part, and especially at the beginning, this insistence owed something to the association of women, salons, and the concept of manners. In a civilized society, women should be treated with courtesy, gentleness, and respect. But increasingly, diverse thinkers came by diverse routes to insist upon women's special kind of excellence and women's special social roles. In so doing, these thinkers were drawing upon a venerable tradition, that of the sexes' separate spheres, and upon more recent arguments, especially those developed by Mme. de Maintenon and the abbé Fénelon, that stressed women's role in the family as "mother-educators." But they were also, and more dramatically, overthrowing long-standing notions of woman as the inferior sex.

Seventeenth-century rationalism, in the hands of Poulain de la Barre, had already produced a passionate and logical argument for the equality of women to men. Seventeenth-century humanism, notably in the hands of Marie de Gournay, had already produced a passionate and learned defense of female excellence.[20] The thinkers of the Enlightenment however, constituted the first group, or intellectual movement, to resolve the long-standing *querelle des femmes* (the quarrel over the excellence or unworthiness of women's nature) in women's favor. Women were declared to be not evil, but especially excellent. This new view derived from related but separate lines of argument about society and sexuality. It also probably owed much of its acceptance to its relation to the philosophes' attack on patriarchalism, even though that attack was not mounted in the name of women.

To the philosophes, patriarchalism meant that body of doctrine that justified the rule of fathers in the names of Church and state. In effect, early modern patriarchalism simply pulled together and systematized long-standing beliefs and practices. But the systematization made the authority of fathers appear all the more arbitrary and odious. In fact, systematic patriarchalism weighed especially heavily on women, whom it subjected to the control of men within households. Thus the crown's centralizing activities included a strong tendency to deprive women of whatever independent legal rights they might previously have had.[21] But the new class of male intellectuals and professionals from whom so many of the Enlightenment thinkers were drawn perceived patriarchalism primarily as the illegitimate domination of some men over others in the name of arbitrary, hierarchical dogmas. They saw the rule of kings, priests, and fathers over honest individuals. They did not, as a rule, support political change or oppose the monarchy. They did vehemently oppose the abuse of royal power, which they called "despotism."

The Enlightenment attacked patriarchalism for its restraints on the exercise and recognition of individual (male) minds and talents, but the attack on patriarchalism in politics naturally developed into an attack on hierarchy in social relations. For the men of the Enlightenment slavery, as the antithesis of freedom, quickly became an important issue. The broad definition of slavery came to include unfree labor, feudal dues and services, *lettres de cachet*, arranged marriages, abuse of paternal power, artificial forms of deference, and more. Among these abuses, *lettres de cachet* attained special notoriety, for they represented the absolute and arbitrary power of the monarch to intervene directly in private lives simply by issuing a letter that ordered an individual's imprisonment. The monarch could also issue a letter and order an imprisonment on the request of a noble father who wished to discipline a wayward son, as in the case of the Marquis de Mirabeau's obtaining a letter for the imprisonment of his son, Honoré de Mirabeau, who was having an affair with a woman of whom his father did not approve. This use of the power of the state to strengthen the power of fathers provides a graphic example of the distinctive patriarchalism of the pre-Revolutionary French monarchy. The attack on patriarchalism primarily concerned relations among men. But it unavoidably raised the specter of women's relation to society. And the British writer, Mary Wollstonecraft, borrowed directly from that political language when she called women slaves of fashion.

During the eighteenth century, the arguments against despotism linked the health of society to political institutions and even justified political institutions in relation to their impact on society. The arguments that were developed by the early members of the Scottish Historical School—notably Francis Hutcheson, Adam Ferguson, and David Hume—and by Montesquieu had their roots in sixteenth- and seventeenth-century arguments against political tyranny, but granted a new importance to social and economic relations as the justification for political relations. The importance of the shift for women cannot be exaggerated. In effect, these thinkers subordinated politics to society and the economy. The "political good" would no longer be seen as an independent category, but would depend upon politics' role in facilitating social and economic relations. Montesquieu, for example, argued that the republic was the appropriate form of government for small, commercial societies and the monarchy for large, landed societies. Hutcheson, Ferguson, and Hume, in their various ways, gave even less attention to political institutions, concentrating instead on moral, social, and economic relations. But all agreed that the position of women in society constituted one important measure of the society's excellence.[22] None of them, however, entertained the notion that women's position might require women's direct participation in politics. Not until the beginnings of the French Revolution had placed political democracy on the agenda would a few daring writers— notably Condorcet, Olympe de Gouges, and Mary Wollstonecraft—claim the rights of citizenship for women.[23]

Women and Sexuality

For Montesquieu, the members of the Scottish Historical School, and countless others, the relation between politics, society, and women's position acquired special importance because of what they considered the visible corruption of their own societies. They tended to equate the growth of cities, of luxury, and of new fashions with female sexuality, which they saw as escaping from the privacy and control of the male-dominated household. Montesquieu especially, in his *Lettres Persanes* (1721), drew the analogy between the corruptions of France and those of eastern despotisms, complete with harems. In effect, the men of the Enlightenment shared with the more conservative critics of their society the belief that somehow women—in practice, aristocratic or elite women—had slipped through the cracks of traditional restraints. They left convent schools only to throw over all traces, including those of their own too early marriages. Having born a child or two, they set themselves to worrying about preserving their looks and attracting lovers. They indulged in luxury, tended to dress indecently, neglected their offspring, and devoted far too much time to social life. On close inspection, the philosophes' views of women's relations to society do not result in an entirely coherent picture. In principle, most philosophes claimed that treating women with courtesy and decency constituted a hallmark of civilized, western society. In practice, most of them also believed that aristocratic women suffered from too much confinement before marriage and too much freedom after. In the wake of the Revolution, the philosophes, in collaboration with women writers, would resolve the contradictions between the favorable and unfavorable views of women with a new model of (bourgeois) female domesticity. Women's roles as mothers would emerge as the cornerstone of this new model.

The men of the Enlightenment, many of whom were themselves bourgeois by origin or isolated professionals by condition, began to display an extraordinary empathy for the children they believed women were neglecting. Led by the ever anxious Rousseau, by the populationists (a group of demographers who, incorrectly, feared that France was becoming depopulated), and by the new breed of physicians, they discovered the virtues of maternal nursing. The English, like the conservative French country nobility, instructed women in the virtues of family life. Combining maternal nursing and the virtues of family life with their own experience of individualism, these authorities preached the related virtues of marriage for love and of women's domestic confinement. The writings that refer to women leave little doubt that men caught in the thralls of their own individualism felt a compelling need for comforting and submissive domestic mirrors. In these concerns and these needs Diderot was as one with Rousseau. Adam Smith, with his customary clear-sightedness, carefully explained that a woman's marital fidelity was essential to man's need to be assured that she preferred him to all others.[24]

The theme of anxious (male) individualism and willing (female) submission attained its clearest expression and its greatest popularity in the works of Rousseau, who provided the quintessential heroine in Julie, of La Nouvelle Héloise (1761), who ruled her domestic universe with smiles bestowed and withheld, just as he provided women with a practical model in Émile's Sophie, who was "made for man's delight."[25] La Nouvelle Héloise, written in the epistolary style popularized by Richardson, details the love affair of Julie with her tutor Saint Preux. Their intimate exchange of ideas leads to love and on to sexual relations. Julie combines the attributes of the pubescent virgin and the fallen woman. Saint Preux, a mere tutor, cannot aspire to marry her. Rather, her father marries her to an older and appropriately wealthy nobleman, the Baron de Warens. As the Baron's wife, Julie enjoys peace in her domestic enclave, which she shares with other women and children. But Saint Preux's return confronts her with the old love that she had never forgotten. Unable to resolve her dilemma, Julie commits suicide; in death as in life, however, her virtue transcends her sins. Like Pamela before her, she exemplifies a titillating, pubescent, almost virginal sexuality that both male and female readers seem to have found irresistible and that the Marquis de Sade would shortly thereafter exploit explicitly in numerous works, notably, and not accidentally, his own Julie.

In Émile (1762), an epistolary novel whose theme is education, Rousseau again presents the relation between a tutor and his student, but here the student is male. The point of the extremely influential Émile, which Mary Wollstonecraft among many deeply admired, was to demonstrate how a young mind could be shaped—to provide a practical exercise in education. But the education of young men inescapably leads to relations with women. In Book V, Rousseau discusses the education of Sophie, the companion he proposes for Émile. But when Sophie forsakes the country for Paris, her education cannot withstand the corrupting influences of fashionable life, and she badly wounds Émile through her pursuit of pleasure, luxury, and other lovers. Both works, then, insisted on women's special combination of power and weakness: the power, through the ability to inspire love, to ruin men; the weakness, through vulnerability to temptation, of their sex. *La Nouvelle Héloise* and *Émile* provide the links between Rousseau's analysis of the modern state in his *Contrat Social* (1762) and his subjective portrait of the modern individual in his *Confessions* (1782).[26]

Rousseau, the son of a modest watchmaker from Geneva, always felt himself an outsider in relation to Paris society, and even to the other philosophes. His friendship with Diderot, whose career his own in many ways most resembled, ended in a bitter estrangement. He lived for years with a serving woman, Thérèse, on whom he apparently depended emotionally, but to whom he never appears to have granted the adoring love he bestowed on various more aristocratic women. For Rousseau, women, sex, and love presented insoluble problems. So did fatherhood. He turned all four of his and Thérèse's children over to a foundling home. In all his human relations, and many of his writings, he manifested an uneasy combination of arrogance and shame. He was less than frank, and less than honest, when he began his *Confessions* with the assertion that he did not wish to present himself as better or worse than other men, just different.

Rousseau's personal history has an important bearing not merely on his own writings, but on the emerging notion of bourgeois individualism which would so decisively shape the Enlightenment's legacy for women—shape women's expectations for themselves and, more important in the short run, shape the attitudes of the men with whom they would live. For however much Rousseau differed from other men, his psychological experience, including the anxiety attendant upon individualism, informed all his writings and found a significant echo among his contemporaries and successors. Knowing his own deep competitiveness, for instance, he guarded against the competitiveness of others. In his *Contrat Social*, he projected a democratic government in which all individuals gave their individual wills over to the "general will." The "general will" constituted his compromise between egalitarian democracy and centralized authority—a kind of submission to a public virtue. His notion of virtue would find committed disciples among such Jacobins as Robespierre and Saint-Just, who presided over the Terror during the French Revolution. Should men's natural inclinations not lead them into the paths of virtue, the government would have to do the job—in the interests of realizing their deeper individual wills. This vision of individualism included a firm commitment to the subordination of women to men within a private domestic sphere, largely as compensation for men's loss of authority over other men. Rousseau captured the essence of that sphere in *La Nouvelle Héloise* in his description of Julie's eating the nuts and fruits that a benevolent (maternal) nature freely offered, instead of the meat that rapacious humans acquired through carnage and domination. Both his political model and his self-portrait depend upon such female submission to the male individual. Long after Rousseau's "radical" political views and outrageous personal behavior had been repudiated, his vision of the bourgeois individual and the docile bourgeois woman would remain compelling to many.[27]

As Rousseau's work so clearly suggests, the men of the Enlightenment defined themselves as individuals by defining women as something else. In this attempt to redefine women, they gradually set the outlines of a new discourse on womanhood. The doctor Pierre Roussel's title for his medical treatise on women, *Le Système Physique de la Femme* ("The Physical System of Woman") captures the spirit of the general project that took shape in a variety of writings on society and the family. Roussel stated explicitly what many others only implied when he began his treatise with the assertion that up until now doctors had incorrectly portrayed woman as an imperfect man when she was, in fact, a completely different creature.[28]

A NEW AGENDA FOR WOMEN

Like the relation between the text and the plates in *L'Encyclopédie*, the relation between the discourse on womanhood and women's lives remained disjointed. Those who fashioned the discourse worried about women's roles as reproducers. They knew, however vaguely, of the increasing numbers of unwed mothers; they feared that population was declining; and they blamed women's use of wet nurses for the death of infants. They were primarily concerned neither with the needs and feelings of women of the popular classes, nor even with the needs and feelings of those of the elite, although they made some effort to accommodate elite women's sensibilities. In their various ways, however, each of these male writers believed that any analysis of, or plan for, society must take account of gender. In developing a universalistic social science, they looked at all women through the lens of gender and, thereby, albeit unintentionally, validated the notion of a general rather than an individual female experience and perception. In fact, the experience and perceptions of French women of the various classes probably remained more different than similar throughout the eighteenth century. Women of the peasantry, the laboring poor, and even the artisan class continued to work long, hard hours; to suffer the hardships of a makeshift economy; to face the dislocations of inadequate or erratic supplies of bread; and to age prematurely. Women of these classes also lived within a rigid role—that of woman—with sharply defined rights and responsibilities. The church, the state authorities, and the folk culture alike reminded them of their distinct nature, their necessary subordination to men, and their special tasks and roles. Women of the bourgeoisie and the nobility also received strong messages about their roles and responsibilities as women, but wealth and status discouraged them from identifying as women with their less fortunate sisters.[29] Elite women, in fact, benefited from the exploitation of women of the lower classes, whom they viewed at best with disdain and at worst as members of a different species.

Both modern feminism and the modern notion of separate spheres, including the cult of motherhood and domesticity, derive from the interaction of these social and intellectual currents. Women had, at least since Christine de Pizan (1365–1429), been arguing in favor of women's intrinsic excellence and thereby had been rejecting the time-honored notion of women's intrinsic inferiority to men. But their arguments remained bound by the particularistic and hierarchical assumptions of pre-Enlightenment thought. During the last quarter of the seventeenth century, Poulain de la Barre, who closely followed the logic of René Descartes, first offered a general, rationalist argument for the equality of women and men, but his argument remained essentially abstract. In theory, the work of the philosophes opened the door to imagining women's equality with men by positing women's interchangeability with men as individuals. Few eighteenth-century men or women followed that line of thought, although Condorcet, Olympe de Gouges, and Mary Wollstonecraft, all of whom wrote treaties in favor of women's rights under the impetus of the French Revolution, constitute important exceptions.[30] But if the Enlightenment thinkers stopped short of the full implications for women's identity of their logic, they did overturn the concept of women's inferiority.

The Enlightenment developed the rudiments of the modern ideology of womanhood, precursors of which, especially the notion of separate spheres, had appeared earlier. But the thought of the Enlightenment linked the notion of womanhood to the new ideal of individualism and, in so doing, grouped all women under the idea of woman, the opposite—companion, helpmeet—of man.[31] Thanks to the intellectual and social currents of the eighteenth century, the ideal of the woman on the pedestal, which had made its first shadowy appearance in the doctrine of courtly love, became associated with the private home and the model for all women.

The new positive view of women was informed by all the cultural and social tensions of the eighteenth century. Although it glorified women as mothers, wives, daughters, custodians of the domestic sphere, it did not necessarily reflect men's easy acceptance of women's own powers and perceptions. The most sentimental and individualistic of the philosophes, notably Diderot and Rousseau, feared and possibly mistrusted women as fully as any of the "misogynists" of earlier periods. Even Montesquieu and Voltaire can be shown to have assumed that the domestic subordination of women was ordained by nature, if not by God. And although female literacy had progressed significantly during the century and although women's education was high on the Enlightenment's agenda for progress, women as a group did not yet command the intellectual resources to make their own case with force. It is not even certain what case they would have chosen to make. Exceptionally talented women such as Manon Phlipon (Mme. Roland), Germaine Necker (Mme. de Stael), and even Mary Wollstonecraft warmly appreciated at least some of Rousseau's writings, as did many less vocal women.[32] Romantic love, enlightened motherhood, and domestic dominion apparently carried strong appeal for large numbers of women, who recognized in them new sources of self-esteem for themselves. Certainly women novelists in France as in Great Britain embraced the model of domestic womanhood and fashioned tales that rewarded women's virtue, as Richardson had rewarded Pamela's, with marriage.

The growing numbers of women novelists also used their talents to make different points about women than did most of their male peers. Novelists as different as Mme. Clarière, Mme. de Stael, Mme. Gacon Dufour, and Charlotte Smith all criticized some aspect of their society and made strong cases for women's need for education. In *Lettres Écrites de Lausanne* (1787) Mme. Clarière linked the celebration of motherhood to a critique of fashionable society and to a demand for women's education. In *De la Nécessité de l'Instruction Pour les Femmes* (1805), Mme. Gacon Dufour made similar arguments, but with an even sharper attack on the nobility's corrupting influence on all human relations. Both women presented motherhood as a vocation that women could — after the initial conception — exercise without the benefit of male assistance. In *Emmeline, the Orphan of the Castle* (1788) and *The Old Manor House* (1793) Charlotte Smith explicitly linked the lack of proper mothering among the aristocracy to male violence and campaigned for universal, middle-class standards of domesticity. And, yet more defiantly, Mme. de Stael, in her novels, *Delphine* (1803) and *Corinne* (1807), celebrated women's intellectual and artistic powers and deplored the cruel punishments that a hostile society inflicted on "great" women. Other female novelists, in growing numbers, propagated similar messages. They were, in the fiction they wrote primarily for other women, appropriating one legacy of the Enlightenment.

The men of the Enlightenment, like so many of their successors, largely mistrusted women's potential for authority, including the intellectual authority of authorship. They did not believe it becoming or even acceptable for women to write and publish on equal terms with men. They even explicitly associated such unfeminine ambition with women's aggressive sexuality — precisely what Mme. de Stael was complaining about. From men's perspective, society could only benefit from the confinement of women's sexuality, which so deeply threatened men's autonomous exercise of individualism. They fashioned an image of woman that denied woman's passion and anger. They willed woman to be the passive object of their desires, the comforting pillow for their anxieties. And they linked that image tightly to their view of bourgeois society. It would appear that at least some of these authors, notably Rousseau and Diderot, were taking revenge on the aristocratic women who had tempted and awed them. In promoting a universal model of bourgeois womanhood, they simultaneously leveled the mighty and elevated the downtrodden.

What the Enlightenment wrought in theory haltingly penetrated social practice. The Enlightenment did not "cause" the changes in women's lives or in society that ultimately resulted in the dissemination of a modern ideal of female domesticity. The impact of high culture—and the Enlightenment was high culture par excellence—on politics and society remains hotly contested. And women did not even play a central role in the forging of that high culture. Did women have an Enlightenment?

Women did not have an Enlightenment: They had many Enlightenments. And their Enlightenments, like the tails of a comet, sprayed in different directions and affected different groups of women differently. Ultimately, women's reality remained overwhelmingly bound by the specific features of their daily lives. The broad conceptualizations of those lives in intellectual discourse rarely touched them directly, although those conceptualizations did contribute to their growing literacy and their growing access to schooling. The Enlightenment's concern with women derived at least in part from social and economic changes that also affected women. The Enlightenment sought new words to describe the things—including the relationships among things—that constituted the world. And the new words that it found— "individual," "reason," "economy," "moral sentiments," "rights," "self," "motherhood," among many—influenced women's subsequent experience in innumerable ways.

For women, as for men, the Enlightenment ended with the outbreak of the French Revolution in 1789. For the previous two decades the Enlightenment proper had been giving way to other currents, notably pre-Romanticism. The growing emphasis on love, sensibility, and domestic happiness combined to endow women's own perceptions with a new importance. This emphasis set the stage for the new model of womanhood that would triumph after the Revolution had destroyed the old, artificial distinctions of status. As men, at least in theory, gained access to the "rights of man and the citizen," women gained a new role as the valued helpmeets of individual men. Yet ultimately the most important aspect of the Enlightenment for women surely lay in its emphasis on individualism as a universal category. For if that individualism initially prescribed the private subordination of each woman to a man, it inescapably also offered women a language of individualism for themselves. The advances that the Enlightenment offered women may have proved limited, but they also proved decisive in making possible women's own expanding discourse about women. In this perspective, Mary Wollstonecraft ranks among the Enlightenment's first, great female heirs. She drew from the currents of Enlightenment thought the many-sided vision embodied in her novels, *Mary, a Fiction* (1788) and *The Wrongs of Woman* (1796) and her treatises, *Thoughts on the Education of Daughters* (1787), and *A Vindication of the Rights of Woman* (1792).

There is a fitting irony in Mary Wollstonecraft's position as heir of the Enlightenment. As did Diderot and Rousseau, she established herself, albeit more precariously than they, as an independent person of letters. Writing on many subjects, she, as did they, wrote in many genres. She, too, drew upon and combined different modes of thought to forge a new voice appropriate to her condition. Her personal history largely confirmed Mme. de Stael's pessimism about society's attitudes towards the great woman.[33] Yet her works embody a moving combination of realism and optimism. For Wollstonecraft extended the Enlightenment's message of individual capacity, responsibility, and rights and applied it to the condition of women in every sense, and she reread the message through the prism of radical English politics. In her fiction, she depicted what we might call women's personal perspective on the pain caused them by male dominance, but she staunchly related that personal experience to the social conditions that produced it. In her thoughts on education for women, she courageously explored the weakness as well as the potential strength of what she took to be women's nature. Society, she believed, had dreadfully warped that nature—had made women "slaves of fashion." In her work on education as in her pathbreaking work on women's rights, she followed Rousseau in accepting women's domestic vocation but departed from him in insisting on women's capacity for intelligent and independent action. Concern with clothing and personal adornment rendered women weak and dependent. A proper education must imbue them with values and standards that they could internalize as a basis for an adult identity. Properly educated, women could become true adults. And, as true adults, women like men were endowed with certain inalienable rights.

Wollstonecraft's work offers a microcosm of the Enlightenment's paradoxical legacy for women. For the Enlightenment powerfully contributed to delineating and justifying the limitations that the emerging bourgeois society would impose on women as members of a gender. The extension of the doctrine of bourgeois individualism to all men initially also established theoretical equality among all women, but relegated them equally to a dependent domestic sphere. Exalting women as naturally loving and nurturing wives and mothers, the male heirs of the Enlightenment repudiated the notion that women, like men, should enjoy political rights—should be citizens. Yet, as both Wollstonecraft and Condorcet precociously perceived, the logic of the bourgeois doctrines of individualism and democracy implied equality between women and men. As increasing numbers of women came to understand those implications, they drew upon the legacy of the Enlightenment to claim the rights of the individual for all women.

NOTES

1. Ian Maclean, *The Renaissance Notion of Woman: A Study in the Fortunes of Scholasticism and Medical Science in European Intellectual Life* (Cambridge: Cambridge University Press, 1980).
2. Joan Kelly-Gadol, "Did Women Have a Renaissance?" Chapter 7 in this volume.
3. For a general discussion of these themes, see, Elizabeth Fox-Genovese and Eugene D. Genovese, *Fruits of Merchant Capital: Slavery and Bourgeois Property in the Rise and Expansion of Capitalism* (New York: Oxford University Press, 1983), Chapter 11, "The Ideological Origins of Domestic Economy."
4. On Émilie du Châtelet, see Linda Gardiner, "Women in Science," in Samia Spencer, ed., *French Women and the Age of Enlightenment* (Bloomington: Indiana University Press, 1984), pp. 181–93. Despite her intellectual accomplishments, du Chatelet was long known primarily as Voltaire's beloved mistress, who died while bearing the child of yet another lover.
5. Edmond et Jules de Goncourt, *La Femme au dix-huitième siècle*, 2 vols. (Paris: Flammarion & Fasquelle, n.d.)
6. See, Diderot, *Oeuvres Esthétiques*, ed. Paul Vernière (Paris: Garnier, 1968), Extracts from "Les Salons," pp. 481–655. Diderot was, in fact, trying to develop a self-consciously bourgeois and realist aesthetic.
7. For a fuller discussion of these themes, see my "Introduction," Spencer, ed., *French Women and the Age of Enlightenment*.
8. We do not have a modern study of any of the leading French *salonnières*, but their lives and views can be glimpsed through their correspondence. See Judith Curtis, "The Epistolières," in Spencer, ed., *French Women and the Age of Enlightenment*, pp. 226–41, for an introduction and references to the sources. See also the dated but informative, Amelia Gere Mason, *The Women of the French Salons* (New York: The Century Co., 1891).
9. Norbert Elias, *The Civilizing Process: The History of Manners*, trans. Edmund Jephcott (New York: Urizen Books, 1978), esp. Part Two, "Sociogenesis of the Concept of *Civilization* in France"; Carolyn Lougee, *Le Paradis des Femmes: Women, Salons, and Social Stratification in Seventeenth-Century France* (Princeton: Princeton University Press, 1977).
10. See, for example, the work of Pierre Roussel, cited below, note 28, and the many treatises of Samuel Auguste Tissot, notably his *De la santé des gens de lettres*, ed. Francois Azouvi (Geneva: Slatkine, 1981).
11. *The Autobiography of Du Pont de Nemours*, trans. and with an introduction by Elizabeth Fox-Genovese (Wilmington: Scholarly Resources, 1984), p. 268.
12. See John Carroll, ed., *Selected Letters of Samuel Richardson* (Oxford: Oxford University Press, 1964); and Denis Diderot, "Éloge de Rousseau," in Vernière, ed., *Oeuvres esthétiques*, pp. 23–48.
13. Diderot began drafting *La Religieuse* as early as 1760, and had completed it by 1770. The idea grew out of an actual event. See the modern edition in Diderot, *Oeuvres Romanesques*, ed. H. Benac (Paris: Garnier, 1962).
14. See, among many, Jean H. Bloch, "Women and the Reform of the Nation," in Eva Jacobs et al., eds., *Women and Society in Eighteenth-Century France: Essays in Honour of John Stephenson Spink* (London: Athlone Press, 1979), pp. 3–18.

15. Sophia, A Person of Quality, *Woman Not Inferior to Man* (London, 1739; repr. 1975).

16. On women's contribution to early childhood education, see, Mme. de Genlis, *Discours sur la suppression des couvents* (Paris: Onfrois, 1790), and her *Adèle et Théodore* (Paris: Maradan, 1804); Mme. Le Prince de Beaumont, *Le Magasin des Enfants* (Paris: Garnier, n.d.); and Samia Spencer, "Women and Education," in Spencer, ed., *French Women in the Age of Enlightenment.*

17. Robert Darnton, *The Business of Enlightenment: A Publishing History of the Encyclopédie 1775–1800* (Cambridge, MA: Harvard University Press, 1979). *Encyclopédie ou dictionnaire raisonné des sciences, des arts et des métiers, par une société de gens de lettres,* ed. Denis Diderot and Jean Le Rond d'Alembert, 17 vols. (Paris: Briasson et al., 1751–1765) and the *Recueil de planches sur les sciences, les arts libéraux et les arts mécaniques, avec leur explication,* 11 vols. (Paris: Briasson et al., 1762–1772). All the articles on women are in Volume 6. See also Sara Ellen Procious Malueg, "Women and the *Encyclopédie,* in Spencer, ed., *French Women and the Age of Enlightenment,* pp. 259–71.

18. Barthez mentioned Marie de Schurman, a female scholar who advocated universal education for Christian women; Boucher d'Argis discussed a number of learned women who had received doctor's degrees from foreign academies— Helene-Lucrece Piscopia Cornara in philosophy (Padua, 1678), la demoiselle Patin in philosophy (Padua, 1732), Laura Bassi in medicine (Bologna, n.d.), and Maria-Gaetana Agnesi in mathematics (Bologna, 1750). On the tradition of learned women, see, J. R. Brink, ed., *Female Scholars: A Tradition of Learned Women before 1800* (Montreal: Eden Press, 1980).

19. Terry Smiley Dock, "Woman in the *Encyclopédie,"* PhD dissertation, Vanderbilt University, 1979.

20. Poulain de la Barre, *De l'égalite des deux sexes* (1673). On Marie Le Jars de Gournay's various works, see, Ian Maclean, *Woman Triumphant: Feminism in French Literature 1610–1652* (Oxford: Oxford University Press, 1977).

21. The best general discussion of women's status remains Léon Abensour, *La Femme et le Féminisme en France avant la Révolution* (orig. ed. 1923; Geneva: Slatkine, 1977). See also, Susan P. Conner, "Women and Politics," in Spencer, ed., *French Women and the Age of Enlightenment,* pp. 49–63, and Adrienne Rogers, "Women and the Law," *loc. cit.,* pp. 33–48.

22. Montesquieu, *De l'Esprit des Lois,* 2 vols. ed. Robert Dérathé (Paris: Garnier, 1973), first published 1748, trans., Thomas Nugent, *The Spirit of the Laws by Baron De Montesquieu* (New York: Hafner Press, 1949). For the views of members of the Scottish Historical School, see Adam Ferguson, *An Essay on the History of Civil Society,* ed. Louis Schneider (New Brunswick, N.J.: Transaction, 1980); Francis Hutcheson, *A Short Introduction to Moral Philosophy,* 2nd ed. (Glasgow, 1753); David Hume, *A Treatise of Human Nature,* ed. L. A. Selby-Bigge (Oxford: Clarendon Press, 1888).

23. Marie Jean de Caritat, marquis de Condorcet, *Essai sur les assemblées provinciales* (1787) and his *Essai sur l'admission des femmes aux droits de la cité* (1790) in *Oeuvres de Condorcet,* ed. A. Condorcet O'Connor and M. F. Arago, 12 vols. (Paris: Firmin Didot Freres, 1847), vol. 10, pp. 119–30, trans. in Susan Groag

Bell & Karen M. Offen, *Women, the Family and Freedom: The Debate in Documents*, 2 vols. (Stanford, CA: Stanford University Press, 1983), I. document 24; Olympe de Gouges, *Les Droits de la femme* (Paris, 1791), repr. and trans. in *Women in Revolutionary Paris 1789–1795*, ed. Darline Gay Levy, Harriet Branson Applewhite, Mary Durham Johnson (Urbana: University of Illinois Press, 1979), pp. 22–26; Mary Wollstonecraft, *A Vindication of the Rights of Woman* (London, 1792).

24. On specific problems, see also, Joan Kelly, "Early Feminist Theory and the *Querelle des Femmes*, 1480–1789," in *Women, History, and Theory*, pp. 65–109; Elizabeth J. Gardner, "The *Philosophes* and Women: Sensationalism and Sentiment," in Jacobs et al., eds., *Women and Society in Eighteenth-Century France*, pp. 19–28; Sheila Mason, "The Riddle of Roxane," *loc. cit.*, pp. 28–41; Robert Niklaus, "Diderot and Women," *loc. cit.*, pp. 69–82; Eva Jacobs, "Diderot and the Education of Girls," *loc. cit.*, pp. 83–96; R. F. O'Reilly, "Montesquieu anti-feminist," *Studies on Voltaire and the Eighteenth Century*, vol. 102 (1973): 143–56. For Adam Smith's view, see my "Property and Patriarchy in Classical Bourgeois Political Theory," *Radical History Review* 4, nos. 2–3 (Spring–Summer 1977): 36–59.

25. The literature on Rousseau now abounds. See, among many, Victor G. Wexler, " 'Made for Man's Delight': Rousseau an Antifeminist," *American Historical Review* 81 (1976): 266–91; Tony Tanner, "Julie and 'La maison paternelle': Another Look at Rousseau's *La Nouvelle Héloise*," *Daedalus* 105 (1976): 23–45.

26. The best modern edition of Rousseau's works is Jean-Jacques Rousseau, *Oeuvres Complètes*, Vols. I–IV, ed. Bernard Gagnebin and Marcel Raymond (Paris: Gallimard, 1959–69).

27. Carol Blum, *A Virtuous Terror* (Ithaca: Cornell University Press, 1986).

28. Docteur (Pierre) Roussel, *Système physique et morale de la femme*, new ed. (Paris, 1813).

29. For a fuller discussion, see my, "Women and Work," in Spencer, ed., *French Women and the Age of Enlightenment*, pp. 111–27; Olwen Hufton, "Women and the Family Economy in Eighteenth-Century France," *French Historical Studies* 9, no. 1 (Spring 1975): 1–22; Martine Segalen, *Love and Power in the Peasant Family*, trans. Sarah Matthews (Chicago: University of Chicago Press, 1983); Natalie Zemon Davis, "Women in the 'Arts mecaniques' of Sixteenth-Century Lyon," *Mélanges Richard Gascon* (Lyon: Presses Universitaires de Lyon, 1979).

30. See note 23 above.

31. See Kelly, "Early Feminist Theory," *loc. cit.*, with which I am differing slightly.

32. See Gita May, "Rousseau's 'Antifeminism' Reconsidered," in Spencer, ed., *French Women in the Age of Enlightenment*, pp. 309–17.

33. Mary Wollstonecraft Godwin, *Thoughts on the Education of Daughters with Reflections on Female Conduct in the more important Duties of Life* (Clifton: Augustus M. Kelley, 1972); Mary Wollstonecraft, *Mary, a Fiction and The Wrongs of Woman*, ed. Gary Kelly (Oxford: Oxford University Press, 1972).

SUGGESTIONS FOR FURTHER READING

The Enlightenment has fueled a massive intellectual industry that has generated not merely innumerable books and articles but a large number of specialized journals. For an introduction, see Peter Gay, *The Enlightenment: An Interpretation*, 2 vols. (New York: Alfred Knopf, 1966 and 1969).

We have no general modern study of French women during the eighteenth century or of women's relation to the Enlightenment. The most comprehensive introduction can be found in Samia Spencer, ed., *French Women and the Age of Enlightenment* (Bloomington: University of Indiana Press, 1985). Eva Jacobs et al., *Women and Society in Eighteenth-Century France: Essays in Honour of John Stephenson Spink* (London: Athlone Press, 1979), contains a fine selection of scholarly essays on historical and literary questions. Vera Lee, *The Reign of Women in Eighteenth-Century France* (Cambridge, MA: Schenkman, 1975), offers a lively overview. Margaret Hunt et al., *Women and the Enlightenment* (New York: The Haworth Press and the Institute for Research and History, 1984), also published as *Women and History*, No. 9 (Spring 1984), consists of specialized essays on Mary Astell, women and the London press, and women and Freemasonry. For a general discussion of women in the thought of the Enlightenment, which follows the conventional model of the history of the idea of woman, see Paul Hoffmann, *La Femme dans la Pensée des Lumières* (Paris: Editions Orphys, 1977), and for a recent interpretive essay on background, Pierre Darmon, *Mythologie de la Femme dans l'ancienne France, XVIe–XVIIe siècles* (Paris: Le Seuil, 1983). Rita Goldberg, *Sex and Enlightenment: Women in Richardson and Diderot* (Cambridge: Cambridge University Press, 1984) offers an interesting discussion of Richardson and Diderot. See also, Arthur Wilson, " 'Treated Like Imbecile Children' (Diderot): The Enlightenment and the Status of Women," in *Woman in the 18th Century and Other Essays*, ed. by Paul Fritz and Richard Morton (Toronto: Samuel Stevens Hakkert & Co., 1976). For a new look at Rousseau's attitudes towards women, see, Joel Schwartz, *The Sexual Politics of Jean Jacques Rousseau* (Chicago: University of Chicago Press, 1984).

On the development of "feminist" thought among women and men, see, David Williams, "The Politics of Feminism in the French Enlightenment," in *The Varied Pattern: Studies in the 18th Century*, ed. Peter Hughes and David Williams (Toronto: A. M. Hakkert, Ltd., 1971); Georges Ascoli, "Essai sur l'histoire des idées féministes en France du XVIe siècle à la Révolution," *Revue de Synthèse Historique* 13 (July–December 1906): 25–57, 99–106, and 167–84; and, for England, Hilda Smith, *Reason's Disciples: Seventeenth-Century English Feminists* (Urbana: University of Illinois Press, 1982) and Katherine M. Rogers, *Feminism in Eighteenth-Century England* (Urbana: University of Illinois Press, 1982).

Among the many works on eighteenth-century literature, Ian Watt, *The Rise of the Novel: Studies in Defoe, Richardson and Fielding* (Berkeley: University of California Press, 1957), remains valuable. For a more recent reading of important texts, see Nancy K. Miller, *The Heroine's Text: Readings in the French and English Novel 1772–1782* (New York: Columbia University Press, 1980). See also, Terry Castle, *Clarissa's Cyphers: Meaning and Disruption in Richardson's Clarissa* (Ithaca: Cornell University Press, 1982), and Madelyn Gutwirth, *Madame de Stael,*

Novelist: The Emergence of the Artist as Woman (Urbana: University of Illinois, 1978).

There has been little work on women and salons in the eighteenth century to match Carolyn Lougee, *Le Paradis des Femmes: Women, Salons, and Social Stratification in Seventeenth-Century France* (Princeton: Princeton University Press, 1977), but see Evelyn Gordon Bodek, "Salonnieres and Bluestockings: Educated Obsolescence and Germinating Feminism," *Feminist Studies* 3, nos. 3/4 (Spring/Summer 1976): 185–99; and Deborah Hertz, "Intermarriage in the Berlin Salons," *Central European History* XVI, no. 4 (December 1983): 303–46. Myra Reynolds, *The Learned Lady in England, 1650–1760* (Boston: Houghton Mifflin, 1920), remains valuable. On women's education, see, Georges Snyders, *La Pédagogie en France au XVIIe et XVIIIe siècles* (Paris: Presses Universitaires de France, 1965); comte de Luppé, *Les Jeunes Filles à la fin du XVIIIe siècle* (Paris: Édouard Champion, 1925); Paul Rousselot, *Histoire de l'éducation des femmes en France*, 2 vols. (n.d.; repr. New York: Burt Franklin, 1971). For general discussions of educational reform, albeit with no reference to women, see, Harvey Chisick, *The Limits of Reform in the Enlightenment: Attitudes toward the Education of the Lower Classes in Eighteenth-Century France* (Princeton: Princeton University Press, 1981), and Roger Chartier, Dominique Julia, and Marie-Madeleine Compere, *L'Éducation en France du XVIe au XVIIIe siècle* (Paris: CDU & SEDES, 1976).

On the general status of French women nothing has replaced Leon Abensour, *La Femme et le Féminisme avant la Révolution* (1923; repr. Geneva: Slatkine, 1977). See also James F. Traer, *Marriage and the Family in Eighteenth-Century France* (Ithaca: Cornell University Press, 1980).

Among the many works on Mary Wollstonecraft, see, Margaret George, *One Woman's Situation: A Study of Mary Wollstonecraft* (Urbana: University of Illinois Press, 1970); Emily W. Sunstein, *A Different Face: The Life of Mary Wollstonecraft* (Boston: Little, Brown, 1975); and, for her intellectual context, Ralph M. Wardle, *Mary Wollstonecraft: A Critical Biography* (Lincoln: University of Nebraska Press, 1966).

On October 5, 1789, thousands of women, principally from the market districts of Paris, marched to Versailles to confront Louis XVI and to protest bread shortages and high prices. Hours later, the National Guard followed the women; the next day, violence erupted when the crowd invaded the palace and clashed with the royal guards. The Royal Family and the National Assembly agreed to take up residence in Paris, and the return march was a triumph for the revolutionaries. (Bibliothèque Nationale)

chapter 11

Women and Political Revolution in Paris

Darline Gay Levy
Harriet Branson Applewhite

For centuries individual women had insisted on their worth in the marketplace, in their homes, in religion, and in the cultural world. Against vicious misogynist attacks and the steady erosion of their legal rights, women did their best to hold their own and demand redress of specific grievances. During the French Revolution, for the first time in history, a few educated women demanded equality from the state. Harriet Applewhite and Darline Levy depict women marching, petitioning, writing pamphlets, and joining in political debates. While sharing revolutionary men's general belief in democracy, women formed a distinct presence in the dramatic mass events that decisively affected the outcome of the Revolution. Market women of Paris marched to Versailles in October 1789. Educated, radical women joined some key Jacobin circles. Masses of women joined the throng on the Champ de Mars in July 1791 and even marched into the King's residence in 1792. But reaction came swiftly in 1793 and fell heavily on women. Even as the Napoleonic Code enshrined the patriarchal family, a tradition of women activists lived on in the writings of early feminists. Applewhite and Levy portray the complex needs and expectations of women in all classes of the social spectrum. The authors' conclusions foreshadow Jane Jenson's essay on the 1980s by highlighting the tensions created when women assert their special concerns and their claims to universal citizenship.

The French Revolution was the most democratic of all the revolutions in the eighteenth-century western world. Although the revolutionaries did not live in a world of modern democratic government, with its mass suffrage, political parties, and interest groups, the institutions and principles that the revolutionaries modified and created were the foundations of the republican tradition in French politics and established the most important precedents for modern democracy. Revolutionaries developed and spread doctrines of human rights, redefined citizenship, and established and practiced principles of popular sovereignty, such as the tenet that the people themselves were the source and ultimate expression of authority and legitimacy in the political system. French revolutionaries established legislatures, local governing bodies, political clubs, a popular press, and other institutions for political participation; and they involved millions of individuals throughout French society in political conflict and civil and international war.

Women were involved in these transformations in all kinds of ways: as members of revolutionary crowds, as radical leaders, and as supporters of the French government. Some donated their jewels to the treasury; knitted stockings, made bandages for the armies, or joined revolutionary festivals. Others were victims of revolutionary change, for example, noblewomen who lost rank and privilege and deeply religious women whose world fell apart when their church was attacked and their faith declared unpatriotic. Women contributed to both revolutionary and counterrevolutionary ideology and discourse as they edited, printed, and distributed journals and political tracts. Women's revolutionary allegiances were complex; their roles were staggeringly diverse. It would be misleading to speak of women's experiences in the revolution and their contributions to its unfolding, as if those experiences were shared by all women. Just as for men, it made a difference whether a woman lived in Paris or in the provinces, was a noblewoman or a domestic servant, kept a market stall or wrote plays, was a devout Catholic or resented the wealth of the church.

During the past twenty years, as historians have reflected on the meaning of all this complexity and diversity, they also have sharpened the lines of a historiographic debate over the interpretation of women's involvement. Should we understand the decisive impact of the French revolution on women largely in negative terms? Were women worse off, or at most no better off, after the revolution, notwithstanding the rhetoric of universal rights, and the experience with republican institutions and new principles of popular sovereignty? Or did the revolution change women's minds, reshape and politicize their behavior and bequeath a legacy of ideology and actions that inspired later generations? And what if we reverse the question? How should we understand the impact of women on the revolution? Were women, and especially women in Paris, drawn into protest exclusively or principally

We wish to dedicate this article to the memory of Annette Kar Baxter, mentor, colleague, and friend.

out of their traditional concern with providing food and other necessities for their families? When subsistence issues came up, were women for the most part untouched or unchanged by the new revolutionary principles and practices, or did they turn violently against them?

The answers to these questions depend in part on the historian's focus: what groups of women is he/she investigating, in what geographic area, engaged in what kinds of activities, over what period of time? Because both the king and the political institutions that were struggling to control the monarchical executive were located in Paris by October 1789, we have centered our narrative and interpretation on women in the revolutionary capital.

Our story can be summarized briefly. In October 1789, Parisian women marched to see the king and the National Assembly at Versailles to protest bread shortages. The women marchers were aware of the role of institutions like the National Assembly.* They had been interacting since the summer with municipal authorities and with the newly formed National Guard, the bourgeois militia organized by the municipality to maintain order and protect property. Now, accompanied by the National Guard, the women escorted the royal family and the legislature back to Paris, where they agreed to take up residence. Throughout 1790 to August 1792, significant numbers of women were involved in the progressive radicalization of politics in Paris and especially in the development of republicanism after the king tried unsuccessfully to flee the country in June 1791, and after the Legislative Assembly declared war against Austria in April 1792.

Women were among the armed demonstrators and marchers, the writers of speeches, the editors and printers of journals, and the activists maneuvering both within and outside of local and national institutions in Paris. These efforts undermined the supports of constitutional monarchy and established a republic. From August 1792 until October 1793, as the Jacobins fought for and won primacy in national politics, radical women in Paris struggled on the extreme left. A certain number of their demands were translated into laws, but eventually women were attacked, forcibly disbanded, and excluded by law from political activities. The Jacobins justified this repression in blatantly misogynist rhetoric. In the months and years following the fall of the Jacobins in July 1794, women lost much of what had been gained, such as the right to divorce. Finally, the Napoleonic code, promulgated in 1804, reinstated women's dependent status.

---

*The name of the French legislature changed four times between 1789 and 1795. The Estates General sat at Versailles from May 6 to June 17, 1789. On June 17, the Third Estate deputies and most of the deputies to the lower clergy (the First Estate) voted to declare themselves the National Assembly. On June 27, the king ordered the remaining clergy (mostly bishops and other high church officials) and the noble deputies (the Second Estate) to join the National Assembly. The National Assembly wrote the first French written constitution, and sat until September 30, 1791. It was replaced by new elections with the Legislative Assembly, set up by the Constitution of 1791 and in session until September 1792. Under the First Republic, the legislature was called the National Convention, in session from September 1792 until 1795.

This account would seem to indicate that the outcome of the French Revolution was just as negative for politically active women in Paris as for many peasant women, religious women, and noblewomen. In spite of the women's acts during the Revolution and the aspirations and ambitions aroused in them by the rhetoric of universal rights to liberty and equality, in the end, patriarchal principles were more firmly in place than ever.

Focusing on women in revolutionary Paris between 1789 and 1794–5, we offer another interpretation of the impact of the French Revolution on them. Women contributed to redefinitions of citizenship, popular sovereignty, and legitimate government. The discourse and the acts of women in the revolutionary capital cannot be dismissed even though the implications of these words and deeds were not fully realized in French politics for more than a century. Women writers were politically savvy, and some made it clear that restructuring relationships between rulers and ruled required facing both the differences between the sexes, as well as their common claims for rights of citizenship, first in a constitutional monarchy and then in a republic. Other women whose words and thoughts were never recorded made their mark on the revolution through their collective behavior: marching, demonstrating, signing or marking petitions, attending revolutionary meetings, and participating in neighborhood self-government. We have relatively little evidence to help us assess their level of revolutionary consciousness, the extent to which they understood abstract issues of government and politics, or the exact intentions that informed their actions. We do suggest that the strength of their numbers, the implications of their actions, the slogans they shouted and the symbols they carried, their connections with the National Guard, and their involvement in acts of armed force all had an impact on political leaders that cannot be discounted in assessing the meaning of the French Revolution for French political history and for women's history. The thousands of women who marched to Versailles from Paris in October 1789, signed petitions concerning the future of the constitutional monarchy on the Champ de Mars in July 1791, and marched through the halls of the Legislative Assembly and the king's residence in the Tuileries in the summer of 1792 forged a link between their actions and the concepts of popular sovereignty, citizenship, and political legitimacy. Their acts demonstrated and dramatized the power of those concepts to restrain, limit, and challenge political authorities.

When we bring women into our interpretation of the French Revolution, we find that, initially, the Revolution seems more democratic than it does when women are ignored: that is, it involved more people exercising greater influence. Although women never received full citizenship rights in any of the revolutionary constitutions and codes, some women penned tracts and petitions that redefined citizenship and made claims for women's citizenship rights. Many women, thousands strong, occasionally tens of thousands strong, participated in the insurrectionary crowd movements of the Revolution, the great revolutionary days—a collective practice of the principle of popular sovereignty. Petitioning, conspicuously displaying revolutionary symbols and emblems—the cockade, the liberty cap—bearing arms, pressuring legislators, attaching themselves to the National Guard, and labeling themselves *citoyennes* (women citizens)—women demonstrated popular sovereignty, and these actions were, for a time, tolerated and even encouraged by revolutionary men.

As women and men identified themselves as citizens and enacted the power of popular sovereignty, they unsettled and challenged the traditional bases of the monarchy's legitimacy. By their actions and by their ideas, they made themselves into sources and arbiters of the legitimacy of those in power at all levels of government—the king, deputies in the national legislature, mayors, neighborhood officials—as the government changed and changed again until, late in 1793, women were finally driven out of the political sphere by force and by law.

Again, when we include women in our interpretation of events after 1793, the revolution seems not only less democratic but also more harshly repressive. When the Church and the army returned to power after 1795 their leaders refused to tolerate women's political activism, but so did the revolutionary Jacobin leaders who were firmly in control in Paris in 1793 and 1794. Jacobin leaders, for all their rhetoric of liberty and equality, gave voice to one of the most sweeping and categorical denials of women's capacity for political activity on record when they passed legislation closing women's clubs in the fall of 1793. They were only too aware of what the implications for male dominance and control would be if women's rights were codified in constitutions and laws.

THE CHALLENGE TO ROYAL LEGITIMACY: FROM OLD REGIME TO CONSTITUTIONAL MONARCHY

Women had long been highly visible actors in the ceremonial, economic, and political life of Paris. Women participated, for example, in festivals associated with the liturgical year and in marches of supplication or thanksgiving for bountiful harvests. Women were also involved when civic order was threatened by religious controversy, subsistence crises, market disturbances, or conflicts between the king and the Parlement of Paris (a law court that had the power to register and promulgate laws). Women participated directly in events that were very centrally related to the reinforcement of public order and the legitimation of royal authority. The *poissardes* (fishwives) of Paris were required to attend the childbirth of a reigning queen in order to certify the legitimacy of the royal heir, and were later present when the infant dauphin was presented at the Hôtel de Ville. In the patriarchal society of the ancien régime (France before the revolution), ruled by a monarchy where a woman could not inherit the throne, an ancient female occupational group had a dramatic role in validating the king on behalf of the people; they added a popular voice and a feminine presence to the rituals by which the monarchy was legitimated.

The legitimacy of Louis XVI and his authority to govern were under challenge from the very beginning of his reign in 1774. These challenges came from many institutions: the parlements, whose power to register laws gave them the power to delay or block them; provincial estates and assemblies, which had some regional authority over law, administration, and taxes; the Church, which had power to tax and to regulate behavior; and many specially privileged groups of people—army officers, seigneurial judges, local administrators—who had some opportunity for political maneuvering.

In addition to these institutional challenges, Enlightenment thinkers were questioning, debating, and reformulating theories about the nature and limits of legitimate authority. Enlightenment writers broadcast new doctrines of natural law, natural rights, and social contract. They demanded reforms in civil and criminal law; they challenged the legitimacy of a monarchy based on hereditary right and divine right; and they questioned defenses of privilege based on models of a hierarchical corporate society. Their discourse contributed to an erosion of the foundations of traditional authority and generated new doubts about the legitimacy of what had been one of the strongest monarchies in Europe.

Women as well as men, and particularly in Paris, were caught up in these challenges to monarchical authority. Their overtures to the king and ministers, their ceremonial marches, and their energetic participation in the street life of Paris were, traditional urban activities. Anxieties about subsistence led them to take leading roles in market disturbances and riots, just as they always had. In the 1770s and 1780s, however, the political setting within which all these activities occurred was itself changing. Attempted reforms and reactions to reform attempts; talk of liberty and rights; charges of despotism; economic crises and bread shortages in Paris; court politics and rumors of scandals—all combined to weaken the foundations of the French monarchy. Women as well as men lost so much respect for the monarch that they came to question the legitimacy of royal authority itself. One window on women's activities is the journal of Siméon-Prosper Hardy, the Parisian bookseller, who reported events like the crowd's failure to shout "Vive le Roi!" ("Long live the King!") as Louis XVI and his queen, Marie Antoinette, reviewed troops of the French Guards and the Swiss Guards on May 8, 1787.[1] During the Feast of the Assumption in 1787, authorities had to present the *poissardes des Halles* (the fishwives of the Halles market) with a police order to force them to go through with their customary ceremonial offering of bouquets to the queen.[2]

In May 1788, after failing in a number of attempts to gain support for new taxes from various groups of notables, the king and his ministers decided to reinstate an old institution that had not met since 1614: the Estates General, an assembly of deputies representing the nobility (Second Estate), the clergy (First Estate), and the common people (Third Estate). The King hoped that this newly revived body would consent to the levying of taxes. The announcement generated great excitement throughout France. There was an enormous outpouring of political pamphlets and tracts. After the dates for elections to the Estates General had been fixed for Spring 1789, electors at the local and provincial level drafted *cahiers de doléances*, official grievance lists for the elected deputies to take to the king, as well as unofficial grievance lists expressing opinions and demands. Women drafted some of these unofficial cahiers.

In the first months of 1789, Paris was stirred up by the political process of naming electors to choose representatives for the Estates General and by shortages of bread and other necessities during a particularly cold winter. Women participated in the Réveillon riots in April 1789, in which workers and residents in the Faubourg Saint-Antoine ransacked the home of the Paris elector and wallpaper manufacturer, Réveillon after he claimed at an electors' meeting in his district that high wages were a costly burden for entrepreneurs. News of this speech infuriated families struggling to pay the high price of scarce bread, the staple of their diet. Women were also active in the conquest of the Bastille on July 14, 1789, and most conspicuously in the destruction of the toll gates surrounding Paris at the time of that insurrection. They were principal participants in the thirty-four marches of supplication and thanksgiving which wound through Paris during August and September, in the aftermath of the violent events of July 1789. In these processions, large numbers of women, accompanied by contingents from the newly formed National Guard, marched in formation and to drumbeat. Typically, the women and their escort of Guardsmen marched to the Eglise Sainte-Geneviève, Nôtre Dame, and the Hôtel de Ville (seat of Paris's municipal government). The line of march symbolically linked the women with both traditional and newly designated protectors of the city of Paris: Sainte-Geneviève, patron saint of Paris, Nôtre Dame, the national church; the Hôtel de Ville, locus of the new representative government; and the National Guard, the new bourgeois military force. The bookseller and diarist Hardy found these imposing demonstrations of popular allegiance and strength patently ridiculous, but they also made him apprehensive.

Many people found there was something terrifying in [the procession's] arrangement, composition, and immensity. Sensitive people found these public acts, which could not be interrupted and of which piety was unfortunately not the full motive, ridiculous. They thought it would have been infinitely wiser for each male and female citizen to thank the Almighty individually . . . rather than collectively.[3]

The alliance between women and the National Guard eventually became a central factor in the weakening of monarchical government and the creation of an armed revolutionary force whose claims for popular sovereignty were ultimately to triumph.

During the summer of 1789, the electoral assemblies in Paris assumed responsibility for conducting local government. Activists in these districts challenged the new municipal leaders. They demanded direct democracy, protested against tax qualifications for the right to vote and for National Guard membership, and insisted on the right to recall unpopular deputies.[4] *Moniteur* (a daily paper covering events in the legislature) printed a petition sent to the National Assembly from the Palais Royal on August 31, which stated: "The veto does not belong to one man, but to 25 million," and again: "Citizens meeting at the Palais Royal believe that ignorant, corrupt and suspect deputies should be recalled."[5] Women did not lead this district-level movement toward direct democracy, but they participated; they spoke at meetings of the Palais Royal, and women marchers organized themselves by districts.[6]

The quintessential women's event of the Revolution was the march to Versailles in October 1789. For some weeks, radical leaders and the Parisian masses had been agitated over bread shortages and high prices, the issue of royal veto power, the king's failure to ratify the Declaration of Rights, the calling up of additional royal troop reinforcements, and finally, the soldiers' insults to the revolutionary tricolor cockade at a banquet for royal bodyguards at Versailles. On October 5, many women gathered at the Hôtel de Ville, armed themselves, and exhorted the National Guard to march with them to the king's palace at Versailles. Seven thousand strong, the women, accompanied by a contingent of Guardsmen, marched to Versailles, confronted the National Assembly and the king with demands for bread and security for Paris, and shouted "à bas Monsieur le Véto" ("Down with Mister Veto")—a protest against those who favored an absolute royal veto over laws. After some hours of hesitation, the king finally accepted the Declaration of Rights and agreed to guarantee subsistence to Paris. General Lafayette arrived that evening from Paris with thousands of National Guard troops. After a restless night, the crowds invaded the Palace of Versailles and clashed with soldiers defending the king. Both sides suffered casualties, and the enraged crowds of Parisians decapitated two royal guardsmen and mounted their heads on pikes. Under pressure from the crowds and General Lafayette, the king and queen and their two children appeared on a balcony; the king announced his decision to return with the crowd to Paris and, surrounded by a turbulent and joyous throng, was driven in his carriage to Paris to take up residence in the Tuileries (the royal palace). The ministers and those elected deputies to the National Assembly who had not resigned agreed to relocate in Paris.

The implications of these critical events intensified the development toward popular sovereignty. After dawn on October 5, a rainy fall Monday, the *tocsin* (alarm bell) began ringing first from the Hôtel de Ville, then from the church of Sainte-Marguerite, and finally all over the city. We can hear the stomp of the poissardes' *sabots* (wooden shoes) and imagine the smell of their damp skirts as they swarmed into the Hôtel de Ville and forcibly kept men out. They were looking for ammunition, but also (according to Stanislas Maillard, a leader of the National Guard), for administrative records, saying that all the revolution had accomplished so far was paper work. They proceeded to claim for themselves the power and the right of insurrection: by drumming the *générale* (a military call to arms), they recruited thousands of other women, and they sounded the tocsin to declare insurrection in progress. Then they marched off to Versailles.

When the young women who actually were granted an audience with the king left his apartments and returned to the palace courtyard with news of Louis XVI's good intentions, the waiting crowds of women threatened them and sent them right back to obtain a written document sealing the king's promise to ensure a supply of bread for Paris. The women who entered the meeting room of the National Assembly voted on motions and occupied the speaker's chair. Such political dramaturgy reflects the French tradition of role reversals on carnival days ("king for a day"); however, the fifth and sixth of October 1789 were not carnival days. The women's acts were direct interventions in the legislative process and symbolic replacements of representatives who did not represent. The women's actions, supported by the National Guard—an armed force on the side of revolution—anticipated later acts by organized crowds of men, women, and children who claimed rights and powers of popular sovereignty and who in fact brought down the throne.

French historian George Rudé interprets these days as events that brought together previously separate revolutionary activities—those centered on economic problems, on the one hand, and those centered on constitutional questions, on the other. Concerns over unemployment and bread supplies and prices had kept tensions in Paris high ever since April. Political issues, chiefly the transformation of the Estates General into a Constituent Assembly, had been settled in July, but deputies were concerned that the king had not yet accepted the Declaration of the Rights of Man and Citizen, the central issue facing the National Assembly early in October.[7] This distinction between economic and constitutional issues is clear, but should not mask the fact that subsistence had long been a political issue between rulers and ruled. During the final decades of the ancien régime, the public—notably women, for whom subsistence was a matter of daily concern and unending anxiety—expected and demanded as a condition of civil obedience, that public authorities, starting with the local police and ending with the king, guarantee subsistence commodities at affordable prices. In the end, nothing less fundamental than the legitimacy of the monarchy was at stake when subsistence matters were raised.

After October 6, authorities moved to suppress collective demonstrations of popular force. City officials decreed martial law for Paris, following the lynching of a baker whom a woman had accused of reserving bread for deputies to the Assembly. Subsequently, hundreds of the deputies were exposed by the women's accusation, which implied that deputies had subordinated the public good to their private interests. This event suggests that women and men in the Paris crowd held deputies directly accountable to the people for their actions. Following the passage of restrictive legislation, two of the Paris districts protested the prohibition of assemblages; they also protested the city officials' failure to consult them before decreeing martial law. These protests amounted to an unequivocal demand for the right of referendum, which authorities did not grant, although they did permit delegations of up to six persons to submit a grievance petition.[8]

The National Assembly, relocated in Paris, began to work in the late fall of 1789 on the details of the new constitution. On December 22, 1789, the Assembly issued a decree that set up electoral assemblies and defined the limits of the franchise. Abstract debates about citizenship now produced a concrete and codified definition. Active citizens were defined as men who met a tax qualification: that they pay "a direct tax equal to the local value of three days' labor."[9] The decree did not set up a category for those not qualifying as active citizens, but the question was discussed in the National Assembly during the October 1789 debates on citizenship.[10] Other people—women, foreigners, domestic servants, and men who did not meet the tax qualification—were considered passive citizens. The definition of passive citizenship allowed for the possibility that men so categorized could become active citizens if their income, reflected in their tax payment, increased. No such possibility existed for women.

The exclusion of women from full legal citizenship was never remedied in any code or constitution throughout the revolution. Nonetheless—and this is the central point of the story we have to tell—many thousands of women in Paris pushed past the legal boundaries to claim citizenship in words and deeds, to erode acceptance of the constitutional monarchy as a legitimate government even as it was being set up, and to take their place alongside men in the ranks of the sovereign people.

During the course of the next year and a half, a political struggle pitted activists in the Paris districts and clubs against the municipal leadership and

National Assembly, whose members were trying to contain the potential force of the sovereign people by limiting the suffrage, by prohibiting collective petitions, and by outlawing strikes. The Paris sections (neighborhood governing bodies that replaced the districts) met regularly, often with galleries open to spectators, and political clubs actively recruited members and consciously took on an educational mission.

Women vigorously challenged restrictions on popular sovereignty, not just as gallery spectators and wives, but as printers, journalists, political organizers, petitioners, and delegates. Together with men, women were embroiled in the crisis over the legitimacy of the constitutional monarchy—a crisis that was building in the spring of 1791 as people increasingly suspected the intentions of Louis XVI.

The minutes of the Cordeliers Club (a radical political club) for February 22, 1791, contained an exhortation to the club by women who called themselves citoyennes of the rue du Regard. The women began by defining themselves as good Rousseauist mothers who taught their children constitutional principles, but they threatened to become militant if men did not fight hard enough for the revolution.

> We have consoled ourselves for our inability to contribute to the public good by exerting our most intense efforts to raise the spirit of our children to the heights of free men. But if you deceive our hope, if the machinations of our enemies blind you to the point of rendering you insensible at the height of the storm, then indignation, sorrow, despair will impel and drag us into public places. There, we shall fight to defend liberty; until you have conquered it you will not be men. Then we shall save the Fatherland, or dying with it, we will uproot the torturous memory of seeing you unworthy of us.[11]

On the night of June 20–21, 1791, the royal family, in disguise, was smuggled out of the Tuileries palace into a waiting coach and driven east toward the Belgian border, intending to meet with French generals, cross the border to the Austrian army, and unleash counterrevolution. They were recognized at the town of Varennes and forced to wait there for an escort of deputies from the National Assembly and then to return to Paris. They entered the city surrounded by an escort of National Guards and rode past a silent and largely hostile crowd lining the route.

The National Assembly temporarily suspended the king's executive authority and debated what to do with him. Paris radicals were not so hesitant. Clubs like the Cercle Social and the Cordeliers reached out to popular societies, whose members were men and women of humble rank, and recruited them to sign petitions challenging the legitimacy of the king as well as that of the National Assembly. Women were actively and directly involved in this political mobilization. The historian Albert Mathiez cites Mlle. Le Maure as author of an address adopted by the Cordeliers and presented to the National Assembly, which protested decrees restricting the right to petition.[12] Women were involved in surveillance (exposing an arms cache) and in urging vandalism against statues of the king in Paris, and signed various petitions demanding consultation on the future of executive authority.[13] Women were part of the voice of the people. Forty-one signatures of women, "women, sisters and Roman women," were appended to the "Petition of the 100," which was delivered to the National Assembly on July 14, 1791. The text of this petition stated: "Therefore, make this sacred commitment to await the expression of this public voice before pronouncing on a question which affects the whole nation and which the powers you have received from [the nation] do not embrace."[14] The petitioners were asking the legislators to defer in this fundamental matter of political legitimacy to the will of the nation concretely expressed in a national vote.

On July 17, an extraordinary convocation of thousands of commoners, women and men, gathered on the Champ de Mars to challenge the deputies in the National Assembly and the Constitution of 1791, which authorized only the legislature to act in the name of the sovereign nation. They gathered peaceably to sign a petition demanding a national referendum on the question of the future of monarchical authority. Late in the afternoon of the seventeenth, the National Guard fired on the assembled crowds, killing and wounding several dozen people. The mass demonstration ended in a bloody confrontation between the political leaders of Paris and the crowd of petition-signers acting on their claim to the right to exercise popular sovereignty in the name of the nation.

Following the bloody silencing of this claim, authorities arrested a number of participants; several politically engaged women were among those detained. One was Anne Felicité Colomb, the owner of the printworks that produced the radical journals *Ami du Peuple* and *L'Orateur du peuple*. Colomb made an extraordinary contribution to the articulation and defense of revolutionary ideology. Her story illustrates the links between clubs, journals, and the new constitutional right to a free press, all of which promoted the cause of republicanism and radical democracy. On December 14, 1790, Colomb had been visited in her shop by a police *commissaire* and a man named Etienne, who had obtained a police order to interrogate her and confiscate all copies of the journals she was printing. Colomb protested against the visit as "illegal, as damaging to the rights of citizens, whose domiciles could be inspected only by a court to which proper authority was assigned [*un tribunal revêtu de pouvoir suffisant*]." She announced she would initiate proceedings against her interrogators "before the appropriate courts and before the Nation, which is concerned about preserving the liberty of all [its] members." Furthermore, she said that she would give the names of the authors of *Ami* and *Orateur* "only at that time and in those places and to whom it is appropriate."[15] On December 18, a court decision went against her, requiring that she cease printing and distributing any paper. She appealed on January 10, 1791, before the Tribunal de Police at the Hôtel de Ville, with the Cordelier Club activist Buirette de Verrières defending her. Her early arguments were restated, and in addition, Colomb wanted Sieur Etienne fined for court costs and damages to her good name and the reputation of her shop. She asked for 10,000 *livres* to go to the poor of Section Henry IV and Section du Théâtre français. She asked the court to invoke Article 11, the free press guarantee in the Declaration of the Rights of Man; and she demanded that her printworks, the authors of *Ami* and *L'Orateur,* and the distributors (*colporteurs*) all enjoy the protection accorded to them by the law, with the understanding that they would be held responsible for abuses of freedom of the press. The court vindicated Colomb and required Etienne to pay a small fine.[16]

On July 20–21, 1791, following the events on the Champ de Mars, authorities arrested and jailed Colomb and others at her printworks. The prisoners proceeded to appeal directly to the National Assembly, and on August 16 the Committee on Investigations of the Assembly wrote to the tribunal of the sixth *arrondisement* (an administrative ward) concerning the prisoners' provisional release, claiming that the records of their arrests and interrogations did not seem to warrant the court's long delay in reaching a decision. The committee informed the court that it had learned that the grievances of the detained parties would be aired before the National Assembly at any moment. On August 17, an officer of the tribunal replied that he was awaiting the results of further investigation.[17]

Colomb was an extraordinarily sophisticated political activist who defined citizenship and popular sovereignty to support her convictions and defend her professional rights. She and others arrested with her were ready to go beyond the courts directly to the National Assembly to do battle for their rights, and may in fact have been trying to discredit the Assembly by demonstrating that these newly guaranteed constitutional rights were being violated in investigations ordered by the Assembly after the events on the Champ de Mars. As a printer for the radical press, Colomb occupied a central position connecting the communications media, the Cordelier Club, and the new courts and legislature.

Also detained by the authorities, on the charge of insulting and threatening a member of the National Guard, was Constance Evrard, a cook and close friend of the political activist Pauline Léon. The minutes of Evrard's interrogation show that this passive citizen and political activist interpreted the Guards' acts on the Champ de Mars as a betrayal of the new and critically important bond and trust which had been developing between the nation's armed forces and citizens in the Paris sections. The wife of the Guardsman reported that Evrard, Pauline Léon, and Léon's mother had denounced her husband as "an assassin, a hangmen, a scoundrel, who was killing everyone on the Champ de Mars." Evrard had threatened to knife him within three days. Evrard herself admitted that she returned from the Champ de Mars on July 17 "outraged at the conduct of the National Guard against unarmed citizens," and that, seeing the Guardsman with his battalion passing by en route to the Champ de Mars, she reproached him for going there.[18]

The interrogation of Constance Evrard demonstrates her extraordinary sensitivity to the potential disaster that the National Guard's treachery could cause. In addition, she identified her personal actions with new concepts, responsibilities, and practices of citizenship and popular sovereignty that the crises of the summer of 1791 had crystallized. She told her interrogators that she had gone to the Champ de Mars and had "signed a petition like all good patriotic women." While admitting that she had not read the petition on the Champ de Mars, she "believes that this petition tends to have the executive power organized in another way." She acknowledged that she sometimes went with groups of people to the Palais Royal and the Tuileries—public places where political news was regularly circulated; she also attended the Cordeliers Club, although she was not a member. Evrard told authorities that she subscribed to the radical journal *Révolutions de Paris*; she had complimented the editor, Prudhomme, on his article on tyrannicides, and told him how enthusiastic she was about this article, adding that "had she been a man, she didn't know how far patriotism would have led her." She also stated that she read the journals of Marat, Audouin, Desmoulins, and "very often the *Orateur du People*"—all radical journals.[19]

During the summer of 1791, the revolutionaries had developed both the theory and the practice of popular sovereignty in revolutionary Paris. Women were among the sovereign people. Women *engaged themselves;* and, equally significantly, revolutionary leaders, determined to demonstrate the full weight of opposition to the constitutional monarchy, accepted and even recruited them as equal participants. For example, one of the men arrested for sedition on July 16 was accused of carrying a petition to the National Assembly, and of reading an invitation to all citizens that included the statement "that all women and children who had attained the age of reason would be received to sign the petition."[20] Notwithstanding their constitutional exclusion from such rights of citizenship as voting and standing for and holding office, the passive citizenry, men and women, behaved as citizens. They participated in revolutionary ceremonies, attended political meetings (as discussants, petitioners, and delegates), wrote political tracts, formulated and communicated revolutionary ideology, and involved themselves centrally in revolutionary *journées* (revolutionary "days"). They wore and displayed symbols which showed their patriotic commitment to the revolution. All these behaviors pressured and influenced authorities and contributed to transforming the French monarchy into the First Republic.

WOMEN AND THE TRIUMPH OF POPULAR SOVEREIGNTY

Between September 1791 and August 1792, some of the revolutionary leaders in Paris tolerated and even encouraged the involvement of women in open challenges to the constitutional monarchy and in acts of popular sovereignty expressive of a progressively more democratic understanding of the meaning of citizenship.

The actual collapse of the constitutional monarchy on August 10, 1792, was the outcome of a battle in the courtyard of the Tuileries between the king's Swiss Guard and a popular armed force. However, it was prepared by a complex series of events that strengthened revolutionary forces and weakened resistance in the king's camp and in the national legislature. On April 20, 1792, the Legislative Assembly voted a declaration of war against Austria, the event that ushered in twenty-three years of nearly continuous war in Europe. Other principal developments were the king's alienation from other revolutionary authorities, with whom he was required to work under the Constitution of 1791, and the public's growing attraction to republicanism, both of which widened the breach between king and people and sharpened the confrontation between the government officials — ministers, deputies, and municipal authorities who continued to operate within constitutional limits — and the fully mobilized insurgents who claimed legitimacy and sovereign authority for the people.

Between March 9 and June 20, 1792, thousands of men, women, and children from the sections and environs of Paris participated in armed processions through the halls of the Legislative Assembly. In each procession, the participants demanded recognition of their legitimate power as the sovereign people, and received that recognition from the legislature. In addition, in the accompanying speeches, and through signs, exclamations, gestures, images, symbols, such as the red cap of liberty and ribbons in revolutionary colors, and line of march, participants enlarged the significance of their actions, and linked them to new definitions of citizenship, national sovereignty, and the legitimacy of rulers. Finally, they conspicuously paraded pikes and sabres, which carried the threat that armed force would be used. This display of military force, in combination with concrete demands and the symbols and words which colored them with a general significance, produced a second revolution, during which the constitutional monarchy collapsed and a republic was established.

The people in arms reclaimed and rebuilt an alliance with official armed forces which had been shattered by the gunfire on the Champ de Mars in July 1791. Astonishingly, radical leaders as well as authorities first questioned but in the end tolerated the presence among the Guardsmen of men and women armed with the pike, the universally recognized weapon of the sovereign people.

In an editorial, "Des Piques," appearing in a February 1792 number of his *Révolutions de Paris*, the journalist Prudhomme called attention to the symbolic and military significance of the pike: "Universally accessible, available to the poorest citizen," the pike was an emblem for independence, equality under arms, vigilance, and the recovery of liberty. "The pikes of the people are the columns of French liberty." Prudhomme conspicuously denied the right of women to bear these arms: "Let pikes be prohibited for women; dressed in white and girded with the national sash, let them content themselves with being simple spectators." In his calculations Prudhomme eliminated the female portion of the 24 million potential pikebearers of France.[21] In fact, women continued to claim and exercise the right to arm themselves — with the pike, weapon of the sovereign people, and with other weapons as well. They thereby met Prudhomme's definition of the revolutionary citizen: independent, free, equal, vigilant, and armed.

On March 6, less than a month after this article appeared, a delegation of "citoyennes de la ville de Paris," led by Pauline Léon, an outspoken revolutionary activist, presented to the Legislative Assembly a petition with more than 300 signatures concerning women's right to bear arms. The petitioners grounded their claim in an appeal to the natural right to defend one's own life and liberty. "You cannot refuse us and society cannot remove from us this right which nature gives us, unless it is alleged that the Declaration of Rights is not applicable to women and that they must allow their throats to be slit, like sheep, without having the right to defend themselves." The delegation requested permission for women to arm themselves with pikes, pistols, sabres, and rifles; to assemble periodically on the Champ de Mars; and to engage in military maneuvers. The Assembly, after much debate, decreed a printing of the petition and honorable mention in the minutes and passed to the order of the day.[22]

While the Legislative Assembly hesitated between dismissing and tolerating women's demands for the right to bear arms, the newly formed, revolutionary Paris city government (the *Commune*) and the Mayor, Jérôme Pétion, took action to honor women's militancy publicly, reward it officially, and instate it as a model of female citizenship. In his speech of April 5 to the Commune, Pétion supported a petition on behalf of Reine Audu, one of the few participants in the women's march to Versailles in October 1789 who had been arrested and imprisoned. He argued that while French customs generally kept women out of combat, it was also the case that "in the moment of danger, when the fatherland is in peril," women "do not feel any the less that they are *citoyennes.*" The council, acting on the petition, decreed a ceremony in which the mayor would honor and decorate "this *citoyenne*" with a sword as "an authentic testimony to her bravery and her patriotism."[23]

In the weeks preceeding the April 9 armed procession a concept of female citizenship emerged that dissolved distinctions between active/passive, male/female citizens; combined women's right of self-defense with their civic obligation to protect and defend the nation; and placed both directly in the center of a general definition of all citizens' rights and responsibilities. Thus the armed women who between March and June 1792 marched in imposing processions, giving dramatic and forceful expression to the potent image of a united national family in arms, at the same time embodied militant citizenship, a driving force in the process of revolutionary radicalization. This moving picture is the clean, sharp inverse of the radical journalists' earlier depictions of unarmed families brutally gunned down by Lafayette's troops as they gathered on the Champ de Mars in July 1791 to sign the petition on the fate of the king. In the days and weeks following the events of July 17, 1791, Jean-Paul Marat had filled the pages of his *Ami du peuple* with provocative images: "The blood of old men, women, children, massacred around the altar of the fatherland is still warm, it cries out for vengeance."[24] The arming of passive citizens, including women, in the spring of 1792 turned upside down this picture of helpless martyrs; it empowered the powerless, it activated an involuntarily pacific (because legally "passive") citizenry, placing the potential force of women behind the radical leadership's escalating estimates of the strength of the national family in arms.

The armed procession of June 20, 1792, reflected turmoil in Paris over the king's dismissal of liberal ministers and his vetoes of two decrees, one authorizing harsh sanctions against clergy who had refused to swear an oath of loyalty to the Constitution and another establishing a camp for 20,000 French troops beneath the walls of Paris. Four days before, on June 16, a delegation from two militant neighborhoods (*faubourgs*) informed municipal authorities of plans to commemorate the fourth anniversary of the Tennis Court Oath—an oath sworn by deputies to the National Assembly not to disband until they had given France a constitution. The key event was to be an armed procession before the Assembly and the king to present petitions. The authorities tried to prevent the march, but the mayor, Pétion, realized that nothing could stop it. He developed a strategy of putting all armed citizens under the flags of the National Guard battalions and under the authority of battalion commanders, thereby legitimating a force composed of National Guardsmen and all citizens, passive along with active, women and children along with men.

On the morning of June 20, thousands of marchers were granted permission to parade through the meeting hall of the Legislative Assembly. Marchers included National Guardsmen, light infantrymen, grenadiers, and troops of the line—all interspersed with women, ("dames and femmes du peuple"), men (porters, charcoal burners, priests with swords and guns, veterans), and children. The marchers carried long pikes, guns, axes, knives, paring knives, scythes, pitchforks, sticks, bayonets, great saws, and clubs. Armed women were described as wearing liberty caps and carrying sabres and blades. The marchers' signs and banners proclaimed loyalty to the constitution,[25] and they meant what they said. In addition, their actions made it clear that the constitution, along with the government, was only the instrument of the will of an armed sovereign people.

These new meanings of sovereignty and legitimacy symbolically inverted the king's executive authority, his right to veto laws, and his role as representative of national sovereignty—all established in the Constitution of 1791. The people, constitutionally prohibited from exercising sovereignty, were doing just that.[26] When the marchers left the Assembly, they charged into the Tuileries and for six hours paraded, armed, before the king, displaying the banners and symbols which identified them as the sovereign nation. The king, in turn, refused to bend his will to that of this "sovereign people," and the mayor and other officers finally persuaded the demonstrators to leave the palace.[27]

Several witnesses were quick to seize the larger import of the day's events. An official of the Department of Paris (the national administrative unit for Paris) commented: "The throne was still standing but the people were seated on it, took the measure of it; and its steps seemed to have been lowered to the height of the paving stones of Paris."[28] These armed marches, repeatedly legitimized by the Assembly's votes to permit and honor them, were successful ceremonial demonstrations of the breadth, scope, and power of a fully mobilized democratic force in revolutionary Paris. The alliance between the women and men of the radical faubourgs and their National Guard, an alliance which had been shattered on the Champ de Mars in 1791, was being reforged on the bases of rebuilt trust and restored unity of purpose. On June 21, a police commissioner reported that in the Faubourg Saint-Antoine people were saying that " . . . the people is the only sovereign, it must make the law WITHOUT CONSTITUTION AND WITHOUT SANCTION [from any higher authority]."[29]

Pétion, the mayor of Paris, called particular attention to the significance of women's involvement in the events of June 20. Under attack for having failed to use force to prevent or disperse the procession, Pétion rushed into print with a self-defense: "Conduct of the Mayor of Paris on the occasion of the Events of June 20, 1792." In it he said that neither he nor anyone else could have commanded the force capable of stopping the march of "such an immense crowd of citizens." "Where was the repressive force capable of stopping the torrent? I say it did not exist." All battalions from the two faubourgs had marched with cannon and arms, followed by large numbers of armed citizens and a multitude of unarmed citizens, Pétion argued. Any force mobilized against the marchers could only have been composed of National Guardsmen, who, in that case, would have been opposing fellow guardsmen; combatting fellow citizens armed with pikes; opposing unarmed men, maybe even their neighbors; confronting women— their sisters, their wives, their mothers; battling with children—possibly their own. "Who would have been able to answer for the lives of these persons who are the most precious to the nation [and] whom it is most important to preserve?" On whom and where would this attacking force have fired? "The very idea of this carnage makes one shiver;" "And to whom would this bloody battlefield have been left?" Three quarters of the National Guard would have refused to fire on their fellow citizens, given that they all shared the marchers' motives; given that the Legislative Assembly already had set precedents when it "tolerated" earlier processions.[30]

The officials of the Department of Paris, who suspended Pétion from office for his failure to prevent the march, acknowledged that he was right about June 20: the presence of women and children in the ranks of the National Guard paralyzed it.[31] In short, authorities of all convictions, who would have had to give the order, perceived that the participants in the processions of June 20—precisely this particular combination of National Guardsmen and their commanders, armed and unarmed men and women and children, their relatives, friends, neighbors—had symbolized a new political and military force, a great national family in arms, which could be vanquished only at unthinkable cost.

The fall of the monarchy on August 10 was the culmination of this movement of popular militancy. Louis XVI, fearing he had lost the loyalty of the National Guard, sought refuge in the Legislative Assembly. Shortly afterwards, an armed populace of National Guardsmen and citizens stormed the Tuileries, overcame the Swiss Guard at the cost of tremendous losses on both sides, and by this bloody victory precipitated the final crisis of the monarchy and its fall.

The new republican authorities moved quickly to control and restrain the men and women who had helped bring them to victory. For example, on August 14, the Legislative Assembly decreed that those receiving government pensions must appear before the city officials to swear fidelity to the nation.[32] Shortly after this decree, the General Assembly of one neighborhood government printed and posted a decree that all male citizens aged fifteen and over and all female citizens over the age of thirteen had to take an individual oath before the section Assembly. The wording of the oath was similar to that decreed by the Legislative Assembly on August 14: "to uphold liberty and equality and to die, if necessary, for both. . . . " The section Assembly declared that it would regard as "bad" citizens and citoyennes those who would not swear it, and that it would refuse entry into its sessions to anyone who had not fulfilled this "civic duty." To enforce this stipulation, certificates would be issued to oathtakers and the registers would be closed on August 25, just before the primary assemblies for the next legislative elections. These authorities recognized that the armed men and women who had just brought down the monarchy could not be dissolved or repressed. The administrative requirement was to regulate them: "It is important to know who are the good citizens and citoyennes who want to bring about liberty and equality, and who are the cowards and traitors who still would dare to

yearn for despotism."[33] Authorities recognized women's full political and
military engagement and developed mechanisms to regulate it, and their
language hints at the potential for turning these regulations into instruments
of repressive control.

The full weight of repression against political women was not felt for
more than a year after the fall of the monarchy. In the spring, summer, and
early fall of 1793, organized women became a force for authorities to
reckon with. The first exclusively female interest group in western politics,
the Society of Revolutionary Republican Women, organized in early 1793
by Pauline Léon and Claire Lacombe, cooperated with and eventually came
into conflict with the radical Jacobin establishment. The Society had close
ties to radical men active in neighborhood politics, the Enragés, and
began to meet under the aegis of the Jacobin Club, which provided them
with a meeting hall. Members of the Society were instrumental in helping to
evict the Girondins (a loosely organized "party" of liberal deputies) from the
National Convention in late May 1793; throughout the summer of 1793
they urged the Convention to more radical curbs on aristocrats, laws regulating supplies and prices in Paris, and legislation in support of the revolutionary armies. In late summer, the Society's radicalism evoked protests from
market women, who opposed price control and who accused the Society of
ruining their commerce. Despite heroic defensive maneuvers by Claire
Lacombe and others, the Convention voted to close the Society in October
1793, on the grounds that its members threatened public order.

The Jacobin leaders who engineered the repression of the Society,
extended the ban to all clubs and popular societies of women and inflated
their rhetoric into a full-blown, misogynist theory of the biological,
psychological, and moral determinants of women's incapacities for political
action. André Amar, the spokesman for the Committee of General Security,
reporting to the Convention on October 28, 1793, began with specific
complaints about market disorders near Saint-Eustache, which the Revolutionary Women allegedly incited, and reported the request of the Section des
Marchés (a self-governing municipal unit) for a prohibition against popular
societies of women. Amar then posed the general question: Should women
exercise political rights and meddle in political affairs? His negative answer
was no longer addressed to the specific issue of the Society's responsibility
for market disorders; rather, in his rationalization of the legislation, Amar
cited women's reproductive responsibilities, their moral weakness, their
inadequate political education, and their nervous excitability. Interestingly,
another deputy (Charlier) commented that police ought to be able to deal
with disorder, and women should not be denied their right to assemble
peaceably. "Unless you are going to question whether women are part of the
human species, can you take away from them this right which is common to
every thinking being?"[34] The debate concluded with the remark by the
deputy Bazire that he did not want to hear any more about principles;

public order was endangered, and that situation called for the absolute prohibition of women's associations.[35]

What is intriguing about this exchange is the deputies' manifest awareness of the implications of sex roles. They recognized what modern historians have sometimes forgotten: that the rights and responsibilities of citizenship had to be defined for women as well as men. No matter what an individual debater's opinion on the immediate matter of the Society for Revolutionary Republican Women, he admitted that women were one factor in the power equation in a city and nation in the throes of revolution and war where the bases of sovereign and legitimate authority were continually being questioned.

The end result was to try to slam the lid back down on the Pandora's box that had been opened by women's revolutionary behavior. Not only were women's societies proscribed, but women were barred from sessions of the Paris Commune and, in the spring of 1794, from popular assemblies. Thus, women's institutional bases of power were destroyed. They were prevented from meeting and organizing so that their political voice could be silenced.

There is some striking evidence that even this legal abolition did not eliminate women's political influence. At a single session of the Jacobin Club, on June 26, 1794, women intervened at several points in an attempt to impose their views. First, Citoyenne Berny expressed her approval of a tableau depicting the deification of Jean-Paul Marat, the martyred radical journalist; the Club recognized her sentiments. Then the president recognized a deputation of wives of some men from Orléans who had been arrested and transferred to a prison in Paris. A member reported that the Committee of Public Safety knew about the arrest and had ordered the transfer. After the Club debated some other issues already scheduled, a member announced that some citoyennes wanted to denounce a member of the Club who was present at the meeting and who embraced the most counterrevolutionary principles. The spokesman demanded that the citoyennes be heard immediately; they indicated the member they were accusing. Tumult ensued. The accused man went out, accompanied by many members, and was taken to the Committee of General Security. Finally, at the end of the session the president announced a patriotic gift from a citoyenne consisting of a package of bandages.[36]

The events of this single session illustrate the range of women's public concerns, the seriousness with which they continued to be taken, and their continuing access to and influence upon an institution like the Jacobin Club, an important part of the power structure of revolutionary government. Eight months earlier, Amar's rhetoric had limited women to such symbolic acts of support as the recognition of revolutionary heroes or the donation of bandages. He did not anticipate women's continuing political activism on other fronts. The wives from Orléans still recognized the Society as a place to which they could turn collectively to submit a grievance and ask for assistance. Although their request was denied, no member questioned their right of access. No one challenged the group of women who denounced a member; no one questioned their accusation, and the accused man was accompanied immediately to the Committee of General Security for questioning. Their word alone was enough to trap their victim; hardly an illustration of female political impotence.

This evidence does not deny the significance and severity of the Jacobin curbs on women's opportunities for political initiative. The Jacobins had destroyed their bases of influence in the neighborhoods and their single-sex club. And even though they were principal actors in the last great revolutionary uprising, the journées of Germinal-Prairial, Year III (1795), that insurrection left no institutional imprint because the organizational base of political influence for the common people had been dissolved. In May 1795 the legislature ordered women to remain in their homes and decreed that groups of more than five women in public would be dispersed, forcibly if necessary.

Under the Napoleonic Code (the national code of laws completed in 1804), women had no political rights, and their legal status was that of dependents. Women could not sign contracts, buy or sell, or have bank accounts in their own names. Divorce, allowed by law since September 20, 1792, was made much more difficult. It would take two more generations, the spread of industrialization, the development of labor organizations, and a second republic to renew political institutions for the popular classes, men and women.

CONCLUSION

To focus on women in revolutionary Paris is to create a different understanding of citizenship, popular sovereignty, and legitimacy and the connections among them. What difference did the presence and even the active participation of women really make to the development of popular sovereignty and new concepts of political legitimacy? Are the historians missing much when they leave women out of their depictions and analyses of the French revolution or include them, if at all, only to add local color?

First, women contributed to revolutionary political ideology. A handful of women writers and activists explored the situation of women and proposed definitions of citizenship that spoke to women's gender-specific needs as well as to their right to full citizenship. The radicalism of their claims for women did not place them, necessarily, on the political left in revolutionary politics. Olympe de Gouges, playwright and publicist in Paris, wrote, in the summer of 1791 as the constitution was being completed, a Declaration of the Rights of Woman. Adopting the form and the language of the Declaration of the Rights of Man and Citizen, she called for full political equality for women, but in addition, demanded legislation for women specifically, for example, laws that would secure property and inheritance rights for women and would establish the right of a mother to legitimate her child regardless of her marital state.[37] De Gouges was not a leftwing radical; she supported the constitutional monarchy and addressed her Declaration to Queen Marie Antoinette. She was arrested in 1793, accused of royalism, tried and found guilty by the Revolutionary Tribunal, and guillotined on November 3, 1793. Another writer, Etta Palm d'Aelders, a Dutch-born revolutionary, was allied with political moderates in 1791 and 1792. She envisioned a network of political clubs that would be concerned with women's needs and special role in society. She also addressed the issue of equal rights for women, particularly on matters of laws about marriage and equal educational opportunity.[38] Contributions like those of de Gouges, d'Aelders, and Anne Félicité Colomb became part of the ideology supporting the liberal tradition in France. Ideas counted in making, explaining, and propagandizing a democratic revolution; and women, in their roles as journalists, pamphleteers, speech-makers, printers, petitioners, and witnesses, actively disseminated their ideas. They understood that liberty, equality, and fraternity had to be redefined to include women. New forms of citizenship and sovereignty would be new pillars of legitimacy supporting a wholly new form of government, whether a constitutional monarchy or a republic.

In addition to ideas, the revolution produced behaviors based on claims to full popular sovereignty that grew out of ancient popular roots. At first, the self-defined citizens supported the monarchy; later they were radicalized through direct collective action and assertions of insurrectionary power. Women were centrally involved in this development of sovereignty. Numbers counted in this radicalization process; not only were thousands of women active in Paris, but revolutionary authorities at all levels actively recruited them.

Force counted also when crowds acted on their belief in popular sovereignty. The journées and smaller-scale acts of violence were powerful agencies of democratization. Legal and constitutional changes did not give political influence to the common people in revolutionary Paris; the threat of force did. Women took part in acts of violence; they turned to the use force because of their supersensitivity to subsistence and security issues. Moreover, they counted in calculations of force as a political resource.

Finally, only a military victory could overthrow the forces committed to the preservation of the constitutional monarchy. On June 20, these forces, particularly the National Guard, were coopted by "the sovereign people"—armed men, women, and children from the radical sections of Paris. Their symbolic victory over the Legislative Assembly and the king anticipated the actual overthrow of the constitutional monarchy by a popular armed force on August 10. This triumph illustrates the paralysis of the military force supporting the ruling authorities. That paralysis must be counted as one of the key elements in the empowerment of popular sovereignty. At a critical turning point in the revolution, the transition from constitutional monarchy to republican government, the authorities in power were unable to turn their guns on the insurgent masses, in part because those masses, with women in their midst, had succeeded so completely in identifying themselves as a great national family in arms, the sovereign people and the French nation.

On one level, real families armed themselves for their own survival, and on another level, symbolically they armed the nation. Moreover, the same women who picked up arms in self-defense also demanded the policing of markets, the distribution of welfare, and the enforcement of Terror. They also claimed the right to bear arms, the right to assemble, the right to free expression, and the right to full political participation. The militancy of all these demands threatened male revolutionaries. Leaders of the republican government accepted the fact that selective extensions of women's roles as wives, mothers, and guardians of morals were required when the fatherland was in danger. Nonetheless, in the fall of 1793, as in the spring of 1795, these leaders moved decisively to repress politicized women absolutely when the men perceived the implications of such empowerment: a world in which women could threaten men's control of political authority.

NOTES

1. Siméon Prosper Hardy, "Mes Loisirs, ou Journal d'événements tels qu'ils parviennent à ma connoissance," vol. 7, 8 mai 1789, p. 78. fol. 475, in Bibliothèque Nationale, MSS, fonds français, no. 6687, our translation.
2. H. Monin, L'état de Paris en 1789: Etudes et Documents (Paris: Jouaust, Noblet, et Maison Quantin, 1889), p. 637.
3. Hardy, "Mes Loisirs," vol. 8, 14 September 1789.
4. R. B. Rose, "How to Make a Revolution: The Paris Districts of 1789," Bulletin of the John Rylands Library of the University of Manchester, 59, No. 21

(1976–77), 426–457; and "The Paris Districts and Direct Democracy, 1789–90," *Bulletin*, 61, No. 2 (1978–79), 422–443.

5. *Réimpression de l'Ancien Moniteur universel* (Paris: Au Bureau Central, 1840), II, p. 399 (31 août 1789).

6. Sigismond Lacroix, *Actes de la Commune de Paris* (7 vols., Paris: L. Cerf, 1894–1898), I, 7 September 1789, p. 499, reports a request to the Commune from female citizens of the district of Saint-Leu for permission for a march to Sainte-Geneviève. Permission was granted.

7. George Rudé, *The Crowd in the French Revolution* (Oxford: Clarendon Press, 1959), pp. 61–79.

8. Jennifer Dunn Westfall, "The Participation of Non-elite Women in the Parisian Crowd Movements of the Opening Year of the French Revolution," unpublished honors thesis, Mt. Holyoke College, 1976, pp. 101, 102, citing Arch. nat., C 32, No. 271.

9. John Hall Stewart, *A Documentary Survey of the French Revolution* (New York: Macmillan, 1951), p. 129.

10. J. Mavidal, E. Laurent, et al., eds. *Archives parlementaries*, de 1787 à 1860, First Series (34 vols., Paris: Imprimerie nationale, 1867–1890) IX October 20, 1789, p. 470.

11. Club des Cordeliers, Société des amis des droits de l'homme et du citoyen, "Extrait des délibérations du 22 février 1791,:" in Bibliothèque historique de la Ville de Paris, 10,065 No. 67, translated in Darline G. Levy, Harriet B. Applewhite, and Mary D. Johnson, eds., *Women in Revolutionary Paris, 1789–1795*. (Urbana: University of Illinois Press, 1979), p. 67.

12. Albert Mathiez, *Le Club de Cordeliers, pendant la Crise de Varennes et le Massacre du Champ de Mars* (Geneva: Slatkine-Megariotis Reprints, 1975; reprint of 1910 edition), pp. 8, 28.

13. Ibid.; Levy, Applewhite, and Johnson, *Women in Revolutionary Paris*, p. 78, 79, 83, 84.

14. Ibid., p. 79.

15. Dossier of Anne Felicité Colomb, Archives nationales, F[7] 2624, plaq. 1, fols. 52–69.

16. Ibid.

17. Section de la Place Vendôme, 20–21 July, 1791, Procès-verbal of the seizure of manuscripts and printed works by Marat and others . . . arrest and imprisonment of Dlle. Colomb, Redelé de Fl [illeg.], and Verrière[s] in Archives nationales, W. 357, no. 750; Letter of the Comité des recherches to the Tribunal of the 6th Arrondissement, 16 August 1791, in Archives nationales, DXXIX[bis]31[b], no. 324; letter from the Interim President of the Tribunal of the 6th Arrondissement, to the Comité des Rapports, 17 August 1791, in DXXIX[bis]34, no. 352.

18. Procès-verbal of the interrogation of Constance Evrard and witnesses, Section de la Fontaine de Grenelle, Sunday, 17 July 1791, in Archives, Préfecture de la Police, Paris, Series Aa, 148, fol. 30.

19. Ibid.

20. Mathiez, *Le Club des Cordeliers*, p. 363.

21. Prudhomme, "Des Piques," *Révolutions de Paris*, Vol. 11, 11–18 February 1792, pp. 293–298.

22. *Archives parlementaires*, XXXIX, 6 March 1792, pp. 423, 424.
23. *Extrait du registre des délibérations du Conseil général de la Commune de Paris*, Vendredi, 5 April 1792 (Paris, 1792).
24. Marat, *Ami du peuple*, no. 524, 20 July 1791, p. 2.
25. *Archives parlementaires*, XLV, 20 June 1792, pp. 406 ff., and esp. 411–419. [Madame Rosalie Jullien] *Journal d'une Bourgeoise pendant la Révolution, 1791–1793*, published by Edouard Lockroy (Paris: Calmann-Lévy, 1881), pp. 134–147. *Le Mercure universel*, 21 June 1792, as cited in Laura B. Pfeiffer, "The Uprising of June 20, 1792," in *University Studies* of the University of Nebraska, Vol. XII, No. 3 (July, 1912), pp. 84,85.
26. Stewart, *A Documentary Survey of the French Revolution*, p. 234.
27. Laura Pfeiffer, "The Uprising of June 20, 1792," pp. 284–323.
28. P. L. Roederer, *Chronique des cinquante jours du 20 juin au 10 août 1792* (Paris, 1832), p. 63.
29. Dumont, commissaire de police, Section de la Rue Montreuil, to the Directory of the Department of Paris, 21 June 1792, in "Journée du 20 juin 1792," *Revue Rétrospective, ou Bibliothèque historique*, 2nd. series, vol. 1 (1835), p. 180.
30. Jérôme Pétion, "Conduite tenue par M. le Maire de Paris à l'occasion des événements du 20 juin 1792", in *Revue Rétrospective, ou Bibliothèque historique*, 2nd series, vol. I (1835), pp. 221 ff.
31. *Extrait des Registres des délibérations du Conseil du Département de Paris, 6 juillet 1792* (Paris, 1792).
32. *Archives parlementaires*, XLVII 10 August 1792, pp. 639–642.
33. *Extrait des Registres des délibérations de la Section du Pont Neuf, Réunie en Assemblée permanente, le 15 août 1792, l'an 4ᵉ de la liberté, le 1ᵉʳde l'égalité*. Paris, n.d. See also F. Braesch, ed., *Procès-verbaux de l'Assemblée générale de la Section des Postes, 4 décembre 1790–5 septembre 1792* (Paris, 1911), pp. 198, 199, n. 2.
34. *Réimpression de l'Ancien Moniteur*, National Convention, Session of 9 Brumaire, Vol. 18, pp. 298–300; translated in Levy, Applewhite, and Johnson, eds., *Women in Revolutionary Paris*, p. 217.
35. Ibid., pp. 213–217.
36. F. A. Aulard, *La Société des Jacobins* (6 vols.; Paris: 1889–1897), VI, pp. 189–192, session of 8 Messidor, An II (26 juin 1794).
37. Levy, Applewhite, and Johnson, eds., *Women in Revolutionary Paris*, pp. 87–96.
38. Ibid., pp. 75–77 and p. 123.

SUGGESTIONS FOR FURTHER READING

Sources in English

Abray, Jane. "Feminism in the French Revolution," *American Historical Review*, 80 (February, 1975): 43–62.

Applewhite, Harriet B., and Darline Gay Levy. "Ceremonial Dimensions of Citizenship: Women and Oathtaking in Revolutionary Paris," *Proceedings of the Fifth George*

Rudé Seminar in French History (Wellington, New Zealand: Victoria University of Wellington, August, 1986).

———. "Women, Democracy, and Revolution in Paris, 1789–1794," in *French Women and the Age of Enlightenment*, ed. Samia I. Spencer (Bloomington: Indiana University Press, 1984).

———. "Responses to the Political Activism of Women of the People in Revolutionary Paris, 1789–1793," in *Women and the Structure of Society: Selected Research from the Fifth Berkshire Conference on the History of Women*, ed. Barbara J. Harris and JoAnn K. McNamara (Durham, N.C.: Duke University Press, 1984).

Dawson, Philip, ed. *The French Revolution* (Englewood Cliffs, N.J.: Prentice-Hall, 1967).

George, Margaret. "The 'World Historical Defeat' of the Républicaines-Révolutionnaires," *Science and Society*, 40, no. 4 (Winter, 1976–77): 410–437.

Hufton, Olwen H. *The Poor of Eighteenth-Century France, 1750–1789* (Oxford: Oxford University Press, 1975).

———. "Women and the Family Economy in Eighteenth-Century France," *French Historical Studies* (Spring, 1975): 1–22.

———. "Women in the French Revolution," *Past and Present*, 53 (November, 1971): 90–108.

Kaplan, Steven L. *Bread, Politics, and Political Economy in the Reign of Louis XV.* 2 vols. (The Hague, Netherlands: M. Nijhof, 1976).

———. *Provisioning Paris: Merchants and Millers in the Grain and Flour Trade During the Eighteenth Century* (Ithaca: Cornell University Press, 1984).

Kates, Gary. *The Cercle Social, the Girondins, and the French Revolution.* (Princeton, N.J.: Princeton University Press, 1985).

Levy, Darline Gay; Harriet Branson Applewhite; and Mary Durham Johnson. *Women in Revolutionary Paris, 1789–1795* (Urbana: University of Illinois Press, 1979).

Levy, Darline Gay and Harriet B. Applewhite. "Women of the Popular Classes in Revolutionary Paris, 1789–1795," in *Women, War and Revolution*, ed. by Carol R. Berkin and Clara M. Lovett (New York: Holmes and Meier, 1980).

Lytle, Scott. "The Second Sex (September, 1793)," *Journal of Modern History.* 26 (1955): 14–26.

Moses, Claire Goldberg. *French Feminism in the Nineteenth Century* (Albany: State University of New York Press, 1984).

Rose, R. B. *The Enragés: Socialists of the French Revolution* (Sydney, Australia: Sydney University Press, 1968).

———. *The Making of the Sans-culottes: Democratic Ideas and Institutions in Paris, 1789–92* (Manchester: Manchester University Press, 1983).

Rudé, George. *The Crowd in the French Revolution.* (New York: Oxford University Press, 1959).

———. *Paris and London in the Eighteenth Century: Studies in Popular Protest* (London: Collins, 1970 and New York, 1971).

Stoddard, Julia C. "The Causes of the Insurrection of the 5th and 6th of October," *University of Nebraska Studies*, 4, no. 4 (October, 1904): 267–327.

Tackett, Timothy. *Religion, Revolution, and Regional Culture in Eighteenth Century France: The Ecclesiastical Oath of 1791* (Princeton, N.J.: Princeton University Press, 1986).

Williams, David. "The Politics of Feminism in the French Enlightenment," in *The Varied Pattern: Studies in the Eighteenth Century*, ed. P. Hughes and D. Williams (Toronto: University of Toronto Press, 1971).

Woloch, Isser. *Jacobin Legacy: The Democratic Movement under the Directory* (Princeton: Princeton University Press, 1970)

Sources in French

Abensour, Léon. *La Femme et le Féminisme avant la Révolution française* (Paris: Plon Nourrit, 1923).

Bourdin, Isabel. *Les sociétés populaires à Paris pendant la Révolution de 1789 jusqu'à la chute de la royauté* (Paris: Librarie du Recueil Sirey, 1937).

Bouvier, Jeanne. *Les Femmes pendant la Révolution* (Paris: Collection Durand, 1931).

Cerati, Marie. *Le Club des citoyennes républicaines révolutionnaires* (Paris: Editions sociales, 1966).

Duhet, Paule-Marie. *Les Femmes et la Révolution, 1789–1794* (Paris: Julliard, 1971)

Garaud, Marcel and Romuald Szramkiewicz, *La Révolution française et la famille* (Paris: Presses universitaires de France, 1978).

Lacour, Léopold. *Les origines du féminisme contemporain. Trois Femmes de la Révolution: Olympe de Gouges, Théroigne de Méricourt, Rose Lacombe* (Paris: Plon, 1900)

Markov, Walter, and Albert Soboul, eds. *Die Sansculotten von Paris: Dokumente zur Geschichte der Volksbewegung, 1793–1794* (Berlin and Paris: Akademie, 1957).

Mathiez, Albert. *Le Club des Cordeliers pendant la crise de Varennes et le massacre du Champ de Mars* (Geneva: Slatkine-Megariotis Reprints, 1975; reprint of 1910 edition)

Michelet, Jules. *Les Femmes de la Révolution* (Paris: Delahays, 1854).

Ozouf, Mona. *La Fête révolutionnaire, 1789–1799* (Paris: Gallimard, 1976).

Portmer, Jean. "Le Statut de la femme en France depuis la Réformation des coutumes jusqu'à la rédaction du Code Civil," in *Recueils de la Société Jean Bodin pour l'histoire comparative des institutions*, vol. 12, pp. 447–497.

Roche, Daniel. *Le Peuple de Paris: Essai sur la culture populaire au XVIIIe siècle* (Paris: Editions Aubier Montaigne, 1981).

British women at work in a match factory in 1902. (© Mary Evans Picture Library/Photo Researchers, Inc.)

chapter 12

Women in the Industrial Capitalist Economy

Laura Levine Frader

The changes in the process of production known as the Industrial Revolution were a dreary experience for working class women. Factory production separated home and workplace, breaking up the family as an economic unit and devaluing women's work in the home. Mechanization created new divisions of labor that widened the gender gap by relegating women to the lowest paid, most unskilled places in the new work hierarchy. Whether in the new factories or in the home industries that supplemented these, women clustered in the production of only a few goods, such as textiles and garments, crowding those fields and depressing wages in them. At the same time, a discourse of domesticity implied that women worked only for pin money, a rationalization for low pay. Toward the end of the nineteenth century, new areas of service opened to women, mainly in clerical and sales work and in the professions of teaching and nursing, all of which provided alternatives to domestic service, which declined. Male workers' fear of cheap female labor retarded organizing, but some joint efforts succeeded and some women's unions were formed. In the end, the forces of oppression also created conditions for opposition and women began to fight for their economic rights.

INTRODUCTION

The development of industrial capitalism from about 1750 through 1914 brought dramatic changes to the European landscape. Capitalist entrepreneurs began to invest in large-scale manufacturing, and wage laborers moved from the household or workshop (where they had worked during the protoindustrial period) to the factory, which became the primary place of work. Workers and their families became more dependent than ever before on the wage as their primary means of subsistence. Large factories, the hallmarks of industrial capitalism in nearly every country, belched forth soot and smoke, blackening the cities that sprang up around them: Manchester, Stockport, and Leeds in England, Roubaix and Lille in France; Berlin and Hamburg in Germany. Women made a major contribution to this transformation by providing much of the cheap labor that enabled industrial capitalism to expand.

Over the course of about a century Europe was transformed. A rapid industrial revolution radically changed the British economy between 1750 and 1850. France, on the other hand, experienced no revolution, but rather the gradual development of industry and trade in the early nineteenth century. In Germany, massive and swift industrialization took place after about 1850. The new technology of industrialization produced extraordinary wealth, but the members of the industrial working class often struggled to eke out an existence as capitalism passed through alternate phases of prosperity and depression.

This essay addresses women's experience of industrialization as wage workers between 1750 and 1914, and looks at how social class, gender, reproduction, and the family shaped that experience. It examines the stages in the development of industrial capitalism, the concomitant changes in agriculture, the growth of manufacturing, and the expansion of the service sector in Britain, France, and Germany.

Some historians have viewed women's wage work under industrial capitalism as a triumph for women, arguing that women gained new freedom, independence from their families, and improvements in their material lives. It is true that over the period discussed here women separated from their families to earn wages and that they worked in new jobs under conditions that differed vastly from those of the early modern economy. Industrial capitalism did not, however, lead to greater freedom or greatly improved material conditions for most women, at least initially. Moreover, women experienced industrial capitalism largely through the filter of their gender and family roles. Cultural definitions of women's roles that stressed the importance of their domestic activities also made their situation in the workplace extremely insecure.

THE COMING OF THE INDUSTRIAL REVOLUTION

In Britain, numerous factors contributed to the swiftness of the industrial revolution. As part of the effort to rationalize agriculture by introducing more efficient farming methods and better fertilizers and equipment (the agricultural revolution), many large farmers put fences around their land and took over village common pastures (enclosures). This practice threw small peasant farmers off the land and, along with population growth, helped to create the "free" labor force necessary to industrialization. The relatively early breakdown of the feudal and guild systems, and the presence of small-scale forms of manufacturing already in place also facilitated the growth of industry. Britain's possession of an immense colonial empire was beneficial: it led to the growth of an urban middle class based on merchant capital and provided the economic benefits of colonies as resources and as markets. Finally, the availability of ports and inland transportation, as well as a strong system of banking and credit, provided the material basis for Britain's enormous industrial transformation. In addition, the growing belief in individual rights, the value of hard work, and the freedom of the individual to act on the basis of self-interest in the marketplace also favored the development of industrial capitalism. By the second half of the nineteenth century, the industrial middle class had gained control of government to further its own economic aims, and Britain's industrial power was uncontested.

In France, the great revolution of 1789 both encouraged and forestalled industrialization. The revolution swept away the restrictive guild system that hampered economic expansion and abolished such remaining vestiges of feudalism as the leisured aristocracy that had been resistant to capitalist activity. The triumph of the bourgeois values of private property, and individual liberty, cornerstones of the revolution, provided the ideological foundations of French industrial capitalism. Other developments, however, posed obstacles to the development of capitalism in France. By freeing land from the grip of the aristocracy, the revolution also created a class of peasants whose solid attachment to the soil prevented the creation of a free labor pool necessary to large-scale capitalist development. The disruption caused by the revolutionary and Napoleonic wars also forestalled economic expansion. Limited access to credit stymied would-be entrepreneurs, and the protectionist constitutional monarchy that succeeded Napoleon's government was dominated by conservative landed interests who discouraged technological innovation. Poor coal resources and inefficient internal transportation also slowed industrialization. Finally, however, between 1840 and the 1860s, the upper–middle class gained more control over government policy, and instituted a number of policies—support for railway building, the negotiation of trade agreements, and the opening of credit resources— that stimulated capitalist development.

A combination of political and economic factors also delayed German industrialization. Until 1871 Germany consisted of a fragmented collection of quasi-independent states with enormous regional variations. Serfdom and guilds, both constraints on the formation of a "free" labor force, survived into the early nineteenth century in some parts of Germany, and a powerful landed aristocracy with little interest in business dominated much of eastern Germany. All of these conditions posed obstacles to the growth of industrial capitalism. The conclusion of internal customs agreements within Prussia in the 1830s; the gradual decline of the guilds by the 1850s; the unification of Germany in 1871 under the powerful monarchy of Kaiser Wilhelm; and strong government support of industry assured by Wilhelm's Chancellor, Otto von Bismarck; all these developments facilitated industrialization. Political and economic compromises between conservative grain growers in the east and industrialists in the west, and the concentration of industry in the hands of a few large industrial monopolies, also allowed for the rapid development of industrial capitalism. By the end of the nineteenth century, Germany actively competed with Britain on the world market.

In spite of these differences in the timing of industrialization, certain features of women's roles and conditions were common to industrial capitalism in all three countries.

New Conditions of Work and Women's Roles

Industrialization fundamentally changed the nature and organization of work, altered the family's role in production, and changed women's economic activities. Within the factory, skilled artisans found themselves replaced by steam driven machines and unskilled laborers. Not only did workers labor for the profits of the capitalist (as they had already begun to do under the early modern economy), they no longer had the freedom to control the timing and pace of work themselves. The clock and the machine now determined when and how fast they worked. Within the factory the worker no longer took pride in the production of an entire piece of cloth from scratch, for example, but now made only part of the finished product. These features of industrial capitalism affected men and women alike, but the reorganization in factories of much production formerly undertaken in the artisan's workshop or household resulted in particular changes for women and their families.

The separation of household and workplace meant the continued limitation of women's economic activities and the continued devaluation of women's place in the economy—developments that had already begun in the early modern economy (see Merry Weisner's essay in this volume). Until well into the nineteenth century in Britain, France, and Germany, the enterprises of manufacturers and small shopkeepers, such as textile manufacturers, clothiers, butchers, and bakers, who combined production and sales, had relied on family labor. Often the factory or shop stood on the same grounds as the owner's home and the wife and children helped with the business. Women assumed a substantial portion of selling, managing, and accounting in early workshops, bakeries, and dairies. As these enterprises expanded and manufacturers tried to increase their profits, however, male assistants with training in management and accountancy, replaced women family members. Prosperous middle-class businessmen bought homes in pleasant, green suburbs far from the urban factory, shop, or workshop, and their wives increasingly retreated to the confines of their homes. Here they occupied themselves with consumption and reproduction rather than production, and in creating havens from the dirty, unhealthy world of industrial capitalism. The development of an industrial economy reinforced the demarcation of male and female spheres and more clearly underlined the ideas about the differences between men's work and women's work that had already begun to emerge in the early modern economy.

In nineteenth-century Britain, France, and Germany, guidebooks and manuals glorified women's maternal and domestic activities and defined women as inherently weaker and more delicate than men. This literature had existed earlier but as literacy increased it drew a wider audience than ever before. In addition, writers idealized the home even more as household and workplace separated. Works such as Mrs. Sarah Stickney Ellis's *Mothers of England* (1843) and John Ruskin's "Of Queen's Gardens" (1865) portrayed the home as a haven from the competition and materialism of the industrial capitalist world: " . . . a place of Peace; the shelter, not only from all injury, but from all terror, doubt, and division."[1] According to the ideal of domesticity—an ideal which continues in our own day—women must take responsibility for maintaining the home as a sanctuary. The good wife should devote herself to pleasing her husband and caring for her home and children, and should cultivate the moral virtues that would sustain the family against the harsh world of industry. These tasks required considerable effort, but, as in the early modern economy, because women received no wages for domestic tasks and child care, most people did not consider such activities as "work." Throughout the nineteenth and early twentieth centuries (and still, today) the domestic ideal strongly influenced middle-class and working-class attitudes towards women's paid work under industrial capitalism. As increasing numbers of women entered the industrial workforce, and as their paid work became more visible, critics deplored working-class women's abandonment of the home and condemned them for contributing to the decline of the family.

If middle-class wives could afford to withdraw from the world of production, the vast majority of working-class women had to earn wages at some point during their lives. In fact, their labor as wage workers created the wealth that permitted middle-class women to live lives of comparative ease and comfort. Working-class women, indeed, experienced the negative consequences of industrial capitalism most acutely, as the situation of women in agriculture indicates.

Changes in Women's Agricultural Work

Since time immemorial, women have tilled the soil, planted, harvested, and sold the products of their labors. But women's agricultural work changed significantly with the coming of industrial capitalism. In Britain, the agricultural revolution, enclosures, and the concentration of large farms led to the decline of small family farms that once depended heavily on women's contributions in dairying, poultry-raising, cheese and butter making, and harvesting. Women who had earlier run their dairies as small businesses no longer made the weekly trip to village and town markets to sell their produce, and if they continued dairying, they did so only for their own families' consumption. Other women, forced off the soil and deprived of land for raising vegetables and livestock, now entered the labor force as industrial or agricultural wage workers, and became entirely dependent on wages. Some, desperate for any work they could get, joined agricultural "gangs," a form of labor subcontracted for farmers by a gang master. Gangs employed unskilled women and children in heavy field work—planting, hoeing and harvesting. Such women, used to laboring on their own plots at their own pace, now found themselves driven by the gang master and obliged to work from sunrise to sunset in pouring rain or biting frost for less wages than men earned for the same work.[2] Many women experienced sexual harassment and brutality from the gang leaders. This system lasted until the 1860s, when reforms of the gangs (1868) and laws establishing compulsory primary school education (1870) made it obsolete. The introduction of agricultural machinery also allowed farmers to do without women's and children's labor in the fields.

French women who tilled the soil did not experience such dramatic changes even after the development of large scale industrial capitalism. As Table 12–1 shows, three to five times as many French women as British women worked in agriculture throughout the nineteenth century, although not all women who performed agricultural labor did so for wages. In contrast to Britain, where small family farms gradually disappeared, the number of small family farms increased in France. French women's labor on the family farm continued to be vital. Rural French women performed many of the same tasks they had performed for centuries: cultivating vegetable gardens, dairying, weaving, spinning. Some made lace to bring in extra income. Contemporary men and women defined these tasks as "women's work," whereas plowing, care of the horses and stable, and heavy cultivation, constituted "men's work." Rural women engaged in the same market activities that had brought them into the world of commercial relations earlier, before the age of industry. In large market towns, they continued to sell their cheese, eggs, and butter; indeed, many still do so today. In addition to work on family farms, French women also worked regularly as wage laborers on vineyards and as harvesters on vineyards and large grain farms. Like British workers, these women usually earned less than half of what male workers earned.

The experiences of rural German women varied according to the sharp regional contrasts of the German economy, the result of centuries-old political divisions. In Prussia, the emancipation of the peasants in the early nineteenth century and land enclosure legislation resulted in the domination of eastern Prussia (Pomerania) by massive farms, whereas western Prussian (Westphalia) remained broken into small peasant holdings and family farms. On the large estates in the east, the production of grain for the market demanded a large and cheap workforce. Here, many women worked as full-time agricultural wage workers to supplement the low wages of their husbands, fathers, or sons, performing the same tasks as the men but for lower wages. In western Prussia, the introduction of labor-intensive crops like potatoes and beets created demand for women's unpaid labor on small family farms. The expansion of small holdings in this region around the middle of the nineteenth century had the same effect here as in France: it reinforced existing patterns of women's work, and in some areas reinforced women's market activities as well. Thus, the situation of women in east Prussia resembled that of rural working-class women in Britain, whereas the situation of women in west Prussia resembled that of French rural women. These changes in agriculture led many women to migrate to towns and cities, where they took jobs in manufacturing.

Manufacturing and Women's Family Roles

As factories began to dominate the skylines of European cities, more women worked outside of the home than ever before, and women's work experience changed dramatically. Throughout the nineteenth century, a relatively large proportion of women workers left household-based production for manufacturing, (see Table 12–2) working most often in areas that were extensions of their traditional household activities. Thus, women who had formerly spun or wove in their homes found jobs in factories, where large-scale production of textiles created a demand for their unskilled, cheap labor. Most of them were single and relatively young, between the ages of sixteen and twenty-one.[3] In working-class families where men's low wages kept the family perilously close to the poverty line, women's and children's work was absolutely necessary for survival. The working-class family economy required that all members of the household contribute wages. Thus, working-class women often had to balance the family's need for income against the responsibility of childrearing differently than they had done prior to industrialization. Before the age of the factory, women who worked in household production could informally adjust income-producing activities to childbearing and child care. A spinner could easily watch a child as she

TABLE 12–1

Percentage of Women Out of All Workers in Each Major Branch of Activity

	BRITAIN							
	1841	1851	1861	1871	1881	1891	1901	1911
Agriculture	5.3	11.2	8.3	7.5	7.0	5.2	5.8	7.3
Mining/Quarrying	3.1	2.8	1.3	2.1	1.3	0.9	0.6	0.7
Manufacturing	26.0	35.0	35.8	35.5	36.1	36.7	34.7	34.6
Commerce, Banking, Insurance[1]	1.1	0	1.5	2.3	3.0	5.5	11.3	17.5
Transport/Communications[2]	2.0	2.9	1.9	2.4	1.7	1.8	1.9	2.4
Service[3]	69.4	72.0	73.2	73.5	73.4	72.9	69.1	65.3
Domestic Service as Percentage of Service	95.0	91.4	91.5	91.3	88.1	87.9	84.9	83.1

	FRANCE					
	1856	1866	1886	1896	1901	1906
Agriculture	29.6	29.7	33.1	32.5	32.3	37.6
Mining/Quarrying	8.8	8.8	11.9	2.6	2.2	2.1
Manufacturing	35.4	34.2	38.2	37.2	38.5	39.7
Commerce, Banking, Insurance[4]	30.9	33.1	35.6	39.4	54.0	39.8
Transport/Communications[5]	4.5	4.8	7.1	22.6	26.1	27.6
Service[6]	43.1	40.2	41.3	40.2	42.8	42.6
Domestic Service as Percentage of Service	77.5	74.6	69.0	56.8	55.4	54.9

spun in her cottage, or could stop work to nurse an infant. Women who worked in factories however, lacked this flexibility. They had to time work more carefully to coincide with periods when they did not have the responsibility of young, dependent children. A married woman with a small child, a single mother, or a sibling with child-care responsibilities could not leave the factory to supervise the child. Once the factory gates closed, she remained locked inside until the evening bell. Such women must have felt a terrible frustration at leaving their young children behind. Married women whose mothers or mothers-in-law lived in their households and could look after infants while mother worked were fortunate indeed. Poor women, on the other hand, who lacked this form of child care sometimes resorted to bringing their infants into the mills in baskets, and, while they worked, kept their little ones drugged and sleepy with brandy-soaked rags or opiates. It is not surprising that comparatively few married women worked in manufacturing over this period. The mother who had to leave factory work upon the birth of a child could earn cash in other ways—by taking in boarders and lodgers or by doing laundry. Once children were old enough to earn wages, they went out to work and mothers remained at home. Women might then return to wage-earning when widowed, or when older children had left the home.[4]

TABLE 12–1 (*continued*)
Percentage of Women Out of All Workers in Each Major Branch of Activity

	GERMANY		
	1882	*1895*	*1907*
Agriculture	30.8	33.2	46.5
Mining/Quarrying	3.7	3.9	3.9
Manufacturing	21.1	22.8	23.9
Commerce, Banking, Insurance[7]	20.6	24.4	30.5
Transport/Communications	3.2	2.9	4.2
Service[8]	27.4	31.8	35.9
Domestic Service as Percentage of Service	26.2	24.5	26.1

[1]Includes women who worked in family-run shops, who did not earn wages.

[2]Women who worked in post offices or as telegraph and telephone operators were most likely included in the government services grouped under "service."

[3]Includes governmental services, liberal professions (teaching), armed services (no women), personal and domestic services.

[4]Includes women who worked in family-run shops. The persistence of small family-run shops in France through the nineteenth and early twentieth centuries meant that considerably more women worked in this sector than in Britain.

[5]Telephone and telegraph workers in France are included in this category.

[6]Includes governmental services, armed services (no women), liberal professions, hotel and cafe workers, and personal domestic service. The smaller proportion of female domestic service workers in France accounts for the small size of this sector by comparison to Britain.

[7]Includes family-run shops in which wives worked.

[8]Includes government services, armed services (no women listed), "services not elsewhere classified" (probably liberal professions such as teaching), and personal domestic service.

SOURCE: Paul Bairoch, *La Population active et sa Structure* (Brussels: Institut de Sociologie de l'Université libre de Bruxelles, 1969), pp. 136–137, 173–175, 189–191.

WOMEN'S WORK EXPERIENCE AND WORKING CONDITIONS

Women and Factory Work

Behind the imposing facade of the factory working women faced degrading and often dangerous conditions, as well as sexual harassment on the job. The existence of such conditions raises serious questions about how liberating factory work was for women. Young women and girls in the large British textile centers of Manchester, Preston, and Stockport often began work as early as five or six years of age, as assistants to parents employed in weaving or spinning, and remained in factory work during adolescence. Selina Cooper, future leader of the radical suffrage campaign in Lancashire, began work at a cotton mill at the age of ten; Sarah Dickenson, a labor and suffrage activist, started work at eleven to help support her family.

TABLE 12–2

Women's Representation in Specific Economic Sectors as Percentage of the Entire Female Labor Force

	BRITAIN				
	1841	*1861*	*1881*	*1901*	*1911*
Agriculture	4.5	5.0	3.1	1.8	2.2
Mining/Quarrying	0.4	0.2	0.2	0.1	0.2
Manufacturing	35.2	44.7	43.3	44.7	44.9
Commerce, Banking, Insurance	0.1	0.1	0.3	1.6	2.9
Transport/Communications	0.2	0.3	0.4	0.6	0.7
Service[1]	57.4	47.2	50.6	49.6	47.2
Other	2.2	2.2	2.1	1.6	1.9
Domestic Service as Percentage of Service	54.5	43.2	45.2	42.2	39.3

	FRANCE				
	1856	*1866*	*1886*	*1901*	*1906*
Agriculture	48.9	48.0	46.0	37.9	43.3
Mining/Quarrying	0.4	0.3	0.5	0.1	0.1
Manufacturing	24.8	25.7	22.2	27.4	26.7
Commerce, Banking, Insurance	5.2	5.6	8.9	11.3	8.3
Transport/Communications	0.2	0.3	0.4	3.0	3.1
Service[1]	20.1	19.8	20.9	20.3	18.5
Other	.4	.4	1.1	0	0
Domestic Service as Percentage of Service	15.6	14.8	14.4	11.6	10.4

	GERMANY		
	1882	*1895*	*1907*
Agriculture	59.5	52.3	55.8
Mining/Quarrying	0.5	0.6	0.6
Manufacturing	23.4	25.7	22.7
Commerce, Banking, Insurance	4.2	5.7	6.7
Transport/Communications	0.3	0.3	0.5
Service	10.4	14.2	13.0
Other	1.7	1.2	.7
Domestic Service as Percentage of Service	2.7	3.5	3.4

[1]Includes domestic service, cafe and hotel service, government services and the professions. The majority of women's jobs in this area in Britain and France were in domestic service.

SOURCE: Paul Bairoch, *La Population active et sa Structure* (Brussels: Institut de Sociologie de l'Université libre de Bruxelles, 1968), pp. 131, 136–137, 167, 173–175, 183, 189–191.

As machine tenders, spinners and weavers, women and girls worked twelve and thirteen hour days in an unhealthy and unsafe environment, under the watchful eye of the shop foreman. Those who worked at wet spinning in flax mills in the 1830s spent most of their working day drenched by a constant spray of water from the spinning frames. Overseers often beat women and their children if they failed to come to work on time, as Hannah Goode and Eliza Marshall charged when they testified before the Parliamentary Commissioners in 1833. Thus, Goode and Marshall and others like them came face to face with the disciplinary power of men over women in the factory, a discipline that compounded the regimentation of the clock and of the machine. Other women described the horribly crushed limbs or dislocated shoulders they suffered at work on large carding or spinning machines, when clothing or hair caught in the machine shafts.[5] Such conditions couldn't have been more different from the household-based workshops familiar to these women before the age of industry.

Fewer French women worked in manufacturing (see Table 12-2) than British women (more French women continued to work in agriculture), but their experience of industrial work strongly resembled that of British women. They too tended spinning frames and looms, in workshops and factories where lateness in arriving at work could mean a beating or loss of wages. In small, quiet provincial towns located near sources of water power, women and girls labored in spinneries, whose dark and damp conditions contrasted sharply with the sunny landscape surrounding them. From dawn to dusk, they worked without artificial light, fourteen to sixteen hours a day in summer, in workrooms whose close, wet air hung thick with cotton dust. Women and girls who worked in silk spinning and weaving suffered from respiratory and lung diseases, including tuberculosis, brought on by the dampness of the workrooms, closed windows, and poor ventilation (designed to prevent air or wind from damaging the delicate silk). Here too, most women began work at an early age in order to contribute to the family economy. Jeanne Bouvier, who later became an important feminist and union organizer, entered a silk factory at the age of eleven to help her family after her father's business failed in the early 1870s. From five in the morning until eight at night, with two hours for meals, Bouvier wound thread on bobbins. "I didn't complain," she wrote in her autobiography, "misery had knocked on our door, and my thirteen hours in the factory would pay me 50 centimes."[6] At this time, a loaf of bread cost between 25 and 30 centimes, and without Bouvier's help, her family would have found survival difficult. But Bouvier's poor factory wages alone could not feed the family; often she crocheted shawls and scarves late into the night to earn extra money. Women like Bouvier clearly did not experience the age of industrial capitalism as a golden age at all.

Some French women who had to help their families but could not find jobs where they lived traveled considerable distances to find work. As agricultural workers, women had often participated in temporary migrations, to harvest grapes, wheat, and fruit. As industrial workers they also left home for months at a time, or even permanently, to work as spinners in the cotton-producing city of Lille, or in the silk-producing center of Lyons, or as servants, laundry workers, and housekeepers in the city of Nîmes.[7] Contemporary observers (and some historians) feared that migration was a sure sign of the breakdown of the family. To be sure, families no longer had complete control over daughters who left home to work elsewhere. These women and girls, however, migrated not to achieve independence or acquire new occupational skills, but to help support their families. Moreover, family ties often determined the migration strategies of individuals who went in search of better wage-earning possibilities; usually relatives or friends who had already moved and settled in a city helped newcomers find work. When Jeanne Bouvier, demoralized and exhausted by thirteen-hour days in the silk factory, left her job, her cousin helped her find work as a maid in Vienne, 17 miles away. Thus, not only did the needs of the family determine women's work patterns, but families provided a cushion when women struck out on their own to find better jobs, much as they do today.

German women also entered textile mills and shoe and garment factories at an early age to contribute to the family economy. The childhood experience of Adelheid Popp, who later became an important Austrian socialist and labor activist, typified that of many German women of her generation. Popp began work at the age of ten and a half in a garment workshop in Vienna, crocheting shawls for twelve hours a day. Later, at the age of twelve, she worked at making pearl and silk trimmings and decorations for the fashionable dresses of wealthy middle-class women. Paid on a piecework basis, she quickly developed the dexterity to increase her output, but to her utter dismay, her employer reduced the piece rates to keep her wages low. Popp also attempted to earn extra money by working at home until late into the night, like Bouvier.[8] In fact, many factory workers extended their work day by four or five hours with home work, after legislation in 1891 restricted women's work day in German factories to eleven hours. When a travelling salesman promised her higher wages in return for sexual favors at fifteen, Popp began to see the power relations of the industrial world intruding with frightening intimacy on her personal life, as they did in the lives of so many young working women. Men's ability to use their physical power over women and girls in the workplace threatened the physical security of female workers as much as the possibility of work accidents.

Women in the Mines

The harsh realities of industrial capitalism stood out in especially sharp relief for women who worked in mining. In the dark coal towns of West Lancashire, Yorkshire, Scotland, and South Wales, mine owners were eager to benefit from women's cheap labor. Faced with few alternative jobs, women and children worked in the pits drawing coal carts through narrow mine shafts by pulling them with chains and belts attached to their bodies, crawling on all fours. Deformed spines, swollen legs, cramps, severe fatigue, and accidents awaited these young women truly desperate for income, until legislation in 1842 excluded them from working underground.[9] Other adult women, "pit brow lasses," demonstrated enormous physical strength as they operated windlasses to raise coal to the surface, then shoveled, raked, sorted, and cleaned coal. They continued this work until well into the twentieth century, when mechanization replaced them.

Emile Zola's novel, *Germinal* (1885), set in the French mining community of Anzin, graphically depicted the work of women and girls who labored on all fours as haulers. Describing the young Catherine, Zola wrote, "She sweated, she panted, her joints cracked, but without a complaint, with the indifference of custom, as if it were the common wretchedness of all to live thus bent double."[10] In fact, French women made up a larger proportion of miners than women in either Britain or Germany (see Table 12–1). In 1874, thirty-two years after British legislators restricted women and children to surface work, French legislation outlawed underground mine work for women and girls. Although nationally few German women worked in mines (see Tables 12–1 and 12–2), in some regions, such as Upper Silesia, labor shortages in metal working and coal mining led mining agents to scour the countryside for cheap labor. They successfully encouraged some women and children to migrate to mining towns from their farming communities.[11]

Gender Division of Labor

Women experienced industrial work in remarkably similar ways in all three countries. Nowhere did new jobs in manufacturing lead to immediate improvements in their lives. The growing division of labor by gender conspired to keep women in an inferior position at work. The development of sophisticated technologies and steam-driven machines meant that women lost certain types of work, such as spinning, that they had performed in the early modern economy. Men now operated the new, heavy machines that were deemed to require more strength. It is true that machines also created new jobs for women. For instance, many women worked tending power looms, displacing male handloom weavers. Even this seemingly positive development for women contained problems however, as women found themselves tied to the endless, repetitive rhythm of the machine.

Everywhere, both men and women experienced poor working conditions, low wages and the fragmentation of tasks. However, the separation of tasks according to gender in industry and the cultural expectations for women that accompanied the gender division of labor meant that women were often worse off than men. Practically speaking, the gender division of labor meant simply that men and women increasingly worked apart. As a French report of 1867 declared, "Family and sewing are the lot of women; wood and metal are for men. . . ."[12] Indeed, women tended to work in textile and garment production, and men concentrated in mining and metallurgy. Even within the factory, a clear division prevailed. Family members who had worked together in factories at an earlier stage of capitalist development now worked in different areas of factory production under industrial capitalism. One result of this change was that men actively excluded women from their trades; this kept women's wages far below men's wages. Wage differences, of course, often reflected real differences in skill, but employers and male craftsmen systematically denied women training for skilled or higher paying jobs. Even when they worked at the same jobs as men, women earned less. The identification of certain jobs with gender came to dictate the wage levels for those jobs. Thus, throughout western Europe and Britain, women earned between one-third and one-half of men's wages in virtually every area in which women worked, just as they had prior to industrialization.[13]

The wage and skill differences that distinguished women's situation from men's in the workplace reflected the dominant cultural perceptions of women's roles referred to earlier. The ideal of domesticity that dictated a life of marriage, motherhood, and household accomplishments encouraged the belief that women should work as supplementary breadwinners, that they only worked for "pin money." Despite the fact that in reality women worked to keep their families from starvation, employers who wished to benefit from women's cheap labor conveniently used these ideas to rationalize paying women at the bottom of the wage scale. Dr. Mitchell, a British Parliamentary subcommissioner, even argued in 1833 that paying women low wages would discourage them from working permanently and would encourage them to return to hearth and home.[14] Women did not leave work because of low pay; on the contrary their need to earn wages, however low, caused them to continue to work under the most exploitative conditions. These conditions overall made women industrial workers especially vulnerable to the power and dominance of men at work. As the miserable situation of women workers under industrial capitalism became more obvious, social reformers grew increasingly concerned about it.

Reform Efforts and Protective Legislation

In all three countries, reformers attempted to protect young women from the cruelty of the industrial system. These efforts often meant the imposition of middle-class views of women's roles on working-class women. Middle-class observers openly expressed their opposition to women's industrial work. Underlying their horror at its moral dimension and their genuine concern over the gruesome conditions in which many women worked was shock at the way in which working-class women deviated from the ideal of domesticity. Reforms reflected the cultural belief that women were weaker or more delicate than men and that they needed special protection. In France, religious orders resurrected an old institution, the convent workshop, where young girls worked under the supervision of nuns. This tried and true form of labor discipline, linking the altar and the machine, governed some one hundred thousand women in the silk-producing region around Lyon by 1906. In other areas, concerns about the vulnerability of young female workers led industrialists to build dormitories for young, single girls, with strict supervision over hours, mobility, and religious observance.[15] Men seldom experienced this form of protection and discipline.

Numerous laws, some outlawing child labor (for both girls and boys) and some regulating women's factory work, attempted to restrict women's presence in the workplace; for reformers believed that this was a sphere in which women did not belong. None of the laws governing adult women applied to men. In Britain, efforts to regulate child labor began as early as 1802, and acts passed in the 1830s and 1840s limited child labor and reduced women's working hours to twelve and then ten per day. The politics of protective legislation involved differences within the middle class. Reformers wanted to restrict women's work because it was incompatible with their ideal of womanhood; middle-class industrialists, however, eager to profit from women's cheap labor, refused to obey these laws. Initially, much factory legislation was ignored; factory inspectors, sympathetic to the industrialists, often turned a blind eye to infractions. By the end of the nineteenth century, French and German reformers had also begun to regulate women's employment and to put an end to working conditions considered to be incompatible with French or German womanhood. Again, such legislation did not control men's work and the reformers in these countries were in part motivated by their desire for working-class women to conform to the ideals of domesticity.

The same concerns lay behind the thinking of radical working-class and socialist leaders who argued for the "family wage." This amounted to an effort to exclude women from wage work altogether by forcing employers to pay male workers enough to support their families. In Britain, tailors and weavers proposed a family wage in the 1820s, 1830s, and again in the 1850s. Some members of the French delegation to the first congress of the International Working Men's Association in 1866 also favored the idea. Much later, just after the turn of the century, French socialist deputy Jean Jaurès argued that "the wage of the working man, the head of the family, must be increased so that what is now a family wage [can be earned by him]."[16] Other socialists in the international congresses of the Socialist Second International pressed for a shorter work day and protective legislation for women almost every year. Appeals for a family wage were motivated by the bourgeois ideal of the family in which domesticated women and their children depended on their husbands' and fathers' support. Thus, patriarchial authority could be preserved.

In fact, protective legislation was a double-edged sword. Arguably, it helped women and children by reducing exhausting work days and by making it easier for children to attend school. Yet such legislation did not really mark a major improvement in women's situation at work. It reinforced gender divisions in the workplace by reinforcing women's subordinate status, since it assumed that women needed protection and restriction whereas men did not. Women thus remained condemned to low-paying, inferior positions. Protective legislation sometimes caused women to lose needed wages, altered the patterns of women's work, and frequently meant that women lost more remunerative jobs, for instance, in higher-paying night shifts. Shortening the work day for women but not for men meant that managers demanded faster work rates from women in order to maintain production levels. In all countries employers who did not disregard the new laws outright attempted to escape these restrictions by hiring women who could work in their homes on a putting-out basis. This form of production did not fall under the scope of protective legislation.

Home-based Production in the Industrial Economy

In the shadow of the urban factory, behind the doors of working-class homes, increasing numbers of women took up industrial home work, with mixed consequences for women. This form of production, which seemed such a contrast to the factory-based development of industrial capitalism, was not actually new. In the early modern economy, women and their families worked together in household production. Most nineteenth-century industrial home work, however, differed from earlier forms of family or household production in that it depended not on the cooperative labor of the entire family but largely on the labor of women. As industrial capitalism developed, many women had continued to work in the "sweating system" of home-based production, doing "slop work" in bookbinding, dress-making and millinery. By the turn of the century, however, women's industrial home work increased. In France it became so widespread that about half of the women in the wage labor force performed industrial work in their homes.[17] All over Europe, in the highly mechanized heavy industries, factories became primarily employers of men; women dominated virtually all forms of home-based production such as the garment trades and their associated small industries, artificial flowermaking, embroidery, shoemaking, and lingerie. Under this system, employers subcontracted work to women who sewed shirts, waistcoats, trousers, and dresses at home. Such employers valued this system because women would accept the low piece-rate wages; moreover, the worker carried the overhead and the employer only had to furnish the raw materials. Women favored this form of wage-earning because it more nearly conformed to cultural expectations of women's home-based role and it provided them with more flexibility in controlling the timing and pace of work. A woman could easily combine wage-earning with domestic responsibilities, leaving her paid work to tend to a child or prepare a meal. Working at her own pace in her own home, she was free from the constraints and discipline of the factory.

The return to this older form of production, however, did not improve women's working lives. Low piece rates and the burden of supporting a family made home workers work just as hard as factory hands. Women who worked in tailoring in Paris in the 1850s could earn more at home than in a factory, but they labored almost without stopping, 365 days a year. In addition to sewing, they had to cook, clean, and care for their children. Such women often worked themselves to exhaustion in order to earn an adequate living. Bourgeois social reformers, who assumed that women belonged in the home, applauded the fact that married women and their single daughters could work within the protective environment of the household or family. Little did these reformers understand that women undertook such work at the price of intense pressure and endless toil.

Domestic Service and the Changing Service Sector

Women who worked in the service sector of the economy saw striking shifts in that sector in the second half of the nineteenth century, as industrial capitalism entered yet another stage of development—the age of the monopoly and the large corporation.

Early in the nineteenth century, "service" meant domestic service. As industrial capitalism expanded, relatively large numbers of women toiled in the homes of the middle class as domestic servants, performing household chores that middle-class ladies would not deign to touch. Service first became a predominantly female occupation in nineteenth-century Britain, where early industrialization drew men out of service into industrial occupations. The results of this shift appeared as early as 1841, as Table 12–1 shows. In France and Germany, a much smaller proportion of women worked as servants, partly because more women worked in agriculture in those countries (see Tables 12–1 and 12–2). In all three countries, the vast majority of servants were young, single women who worked for a relatively brief period of their lives, en route to marriage or other occupations.

Despite the contemporary view of service as a higher-status occupation than factory work, in reality the servant's position was not as enviable as her uniform and starched white apron suggested. Service meant constant deference to and dependence on the servant's employer. Servants had little rest from fifteen- to eighteen-hour days spent in an endless round of cooking, washing, and child care, as they performed the rituals of ordering and cleansing the middle-class home. Still more serious, deference to an employer's wishes or whims made young working-class women especially vulnerable to sexual harassment from male employers. Finally, domestic service embodied one of the most glaring contradictions of the ideal of domesticity: the exploitation of working-class women by bourgeois women whose wealth could buy them leisure and respite from domestic toil. Hannah Cullwick, a Victorian servant, poignantly described the chasm that separated servants from their bourgeois mistresses.

i often thought of Myself and them, all they ladies sitting upstairs and talking and sewing and playing games and pleasuring themselves, all so smart and delicate . . . and then me by myself in that kitchen, drudging all day in my dirt, and ready to do anything for 'em whenever they rung for me—it seems like [being] a different kind o creature to them. . . . [18]

Over the nineteenth century, fewer and fewer women toiled in middle-class households as servants, as the industrial capitalist societies and economies of western Europe transformed and the definition of service changed. This development was especially evident in Britain and France (see Table 12–2), where new jobs opened for women before World War I. Three developments affected women's movement from domestic service into other areas. First, compulsory education laws requiring school attendance until the age of fourteen meant that young girls who had previously gone into service at the age of ten or eleven remained in school. Those over fourteen now saw their educational level raised; the new educational requirements also created a demand for teachers. Young women armed with the proper diploma or certificate could now take jobs that required literacy. Second, the emergence of large corporations and the growth of huge urban department stores increased the demand for clerks, secretaries, and salespeople. Third, inflation throughout Europe at the end of the nineteenth century made it more difficult for middle-class households to hire servants. Young women began to withdraw from domestic service and turned to new jobs in commerce, banking, insurance, and communications, as Table 12–2 suggests.

As a result of these changes more women worked as white-collar workers than ever before. In France, for example, department stores like the Bon Marché and the Magasin du Louvre in Paris hired so many women that the retail sector quickly became the largest white-collar employer of women, with teaching following a close second.[19] In Britain and Germany, the growth of large-scale distributive trades also brought large numbers of women behind the counters of shops and department stores.[20] By World War I women had gradually come to dominate elementary school teaching all over Europe. Moreover, now middle-class women as well as lower-class women began to enter teaching by the turn of the century.

Some middle-class women also made their way into the nursing profession, as the story of Florence Nightingale illustrates. Nightingale, born into a comfortable bourgeois family, rebelled against the domestic pursuits to which most women of her class were confined. She sought fulfillment in nursing at a time when most nurses were men and when intimate contact with the body was considered improper for delicate middle-class ladies. In the early 1850s, she trained abroad and in Britain, and then served as an army nurse during the Crimean War (1854–1856). In an aggressive and far-reaching campaign to reform nursing, she transformed the profession by making education more rigorous, and by drawing in other young women. The fact that young middle-class women began to enter the ranks of teachers and nurses reflected a shift in the ideals of domesticity. Cultural norms still demanded that women be nurturers and teachers in the home, but these values expanded to allow middle-class women to take those roles into the public world as well.

Working-class women moved into other areas of the expanding service sector in large numbers. Offices, which had been dominated by male clerks in the early nineteenth century, underwent a striking transformation in the second half of the century, when the feminization of office work occurred virtually everywhere. Women became clerical workers as male clerks moved into other occupations and women's educational levels rose. Gradually, women also took jobs as post office, telegraph, and telephone workers; in France, they made up the vast majority of telephone operators by the turn of the century.[21]

As significant as these developments were, they did not constitute a revolutionary leap forward for women. For one thing, as Table 12–2 shows, women who worked in offices in commerce, banking, and communications constituted a small minority of working women. Moreover, these women continued to experience working conditions not so different from those in industry. Most department store salesgirls stood for twelve to fourteen hours a day, subject to a discipline and control similar to that for young women in convent workshops or for domestic servants. Women in the new service-sector jobs continued to find themselves restricted to the lowest-paid levels of the enterprises. The feminization of telephone, telegraph, and clerical work caused downgrading in positions and the segregation of women in jobs defined as "women's work," with a corresponding decline of wages. It is true that the constraints of Victorian domestic ideals loosened sufficiently to allow some middle-class women into the professions and white-collar work, but those very ideals continued to justify the allocation of unskilled, low-paid work to women. The assumption remained that women worked only for pin money and should eventually leave work for marriage and motherhood. Despite the persistence of these cultural ideals of gender roles, women did not withdraw from wage work; moreover, not all women passively accepted exploitation under industrial capitalism, or submission within the power relations of the factory or workshop.

ORGANIZATION AND PROTEST

Women's efforts to protect themselves from the worst evils of industrial capitalism are as old as the industrial system itself. However, the same features of industrial capitalism that made their lives so difficult — the gender division of labor, their unskilled status, and their vulnerability before the power of male employers — also posed obstacles to those efforts.

During the early years of industrialization in Britain, women reacted violently against the introduction of machinery by engaging in brief but dramatic episodes of machine-breaking. In 1799, women in Lancashire destroyed spinning jennies that threatened to displace hand spinners. Later, in Britain, France, and Germany, they organized in labor unions and some joined the growing socialist political movements that developed in those countries—movements that struggled to obtain workplace reforms for women and supported women's rights, including female suffrage.

Numerous obstacles prevented women from organizing, however. Skilled male workers consistently excluded women from their labor organizations during much of the nineteenth century. These men feared that unskilled, poorly paid women would weaken their bargaining position with employers; they also resented employers' use of women as strikebreakers. Women's low status in the workplace meant that it was easy to dismiss and replace them if they organized against an employer. Those women who performed industrial home work, isolated from one another in their homes, lacked a sense of solidarity with other women like themselves. Furthermore, women who worked a double day, performing wage labor and then returning home to cook, clean and wash, hardly had the time for union meetings after work. Finally, in some countries, church efforts to provide a different form of solace to working women drew some away from organized labor.

In spite of obstacles, some women did organize. In Britain, early unions such as the Lodge of Female Tailors and the Grand Lodge of Operative Bonnet-Makers formed in the early 1830s. By 1886, the National Women's Trade Union League, formed in 1874, had succeeded in organizing between thirty and forty women's unions. Ultimately, new industrial unions geared to organizing the unskilled opened their ranks to women. By World War I, women counted for about 12 percent of organized workers in Britain.[22]

A few French women overcame the obstacles to unionizing and formed labor associations of their own. In 1848 and 1869 women in the silk-producing center of Lyons went on strike. In 1869 they joined the International Working Men's Association. After 1884, when the government legalized labor unions, French women organized, but only sporadically. Women constituted a small minority of the organized workers in France before the war (less than 9 percent), but their unions increased in the those years, and the numbers of organized women workers actually tripled between 1900 and 1911.[23] The story of Emma Couriau illustrates the extent to which the French labor movement, dominated by men, had begun to change its attitude towards women. Couriau began work as a typographer in Lyons in 1912; she was paid at union wages but the local typographer's union refused to admit her, on the grounds that women really belonged at home. Major (male) labor leaders all over France, who realized the importance of women's participation in labor struggles however, sided with Couriau.[24] Buoyed by their support, she began to organize women typographers into their own union. Regrettably, her efforts came to a halt with the onset of the war, as did the efforts of German women, whose organizing efforts had gained momentum since the turn of the century.

That so few women organized against the injustices of industrial capitalism shows how difficult it was to overcome the evils of that system. The stories of those who did fight those injustices, however, show that working-class women did not all conform to Victorian stereotypes of docility or timidity when it came to defending their rights in the workplace. Women who organized and protested did not demand equal pay or equal rights with men, nor did they attempt to displace men in the workplace. Just as the needs of the family influenced the patterns of women's working lives, so too, family needs motivated and shaped women's protest. Women often challenged male authorities in the workplace, but protest usually occurred as women fought to preserve their right to work—with dignity, in humane conditions—in order to contribute to the survival of their families.

CONCLUSION

Industrial capitalism brought a new era of economic development to western Europe, with the growth of new technologies, new forms of mechanization, and the production of enormous wealth. Capitalism transformed women's lives, and it probably could not have developed without women's "free," cheap labor. Yet the majority of women did not reap the benefits commensurate with their contribution. Although industrialization promised enormous economic and social progress, it did not result in rapid or major improvements in women's social status, material conditions, or position in the workplace. In Britain, France, and Germany, industrial capitalism perpetuated and amplified developments that had already begun to change women's lives during earlier stages of capitalist development. Women continued to withdraw from productive activities, to see their economic contribution devalued, and to experience a still more acute gender division of labor than in the early modern economy.

Throughout this period of dramatic change, entrenched cultural expectations of women's family roles strongly influenced women's experience of work in the industrial capitalist economy. First, women worked out of the necessity to help support their families, not out of the desire for personal autonomy. In the interest of family survival they entered factories and workshops, faced dangerous and unhealthy working conditions, and migrated to distant towns for work. The wage-earning textile operative, whether she worked in Preston, Lille, or Hamburg, experienced little freedom on her starvation wages, and little leisure time in the few hours of the day that remained after work. Indeed, one of the ironies of industrial capitalism was that the values of individual rights, self-interest, and independence that operated so forcefully for the middle class in the market place had scarcely any application to working-class women's lives. Indeed, these values differed profoundly from the notion of the working-class family as a community in which each person contributed his or her part.

Second, women's reproductive role and the ideology of domesticity that glorified it combined with the grinding discipline of the factory to shape women's experience of industrial capitalism. Employers used what they believed to be women's primary role in reproduction to justify women's secondary role in production. The assumption that marriage and maternity constituted the most appropriate activities for women indicated that women did not really belong in the workplace. It not only kept women in inferior positions in the factory, but led some social reformers to try to remove them from the workplace altogether. In addition to low wages, loss of control over the pace of work, and confinement to unskilled labor, women emerged with a terrible heritage of subordination within the power relations of the workplace—a subordination that reflected and reinforced women's inferior status in the overall social system. To be sure, women exhibited extraordinary flexibility in juggling the competing demands of family and work and in their ability to perform a diverse range of tasks. But this strength was also a liability, for women's ability to "cope" and adjust often prevented them from pressing forward with demands and inhibited change.

For the vast majority of working-class women, then, their experience of industrial capitalism appeared as dark and dreary as the industrial cities in which they toiled. Yet, from that largely dark and dreary time, one positive light emerged. The very forces that oppressed women also created the conditions through which they forged links with one another and organized to fight oppression. The few women who did join the labor movement showed that some women resisted being swept blindly along by the larger forces of economic change. In so doing, they provided a foundation from which, later in the twentieth century, working women could challenge the constraints of class, gender, and the power relations of the industrial world.

NOTES

1. Mrs. Sarah Stickney Ellis, *The Mothers of England* (London: Peter Jackson, 1843); John Ruskin, "Of Queen's Gardens," in *Sesame and Lilies* [1865] (New York: John Wiley and Son, 1880), p. 91.
2. Erna Olafson Hellerstein, Leslie Parker Hume, and Karen Offen, eds., *Victorian Women* (Stanford, Calif.: Stanford University Press, 1981), p. 361.
3. Michael Anderson, *Family Structure in Nineteenth Century Lancashire* (New York: Cambridge University Press, 1971), p. 71; Louise A. Tilly, "Individual Lives and Family Strategies in the French Proletariat," *Journal of Family History* 4(Summer, 1979):146.
4. Louise A. Tilly, "Structure de l'emploi, travail des femmes et changement démographique dans deux villes industrielles: Anzin et Roubaix, 1872–1906," *Le Mouvement Social* 105 (October–December, 1978): 43–48; Louise A. Tilly and Joan W. Scott, *Women, Work and Family* (New York: Holt, Rinehart and Winston, 1978), pp. 123–136, 194–205.
5. Hellerstein, Hume, and Offen, *Victorian Women*, pp. 386–391.
6. Jeanne Bouvier, *Mes Mémoires*, edition prepared by Daniel Armogathe and Maïté Albistur (Paris: Maspero, 1983), pp. 56–57. Although legislation in 1840 forbade children under twelve from working more than eight hours a day, it was not rigorously enforced. Thus, Bouvier was able to work five hours over the legal norm as late as 1876.

7. Leslie Page Moch, *Paths to the City: Regional Migration in Nineteenth Century France* (Beverly Hills: Sage, 1983), pp. 186–187. British and German women undoubtedly embarked on long-term migrations to find jobs, but their migration patterns have been less well documented than those of French women.

8. Adelheid Popp, *La Jeunesse d'Une Ouvrière* [*Die Jugendgeschichte einer Arbeiterin* (Munich, 1909)], trans., Mina Valette (Paris: Maspero, 1979), pp. 27–29.

9. On the experience of women and children in British mines, see Angela V. John, *By the Sweat of their Brow: Women Workers at Victorian Coal Mines* (London and Boston: Routledge and Kegan Paul, 1980).

10. Emile Zola, *Germinal*, translated and introduced by Havelock Ellis (London: Dent; New York: Dutton, 1933), p. 31; quoted also in Tilly and Scott, *Women, Work and Family*, p. 85.

11. David Crew, *Town on the Ruhr. A Social History of Bochum 1860–1914* (New York: Columbia University Press, 1979), pp. 51–54; Lawrence Shofer, *The Formation of A Modern Labor Force: Upper Silesia 1865–1914* (Berkeley: University of California Press, 1975), pp. 27, 68.

12. Cited in Michelle Perrot, "De la Nourrice à l'Employée," *Le Mouvement Social* 105 (October–December, 1978): 7.

13. Ivy Pinchbeck, *Women Workers and the Industrial Revolution 1750–1850* [1930] (London: Virago, 1981), pp. 190–194; Tilly and Scott, *Women, Work and Family*, pp. 45, 162; Shofer, *Formation of a Modern Labor Force*, pp. 103–107; Jean Quataert, *Reluctant Feminists in German Social Democracy 1885–1917* (Princeton, N.J.: Princeton University Press, 1979), p. 33.

14. Pinchbeck, *Women Workers*, p. 194.

15. Perrot; Georges Duveau, *La Vie Ouvrière en France Sous le Second Empire* (Paris: Gallimard, 1946), pp. 291–292.

16. Quoted in Tilly and Scott, *Women, Work and Family*, p. 132.

17. Marilyn Boxer, "Women in Industrial Homework: The Flowermakers of Paris in the Belle Epoque," *French Historical Studies* 12 (Spring, 1982): 406.

18. Hellerstein, Hume, and Offen, *Victorian Women*, p. 351.

19. Theresa McBride, "A Woman's World: Department Stores and the Evolution of Women's Employment, 1870–1920," *French Historical Studies* 10 (Fall, 1978): 671; Claudie Lesselier, "Employées des Grands Magasins à Paris Avant 1914," *Le Mouvement Social* 105 (October–December, 1978): 109–126.

20. Lee Holcombe, *Victorian Ladies at Work: Middle-Class Working Women in England and Wales* (Hamden: Archon, 1973), pp. 103–140.

21. Susan Bachrach, "Dames Employées: The Feminization of Postal Workers in Nineteenth Century France," *Women and History* 8 (Winter, 1983); Holcomb, pp. 165, 166–168.

22. Barbara Drake, *Women in the Trade Unions* [1921], Introduction by Noreen Branson (London: Virago, 1984), pp. 21–22 and Table 1; Norbert Soldon, *Women in the British Trade Unions* (Dublin: Gill and McMillan; Totowa, N.J.: Rowman and Littlefield, 1978), p. 145.

23. Madeleine Guilbert, *Les Femmes et l'Organisation syndicale avant 1914* (Paris: CNRS, 1966), pp. 29, 32–33.

24. Charles Sowerwine, "Workers and Women in France Before 1914: the Debate Over the Couriau Affair," *Journal of Modern History* 55 (September, 1983): 414–444.

SUGGESTIONS FOR FURTHER READING

In addition to the works cited above, an abundant literature charts women's experience in the development of industrial capitalism. The emergence of an ideology of domesticity is examined by Catherine Hall, "The Early Formation of Victorian Domestic Ideology," in *Fit Work for Women*, ed. Sandra Burman (London: Croom Helm, 1979), pp. 15–32; and James McMillan, *Housewife or Harlot. The Place of Women in French Society, 1870–1940* (New York: St. Martin's Press, 1981). A fresh look at leisured middle-class women is taken by Bonnie G. Smith, *Ladies of the Leisure Class: the Bourgeoises of Northern France in the Nineteenth Century* (Princeton, N.J.: Princeton University Press, 1981).

Two recent works that examine the impact of agricultural change on rural women are: K. D. M. Snell, *Annals of the Laboring Poor: Social Change and Agrarian England 1660–1900* (New York: Cambridge University Press, 1985); and W. R. Lee, "The Impact of Agrarian Change of Women's Work and Child Care in Early Nineteenth Century Prussia," in *German Women in the Nineteenth Century: A Social History*, ed. John Fout (London: Holmes and Meier, 1984). French women's migration in the context of industrialization has received more attention than that of British or German women. Two good treatments are, William Sewell, Jr., *Structure and Mobility, The Men and Women of Marseille 1820–1870* (New York: Cambridge University Press, 1985); and Leslie Page Moch and Louise A. Tilly, "Joining the Urban World: Occupation, Family and Migration in Three French Cities," *Comparative Studies in Society and History* 27 (January, 1985): 33–56, both of which emphasize the importance of family strategies in women's migration.

Relatively little work has appeared as yet on the problem of protective legislation for women, but a good start is made by Mary Lynn Stewart-McDougall, "Protecting Infants: the French Campaign for Maternity Leaves, 1890s–1913," *French Historical Studies* XIII (Spring, 1983), which shows that concerns about the French birth rate, rather than women's welfare, motivated the French to grant maternity leaves. More attention has been given to the place of women's industrial home work in the process of industrialization. Particularly useful are Jean Quataert's recent examination of the ambiguities of household and market production in "The Shaping of Women's Work in Manufacturing Guilds, Households and the State in Central Europe 1648–1870," *American Historical Review* 90 (December, 1985): 122–1148; Quataert, "Social Insurance and the Family Work of Oberlausitz Home Weavers in the Nineteenth Century," in *German Women in the Nineteenth Century: A Social History*, ed., John Fout (London: Holmes and Meier, 1984); and Joan W. Scott, "Men and Women in the Parisian Garment Trades: Discussion of Family and Work in the 1830s and 1840s," in *The Power of the Past: Essays for Eric Hobsbawm*, eds., Pat Thane, Geoffrey Crossick, and Roderick Floud (New York: Cambridge University Press, 1984) who shows that not all French artisans favored the "family wage."

A number of works have provided valuable insight into the patterns of women's work over women's life cycle, and the importance of women's work within the family economy: Louise A. Tilly, "The Family Wage Economy of a French Textile City: Roubaix 1872–1906," *Journal of Family History* 4 (Winter, 1979); and Laura Oren, "The Welfare of Women in Labouring Families: England, 1860–1950," in Mary S. Hartman and Lois Banner, eds., *Clio's Consciousness Raised* (New York:

Harper and Row, 1974). Two classic works on the subject that bring alive women's experiences in their own words are: Margaret Llewelyn Davies, *Maternity: Letters from Working Women* [1915] (London: Virago, 1978) and Davies, *Life As We Have Known It* [1931] (London: Virago, 1977).

Historians have added much to our understanding of women's activity in the labor and socialist movements. For England, Barbara Taylor's *Eve and the New Jerusalem* (London: Virago, 1983) is especially noteworthy for its examination of women in the early socialist and trade union movements; on France, Marie-Hélène Zylberberg-Hocquard, *Femmes et Féminisme dans le Mouvement syndical français* (Paris: Editions Ouvrières, 1981) and Charles Sowerwine, "Workers and Women in France Before 1914: the Debate over the Couriau Affair," *Journal of Modern History* 55 (September, 1983): 414–444, are both excellent recent analyses, especially the latter, which looks at the problem of gender politics within the French labor movement. See also Sowerwine, *Sisters or Citizens. Women And Socialism in France Since 1876* (London: Cambridge, 1982); and Patricia Hilden, *Working Women and Socialist Politics in France* (London: Cambridge, 1986).

Finally, on all of these issues, several recent documentary collections provide valuable sources: John Fout and Eleanor Riemer, eds., *European Women, A Documentary History 1789–1945* (New York: Schocken, 1980); Erna Olafson Hellerstein, Leslie Parker Hume and Karen Offen, eds., *Victorian Women* (Stanford, Calif.: Stanford University Press, 1981); and Susan Groag Bell and Karen Offen, eds., *Women, the Family and Freedom*, 2 vols. (Stanford, Calif.: Stanford University Press, 1983).

Les Divorceuses by French lithographer Honoré Daumier depicts a French women's rally concerning the right to divorce. (Bibliothèque des Arts Décoratifs/Jean-Loup Charmet)

chapter 13

Liberty, Equality, and Justice for Women: The Theory and Practice of Feminism in Nineteenth-Century Europe

Karen Offen

Although Americans tend to emphasize English suffragists' uncompromising insistence on fundamental equality, Karen Offen reminds us of the variety among women's rights advocates in other European settings. Across the European continent, women in authoritarian states advanced their claims to equality in relation to other movements that worked for national liberation, unification, and political reform. To them, community cohesion and family protection seemed at least as vital as women's equality. Like the women described by Margaret Strobel who ventured into the Third World under the auspices of Empire, these "relational feminists" saw their concerns as part of broader nationalist ideals. Offen examines the many ways in which women's rights advocates used the belief in a special feminine nature as a wedge into public activity. After several generations, feminists had made little headway. Then, at the turn of the century, they faced twin threats from a new direction. Respected geneticists declared women innately inferior, and demographers spread panic about low birthrates among the "most desirable" Europeans. This double challenge inspired a few feminists to fight back and defend their vision of freedom and fulfillment. While a few English radicals made headlines, in other European nations feminists defended their faith in separate spheres as the most secure basis for healthy families and communities.

Between the French Revolution and World War I the western world witnessed an unprecedented surge of analysis, debate, and action on behalf of women's emancipation by both women and men. They aimed to abolish the privileges of the male sex, uproot the prejudices that disadvantaged women, and restructure the social relations of the sexes within the family and in society.

The eruption of politically formulated demands for women's emancipation coincided with the outbreak of the French Revolution in 1789, a major political event of modern times. The 1790s witnessed publication of a number of major arguments for change—the Marquis de Condorcet's *Plea for the Citizenship of Women* (France, 1790), Olympe de Gouges' *Declaration of the Rights of Woman* (France, 1791), Etta Palm d'Aelders's *Appeal to Frenchwomen Concerning the Regeneration of Morals and the Necessity for Women's Influence in a Free Government* (France, 1791), Mary Wollstonecraft's *Vindication of the Rights of Woman* (Great Britain, 1792), and Theodor Gottlieb von Hippel's *On Improving the Status of Women* (Prussia, 1792)—all of which evoked much comment.

The chorus of protest continued. In 1795 came the Marquis de Condorcet's *Sketch For a Historical Picture of the Progress of the Human Mind*, calling for "annihilation of the prejudices that have established an inequality of rights between the sexes." In 1808 the French social critic Charles Fourier wrote that "The extension of women's privileges is the general principle for all social progress." In 1817 the British poet Percy Byshhe Shelley pondered the question, "Can man be free if woman be a slave?" At midcentury Fourier's countryman, the poet Victor Hugo, prophesied that the nineteenth century would proclaim the right of woman, the eighteenth century having proclaimed the right of man. By 1900 advocates of ideas about reorganizing male-female relations and the male-dominated family had stimulated not only the growth of consciousness, but also the development of a comprehensive theoretical critique of women's subordinate status and the formation of a loosely organized political movement of women and men dedicated to the emancipation of women.[1]

During the 1890s these ideas and the movement that sought to realize them came to be known throughout Europe as feminism. The vocabulary itself was French. The words *feminism* and *feminist*, popularized in France in the late nineteenth century, spread rapidly into other European languages to describe both the ideas and the movement. But the ideas and the growth of organized movements for women's emancipation preceded the birth of the words, and consciousness of women's oppression through their subordination to men, elaborated in the midst of the Enlightenment critique of European social and political institutions, preceded both. Throughout most of the nineteenth century Europeans argued over "women's emancipation" and the "woman question," terms that aptly suggested the focus of the debate in a still monarchical, authoritarian, and male-centered culture in which an unresolvable tension existed for women between the demands of the family and the call of freedom. The new words gave focus and meaning to a preexisting analysis and critique.[2]

European thinkers and activists made vital contributions to the development of feminism throughout the world. The debate over these issues raged in religious and political tracts and speeches, in newspapers, periodicals, poems, novels, plays, and books of every description. By the beginning of the twentieth century, organized women's movements existed in France, Germany, the Low Countries, the territories of the Austro-Hungarian Empire, Switzerland, Scandinavia, European Russia, Italy, and other parts of Mediterranean Europe.[3] The very vocabulary of European feminist discourse, along with its forms of political agitation—publications, petitions, demonstrations, and even media events—had begun to spread to the Middle East and to Asia. The majority of member-nations of the first international organization of women, the International Council of Women, founded in 1888 by American suffragists, were European. The International Woman Suffrage Alliance, founded specifically to promote the cause of women's suffrage throughout the world, likewise enjoyed extensive European participation. Thousands of women journeyed by steamship and railroad to the conventions of these organizations, held every five years in London, Paris, Berlin, Budapest, and other major European cities. In the absolute and constitutional monarchies and even in the few male-dominated democratic or republican nation-states of pre–World War I Europe, both the ideas of the feminists and their political activity conjured visions of a world turned upside down and evoked correspondingly strong opposition. By the early twentieth century, the Swedish author and women's advocate Ellen Key observed that "The struggle that woman is now carrying on is far more far-reaching than any other; and if no diversion occurs, it will finally surpass in fanaticism any war of religion or race."[4]

VARIETIES OF FEMINISM IN NINETEENTH–CENTURY EUROPE

It is impossible to judge the historical significance of European feminism solely in terms of contemporary American understanding of equal rights and individual liberty. If feminism is potentially individualistic in theory, (that is, committed to the maximum self-realization for every individual) it has not invariably been so in historical actuality. Despite common ideological roots and similarities in vocabulary and rhetoric, the Anglo-American arguments for women's emancipation through the exclusive acquisition of personal rights, which some writers today refer to as "liberal," "liberal individualist," or "bourgeois" appear to be as atypical in the overall framework of western thought as are Anglo-American political theory and institutions themselves. In the nineteenth century, most western European feminist thinkers—with the possible partial exception of the English—shied away from individualistic and legalistic arguments; they were still far more preoccupied with community cohesion than with individual liberty. As they chipped away at male-centered thinking about society, they downplayed, sidestepped, or even rejected individual rights arguments for women's emancipation, even as they spoke freely of "liberty" and "equality." Instead, they emphasized the roles and duties of individuals, the complementary and interdependent relationship between women and men, and women's distinctive nature and contributions to society as a sex, especially as mothers. Even those feminist thinkers who argued for greater personal autonomy for women generally cast their arguments in terms of women's relationships to others and their responsibilities to a broader collectivity—in some cases the nation and in others the working class. In either case they considered the family, not the individual, to be the primary social and political unit. And they emphasized what we now refer to as an ethic of care, over an ethic of competition.

This mode of argument can be understood as *relational feminism*. Nineteenth-century advocates of relational feminism insisted on the physiological and cultural distinctions between the sexes and adhered to the concepts of womanly or manly "nature" and to a sharply defined sexual division of. labor both in the family and throughout society. The premise that there exist distinct and different male and female natures led to a conception of social organization that implied distinct and different duties for women *and* for men. Relational feminists insisted on the centrality of the complementary couple and/or the mother/child dyad to analysis of women's plight and the search for solutions. They sought to reconfigure prevailing images of women (notably, the Christian association of woman with sin) through "the rehabilitation of womanhood" and to equalize the power of women and men in society. But they wished to accomplish this without eroding or eliminating distinctive and, to them, desirable gender differences. They wished to preserve cooperation between women and men in all aspects of social and political life, even as they sought to dismantle patriarchal institutions and restructure society in its totality. The arguments of most nineteenth-century European advocates of women's emancipation, including most socialist feminists as well as the "bourgeois" feminists they condemned so vigorously from the 1890s on, can be classified under the broader heading of relational feminists.[5]

The second mode of argument in nineteenth-century Europe is more familiar to us. It is called *individualist feminism*. More radical than relational feminism in its claims and social consequences, its advocates focused more exclusively on demands for women's "natural" rights, for freedom from social restraint and opportunities for personal development for women (and for men), and for self-determination, or autonomy, as the essential condition for the growth and development of human potential.

Partisans of individualist feminism tended to minimize or even ignore the social and political implications of women's relationships to children, to men, and to the society in which they lived. This was no doubt due to the fact that such arguments had first been developed with reference to property-holding male heads of households, which is how theorists in previous centuries had understood "the individual." But to critics, individualist feminism seemed to call for women's independence from men and children and also to reveal hostility toward them both and to any relationships or responsibilities that might infringe on women's personal liberty. Relational feminists in western Europe identified this approach with Anglo-American thinkers, particularly John Stuart Mill and his successors, and they distanced themselves from it. They accused the individualist feminists of treating women only as asexual, abstract beings. They viewed such ideas as self-indulgent and antisocial, hostile to the collective interest of a well-ordered society.

Thus, the terms *feminism* and *feminist* as used in this chapter will designate a spectrum of advocates of female emancipation, ranging from relational to individualistic. Some advocates combined both types of arguments in subtle and inconsistent blends. As today, nineteenth-century feminists made their case in a number of different national political, economic, and cultural settings, which affected the tone and terms of their arguments; as advocates of change they were rarely in a position to dictate circumstances, and, as a result, their arguments often have an opportunistic ring. Overall, however, European women and men who fought for the emancipation of women shared several common attitudes that allow us to employ a historically valid definition of feminism that transcends the particularities of time and place. First, they consciously recognized the validity of female experience. Second, they analyzed women's subordination as a problem of institutional injustice (not as a purely personal problem). Third, they sought the elimination of such injustices by attempting both to enhance the relative power of women and to curb the coercive power, whether political, economic, or cultural, available to men. Despite these common attitudes, within a given society the feminists' analyses did not always lead to the same priorities, strategies, or tactics on behalf of change in women's status. Both intranationally and internationally, they often disagreed with one another about solutions, much as feminists still do today.

THE POLITICAL AND ECONOMIC CONTEXT OF NINETEENTH-CENTURY FEMINISM

The historical development of feminism in Europe accompanied the growth and democratization of nation-states, the spread of literacy through mass education, and the expansive growth of an urban and ultimately industrial-

ized capitalist market economy. Its roots are, therefore, intertwined with the
political, intellectual, and socioeconomic history of early modern Europe
since medieval times. The vocabulary of feminism—liberty, equality, emancipation, liberation, justice, sisterhood—is directly appropriated from the
vocabulary of the European Enlightenment and the French Revolution.

Thus, it was no accident that the cluster of works by Condorcet,
Gouges, Wollstonecraft, Hippel, and others coincided with the French
Revolution. Throughout the revolutionary years, women and their male
champions vigorously pressed their claims, only to find them overruled by
the new revolutionary male elites.

The course of early nineteenth-century European feminist thought and
action cannot be understood without reference to the events of the revolutionary years, the ensuing Napoleonic wars of conquest, and the counterrevolutionary reaction that followed Napoleon's final defeat at Waterloo.
These events shook the political and social system of Europe to its foundations. This revolutionary and counterrevolutionary experience served as
the crucible for nineteenth-century conservative, liberal, radical, and socialist
thought and action. It also served as the crucible for feminist thought and
action (which could likewise be divided according to conservative, liberal,
radical, and socialist factions) and dictated the dominant relational pattern
of early nineteenth-century European feminist thought, especially on the
Continent.

Many men who concluded the settlements of 1815 still remembered
the consequences of the Declaration of the Rights of Man in 1789 and the
corresponding demands for the rights of woman; they also remembered the
extraordinary phenomenon of women's political activity in the revolution,
and they considered justifiable its ruthless repression during the Terror in
1793. They took note, too, of the revolutionary French government's attempt
to reconstruct and appropriate the family as a bulwark of the secular state
by institutionalizing civil marriage and divorce and by equalizing inheritance laws for daughters and sons, thereby ending the favor shown to
firstborn males. Nor could they passively ignore the concurrent challenge to
institutionalized marriage sounded by European male writers exploring the
boundaries of freedom in passionate love, including Frederich von Schlegel's
Lucinde (Germany, 1799), Etienne de Senancour's *On Love* (France, 1805),
Charles Fourier's *Theory of Four Movements* (France, 1808), and Johann-
Wolfgang von Goethe's *Elective Affinities* (Germany, 1809).

The treaties that ended the wars in 1815 reestablished a precarious
European peace. But the victorious monarchies of Continental Europe (Prussia,
Russia, and Austria) could not rest content with treaties. Led by Prince
Metternich, the Austrian chancellor, they also initiated a campaign to
suppress the revolutionary energies that had emanated from France into the
rest of Europe; this counterrevolutionary campaign attempted to exert strict
control over public speech and association (clamping down on the press and

political meetings) and over personal liberties as well. Even England, clearly the most politically liberal of the victor nations, was affected by this repressive climate, though the British did not participate as ruthlessly in counterrevolutionary activities as their Continental partners. Throughout the 1820s, in Restoration France, the Austro-Hungarian Empire, or Imperial Russia, whenever tensions increased, authorities quickly suppressed all reformist and radical publications and watched suspiciously for any signs of hostile political activism. The continental victors sought to consolidate the social order by strengthening centralized, hierarchical, male-dominated political authority in the family and in the polity, often calling on the coercive authority of established religions to support their efforts to control "antisocial" behaviors. Such behaviors included threatening activity by women who protested against their oppression.

The years before and after the French Revolution had produced an abundance of prescriptive laws and "scientific" publications by authors who sought to construct rigid boundaries between the public and private spheres and to establish new rationales for women's subordination in the family. Such efforts included tracts positing a vital role for women in the domestic economy of the household, medical treatises on their reproductive functions, and tracts discussing their proper education; they ranged from the Napoleonic legal code itself (which was adopted in many other areas of Europe) to Hannah More's cautionary tales for girls. In the wake of the French Revolution, political theorists such as Johann-Gottlieb Fichte and Georg-Wilhelm-Friedrich Hegel in Germany and Joseph de Maistre and Louis de Bonald in France drew on this literature to counter revolutionary claims by insisting on the necessary subordination to men of women and children in the family unit on behalf of the modern state.[6] In order to gain even the slightest success in such a political climate, and to avoid prosecution by nervous public authorities, most early nineteenth-century advocates of change in women's status—female and male alike—were concerned to present even the most modest claims for women's education in a manner that did not "smell" revolutionary or appear subversive to the existing order. Only a few were as daring as the irrepressable novelist and political activist Germaine de Staël, whose defiance of Napoleon had resulted in her exile from France. Her novels *Delphine* (1804) and *Corinne* (1807) introduced a new generation of European readers to a radical critique of marriage and female education from the perspective of a gifted, daring, and rebellious woman.

In the late 1820s and early 1830s, calls for the emancipation of women again resurfaced, particularly in Great Britain and France. These calls pressed by a new generation of women and men, ranged from pleas for major changes in women's legal status and for their access to substantive formal education to full-blown demands for economic freedom and political rights, moral reform, and sexual liberty. The pros and cons of women's emancipation preoccupied most major European thinkers and generated considerable anxiety. Even conservative men, including some who exercised great authority over European public opinion, recognized the revolutionary potential of the claims being made on women's behalf. The widely read French Catholic writer François-René de Chateaubriand, who had lived through the revolutionary years, spoke for many when in 1834 he acknowledged the emancipation of women as one of the major challenges to the postrevolutionary European sociopolitical order. He viewed it, along with the economic injustices of wage labor and the redistribution of fortunes, as a key issue in the emergence of a new society, no longer organized "around groups and by families." "What aspect will [the new society] offer," he asked, "when it is individualized, the way it seems to be becoming, the way one can already see it in formation in the United States?" Chateaubriand's younger colleague, Alexis de Tocqueville, in volume two of his study, *Democracy in America* (1837), attempted to mitigate such fears of American-style individualism among the French by lauding the counterbalancing superiority of American women. For the benefit of his French audience, he applauded what he understood to be the American understanding of sexual equality, in which each sex seemed to him to have its distinctive sphere of activity and respected the other. "The Americans," he wrote enthusiastically, "have applied to the sexes the great principle of political economy which governs the manufactures of our age, by carefully dividing the duties of man from those of woman in order that the great work of society may be the better carried on." Little could Tocqueville foresee the intensity with which this assertion of a new rationale for a sexual division of labor would be enforced and contested, both in the New World and the Old World.[7]

Tocqueville's remarks remind us that in the 1830s continental Europe, like England a few decades earlier, had entered a period of major economic development, centered in mechanized and increasingly centralized manufacturing in the textile and metal-processing industries. In England, France, Belgium, Switzerland, and some German states, reformers voiced concern over the extent of participation by women and children in the new industrial labor force. Stories of the exploitation of workers of both sexes by manufacturers and allegations of promiscuity and sexual harassment resulting from the mixing of the sexes in factories and workshops aroused severe public criticism. Opponents of women's employment reiterated that the sexes must occupy separate spheres and that the place of women was not in the paid labor force, just as it was not in political life, but in the household, under male protection and control.

The development of industrial production and expansion of a cash economy introduced severe strains on the household subsistence economy, and confirmed the shift in thinking about the sexual division of labor that had been gathering ideological momentum during the eighteenth century. Like the counterrevolutionary political theorists who insisted on women's exclusion from political life, counterrevolutionary economic theorists sought to bolster women's subordination in the family by insisting that the male head of household must support his wife and children with money earned outside the home, while the wife managed the household and raised the children. Such theorists urged daughters to complete their domestic apprenticeships with their mothers, rather than seek outside employment. In the cities and large towns of early nineteenth-century Europe where the cash economy had developed most fully, such prescriptions were for most people merely attractive ideals, impossible to realize under prevailing conditions. As competition for jobs increased and wages fluctuated, many poorer families depended increasingly on the pooled income of several wage earners, including women and most children over the age of seven. Few working-class people could live according to the new ideal of separate spheres, though increasing numbers of skilled workers aspired to realize it. As cash payments to landless laborers increasingly displaced the barter economy that characterized bound, or serf labor, women's household tasks, which did not bring in cash, were effectively redefined as noneconomic. As a result the actual chores performed by most city women, from hauling water to cooking meals and doing laundry, became economically invisible and culturally devalued. Single adult middle-class women (a new historical phenomenon) confronted the prospect of having to support themselves, as family fortunes waxed and waned with the unpredictable cycles of the new market economy. Meanwhile their married sisters, at least the more prosperous, might retreat into the elaboration and refinement of complex domestic households. Only landed wealth seemed to offer security either to women or to men in these times of boom and bust, but in most European countries such wealth was still controlled by a very few families.[8]

The combined effect of political repression with unprecedented socio-economic change insured that most nineteenth-century continental European feminists would couch potentially radical arguments for an end to women's subordination in the least threatening terms. Most cautiously emphasized women's social roles and insisted on women's special nature as a positive social force. Although they appealed to principles of liberty and equality, they took care to reassure (not always successfully) their adversaries that the changes they proposed would improve, not explode, the social order. In western Europe particularly, feminists elaborated on these principles with reference to the late eighteenth-century images of the mother-educator and the womanly-citizen, and proposed concrete reforms that would enhance women's "equality in difference."[9]

Inevitably, there were exceptions. In England during the 1820s agitation for change in the position of women reverberated in radical political and religious circles, accompanying agitation for reform of the parliamentary franchise and extension of manhood suffrage. In 1825 William Thompson and Anna Doyle Wheeler published their important tract, *Appeal of One Half the Human Race Against the Pretensions of the Other Half—Men—to*

Retain Them in Political and Thence in Civil and Domestic Slavery. Members of radical Protestant sects known as Dissenters, Unitarians, and Quakers, as well as the disciples of the textile king, social reformer, and trade union organizer Robert Owen, began to address the woman question in their publications.[10]

The question of political rights for propertied single women quickly arose and was as quickly dispatched. In 1832, when the British Parliament passed the landmark Reform Act, each paragraph dealing with parliamentary suffrage carried the preface, "every male person of full age, and not subject to any legal incapacity . . . " These words excluded single women property owners and all married women from political rights. Despite continued agitation, only one significant legal reform, establishing limited rights for mothers to custody of their own children, was realized before the 1850s.[11]

In the late 1830s, the redoutable Sarah Stickney Ellis began to preach the doctrine of women's conscious subordination to breadwinning men in her many books on the daughters, wives, and mothers of England. Eloquent protests in works such as Marion Kirkland Reid's tract *A Plea for Women* (1843), Charlotte Brontë's novels *Jane Eyre* (1847) and *Shirley* (1849), and Elizabeth Barrett Browning's novel in blank verse, *Aurora Leigh* (1856) testify to the fact that by midcentury women were finding their own voices to combat the counterrevolutionary prescriptions of the Mrs. Ellises. Meanwhile, other women and their allies busied themselves by founding professional schools to educate young middle-class women as teachers and governesses, and England became the first nation in the world to regulate the paid employment of women and children in manufacturing.

On the Continent, feminist theory and action found its greatest stimulus in Paris, where in the early 1830s a new revolution replaced the Bourbon monarchy with a constitutional monarchy complete with a charter of rights. In the ferment of this political upheaval, social critics and Romantics writers once again raised questions about women's status that would be diffused and discussed by women and men in intellectual circles throughout the rest of Europe. British radicals from Anna Doyle Wheeler to John Stuart Mill found new ideas in France, which they introduced to their contemporaries in England. Despite censorship, this intellectual ferment spread to Germany, the Scandinavian countries, the Italian states, and Russia. Critics restated many eighteenth-century notions, particularly the challenge to the principle of male legal control over women in marriage, which in effect treated all married women as a distinct and subordinate class. They also included the critique of marriage itself as legalized prostitution, meaning a strictly commercial transaction of support in exchange for sex. Everywhere feminists reiterated the demand for female education, the reorganization of the household, the defense of women's trades against the intrusion of men, and the assertion of women's right to work.[12]

French novelists of the Romantic school—especially George Sand (Amantine-Lucile-Aurore Dupin, baroness Dudevant), author of the controversial and widely read books *Indiana* (1832) and *Lélia* (1836)—and the utopian socialist reformers known as the Saint-Simonians and Fourierists once again raised the explosive theme of "free love." Advocates of free love proposed that men and women ought to form couples according to sexual or emotional inclination rather than according to the dictates of class-based, family, sociopolitical, or economic needs; in the metaphor of the time, free love was couple-based, not clan-based. Free love enthusiasts insisted that this practice would lay the foundation for better marriages, but their opponents denounced it as a coded call for sexual promiscuity and the destruction of the family, by which they meant the patriarchal family. Prosper Enfantin, the acknowledged leader of the mostly well-educated Saint-Simonian men, not only advocated free love but also contradicted Catholic doctrine on carnal sin by urging a "rehabilitation of the flesh." This scandalized many members, even some of the sect's male leadership. It led to government prosecution for outrages to public morality. Enfantin also called for women to speak out on the conditions of their own emancipation. In response, a small group of Saint-Simonian women founded a women's paper, which was called successively *La Femme nouvelle* ("The New Woman"), *L'Apostolat des femmes* ("Women's Apostolate"), *La Tribune des femmes* ("The Women's Tribune"), and *La Femme libre* ("The Free Woman"). This group included Suzanne Voilquin, Désirée Gay, and Jeanne Deroin, all young working women who signed their articles with first names only—"Jeanne-Victoire," "Jeanne-Désirée," and so forth. They downplayed Enfantin's free love doctrines, insisting instead on the greater importance of women's economic independence from men. Even as they argued specifically for women's right to work and to be self-supporting, they also focused on defending traditional sectors of women's employment, such as selling ribbons, from male interlopers.[13]

Though they disagreed on matters of sexual emancipation, both Saint-Simonian women and men emphasized the complementarity of the sexes. Both viewed the male-female couple as the *social individual*, but the Saint-Simonian women saw maternity as the common denominator for female solidarity. Women were not simply part of a greater whole; through maternity they possessed a unique quality that could be turned to good account in arguments for women's emancipation. Jeanne-Désirée made this claim in an early issue of the *Apostolat des femmes*: "Women's banner is universal, for . . . are they not all united by the same bond, MATERNITY?" Suzanne Voilquin felt even more strongly on this count, as is evident from her later *Souvenirs*. Flora Tristan, although she was not directly associated at the time with the Saint-Simonians or the women's paper, likewise emphasized the social importance of motherhood as a vehicle for freeing women. It was *LA MÈRE*—the Mother—whose revelation the Saint-Simonians awaited and whom they finally went to the Orient in 1834 to find. This single-minded emphasis on motherhood as the central feature of women's difference, incorporating both the physiological capacity for childbearing and the importance of their social role as mother-educators, was one of the most striking features of French feminist thought in the 1830s. Women reformers elaborated at length on the political implications of this social role.[14]

The educational claims made by other French women prior to 1848 likewise centered on maternity and its social implications. Such claims originated in the more modest arguments of seventeenth- and eighteenth-century advocates of formal education of girls. In Protestant countries, the Reformation had actually enhanced the opportunities for primary education for girls because of its emphasis on the need for literacy for Bible reading; leaders of the Catholic Counter-Reformation likewise promoted women's education, with an eye to encouraging women's religious piety, and established teaching orders of nuns, such as the Ursulines, which founded many girls' schools. In France, the sociopolitical utility of educating women for the family and the state had received increasing emphasis since 1687, when Archbishop Fénelon published his *Treatise on the Education of Daughters*. By the 1760s, male critics ranging from Jean-Jacques Rousseau to the Physiocrat Nicholas Baudeau had discussed the importance to the state of educated women. Such writers were not primarily concerned with women's own needs but like their church-minded rivals, recognized the vital role of mothers for the production of upstanding *male* citizens. Indeed, Baudeau advocated the establishment of national schools to educate French women (according to their respective ranks) as *citoyennes*, wives, and mothers. Outside France, such arguments influenced a number of the minor princes in southern Germany, as well as the enlightened despots, Catherine the Great in Russia and Frederick the Great in Prussia, both of whom established educational institutions along French lines for daughters of the elite in their respective countries. In the early stages of the French Revolution, legislators and social critics, including Condorcet, proposed a number of plans for the nationwide education of girls. These plans failed as crisis after crisis impeded the peaceful progress of the Revolution.[15]

In the wake of the Revolution, however, emphasis on the mother-educator increased throughout Europe as women were effectively shut out of postrevolutionary political life. Early nineteenth-century French educators wrote many tracts elaborating this idea. Following the important published contributions of Marie-Jeanne de Campan, Pauline Meulan Guizot, and Claire de Rémusat in the 1820s, even male advocates began to make extravagant claims in its support, as in Louis Aimé-Martin's influential tract, *The Education of Mothers; or the Civilization of Mankind by Women* (1834). The mother-educator idea was strategically important because it provided women with a serious—and quasi-political—purpose in life. Women themselves found the new role appealing because of the social power it accorded them. Some aristocratic women viewed it as a meaningful alternative to the dissipation of pre-revolutionary court and social life. For urban women of the middle and lower-middle classes, the new ideal of the mother-educator had a dignity and value that could counteract the devaluation of the many other vital but less inspired chores that fell to them. It also gave women an argument for demanding formal educational opportunities and special institutions for their sex, and for acquiring training as teachers. As citizen-mothers, they were able to make many claims on the state.[16]

The notion of the educated mother as educator of citizens greatly influenced thought on women's emancipation throughout Europe and America, especially in areas where nation-building was in progress. In various nationalist movements, Polish, Italian, Ukrainian, and Finnish, women writers repeatedly staked their own claims to full citizenship on their sociopolitical utility to the nation as mother-educators. These writers claimed for mother-educators the vital role of keeping the national language alive, or of helping to revive it in the face of suppression. Polish nationalist Klementyna Tanska Hoffmanova urged mothers to teach their children Polish and wrote of Polish women's role and duties. Later in the century, Hoffmanova's disciple, Natalia Kobryns'ka, made similar appeals in the cause of Ukrainian nationalism. In 1906 Alexandra Gripenberg applauded the successful efforts of Finnish mother-educators in gaining full citizenship, including voting rights, in the new charter given to Finland by the Russian Tsar.

Throughout the first half of the nineteenth century, women and men used these appeals and other, more general, arguments to invoke the importance of female cultural influence in advancing women's interests both among secular rationalists and within more progressive sectors of the Judeo-Christian religious tradition. In France, after the Saint-Simonian controversy had died down, supporters of female emancipation felt obligated to emphasize the moral respectability of their ideas. In 1848–49, the French dramatist Ernest Legouvé summed up the arguments for radical change in the legal, educational, and economic status of women in his *Moral History of Women*. Many German women invoked the idea of women's importance as culture-bearers. This proved to be as potent a political tool for religiously identified women in Germany as it had been in France for the secularizers.

By midcentury, however, partisans of female subordination were using the same notion to support their policies. Pope Pius IX, fleeing from the revolution in Rome in 1849, invoked the positive power of educated and influential womanhood when he called for promulgation of the dogma of the Immaculate Conception of Mary. As men defected from the church, the pope seemed especially anxious to retain women's allegiance in a time of revolutionary upheaval; he understood and hoped to harness the power of Christian mothers in forming souls for the church. Though they were poles apart politically, both the pope and the ardent secular philosopher-sociologist Auguste Comte testified to their belief in the importance of female influence for the regeneration of European political and cultural life. Unlike the feminists, however, neither was led to argue for women's emancipation by this belief. In the highly politicized atmosphere of midnineteenth-century Europe, the reinvigorated and elastic notions of women's influence and separate spheres could and would henceforth serve both revolutionary and counterrevolutionary ends.[17]

FEMINIST THOUGHT AND ACTION IN THE REVOLUTIONS OF 1848

In 1848 revolutions once again broke out. Beginning with the ouster of Louis-Philippe in Paris, revolutionary activities also erupted in Berlin, Vienna, Frankfurt, and other major European cities. Once again, demands for women's emancipation became part of the revolutionary political agenda.

Two women exemplify the possibilities and limitations of continental European feminist thought and action in the years from 1848 to 1851. The Frenchwoman Jeanne Deroin (1805–1894) and her somewhat younger German counterpart Louise Otto (later Otto-Peters; 1819–1895) from Saxony illustrate the ways in which the cause of women's emancipation was wedded to the political and intellectual history of the times. Their respective approaches also provide insight into the national differences that emerged in the course of the nineteenth century. Both women took active roles in the revolutionary events of midcentury Europe; both published women's periodicals during the revolutionary years, Deroin in Paris, and Otto first in Meissen, then in Gera. Both asserted women's claims to liberty, equality, and justice as staunchly as they insisted on the difference of women from men without perceiving these claims as contradictory in the least. Both were radicals with reference to their respective societies, and both can be viewed as relational feminists. Deroin advocated women's suffrage, while Otto advocated improvement of women's educational and economic situation.

Jeanne Deroin was a Parisian working-class woman who, although married and a mother, used her given name rather than that of her husband Desroches. As noted earlier, she had participated in the Saint-Simonian movement during the 1830s and had absorbed many of the teachings of Charles Fourier concerning the reorganization of the household and social work. She considered herself a democratic socialist, but her first priority was the cause of women.[18]

Writing in the women's newspaper, La Voix des femmes ("Women's Voice"), founded shortly after the outbreak of the Paris revolution, Deroin called for women's formal participation in public affairs. The provisional government had established universal manhood suffrage; thus France had become the first ostensibly democratic European nation. But this democracy was all male. The leaders of the provisional government sneered at proposals to extend the vote to women, and the fact that the newly enfranchised men elected an assembly that was not even sympathetic to the revolutionaries ended all hope of significant social or political change. By June 1848 (after weeks of civil disruption) the new assembly abruptly closed all political clubs, including those organized by women.

This action effectively ended all organized female political activism, but Deroin persisted. Even after the male voters elected Louis-Napoleon (heir of the Bonaparte dynasty) President of the Republic, she continued to press for women's inclusion in political life. In 1849 she founded her own periodical, L'Opinion des Femmes ("Women's Opinion"), and in a serialized essay on "woman's mission," she presented her vision of what women's participation in the public sphere ought to accomplish.

The first priority of democratic government, she argued, must be to end the struggle between women and men. Only by abolishing male privilege (in this case, male political privilege), she insisted, could the new government achieve the realization of a truly new society. To Deroin, privileges of sex were even more insidious than those of class. "The abolition of the privileges of race, birth, caste, and fortune cannot be complete and radical unless the privilege of sex is totally abolished," she wrote. Deroin argued that only by achieving full citizenship could women participate properly in the reconstruction of French society.

In Deroin's view, women and men made distinctive contributions to society. She insisted on the complementarity of the sexes, and she based her arguments for women's participation in political affairs on sexual complementarity and women's difference (both biological and social) from men, in particular, on women's "sacred function as mother" and her "sublime humanitarian maternity." In Deroin's estimation, women had not only a right but a duty, given their maternal role, to intercede in both civil and political life in order to carry out the duty of watching over the future of her children.

Violence and repression must henceforth yield to participatory government. Women, Deroin argued, must be called on to "teach everyone how fraternity should be practiced," to show men the way of transcending secular quarrels between individuals, between families, and between nations. Women had nothing less than an apostolic mission to "realize the kingdom of God on earth, the reign of fraternity and universal harmony." Deroin never clearly elaborated her reasons for insisting on women's ability to achieve these goals; in the circumstances of male revolutionary violence, she seems to have considered women's moral superiority self-evident.[19]

Deroin did more than make claims for women's participation in the public sphere, however; she acted on her ideals. In early 1849, she petitioned the Democratic-Socialist party to become a candidate for the Legislative

Assembly. Deroin's candidacy was unsuccessful, but she merits a distinctive place in history for her synthesis of ideals and activism. Not only was she the first European woman to declare her candidacy for public office under a democratized regime, but she was also one of the first women to be arrested and imprisoned for her efforts to organize joint associations of male and female workers (yet another form of prohibited political activity in mid-nineteenth century France). In 1852 Deroin fled to England, along with other men and women who actively opposed the consolidation of Louis-Napoleon's grip on political power. She spent the remainder of her life in London.[20]

In the revolutionary climate of midnineteenth century Germany, feminist activists used different arguments, although, as in France, they emphasized women's difference as a central tenet. The central theme was German womanliness, rather than social motherhood. In German feminist discourse, arguments often carried an undeniably nationalist overtone. German feminists emphasized the distinctive contribution women, as women, could and must make to the building of the German nation, a very important political goal prior to the forced unification of the many German principalities with Prussia in 1871 under Otto von Bismarck. The arguments put forth by Louise Otto, a well-educated single woman of upper-middle-class background who, like Deroin, had become a political radical, exemplify this particular type of relational feminism.

Based in Saxony, one of Germany's most industrialized regions, Otto edited the longest-lived of several German revolutionary women's publications, the *Frauenzeitung* ("Women's Newspaper"). Since the mid-1840s she had crusaded for systematic reform of the education of middle-class women and for improvements in the condition of working women in the region's industrial cities. Marriage, in Otto's view, was a degraded institution, merely "a support institution for the female sex." She scorned women's "characterlessness" in a culture where the building of character (*Bildung*) was considered so extremely important for educated men. Far more than Deroin, and reflecting the spirit of German philosophy since Kant (though Kant would hardly have applied such ideas to women), Otto emphasized "independence," not only of a moral nature ("the exercise of judgement") but also of a material, or economic nature ("the exercise of action").[21]

Of particular significance to Louise Otto was her oft-repeated concern with "true womanliness," which epitomized for her a quality quite different from, and far more potent than, the characterlessness she objected to in so many German women. Her arguments for true womanliness carried a defensive tone, however; she constantly issued disclaimers against those who (as she put it) discredited the emancipation of woman "by devaluing woman to become a caricature of a man." This had become a sore point among German feminists, exacerbated by a recent wave of "Georgesandismus"

—the aping by certain self-proclaimed "emancipated women" in Germany of the unusual and much-publicized habits of the French writer George Sand. These habits included wearing male dress (illegal in France without a police permit), smoking, and engaging in liaisons with men to whom one was not married. In their reaction to Georgesandismus, German feminists at midcentury often demonstrated a peculiarly self-righteous and straight-laced quality. Otto's true woman was above all else, virtuous, courageous, moralistic, patriotic, and peaceable—all the things German men allegedly were not.[22]

Well before the revolutions of 1848, and in spite of a hostile political climate, the voices of European feminists made themselves heard. Some women and some men sympathetic to women's emancipation articulated a distinctive consciousness of women's subordination. They expounded the full range of criticisms that would characterize the movement for women's emancipation during the remainder of the century. They set forth their visions of a new society in which women, free from male domination, were men's equals. They criticized male-established marriage institutions and women's legal, economic, and sexual dependence in marriage. They attacked male definitions of womanhood, and rehabilitated the idea of womanhood by emphasizing women as mother-educators and women's distinctive contributions to society. They argued for women's right to economic independence and for a restructuring of the newly emerging world of extra-household employment so that it did not disadvantage women, especially as concerned childbearing. They objected to the sexual double standard that preserved the "virtue" of privileged women at the expense of poor women, and, finally, they criticized male control of political life, and claimed political representation for women based squarely on their differences from men and on the potential contribution they could make to the public weal as "republican mothers" by "domesticating the public sphere." All these ideas developed within a framework of relational feminist arguments in repressive political environments.

THE DEVELOPMENT OF ORGANIZED WOMEN'S MOVEMENTS

Although the essential elements of a feminist critique of European society can be clearly identified by 1848, the development of an organized political movement for women's emancipation came later. Not surprisingly, in light of the repressive political climate of Europe, the most success-ful initial efforts to organize took place outside Europe, in the United States. As early as 1851, Harriet Taylor Mill expressed her admiration at the activism of the American women who had convened at Worcester,

Massachusetts, in pursuit of their rights. Not until the late 1850s and 1860s did equivalent organization on behalf of women's emancipation begin in Europe.[23]

From that time forth, however, many such initiatives sprang up. In western Europe, the leaders were mostly (though not exclusively) upper middle-class women who were well connected to the governing male elites. The epitome of such a feminist activism blossomed in England: a concerted movement for women's suffrage side-by-side with organized campaigns to reform the laws that governed married women's property, to eradicate legalized prostitution, and to achieve the admittance of women to British universities and medical schools. In France, with the liberalization in 1867 of laws on the press and association, the first significant organizations for reform of women's legal status were formed; and in Germany, a group of women and men led by Louise Otto founded the General Association of German Women, dedicated to improvements in women's educational and economic status. In Imperial Russia, where tsarist absolutism did not allow the possibility of democratic political participation even for men, no actual organized western European-style movement sprang up. Even so, Russian women became the first in Europe to obtain government-sponsored access to secondary and higher education. Agitation for women's emancipation among the radical intelligentsia in Russia accompanied the freeing of the serfs (to Whose plight the situation of women was often compared) and led subsequently to extensive participation by educated women in movements for the revolutionary overthrow of the tsarist regime.

Although conditions specific to each country governed the shape political activity on women's behalf would take, the new wave of activism that erupted in the 1860s manifested many features common to all. Concerns for women's education and possibilities for employment were central. In London these concerns led to the formation of the Society for Promoting the Employment of Women (1859); in Paris to the founding in the early 1860s of Elisa Lemmonier's schools for girls' vocational education; in Germany to the establishment of the paternalistic Lette-Verein (1865); and in St. Petersburg to plans for a Society for Women's Work. Some of the most successful initiatives for change in each country ultimately emerged from philanthropic activity by women's groups.

Concerted efforts to change women's civil and political status under the law were especially evident in Britain and in France during the 1860s. Although a major reform—the transfer of divorce proceedings from ecclesiastical courts to civil courts—had been enacted in England in 1857, the legal standing of married women was still nonexistent. According to English common law, adult women once married lost all authority over property, whether property they brought to marriage or their own earnings. For instance, at one notable trial, the court charged the thief with "stealing from the person of Millicent Fawcett a purse containing £1 18s. 6d., the property of Henry Fawcett." (Millicent Garrett Fawcett eventually became a leader of the British movement for women's suffrage.) British feminists, headed by Barbara Leigh Smith Bodichon, established a Married Women's Property Committee, and by persuading sympathetic Members to introduce legislation, provoked a full-scale debate on the subject in Parliament. This agitation ultimately led to the passage in 1882 of a sweeping Married Women's Property Law. In 1869 John Stuart Mill published his famous treatise *The Subjection of Women*. This work, which no one could ignore because of Mill's international reputation as a political theorist, has become a classic text in the history of feminist thought. At the time it triggered much criticism as well as much acclaim; despite the criticism, it was quickly translated (in many cases by women) into many languages, including Danish and Polish.[24]

In France, the subordinate legal status of married women provoked concerted agitation for change under the leadership of Maria Deraismes and Léon Richer. Both were closely identified with the anticlerical republican opposition to the Second Empire of Napoleon III and were therefore well-connected to the elite of the succeeding regime, the Third Republic. In 1868 Richer established a periodical, *Le Droit des femmes* ["The Right(s) of Women"], which insistently promoted changes in the legal, educational, moral, and economic position of women for well over twenty years. In 1878 Richer and Deraismes convened the First International Congress on Women's Rights, which met in Paris. Representatives of twelve nations attended this congress. Despite this promising beginning, the Republic's establishment of secondary girls' schools (1880) and teacher training institutes, and the enactment of divorce legislation (1882), the political uncertainties in 1880s France worked against further changes in women's status. It was only in the 1890s, under a new generation of leaders, that feminist agitation for major legal reform in women's status began to achieve any additional successes. No thorough overhaul of the legal status of married women took place in France until the middle of the twentieth century.[25]

The development of an organized movement in Italy followed on the heels of efforts to achieve national unification, which succeeded in the early 1860s. The pioneer reformer Anna Maria Mozzoni focused on promoting a liberal treatment of women in the new legal code, while other women reformers zealously promoted women's education for patriotic motherhood in the interest of the new nation. This pattern would recur in the context of other European nationalist movements.

Agitation to promote women's suffrage resurfaced again in western Europe during the 1860s. In England, during consideration of the Second Reform Act in 1867, John Stuart Mill, then in Parliament, introduced a measure to amend the parliamentary suffrage extension bill by substituting the word *person* for *man* wherever it appeared in the bill. Although this measure failed, in 1870 English women won the right to vote in local elections.

In France, discussion of votes for women emerged again during this period, only to be squelched again in the wake of France's defeat by Germany in 1870. The ensuing revolt and the short-lived reign of the Paris Commune, in which many women took part, caused another wave of reactionary fears, including fear about the inclusion of women in political life. Despite the valiant efforts of Hubertine Auclert to obtain the right to vote for French-women, the suffrage issue remained too controversial to arouse much support before the early twentieth century. Anticlerical men of the Third Republic resisted women's suffrage because they feared that women would support the monarchist Catholic opposition. After German unification in 1871 the subsequent establishment of an indirect national system of male suffrage for the Reichstag, Hedwig Dohm and others argued for women's right to vote but did not attract a significant following.

Efforts to establish international links in the women's movement also blossomed in the late 1860s. In conjunction with a movement to promote European peace and solidarity across national lines, Marie Goegg of Switzerland attempted to establish an international women's network. Many of the leading European advocates of pacifism and international cooperation also supported women's rights and reforms. The debate over the woman question likewise surfaced in the congresses of the International Working Men's Association. These meetings, attended by a mixture of progressive middle-class intellectuals and skilled workers, engendered heated debate of women's role in the labor force and in the family. Few of the working men present supported the principle of women's right to work. They preferred the notion of a "family wage," that would allow men to earn enough to support their wives and children.[26]

The 1880s witnessed a change in the context of the debate on the woman question and in the character of the demands made for women's emancipation. In the course of the nineteenth century, the woman question, like the so-called social question, had become an integral feature of the vast European debate over changing sociopolitical circumstances. The complex mixture of interrelated problems stemming from industrialization, working-class agitation, demographic changes, and the emerging political challenge of socialism intensified the debate. During the 1870s and 1880s, European governments had begun to confront issues raised by the employment of working-class women in industrial manufacturing. But since most working women did not work in factories, their work was not easily regulated. For these women, employment meant long hours, unhealthy working conditions, and inferior pay with little sense of personal reward. Especially in France, but increasingly after 1900 in Germany and Great Britain, members of the educated classes, including doctors as well as politicians, began to worry over the possible adverse consequences for their countries of new population patterns. Birth rates were falling off significantly and mortality rates, especially high among infants and small children, were becoming a major public concern. In some countries, especially in Scandinavia, heavy emigration was depleting the population. National governments were becoming concerned about the production of future generations of workers and soldiers. Opponents of women's emancipation interpreted even the assertion of women's right to paid employment (let alone the demand for women's right to pursue the better-paid "masculine" professions) as a threat to the demographic and economic well-being of the nation-state. Working women, they argued, did not bear and could not raise healthy children. Women's claims for rights threatened to interfere with women's "responsibilities" to society and the state.[27]

In this changing context, European novelists and dramatists began to explore the "new woman" and the problem posed for society by women's "egotism," as women's search for freedom and self-realization was often labelled. In the play, A Doll's House (1879), which created a sensation throughout Europe in the years that followed, the Norwegian dramatist Henrik Ibsen sympathetically portrayed a woman caught in marriage to a mediocre man and her decision to abandon husband and children in order to "find herself." The uproar generated by Nora's decision to walk out at the end of Act III epitomized the general touchiness of public opinion on the subject of women's emancipation, and on at least one occasion, Ibsen rewrote the last scene before the play could be produced. In her Story of an African Farm (1883), the novelist Olive Schreiner created the character of Lyndall, who boasted that she was "not in so great a hurry to put [her] neck beneath any man's foot." Other "new woman" novels followed, many of which attacked the existing institution of marriage; they attracted an enthusiastic readership, especially among women. In England, Mona Caird's articles in the Westminster Review criticizing the institution of marriage "stirred the press to white heat both in England and America," according to the American observer Elizabeth Cady Stanton. At the same time, essayists and social critics such as Karl Pearson, Eleanor Marx, Havelock Ellis, August Bebel, and Friedrich Engels reintroduced exploration in print of the links between sexuality, socioeconomic and family structures, capitalism, and the state. All these writers probed the social consequences of women's emancipation, and although many authors seemed sympathetic to women's strivings, few of them were optimistic about the consequences for society of women's efforts to achieve self-realization. Nevertheless, the fictional creations contributed significantly to the diffusion of individualist feminist arguments.[28]

Aside from demands for political equality for women, only rarely before 1880 had any advocates of women's emancipation argued for more than moral or intellectual equality for women and ending their legal and economic subordination in marriage. Motherhood and womanliness, as we have said, lay at the base of all arguments, and concepts of "woman's nature" and "woman's role" fostered arguments for radical change. Before 1880, only the Fourierists had proposed a non–sex-typed, non–role-based notion of human social equality for women, or the sharing of "women's work"—housework or childcare—by men. After 1880, this situation began to change; even the concept of woman's nature began to find its challengers, and "new women" were charged by their critics of pursuing a masculine vision of individualism. New, more radical definitions of the problem and proposals for change engendered a new wave of overt opposition to women's emancipation and dampened the enthusiasm of earlier supporters. Social Darwinist writers, such as Patrick Geddes and J. Arthur Thomson in Britain, invoked evolutionary theory to justify the sexual division of labor. "What was decided among the prehistoric Protozoa," they wrote, "cannot be annulled by Act of Parliament." Opponents of social change tried to discredit all arguments for women's emancipation by alleging that every claim for women's equality was necessarily individualistic, or egotistic, and that the realization of such claims would lead to social and political anarchy. "Woman wants to become self-reliant," Friedrich Nietzsche sneered in 1886, "and for that reason she is beginning to enlighten men about 'woman as such': *this* is one of the worst developments of the general *uglification* of Europe." Indeed, opponents of women's rights increasingly talked about the threat of individualist feminist arguments, including the threat that unmarried independent women might become a "third sex." To frighten off prospective supporters, some opponents of female emancipation warned that emancipated women threatened men's virility and, therefore, national security. "The German man is manly, and the German woman is womanly," the British Minister of War pointed out in 1910 to an anti–women's suffrage audience in Manchester. "Can we hope to compete with such a nation as this, if we war against nature, and endeavour to invert the natural roles of the sexes?"[29]

THE FLOWERING OF FEMINISM

During the 1890s the words feminism and feminist entered widespread usage. A new generation of European feminist theorists and women political leaders emerged. This generation included increasing numbers of highly educated, self-assured, and often politically radical young women, with university degrees in letters, law, and medicine, who felt little need to apologize for any presumed intellectual inferiority. It also included middle-aged, more conservative women who had come to recognize, through philanthropic activity in aid of the deviant and the dispossessed, the systematic injustices that women suffered in male-dominated societies. Through their charitable work, these women had acquired organizational skills and a far-reaching network of contacts. They set about organizing internationally and setting a new agenda of demands on behalf of their sex, in addition to the many still unanswered claims.

Many of the most radical members of this new generation of feminists continued to emphasize women's biological and social difference from men and underscored motherhood as the focal point for female solidarity. They argued for special rights for women, as well as equal rights with men. Though theoretical and literary feminists articulated ideas that were often extraordinarily individualistic, the activists found themselves—due to political circumstance—having to proceed cautiously in order to wrest desired reforms from an often reluctant, male-dominated political power structure, which their socialist counterparts scorned as "the bourgeois state." In countries like Russia, a reformist feminist movement emerged only timidly in the early twentieth century. Further west, however, the women's movement took on substantial proportions. Indeed, the growth of a full-blown organized women's movement and the explosion of feminist publications in western Europe between 1890 and 1914 constitute one of the most significant new features in the European political landscape. The movement's rapid growth can be directly attributed to the more relaxed and democratic political environment of the late nineteenth century, which increasingly permitted, in spite of much official reluctance, more freedom for political association and less restricted public speech.

In France, for example, various groups within the women's movement campaigned for reform of the Civil Code and for the right of married women to control their own earnings. Some wanted to give unmarried mothers the right to sue the fathers of their children for child support, while others called for state subsidies for all mothers, married and unmarried alike. Others hoped to abolish government-regulated prostitution. They differed widely concerning protective labor legislation for women. In Germany, movement members sought more protective labor legislation, an end to legalized prostitution, and control of the spread of venereal disease. Radical women in the *Bund für Mutterschutz* (Mother's Protection League) proposed that programs for the "protection of mothers" include unmarried as well as married women, and demanded a new sexual ethic. Throughout Europe, some feminists sought to achieve measures similar to those embodied in the German program for maternity insurance and leaves for working women, while others opposed legislation that "protected" women in ways that might disadvantage them in the struggle for full equality. Others founded unions for women in the workforce.

It should be clear from this overview that women's suffrage was far from the only feminist political issue of note in the first decade of the twentieth century. But it was becoming increasingly clear to feminist activists on the European continent, as it had become clear in the English-speaking world several decades before, that male-dominated governments, especially newly democratized governments responsive only to male voters, were extremely resistant to making dramatic changes in existing institutions for the benefit of women who were politically powerless. In the democratic states of western Europe, therefore, feminist women and their male allies worked to obtain formal political power for women equivalent to that available to men. Only after World War I did most succeed. After a celebrated campaign, women in England, in Germany, and in many other European nations (the notable exceptions being France, Italy, and Switzerland) all obtained some degree of political rights by 1920.[30]

The crusade for women's suffrage—especially the militant campaign led by the Women's Social and Political Union (WSPU) in England—riveted world attention during the early twentieth century. In this campaign, orchestrated by Emmeline Pankhurst, her daughters, and many middle-class and working-class women, the prevailing ideal of feminine propriety (though not femininity) was renounced. As Emmeline Pankhurst put it in her court testimony of 1908, "We have tried to be womanly, we have tried to use feminine influence, and we have seen that it is of no use . . . ; we are here not because we are law-breakers; we are here in our efforts to become law-makers."[31] The British women's campaign for the vote ranks as the feminist movement's first great media event, and the repressive measures instituted by the British government against the suffragettes aroused the sympathy of women around the world.

Late nineteenth-century advocacy of women's emancipation ran the gamut from moderate single-issue campaigns for reform to sweeping radical critiques of the entire sociopolitical status quo. By 1900 the successors of Deroin and Otto were conducting far more open discussions of women's sexuality and the politics of reproduction; some even claimed woman's right to exercise independence in matters of love. The notions of woman's difference and her educational mission continued to buttress the demands of relational feminists for the development of educational institutions for women, but now also served as a basis for a far more explicit, more insistent attack on patriarchal institutional arrangements, including capitalism, and on the "masculinist" state itself. Since it is impossible here to deal in depth with all the variations of this attack, what follows is a brief introduction to several of the most singular and influential new contributions by women to European feminist thought between 1890 and 1914.

Swedish writer Ellen Key (1849–1926) made perhaps the most controversial contribution to Continental feminist thought in this new context. Key did not confine her theoretical work to short articles and newspapers, as had the women of 1848. She published several important books: *The Century of the Child* (orig. in Swedish, 1900), and *Love and Marriage* (orig. in Swedish, 1904). Key's works found many enthusiastic readers; they were circulated, quoted, translated, and argued about throughout Europe, and had a major impact on leaders of the women's movements in Germany and France as well as in Scandinavia.

Key's arguments derive from the explication of the social value of motherhood by Jeanne Deroin and other early nineteenth-century advocates of women's emancipation. Key gave them a distinctive twist. Although she spoke of women's biological nature and the traditional division of labor between the sexes in the family, according to which women were the childbearers and childrearers, she diverged from earlier arguments at a critical point—on the question of state-organized and -subsidized childcare for women in the workforce. Proposals for such measures, common to social visionaries from Plato to Charles Fourier, came under serious scrutiny throughout western Europe as national governments began to investigate the social consequences of women's employment.

Ellen Key examined at length the problem posed for women by motherhood in western society. The strategic significance of Key's analysis lay in her attempt to synthesize a rigorously relational approach to social analysis (based on women's difference) with deeply felt individualist claims for women's right to fulfillment and self-realization. Key proposed that women could achieve their maximum development as individuals through their contributions to society as mothers. But she also argued that the conditions for motherhood must be totally restructured in order for such a synthesis to occur, and that motherhood must be revalued, sanctioned, as it were, both politically and economically, by the nation-state. Economic support of individual women during their childbearing years by individual men, which she viewed as the immediate cause of women's subordination, should be the responsibility of the government. Child care should take place in the home, supported by the collectivity, but in the biological mother's charge; it should not become a direct responsibility of the collectivity as Fourier and others had insisted. Indeed, Key argued—expanding upon earlier "republican motherhood" arguments—that the state should recognize formal training of women for this role as the equivalent of military service for men. She also called boldly for open recognition of the sexual side of love, including women's sexual pleasure, a feature of her arguments that endeared her to commentators such as Havelock Ellis in England but scandalized defenders of traditional morality.

In the population-conscious political climate of Third Republic France, Nelly Roussel (1878–1922) developed a related line of argument, once again based on women's social position as mothers. Herself married (unlike Ellen Key) and the mother of three, Roussel identified herself as a free thinker. She discussed the plight of women in speeches and articles and was closely associated with Marguerite Durand, publisher of the French women's daily newspaper, La Fronde. [32]

Nelly Roussel emerged as a powerful public speaker for the French women's rights movement in 1903. Defying the politicians who urged harsh measures to raise the French birthrate, she eloquently advocated women's right to control their own fertility. She called for a complete revision in the French laws governing marriage, at a time when the government of the Third Republic was becoming increasingly concerned about the decline in the national birthrate. She appealed to women of all classes to "declare war on today's society." In one celebrated oration, she even invoked the threat of a birth-strike against the patriarchal state:

> Beware, oh Society! The day will come . . . when the eternal victim will become weary of carrying in her loins sons whom you will later teach to scorn their mothers or daughters destined—alas!—to the same life of sacrifice and humiliation! The day when we will refuse to give you, ogres, your ration of cannon-fodder, of work-fodder, and fodder for suffering! The day, at last, when we will become mothers *only when we please.* . . .

Like Ellen Key, Roussel based her claims for women's emancipation on the social value of motherhood, and she too demanded that the terms for mother-hood be made far more favorable to women. She also argued in relational terms, emphasizing the political implications of the relationship between women, children, and the male-dominated and increasingly militaristic nation-state. She too demanded the establishment of motherhood as a "social," or state function and called for sex education for girls before they entered marriage.

Roussel was first and foremost a women's advocate. She took every opportunity to criticize *masculinisme*, a term she used to describe male supremacy. She addressed her arguments to women of every class, and worked closely with French proponents of birth control in efforts to reach women of the working class. She opposed French socialists who, in their single-minded insistence on placing class interests above all others, cautioned against cooperation on women's issues between socialist feminists and bourgeois feminists. She also criticized socialist opposition to birth control. From Roussel's perspective, all women were oppressed and women of all classes should pursue the same goal—emancipation. Women, she insisted, had far more in common than did men of different classes, because whatever their class, they shared a common oppression. Women were, in her view, still the "eternal victims."

Even more controversial were the arguments of Christabel Pankhurst (1880–1958), who became the chief theorist and tactician of the militant British WSPU. The eldest daughter of Emmeline and Richard Pankhurst, she studied law and received a degree, though she could not become a member of the bar. Christabel Pankhurst became incensed about the sex scandals that rocked Britain during the period of persecution of the suffragettes and penned a scathing attack on male vice and its consequences for innocent women. Her solution: "Votes for Women and Chastity for Men."[33]

CONCLUSION

By the early twentieth century, European feminist theorists were exploring in depth virtually every issue we are familiar with today. Feminist activists had organized to work for political and socio-economic change in women's position along a broad front. Both theorists and activists found inspiration for their protests and a vocabulary for articulating a feminist consciousness in the Enlightenment language of liberty, equality, and justice. But the contours of their thought and action in the nineteenth century were bounded by historical circumstances, and they had not yet acquired the formal power to reshape these. This may explain why their most persuasive arguments for the achievement of particular reforms featured a relational logic.

Both nineteenth-century European feminist thinkers and their opponents agreed that the social relation of the sexes was the very glue that held organized society together and that marriage and sex/gender roles were inherently political. Although most accepted a sexual division of labor in society, they rejected the public/domestic division of spheres as inappropriate and argued that women's influence must be felt throughout society. Most Continental feminists in this era insisted on the importance of bio-physiological differences between the sexes and on what Adrienne Rich has since derogated as "compulsory heterosexuality," and in fact, many (though by no means all) political progressives who supported women's emancipation also argued for universal marriage as their social ideal. Most viewed motherhood as women's particular responsibility. Indeed, for many, maternity had become not only the strategic common ground for women's solidarity but also the vehicle for their liberation. Most nineteenth-century feminists also insisted (far more than we find comfortable doing today) on the close relationship between the family and the state; indeed, they held an optimistic view of the potential for harnessing state power on women's behalf. This optimism remained intact even as emancipators envisioned a radical reorganization (through democratic means) of existing heterosexual relations, familial institutions, and the socio-economic structure—a vision diametrically opposed to that enforced by most late nineteenth-century states.

European feminist theory and practice remains to this day far more overtly conscious of state power and the political centrality of the family to the state than does its Anglo-American counterpart. Nineteenth-century European feminist theorists questioned the political structure of society from marriage to monarchy and increasingly challenged the practices and assumptions of the new capitalist economic order that seemed to bolster the male-dominated structures. Their own assertions about the way in which the entire post-revolutionary order should be revised and reconstructed were based on their prior understanding of "nature" and "culture," on a successful reinterpretation of women's importance as culture-bearers, and on their perception of the seeming fragility of the intricate web of relationships that bound individuals together into societies. Years ago Theodore Roszak remarked that "a major shift in sex relations . . . is bound to produce a severe cultural trauma."[34] The history of feminism in the nineteenth century (and into the twentieth century) demonstrates the truth of Roszak's proposition. Indeed, to end women's subordination requires a far more radical reconceptualization of the social order than ending the reign of kings, which in European history had been envisioned as strictly a male affair.

NOTES

1. Marie-Jean-Antoine-Nicolas Caritat, marquis de Condorcet, *Esquisse d'un tableau historique des progrès de l'esprit humain* (orig. publ., 1795; Paris: Editions Sociales, 1966), pp. 274–75; Charles Fourier, *Théorie de Quatre Mouvements et des destinées générales* (orig. publ., 1808; reprinted Paris: J. J. Pauvert, 1967), p. 147; Percy Bysshe Shelley, *The Revolt of Islam* (1817), Canto II, verse 43; Hugo, "Sur la Tombe de Louise Jullien" (1853), *Oeuvres complètes de Victor Hugo*, (Paris: Editions Hetzel-Quantin, 1880–89), vol. 44, p. 92.

   For further documentation of European feminist thought and action in English translation, including Condorcet, Gouges, Hippel, Fourier, and many of the other texts on which the following analysis is based (and an extensive bibliography of relevant works published prior to October 1982) see Susan Groag Bell and Karen M. Offen, *Women, the Family, and Freedom: The Debate in Documents, 1750–1950*, 2 vols. (Stanford, Calif.: Stanford University Press, 1983). In addition, see the bibliographical essay at the end of this chapter. Wollstonecraft's *Vindication of the Rights of Woman* is available in a number of recent re-editions.

2. For further discussion, see Karen Offen, "Sur les origines des mots 'féminisme' et 'féministe,'" forthcoming in *Revue d'histoire moderne et contemporaine* (Paris). The first known use of the word in French (by Alexandre Dumas fils, 1872) was pejorative, but in 1882, the French women's suffrage advocate Hubertine Auclert claimed the word feminist to describe herself and other advocates of women's emancipation. The first documented use of the words I have found in English dates from 1894; in Spanish, 1896; in Russian, 1898, and in German, 1902.

3. In 1884 Theodore Stanton edited a collection of essays covering fifteen nations and two regions (Bohemia and the Orient). See his *The Woman Question in Europe* (New York: G. P. Putnam's Sons, 1884). By 1901, when Helene Lange and Gertrud Bäumer assembled their history of the women's movement, they included contributions from seventeen nations, including Greece, Spain, and Portugal. *Die Geschichte der Frauenbewegung*, vol. 1 of *Handbuch der Frauenbewegung*, ed. Helene Lange and Gertrud Bäumer (Berlin: W. Moeser Buchhandlung, 1901).

4. Ellen Key, *Love and Marriage*, tr. Arthur G. Chater (New York, 1911), p. 214. Orig. publ. in Swedish, 1904.

5. The "bourgeois"/"socialist" distinction dates from the founding in 1894 of the German *Bund Deutscher Frauenverein*, which excluded the feminist women

associated with the German Social Democratic Party. For an analysis of the mutual attractions and differences between partisans of both groups, see Richard J. Evans, "Bourgeois Feminists and Women Socialists in Germany, 1894–1914: Lost Opportunity or Inevitable Conflict?" *Women's Studies International Quarterly*, 3, no. 4 (1980), 355–376. Not surprisingly, the terminology spread throughout the socialist parties represented in the Second International and colors subsequent historical scholarship, though the lines between bourgeois and socialist were never drawn as sharply in the women's movements outside Germany.

6. Pertinent sections of the Napoleonic Code and the works of More, Maistre, and Bonald can be consulted in Bell & Offen, *Women, the Family, and Freedom*, vol. 1. On Hannah More, see Mitzi Myers, "Reform or Ruin: A Revolution in Female Manners," in *Studies of Eighteenth-Century Culture*, 11, ed. Harry C. Payne (Madison, Wisc.: University of Wisconsin Press, 1982), 199–215. For More's French counterparts, see Barbara Corrado Pope, "Revolution and Retreat: Upper-Class French Women after 1789," in *Women, War, and Revolution*, ed. Carol R. Berkin and Clara M. Lovett (New York: Holmes & Meier, 1980).

 For discussion of the literature on domestic economy and the character of the sexes in Great Britain, France, and Germany from the later eighteenth century on, see Karin Hausen, "Family and Role-Division: The Polarisation of Sexual Stereotypes in the Nineteenth Century—An Aspect of the Dissociation of Work and Family Life," (1976) in *The German Family*, ed. Richard J. Evans and W. R. Lee (Totowa, N.J.: Barnes & Noble, 1981); Peter Petschauer, "From Hausmütter to Hausfrau: Ideals and Realities in late Eighteenth-Century Germany," *Eighteenth Century Life*, 8, no. 1 (October 1982), 72–82; Catherine Hall, "The Early Formation of Victorian Domestic Ideology," in *Fit Work for Women*, ed. Sandra Burman (New York: St. Martin's Press, 1979); Elizabeth Fox-Genovese, "The Ideological Origins of Domestic Economy," in Elizabeth Fox-Genovese and Eugene Genovese, *Fruits of Merchant Capital: Slavery and Bourgeois Property in the Rise and Expansion of Capitalism*, (New York: Oxford University Press, 1983); and Marion W. Gray, "Prescriptions for Productive Female Domesticity in a Transitional Era: Germany's *Hausmütterliteratur*, 1780–1840," forthcoming in *History of European Ideas*, special issue on women's history, 1987.

7. Chateaubriand, "L'Avenir du monde," *Revue des deux mondes*, 15 April 1834, 236–237; Tocqueville, *Democracy in America*, II (New York: Vintage, 1959), pp. 222–225.

8. For further discussion of the process whereby women's work became marginalized and increasingly invisible, see Leslie Parker Hume and Karen Offen, "The Adult Woman: Work," and accompanying documents in *Victorian Women: A Documentary Account of Women's Lives in Nineteenth-Century England, France, and the United States* (Stanford, Calif.: Stanford University Press, 1981).

9. For the Anglo-American tradition, see especially Ruth Bloch, "Untangling the Roots of Modern Sex Roles: A Survey of Four Centuries of Change," *Signs: Journal of Women in Culture and Society*, 4, no. 2 (Winter 1978), 236–52.

10. See Barbara Taylor, *Eve and the New Jerusalem: Socialism and Feminism in the Nineteenth Century* (London: Virago, 1983) and the many other works cited in the bibliographical essay below.

11. "An Act (2 William IV, c. 45) to Amend the Representation of the People in England and Wales, 7 June 1832," in *English Historical Documents*, ed. David C. Douglas, vol. 11 (1783–1832), ed. A. Aspinall & E. Anthony Smith (1959), doc. 303, articles XIX and XX. The efforts of Caroline Norton, who fought back when her husband charged her with adultery and absconded with their children, resulted in changing the law on child custody; see her tract, *The Separation of Mother and Child by the Law of 'Custody of Infants', Considered* (London, 1838). For background see Françoise Basch, *Relative Creatures: Victorian Women in Society and the Novel* (New York: Schocken, 1974).

12. Scholars who have examined the cross-fertilization of controversial ideas in nineteenth-century Europe generally agree that they spread outward from France. See, among others, Iris Wessel Mueller, *John Stuart Mill and French Thought* (Urbana, Ill.: University of Illinois Press, 1956); Gail Malmgreen, *Neither Bread Nor Roses: Utopian Feminists and the English Working Class, 1800–1850* (Brighton, England: Studies in Labour History Pamphlet, 1977); Patricia Thomson, *George Sand and the Victorians* (London: Macmillan, 1977).

13. Claire G. Moses, *French Feminism in the Nineteenth Century* (Albany, N.Y.: State University of New York Press, 1984), chaps. 3 and 4.

14. The emphasis on sexual complementarity and motherhood in the 1830s cannot be overestimated. The article by "Jeanne-Désirée" appeared in *L'Apostolat des femmes*, no. 5, 3 Oct. 1832. Translated excerpts from the respective texts of Flora Tristan and Suzanne Voilquin can be consulted in Hellerstein, Hume, and Offen, *Victorian Women*, pp. 170 and 247.

15. Phyllis Stock, *Better Than Rubies: A History of Women's Education* (New York: G. P. Putnam, 1978); Jean H. Bloch, "Women and the Reform of the Nation," in *Women and Society in 18th Century France: Essays in Honor of J. S. Spink*, ed. Eva Jacobs et al. (London: The Athlone Press, 1979), and Jean Perrel, "Les écoles de filles dans la France d'Ancien Régime," *Historical Reflections/Réflexions Historiques*, 7, nos. 2/3 (1980), 75–83. For the appropriation of French ideas on women's education by reforming German and Russian rulers, see Joseph L. Black, "Educating Women in Eighteenth-Century Russia," in *Citizens for the Fatherland: Education, Educators, and Pedagogical Ideals in Eighteenth-Century Russia* (Boulder, Colo.: East European Quarterly, 1979); Carol S. Nash, "Educating New Mothers: Women and the Enlightenment in Russia," *History of Education Quarterly*, 21, no. 3 (Fall 1981), 301–316; Peter Petschauer, "Improving Educational Opportunities for Girls in Eighteenth-Century Germany," *Eighteenth Century Life*, 3, no. 2 (Dec. 1976), 56–62; and Joanne Schneider, "Enlightened Reforms and Bavarian Girls' Education," in *German Women in the Nineteenth Century*, ed. John C. Fout (New York: Holmes & Meier, 1984). Sylvana Tomaselli, "The Enlightenment Debate on Women," *History Workshop*, no. 20 (Autumn 1985), 101–124.

16. For Aimé-Martin and his text, see *Women, the Family, and Freedom*, I, Part II, doc. 43. For the debate on women's education in France during and after the Revolution, see especially Barbara Corrado Pope, "Revolution and Retreat: Upper-Class French Women after 1789," in *Women, War, and Revolution*, ed. Carol R. Berkin and Clara M. Lovett (New York: Holmes & Meier Publishers Inc., 1980), and *Women, the Family, and Freedom*, I, Part I. For Germany, see

Ann Taylor Allen, "Spiritual Motherhood: German Feminists and the Kinder-garten Movement, 1848–1911," *History of Education Quarterly*, 22 (Fall 1982), 319–339. For England, see Carolyn Steedman, "The Mother Made Conscious': The Historical Development of a Primary School Pedagogy," *History Workshop*, no. 20 (Autumn 1985), 149–163.

17. Karen Offen, "Ernest Legouvé and the Doctrine of 'Equality in Difference' for Women: A Case Study of Male Feminism in Nineteenth-Century French Thought," *Journal of Modern History*, 58, no. 2 (June 1986), 452–84, and Stéphane Michaud, *Muse et madone: Visages de la femme de la Révolution française aux apparitions de Lourdes* (Paris: Editions du Seuil, 1985). Riv-Ellen Prell, "The Vision of Woman in Classical Reform Judaism," *Journal of the American Academy of Religion*, 50, no. 4 (Dec. 1982), 575–89. Catherine Prelinger, "Religious Dissent, Women's Rights, and the *Hamburger Hochschule für das weibliche Geschlecht* in Mid-Nineteenth Century Germany," *Church History*, 45, no. 1 (March 1976), 42–55.

18. Moses, *French Feminism*, ch. 6; Geneviève Fraisse, "Les Femmes libres de 48, moralisme et féminisme," *Les Révoltes logiques*, no. 1 (Winter 1975), 23–50; and Michèle Riot-Sarcey, "La Conscience féministe des femmes de 1848: Jeanne Deroin et Désirée Gay," in *Un Fabuleux Destin, Flora Tristan: Actes du Premier Colloque International Flora Tristan, Dijon, 3 et 4 mars 1984* (Dijon: Editions Universitaires de Dijon, 1985), 157–165.

19. Deroin's "Mission de la femme dans le present et dans l'avenir" appeared in the issues of 28 January, 10 March, and 10 April 1849, translated in Bell and Offen, *Women, the Family, and Freedom*, I, doct. 77.

20. Deroin's arguments are translated in ibid., I, docts. 84–85.

21. Ruth-Ellen Boetcher Joeres, "Louise Otto and her Journals: A Chapter in Nineteenth-Century German Feminism," *Internationales Archiv für Sozial-geschichte der deutschen Literatur*, 4 (1979), 100–129.

22. On *Georgesandismus* outside France, see Martin Malia, "Realism in Love: George Sand," *Alexander Herzen and the Birth of Russian Socialism 1812–1855*, chap. 11 (Cambridge, Mass: Harvard University Press, 1961). Public attention focused as much on George Sand's well-publicized love affairs and her habit of wearing mannish attire and smoking in public, as on the content and depth of her critique of marriage. In Berlin, Louise Aston took up similar behaviors; see Hans Adler, "On a Feminist Controversy: Louise Otto vs. Louise Aston," *German Women in the Eighteenth and Nineteenth Centuries*, ed. Ruth-Ellen Boetcher Joeres and Mary Jo Maynes. (Bloomington, Ind.: Indiana University Press, 1985).

23. Harriet Taylor Mill, Review essay on *The New York Tribune for Europe* (issue of 29 October 1850), *Westminster Review*, no. 109 (July 1851), re-printed, with J. S. Mill's introduction, as "Enfranchisement of Women," in John Stuart Mill and Harriet Taylor Mill, *Essays on Sex Equality*, ed. Alice S. Rossi (Chicago: University of Chicago Press, 1970); also in *WFF*, I, doct. 88.

24. See Lee Holcombe, *Wives and Property: Reform of the Married Women's Property Law in Nineteenth-Century England* (Toronto: University of Toronto Press, 1982).

25. See especially Patrick Kay Bidelman, *Pariahs Stand Up! The Founding of the Liberal Feminist Movement in France, 1858–1889* (Westport, Conn.: Greenwood Press, 1982).

26. For the First International Workingmen's Association debates, see Boxer, "Socialism Faces Feminism."

27. Karen Offen, "Depopulation, Nationalism, and Feminism in Fin-de-Siècle France," *American Historical Review*, 89 (June 1984).

28. Mona Caird's articles appeared in the *Westminster Review*, vol. 130 (July–Dec. 1888), 186–201 and 617–636. Quote from Stanton in Elizabeth Cady Stanton, *Eighty Years and More: Reminiscences, 1815–1897* (New York, 1897; reprinted New York: Schocken Books, 1971), p. 409.

29. Patrick Geddes and J. Arthur Thomson, *The Evolution of Sex* (New York: Scribner's, 1889), p. 267; Friedrich Nietzsche, *Beyond Good and Evil* (1886), in *Basic Writings of Nietzsche*, tr. and ed. Walter Kaufmann (New York: Random House, 1968); in Bell & Offen, *Women, the Family and Freedom*, II, doc. 6; Evelyn Baring, First Earl of Cromer, speech at Manchester, as reported in the Anti-Suffrage Review (November 1910), p. 10.

30. Steven C. Hause and Anne R. Kenney, "The Limits of Suffragist Behavior: Legalism and Militancy in France, 1876–1922," *American Historical Review*, 86, no. 4 (Oct., 1981), 781–806.

31. *Votes for Women*, 29 October 1908, p. 1.

32. Maïté Albistur and Daniel Armogathe eds., *Le Grief des femmes* (1978); and *Nelly Roussel: L'Eternelle sacrifiée*. Two Roussel texts are translated into English in Bell & Offen, *Women, the Family, and Freedom*, II, docs. 29 and 42. The quote below is from doc. 29, a speech Nelly Roussel delivered in 1904 at a mass meeting called to protest the centennial of the French Civil Code.

33. David J. Mitchell, *Queen Christabel: A Biography of Christabel Pankhurst* (London: Macdonald and Jane's, 1977), and Elizabeth Sarah, "Christabel Pankhurst: Reclaiming Her Power," in *Feminist Theorists: Three Centuries of Key Women Thinkers*, ed. Dale Spender (New York: Pantheon, 1983).

34. Theodore Roszak, "The Hard and the Soft: The Force of Feminism in Modern Times," in *Masculine/Feminine: Readings in Sexual Mythology and the Liberation of Women*, ed. Betty Roszak and Theodore Roszak (New York: Harper & Row, 1969), p. 88.

SUGGESTIONS FOR FURTHER READING

The history of modern European feminism resembles a vast unfinished patchwork quilt. The scholarly literature is spread over a widely scattered range of journals and publishers, and not all of it is informed by feminist analysis. Many pieces are still missing and many questions remain unanswered. Even so, the overall design is becoming clearer as scholars fill in one hole after another. These suggested readings focus only on scholarship on the history of European feminism published in English within the last ten years (1976–1986).

Most studies to date focus on developments in individual nations, but a few attempt to develop a comparative cross-national synthesis. The most successful to date is

Jane Rendall, *The Origins of Modern Feminism: Women In Britain, France, and the United States, 1780–1860* (New York: Schocken Books, 1984). An attempt to develop a comparative Anglo-American analysis is Olive Banks, *Faces of Feminism: A Study of Feminism as a Social Movement* (New York: St. Martin's Press, 1981). Priscilla Robertson's *An Experience of Women* (Philadelphia: Temple University Press, 1983) contains a vast amount of interesting information on non-conforming nineteenth-century women in England, France, Italy, and Germany, but her analysis remains untainted by the insights of contemporary feminist historiographical inquiry. A provocative though uneven analysis is provided by Marielouise Janssen-Jurreit, *Sexism: The Male Monopoly on History and Thought,* translated from the German by Verne Moberg (New York: Farrar, Strauss, Giroux, 1982). Dale Spender, *Women of Ideas (and what men have done to them)* (London: Routledge and Kegan Paul, 1982) provides a fresh personal approach to a number of European feminist thinkers.

Three interpretative documentaries attempt a broader range of coverage on modern European women's history, making available in English translation many European feminist texts: Eleanor S. Riemer and John C. Fout, eds., *European Women: A Documentary History, 1789–1945* (New York: Schocken Books, 1980); Erna Olafson Hellerstein, Leslie Parker Hume, and Karen M. Offen, eds., *Victorian Women: A Documentary Account of Women's Lives in Nineteenth-Century England, France, and the United States* (Stanford, Calif.: Stanford University Press, 1981), and Susan Groag Bell and Karen M. Offen, eds., *Women, the Family, and Freedom: The Debate in Documents, 1750–1950,* 2 vols. (Stanford, Calif.: Stanford University Press, 1983). Each of these volumes contains extensive essays, notes, and further bibliography.

Several valuable collections of articles, all with a cross-national selection of pertinent scholarship, include: Berenice A. Carroll, ed., *Liberating Women's History: Theoretical and Critical Essays* (Urbana, Ill., University of Illinois Press, 1976); Marilyn J. Boxer and Jean H. Quataert, eds., *Socialist Women: European Socialist Feminism in the Nineteenth and Early Twentieth Centuries* (New York: Elsevier, 1978); Carol R. Berkin and Clara M. Lovett, eds., *Women, War, and Revolution* (New York: Holmes & Meier, 1980); Jane Slaughter and Robert Kern, eds., *European Women on the Left: Socialism, Feminism, and the Problems Faced by Political Women, 1880 to the Present* (Westport, Conn.: Greenwood Press, 1981); and Judith Friedlander, Blanche Wiesen Cook, Alice Kessler-Harris, and Carroll Smith-Rosenberg, eds., *Women in Culture and Politics: A Century of Change* (Bloomington: Indiana University Press, 1985). On the history of feminism, see Elizabeth Sarah, ed., *Reassessments of "First Wave" Feminism* (Oxford and New York: Pergamon Press, 1982); and the articles in Dale Spender, ed. *Feminist Theorists: Three Centuries of Key Women Thinkers* (New York: Pantheon, 1983).

There is as yet no comprehensive scholarly study of the international movement for women's rights that takes account of the last decade of scholarship. The best study to date remains Richard J. Evans, *The Feminists: Women's Emancipation Movements in Europe, America, and Australasia, 1840–1920* (London: Croom Helm, 1977). See also Edith F. Hurwitz, "The International Sisterhood," in *Becoming Visible: Women in European History* (1st ed., 1977), pp. 325–345, and Rebecca L. Sherrick, "Toward Universal Sisterhood," in Sarah, ed., *Reassessments of "First Wave" Feminism* (cited above), pp. 655–661. On women in the international peace movement, see Sandi E. Cooper, "The Work of Women in Nineteenth-Century Continental European Peace Movements," *Peace and Change*, 9, no. 4 (Winter 1984), 11–28.

Historical treatment of European feminist developments at the national level varies widely. To date, the major Western European countries—and Russia—have received most attention, a pattern characteristic of most historical writing on Europe. But a few studies dealing with other nations are now available.

France

English-language scholars have shown great interest in the theory and practice of nineteenth- and early twentieth-century French feminism. Claire Moses and S. Joan Moon have both made important contributions to the understanding of feminist thought and action during the first half of the nineteenth century. See Moses, "Saint Simonian Men/Saint-Simonian Women: The Transformation of Feminist Thought in 1830s France," *Journal of Modern History*, 54 (June 1982), 240–267, and *French Feminism in the Nineteenth Century* (Albany: State University of New York Press, 1984).

Jonathan Beecher's new biography *Charles Fourier* offers new insights into the contribution of the most influential of the early nineteenth-century male feminist social critics (Berkeley: University of California Press, 1986). The collection of Fourier texts edited by Beecher and Richard Bienvenu, *The Utopian Vision of Charles Fourier: Selected Texts on Work, Love, and Passionate Attraction* (Boston: Beacon Press, 1971) should also be consulted. The contribution of another prominent French male feminist of the 1840s is examined by Karen Offen, "Ernest Legouvé and the Doctrine of 'Equality in Difference' for Women: A Case Study of Male Feminism in Nineteenth-Century French Thought," *Journal of Modern History*, 58 (June 1986), 452–84.

For the later nineteenth century, readers should see Patrick Kay Bidelman, *Pariahs Stand Up! The Founding of the Liberal Feminist Movement in France, 1858–1889* (Westport, Conn.: Greenwood Press, 1982); Moses, *French Feminism* (cited above); James F. McMillan, "Clericals, Anticlericals, and the Women's Movement in France under the Third Republic," *The Historical Journal*, 24 (June 1981), 361–376; and various articles by Karen Offen, "The Second Sex and the Baccalaureat in Republican France, 1880–1924," *French Historical Studies*, 13 (Fall 1983), 252–86; "Depopulation, Nationalism, and Feminism in Fin-de-Siècle France," *American Historical Review*, 89 (June 1984), 648–76; and "Toward an Historical Definition of Feminism: The Case of France," *Signs: Journal of Women in Culture and Society* (forthcoming). See also Offen, *The Woman Question in Third Republic France, 1870–1914* (Stanford, Calif.: Stanford University Press, forthcoming).

Steven C. Hause, with Anne R. Kenney, have made a major contribution to understanding the French women's suffrage movement in *Women's Suffrage and Social Politics in the French Third Republic* (Princeton, N.J.: Princeton University Press, 1984). See also their comparative analysis, "The Limits of Suffragist Behavior: Legalism and Militancy in France, 1876–1922," *American Historical Review*, 86, no. 4 (October 1981), 781–806.

Much information concerning nineteenth-century feminist campaigns for women's educational and economic opportunities can be found in Laura S. Struminger, *What Were Little Girls and Boys Made Of?: Primary Education in Rural France 1830–1880* (Albany: State University of New York Press, 1983); Linda L. Clark, *Schooling the Daughters of Marianne: Textbooks and the Socialization of Girls in Modern French Primary Schools* (Albany: State University of New York Press, 1984); and Mary Lynn Stewart (McDougall), "Protecting Infants: The French Campaign for Maternity Leaves, 1890s–1913," *French Historical Studies*, 13 (Spring 1983), 79–105.

A staunch defense of the socialist contribution to French feminism is Charles Sowerwine, *Sisters or Citizens? Women and Socialism in France Since 1876* (Cambridge, England: Cambridge University Press, 1982). See also his article, "Women and Workers in France Before 1914: The Debate over the Couriau Affair," *Journal of Modern History*, 55, no. 3 (Sept. 1983), 411–441.

Germany

Recent historical writing on German feminism focused initially on its connections to socialism, turning subsequently to consideration of the middle-class ("bourgeois") women's movement and to literary feminism. On the problematic German socialist-feminist connection, see, in addition to the books by Thönnessen and Quataert cited by Charles Sowerwine in this volume, Karen Honeycutt, "Socialism and Feminism in Imperial Germany," *Signs: Journal of Women in Culture and Society*, 5, no. 1 (Autumn 1979), 30–41; and Richard J. Evans, "Bourgeois Feminists and Women Socialists in Germany, 1894–1914: Lost Opportunity or Inevitable Conflict?" *Women's Studies International Quarterly*, 3, no. 4 (1980), 355–376, and "Theory and Practice in German Social Democracy 1880–1914: Clara Zetkin and the Socialist Theory of Women's Emancipation," *History of Political Thought*, 3, no. 2 (Summer 1982), 285–304.

On the development of the bourgeois women's movement and its various issues in Germany after 1894, see Richard J. Evans, *The Feminist Movement in Germany 1894–1933*. (London and Beverly Hills, Calif.: Sage Publications, 1976), and two articles by Amy Hackett, "The German Women's Movement and Suffrage, 1890–1914: A Study of National Feminism," in *Modern European Social History*, Robert Bezucha, ed. (Lexington, Mass.: D. C. Heath, 1971); and "Feminism and Liberalism in Wilhelmine Germany, 1890–1918," in *Liberating Women's History*, Carroll, ed. (cited above). A new biography of Lily Braun, who had a foot in both camps, has been published by Alfred G. Meyer, *The Feminism and Socialism of Lily Braun* (Bloomington: Indiana University Press, 1985).

Two new collections of English-language articles on German women's history contain pertinent analyses: John C. Fout, ed., *German Women in the Nineteenth Century: A Social History* (New York: Holmes & Meier, 1984), and Ruth-Ellen Boetcher Joeres and Mary Jo Maynes, eds., *German Women in the Eighteenth and Nineteenth Centuries: A Social and Literary History* (Bloomington: Indiana University Press, 1986). A third collection, *When Biology Became Destiny: Women in Weimar and Nazi Germany*, Renate Bridenthal, Atina Grossmann, and Marion Kaplan, eds. (New York: Monthly Review Press, 1984), contains several articles that cover early twentieth century feminist activity.

The religious origins of German feminism have been investigated by Catherine Prelinger in several articles including those in the Joeres and Maynes and Fout books cited above; also see "Religious Dissent, Women's Rights, and the *Hamburger Hochschule für das weibliche Geschlecht* in Mid-Nineteenth Century Germany," *Church History*, 45, no. 1 (March 1976), 42–55. See also Ann Taylor Allen, "Spiritual Motherhood: German Feminists and the Kindergarten Movement, 1848–1911," *History of Education Quarterly*, 22 (Fall 1982), 319–339.

English-language scholarship on feminism after unification of the German nation in 1871 has exploded in recent times. In addition to the work of Richard Evans on the bourgeois and socialist feminist movements, one must consult the articles of James C. Albisetti on the educational and professional advancement of middle-class German women: "Could Separate Be Equal? Helene Lange and Women's Education in Imperial Germany," *History of Education Quarterly*, 22 (Fall 1982), 301–317; "The Fight for Female Physicians in Imperial Germany," *Central European History*, 15 (June 1982), 99–123. The Society for the Protection of Mothers has attracted considerable scholarly interest; see Ann Taylor Allen, "Mothers of the New Generation: Adele Schreiber, Helene Stöcker, and the Evolution of the Idea of Motherhood, 1900–1914," *Signs*, 10 (Spring 1985), 418–438; and Amy Hackett, "Helene Stöcker: Left-Wing Intellectual and Sex Reformer," in Bridenthal, Grossmann, and Kaplan, eds., *When Biology Was Destiny* (cited above). On Hedwig Dohm, see Renate Duelli-Klein, "Hedwig Dohm: Passionate Theorist (1833–1919)," in *Feminist Theorists*, Spender, ed. (cited above).

Great Britain

The historical literature on British feminism has reached a sophisticated level of analysis. Ray Strachey's *The Cause* (originally published in 1928; reprinted, 1978) retains its value as a lively and well-informed introduction to the British women's movement. The contributions of various individuals to "The Cause" are now being re-evaluated: see, among other works, the essays on Harriet Martineau, Barbara Bodichon, Josephine Butler, Millicent Garrett Fawcett, Olive Schreiner, Vida Goldstein, Christabel Pankhurst, Virginia Woolf, and Vera Brittain in *Feminist Theorists*, Spender, ed. (cited above).

Barbara Taylor's *Eve and the New Jerusalem: Socialism and Feminism in the Nineteenth Century* (London: Virago, 1983) affords a splendid introduction to the 1820s and 1830s. See also Kathleen E. McCrone, "William Thompson and the Appeal of One Half the Human Race . . . ", *Atlantis*, 5 (Spring 1980), 34–51; and the myopically British re-evaluation of the Benthamites' contribution by Terence Ball, "Utilitarianism, feminism and the Franchise: James Mill and his Critics," *History of Political Thought*, 1, no. 1 (Spring 1980), 91–115; and Nella Fermi Weiner, "Of Feminism and Birth Control Propaganda, 1790–1840," *International Journal of Women's Studies*, 3, no. 5 (1980), 411–430. Balance is restored by Gail Malmgreen's *Neither Bread Nor Roses: Utopian Feminists and the English Working Class, 1800–1850* (Brighton, England: John Noyce, 1978), which stresses the cross-fertilization of British and French ideas and influences. Malcolm L. Thomis and Jennifer Grimmett, *Women in Protest 1800–1850* (New York: St. Martin's Press, 1982), explore various forms of women's political self-expression prior to 1850.

On developments in the mid-to-late nineteenth century, Judith R. Walkowitz, *Prostitution and Victorian Society: Women, Class, and the State* (Cambridge, England: Cambridge University Press, 1980) is indispensable. See also the insightful articles: Barbara Caine on the middle-class movement, "John Stuart Mill and the English Women's Movement," *Historical Studies*, 18 (April 1978), 52–67; A. P. W. Robson, "The Founding of the National Society for Women's Suffrage 1866–1867," *Canadian Journal of History*, 8, no. 1 (March 1973), 1–22; Andrew Rosen, "Emily Davies and the Women's Movement, 1862–1867," *Journal of British Studies*, 19, no. 1 (Fall 1979), 102–121; and two articles by Carol Bauer and Lawrence Ritt, "A Husband Is a Beating Animal'—Frances Power Cobbe Confronts the Wife-Abuse Problem in Victorian England," *International Journal of Women's Studies*, 6, no. 2 (March/April 1983), 99–118, and "Wife Abuse, Late Victorian English Feminists, and the Legacy of Frances Power Cobbe," *International Journal of Women's Studies*, 6, no. 3 (May/June 1983), 195–207. See also Carolyn Steedman, " 'The Mother Made Conscious': The Historical Development of a Primary School Pedagogy," *History Workshop*, no. 20 (Autumn 1985), 149–163. A classic is J. A. Banks and Olive Banks, *Feminism and Family Planning in Victorian England* (New York: Schocken Books, 1964). See also Sheila Jeffreys, *The Spinster and Her Enemies: Feminism and Sexuality, 1880–1930* (London and Boston: Pandora Press, 1985).

The early twentieth-century British suffrage movement, whose militancy electrified the world, has attracted abundant attention from scholars. See, in particular, Andrew Rosen, *Rise Up, Women! The Militant Campaign of the Women's Social and Political Union, 1903–1914* (London: Routledge & Kegan Paul, 1974); Brian Harrison, *Separate Spheres: The Opposition to Women's Suffrage in Britain* (New York: Holmes & Meier, 1978); Jill Norris and Jill Liddington, *One Hand Tied Behind Us: The Rise of the Women's Suffrage Movement* (London: Virago, 1978), which studies the radical working-class force behind women's suffrage; Leslie Parker Hume, *The National Union of Women's Suffrage Societies, 1897–1914* (New York: Garland Press, 1982); and Les Garner, *Stepping Stones to Women's Liberty: Feminist Ideas in the Women's Suffrage Movement 1900–1918* (London: Heinemann, 1984).

Valuable collections of primary texts on British feminism include Carol Bauer and Lawrence Ritt, *Free and Ennobled: Source Readings in the Development of Victorian Feminism* (Oxford and New York: Pergamon, 1979); Patricia Hollis, ed., *Women in Public: The Women's Movement. Documents of the Victorian Women's Movement (1850–1900)* (London: G. Allen & Unwin, 1979); Janet Horowitz Murray, *Strong-Minded Women and Other Lost Voices of Nineteenth-Century England* (New York: Pantheon, 1982); and Elizabeth K. Helsinger, *The Woman Question: Society and Literature in Britain and America, 1837–1883*. 3 vols. (New York: Garland, 1983).

Italy

Most of the recent scholarship on the nineteenth-century Italian women's movement in Italian is inspired by the contributions of the late Franca Pieroni Bortolotti. In English one should consult the articles by Judith Jeffrey Howard: "The Civil Code of 1865 and the Origins of the Feminist Movement in Italy," in *The Italian Immigrant Woman in North America*, Betty Boyd Caroli, Robert F. Harney, and Lydio F. Thomasi, eds. (Toronto: The Multicultural History Society of Ontario, 1977); and

"Patriot Mothers in the Post-Risorgimento: Women After the Italian Revolution," in *Women, War, and Revolution*, Berkin and Lovett, eds. (cited above). See also Mary S. Gibson, "Prostitution and Feminism in Late Nineteenth-Century Italy," in *The Italian Immigrant Woman*, Caroli, Harney, and Tomasi, eds. (cited above). A recent work with a more contemporary focus, but which also provides some nineteenth-century background, is Lucia Chiavola Birnbaum, *Liberazione della donna: Feminism in Italy* (Middletown, Conn.: Wesleyan University Press, 1986). On the feminist conflicts with organized socialism, see Claire Lavigna, "The Marxist Ambivalence Toward Women: Between Socialism and Feminism in the Italian Socialist Party," in *Socialist Women*, Boxer and Quataert, eds. (cited above).

Russia

The indispensable English-language works on feminism in nineteenth-century Russia include Richard Stites's masterful study, *The Women's Liberation Movement in Russia: Nihilism, Feminism, and Bohshevism, 1860–1930* (Princeton, N.J.: Princeton University Press, 1978); and Linda Edmondson, *Feminism in Russia, 1900–1917* (Stanford, Calif: Stanford University Press, 1984). Two articles clarify developments in the 1860s: Barbara Heldt Monter, "*Rassvet* (1859–1862) and the Woman Question," *Slavic Review*, 36, no. 2 (March 1977), 76–85, and Cynthia H. Whittaker, "The Women's Movement During the Reign of Alexander II: A Case Study in Russian Liberalism," *Journal of Modern History*, 48, no. 2 (June 1976; on-demand supplement). Also of value for understanding the national particularities of women's liberation in the Russian context is Barbara Alpern Engel, *Mothers and Daughters: Women of the Intelligensia in Nineteenth-Century Russia* (Cambridge, England: Cambridge University Press, 1983). Rose L. Glickman, *Russian Factory Women: Workplace and Society, 1880–1914* (Berkeley: University of California Press, 1984), includes analysis of the socialist/feminist differences. For the twentieth century, the figure of Alexandra Kollontai is central. See her two biographies: Barbara Evans Clements, *Bolshevik Feminist: The Life of Aleksandra Kollontai* (Bloomington: Indiana University Press, 1979); and Beatrice Brod Farnsworth, *Aleksandra Kollontai: Socialism, Feminism, and the Bolshevik Revolution* (Stanford, Calif.: Stanford University Press, 1981).

Scandinavia

Scandinavian feminists have made internationally-important contributions to the development of European feminism. None was perhaps as important as the Swedish writer Ellen Key. For two opposing interpretations, see Cheri Register, "Motherhood at Center: Ellen Key's Social Vision," *Women's Studies International Forum*, 5, no. 6 (1982), 599–610, and Torborg Lundell, "Ellen Key and Swedish Feminist Views on Motherhood," *Scandinavian Studies*, 56, no. 4 (Autumn 1984), 351–369.

On Finland, see Riitta Jallinoja, "The Women's Liberation Movement in Finland: The Social and Political Mobilisation of Women in Finland, 1880–1910," *Scandinavian Journal of History*, 5, no. 1 (1980), 37–49. For Norway, see Ida Blom, "A Centenary of Organized Feminism in Norway," in Sarah, ed., *Reassessments of "First Wave" Feminism* (cited above), and "The Struggle for Women's Suffrage in Norway, 1885–1913," *Scandinavian Journal of History*, 5, no. 1 (1980), 3–22.

Eastern and Southeastern Europe

Until recently, the debate on the woman question and the development of feminism in eastern and southeastern Europe have been little studied by historians. Our knowledge is greatly enhanced by the pioneering contributions of Martha Bohachevsky-Chomiak, "Socialism, Feminism, and Nationalism: The First Stages of Women's Organizations in the Eastern Part of the Austrian Empire," in *Women in Eastern Europe and the Soviet Union*, Tova Yedlin, ed. (New York: Praeger, 1980), and "Natalia Kobryns'ka: A Formulator of Feminism," in *Nationbuilding and the Politics of Nationalism: Essays on Austrian Galicia*, Andrei S. Markovits and Frank E. Sysyn, eds. (Cambridge, Mass.: Harvard University Press, 1982). See also Bohachevsky-Chomiak's forthcoming book, *Feminists Despite Themselves: Women in Ukrainian Community Life, 1884–1939* (in press, University of Alberta Press). For Poland, see Bogna Lorence-Kot, "Klementyna Tanska Hoffmanowa (1798–1845), Cultural Nationalism and a New Formula for Polish Womanhood," *History of European Ideas* (forthcoming, 1987). Feminist developments in Slavic-language areas in eastern and southern Europe during the late nineteenth and early twentieth centuries can be followed in the articles in Sharon L. Wolchik and Alfred G. Meyer, eds., *Women, State, and Party in Eastern Europe* (Durham, N.C.: Duke University Press, 1985).

Sent by the British government or missionary societies, European women served in the British colonies as nurses and, less frequently, as doctors. The dispensary at Msalabani, present-day Tanzania, c. 1890. (United Society for the Propagation of the Gospel, London)

chapter 14

Gender and Race in the Nineteenth- and Twentieth-Century British Empire

Margaret Strobel

European women participated not only in the politics of their own nations, but also in the empires acquired by those nations. Around the globe, they played ambiguous roles as members of a sex considered to be inferior within a race that considered itself superior. This contradictory position brought ambivalent results. On the one hand, European women advanced the interests of the colonizers by maintaining social distance between the Europeans and the colonized. This is evident in various forms of cultural imperialism, such as missionary work, anthropological study, and "reform" of indigenous practices that were viewed as harmful by western standards. On the other hand, European women sometimes identified with the oppressed and, although they rarely questioned the practice of imperialism itself, sought to ameliorate some of its worst effects. In either case, women traveling to the colonies often gained opportunities lacking at home and played a central role in shaping the social relations of imperialism.

European[1] women had a complex, varied, and often contradictory relationship to the African and Asian territories controlled by Britain in the nineteenth and twentieth centuries. As members of the inferior sex within the superior race (to use contemporary formulations), women were afforded options by imperialism that male dominance in the colonies then limited.

As participants in British expansion, European women benefited from the economic and political subjugation of indigenous peoples and shared many of the accompanying attitudes of racism, paternalism, ethnocentrism, and national chauvinism. For most women, life in the colonies provided opportunities not found in Europe, where their options were limited by their social class, a "shortage" of marriageable men, difficulty in finding adequate employment, or the lack of "heathen souls" to be converted. At the same time, women continously experienced, sometimes challenged, and sometimes reproduced the economic, political, and ideological subordination of women. As wives of colonial officials, they subordinated their lives to a male-centered administrative environment. As educators of indigenous women, they reproduced the Victorian notions of domesticity and female dependence. Even missionary women, whose commitment to career and calling was a challenge to those very notions, accepted the patriarchal ideology and bureaucracy of the church and transmitted conventional European gender roles to African and Asian women.

By the twentieth century, some European women attacked aspects of the racial, political, and economic inequalities of the colonial relationship. But the vast majority of European women supported and contributed to the imperial venture.

British imperialism in Africa and Asia reached its height between 1850 and World War Two. The British government took over administration from the British East India Company following the Army Mutiny of 1857. Thereafter Britain governed two-thirds of the subcontinent directly, until it granted independence to India and Pakistan separately in 1947. From the midnineteenth century on, India had a sizeable European community, although men outnumbered women.

Britain's relationship with Africa similarly began in trade and ended in formal colonial rule. Following the partition of Africa in 1885, European rivals established colonial administrations by military conquest or cooptation of African political representatives. In most areas a small core of white men administered the colony. Where Britain encouraged white settlers, for example Kenya, Northern Rhodesia/Zambia, and Southern Rhodesia/Zimbabwe, the European population was tiny and largely male until after World War One. South Africa's history differs. The Afrikaners (Boers), descendants of the seventeenth-century Dutch settlers, had a demographically balanced population when British capitalists and settlers, disproportionately male, came in substantial numbers in the nineteenth century. South Africa became a self-governing (by whites) country in

1910; the rest of colonial Africa gained its independence beginning in the 1950s.

Effective control of the colonies required an ideology, accepted by at least a portion of the colonized, that legitimized British rule, namely, the superiority of European, Christian civilization. The spread of western education and medical skills obscured exploitative economic relations and the absence of political rights for colonized peoples at the same time that it led to real improvements in their lives. Excluded from the military and—until the very end of the colonial period—from key positions in the political administrative structure, women helped legitimize colonialism as teachers, nurses, the wives of administrators, and/or ameliorators of the worst manifestations of indigenous and colonial oppression. Interestingly, the patriarchal ideology that assigned these helping roles to women also masked the exploitation of imperialism by identifying the imperial power as the "mother country" and, by inference, the colonies as immature and untrained children.

Did European women in the colonies threaten the imperial relationship? Many scholars claim they did. Three components of this myth are relevant: British attitudes toward mixed-race sexual relations; rituals that maintained social boundaries between races; and the subordination of the domestic sphere to the public realm of imperial life. While examining the sexist bias of the myth, we will explicate the racial and gender dynamics of colonial society. In the remainder of the chapter, we will look at several roles women played in the colonies—job-seekers, missionaries, anthropologists, and reformers—and ask how women's activities advanced or subverted the imperial mission and how the imperial context reinforced or undermined female gender roles.

THE MYTH OF THE DESTRUCTIVE FEMALE: SEXUALITY, RITUAL, AND HOME

Most of the histories that mention European women's arrival in the British colonies at all claim that European women contributed to the deterioration of the relationship between the European administrator and those he governed. According to this myth, "vulnerable" European women provoked the sexual appetites of indigenous men, while as wives they replaced indigenous concubines (from whom male administrators had previously learned much about local society and culture) and drew the attention of the men away from their official responsibilities. In addition, historians describe British wives as racists who distanced themselves from the local population. It is true that the arrival of women in substantial numbers made possible the creation of an exclusive social group, and that the women, in their social roles as wives and hostesses, maintained the hierarchy within the European community and its social distance from the indigenous peoples by elaborate rituals.

Rather than blaming European women for the growing rift between white and nonwhite populations in the empires, recent historians tend to see their arrival as coinciding with other developments in colonial society: heightened racial prejudice, the growth of evangelical Christianity with its ethnocentrism and attack on nonmarital liaisons, and the increased size of the European population generally. And, where settlement was the goal (in parts of Africa and, earlier, in North America) rather than rule (in India, most of Africa, Southeast Asia, and the Pacific Islands), women's arrival seems to have been valued more by their contemporaries and by later scholars. However, because it is so widespread and unquestioned, the components of this myth—sexist assumptions about sexuality, ritual, and domestic life—merit examination for what they reveal about the dynamics of British colonial society.

The myth of the destructive female contains two elements that pertain to sexuality: concubinage and the protection of European women. Officials justified access to concubines and indigenous prostitutes on the grounds of keeping men virile and heterosexual, essential components of rule that reflected imperial power. Moreover, in interfering with the European male's access to indigenous concubines, European women purportedly contributed to the creation of greater distance between the communities. In the early colonial days, European men commonly took concubines. The perils of transition when one's wife appeared are illustrated by a story that circulated in West Africa about 1910:

> One D. C. [District Commissioner arrived with] his new spouse [at] his boma late at night and promptly went to bed. About four in the morning his cook walked boldly into the room, lifted the mosquito net sheltering the exhausted sleepers, soundly slapped the lady on her bottom and said, "Leave now missy, time to go back to the village."[2]

Concubinage entailed physical proximity and intimacy in a context of inequality. The same can be said of the mistress/servant relationship, but historians have not credited it with developing ties to the indigenous community. To single out European women's dislike for concubinage as a cause of increasing social distance is to leave unquestioned the inequality of the colonizing male/colonized female concubine relationship. Only if one ignores the element of subordination in a concubinage relationship can it be read as closeness. In fact, it was the attitudes of superiority exhibited by Europeans in the colonies, male and female, that created the social distance. Moreover, as racial prejudice deepened toward the turn of the century, the need to reinforce social distance overcame official concerns about sexual access for European men. Thus in 1909, when there were still few European women in the British colonies other than India, the Colonial Secretary prohibited liaisons between officials and indigenous women.

According to the myth, not only did European women inhibit the valuable institution of concubinage; they also aroused the sexual appetites of indigenous men from whom they then had to be protected. This situation of sexual competition increased the distance between European and indigenous men. The contradictory nature of this formulation clearly reveals the sexism of the myth itself. If concubinage enhanced the relationship of colonizer and colonized, then why should not voluntary sexual liaisons between European women and indigenous men do the same? Such relationships were not common, but they prompted sharp response. In 1893 the Maharaja of Patiala married Miss Florry Bryan; this disturbed Lord Curzon, the Viceroy of India. Not only did the marriage transgress against the social distance between Europeans and indigenous people mandated by imperial ideology, but the Maharaja's high social status and his wife's working-class background confused even more the racial, sexual, and class hierarchies of empire. Even in the absence of marriage across class lines, such relationships raised concern. In turn-of-the-century South Africa, officials, in order to prevent African migrant workers from frequenting white prostitutes, passed laws that forbade intercourse between black men and white women. Such voluntary relationships offended imperial minds because they forced a contradiction between two notions central to the racist and sexist ideologies of the time: whites should be superior to people of color and men superior to women.

The aroused sexual desires of indigenous men, Europeans feared, might lead to sexual assaults on European women—the dreaded "Black Peril." Ironically, European men seemed to feel more threatened than European women by this "danger." In Papua, New Guinea, men, not women, pushed for the passage of the harsh White Women's Protection Ordinance in 1926 — the death penalty for rape or *attempted* rape by a New Guinean man. Moreover, excolonial women's reminiscences do not mention fear of indigenous men. On the other hand, in 1907 the Associated Women's Organizations of the Transvaal requested the government to enact segregation as a protection against assaults on (European) women. Whether or not women participated in efforts to prevent real or imagined assaults, the notion that they needed male protection fit nicely into the racist and sexist ideologies of the day.

In addition to such racist ideas about sexual relations between Europeans and indigenous people, the myth of the destructive female embodies the stereotype of petty, frivolous, racist, unproductive, and dependent women who contributed nothing to either the imperial enterprise or to indigenous peoples. Typically, the wife of a colonial administrator, settler, or army officer is pictured as living a life of leisure, consisting of dinner parties, banal conversation, and petty jealousies about her own and her husband's status. This stereotype can be challenged in two ways: its inaccuracy, which the portraits in the subsequent sections establish, and its conceptual male-centered bias, which distorts and subordinates female experience.

Colonial society charged women with enacting the social rituals that defined the boundaries between Europeans and indigenous people and the hierarchy among Europeans, but it subsequently stigmatized such activities as trivial. The social life described here reached its height in the late-nineteenth century in India and between the world wars in the remaining colonies when the colonial enterprise was relatively unquestioned. A regal and commanding style necessarily accompanied political domination, and such rituals as dressing formally for dinner helped Europeans define the differences between themselves and the colonized. The widowed wife of a colonial officer, Sylvia Leith-Ross, describes herself and a colonial official dressing for dinner in 1913 on a steel canoe on a Nigerian river: "When you are alone, among thousands of unknown, unpredictable people, dazed by unaccustomed sights and sounds, bemused by strange ways of life and thought, you need to remember who you are, where you come from, what your standards are."[3] If some rituals helped maintain a sense of cultural identity, others emphasized internal stratification. The apparently trivial pursuit of "calling" can be seen in this light. The practice of leaving calling cards at each European household, from the top of the hierarchy on down, inaugurated the rainy season in India, when the British returned to the plains from the cooler hill stations. Thus, women performed important functions in organizing and executing the social life that appears to us, in a less formal time and place, unduly rigid and formal, if not silly.

Although a woman's role in colonial society included identifying social boundaries and hierarchy, she did so in a profoundly male world. For many women, a wife's position in the colonial hierarchy derived from her husband's; she had no independent place. This fact has implications that shed light on the stereotypical behavior of colonial women. Colonial administrators' wives often had to engage in trivial conversation, for example, while entertaining, to avoid revealing privileged information. Moreover, since a woman's position in the social hierarchy depended on the course of her husband's career, she was limited in the extent to which she could express intimacy or solidarity with other women above or below her, which helps to explain her apparent competitiveness with other women.

The diary of Laura Boyle vividly reveals the implications of having one's status and role derive from that of one's husband. Written in 1916 while her new husband was stationed in a northern area of the Gold Coast (now Ghana), where no white woman had been since the turn of the century, the initial portion of the diary describes their joint travels in the bush and her observations of African society. After the government promoted him and transferred them to the Secretariat in Accra, her observations run to sports and cultural activities. "It is all very different from the daily opportunities in Wenchi," she noted then, "where we both could take a share of the problems in 'bush' administration." In Accra she supervised the servants, while he worked at the office.[4]

In colonial administrative structures, the female hierarchy usually paralleled the male hierarchy. The highest ranking wife set the standard and tone for the female portion of colonial society. Exercise of this leadership might range from mundane decisions that female dinner guests need not wear white gloves in hot weather to more substantive encouragement of welfare efforts. A wife who did not act in a manner appropriate to her husband's rank upset the entire community by disrupting the social order. Even in smaller European colonial communities, elaborate rituals prevailed. Social control of the behavior of other Europeans through gossip or ostracism helped maintain the sense of security of the outnumbered European community.

As noted earlier, the empire was a man's world. Imperial structures and processes made few accommodations to the female roles of wife, mother, and homemaker, even though these activities both provided material benefits for the husband and children and helped to maintain the social boundaries that separated the European community from the indigenous one. Indeed, the task of homemaker and mother had even greater implications for preserving "civilization" when carried out in the outposts of the empire. Women's reminiscences overflow with tales of housekeeping, while men's deal with the public actions of imperial officers, accurately reflecting the social division of labor.

Indeed, homemaking in the colonies, particularly in the early days, challenged a woman's ingenuity and fortitude. Flora Annie Steel and Grace Gardiner's *The Complete Indian Housekeeper and Cook* (1888) offered advice on a myriad of topics, from the number of camels it took to move the household to the hills for the hot season, to wetnursing, to remedies for tropical diseases. Health was a constant concern. Malaria and blackwater fever took their toll of both children and adults. Sylvia Leith-Ross noted that of the group of five with whom she traveled from Liverpool to Nigeria in 1906, she alone remained alive thirteen months later. African and Asian women experienced health hazards and raised families under even more difficult conditions, of course. But the change from a European life style shocked many emigrants who sought to reproduce it as best they could.

The exigencies of life in the tropical colonies forced changes in family life. Unlike their sisters in Britain, women in Victorian India drew upon non-kin from their community for support. Restricted by Victorian conventions, women frequently chose female midwives over male physicians. Racial prejudice prescribed the use of European midwives, who came from lower-class backgrounds. Indeed, the British colonials believed non-European physicians were unfit to attend European births. Due to local health conditions miscarriages were common; tropical diseases caused a high infant mortality rate. Among the British in Bengal, for example, infant mortality more than twice exceeded that of England for the period from 1860 to 1869.

British official attitudes toward the domestic sphere changed over time, but they initially articulated the third element of the myth of the destructive female: the idea that a home and family distracted an administrator from his work. Not until 1920 did the Secretary of State for the Colonies decree that married life should be the norm for administrators in colonies other than India (where a substantial British community already existed). Elsewhere, until the 1940s a man expected to marry only after his second or third tour of duty. The practice of sending children back to Britain for schooling continued until after World War Two. Thus, although many wives of men in the Colonial Service sought to fulfill the traditional female roles of mother, wife, and homemaker, they did so under severe strains and with little official support.

The perquisites of being a European in the colonies included having servants, a luxury not available in the twentieth century to the largely middle class group from whom colonial administrators came, and certainly not to the working classes from which some settlers came. Granted, homemaking in the colonies was more difficult than in Britain, but Europeans lived at a much higher standard of living than the vast majority of colonial subjects. Even otherwise impoverished white settlers in Africa had servants. Living as an administrator's family in a remote part of presentday Ghana in 1916, Laura and David Boyle had six male and female house servants and twelve men working outside. Having servants not only lessened the burdens of housekeeping, it offered many women their most salient interaction with indigenous people. European women developed a distorted view of local people's lives and culture based upon this profoundly unequal relationship. European women's most intense relationships with indigenous people focused upon a single part of the social structure, because servants generally came from impoverished and low status or low caste groups. Moreover, Europeans rarely saw servants in the latters' own surroundings, and servants had every reason to mask their real selves.

Not surprisingly, much of the racism or paternalism found in memoirs of colonial women focuses upon servants and substantiates this aspect of the charge leveled at them as "destructive women." Yet colonial men expressed the same racism through their own work as administrators, business owners, or settlers. Elizabeth Melville's *A Residence at Sierra Leone* (1849), communicates a common attitude toward African servants, found with little variation everywhere and throughout the decades. Concerned with the "trivial matter" of daily life and housekeeping, the narrative bemoans the "indolence, stupidity, and want of tidiness of the African" and the problems of locating and training servants.[5] Where it occurs, such noncooperation is, of course, a standard technique of resistance on the part of subordinates. In many cases cultural differences made difficult the transformation of indigenous men and women into servants for European households. Many memoirs, while noting difficulties with servants, record a paternalistic affection for particular servants and occasional concrete assistance to them. The author Isak Dinesen, for example, went to unusual lengths to provide for her servants when she left her failed coffee farm in Kenya.

In summary, the sexist bias of the myth of the destructive female obscures the real role played by European women in the empire. To the extent that their arrival inhibited the practice of concubinage, it struck a blow at a racially and sexually unequal relationship that has been romanticized to represent harmony between the colonizer and colonized. In carrying out the social rituals that have been characterized as petty, women identified the boundaries between ruler and ruled and the hierarchy within the European community that lay at the heart of imperial relations. In establishing homes in the face of official disinterest or even discouragement, women contributed to the improved health and happiness of male officials and the solidification of a strong European community. Thus, colonial women, far from losing the empire, were central to its continuation. Unfortunately, the rising nostalgia for the Raj that is exhibited in films, television shows, and collections of reminiscences provides little critique of the sexist nature of empire nor its fundamental exploitation of colonized peoples.

The women described above largely represent those who came as dependents to their husbands. But, in addition to the many dependent wives who developed an interest in working with African and Asian people, other women came to or grew up in the colonies with their own agendas, which fit the imperial design to a greater and lesser degree. Patriarchal structures and ideologies shaped their lives as well. It is to this interplay of imperial mission and gender imperatives that we now turn.

DOMESTIC SERVANTS: WHITE WOMEN AND THE IMPERIAL MISSION

Particularly after World War One, but earlier in India, women—from prostitutes to doctors—came to the colonies seeking employment to escape economic conditions or sexist discrimination back home. The experiences of one such group of white women, those recruited to South Africa as domestic servants, reveals most clearly the harmony of imperial and gender ideology.

Although most domestic servants in Africa were Africans, many of the women who emigrated from Britain throughout the latter half of the nineteenth century ended up in South Africa as domestics. By the 1880s and 1890s, several groups united under the British Women's Emigration Association (BWEA). Their recruiting propaganda stressed the possibilities for genteel domestic service, potential marriage, civilizing the world, and promoting British values in the colonies.

The causes for female emigration lay in demographic imbalance and limited employment for women in Britain. Because of male migration to the colonies, the ratio of women to men in Great Britain increased steadily from the midnineteenth century, from 1042:1000 in 1851 to 1068:1000 in 1911. The notion of "surplus" women of marriageable age is, of course, ideologically determined: a patriarchal ideology that prescribed for women the roles of mother, wife, and household manager could conceive no positive outcome for single women. In addition, lower-middle-class and middle-class single women competed for the same narrow range of employment. The differential in wage levels also helped recruitment. White domestics in South Africa might earn as much in two months as their counterparts in England could earn in a year.

The colonies needed female immigrants for demographic, ideological, and employment reasons. In contrast to the belief elsewhere that European women destroyed the empire, here they were considered essential to it. The successful transplantation of British civilization and the assurance of enough white labor required large numbers of white women. Particularly in South Africa after the Anglo-Boer War, the colonial state encouraged the "surplus" women of Britain to immigrate. The rhetoric of the time combined imperial and patriarchal goals. Ellen Joyce, a BWEA pioneer, stated that "the possibility of the settler marrying his own countrywoman is of imperial as well as of family importance." Put more bluntly: "We cannot assimilate the Boers at present if at all. . . . If we cannot assimilate them we must swamp them."[6] In addition, the colonial state sought to replace African male servants with white female servants to free the former for work in the Rand goldfields of the Transvaal.

Although many women emigrated, recruitment ultimately failed to satisfy the demand for servants. Between 1902 and 1912, approximately 1,500 white female domestics came to the Transvaal. Once there, however, the women deserted service for other occupations or for marriage. The racial ideology clearly dictated that the lowest work should be done by Africans, and employment in other typically female occupations as waitresses, clerical workers, or to a lesser extent, factory operatives attracted emigrants after a year of domestic service. Still, although a servant's marriage represented a loss to the employer, it counted as a success for the colonial state, which sought to increase the English population. For the individual woman, marriage meant entry into a relatively privileged white society.

In the institution of domestic service in South Africa, then, we see imperial and patriarchal forces reinforcing each other. European mistresses had their oppression as women meliorated by the availability of domestic servants. The mistress/servant relationship, often European women's only significant contact with indigenous people, reinforced the ideology of racial superiority. The colonial state's recruitment of white female labor was based on the patriarchal definition of domestic service as (white) women's work, the patriarchal glorification of matrimony, and the imperialist "ideal" of spreading British values and civilization. Domestic service was, for many white women in South Africa, a way to gain a share of white privilege. For African men and women, it remained, as it does today, an institution of exploitation and oppression.

FEMALE MISSIONARIES

Missionaries came before formal colonial government in Africa and in British India. They played a crucial role in dissolving and transforming the societies and cultures of the peoples with whom they interacted, linking colonized peoples to the colonizers socially and culturally. Not that missionaries worked hand in glove with colonial governments; indeed, they often challenged colonial policies. Where colonial governments, conscious of the need to keep the peace, wished not to disturb local customs, missionaries sometimes forced discussion of such issues as clitoridectomy (the removal of all or part of the clitoris). In this sense, because they were concerned with souls and beliefs, they intruded more than European administrators or settlers into indigenous culture, combining some understanding of their converts' society with a firm commitment to European Christianity and gender norms. For all their ethnocentrism, missionaries lived among their Christian converts. This lifestyle challenged the maintenance of social boundaries and often isolated missionaries from the rest of the European community. For more sensitive missionaries, for example Elise Kootz-Kretschmer in Tanganyika, living among indigenous peoples called into question their own notions of western superiority.

Female missionaries actively engaged in these cultural aspects of imperialism. In pursuing careers abroad, they modeled an alternative role to that of wife, mother, and homemaker. Yet, as helpers and spreaders of "civilization," they conformed to Victorian gender norms and indeed taught the domestic ideology to their converts.

Female missionaries played a special role in societies like India, where male foreign missionaries had little access to indigenous women. Female missionaries reached Indian women by offering education—in the homes of prominent families for upper-caste women and in public schools for the lower castes. In Bengal, these efforts in *zenana* education (titled after the name for the women's section of the house) began in the 1820s. Successful conversion occurred primarily among the lower castes and widows, groups who had the most marginal positions in Hindu society. More privileged Indians correctly suspected missionaries to be interested in education largely in order to gain converts. Christian teachings and handicrafts dominated the content of early women's education. By the 1890s, the first two British female doctors arrived in India, sent as part of the Zenana Mission Movement; they added medical education to the curriculum.

The most famous British female missionary in Africa, Mary Slessor, lived for forty years in southeastern Nigeria. Her career advanced the empire perhaps more than Christianity. Slessor made few actual converts but had enormous influence among the Efik and Ibibio peoples with whom she lived. She opposed such indigenous practices as slavery, human sacrifice upon the burying of an important person, poison ordeals, and the putting to death of twins, whose birth was thought to be dangerous to the community. With the establishment of the British Niger Coast Protectorate, Slessor was appointed Vice Consul and District Magistrate. Living under the same conditions as local people, Slessor's commitment promoted a reciprocal trust and affection. Ironically, this relationship aided the extension of colonial rule, occasioned in 1901 by the military suppression of an important local oracle involved in the slave trade. At the same time that she aided imperial expansion, Slessor worked to undermine discrimination against women both locally and in Britain. Her efforts brought significant change in the lives of women among whom she lived, particularly the unfortunate mothers of inauspicious twins. At home her defense of women's rights extended to support for the role of women within mission work.

Other female missionaries came into direct conflict with the church over women's issues. Teresa Kearney, who became Mother Kevin, arrived in Uganda in 1903 as a Franciscan nun to join the mission settlement organized by the White Fathers. As she worked establishing schools and convents in the area, Mother Kevin came to disagree with the Catholic hierarchy over the need to provide medical missionaries trained in obstetrics. The Vatican did not lift the ban on obstetrical work by religious missionaries until 1936, after years of lobbying by Mother Kevin and the decisive intervention by an influential male ally.[7]

Steeped in the patriarchal ideology of Victorian Christianity, European female missionaries in Africa, as in India, generally focused upon providing education for indigenous women who might become appropriate wives for westernized local men, especially clergy. The Homecraft Village School, established in Southern Rhodesia in 1943, clearly was organized for just this purpose. The potential minister's wife needed to adopt new values, modeled on European gender roles: self-reliance and independence as distinct from loyalty to the extended family; monogamy; physical and social mobility; familiarity with a "modern" home; and the use of money.

Even though they furthered the expansion of western culture and at times directly aided the colonial administration, on the whole missionaries questioned the imperial agenda more than they questioned Victorian gender norms. In their role as self-appointed (or government-appointed) representatives of the "natives," missionaries often criticized imperial officials and such practices as forced labor. On the other hand, although female missionaries performed serious work, acknowledged by their religious community, mission structures rarely accorded women positions of authority over males *and* females. In addition, the content of their teachings, even where spiritually equality was stressed, reproduced an ideal of female domesticity imported from home. Even the reforms they proposed specifically to aid women, most notably the elimination of polygyny, rarely came from a feminist impulse. More often, these reforms reflected missionary desires to establish Christian families along a European model.

The activities of missionaries raise fundamental questions about the morality of externally inducing social change and about the relationship of "humanitarian" work to imperialism. The same issues appear with regard to anthropologists and reformers, to whom we turn next. On the one hand, such humanitarian efforts were part of the process of imperialism, the transformation of indigenous societies in the interest of European economies and politics. Undoubtedly, imperialism distorted the development and history of indigenous peoples; earlier European intervention had even significantly intensified some of the evils that Europeans later sought to stamp out, for example, slavery and the slave trade. Yet indigenous societies generated their own forms of oppression. Women suffered from such indigenous practices as *sati* (the burning of a widow on her husband's funeral pyre) in India and clitoridectomy or infibulation (the sewing up of the vulva to maintain virginity or chastity) in parts of Africa. At times, European women and men attempted to intervene in these situations or in the relationship between the colonial government and indigenous peoples; such people saw themselves, with more or less arrogance, helping local people. In many cases, European intervention, combined with local efforts at change, resulted in concrete improvements for women: fewer women were burned or had their genitals cut. At the same time, these and other reforms, like women's education, often caused indigenous people to identify more closely with western culture. Thus the process of externally-induced reform itself can be seen as part of cultural imperialism. Carried out, as they were, in the absence of a critique of colonialism, such reforms mistakenly identified women's problems as the result only of indigenous patriarchal relations, rather than the result of the interaction of these relations with colonial exploitation and gender oppression.

FEMALE ETHNOGRAPHERS AND ANTHROPOLOGISTS

With the establishment of a foreign mission by a church organization or the establishment of colonial rule by a European government came the need to understand the peoples and societies of Africa and Asia. As missionaries or as wives of colonial officers, women at times became ethnographers, studying systematically the mores and institutions of an indigenous group, or, more particularly, of the women of such a group. As a discipline, anthropology sought to understand a society on its own terms. In practice, particularly in Africa beginning in the interwar period, anthropologists worked closely with administrators to promote change.

In the first quarter of the twentieth century, the interest in having a woman's perspective came from two sources. First, the European feminist challenge to political and social practices prompted intellectual questioning as well. Writing in the midst of the pre–World War One suffrage struggle in

Britain, D. Amaury Talbot, author of *Women's Mysteries of a Primitive People; The Ibibios of Southern Nigeria* (1915), saw her study as a way of understanding changes in women's position. Without aligning herself with the feminist movement, she notes its challenge to the status quo. Second, anthropology's claim to view society as a whole made more likely the systematic study of women's roles. Since local custom generally denied male anthropologists access to local women, female anthropologists performed essential functions within the discipline.

The male bias of much anthropological work gives evidence that anthropology did not escape the patriarchal perspectives of the broader European society. Some female anthropologists who should have become prominent did not. Daisy Bates, who spent fifty years among Australian aborigines, had her material appropriated by a famous male colleague, A. Radcliffe-Brown.[8] Other women, who perhaps never aspired to be anthropologists, aided their husbands' research. The classic works of the period by male anthropologists acknowledge their wives' contribution only in the preface, not on the title page.

Some British anthropologists combined a concern for social problems with an interest in the study of indigenous women. Audrey Richards produced a number of basic ethnographic accounts of indigenous people in presentday Zambia, one of which, *Chisungu*, (1956) ranks among the best studies of female life cycle rituals. Nonetheless, an assessment of her career involves coming to terms with a radical critique of anthropology itself. "If she had greater faith than is common nowadays in the will and the power of governments given the right information to solve these problems [arising from social change]," states her memorialist, capturing the spirit of the period, "she was by no means their unwitting tool." Yet an African critic less charitably attacks her work: "The *neogenocidal* implications of the *involuntary migration of* . . . Bemba males to European mines to earn money for colonial taxes are not considered in her classic study of the deterioration of Bemba nutrition (1939)."[9]

Emerging as a field in the late nineteenth century, anthropology represented a step beyond the bald ethnocentrism of unexamined imperialism. Colonial administrators suspected it to be a leftist ideology because it fostered an identification with indigenous peoples. Indeed, many anthropologists empathized with the plight of colonized peoples and sought to ameliorate their conditions. However, they rarely saw colonialism itself as the root of the problems people faced. Because anthropological analyses aided in the administration, rather than the liberation, of colonized peoples, anthropology as a field became scorned in newly independent Africa. The criticisms raised of anthropology during the colonial period must be shared by female anthropologists as well.

The field of anthropology, and in its applied form, colonial administration, provided exciting work and meaningful careers for a number of women of

Richard's generation. Yet gender discrimination limited even these women's opportunities. Dame Margery Perham, as influential as any man in the field of colonial administration, would undoubtedly have been appointed a colonial governor had she been a man. As a woman she served, in her travels in the colonies and in her official training seminars for the Colonial Service, as consultant and guide for male administrators: "a builder of empire builders."[10]

EUROPEAN REFORMERS

If any women can be said to have threatened imperial rule, it is the reformers, such as those who actively campaigned for Indian independence, risking imprisonment. Others, in postcolonial South Africa, participated in legal and illegal efforts to dismantle the racial segregation and economic exploitation resulting from white rule. Many others participated in less radical reform efforts that at least softened the effects of colonialism and breached the social boundaries that colonialism erected between ruler and ruled.

European women were active in Indian reform movements in the nineteenth century; in Africa, the 1940s and 1950s mark a turning point in both the involvement of European women in African women's issues and the formation of African women's organizations modeled after European voluntary associations. As World War Two hastened the demise of the empire, two important changes occurred within the Colonial Service. First, the colonial mission shifted to an emphasis on trusteeship and development. In addition, after agitation by British feminists, the Colonial Office in 1938 dropped its ban on admitting women and, in the late 1940s, the Colonial Service significantly increased its recruitment of women as education and social welfare officers. It is likely that both the ideological change and the presence of female development officers spurred the efforts of European women in the colonies to help African women.

In Kenya such efforts supported both the imperial mission and European gender norms. Administrators' wives and female white settlers organized classes in sewing and homecrafts for African women in rural areas in the period following World War Two. Since African women are farmers, they would have benefited more from agricultural extension services. Whether female white settlers were unable to provide help on agricultural topics or were merely blind to the need for such help because of European gender ideology, African women remained without the kind of assistance they needed most. Nonetheless, the groups prospered. By 1951, existing "Women's Institutes" had become the model for the development of Maendeleo ya Wanawake (Women's Progress), now a major national women's organization. The Department of Community Development, using European volunteers, encouraged the growth of Maendeleo ya Wanawake. By the mid-1950s, the Kikuyu insurrection known commonly as Mau Mau had forced settlers and administrators alike to entertain the notion of independent majority rule for Kenya. Administrators viewed the women's clubs as a key to luring some Kikuyu women away from supporting the guerillas.

The ethnocentrism and maternalism of reformers at the center of the empire matched that of colonial women. An example is the controversy that developed in the 1920s in Kenya over the operation of clitoridectomy performed on Kikuyu girls. The dispute, which led to feminist lobbying efforts in Britain, illustrates the presence of indigenous practices harmful to women, European paternalism on behalf of indigenous women, and European blindness to the colonial political and cultural context. Significantly, within the British community, the controversy pitted local male administrators known for their political sympathy to Africans (who advocated allowing a hygienic form of the operation) against British female feminists without direct experience in Africa (who called for its elimination), with the missionary community falling at various points in between.

Missionaries and their converts among the Kikuyu raised medical objections to clitoridectomy. It was painful; unhygienic operations led to infection; the resulting scar tissue made childbirth difficult. The controversy split the Kikuyu community. Some church elders attacked clitoridectomy. Other Kikuyu leaders denounced mission intervention as a form of cultural imperialism. Jomo Kenyatta, later the first President of an independent Kenya, wrote a defense of the operation in *Facing Mount Kenya* (1938), itself an anticolonialist landmark as the first ethnographic study done by an African scholar.

While the controversy raged among Africans and Europeans in Kenya, British women pressured for parliamentary investigations. The Duchess of Atholl, a Member of Parliament with missionary friends, joined Eleanor Rathbone and two non-Members in conducting investigations based on testimony from medical experts, missionaries, and others, including Kenyatta. The group ultimately did not succeed in prohibiting the operation through legislation.

Eleanor Rathbone lobbied in London on behalf of Indian women as well. We have no knowledge of how most Kikuyu women felt about their self-appointed benefactors, but Indian spokeswomen generally did not appreciate Rathbone's role. In 1918 Rathbone became president of the National Union of Societies for Equal Citizenship (NUSEC), which exemplified the moderate wing of the suffrage movement in Britain. In 1927 she pressed NUSEC to work for the improvement of Indian women's status, notably around the issues of women's suffrage and raising the legal age for marriage. She especially blamed the low status of Indian women on the British government for its refusal to intervene in indigenous customs that hurt women. However, her efforts on their behalf met resistance from female

Indian leaders, who shared many of her goals but found her to be ignorant of the realities of Indian women's lives. She had visited India only once and derived much of her knowledge from a negative and controversial exposé written by an American woman. Although many appreciated Rathbone's concern, by the 1920s Indian women were prepared to speak for themselves. Moreover, they resented the reinforcement of imperial authority that Rathbone's activity represented. Finally, as nationalists, they disagreed with her strategically, placing greater importance on the goal of Indian independence over short-term gains on women's issues.

Living most of her adult life in India, Margaret Cousins devoted her life to the causes of national independence and women's rights, without apparent conflict. She and her husband came to India during World War One. A committed feminist, Cousins in 1927 brought together the All-India Women's Conference, originally an organization to discuss Indian women's educational needs, which became permanent and nationally based. She became its president in 1936. Imprisoned for a year for nationalist activity, Cousins increasingly withdrew from direct involvement, instead entrusting leadership to Indian women.

Like Cousins, Olive Schreiner, a child of missionary parents, was also active both as a feminist and as a critic of British imperialism. She denounced British treatment of the Boers in turn-of-the-century South Africa and, later, British involvement in World War One. As political unification of the English and Boers proceeded following the Anglo-Boer War, she moved away from the racial attitudes of most whites to advocate suffrage for Africans, albeit limited suffrage. Although Schreiner's attitude towards Africans was patronizing, she saw the need for white and African workers to unite in the class struggle, which she believed would replace the English-Boer conflict. An ardent feminist, she nonetheless resigned from the Women's Enfranchisement League when, in the first decade of this century, it advocated the vote for white women only. However, her feminism subsequently found its expression basically in terms of white women's issues and lives, not those of African women, whose needs and political expressions differed drastically from her own. Arousing little response among South African white women, she leaned toward intellectual allies in Britain. The culmination of years of Schreiner's thinking on the Woman Question, *Woman and Labour* (1911), proved to be one of the influential feminist works of the early twentieth century.

In a country as conservative and repressive as South Africa, the vast majority of white women have rarely moved outside of domestic roles to embrace any political activity. Always a small minority, progressive white women have opposed white privilege. The 1930s witnessed active trade union organizing. The electoral victory of the Afrikaner Nationalist Party in 1948 and its implementation of apartheid spawned massive multiracial nonviolent resistance in the 1950s. Equally massive repression drove activists underground until the workers' and students' rebellions of the 1970s and 1980s. In all these movements women played a part, although feminist issues were subordinated to the antiracist, antiapartheid struggle. Helen Joseph and Ray (Alexander) Simons, among others, organized trade unions and were banned and placed under house arrest for their antiapartheid work. Betty Sacks and Hilda (Watts) Bernstein worked through the Communist Party of South Africa (CPSA), as did Ruth First, the victim in 1982 of a letter bomb sent by the South African security forces. These and other white women joined black Africans, Asians, and Coloured (mixed race) women and men in the nonracial African National Congress (ANC).

From its founding in 1954, the nonracial Federation of South African Women, led by members of the ANC's Women's League, actively resisted the imposition of pass laws on African women, who had been exempt until 1950. In 1956, 20,000 women, mostly black Africans, delivered petitions to the Prime Minister, walking to his office in groups no larger than three, since the government had banned processions that day. This disciplined display of nonviolent resistance, like other such efforts against apartheid, failed, and its leaders of all races were banned or imprisoned.

Another small group of liberal women, members of Black Sash, risked ostracism though not imprisonment for their work to alleviate the oppression of apartheid. Moderate or conservative in the context of U.S. politics, their activities are viewed by most white South Africans as radical and are scorned by most young African militants as hopeless and inadequate responses to apartheid. Black Sash originated at a tea party of English-speaking white women in 1955. With little political experience, these housewives viewed with alarm the efforts of the (Afrikaner) Nationalist Party to erode further the limited voting rights of Coloured men. Acting out of Anglo-Boer rivalry more than a concern for racial justice, they founded the Women's Defence of the Constitution League and stood in silent vigil through two nights at the government offices, withstanding the threats, rocks, and garbage thrown at them by gangs of young Afrikaner men. Later, they took for their organization the name of the black sashes they wore to mourn the "death" of the Constitution.

True to the racial ideology of white South Africa, Black Sash began as a white organization. In the late 1950s when the organization completely failed to effect political change, it established Advice Offices to counsel black Africans caught in apartheid's maze of prohibitions. This hands-on work exposed the socially conservative white women to the realities of black life and transformed their views of society. Black Sash became a multiracial organization in 1963, but in transforming it lost its white base. Its membership fell from 10,000 in the 1950s to 1,100 by 1981.

Today Black Sash continues, where virtually all other organizations opposed to apartheid since the 1950s have been banned and their leaders imprisoned or forced into exile, because it scrupulously adheres to the law.

In addition, says current president Sheena Duncan, "The government don't think we're effective enough to worry about because we're women. . . . It's almost impossible for a member of the Nationalist Party or the Dutch Reformed Church to take any woman seriously."[11] In the upsurge of antiapartheid struggle in the 1980s, Duncan has sided solidly with the militants (the ANC and the United Democratic Front) and against those proposing accommodation.

CONCLUSION

The women described here all lived through a period when European hegemony—economic, political, and ideological—overpowered what we now call the Third World. They operated within institutions, cultural patterns, and personal relationships profoundly shaped by notions of male superiority and the reality of male power over females. For all their differences, we can discern the ways in which imperialism and male dominance shaped common patterns in their lives. Their participation in the colonial process brought them benefits. Being white generally meant access to land, a higher standard of living, or the protection of the colonial government. Many came to the colonies seeking jobs that were unavailable back home. The colonial enterprise itself created careers for some as anthropologists and members of the Colonial Service. The vast majority of these women failed to develop a full critique of imperialism, either of its political and economic facets or of the racist and paternalist ideology behind the notion of the "white man's burden." African and Asian women needed their own indigenous institutions; European women could not create these, although they served as midwives to several.

If imperialism gave them benefits as Europeans, male dominance limited their options as women. For the most part, the sexual division of labor that shaped their lives in Britain governed their activities in the colonies. The roles of mother and wife dominated most women's lives. Those who worked outside the home took typically female jobs. Indeed in the public sphere, only unusual women participated in overtly political activities; the rest rarely ventured past providing charity, a task typical of females in socially superior positions.

In one sense, European women's marginal status within a male-dominated colonial society and structure provided an opportunity. People outside the dominant culture have a different perspective that derives from their different experience and position within the social structure. Perhaps European women's marginal position within the dominant colonial society enabled them to see aspects of imperialism differently. European women frequently saw the needs of indigenous women where male administrators were blind to them. Some chose to use their skills, enhanced power, and status as members of the colonizing society on behalf of indigenous people with the result, if not always the conscious goal, of the dismantling of the empire.

NOTES

1. I use the term European for two reasons. First, the women in British colonies came from various European countries, and second, Africans refer to whites as a group (including North Americans) as Europeans.
2. L. H. Gann and Peter Duignan, *The Rulers of British Africa, 1870–1914* (Stanford: Stanford University Press, 1978), pp. 241–242.
3. Sylvia Leith-Ross, *Stepping-Stones: Memoirs of Colonial Nigeria, 1907–1960* (London and Boston: Peter Owen, 1983), p. 69.
4. Laura Boyle, *Diary of a Colonial Officer's Wife* (Oxford: Alden Press, 1968), p. 156.
5. Cited and quoted in Catherine Barnes Stevenson, *Victorian Women Travel Writers in Africa* (Boston: Twayne Publishers, 1982), pp. 16–17.
6. BWEA Annual Report 1900, p. 12, and *The Saturday Review*, 20 September 1902, both cited in Jean Jacques Van Helten and Keith Williams, " 'The Crying Need of South Africa': The Emigration of Single British Women to the Transvaal, 1901–10," *Journal of Southern African Studies* 10, no. 1 (1983), pp. 22–23.
7. Caroline Oliver, *Western Women in Colonial Africa* (Westport, Conn.: Greenwood Press, 1982), pp. 145–188.
8. Ruby Rohrlich-Leavitt, Barbara Sykes, and Elizabeth Rutherford, "Aboriginal Woman: Male and Female Anthropological Perspectives," in *Toward an Anthropology of Women*, ed. Rayna R. Rapp (New York: Monthly Review Press, 1975), pp. 124–126.
9. J. S. La Fontaine, "Audrey Isabel Richards, 1899–1984," *Africa*, 55 no. 2 (1985), p. 201; Omafume F. Onoge, "The Counterrevolutionary Tradition in African Studies: The Case of Applied Anthropology," in *The Politics of Anthropology: From Colonialism and Sexism Toward a View from Below*, ed. Gerrit Huizer and Bruce Mannheim (The Hague: Mouton, 1979), p. 53.
10. A. H. M. Kirk-Greene, "Margery Perham and Colonial Administration: A Direct Influence on Indirect Rule," in *Oxford and the Idea of Commonwealth*, ed. D. K. Fieldhouse (London: Croom Helm, 1982), p. 139.
11. June Goodwin, *Cry Amandla!: South African Women and the Question of Power* (New York and London: Africana Publishing, 1984), p. 142.

SUGGESTIONS FOR FURTHER READING

The following are in addition to sources cited in the notes.

The Myth of the Destructive Female: Sexuality, Ritual, and Home

The myth is presented or refuted in: Percival Spear, *The Nabobs* (London: Oxford University Press, 1963), p. 140; Janice N. Brownfoot, "Memsahibs in Colonial Malaya: A Study of European Wives in a British Colony and Protectorate 1900–1940," in *The Incorporated Wife*, ed. Hilary Callan and Shirley Ardener (London: Croom Helm, 1984), pp. 186–87; James Boutilier, "European Women in the Solomon Islands, 1900–1942: Accommodation and Change on the Pacific Frontier," in *Rethinking Women's Roles: Perspectives from the Pacific*, ed. Denise O'Brien and Sharon W. Tiffany (Berkeley: University of California Press, 1984), pp. 173–200. On sexual relations, see Kenneth Ballhatchet, *Race, Sex, and Class Under the Raj: Imperial Attitude and Politics and Their Critics, 1793–1905* (New York: St. Martin's Press, 1980); Amirah Inglis, *The White Woman's Protection Ordinance: Sexual Anxiety and Politics in Papua,* (London: Sussex University Press, 1975); Charles Van Onselen, "The Witches of Suburbia," *Studies in the Social and Economic History of the Witwatersrand, 1886–1914, Volume Two, New Nineveh,* (London: Longman, 1982), pp. 1–73.

On life in the colonies, Charles Allen has produced three books drawn from interviews with former colonial residents: *Plain Tales from the Raj; Images of British India in the Twentieth Century* (New York: St. Martin's Press, 1976); *Tales from the Dark Continent* (New York: St. Martin's Press, 1979); and *Tales from the South China Seas; Images of the British in Southeast Asia in the Twentieth Century* (London: Andre Deutsch, 1983). Each successive book treats women with more sympathy and understanding. Other works include Pat Barr, *The Memsahibs: The Women of British India* (London: Secker and Warburg, 1976); Beverley Gartrell, "Colonial Wives: Villains or Victims?," in Callan and Ardener, cited above, pp. 165–185; James Fox, *White Mischief* (1982; Harmondsworth: Penguin, 1984) [Kenya]; and Boutelier, cited earlier.

Biographies and autobiographies provide information on life in the colonies: Violet Powell, *Flora Annie Steel, Novelist of India* (London: Heinemann, 1981); Ruth First and Ann Scott, *Olive Schreiner* (New York: Schocken, 1980); Hylda Richards, *Next Year Will Be Better* (1952; Lincoln: University of Nebraska Press, 1985); Alyse Simpson, *The Land That Never Was* (1937; Lincoln: University of Nebraska Press, 1985); Elspeth Huxley, *The Flame Trees of Thika* (New York: William Morrow, 1959); Judith Thurman, *Isak Dinesen* (New York: St. Martin's Press, 1982); Joan Alexander, *Voices and Echoes: Tales from Colonial Women* (London: Quartet Books, 1983).

For more theoretical discussions of colonial society and culture, manners and mores, and the political functions of pomp and ceremony, see Hilary Callan, "Introduction," in Callan and Ardener, cited above, pp. 1–26; and an excellent analysis by Helen Callaway, *Gender, Culture, and Empire: European Women in Colonial Nigeria* (Urbana: University of Illinois Press, forthcoming).

Job-Seekers

James A. Hammerton's *Emigrant Gentlewomen; Genteel Poverty and Female Emigration, 1830–1914* (London: Croom Helm, 1979) discusses the general phenomenon of emigration. See Van Onselen, cited above, for South Africa.

Missionaries, Anthropologists, and Reformers

For India, Meredith Borthwick touches on European women in *The Changing Role of Women in Bengal, 1849–1905* (Princeton: Princeton University Press, 1984); for Mary Slessor and Mother Kevin, see Caroline Oliver, *Western Women in Colonial Africa* (Westport, Conn.: Greenwood Press, 1982).; for exceptions to the patterns outlines here see Charles W. Forman, " 'Sing to the Lord a New Song': Women in the Churches of Oceania," in O'Brien and Tiffany, cited above, pp. 153–172; and Marcia Wright, *German Missions in Tanganyika, 1891–1914: Lutherans and Moravians in the Southern Highlands* (London: Oxford University Press, 1971).

For anthropology, see Margery Perham's own *African Apprenticeship: An Autobiographical Journey in Southern Africa 1929* (New York: Africana Publishing Company, 1974).

For reformers in India, see various works by Barbara N. Ramusack, "Catalysts or Helpers? British Feminists, Indian Women's Rights, and Indian Independence," in *The Extended Family: Women and Political Participation in India and Pakistan*, ed. Gail Minault (Columbia, Mo.: South Asia Books, 1981), pp. 109–15; "Women's Organizations and Social Change: The Age-of-Marriage Issue in India," in *Women and World Change: Equity Issues in Development*, ed. Naomi Black and Ann Baker Cotrell (Beverly Hills, Calif.: Sage Publications, 1981), pp. 198–216. Mary D. Stocks' *Eleanor Rathbone: A Biography* (London: Victor Gollancs, 1949) places Rathbone's colonial efforts in the context of her total career.

For reformers in Africa, see Deborah Kirkwood, "Settler Wives in Rhodesia: A Case Study," in Callan and Ardener, cited above, pp. 143–164; Audrey Wipper, "The Maendeleo ya Wanawake Movement in the Colonial Period: The Canadian Connection, Mau Mau, Embroidery and Agriculture," *Rural Africana*, no. 29 (Winter 1975–76), pp. 195–214; and Jocelyn Murray, "The Kikuyu Female Circumcision Controversy with Special Reference to the Church Missionary Society 'Sphere of Influence' " (PhD Diss., UCLA, 1974).

For South Africa, Beata Lipman, *We Make Freedom: Women in South Africa* (London: Pandora Press, 1984); Cherry Michelman, *Black Sash: A Case Study in Liberalism* (London: Oxford University Press, 1975); Cheryl Walker, *Women and Resistance in South Africa* (London: Onyx Press, 1982); Helen Joseph, *Side by Side* (London: Zed Press, 1986).

Clara Zetkin (left) and Rosa Luxemburg in 1913. Zetkin was then editor of the German socialist women's newspaper, with a circulation of 112,000, and secretary of the International Socialist Women's Movement; Luxemburg was one of the most prominent leaders of the left of the German Socialist party. (Snark/Art Resource)

chapter 15

The Socialist Women's Movement from 1850 to 1940

Charles Sowerwine

*In the late nineteenth century, European socialist parties committed them-
selves to women's emancipation, beginning with full political rights. Based
on the theories of Karl Marx and Friedrich Engels, these parties linked
working-class women's double oppression in industry and in the family to
the particular economic dependency imposed by capitalism. In a socialist
society, they argued, the basis for male domination would fall away. Germany's
strong socialist party, with its separate women's organization, succeeded in
attracting many female members, while France's and Italy's faction-ridden
socialist movements divided women. By contrast, England's socialist and
labor movements allied with an autonomous mass-based radical women's
suffrage movement. Whatever the form socialist feminism took, it reached
more women than did liberal feminism with its narrower class base and
inhospitable liberal parties, although it did not achieve its program in its
own time.*

In the quarter-century before 1914, European socialism developed from small divided movements in different countries into a set of powerful national parties. During the same period, feminism also developed into a powerful movement, which was clearly on the road to success in many countries, especially Britain, and had already obtained the vote in Norway and Finland (not to mention Australia, New Zealand, and some American states).

The great mass of working-class women, however, remained untouched by the suffrage movements, where middle-class women held sway. Working-class women had political concerns, but these arose more from their economic hardship than from their subordination to men. Middle-class or "bourgeois" feminists (as the socialist women called them) had trouble reaching working-class women; so did well-to-do women, who had different concerns and often intimidated working-class women. Conversely, male socialists had trouble reaching women, even working-class women: they too had different concerns and—as men—they often intimidated women. While class differences proved unbridgeable for the feminists, however, the socialists often succeeded in organizing women, but only when they fostered special, separate groups for socialist women.

More than theory or leadership, the existence of such groups determined the success or failure of the socialist women's movement in each country. In Germany, where repressive laws forced the party to develop a separate women's organization, it became the largest and most radical women's movement in Europe, if not in the world; it had 174,751 members by 1914. In France, where democracy and a greater degree of equality for women allowed the party to practice a policy of integration of women into the regular party sections, no effective women's organization emerged, and the party recruited few women. The socialist women's movements in other countries fell between these two extremes.

In varying degrees, all socialist women's groups sought women's political and economic equality, fair wages, and reasonable working conditions in the short term; in the long term they all sought the victory of socialism, economic independence for women, and new, "higher" forms of work and family life. Not only did their goals vary considerably within this broad framework, however, but also their organization, structure, and relation to the party as a whole varied from country to country.

The development of the socialist women's movement did follow a broadly similar pattern across Europe, however. Early socialist-feminist groupings associated with utopian socialism of the first half of the nineteenth century gave way to socialist parties under the First International (1864–1876), in which conservative artisans fought a growing Marxist influence over such issues as women's rights. With the triumph of Marxism in socialist parties by the end of the century came strong theoretical support for women's rights. Separate socialist women's groups, however, arose only in the 1890s: the socialist women's movement flowered under the umbrella of the Second International, from 1889 to 1914. During World War I, national divisions tore apart both the Socialist International and the socialist women's movement. The choice between socialism and communism further divided the socialist women's movement. Finally, fascism and war swept it away.

INDUSTRIALIZATION AND THE VISION OF KARL MARX

Socialism as a movement developed before Marx began writing. Early or "utopian" socialism emerged during the first half of the nineteenth century. Many of these early socialists—men and women—were also feminists, and they created the small but significant socialist-feminist movement discussed in Karen Offen's essay. Among them were disciples of Robert Owen such as William Thompson and Anna Wheeler; disciples of Charles Fourier and Count Saint-Simon such as Suzanne Voilquin; or independent socialist feminists, such as Flora Tristan.[1]

Artisans formed the main constituency of the early, utopian socialist movements, but as industrialization progressed more rapidly, beginning in France during the 1850s, artisans became frightened of being made into factory laborers. They often turned against working women, who seemed to be the cause of their misfortunes. Industrialists paid women less than half men's wages; women therefore appeared to threaten men's jobs. Thus many artisans fought for a return to the protoindustrial household economy, with its most narrow definition of the role of women: "Woman's place is in the home [*la femme au foyer*]."

The artisans' vision was increasingly shaped by the folk memory of the household economy. As one woman put it at the 1876 Workers' Congress in France, "it would be more natural for men to provide a living for their wives and daughters"—as in the small shop or farm—than for all to be dependent on capitalists.[2] Pierre-Joseph Proudhon (1809–1865) articulated the sentiment of these artisans. He is best remembered for his comment, "women must be housewives or harlots, there is no other choice."[3] As capitalism took off in Germany, a decade or so after France, members of the pre-Marxist labor movement led by Ferdinand Lassalle (1825–1864) echoed these sentiments, although in more muted form.

Clear theoretical understanding and acceptance of women's liberation began only when a thinker emerged who could demonstrate the beneficial possibilities of industrialization, the need to develop and use democracy to fight for workers' rights, and the potential for women's independence inherent in their wage earning for themselves. That thinker was Karl Marx (1818–1883). Some have argued that Marx's concentration on the political and industrial struggle of the working class constituted a contraction of socialist ideals, in which the early utopian socialists' broad vision of the emancipation of women was reduced to a narrower vision of political and economic equality, without full understanding of the oppressive nature of the family.[4] Others, however, have argued that the scope of Marx's analysis of capitalism as a whole implied a broadened vision, similar to that inherent in women's liberation movements today.[5]

Certainly Marx's analysis of capitalism and the family provided a platform for the emancipation of working-class women unique in the nineteenth century. Marx and his collaborator, Frederick Engels (1820–1895), together developed the first analysis of women's double oppression. Women were clearly oppressed in their relations with men. "Marriage," Marx argued in the *Economic and Philosophic Manuscripts of 1844*, "is a form of exclusive private property."[6] Forty years later, Engels made this point in a famous aphorism: "Within the family, he is the bourgeois, and the wife represents the proletariat."[7] Moreover, to this historic oppression was being added another that fell upon those women drawn into the economic world created by capitalist industrialization. These women were subjected to the same exploitation as men but at the same time to a "double oppression": employers could pay women a "supplementary wage," half the wages of men; the family would keep them alive despite insufficient wages. In this way women's dependence on men facilitated and increased their exploitation by capitalists. This analysis led Marx and Engels to argue a long-term strategy for women's liberation: first women should obtain political equality; then they should use political equality in the struggle for economic equality and economic independence from men. Only after men and women achieved equality within capitalism could they fight together for the full self-realization which socialism alone would bring.

Marx and Engels both maintained that political equality between the sexes was the necessary precondition to the struggle for full human emancipation. Both used the suffrage situation as an analogy. They had begun their political careers as republicans and they never repudiated their commitment to "the democratic republic." Voting rights in a republic did not constitute social and economic emancipation, but democracy did provide "the clear field on which the fight can be fought out." The possession of political rights would highlight women's oppression in more fundamental areas. As Engels put it in *The Origin of the Family, Private Property and the State*, first published in 1884:

> The peculiar character of the supremacy of the husband over the wife in the modern family, the necessity of creating real social equality between them and the way to do it, will only be seen in the clear light of day when both possess legally complete equality of rights. Then it will be plain that the first condition for the liberation of the wife is to bring the whole female sex back into public industry, and that this in turn demands that the characteristic of the monogamous family as the economic unit of society be abolished.[8]

Engels, like Marx (on whose notes Engels drew in writing *The Origin of the Family*), believed that capitalism would give women economic independence and thus enable them to become independent of men.

Although it was theoretically enticing, this strategy posed more problems for working-class women in the nineteenth century than for aspiring women executives in the twentieth. Wage labor may have laid the basis for economic independence, but it caused horrendous hardship. Marx and Engels realized this; they did not preach for or against wage labor for women, but only noted that women's ability to sell their labor would lay the basis for their economic and hence personal independence from men.

> However terrible and disgusting the dissolution of the old family ties within the capitalist system may appear, large-scale industry, by assigning an important part in socially organized processes of production, outside the sphere of the domestic economy, to women, young persons and children of both sexes, does nevertheless create a new economic foundation for a higher form of the family and of relations between the sexes.[9]

Laying the economic foundation did not in itself build the "higher form . . . of relations between the sexes"; that required political action, for which women needed political rights on the same basis as men.

August Bebel (1840–1913), one of the principal leaders of the German socialist movement and a follower of Marx, tried to provide a platform for the socialist women's movement in his book, *Woman and Socialism*. First published in 1879, five years before Engels' *Origin of the Family*, it was drastically revised in 1891 to take account of Engels' work. In this form it became one of the most popular works of the socialist movement. It ran through fifty editions and fifteen translations before World War I.

In his book Bebel supported all the standard feminist demands, including the right to vote, the right to enter universities and to practice professions, and the right for women to divorce and for married women to own their own property.[10] In doing so he brought such demands to the fore in the nascent socialist movement. The book went even further than mainstream feminists. It posed radical new demands, such as the right to dress freely and the right to sexual satisfaction. And it went further than most feminists in dismissing the idea that women had a "natural calling" to raise families; that idea, Bebel said, was "twaddle."[11] Even more fundamentally, the book argued that the domination of women by men was rooted not in biology but in history and was thus capable of resolution *in history:* "conditions . . . finally grow into custom; heredity and education then cause such conditions to appear . . . 'natural.' Hence . . . woman . . . accepts her subordinate position as a matter of course."[12]

The book had a great impact on working-class women: someone had written about them! The book was thick and "scientific." Moreover, it was not written by just anyone, but by one of the two principal leaders of the socialist movement: it demonstrated not just individual concern for women's problems but the concern of the whole party of the working class. Clara Zetkin later called it "more than a book . . . an event—a great deed."[13] Jean Quataert quotes the instructive reaction of one woman, Ottilie Baader, who would later be a leader in the German socialist women's movement:

> News came of a wonderful book that . . . Bebel . . . had written. Although I was not a Social Democrat I had friends who belonged to the party. Through them I got the precious work. I read it nights through. It was my own fate and that of thousands of my sisters. Neither in the family nor in public life had I ever heard of all the pain the woman must endure. One ignored her life. Bebel's book courageously broke with the old secretiveness. . . . I read the book not once but ten times. Because everything was so new, it took considerable effort to come to grips with Bebel's views. I had to break with so many things that I had previously regarded as correct.[14]

European Socialist Parties and Feminism

The socialist movement as a whole did not immediately accept the principle of equality for women. The early utopian socialists had not founded enduring movements. Only in the 1860s and 1870s did the International Workingman's Association or First International (1864–1876) lay the foundations of lasting socialist movements. These, however, were initially dominated not by Marx and his followers, but by artisans who resisted proletarianization. The artisans' viewpoint was voiced by the second generation of utopians, men like Proudhon and Lassalle, who were hostile to wage labor for women, at least in the factory, and at best unenthusiastic about allowing women into politics. As industrialization progressed, however, wage-earners streamed into the socialist parties. They found Marx's vision of collective struggle more relevant than Proudhon's nostalgia for the old household economy and tended to vote for Marxist positions. With the support of the wage earners, Marxist intellectuals and bourgeois feminists introduced women's equality into socialist platforms more or less at the same time that the Marxist viewpoint gained predominance, over the opposition of the representatives of the artisans.

The German Social Democratic Party (Sozialdemokratische Partei Deutschlands or SPD) was founded in 1875. Its first draft program included the vote "for all citizens," which—it was argued—included women. But when Bebel proposed making it clearer by adding "citizens of both sexes," the congress rejected his proposal by 62 to 55. After 1878, Bismarck's antisocialist laws forced the party to go underground. By the time it reemerged after the repeal of these laws in 1890, Bebel's and Engels' books had circulated widely and had helped the party articulate a position in favor of equality for women. Moreover, Bebel now dominated the party, together with Wilhelm Liebknecht (1826–1900) and Karl Kautsky (1854–1938); all three were followers of Marx and Engels, correspondents of Engels, and supporters of women's rights.

Under their leadership, the 1891 SPD Congress at Erfurt voted overwhelmingly in favor of universal suffrage "without distinction of sex" and "abolition of all laws which place the woman, whether in a private or public capacity, at a disadvantage as compared with the man." The "Erfurt Program" became one of the key texts of socialists everywhere. Kautsky predicted that with the coming of socialism:

> Woman will cease to be a worker in the individual household, and will take her place as a worker in the large industries. . . . By working side by side with man in the great co-operative industries woman will become his equal and will take an equal part in the community life. She will be his free companion, emancipated not only from the servitude of the house, but also from that of capitalism."[15]

The French Socialist Party evolved in much the same way. During the Second Empire (1852–70) and immediately after, Proudhon articulated the concerns of artisans threatened by proletarianization. They took the household economy as their ideal and sought to keep women out of wage labor. During the same period, however, the industrial revolution was spreading through France. Gradually workers began to search for ideas more relevant to their emerging situation as wage laborers. During the 1870s the labor movement slowly re-formed after the disastrous failure of the Paris Commune of 1871, the revolt supported by the International in which 25,000 insurgents lost their lives. Marxists began to propagandize on the basis of accepting the development of industry, seeking to reform it or collectivize it, and supporting women's rights.

The young militant feminist Hubertine Auclert (1851–1914) got involved with these Marxists and her small feminist organization became a constituent member of their "Workers' Party," which would become the French Socialist Party. Auclert went to the 1879 Workers' Congress to fight for women's rights. She not only obtained support for women's suffrage and full legal equality, but also presented a bold vision for the future:

> Men and women . . . will govern this society together and will share in the exercise of the same rights, in public life as in private . . . in all circumstances, women will have their freedom of action like men. . . . Women will take the roles and the places in society to which their vocations call them.[16]

Auclert and her feminist group did not long remain in the Workers' Party. The following year, the party split between the Marxists and the mutualists, or Proudhonists. Even though the mutualists violently opposed women's rights, Auclert's group sided with them, because the Marxists attacked private property. The feminists agreed with the mutualists that private property and the family should be "the basis of society" and this seemed more important to them than the mutualists' opposition to women's rights. The split that would separate bourgeois feminism from socialist feminism was opening up. While the feminists allowed their concern for property to override their commitment to women's rights, the Marxists reaffirmed their commitment to equality for women at their congresses of 1880 and 1882.

THE GERMAN SOCIALIST WOMEN'S MOVEMENT

While such issues could be debated openly in democratic France, imperial Germany repressed socialist activity. Even after the legalization of the SPD in 1890, many provinces of Germany severely restricted or even prohibited women's political meetings. The SPD recognized the need to draw women into its ranks, if only to prevent socialist men from being undercut at home. Given the restrictions on women's activities, however, involving them could only be by special, "nonpolitical" groups for women. For this reason the party statutes drawn up in 1890 provided for women "to elect female delegates to party conferences at special women's meetings." The 1892 conference provided for permanent women's representatives, called spokespeople; this was a significant choice of words, as "spokesman" had no feminine equivalent in German. Ottilie Baader (1847–1925) was elected "central Spokesperson for the women comrades of Germany" at the SPD's 1900 conference.[17]

The SPD created an organizational structure for women independent from that of men, so that women had their own groups in which they could feel secure and develop their talents without fear of male disapproval or ridicule. This separate organizational structure is the key to the success of the German socialist women's movement. By 1908, there were 407 female spokespersons in the party hierarchy, with Baader at the top. The circulation of *Die Gleichheit* (*Equality*), the women's newspaper of the party, edited by Clara Zetkin, had soared to over 70,000; nearly 30,000 women had joined the party. By 1914 there were 174,751 women members, double the *total* membership of the French Socialist Party. The German socialist women's movement was by far the largest such movement and the standard by which all other socialist women's movements were judged. Indeed, between 1890 and 1914 it was the largest movement of women of any political coloration on the Continent.

Clara Zetkin (1857–1933) articulated the radical orientation of the great numbers of women who entered the party through its separate organization for women. Zetkin came to sudden prominence with her speech to the founding congress of the Second International held in Paris in 1889. This speech was so successful that the SPD published it; it became one of the key texts of the socialist women's movement.

In her speech Zetkin built on the analyses of Engels and Bebel. She assumed that socialists must support the feminist struggle; indeed, she declared that in Germany, given the weakness of the middle-class democratic movement, the socialists would have to lead the struggle for women's rights. But working-class women, she reminded her listeners, were not only "slaves" to men—they were slaves to capitalists. Since the bourgeois women of the feminist movement shared the class interests of the capitalists, Zetkin rejected any collaboration between socialists and bourgeois feminists. Socialist women must seek the destruction of capitalism in order to attain economic independence, which in turn would lead to full emancipation.

> Just as the workers are subjugated by the capitalists, women are subjugated by men and they will continue to be in that position as long as they are not economically independent. The quintessential prerequisite for their economic independence is work. . . . Once women have attained their economic independence from men, there is no reason why they should remain socially dependent upon them.[18]

Returning to Germany and developing contacts with the mass movement of socialism there, Zetkin modified her ideas somewhat. She found that women were joining the SPD not, as Marx and Engels had expected, because they were becoming independent of men, but because they were wives or daughters of SPD members; moreover, an experiment between 1892 and 1894 with equal opportunity for women within the party (where legal) convinced her that women needed separate groups with their own aims. By the 1896 party congress, she had muted her critique of the family and had come to view feminism as "completely justified." But she never ceased to proclaim that for proletarian women suffrage was only the first step in the struggle. Indeed, when moving her resolution for women's suffrage at the 1907 International Socialist Congress, she made this point in virtually the same words Engels had used:

> The granting of suffrage to the female sex does not eliminate the class differences between the exploiters and the exploited. . . . It also does not eliminate the conflicts which are created for women as members of their sex. . . . On the contrary: The complete political equality of the female sex prepares the ground on which the conflicts will be fought.[19]

Zetkin incorporated these ideas into the party program at the Gotha Conference in 1896. As editor of *Die Gleichheit* from 1891 until 1917, she expounded these ideas ceaselessly. On this theoretical basis she undertook the practical task of building a socialist women's movement. Zetkin's leadership did not go uncontested, however. While she worked in harmony with Ottilie Baader and others, she had to fight a lengthy battle with Lily Braun before she could assume complete sway over the movement.

Braun (1865–1916) was an aristocrat, but her humanitarian impulses led her to become a feminist and, in 1896, to join the SPD. Her background and support for the revisionist or anti-Marxist school of Eduard Bernstein soon brought her into conflict with the other major figures of the German socialist women's movement, most of whom came from lower middle-class or working-class origins and took hard-line Marxist positions in the revisionist debate that shook the party at the turn of the century.

In 1901, Braun published two essays that were attacked as heretical by Baader and Zetkin. The first, *Women's Labor and Household Co-operatives*, called for the organization of cooperative households, with community kitchens, to reduce the burdens upon women at home. To Zetkin, this was an assent to the capitalist order and a recommendation of reform instead of revolution, which she rejected outright. The second, *The Women's Question*, although quite in keeping with accepted party theory, suggested that there was room for collaboration with bourgeois feminists, a notion which the other women rejected violently, although Bebel called Braun's work "objective" and "scientific."[20]

Zetkin thought that Braun's organizational proposal showed that she was one of those "who lived a quiet bourgeois life, who cannot work in the propaganda struggle, [who is] unwilling to fight within the party itself." She summed up her view of Braun by calling her one of "the ethically coiffed and perfumed salon socialists." By 1901, Zetkin had cancelled Braun's column in *Die Gleichheit* and soon other women had excluded her from their meetings. Braun returned to the bourgeois wing of the feminist movement, becoming secretary of the League for the Protection of Motherhood and Sexual Reform in 1906.[22] With the defeat of Braun, Zetkin and Baader became the uncontested leaders of the German socialist women's movement and drew clear lines between socialist and bourgeois feminism.

In 1908 the laws preventing German women from joining political parties were repealed. Since women could now enter the party freely on the same basis as men, the SPD dissolved its separate hierarchy of women's organizations. Zetkin, however, argued that women still needed separate organization. In a compromise solution, the old central bureau of women became a women's bureau subordinate to the national party executive. Instead of Zetkin or Baader, however, the party appointed the younger and less known Luise Zietz (1865–1922) as women's representative on the executive, possibly in the hope that Zietz would compromise more readily on women's issues.

Nevertheless, legality enabled the movement to flourish. Within a year the number of women in the party more than doubled, reaching over 62,000, or nearly 10% of the total membership. At Zetkin's suggestion, the 1910 International Socialist Congress designated 8 March each year for International Women's Day; beginning in 1911, the Germans and Austrians made this day the occasion for major demonstrations that resulted in greater visibility to the socialist women's movement. At the beginning of World

War I, *Die Gleichheit* had a circulation of 112,000 and 174,751 women were registered as members of the party, constituting 16.1 percent of the total membership. The separate organizational structure had accomplished its main task: it had enabled a large body of dedicated women to develop their political skills. These women formed a nucleus within the party that was ready to attract and welcome large numbers of recruits when political party membership for women became legal.

THE FRENCH SOCIALIST PARTY AND THE WOMEN'S MOVEMENT

The French case clearly demonstrates the problems caused by the lack of an autonomous women's organization. The French Socialist Party had the lowest women's membership of all Second International parties. The party was unified only in 1905 as the French Section of the Workers' International (Section Française de l'Internationale Ouvrière, or SFIO). The SFIO did not create a women's organization until 1913. By the beginning of World War I the women's organization had attracted three hundred women in Paris, but had not yet reached beyond the capital. Total membership in the party (men and women combined) in 1914 was 90,725, while the SPD in Germany had over a million members. Women composed no more than three percent of the national party membership. Earlier efforts to organize a French socialist women's movement had failed, often because of party schisms; during the 1890s, there had been as many as five competing socialist parties in France! The fundamental problems of the French socialists, however, were the lack of a theoretical base, of a newspaper, and especially of a separate organization for women.

Separate socialist women's organizations had been formed in France on several occasions and had enjoyed some success, but none had survived for long. Only in 1899 did there emerge the Feminist Socialist Group, which prefigured the French socialist women's movement and provided two of its most important leaders: Louise Saumoneau (1875–1950) and Elisabeth Renaud (1846–1932). Renaud, the daughter of a worker in a watch factory, had been a governess in St. Petersburg before returning to France and marrying a printer who died after five years, leaving her two children and numerous debts. To support herself and her family, she ran a boarding house and gave French lessons to foreigners. By 1897 we find her a significant if minor figure in Parisian socialist circles; her Friday afternoon teas were frequented by many socialists. In 1898, Renaud and her friends left the hard-line Marxist party of Jules Guesde (1845–1922) for the new Independent Socialist Party of Jean Jaurès (1859–1914).

Saumoneau was a seamstress who came to socialism on the rebound from feminism. Arriving from the provinces in February 1897, she left her work one Wednesday afternoon (thus giving up half her daily pay) to attend a meeting of a feminist group. Ill at ease among the bourgeois women, whom she saw as employers and customers rather than sisters, she listened to a long debate on the morality of the custom of bestowing a dowry. In families like hers there were no dowries. Reflecting bitterly on the irrelevance of the debate and her lost wages, she determined to create a movement for working-class women like herself. Her quest led her to Renaud. Together with two other women in the garment trade, they founded the Feminist Socialist Group in July 1899. Their manifesto called for a socialist women's movement on the lines of Zetkin's. It outlined the "double oppression of women, exploited on a large scale by capitalism, subjected to men by laws and *especially* by prejudice."[22]

Two events destroyed the precarious equilibrium between feminism and socialism implicit in the original manifesto. In the first place, Saumoneau and Renaud attended the 1900 feminist congress as delegates of their group. There they proposed that domestics have a full day off a week. This gave rise to a bitter debate:

> Madam Wiggishoff: . . . You're asking for an entire day off. But where will these little girls of fifteen or sixteen go? Where will they eat?
>
> Madam Renaud: At your house.
>
> Madam Wiggishoff: So I'm to cook lunch for my maid? I'm not a saint and its more than likely that her lunch won't be ready.

This exchange was typical of a long and bitter debate. The congress had, the socialist women reported, "established much better than we could have ourselves the barrier which separates bourgeois feminism from socialist feminism."[23] The second factor which destroyed the group's equilibrium was a personal and political falling-out between Renaud and Saumoneau. After 1902, they never spoke to each other again.

Nevertheless, the group enjoyed some success. At the beginning of 1900 it became a constituent part of Jaurès' Independent Socialist Party, created a union of seamstresses, and developed sister groups in three different working-class neighborhoods of Paris. In 1901 the four groups together began publishing a monthly newspaper modeled on Zetkin's *Die Gleichheit*. By 1902, the groups had one hundred members in Paris, a respectable number in view of the factional difficulties (there were still three competing parties); there were probably no more than two hundred socialist women in the Paris region upon the founding of the unified party in 1905.

After the split between Saumoneau and Renaud, Renaud left the group to Saumoneau. The four groups shrank to one, led by Saumoneau, who violently opposed feminism—for her all feminists were bourgeois—and even doubted the wisdom of having separate women's groups within the socialist party for fear they might be infiltrated by feminists! The contradictions inherent in this position and Saumoneau's abrasive personality undercut the group's application to join the newly unified Socialist Party—the SFIO—at its founding in 1905. After protracted debate, the SFIO refused to admit the group to its ranks. This result went beyond questions of personality: the party thus rejected the German structure of separate women's organizations. The party would accept women on the same basis as men, and only on that basis. The absence of a separate organization for women resulted in a low percentage of women in the party from its inception through World War II. The party did more for women and women's suffrage than any other party in France, but it did not organize women.

Yet the French Socialist Party had the same potential to organize women as the SPD. Recent studies have shown that the feminist movements of France and Germany were roughly comparable in ideology, class background, and numbers.[25] It seems likely therefore that the difference between the women's movements of the two parties resulted not from major differences in the countries, but from differences in the parties' situations and organizations and in their theoretical and practical approaches to women.

Only in January 1913 did a newcomer to the French Socialist Party, Marianne Rauze (1875–ca. 1950), bring together most of the leaders remaining from the original Feminist Socialist Group and get them to agree to found a Socialist Women's Group. Saumoneau, however, more opposed than ever to the formation of a separate group controlled by women whom she suspected of feminism, had it written into the new organization's statutes that membership in the party was a *prerequisite* for joining the group. Thus the group could not recruit women directly; they had to be recruited through the party. As an auxiliary organization for women already in the party, the group could never function as a separate hierarchy, the way the German movement had done so successfully. Moreover, Saumoneau's hostility to bourgeois feminism had become so bitter that it soon drove out the moderate members of the group. She refused even to support the case of a woman printer barred from her work by male trade unionists, arguing that to do so would give aid and comfort to the feminists.

Yet Saumoneau won all these battles because a majority of working women in the group, especially seamstresses, identified with her more than with the apparently bourgeois women who opposed her. Saumoneau was able to tap their energies, so that the French socialist women held their first International Women's Day in March 1914, with Saumoneau presiding at a rally where over two thousand men and women heard speeches by various party personalities. To Saumoneau's great delight, Clara Zetkin sent a telegram: "A socialist women's day at Paris, that's good news indeed."[25] But these promising beginnings were cut short by the war.

SOCIALISM AND WOMEN IN ENGLAND

England had no movement comparable to the German socialist women's movement and yet we cannot speak of the failure of socialism to reach women in the same way as we can in the case of France. Three factors make the English situation particularly complex. First, English socialists did not create a unified party on the Continental model. Only in 1900 was the Labour Representation Committee founded, an umbrella organization which gradually drew in the existing parties and trade unions and could, by 1907, call itself the Labour Party. Its constituent groups remained independent, however. In 1907 and again in 1910, Britain was the only western European nation not to send a unified delegation to the International Socialist Congress; instead, delegations went from the Social Democratic Federation (SDF) of H. M. Hyndman (1842–1921), the Independent Labour Party (ILP) of Keir Hardie (1856–1915), the Fabian Society, and the Labour Party itself. Moreover, reformist trade unionists far outweighed socialists in the Labour Party.

Second, Britain was an effective parliamentary democracy and the suffrage was therefore of vital significance, but, unlike France (where universal male suffrage had been introduced in 1848), Britain still had a property suffrage, which disenfranchised one-third of the adult male population. The right to vote was dependent upon registration at a fixed residence and payment of at least four shillings a week rent or equivalent. This meant that if women obtained the franchise on the same basis as men, most married women would be disqualified. Sylvia Pankhurst estimated that in such an event only one woman in thirteen would vote.[26]

Third, Britain, unlike Germany and France, had a mass-based, radical women's suffrage movement. Although bourgeois women dominated the leadership of the British as of the Continental feminist movements, the British suffragette movement (so-called to distinguish it from the suffragists, who demanded universal adult suffrage and refused to support women's suffrage based on the existing limited franchise) undertook direct action and mobilized support from working-class women, at least in some areas. Jill Liddington and Jill Norris have demonstrated that significant numbers of working-class women actively supported the women's suffrage movement in Manchester, often combining this with trade union or Labour Party militancy. Studies of Germany and France and indeed of Europe as a whole have certainly unearthed nothing comparable. The British could undertake direct action without endangering the existing social order, whereas continental feminists feared that direct action might undermine the existing social and political order. Two revolts and three wars had drastically altered French and German society within living memory, while in Britain the existing order seemed secure. This security gave advocates of women's suffrage greater freedom of action.

None of the three parties that later merged into the early Labour Party had women's organizations before 1906. In that year, the Women's Labour League was founded, largely upon the initiative of Margaret MacDonald (1870–1911; wife of the ILP leader, Ramsay MacDonald), but it existed mainly to support Labour candidates. Liddington and Norris suggest that working-class women who had been active for the suffrage refused to support Labour until the party made a firmer commitment to women's suffrage. Other women hesitated to join the league for fear that, in the absence of the theoretical backbone which characterized Zetkin's movement in Germany, it might only be, as one ILP activist later put it, "a permanent social committee." The league never developed into a significant force. A similar women's committee set up by the SDF in 1906 also came to little.[27]

The British path did not lead toward organizations comparable to Continental socialist women's movements, but rather toward an alliance of Labour and feminism, which was dependent on the Labour Party's making a commitment to women's suffrage. Before the development of the Labour Party, the various organizations which would compose it had a mixed record on women's rights. At one extreme, the SDF, under Hyndman's influence, was hostile to women's suffrage. At the other extreme, the ILP and the Fabian Society supported it; the Society, however, was not and did not aspire to be a mass movement. Of parties aspiring to a mass base, only the ILP under Keir Hardie consistently supported women's suffrage, and even that support developed slowly.

Only after the turn of the century did the ILP take a formal position in support of votes for women. Isabella Ford (ca. 1860–1924), "a prosperous Quaker lady," as Sylvia Pankhurst (1882–1960) described her,[28] and an ardent supporter of women's suffrage, joined the party executive in 1903. In 1904, Emmeline Pankhurst (Sylvia's mother, 1858–1928) also joined the executive, and the party instructed the executive to introduce a bill for the extension of the suffrage to women on the same property basis as men already enjoyed (or did not enjoy) it. But as the nascent Labour Party filled with trade union representatives, who had hardly been anxious to welcome women into their ranks, it shied away from supporting women's suffrage if it meant that only well-to-do women would be enfranchised while many working-class men and most working-class women remained without the vote. At the 1905 Labour Party conference and again in 1906 an SDF representative defeated the ILP position.

The ILP, nevertheless, at its 1907 conference renewed its support for women's suffrage on the same property basis as men's. This position was taken by no other party, socialist or otherwise, and earned the ILP a rebuke from Clara Zetkin at the 1907 International Conference of Socialist Women; to enfranchise bourgeois women, as she and the conference saw it, was anti-socialist.[29] Keir Hardie continued to press for women's suffrage with all the force at his command; at the 1907 Labour Party conference, he even threatened to withdraw from the party because of its refusal to endorse women's suffrage rather than adult suffrage. For Hardie and the ILP, women's suffrage was a question of conscience; even if only propertied women voted while working-class men did not, a partial reform in this direction was preferable to the status quo.

At the end of 1911, the ILP, in Liddington's words "still very much the conscience of the Labour Party," resolved "that proposals for franchise extension which do not confer citizenship upon women should be definitely opposed."[30] This solved the old problem. Those who had hitherto refused to support a franchise for propertied women could not in good conscience accept the government's grant of unrestricted suffrage to men without granting it to women. Thus, in 1912, the Labour Party as a whole accepted a resolution similar to that of the ILP. The following year, both the ILP and the Labour Party reinforced their commitment to oppose any extension of the suffrage which did not include women. Consequently, from 1912 until the war, the National Union of Women's Suffrage Societies and the Women's Freedom League joined together to support Labour, although the Women's Social and Political Union (WSPU, the Pankhursts' group) remained aloof, having broken with Labour in 1907. Thus, if Britain did not develop a socialist women's movement, it did follow another route in keeping with the spirit of Engels' arguments. Engels had certainly approved of alliances between the proletariat and the bourgeoisie to obtain the republic; the alliance between Labour and feminism in the Indian summer of Edwardian England had the same logic behind it.

SCANDINAVIAN SOCIALIST WOMEN'S MOVEMENTS

The potential for an alliance between socialists and feminists was also demonstrated in Finland, although here nationalist liberals were crucial to the success of the coalition. Together with the socialists, they supported women's suffrage as early as 1904 and during the Russian Revolution of 1905 obtained a new constitution providing for universal suffrage for men and women. The women's movement of the Finnish Social Democratic Party was instrumental in bringing the party to demand unrestricted suffrage for women as well as for men. Women could join the party on an equal footing with men, but they chose to create a parallel organization along the lines of that in Germany.

Although the party unified only in 1903, by the end of 1905 it included 9,577 women, almost 21 percent of the total membership, most of them in the party's forty-three women's sections. By 1908, fortified by the new freedom for women to participate in politics, the party had 16,828 women members, nearly 24 percent of the total membership, and women occupied thirteen of the eighty-three socialist seats in parliament. This success resulted from the strength and autonomy of the women's movement, as in Germany, and not simply from women's suffrage: in Norway, the other European nation to establish women's suffrage before 1914 (though on a more restricted basis than for men), the Socialist Women's Movement was weaker than one would expect.[31]

THE SECOND INTERNATIONAL (1889–1914) AND THE AUSTRIAN SOCIALIST WOMEN'S MOVEMENT

With the exception of England, all the other European socialist women's movements ranged between the French and the German models. The stance of these other parties with regard to women was largely determined by the Second Socialist International, which in turn was dominated by the SPD. From its founding congress in 1889, the International had stipulated "that it is the duty of workers to admit women into their ranks, on an equal footing." This resolution assured women the right to join the socialist parties, and until after World War I no other parties accepted women members (though some nonsocialist parties did accept women in auxiliary groups).

Subsequently, the International sought to resolve the dilemma between equality and protective legislation for women. The founding congress of 1889 accepted the principle of equal pay for equal work, but also argued for special protection for women. Only at the 1893 congress did the International resolve this ambiguity. On the one hand, it passed a resolution put forward by Anna Kuliscioff of Italy demanding "equal pay [for women] for equal work" and specifying that protective measures for women should not result in loss of employment opportunity; on the other hand, it passed a resolution put forward by Louise Kautsky of Germany spelling out the measures it had in mind for women workers; these included the eight-hour day, a prohibition of night work and of work in jobs "which are detrimental to their health," and the prohibition of work by pregnant women two weeks before and four weeks after childbirth.[32]

The socialists did not fully spell out their commitment to equality until 1900, when the Paris congress of the International finally addressed itself explicitly to women's suffrage, which it then proclaimed "a necessity for both sexes."[33] Putting this commitment into practice was still, however, a matter for debate in each national section.

The first problem occurred in Belgium. In 1901, the Belgian Socialist Party seemed on the way to obtaining unrestricted manhood suffrage in lieu of the property suffrage then in force. A right-wing Member of Parliament got together the votes for a trap: he offered an amendment for universal suffrage for *both* sexes. He knew that many of the centrist democrats who favored universal men's suffrage feared women's suffrage because they believed women to be under the influence of reactionary priests; with this amendment, the bill would lose. The Belgian socialist women's movement decided to suspend agitation for women's suffrage so as not to jeopardize the bill for men's suffrage.

As a result, the German delegation raised the question of women's suffrage again at the 1904 International Socialist Congress. The congress passed a very forceful and explicit resolution on "universal suffrage for women" so that no party would fall into the Belgian trap. Nevertheless, the Austrian Socialist Party soon repeated the Belgian fiasco.

The Austrian socialist women's movement sought to emulate the German, but lacked the most vital aspect of the German movement, the separate organizational structure for women. The Austrian movement began in the early 1890s, when a small number of Viennese women began meeting as a "working women's educational society." In 1892, the party began to publish a journal for women, the *Arbeiterinnenzeitung* ("Working Women's Newspaper"), edited by Adelheid Popp (1869–1939), the founder and uncontested leader of the Austrian movement. The Austrian movement still lagged far behind the German (although it was far ahead of the French) when a crisis occurred. After the Russian Revolution of 1905, the leadership of the Austrian party began a campaign for universal suffrage. Fearing a backlash if it included the suffrage for women at the same time, the leadership decided to demand only unrestricted male suffrage for the time being. The women's movement accepted this decision in the interests of party harmony and on the basis of the primacy of class loyalties.

For this Clara Zetkin attacked them violently at the first International Conference of Socialist Women, held in conjunction with the 1907 International Socialist Congress. As Zetkin and Baader put it in their draft resolution, "in the fight for the equality of the female sex," the socialists "must not let themselves be overtopped by any bourgeois party, not even the bourgeois women's movement." Zetkin recognized that women might well vote more conservatively than men, which was one of the arguments for postponing women's suffrage, but she pointed out that when women had the suffrage they would participate in the political struggle and learn to support their class interests. Moreover, she argued, to postpone their claim left the impression that they had less right to vote than men; this women should never accept. Bargaining with principles never worked, she argued. Led by Popp, the Austrian women defended themselves as best they could, but the conference supported Zetkin. It passed a strong resolution stating that "the socialist parties of all countries have a duty to struggle energetically for the introduction of universal suffrage for women."[34]

To ensure her victory, Zetkin went on to put a resolution to the full congress of the International declaring that "wherever a struggle is to be waged for the right to vote, it must be conducted only according to Socialist principles, i.e., with the demand for universal suffrage for both women and men." "Every voting rights battle," she commented, "must also be fought as a battle for women's suffrage."[35] The Austrian socialist leader, Victor Adler (1852–1918), proposed an amendment to Zetkin's resolution allowing each national section to determine for itself the right time to begin the struggle for women's suffrage. This would have legitimated the Austrian party's conduct and vitiated the effect of the women's resolution. A French delegate, Dr. Madeleine Pelletier, led the fight against Adler's amendment, making so violent a speech that he withdrew it and the resolution passed as Zetkin had presented it. Subsequently, no national section could subordinate the struggle for women's suffrage to that for men's suffrage without violating a formal resolution of the International. To ensure implementation of this resolution and to spread throughout the parties of the International the German structure of socialist women's organization, the congress voted to set up an independent women's secretariat with Zetkin at its head.

The International's decision galvanized the Austrian women's movement. The following year, in 1908, the Austrian socialist women held a conference at which they agreed that women's suffrage was an inalienable right. The party leadership, chastened perhaps by the drubbing it had received at the international congress, accepted this and went ahead to establish the system of women's spokespersons which had operated so effectively in Germany. As a result, the movement began to grow very rapidly and attained a membership of 15,000 by 1910.

THE ITALIAN SOCIALIST WOMEN'S MOVEMENT

If the Austrian socialist women's movement resembled the German, the Italian socialist women's movement resembled the French; despite some fitful efforts in the 1890s, it was not until the eve of World War I that a serious attempt was made to create a movement modeled on Zetkin's. The Italian Socialist Party, however, differed from the French in being founded as a unified party much earlier—in 1892—and in including among its leaders two dynamic women, both Russians! On the one hand, Angelica Balabanoff (1878–1965) was one of the principal leaders of the left faction of the party. She did not, however, much concern herself with women's issues, preferring instead to act on the national and international stage. On the other hand, Anna Kuliscioff (1854?–1925) played a central role in the founding of the Italian Socialist Party and in all the party's efforts to organize women.

Forced into exile from Russia in 1877, Kuliscioff went to Italy, where she lived with an Italian socialist; they had a daughter in 1881. Finding her companion unable to treat her as an equal, Kuliscioff left him and studied medicine, subsequently practicing in a working-class district of Milan and specializing in gynecology. These experiences and her reading of Marx and Engels led her to socialism. In 1884, she met Filippo Turati (1857–1932), with whom she spent the remainder of her life; they were key figures in the

Italian Socialist Party from its founding in 1892 until its shift to the left in 1912. Although she also remained active in the Italian feminist movement until the late 1890s, she did not make use of her position in the party leadership to press feminist issues until much later.

In a paper presented in 1890, she had made a profound commitment to socialist feminism, echoing Engels' approach: the family, she argued, "will undergo profound modifications which are not yet able to be defined precisely;" "the former domestic relationships based on male domination and on the nuclear family home will be dissolved and a more elevated form of the family, founded upon spontaneity and equality will be prepared."[36] But this did not lead her to introduce feminism into socialism, for reasons which she articulated more clearly than any other socialist feminist leader. Writing in the party magazine in 1897 she argued, "The present feminism of the middle class is merely a reproduction of the revolutionary movement of the male middle class a century ago. Freedom for woman, conquered during the period of its [the middle classes'] economic monopoly, can only be freedom for the middle class woman." Like Engels, she did not mean by this that feminism was unacceptable; on the contrary, the conquests of the revolutionary bourgeoisie, as embodied in the French revolution, were foundations on which the working class had to build. But "socialism and feminism, if they can be parallel social currents, cannot be one sole cause."[37]

Kuliscioff's work in Milan led her, however, to see the need for women's groups and to involve herself with the Milanese Socialist Women's Group, founded in 1897, initially to support the Socialist Party in the elections of that year. Subsequently the group enlarged its sphere of activity, organizing working men and women in support of Kuliscioff's bill to protect women and children workers. While this did not lead to the independent organization of women, it did lead to a massive campaign of meetings, well attended by women, culminating in 1902 in over three hundred meetings throughout Italy and final passage of Kuliscioff's bill by Parliament.

Only after the 1907 International Socialist Congress had passed Zetkin's hard-hitting resolution for women's suffrage did Kuliscioff begin to push the party to support women's suffrage. During 1910, she attacked her partner Turati and other leaders of the party for failing to support women's suffrage. At the 1910 party congress, she presented a resolution enjoining the party to undertake "agitation for the vote for women . . . as an altogether indispensable, utilitarian and idealist necessity to the life and development of the party."[38] The resolution passed; the next step was to organize women.

Kuliscioff pointed out to the 1910 congress that there were fewer women proportionately in the Italian party than in the German and Austrian parties, although she did not give specific figures. The 1911 congress voted funds for a women's newspaper and designated Kuliscioff as editor. In June 1912, at the national party congress and at the first national conference of socialist women (held in conjunction with the congress), Kuliscioff led the effort to found a National Socialist Women's Union and was the most important personality of the three-woman executive committee elected there.

The same congress, however, saw the victory of the left faction, then led by Balabanoff and the young Benito Mussolini (1883–1945), whom Balabanoff—to her everlasting regret—had installed as editor of the party newspaper (he did not begin his swing toward fascism until the war broke out). The left faction expelled some moderate leaders and took control of the party away from Turati, Kuliscioff, and their group. By the end of the year, Kuliscioff had resigned both as editor of the newspaper and as member of the executive of the women's group.

Balabanoff replaced Kuliscioff on the women's executive, but she did not think the matter important enough to mention it in her autobiography.[39] She had argued in 1904 against creating "a feminist socialism since for us the so-called feminist problem does not exist." She was not indifferent to the need to organize women—in 1904 and 1905, she took a major part in a campaign to organize Italian working women in Switzerland—but she concerned herself primarily with ongoing—male—politics.[40] In 1921, the party split, the left wing breaking off to found the Italian Communist Party. Balabanoff had already committed herself to communism and the Russian Revolution; Kuliscioff stayed in the Socialist Party with Turati, but the following year the remaining socialists split, expelling Kuliscioff, Turati and their faction as too right-wing. The coming to power of fascism brought an end to a movement which had shown promise, if so briefly, before World War I.

THE SOCIALIST WOMEN'S MOVEMENTS FROM WORLD WAR I TO WORLD WAR II

Indeed, throughout Europe the war posed a new problem for socialism and in particular for the socialist women's movements, by cutting across sex and faction lines. Clara Zetkin, on the left of her party like Balabanoff, strongly opposed the war. On November 7, 1914, Zetkin issued an appeal to socialist women to struggle for peace: "When the men kill, it is up to us women to fight for the preservation of life. When the men are silent, it is our duty to raise our voices on behalf of our ideals."[41] In France, Louise Saumoneau distributed Zetkin's appeal in a clandestine brochure early in 1915. Socialist women in other countries soon followed suit.

On the basis of this appeal, Zetkin organized an international conference of socialist women at Berne in March 1915, six months before socialist men of the left held a similar conference at Zimmerwald (also in Switzerland). Although the majority of the twenty-eight delegates (including Balabanoff, who did all the translating for the conference) were from neutral countries, several were from Germany and England, a number from Russia (including four Bolsheviks), and one from France: Louise Saumoneau. The Berne Conference showed the potential power of socialist women, but it was not followed by any further action; instead, the socialist women of the various parties devoted their energies to their factions, in working for or against the war as they saw fit. At the end of the war, the socialist women's movement lay in ruins.

Clara Zetkin had joined the antiwar German Independent Socialist Party (USPD) along with Rosa Luxemburg (1870–1919) and Karl Liebknecht (1871–1919). When the government, composed of leaders from the old prowar SPD, put down the left-wing "Spartacist" revolt against the Weimar Republic at the beginning of 1919 and allowed the murder of Liebknecht and Luxemburg to go unpunished, Zetkin became deeply embittered. Joining Lenin's Third International, she gave the remaining years of her life to communism. Popp took over Zetkin's position in the Second International when it was reconstituted, but the reconstituted Second International was only a ghost of its former self and, in virtually all European countries except Austria, the reconstituted socialist women's movement was no longer a powerful and independent force on the left of the party but a women's auxiliary of an essentially male party.

Even without Zetkin the German SPD attracted great numbers of women in the euphoria immediately following the revolution that overthrew the Kaiser and installed the Weimar Republic with SPD leaders at its head. In 1919, women made up more than 20 percent of the membership, a new high point. But many women soon left the party, disappointed by the conservatism of the SPD government. In 1923, the number of women had dropped to 130,000, or just over 10 percent of the membership, but from this point until Hitler's accession to power, it increased, reaching a high point in 1931 of 230,351 members, or 22.8 percent of the total membership. The party elected nineteen women members of parliament in 1919; the number of women in parliament dropped to a low point of eleven in 1924 before reaching a further high of twenty in 1928. In contrast to the years before the war, the party newspapers emphasized motherhood and traditional feminine roles instead of Marxist theory, but this did not ensure success or even increased diffusion: no party newspaper obtained the circulation which *Die Gleichheit* had enjoyed in the years before the war.

In France, the SFIO had voted to join the Third International and thus became the Communist Party in 1920. Those who sought to continue the SFIO independently of the International had to start anew. Louise Saumoneau, unlike Zetkin, shrank from joining the Third International and returned to the SFIO. She and the other leaders of the prewar women's movement reconstructed it on the old lines and reproduced the old failures. In 1930, the prewar Socialist Women's Group was reconstituted as the National Committee of Socialist Women, with a national mandate and support from the party hierarchy. Nevertheless, it still did not recruit women directly, but only offered an additional activity to women already in the party. Thus it had no effect on the numbers of women in the party, which reached a high point of 9,568, still only 3.34 percent of the total membership. This was at the beginning of 1938, following the party's success in the 1936 elections, which put it at the head of a coalition government called the Popular Front. The women's movement, however, made no effort to seize the opportunity presented by the party's being in government and never mentioned women's suffrage while the socialists were in power, although three socialist women leaders served as under-secretaries of state.

In Italy, as we have seen, things went from bad to worse. Only in Austria did the socialist women's movement make progress after the war, because in Austria the party remained largely unified and women enjoyed the suffrage. Under Popp's leadership, the Austrian movement continued to flourish, while the split between socialism and communism significantly weakened other socialist women's movements. By 1925, the Austrian movement had 165,000 members, constituting 29.7 percent of the total party membership. By this time, the party was taking very advanced positions, with the socialist women fighting not only for protective legislation for women workers, but also for changes in the household and even for birth control and abortion. Popp and her movement drew upon the strength of the working-class movement in "Red Vienna." But the fascists destroyed the Austrian Social Democratic Party in 1934 (Popp was among the leaders arrested) and smashed the last strong socialist women's movement remaining on the Continent.

CONCLUSION

The socialist women's movement did not achieve its program in its own time. Political equality came only after World War I (in some countries only after World War II) and fascism rolled back many women's gains. Economic equality remained a battle to be fought even after World War II, and complete equality still eludes the grasp of both women and workers. The short-term goals of better wages and conditions were partially fulfilled by the trade union movement, but the long-term goals of socialism—economic independence for women and "higher" forms of work and family life, transcending "the monogamous family as the economic unit of society" and establishing the freer, more just and more community-oriented society promised by socialism—seem as elusive as ever.

Yet the socialist women's movement left a positive legacy. First, even in the countries where the socialist women's movement was weakest, it reached more women than the bourgeois feminists ever hoped to reach. To be sure, feminism was weak on the Continent, but even in their strongest moments the feminists were held back by their class background and found themselves unable to make contact with working-class women. The socialist parties did reach working-class women, however few, and even when taking their harshest line against bourgeois feminism, as in France, they nevertheless taught working-class women independence and self-respect and gave them a voice of their own, much as the American abolitionist movement did for the early American suffragists.

Second, the socialist women's movement provided a strategy for equality: in welcoming economic independence, however painful it seemed at the time, the movement foreshadowed the demands of socialist feminism today.

Third, the socialist parties gave women a platform to act effectively in politics, at a time when other parties would not even admit women to their ranks. Even leaders who, like Angelica Balabanoff and Rosa Luxemburg, refused to work in the socialist women's movement still provided inspiration for other women as role models. Luxemburg, for instance, preferred to deploy her enormous intellect on the wider stage of the practical and theoretical issues in the party as a whole, but she nevertheless inspired German socialist women, from her close friend and comrade Clara Zetkin to rank-and-file militants.

The most lasting legacy of the socialist women's movement is thus the development of separate organization for working-class women and a consequent articulation of their distinct concerns. This is what characterized the most successful national movements. This success bore fruit when women voted: those parties which had developed effective women's organizations had a head start on those which had failed to do so.

The ability of the socialist parties to attract women now more than ever affects their success as a whole. The German and Austrian SPD have often been in power as part of coalition governments since World War II, partly because of their strong blocs of women members. The French socialists have been successful only in coalitions, first with the center and then with the communists. To be sure, this is in large measure a result of party fragmentation, but it is also a result of the party's failure to implant itself among women; the ghost of Louise Saumoneau still plagues the French socialists, while the heritage of Zetkin and Baader still aids their less radical heirs.

NOTES

1. See Offen, Chapter 13 in this volume.
2. Quoted in Charles Sowerwine, *Sisters or Citizens? Women and Socialism in France since 1876* (Cambridge: Cambridge University Press, 1982), p. 22.
3. *Women, the Family, and Freedom: The Debate in Documents*, ed. Susan Groag Bell and Karen Offen (Stanford: Stanford University Press, 1983), I, 191.
4. Harold Benenson, "Victorian Sexual Ideology and Marx's Theory of the Working Class," *International Labor and Working Class History*, 25 (Spring 1984),

1–23; Barbara Taylor, "Lords of Creation: Marxism, Feminism and 'Utopian' Socialism," *Radical America*, 14 (July–August 1980), 41–49. Taylor's views are more nuanced in the superb introduction to *Eve and the New Jerusalem: Socialism and Feminism in the Nineteenth Century* (London: Virago Press, 1983), pp. ix–xviii.

5. Leslie Goldstein, "Mill, Marx, and Women's Liberation," *Journal of the History of Philosophy*, 17 (July 1980), 319–334; Lise Vogel, *Marx and the Oppression of Women* (New Brunswick, N.J.: Rutgers University Press, 1983), pp. 41–72.

6. Karl Marx, "Economic and Philosophical Manuscripts of 1844," in *Marx's Concept of Man*, ed. Eric Fromm; trans. T. Bottomore (New York: Frederick Ungar Publishing Co., 1961), p. 125.

7. Frederick Engels, *The Origin of the Family, Private Property and the State*, ed. Eleanor Burke Leacock; trans. Alec West (New York: International Publishers, 1972), p. 137.

8. *Ibid.*

9. Karl Marx, *Capital: A Critique of Political Economy*, trans. Ben Fowkes (Harmondsworth, Middlesex, England: Penguin, 1976), Vol. I, pp. 620–21.

10. August Bebel, *Woman Under Socialism*, trans. Daniel De Leon (New York: Labor News Press, 1904; reprint, New York: Schocken Books, 1971), pp. 187–188, 216–224.

11. *Ibid.*, pp. 39, 80, 119, 140, 182.

12. *Ibid.*, p. 9.

13. *Clara Zetkin: Selected Writings*, ed. Philip S. Foner; trans. Kai Schoenhals (New York: International Publishers, 1984), p. 79.

14. Quoted by Jean H. Quataert, "Unequal Partners in an Uneasy Alliance: Women and the Working-Class in Imperial Germany," in *Socialist Women: European Socialist Feminism in the Nineteenth and Early Twentieth Centuries*, ed. Marilyn J. Boxer and Jean H. Quataert (New York: Elsevier, 1978), p. 120.

15. Karl Kautsky, *The Class Struggle (Erfurt Program)*, trans. William E. Bohn (New York: Norton, 1971), pp. 127–128.

16. Quoted in Sowerwine, *Sisters or Citizens?*, p. 26.

17. Werner Thönnessen, *The Emancipation of Women: The Rise and Decline of the Women's Movement in German Social Democracy 1863–1933*, trans. Joris de Bres (London: Pluto Press, 1973), pp. 48, 62. The original German word is *Vertrauensmann;* it was changed to *Vertrauensperson.*

18. Foner, ed., *Zetkin: Selected Writings*, pp. 46–47.

19. *Ibid.*, pp. 76, 99.

20. Quoted in Jean H. Quataert, *Reluctant Feminists in German Social Democracy, 1885–1917* (Princeton: Princeton University Press), p. 125.

21. Quotes *ibid.*, pp. 110, 116.

22. Quoted in Sowerwine, *Sisters or Citizens?*, p. 85 (emphasis in original).

23. Quotes *ibid.*, pp. 77, 79.

24. Richard J. Evans, *The Feminist Movement in Germany* (Beverly Hills, Calif.: Sage Publications, 1976); Steven C. Hause with Anne R. Kenney, *Women's Suffrage and Social Politics in the French Third Republic* (Princeton: Princeton University Press, 1984).

25. Quoted in Sowerwine, *Sisters or Citizens?*, p. 139.

26. Sylvia Pankhurst, *The Suffragette Movement: An Intimate Account of Persons and Ideals* (London: Longman, 1931; reprint, London: Virago, 1977), p. 242. For an account of the suffrage system see Neal Blewett, *The Peers, the Parties, and the People: The General Elections of 1910* (London: Macmillan, 1972), pp. 357–371.

27. Jill Liddington, *The Life and Times of a Respectable Rebel: Selina Cooper (1864–1946)*, (London: Virago, 1984), p. 178; Jill Liddington and Jill Norris, *One Hand Tied Behind Us: The Rise of the Women's Suffrage Movement* (London: Virago, 1978), pp. 235–236; Hannah M.W. Mitchell (1871–1956), *The Hard Way Up: The Autobiography of Hannah Mitchell, Suffragette and Rebel* (London: Faber, 1968; reprint, London: Virago, 1977), p. 189.

28. Pankhurst, *The Suffragette Movement*, pp. 167–169.

29. *Zetkin: Selected Writings*, p. 104.

30. Liddington, *Respectable Rebel*, p. 223.

31. L'Internationale ouvrière & socialiste, *Rapports soumis au congrès socialiste internationale de Stuttgart (18–24 Août, 1907)* (Brussels: Bureau socialiste internationale, 1907), II, 153, 163, 171; "Report of the Social Democratic Party [Finland]," *Reports on the Labour and Socialist Movement. Presented by Affiliated Parties to the International Socialist Congress of Copenhagen, August 28th–September 3rd, 1910*, in *Histoire de la IIe Internationale, Congrès Socialiste Internationale, Copenhague, 28 Août–3 Septembre 1910* (Geneva: Minkoff Reprint, 1982), pp. 1841–1844, 1867–1868; "Norway," *ibid.*, pp. 1875, 1880.

32. *European Women: A Documentary History, 1789–1945*, ed. Eleanor S. Riemer and John C. Fout (New York: Schocken Books, 1980), p. 92.

33. Quoted in Sowerwine, *Sisters or Citizens?*, pp. 196.

34. *Proposals and Drafts of Resolutions Submitted to the International Socialist Congress of Stuttgart (18–24 August 1907)* (Brussels: International Socialist Bureau, 1907), pp. 567–571; "Anhang: Erste internationale Konferenz sozialisticher Frauen," in *Internationaler Sozialistenkongress zu Stuttgart, 18 bis 24. August 1907* (Berlin: Verlag Buchhandlung Vorwärts, 1907), p. 128 and passim; *Women, the Family, and Freedom*, II, 231–232.

35. *Zetkin: Selected Writings*, pp. 98, 105.

36. Quoted in Claire LaVigna, "The Marxist Ambivalence Toward Women: Between Socialism and Feminism in the Italian Socialist Party," in Boxer and Quataert, *Socialist Women*, p. 170.

37. Quoted *ibid.*, pp. 148–149.

38. Quoted *ibid.*, p. 159.

39. Angelica Balabanoff, *My Life as a Rebel* (New York, 1938; Bloomington: Indiana University Press, 1973); on the other hand, she deemed the victory of her faction at the congress to be worthy of four pages: *ibid.*, pp. 95–98.

40. Nancy G. Eshelman, "Forging a Socialist Women's Movement: Angelica Balabanoff in Switzerland," in *The Italian Immigrant Women in North America*, eds. Betty Boyd Caroli, Robert F. Harney and Lydio F. Tomasi (Toronto: Multicultural History Society of Ontario, 1978), p. 67.

41. *Zetkin: Selected Writings*, p. 116.

SUGGESTIONS FOR FURTHER READING

The utopian socialist feminists are covered in two excellent monographs: for Britain, Barbara Taylor, *Eve and the New Jerusalem: Socialism and Feminism in the Nineteenth Century* (London: Virago Press, 1983); for France, Claire Goldberg Moses, *French Feminism in the Nineteenth Century* (Albany: State University of New York Press, 1983). Students should read key original texts: *The Utopian Vision of Charles Fourier: Selected Texts on Work, Love, and Passionate Attraction*, ed. and trans. Jonathan Beecher and Richard Bienvenu (Boston: Beacon Press, 1971); Flora Tristan, *The Workers' Union*, trans. Beverly Livingston (Urbana: University of Illinois Press, 1983); and William Thompson [& Anna Wheeler], *Appeal of One-Half the Human Race* (London, 1825; London: Virago, 1983).

An excellent introduction to Marxism and women is Lise Vogel, *Marx and the Oppression of Women* (New Brunswick, N.J.: Rutgers University Press, 1983). The key primary texts are Frederick Engels, *The Origin of the Family, Private Property and the State*, ed. Eleanor Burke Leacock; trans. Alec West (New York: International Publishers, 1972), and August Bebel, *Woman under Socialism*, trans. Daniel de Leon (New York .Labor News Press, 1904; reprint, New York: Schocken Books, 1971). A useful survey of Marxian socialist feminism is Alena Heitlinger, "The Historical Development of European Socialist Feminism," *Catalyst*, 10–11 (1977), 125–151.

For the German movement, Werner Thönnessen, *The Emancipation of Women: The Rise and Decline of the Women's Movement in German Social Democracy 1863–1933*, trans. Joris de Bres (London: Pluto Press, 1973), provides a straightforward introduction. More sophisticated treatment is provided by Jean H. Quataert, *Reluctant Feminists in German Social Democracy, 1885–1917* (Princeton: Princeton University Press, 1979). While Richard J. Evans' important study remains untranslated, students will find his three articles informative and provocative: "German Social Democracy and Women's Suffrage 1891–1918," *Journal of Contemporary History*, 15 (1980), 533–557; "Politics and the Family: Social Democracy and the Working-Class Family in Theory and Practice before 1914," in *The German Family: Essays on the Social History of the Family in Nineteenth- and Twentieth-Century Germany*, ed. Richard J. Evans and W. R. Lee (London: Croom Helm, 1981), pp. 256–288; and "Theory and Practice in German Social Democracy 1880–1914: Clara Zetkin and the Socialist Theory of Women's Emancipation," *History of Political Thought*, 3 (1982), 285–304. Finally, students should consult the excellent work of Karen Honeycutt, "Clara Zetkin: A Socialist Approach to the Problem of Women's Oppression," in *European Women on the Left: Socialism, Feminism, and the Problems faced by Political Women, 1880 to the Present*, ed. Jane Slaughter and Robert Kern (Westport, Conn.: Greenwood Press, 1981), pp. 13–28. Students will like *Clara Zetkin: Selected Writings*, ed. Philip S. Foner; trans. Kai Schoenhals (New York: International Publishers, 1984). While we lack a good English-language biography of Clara Zetkin, an enjoyable biography of Lily Braun which tells her side of the story is Alfred G. Meyer, *The Feminism and Socialism of Lily Braun* (Bloomington: Indiana University Press, 1985).

For the French movement, the argument made in this essay is developed in Charles

Sowerwine, *Sisters or Citizens? Women and Socialism in France since 1876* (Cambridge: Cambridge University Press, 1982), which also deals with the International and with the socialist women's opposition to World War I. An introduction to the French movement in its European context is Charles Sowerwine, "The Organization of French Socialist Women, 1880–1914: A European Perspective for Women's Movements," *Historical Reflections*, 3, No. 2 (Winter 1976), 1–24. Marilyn J. Boxer emphasizes the socialists' sexism rather than organizational structures in her "Socialism Faces Feminism: The Failure of Synthesis in France, 1879–1914," in *Socialist Women: European Socialist Feminism in the Nineteenth and Early Twentieth Centuries*, ed. Marilyn J. Boxer and Jean H. Quataert (New York: Elsevier, 1978), pp. 75–111, and in her "When Radical and Socialist Feminism Were Joined: The Extraordinary Failure of Madeleine Pelletier," in *European Women on the Left*, eds. Slaughter and Kern, pp. 51–74.

For the complexities of party politics and women's movements in England, see: Sandra Holton, *Feminism and Democracy: Women's Suffrage and Reform Politics in Britain 1900–1920* (Cambridge: Cambridge University Press, 1986), a particularly balanced and sensitive study; Les Garner, *Stepping Stones to Women's Liberty: Feminist Ideas in the Women's Suffrage Movement 1900–1918* (London: Heinemann, 1984); the pioneering study by Jill Liddington and Jill Norris, *One Hand Tied Behind Us: The Rise of the Women's Suffrage Movement* (London: Virago, 1978); and Jill Liddington's splendid biography of a middle-level militant: *The Life and Times of a Respectable Rebel: Selina Cooper (1864–1946)* (London: Virago, 1984).

For the Scandinavian movements, the only readily available source is Richard J. Evans, *The Feminists: Women's Emancipation Movements in Europe, America and Australasia 1840–1920* (London: Croom Helm, 1977). For Austria, see Ingrun Lafleur, "Five Socialist Women: Traditionalist Conflicts and Socialist Visions in Austria, 1893–1934," in *Socialist Women*, ed. Boxer and Quataert, pp. 215–248, and especially Adelheid Popp's moving account of her youth and conversion to socialism, *The Autobiography of a Working Woman*, trans. F. C. Harvey (London, 1912; reprint, Westport, Conn.: Hyperion, 1981).

For Italy, more is available. I have relied heavily on Claire LaVigna, "The Marxist Ambivalence Toward Women: Between Socialism and Feminism in the Italian Socialist Party," in *Socialist Women*, ed. Boxer and Quataert, pp. 146–181. Students may also consult Beverly Tanner Springer, "Anna Kuliscioff: Russian Revolutionist, Italian Feminist," in *European Women on the Left*, ed. Slaughter and Kern, pp. 13–28, and Jane Slaughter, "Humanism versus Feminism in the Socialist Movement: The Life of Angelica Balabanoff," in *European Women on the Left*, ed. Slaughter and Kern, pp. 179–194. Although Balabanoff does not discuss women's issues in her autobiography, it is still well worth reading: *My Life as a Rebel* (New York: 1938; reprint, Bloomington: Indiana University Press, 1973).

A Russian women's demonstration in 1917. (Sovfoto)

chapter 16

Women and Communal Strikes in the Crisis of 1917–1922

Temma Kaplan

Women in the working classes in rapidly growing cities confronted both the age-old problems related to caring for their families and new hardships associated with industrialization. Even when they did not participate in wage labor, as Laura Frader demonstrates, women provided support for their families. Temma Kaplan's essay continues the narrative of women's struggles and relates them to mass strikes in the twentieth century. In times of crisis, women's special responsibilities to their communities and families gave them a different set of needs and a unique vantage point from which to evaluate the situation. Economic depression, often exacerbated by wartime deprivation, induced women in poor urban areas to demonstrate for food, governmental reform, and justice. Unlike the radical women described by Richard Stites and Charles Sowerwine, these women had little prior direct political involvement, but acted out of what Kaplan calls "female consciousness." Having fulfilled their obligations as mothers, wives, and family members, desperate women felt a sense of entitlement to demand the minimum subsistence necessary to continue to carry out their roles. In settings as diverse as St. Petersburg, Milan, Málaga, and Veracruz, women from the working classes acted in crisis, defending their traditional rights and advocating a vision of a just social order.

During World War I and its aftermath, poor women throughout the world often engaged in communal strikes. *Communal strikes* were insurrections in which the women of a neighborhood began by demanding food, fuel, or moderately priced housing until they succeeded in rousing massive support from the men of their class. Together they forced their governments to take action. If men and women in most cultures and historical periods have learned from childhood that women have a special duty to maintain the lives of their families and friends, women have often presumed that they have the right to get food and provide housing even when shortages make those tasks nearly impossible—the situation that existed around World War I. I have called the awareness by which such women and certain male authorities recognized the prerogatives of poor women "female consciousness."[1]

Political participation by poor women during World War I was limited to communal strikes and to some involvement in campaigns for the right to vote in countries like Great Britain.[2] Women had the right to vote only in Norway and Finland until the Provisional Government in Russia, formed as a result of the February Revolution, granted female suffrage in 1917. Since few working women entered trade unions in Europe until after the war, the modern communal strike was the principal form of female political activity in the era of World War I, and the effective militancy women displayed in this era requires explanation.

THE NATURE OF FEMALE CONSCIOUSNESS
IN THE URBAN WORKING CLASS

Working-class women had informal ties that they activated in times of crisis. When these women demonstrated against bakers, landlords, coal merchants, or others who the women believed were speculating on the price of necessities, they followed familiar social paths and allied with women they saw every day. Despite the apparent spontaneity of the kinds of mass movements in which poorer women engaged during World War I, there was a pattern to their activities that followed the grids of everyday life. These women were neighbors, who cared for each other's children, and were familiar with one another because they went to the same churches and markets. Elite and middle-class women, of course, had also been socialized to believe that women had certain obligations and privileges; however, they seldom created the dense web of relationships with neighbors that poor women did at the public markets, in wash houses, or at the fountains (before the introduction of running water).

My thanks to Victoria de Grazia, Dana Frank, Lynn Mally, Paul Mattick, Robert Moeller, Bennett Sims, and Meredith Tax for suggestions they have made along the way. This chapter is part of a larger study that was supported in 1982–1983 by a Rockefeller Humanities Fellowship.

The working-class women who participated in the movements discussed here lived in cities in which irregularities in food supplies and housing were exacerbated by repeated revolutions and wars. The cities where the actions took place combined two special qualities that were prerequisites for communal strikes: neighborhoods stood close to workplaces; and government officials were visible enough that the women themselves could make contact with the state without venturing too far from the safety of their own neighborhoods. When their workplaces were near their homes, those women who worked for wages found their principal allies in other women of their class, with whom they shared responsibilities for preserving their communities. In cities where residence and work were nearby and authorities were known by face and thus thought to be personally accountable, the working-class women's area of operation was the marketplace and surrounding neighborhood streets rather than the factory floor. Under these conditions, women acted in concert with neighbors against governors rather than with fellow workers against employers.

By the seventeenth century, every government in Europe knew that unless the government purchased grain to feed the poor in the cities, the threat of shortages would lead to protests. In the late eighteenth centuries, however, authorities preferred to allow prices of bread to fluctuate according to market values. When costs rose and the poor began to suffer, the governments repressed the populace rather than placating them with subsidized bread prices. When men and women rose up to demand subsidies, they claimed a right to a fair share of food according to a "moral economy."[3]

Although demands for necessities often resulted in massacres, authorities sometimes reacted more sympathetically to women than to men. When crowds consisted only of women or of men dressed as women (as in the Rebecca Riots in mid-nineteenth-century Wales or in the Maria of the Fountain movement in Portugal), the participants assumed that women had privileges beyond those guaranteed by law.[4] Such crowds often spoke of community rather than of individual rights. The female consciousness of these men and women empowered them to claim special benefits that balanced women's special duties as wives, mothers, and preservers of their societies with rights to act against authorities in the name of the greater good of the community.

Before the late nineteenth century, collective action in pursuit of subsistence issues was cyclical. Periodic shortages led to periodic uprisings. In the mid-nineteenth century, men of the popular classes found a way to break the cycle through sustained political effort in the form of unions and parties, which focussed on working conditions and political rights rather than on the family and neighborhood. These men formulated strategies that would enable them to plan for future economic and political redistribution of resources. But in the course of changing emphasis, they lost track of many of the daily subsistence issues with which working-class women were most concerned.[5]

In 1864, with the establishment of the First International Workingman's Association, a loose confederation of largely male unions, socialist clubs, newspapers, and cooperative societies in Europe and America, the male struggle for radical adjustments in society assumed new organizational form.[6] Strategies for long-term changes in economics and politics replaced so-called utopian ideas about the possibilities of perfecting human beings, families, and whole communities. Despite concern about female and child labor among men in the First International, few women themselves affiliated with the organization.

Communal strikes, beginning in the latter third of the nineteenth century, differed from earlier insurrections insofar as they occurred where unions and working-class political parties already existed; this difference moved the principal arena of male politics from the community to the workplace or the state. But even those women who worked outside the home continued to organize collectively in their neighborhoods. While socialist men focussed their attention after the turn of the century on transforming society, working class women became the principal guardians of existing communities.

Communal strikes seldom began with political demands. Instead, they almost invariably were cries of protest by women against conditions that made it impossible for them to protect life. The dislocations of World War I left working-class women to defend their communities while many working-class men died as soldiers or fought as socialists and anarchists to transform political and economic systems. When working-class women took collective action, they were aroused about more immediate issues—social concerns of everyday life such as food, fuel, and shelter. These women never created permanent associations based on female consciousness in the way that their male allies developed revolutionary organizations based on the principles of anarchism and socialism; nevertheless, female consciousness contributed to a continued sense of community in twentieth-century Europe.

WOMEN'S ACTIVITIES IN LAUNCHING THE FEBRUARY 1917 REVOLUTION IN RUSSIA

World War I disrupted food supplies and cut into fuel provisions everywhere in Europe. The year between February 1917 and January 1918 witnessed urban rebellions caused by food and fuel shortages. Typical were those in Petrograd, Russia; Turin, Italy; and Malaga, Spain. The rapid urbanization that characterized European cities from the late nineteenth century on culminated during World War I epoch in high rents, housing shortages, and diminished fuel supplies. The same cycles of war and revolution that overtook Europe also swept Asia, Africa, and Latin America.

In February 1917, after three years of war during which over two million Russian soldiers died, the Russian government failed to supply food and fuel to its civilian population. Because of this failure, women in Petrograd launched a communal strike that in its final stages culminated in the overthrow of the Tsarist autocracy, against which there had been revolutionary activities for decades. In 1905, militant action had resulted in a massacre following which the government was forced to establish a parliament, known as the Duma; however, this body was actually powerless. The upheaval that began with a communal strike in 1917, however, removed the Tsar and resulted in the creation of a Provisional Government, which was meant to lay the foundations of a liberal political system in Russia. The Provisional Government was unstable, and was toppled by the Bolsheviks in October of 1917. Acting in advance of the unionized working class, women precipitated the fall of the Tsar in February 1917 with demands for bread. They thus initiated a revolutionary process that led to the Bolshevik Revolution.

Hunger was epidemic in early 1917—just as hardships due to unemployment had been in 1905—and the St. Petersburg population remembered what had happened then. On Bloody Sunday, January 6, 1905, a crowd carrying icons and led by an Orthodox Priest, Father Gapon, gathered in the plaza in front of the Tsar's Winter Palace in St. Petersburg to petition for relief. The Tsar's soldiers mowed them down, killing 1,000 and wounding countless others; among the victims were numerous women and children.[7]

Between the 1905 Russian Revolution and the end of the first year of World War I in 1915, rents more than doubled in Petrograd, (the name that replaced St. Petersburg from 1914 to 1924, when the city was renamed Leningrad.) Food prices, particularly the cost of flour and bread, rose between 80 and 120 percent in most European cities. The price per pound of rye bread, the staple of working class diets in Petrograd, rose from 3 kopeks in 1913 to 18 kopeks in 1916. Even soap, necessary to maintain clean clothes and human dignity, rose 245 percent in 1917 Petrograd.[8] The failure of governments to ration scarce resources and the widespread belief that speculators benefited from the misery of the poor challenged the ability of states throughout Europe to govern.

Merchants speculated in grain, fuel, and meat prices, while factories from Russia to Spain dismissed workers for lack of fuel to run the plants. Male and female wage earners who faced layoffs often went on strike. Between January and February 1917, more than half a million Russian workers, mostly in Petrograd, left their jobs, and households suffered from poverty and scarcity.

The police reported at the beginning of 1917 that Petrograd was a powderkeg.

It is believed that the slightest disturbance, on the smallest pretext, will lead to uncontrollable riots with thousands of victims. In fact, the conditions for such an explosion already exist. The economic conditions of the masses, in spite of large raises in wages, is near the point of distress. . . . Even if wages are doubled, the cost of living has trebled. The impossibility of obtaining goods, the loss of time spent queueing up in front of stores, the increasing mortality rate because of poor housing conditions, the cold and dampness resulting from lack of coal . . . —all these conditions have created such a situation that the mass of industrial workers is ready to break out in the most savage of hunger riots.[9]

The report neglected to note that all the conditions presumed to lead to an uprising fell into that sphere where the needs and obligations of all women gave them special rights to be outraged.

Most of the female 55 percent of the labor force of Petrograd in 1917 worked in unskilled positions, especially in the textile industries. After eleven- or twelve-hour shifts, the women returned home to wash, mend, take care of children, and get food. They joined their mothers, sisters, and daughters on the bread lines. A contemporary wrote in the Bolshevik women's newspaper that women had to ask themselves:

And with what will you feed them when goods grow continually dearer and the earnings are so small? . . . Exhausted, sick from unhealthy, endless mill work, knowing no peace at home, from morning to night, day in and day out, month after month, the worker mother drudges and knows only need, only worry and grief. Her life passes in gloom, without light. . . . [10]

Russian women used the occasion of International Woman's Day (March 8 in the West but February 23 on the Julian calendar, observed in Russia) to call a meeting for "Bread and Peace," which provoked a communal strike. International Women's Day began as a means to unite the working-class community around a set of common goals, including the recognition of women's rights corresponding to their traditional obligation to feed their loved ones. From the inauguration of International Women's Day in the United States in 1909, Western Europe in 1911, and Russia in 1913, the day had become an opportunity to celebrate female consciousness and to assert women's rights to defend the working-class community.[11]

On International Women's Day, February 23, 1917, women of the militant Vyborg District, the most incendiary part of Petrograd, organized a strike in the textile mills. They convinced even those women who had earlier preferred not to go on strike to join them, and together they marched to the breadlines. Only then, after the women had gathered their forces in the streets and asserted their control over the crowd, did the insurrection spread to the huge machine shops whose male workers gave the district its well-deserved reputation for radicalism. Outside the shops, women shouted,

"Down with war and high prices! Down with starvation! Bread for Workers! Bread!" Singing revolutionary songs, the women ransacked bakeries and grocery shops, while the men went to the other local factories and demanded of male workers that they support the struggle for bread that the women were already leading. Together, men and women marched down the sumptuous street known as the Bolshoi Prospekt, where members of the nobility, merchants, and government officials had their homes. Along the same street stood the academies, sections of the university, a high school, and a women's adult education center. The women already knew that the students, experienced agitators, would give them support. The Vyborg District's proximity to the centers of power, connected as it was by a bridge across the Neva River to the Winter Palace, the Admiralty, and Army Headquarters, had made women of Vyborg believe that they were unusually knowledgeable about the politics of the Russian state. The women's sense that their governors were people with whom they had a relationship meant that they held the government—not just the merchants—responsible for high costs and shortages.

The patterns of mobilization repeated themselves in other major working-class neighborhoods, such as those on Vasilevsky Island and in the Petrograd District. The poorest working-class women on Vasilevsky Island had the experience of mingling with lower-middle-class women of the artisan class. Because both groups of women shopped in the same markets, they knew each other by face and could call upon each other in times of scarcity. The Petrograd District consisted of seven islands, with the working-class neighborhoods on the west and northeast shores. Over 2,000 women worked producing medical supplies there and countless others worked in three large textile mills.[12] After working all day, these women stood together in bread lines in the hopes of securing food for their families. Through these shared experiences the working-class women of these districts intensified their female consciousness in the struggle to save their communities.

Throughout Petrograd, in the days succeeding International Women's Day, women took action. They marched from the working-class suburbs to the Tauride Gardens in front of the Duma, symbolic center of political power in the Russian state, where the workers from the metallurgical factories joined them. From neighborhoods on the other side of the Neva from the Duma, women marched to the jails, particularly the Peter Paul Fortress, to liberate their male relatives, many of whom were political prisoners because of their membership in unions or socialist groups. And many other women looted food shops. Through their neighborhood networks, women knew good from bad retailers, so women's activities in attacking known speculators in their neighborhoods amounted to a form of direct democratic distribution of scarce resources.

All political parties in Petrograd opposed the decision to launch a strike on International Women's Day, because they all knew that the working class was not prepared to carry out a full revolution at that time; party leaders were afraid that precipitous action might result in slaughter or massive arrests.[13] The majority of working-class women, on the other hand, did not belong to the unions and political groups, although the men in their families did. Whereas the men had increasingly been drawn to the organized Left, where leaders formulated economic and political strategy, the women continued to focus their attention on immediate, local needs, the strongest of which was the desperate need for food. The women attempted to provide for their families and neighbors without any thought for women's suffrage or rights for women to participate as men's equals in any future government. And when men joined them, they did so as joint participants in a working-class community that the women helped shape according to the dictates of female consciousness.

The February Revolution took place in two stages. First there was a communal strike, which women organized and in which their demands for food and peace were central. Then there was the revolutionary phase, in which male-dominated unions and political parties took over and transformed the protest into a full-scale revolution. By the third day of citywide strikes, the demand for bread had been almost abandoned in favor of overtly revolutionary slogans.

Officials estimated that 87,000 workers walked off the job on International Women's Day and that the number of demonstrators grew to 200,000 and then to over 300,000 on February 24 and 25. The numbers may have been far larger since the statistics do not account for the women on bread lines who swelled the ranks of activists. As so often happens, mobilization provided the opportunity for political education. Initial calls for peace and bread grew more specific and the crowd extended its call to include demands for the eight-hour day, a Constituent Assembly, and a Republic.

Crowds, including large numbers of women, had taken over Nevsky Prospekt in downtown Petrograd. On February 25, two days after the insurrection began, the Tsar telegraphed General S. S. Khabalov of the Petrograd Military District, ordering him to shoot, if necessary, in order to end the women's rebellion. Khabalov summarized the problems authorities throughout the world faced when confronted with women's consumer demands. He, like they, understood that women as mothers had certain prerogatives in extreme situations where food was scarce. As Khabalov later wrote:

> This telegram, how could I say it, to be frank and sincere, was for me like a sledge-hammer blow. "To stop as of tomorrow." How? What was I going to do? How "stop"? When they asked for bread, we gave bread, and that was the end of it. But when the flags are inscribed "down with the autocracy" it's no longer a question of bread. But what then? The Tsar had ordered—we had to shoot.[14]

On February 26, the police, who had until then been incapable of action, fired into the crowds now under male leadership gathered at the Prospekt. In retaliation, people began to set fire to police stations. By Monday, February 27, almost the entire working class had gone out into the streets, where they tried to convince the soldiers to hold their fire and come over to their side.

Once the masses which included women confronted the state, the major questions were whether the troops themselves had lost faith in the legitimacy of the government. By February 1917, the massive losses that the Germans had inflicted on the Russian army had discredited the Tsar even with the soldiers. The desperate women of the working-class no longer appeared to be making political demands; what they asked seemed only reasonable. Poor women of Petrograd beseeched soldiers to lay down arms and come over to their side in the name of the higher social good represented by women acting for the whole society. The Tsar ordered Cossacks to attack the female crowds, and they approached. According to Aleksei Tarasov-Rodionov, a Tsarist officer who was an eyewitness:

> The only sound that could be heard was the resonant ring of the approaching hoofs. Then a girl walked out from the crowd. She wore a dark padded jacket and huge shoes with galoshes. A simple knitted shawl of the same color as the Cossacks' coat was bound tightly over her head. She crossed over toward the Cossacks, walking swiftly and lightly. She was quite close to the Cossack officer. A thousand eyes followed her and a thousand hearts were numb. Suddenly, she threw away some wrapping paper—and held out a bouquet of fresh red roses to the officer. The officer was young. His epaulettes flashed gayly. His saber, polished like a mirror, was firmly held in a strong hand—but suddenly the blade wavered helplessly and dangled, flashing but harmless, from the supple white-gloved wrist. The officer leaned over and took the nosegay. A mad riotous shout went up—such a shout as I had never heard and never expect to hear again. It was a wild bellow of uproarious joy.[15]

This mythical account, based on folk stories about maidens and gallant officers, tied the past to the future in which the army support for the Bolshevik Revolution in October constituted a crucial element in the victory. In February 1917, there was scarcely a morsel of bread in Petrograd; there certainly were no red roses. But the story indicates the importance that chroniclers inadvertently attributed to female consciousness—in this case, in recognizing that women can act safely where men would get shot down, especially when the issues concern survival. In fact, from the first day, troops had mutinied all over Petrograd—because they would not shoot at the women and because they themselves had become revolutionaries.

Women, acting according to female consciousness, contributed to the overthrow of the Tsar by February 27. Their demands, made in the name of the community rather than for a class, party, or union, won support from male workers and led to an army mutiny against the Tsar. The weak liberal government that ruled for eight months fell during the October 1917 Revolution, during which the Bolshevik Party was able to lead the working class in the creation of the Soviet Union, the first socialist state.

AUGUST 1917, TURIN, ITALY

Italy, like Russia in 1917, displayed characteristics associated with many Third World countries today. Cycles of war and revolution and the irregularities of food supplies for the cities presented constant threats to the working-class community. Italy had been unified as a constitutional monarchy only in 1861, and, even by 1917, regional allegiances still prevailed over a sense of citizenship in a single nation. People in the southern provinces, including Sicily and Sardinia, felt no tie to people in the north; the people of the different regions even spoke different languages. The technologically backward, often absentee landowners of the south derived their income from grain production, but they could compete for Italian markets only if their crops were subsidized. In order to keep the nation together, the Italian state protected grain, thus insuring the incomes of southern landowners. This policy also assured that the cost of bread, the staple of working-class diets, would remain high. To an unusual degree, the price of bread was a constant irritant, capable of provoking ordinary women to take action to preserve their families' livelihoods.[16]

Turin, along the Po River in the foothills of the Alps, resembled other Italian cities with their dispersed houses and red tile roofs despite the concentration of heavy industry. Like Petrograd, Turin housed its country's metallurgical industry. In 1919 and 1920 metalworkers, including auto workers at the Fiat plant, seized the factories of Turin and organized factory councils modeled on the democratic workers' organizations called *soviets* that had emerged in Revolutionary Russian factories. Many observers thought that a revolutionary epoch had begun in Italy. But the sit-ins and the creation of factory councils in Turin were in fact the culmination of a longer revolutionary tradition. The successful confrontations with the government at the workplace had been preceded by years of grass roots political activity and organization by working-class women and men.

Women contributed to the growth of a revolutionary tradition in Italy before 1920. On May Day 1898 in Milan, an uprising over the cost of food engaged countless women.[17] In Genoa in 1900, all the dockers and other workers put down their tools, and women of the community joined them in the public squares, where they confronted police. Similar strikes followed in Turin and Florence in 1902 and in Rome in 1903. In all these strikes, it was common to place women in the front lines in the hope that police and soldiers would recognize their right to fight for bread to feed their children.

World War I exacerbated the antagonism between the Italian government and the working class. By January 1917, in the industrial cities of northern Italy, the price of flour had risen 88 percent, wine 144 percent, and potatoes 131 percent over 1910 prices.[18] In the period from 1915 to 1917, the Italian draft drew men away from Milan and Turin, the only major industrial cities in the country. The people who remained in the factories suffered from loss of rights because the government had militarized labor. Attempted strikes were tantamount to insurrection and could result in executions. For those women who found work in factories, ten- or twelve-hour shifts were followed by four and five hours in bread lines. At the Pirelli rubber plant in Turin, women constituted half of the 3,000 new workers hired between November 1914 and March 1916.[19] Their mothers and sisters who did not work outside their homes suffered along with female wage laborers from shortages and inflation. Since male and female workers labored in sex-segregated units, and since labor organizing was illegal during the war, the women who became industrial laborers were not involved in economic strikes at the workplace. However, prompted by female consciousness, they continued to act in concert with other women from their residential neighborhoods. Although women were unlikely to rebel on the factory floor, they were capable of mobilizing in pursuit of cheap food by turning their own streets into arenas for struggle.

At the beginning of March 1917, just after International Women's Day was celebrated in secret in many belligerent countries, a socialist women's collective in Turin hung posters on the walls of working class neighborhoods. The posters asked:

> Hasn't there been enough torment from this war? Now the food necessary for our children has begun to disappear. It is time for us to act in the name of suffering humanity. Our cry is "Down with arms!" We are part of the same family. We want peace. We must show that women can protect those who depend on them.[20]

As shortages grew worse in August 1917, crowds of women occupied public spaces and demonstrated at the town hall, calling for an end to the war and for improved food supplies.[21] Once again, as in Petrograd, the proximity of the working-class neighborhoods to administrative centers made possible a communal strike in pursuit of demands consistent with female consciousness. Although the mayor agreed to do what he could, it was not enough. The bakers in Turin were reluctant to use all their stores of flour for the daily preparation of common bread. As early as April 1917, local authorities had suggested rationing 250 grams of flour a day for each person in the urban areas, but it was difficult to get grain from the peasants to feed the troops, let alone the people in the cities. For that, local officials needed the help of the national government. Between August 9 and 11, preparation of bread in Turin proceeded irregularly; on August 9, twenty-seven bakeries had shut down in working-class neighborhoods like San Donato, and many women found that the short supplies had gone. There is some evidence that the national authorities manipulated shortages to discredit the city officials, who belonged to an opposing party. From the perspective of the working-class women, however, who and what caused the shortages made no difference. What mattered to them was the necessity to feed their own families.

The big crisis came on Tuesday, August 21, when more than eighty bakeries closed with signs saying "Out of Bread." Women gathered together and, with their children, marched beyond their working-class neighborhoods to protest in the plaza in front of the city hall. They were desperate and furious. It angered them that bakers had sufficient flour to bake the expensive sweet rolls (with raisins) that only the rich could afford to buy, while working-class women could not get bread for themselves or their families.

By the morning of August 22, the demonstrations over short supplies of flour caused the local government to order more from neighboring provinces. Outraged and hungry crowds, led by working-class women, vandalized trolleys. Local officials telegraphed the Minister of Interior to send emergency supplies or face an uprising in the city. On the same day, 2,000 male railroad employees followed the women's lead and went out, proclaiming that they would not work if they had no food to eat. The government took the threat of labor unrest seriously, and attempted to appease the suffering working class, by rushing flour to the city by the morning of August 23. But flour came too late; the powerful metalworkers union, including the Fiat workers, joined the women in protest against the outrageous shortages and walked off the job—back into their communities. The mobilization of the women had provoked the men to act.

What emerged was a communal strike, in which the locus of political and economic action became the streets of the working-class neighborhoods. The women made their work providing meals a matter of collective action, and, on August 23, when the women had received inadequate responses to their demands, they began to construct barricades in the southern working-class districts of San Paolo and Nizza and in the northern Milan district. The men soon joined them in the neighborhood, rather than sitting-in at the factories as they would do in 1919 and 1920.

By the evening of August 22, with barricades up throughout the working class sections of town, the police and army attacked. Despite entreaties, they did not, as in Russia in February 1917, come over to the popular side. Thirty-seven people were hospitalized and over 200 landed in jail, but the fighting went on in the Nizza, San Paolo, and Milan districts. Women and men in Nizza threw handmade bombs at the attackers, wounding several. By August 27, 1,500 had been arrested. The majority of male workers returned to the job on Monday, August 27, but the women remained away from their factory jobs because bread had become scarce again, especially in the working-class areas.

The women who protested were at first preoccupied with the availability of food; however, they also demanded an end to the war and the return of the troops so that married women would not have to work in the factories. By the time the uprising had ended on August 28, it had changed from a bread riot into a coordinated effort of the masses to end the war. Many of the survivors were jailed on charges of spreading discord and pacifism.[22] The war continued, but the communal strike established a lasting feeling of resistance in Turin. Although it is only mentioned in passing in most histories of the Italian Left, the communal strike of 1917, which women initiated, made a vital contribution to the development of revolutionary consciousness in Italy.

WOMEN'S COLLECTIVE ACTION IN SPAIN

Even nonbelligerent countries such as Spain experienced war-related shortages that contributed to the eruption of communal strikes. Spain too had experienced waves of wars and revolutions; it had even been a republic for about one year from 1873 to 1874. Spain was a constitutional monarchy ruled by strong prime ministers. Despite universal male suffrage, the poor had no say in elections. The elections were fixed by the large landowners of the south, including the areas surrounding Malaga. As in Italy, the government tried to placate these absentee landlords, who refused to invest in the mechanized reapers that made the grain from the United States, Canada, and Australia cheaper, despite shipping costs, than any wheat, oats, barley, or rye produced in Europe. Again, as in Italy, Spanish government tariffs, made to keep out cheap foreign grain and to enrich the Spanish landowners, pushed bread prices high, thus contributing to constant unrest in the urban working classes.

Beginning in the mid-nineteenth century, communal strikes had occurred throughout Spain's southern region of Andalusia. In each case, people seized their own city, established a democratic government, and defended it until the inefficient state managed to move the army in to put down the urban insurrection. From 1868 to 1923, a long struggle to establish democratic rights for workers in industry and agriculture had engaged working-class women.

Since the late nineteenth century, Malaga had been a center of anarchism, a movement by which people tried to achieve direct democratic control of their city and region.[23] A socialist theory that opposed all political bureaucracies and states, anarchism had grown well in the soil of Malaga Province, which also produced grapes for raisins and wine. A more powerful government, with larger garrisons of troops distributed throughout the countryside, might have prevented anarchism from flourishing in Andalusia. But given the weakness and impoverishment of the Spanish state, whose army was overloaded with officers and whose soldiers could not always be paid, anarchism became a sustained revolutionary tradition of popular democracy, which persisted until the Spanish Civil War of 1936–1939.

Malaga was a Mediterranean harbor city, heavily dependent on the British wine market. This dependence made Malaga's citizens sometimes painfully aware of the shifting economic changes World War I had brought. Despite propaganda from both the Allies and the Triple Alliance, Spain remained outside the actual fighting in World War I. Since there was no conscription, the local population of Malaga did not suffer from the draft. Nor was economic need linked to a peace movement. There were general food shortages, however because of the markets for food abroad, to supply the troops of belligerent countries. Because food was moved out of Malaga for sale on international markets, bread was scarce and prices high. Women in Malaga, far from the fighting, suffered from the fact that belligerents would pay high prices for even such humble food as the anchovy, their main protein source. And although these women had little understanding of the political and economic forces that caused the suffering, female consciousness roused them to action.

Among the working class whose neighborhoods were near the harbor and close to the government offices, rumors began to circulate about increased exports of fish. On the evening of January 14, 1918, women of Malaga decided to take matters into their own hands. They marched through the streets denouncing speculators and hoarders. They went to the fancy residences and resort hotels and called out the maids and the laundresses to join them in their women's cause of regulating food supplies. Then they moved to the station and auctioned huge boxes of fish to one another at thirty cents a kilo for fresh anchovies. They took sacks of potatoes off the trains scheduled to take the food to markets that could command higher prices than the women in Malaga could spend. Then they marched to the regional governor's offices and demanded that he reduce the prices of potatoes, fish, and olive oil. He promised to do this the next day, but the women were sceptical, and they moved from his offices to the storehouses for fish in order to prevent merchants from moving them to the railroad and shipping them out during the night.[24]

At 1:00 P.M. on the afternoon of January 15, hundreds of women gathered on the Alameda, the main street of the city. They marched to official centers, which they found shut against them. They drove off the children and the men who hoped to join them, yelling, "Only the women!" presumably because their female consciousness led them to believe that officials would not hurt them for fulfilling their obligations as mothers to feed their children. By 3:30 P.M., hundreds more women had increased the original crowd. The Civil Guard dispersed those who had occupied the central administrative districts on Larios Street, Granada Street, and at the

Plaza of the Constitution, near the port. Later the women, representing all classes, returned and reassembled in even larger numbers. What had begun with poor women trying to protect the city's food so that there would be enough for their families turned into a movement to uphold the rights of all women to intervene in government affairs when authorities failed to assure women's ability to provide for their households. As the women moved toward the governor's office to remind him of his promises, they encountered the Civil Guard, who attempted—without success this time—to turn them back. Josefa Caparros died of gunshot wounds during the demonstrations, and the women made a cortege for her, treating her death as a murder and an attack on all women.

The Spanish troops shot at the women when they were ordered to do so. In Spain as in Italy, the government made special efforts to rotate soldiers outside their regions, to reduce the possibility that the soldiers would actually know the workers or women whom they might confront. In Italy, it was customary to use soldiers from the South, who scarcely understood the northern dialect, against movements in Turin. The Spanish government successfully did the same. When women shouted to the soldiers, "We are your wives! We are your sisters! We are your daughters!" their appeals were ineffective because of the regional differences of dress and dialect.

In the record cold winter of 1917–1918, food riots occurred in Spain from Barcelona to Alicante and from Valencia to Valladolid. Thousands of women marched to demand control of food and fuel produced in their area, to prevent food from escaping to markets where merchants could reap huge profits.[25] Despite widespread women's rebellions throughout Spain in January and February 1918 and the concomitant imposition of martial law, the government was never in danger of falling.

In Madrid, Catalonia, and the Basque country, socialists and anarchists had organized general strikes in the summer of 1917. At the same time Spanish soldiers had formed committees to demand higher pay, and congressional delegates from the Spanish Congress (the Cortes) had demanded the creation of a new constitution. Five months before the women's strikes, then, socialists and anarchists urged male workers to lay down their tools and stop working; however, the socialists and anarchists were not demanding immediate relief in the form of food or fuel as the women, acting according to female consciousness, did in the winter of 1918.

Following the women's communal struggles in January 1918, there were other insurrections in Spain. In March 1919, for example, communications and transport workers in Barcelona mobilized; many male workers were ready to overthrow the government, although their labor leaders thought they were not powerful enough to win.[26] Women did not join the mobilization in 1919, and journalists even commented that women were scarcely seen in the streets except hurrying home from market. Since there were no special shortages that would provoke those with female consciousness to view their communities and families as threatened, the women carried on their domestic life. As they had in summer 1917, the unions failed to link economic issues to the broader social concerns that had galvanized working class women in Malaga, Barcelona, and elsewhere. At no time had the communal strikes in which working class women engaged been linked in strategy to other socialist or anarchist plans of action. The gallant struggles of the women of Malaga, Barcelona, Valladolid, and Valencia remain largely invisible to this day.

CRISIS OVER RENTS IN VERACRUZ, MEXICO

Mexico, whose fortunes have been tied to European events since the dawn of the modern period, experienced a number of communal strikes that were, like those in Europe, led by working-class women. One such communal strike occurred when women tried to contribute to the quality of life in Veracruz, Mexico, in July 1922.[27]

Against the background of the Mexican Revolution (which went on in different phases from 1910 to 1927), the cost of living had escalated in Veracruz. Shipping in this commercial capital of the Mexican Republic had drawn many new workers to the city since the Revolution had disrupted rural life and had driven men and women from the countryside. This migration had provided numerous customers for greedy landlords, who drove the rents sky high. Rentals went from ten to thirty pesetas a month as inflation rampaged. As long as the working class found work, they paid the unreasonably high rents, but after the shipping boom caused by World War I subsided, unemployment spread and many could not pay the inflated rents.

The ensuing evictions disrupted personal ties among neighbors and robbed people of what little security they had in the new city. There was widespread misery and increased political activity by the Left. These conditions, combined with the proximity of working-class neighborhoods to the harbor and the government centers, made a communal strike a strong possibility.

In January 1922, 3,000 men and women came together at an open-air meeting to discuss the housing crisis. A group of women and Heron Proal, a utopian socialist tailor with anarchist ideas, emerged as the leaders of the Revolutionary Tenants' Union. They called a rent strike, which, by March 3, had engaged 80 percent of the population, including a large percentage of widows, wives of sailors, and wage-earning women. Mass meetings at which people performed plays about their political situation served to educate the masses and enhance their sense of solidarity. The rent strikers demanded immediate rollbacks in rent. They also called for recognition of the Tenants' Union, which would play a role in determining fair rents and leases.

Among the most active people on the organizing committees that combed the working-class neighborhoods drumming up support were the women, who, everyone agreed, became the lifeblood of the Veracruz strike.[28] When authorities threatened violence, the rent strikers called an illegal public meeting at Francisco Ferrer Park—named for the Spanish anarchist executed in Barcelona in 1909—on July 5, 1922.

As the clock on the Women's Hospital struck 8:00 P.M., Proal (the only man involved in the leadership of the struggle) appeared, surrounded by a group of women dressed in red. Fighting broke out as the police and army attacked, beating everyone they could reach. Forty women shouted, "Viva la Revolucion Social!" ("Long live the Social Revolution!"), as 2,000 of the crowd echoed their cry. Like their Russian sisters, but with less success, they tried to win the soldiers by calling "Viva el hermano soldado!" ("Long live our soldier brothers!").

As the soldiers raised their rifles, the women led the crowd to confront them. A woman named Simona Aguirre ran ahead with her red flag and approached Colonel Lopez Manzano's car. Soldiers blocked her way. One knocked her down and pulled her flag from her hands, and the crowd surged forward to defend her. The soldiers fired into the crowd, killing and wounding a few people and arresting all the union leaders they could find.

For months after the strike women led the community in periodic demonstrations. Dockers and sailors sporadically went out on strike in 1922 and 1923. Veracruz was one of the centers of union militancy and left wing activity in Mexico. Many male dockworkers of Veracruz belonged to anarchist, socialist, or communist parties. The city was a radical hotbed, but as in European countries, the female textile workers, who constituted a large proportion of all the industrial workers, were not enrolled in trade unions.

Demonstrators came from all the political groups. Marchers, dressed in red, included men as well as women and children. Women's batallions generally carried red flags, behind which men carried signs with portraits of Lenin, Trotsky, Marx, and Bakunin. Tough men, bringing up the rear, had prepared themselves to defend the peaceful paraders. Unlike the women of Malaga, the women of Veracruz permitted men to join their political demonstrations, and thus risked additional attacks from police and soldiers, who viewed men as more threatening than women, even though none of the demonstrators was armed.

By 1923, women and men in Veracruz had won a rent ceiling that limited rent increases to 6 percent a year and the right to a year's lease at a fixed price. A law was passed establishing rent boards of tenants and landlords that ruled on health standards, but women did not ask for or gain any place on the boards.[29] Members of the Tenants' Union, who saw in the victory for rent control an opportunity to participate in the government, excluded the women who had won the victory. Inspired only by female consciousness, the women activists made no attempt to assure themselves the right to sit on the governing boards that would regulate their housing. The exclusion of these women deprived the leftist parties, and the city as a whole, of the benefits of their skills, developed in a major grass roots movement.

CONTRADICTORY IMAGES OF WORKING WOMEN

In Petrograd, Turin, Malaga, and Veracruz, the experience of working-class women dramatically demonstrated the contradictions between the idealized images of women as self-sacrificing nurturers that most societies held and the reality of poor women's lives. Under normal circumstances, women of the popular classes never challenged the state, never called for a new political order, and never attacked authorities. The women's obsession was survival, not political or economic change. When periods of extreme scarcity drove women to expose their bodies to bullets in order to win resources necessary for their family's survival, however, these women made it clear that something was very wrong.

Socialist and anarchist ideas permeated the neighborhoods where men and women engaged in communal strikes during the era of the World War I, but it was their female consciousness that actually provoked the women to act. Without the concept of female consciousness, the political implications for women of the communal strikes that occurred during and after the World War I disappear, as they have from most histories of the period. Women who accepted the roles their societies defined for them—women who wanted to be good wives, mothers, sisters, and daughters—sometimes had to confront police or armies because of their need to provide for their loved ones. Working-class men normally overlooked the centrality of women's everyday struggle for community survival to anarchist or socialist goals. Improvements in labor conditions, political arrangements, or the conduct of war—these were the issues around which the men organized during the period. It was only when women engaged in collective action to secure food, fuel, or moderate rents, that the men recognized the relevance of women's efforts to their own goals. Understanding the role of female consciousness in the communal strikes of the era helps reveal how working-class women and men overcame different priorities to unite in social movements in the first decades of the twentieth century.

NOTES

1. Temma Kaplan, "Female Consciousness and Collective Action: The Barcelona Case, 1910–1918," *Signs*, 7, No.3 (1982), 545–66.

2. The major study of a national women's suffrage movement that provides comprehensive material on the participation of working-class women is Jill Liddington and Jill Norris, *One Hand Tied Behind Us: The Rise of the Women's Suffrage Movement* (London: Virago, 1978).

3. Olwen Hufton, "Women in Revolution, 1789–1796," *Past and Present*, 53 (1971), 90–108; E. P. Thompson, "The Moral Economy of the English Crowd in the Eighteenth Century," *Past and Present*, 50 (1971), 76–136.

4. George Rude, " 'Captain Swing' and 'Rebecca's Daughters' " in *The Crowd in History, 1730–1848* (New York: John Wiley, 1964), pp. 149–163; Joyce Riegelhaupt, "Maria das Fontes," Unpublished paper delivered for the Women's Studies Series, Princeton University (Spring 1981).

5. A discussion of how integral women's issues were to the Left before the advent of "scientific socialism" appears in Barbara Taylor, *Eve and the New Jerusalem: Socialism and Feminism in the Nineteenth Century* (New York: Pantheon, 1983).

6. A brief overview of the history of the three Internationals appears in *The Revolutionary Internationals, 1864–1943*, ed. Milorad M. Drakovitch (Stanford, Calif.: Stanford University Press, 1966).

7. Laura Engelstein, *Moscow, 1905: Working-Class Organization and Political Conflict.* (Stanford, Calif.: Stanford University Press, 1982), p. 64. The 1905 Revolution provoked Rosa Luxemburg to write *The Mass Strike, the Political Party, and the Trade Unions*, trans. Patrick Lavin, 1st ed. 1906 (New York: Harper and Row, 1971).

8. Dale Ross, "The Role of the Women of Petrograd in War, Revolution, and Counter-Revolution, 1914–1921," Unpublished Doctoral Dissertation (New Brunswick, N.J.: Rutgers University, 1973), pp. 23, 28; *Encarecimiento de la vida durante la guerra. Precios de las subsisténcias en España y en el extranjero, 1914–1918* (Madrid: Instituto de Reformas Sociales. Secciones la y 3a técnico-administrativas, 1918), p. 49.

9. Cited in Marc Ferro, *The Russian Revolution of February 1917*, trans. J. L. Richards (Englewood Cliffs, N.J.: Prentice-Hall, 1972), p. 32.

10. Cited in David Mandel, *The Petrograd Workers and the Fall of the Old Regime. From the February Revolution to the July Days, 1917.* Centre for Russian and East European Studies of the University of Birmingham, (London: Macmillan, 1983), pp. 25–26.

11. Temma Kaplan, "Commentary on the Socialist Origins of International Women's Day," *Feminist Studies* 11 (Spring 1985), 163–172.

12. Mandel, *The Petrograd Workers*, pp. 48–59.

13. Ferro, *The Russian Revolution*, pp. 38–39.

14. Quoted in Ferro, *The Russian Revolution*, p. 38.

15. Aleksei Tarasov-Rodionov, *February 1917*, (New York: Covici-Friede, 1931), pp. 46–47. Another discussion of the Cossack's reluctance to attack the demonstrators can be found in Tsuyoshi Hasegawa, *The February Revolution: Petrograd, 1917* (Seattle: The University of Washington Press, 1981), p. 225.

16. For an overview, see Giuliano Procacci, *History of the Italian People*, trans. Anthony Paul. 2nd ed. (Harmondsworth, England: Penguin Books, 1978), pp. 324–400.

17. Louise A. Tilly, "I Fatti di Maggio: The Working Class of Milan and the Rebellion of 1898," *Modern European Social History*, ed. Robert J. Bezucha (Lexington, Mass.: D.C. Heath, 1972), pp. 124–158.

18. *Encarecimiento de la vida*, p. 45.

19. The best studies of women's work in Italy during the war years can be found in Alessandro Camarda and Santo Peli, *L'Altro Esercito. La Classe operaia durante la Primera Guerra Mondiale* (Milan: Feltrinelli Editore, 1980), pp. 26–56, 90–97, 146–155, and Stefano Musso, *Gli operai di Torino 1900–1920* (Milan: Feltrinelli Editore, 1980), pp. 121–184.

20. Paolo Spriano, *Storia del Partito Comunista Italiano* (Turin: Einaudi, 1976), III, p. 393.

21. The following narrative comes from *L'Italiano-Gazzetta del Popolo* (Turin), March–August, 1917; and Alberto Monticone, "Il Socialismo Torinese ed i Fatti dell'Agosto 1917," *Rassegna Storica del Risorgimento*, 45 (January–March, 1958), 1–40.

22. Renzo del Carria, *Proletari senza rivoluzione. Storia delle classi subalterne in Italia* (Rome: Savelli, 1966), II, p. 29.

23. For a detailed account of the development of anarchism in Malaga, Cadiz, and Seville provinces, see Temma Kaplan, *Anarchists of Andalusia, 1868–1903* (Princeton, N.J.: Princeton University Press, 1977).

24. Descriptions of the communal strike in Malaga can be found in "El hambre nacional. Protestas violentas," *El Socialista* (Madrid) January 15–30, 1918; and *El Sol* (Madrid) January 22–30, 1918; and María Dolores Ramos, "Crisis de subsistencias y conflictividad social en Málaga: Los sucesos de enero de 1918," *Baetica: Estudios de Arte, Geografía e Historia*, 6 (1983), 441–466. There are no references to this or any other consumer rebellion in Spain in any of the major histories of the period.

25. For consideration of these events in Barcelona see Kaplan, "Female Consciousness," pp. 560–564.

26. The most comprehensive account of this period can be found in Gerald H. Meaker, *The Revolutionary Left in Spain, 1914–1923* (Stanford, Calif.: Stanford University Press, 1974).

27. The discussion of Veracruz comes from Leafar Agetro, *Las luchas proletarias en Veracruz. Historia y autocrítica* (Veracruz: Ediciones revolucionárias, 1942).

28. Agetro, *Las luchas*, pp. 69–75.

29. Agetro, *Las luchas*, pp. 75–90.

SUGGESTIONS FOR FURTHER READING

Marc Ferro. *The Russian Revolution of February 1917*. Trans. J. L. Richards. Englewood Cliffs, N.J.: Prentice-Hall, 1972.

Rose L. Glickman. *Russian Factory Women: Workplace and Society, 1880–1914*. Berkeley: University of California Press, 1984.

Olwen Hufton. "Women in Revolution, 1789–1796." *Past and Present,* 53 (1971), 90–108.

Temma Kaplan. *Anarchists of Andalusia, 1868–1903.* Princeton, N.J.; Princeton University Press, 1977; "Class Consciousness and Community in Nineteenth-Century Andalusia." *Political Power and Social Theory,* 2 (1981), 21–57; "Commentary on the Socialist Origins of International Women's Day." *Feminist Studies,* 11 (Spring 1985), 163–171; "Female Consciousness and Collective Action: The Case of Barcelona, 1910–1918." *Signs,* 7, No.3, (1982), 545–66.

Rosa Luxemburg. *The Mass Strike, the Political Party and the Trade Union.* Trans. Patrick Lavin. 1st ed., 1906. New York: Harper & Row, 1971.

David Mandel, *The Petrograd Workers and the Fall of the Old Regime. From the February Revolution to the July Days, 1917.* Centre for Russian and East European Studies of the University of Birmingham. London: Macmillan, 1983.

Gerald H. Meaker. *The Revolutionary Left in Spain, 1914–1923.* Stanford, Calif.: Stanford University Press, 1974.

Giuliano Procacci. *History of the Italian People.* Trans. Anthony Paul. 2nd. ed. Harmondsworth, England: Penguin Books, 1978.

George Rude. *The Crowd in History, 1730–1848.* New York: John Wiley, 1964.

E. P. Thompson. "The Moral Economy of the English Crowd in the Eighteenth Century." *Past and Present,* 50 (1971), 76–136.·

Barbara Taylor. *Eve and the New Jerusalem: Socialism and Feminism in the Nineteenth Century.* New York: Pantheon Books, 1983.

Louise A. Tilly, "I Fatti di Maggio: The Working Class of Milan and the Rebellion of 1898." *Modern European Social History.* Ed. Robert J. Bezucha. Lexington, Mass.: D. C. Heath, 1972, pp. 124–158.

March 8—Women's Emancipation Day—a poster by Adolf Strakhov, 1920. (From Mikhail Guerman, *Art of the October Revolution* [New York: Abrams, 1979], plate 75. Reprinted with permission of Aurora Publishers, Leningrad)

chapter 17

Women and the Revolutionary Process in Russia

Richard Stites

The history of women in Tsarist Russia and the Soviet Union defies generalization. Dramatic contrasts in education and class, combined with the sudden transformation from reactionary monarchy to Communist dictatorship, placed women in diverse situations. For the fortunate daughters of wealthy and noble families under Tsarist rule, foreign study offered an escape. But several young women used their privilege to fight for a just society. Unlike the leisured women discussed by Karen Offen or the Socialist women described by Charles Sowerwine, Russian women had no access to legitimate reformist organizations. Many chose exile or clandestine activities. A few became terrorists. Richard Stites depicts the shock of upheaval in the wake of the 1917 October Revolution. Suddenly everything seemed possible: fair wages, birth control, divorce reform, communal childrearing, and sexual freedom. However, such emancipatory reforms, difficult even in a stable society, proved impossible in a nation facing economic collapse, political turmoil, and civil war. Under Stalin, rapid and forced industrialization left no leeway for social experiments; and World War II brought renewed pressure on women to work in war production and at the same time bear many children to compensate for the devastating loss of life. For the postwar years, Stites draws a complex balance sheet, weighing solid gains for women in wages, education, and family support against early utopian expectations and against women's achievements in other Western nations.

By the middle of the nineteenth century, the Russian Empire, out of which arose an extraordinary range of women's movements, was considered—and knew itself to be—a backward country, sprawling in territory, economically primitive, and militarily inferior to the major industrial powers of the West. St. Petersburg, the capital of this immense eastern empire, was a Westernized city housing an antiquated autocracy in which the emperor-tsar held sway over the land with the aid of a corrupt and occasionally brutal bureaucracy. A tiny portion of the population—mostly from the gentry, or nobility—constituted the educated elite, who dressed like Europeans and spoke foreign languages. The vast majority of the people, however, lived on the land as serfs—unfree peasants or servants of the gentry and the state.

When the winds of economic and political change, whipped up in Europe by industrialization and the French Revolution, began to blow over Russia, small groups of alienated members of the gentry class began to conspire or agitate for a variety of reforms and outright revolutionary transformations. When the autocracy decided to modernize society by abolishing serfdom and launching other reforms in the 1860s, these tiny currents swelled into a big stream of opposition and social rebellion. Women's movements are often born in the midst of general crises or large-scale historical changes. And so it was in Russia that in the 1860s, feminist, nihilist, and radical women appeared on the historical stage, beginning a continuous movement for liberation that lasted down to 1917. How did this happen?

BEFORE THE REVOLUTION

Russian society before 1917 was a world of patriarchal power, deferential ritual, clear authority patterns, and visible hierarchy with stratified social classes or estates. At the pinnacle of the state, the tsar-emperor (called *batyushka* or little father by the common folk), considered Russia as a family estate or patrimony and his subjects as children—virtuous, obedient, and loyal. The imperial bureaucratic order of ranks, chanceries, uniforms, and rigidly ordered parades constituted a visual celebration of authoritarianism. To subjects of all classes of the empire, every official building— with its geography of guarded entrances, pass booths, waiting areas, office gates—represented authority, inequality, and the demand for deference. Far from the capital and the towns, in the vastness of rural Russia, a simpler absolutism prevailed in the village cabins where the male head of household wielded domestic power that contrasted sharply with the more or less egalitarian land distribution customs of the village community. The Russian Orthodox Church reinforced values of obedience and subordination at every level in its liturgical idiom, its symbols, its organization, and its political ethos of support for a conservative order. The women dwelling within this ancient authoritarian world felt the additional weight of male power and suffered from the sexual division of labor and open inequality between the sexes.

Radical Thought and Feminism

The Russian intelligentsia, which emerged out of the educated gentry class in the early nineteenth century, constituted a small but influential element of rebellion against the authoritarian, patriarchal culture. Perceived family "despotism," an archaic political order, serfdom, and the inequality everywhere visible combined in various ways to inspire the psychological revolt of an entire generation of young people in the 1860s. Young women of the educated classes, heretofore excluded from public life, began to join forces with men in various expressions of their revolt against society.

Friends and foes alike called this revolt "nihilism"—a negation of old ways, especially those that demanded obedience and conformity. Nihilist men accepted women as equals and together they created a kind of symbolic and behavioral counterculture evidenced by rude manners, disrespect for conventions, residential communes for both sexes, common law marriages, generational anger, cultural iconoclasm, and rebellious forms of dress and personal appearance. Nihilism was an unofficial slap in the face to official authority.

Nihilism represented more than negation, however. In the hands of radical popularizers and shapers of the nihilist outlook such as Nicholas Chernyshevsky, it represented training for the future. In a spectacularly successful novel *What is to be done?*—written in prison in 1862—Chernyshevsky outlined a rebellious, rational, and nondeferential personality that would change Russia; described a utopian socialist future; and made the emancipation of women the central motif and metaphor of the novel.

Chernyshevsky's *What is to be done?* must be read as more than just a manifesto of the time. It signaled the power of utopian revolutionary thought in Russia and women's role in it. As did the French utopian socialist Charles Fourier, Chernyshevsky made women's equality central to his socialist vision; provided a concrete plan of labor, life, and residential space in his commune of the future; and granted sexuality a significant place in the cycle of work, love, and rest.

While the visions of Fourier and other French utopians dimmed in the later nineteenth century, the utopian element in the Russian revolutionary movement never disappeared and remained very visible in the first decade of Soviet power. Women were especially attracted to Chernyshevsky's novel because it taught independence and a way to attain stature and dignity. "I want to be independent," exclaims the heroine, "and live in my own way."[1] For many women, in fact, professing nihilism was a stage in personal growth, an act of social or family rebelliousness, and not at all political in the larger sense of the word. In the course of the 1860s, genuinely radical women began to emerge, dedicating themselves to conspiracy and underground revolutionary work.

The Russian radicals of the 1860s and 1870s—generally known as Populists—fought to overthrow the tsarist autocracy, introduce popular self-government, and establish some form of agrarian socialism on the land. An exceptionally large radical movement in nineteenth-century European history, Populism attracted thousands of young people of the educated classes who dedicated their lives and often gave their freedom on behalf of liberating the people. These young idealists' vision of the future was radiant and their standard of personal morality—with some exceptions—very high. Women were welcomed into this underground profession, accepted as equals, and encouraged to use whatever skills they had acquired.

No other radical movement of the time in Europe contained such a large proportion of women in its ranks. Although they rejected feminism as a movement, many radical women passed through a very important phase of women's consciousness that enabled them to connect problems of personal, sexual, or family oppression with the perceived generalized oppression of the regime. Women embarked with passion onto the path of political struggle, spreading socialist propaganda among the peasants and later turning to individual assassination and terror. They paid the same price as did their male comrades—with their freedom and with their lives. The hanging of Sofya Perovskaya—the daughter of a general—for organizing the assassination of Tsar Alexander II in 1881 dramatically punctuated this phase of radical women's struggle. Women paid in other ways too: through their dedication to revolution, they often lost the comforts of love and sexuality; and by refusing to add feminism to the Populist agenda, they made it easier for others to forget it altogether.[2]

Women who chose not to challenge the regime and its entire patriarchal structure but who nonetheless wished to improve the lot of women organized the Russian feminist movement (ca. 1860–1917). Feminist women shared the class background (largely gentry) of the nihilists and radicals, but did not call for the destruction of the existing social system. They worked for women's rights—not for the rights of peasants or workers, and not on behalf of a socialist vision. In the four decades or so after 1860 feminists agitated, with considerable success, for permission to form legal societies, engage in charity work, and open university level and medical courses for women. These courses produced impressive numbers of physicians, teachers, lawyers, and engineers. At the dawn of the twentieth century, feminists turned their attention to the national suffrage issue and continued to press for and win reforms in the status of women in the realm of property rights, divorce, freedom of movement, and other matters that primarily affected women of the gentry and the professional classes of Russia. From 1905 to 1917, no fewer than four feminist parties struggled unsuccessfully in the political arena. Thus all women (and millions of men) remained without representation in the central government. Russian feminism, in the words of its most eloquent historian, was "a movement for women's civil and political equality, whose supporters trusted that a better world could be created without resort to violence, and a constitutional solution be found to Russia's ills."[3]

Industrialization

The industrialization of Russia in the 1890s brought new social tensions, new ideologies, and new currents and crosscurrents to the political landscape of imperial Russia. The peasantry, long dormant even in the face of Populist agitation, now began to stir: sporadic revolts in the early years of the century blossomed into insurrection by 1905 and 1906. Urbanization and the growth of factories enlarged the proletariat and made it into the favored target of socialist organizers, who found it far more amenable than the peasantry to its messages of class solidarity and revolt. An important segment of this new proletariat, women workers, added a new dimension to the interaction of revolution and women's rights. Men and women of the factories launched strikes and protest demonstrations on an ever-increasing scale, which culminated in the Revolution of 1905, a complex movement that consisted of mutinies, jacqueries, strikes, and other displays of public disorder and opposition to the tsarist autocracy. By the end of the year, the tsar found himself forced reluctantly to grant a constitution and open Russia's first parliament in modern history—the State Duma (1906–1917), based on limited male suffrage.

How did all these changes in political and economic life affect the lives of women? Peasants, as usual, were the least affected. Rural families were subjected to a certain amount of destabilization by the pull of industrialization. Wives often remained in the villages to run the household and maintain its economy without the presence of their husbands. Other peasant women— responding to a series of land reforms from 1906 to 1910—joined their husbands in withdrawing from the village communes and setting up independent farmsteads. Some women migrated to the cities to join the urban proletariat, but the bulk of independently employed urban women were domestic servants, overwhelmingly of rural origin, largely illiterate and unskilled, and "easy targets for economic and sexual exploitation." This neglected stratum of women (32 percent of St. Petersburg's working women in 1900 and 25.2 percent of Moscow's in 1912) predominated among mothers (mostly unmarried) who abandoned children and among prostitutes.[4]

The female proletariat was the object of new kinds of exploitation, including poorly regulated, miserable factory conditions and sexual harassment by bosses, as well as a variant of the old: mistreatment at the hands of their proletarian husbands. Their situation was one of double exploitation. "Women workers wrote incessantly and openly about the hostility they endured from male workers, making it clear that this hostility was as much a feature of the normal daily exchange between men and women workers as was the humiliating treatment they endured from male supervisory personnel".[5] This situation drew the attention of the new groups and parties of women—feminist and socialist—who vied for the loyalties of women workers and tried to mobilize them for their own programs. In this way industrialization had brought about what had been lacking in the old rural order: the possibility of a political alliance between women of the upper and the lower classes.

Political Parties

The political parties of late imperial Russia reacted to the question of women's rights in much the same way as their counterparts in Western Europe—their views on this issue being a litmus test for their outlook on social change and mass interests. Those on the right displayed outright hostility to any kind of feminist platform, identifying legitimate politics with the male sex and proclaiming as their program Faith, Tsar, and Fatherland. The liberal parties in the center—the Kadets, or Constitutional Democrats, most prominent among them—initially wavered on the question of votes for women in the Duma but by 1906 supported the more moderate of the feminist parties. The socialists—like the Populists earlier and like their counterparts in Western Europe—proclaimed support for women's equality, including political equality, maternity protection, and equal economic rights.

The socialist parties also included women activists at many levels, some of whom would become prominent political figures during the Revolution of 1917. Of the three major socialist parties—Socialist Revolutionary, Social Democrat-Menshevik, and Social Democrat-Bolshevik—the first eventually became the largest and most variegated. Heirs to the Populist tradition of the nineteenth century, the Socialist Revolutionaries continued to focus on peasant agrarian socialism and an alliance of the "social trinity": peasant, worker, and intelligentsia. Loose in organization and weak in theory, the Socialist Revolutionary party periodically fell back upon terror as its main weapon. Its best-known women were Ekaterina Breshko-Breshkovskaya (1844–1934), a veteran Populist of the 1870s who tried in the 1905 period to promote a theory of "agrarian terror" that included assaults on landlords in the countryside; and Maria Spiridonova (1886–?), a young schoolteacher who achieved fame first by her assassination of a general in 1906 and then in 1917 as the leader of the Left Socialist Revolutionary party. The Socialist Revolutionaries—like the Anarchist groups—could deploy a large number of female terrorists, but women played a minimal role in the organizational and theoretical work of the party.

The Marxists (Social Democrats) had split into Mensheviks and Bolsheviks in 1903. Both enrolled large numbers of women but in neither did many women rise to leadership positions. Among the Mensheviks, Vera Zasulich was the best-known woman (her fame arose from an attempted assassination she had performed in the 1870s) but her political influence remained strictly secondary.[6] The most important activist women among the Bolsheviks—Roza Zemlyachka and Elena Stasova—were tough organizers, but not leaders or theoreticians. In all the socialist parties the leadership remained in the hands of men, men who spent most of the years from 1905 to 1917 in the émigré centers of Western Europe. Two of the best-known Bolshevik women, Nadezhda Krupskaya (Lenin's wife) and Inessa Armand (their friend), made their mark as loyal assistants of the party leader, Lenin, in the emigration years.[7]

The presence of women in the major socialist parties did not advance the cause of women's rights in Russia. Less than ten percent of the delegates to Socialist Revolutionary conferences in the peak years from 1905 to 1908 were women; the percentages were even lower in Marxist and Social Democratic parties.[8] Even if more women had risen to the top of these organizations, however, the picture would not have changed. Women constituted one-third of the Executive Committee of the People's Will of the 1870s, for example, yet those women displayed almost no interest in the issue of women's rights as such. The same mood prevailed in the generation of 1905; revolutionary women put what they called the "common cause" above what they saw as lesser issues. Vera Zasulich, when asked to help in forming a women workers' club, refused.

The most notable exception, Alexandra Kollontai, had to fight on many fronts when she set about combining the advocacy of women's rights with socialism: against her feminist competitors, against indifference in her own party (she was at first a Menshevik and later a Bolshevik), and against the prevailing opinion of the conservative society. Kollontai, a general's daughter, had come to a feminist consciousness through personal experience— the conflict of work and family. Like many European socialist women, particularly Clara Zetkin (see Chapter 15), Kollontai believed that women had special problems that Marxist programs did not sufficiently address. She opposed the feminists as bourgeois; she believed that women workers should rally to the proletarian banner; but she also insisted that working women needed their own self-awareness—as workers and as women. Out of this set of beliefs arose the Proletarian Women's Movement.[9]

In the years from 1905 to 1908 Kollontai fought to create a socialist-feminist movement in order to win away proletarian women of St. Petersburg from the feminists who were trying to organize them into an "all-women's" movement. For three years, Kollontai and a few associates agitated among the factory women, taught them Marxism, and attempted to show them that their principal enemy was the bourgeoisie, not men. In this struggle, Kollontai opposed the bourgeois (as she perceived it) program of the feminists with her own vision of socialist feminism—a combination of gender and class awareness, a recognition of the double exploitation of working-class women (as workers and as women), and an honest facing of the issue of abusive proletarian husbands and insensitive socialist males. Although Kollontai exaggerated the selfish class character of Russian feminists, she did in fact go beyond them and beyond her own comrades in the socialist movement in trying to draw attention to these issues. Police harrassment in 1908 forced her to leave the country, and during her years in Western Europe Kollontai deepened her understanding of the woman question through study and personal experience.

The Eve of Revolution

On the eve of war and revolution, the woman question in tsarist society remained a public issue. Thousands of women graduates of universities had entered professional life; hundreds languished in jail or in Siberia for their chosen profession as revolutionaries. The female terrorist was the Russian counterpart to the British suffragette—but far more violent. Organized feminists continued to agitate for important reforms in the status of women and won considerable legislative victories in legal, educational, and property rights—though mainly for women of the middle and upper classes.[10] The female work force continued to grow and to feel the rigors of industrial life and of relative neglect by the rest of society. With the revival of the militant labor movement around 1912, Mensheviks and Bolsheviks alike reactivated their efforts to organize women workers. International Women's Day, established in Europe in 1910, was celebrated by adherents of both factions for the first time on Russian soil in 1913, and a newspaper, *The Woman Worker*, was established in 1914. During World War I much of the machinery for organizing women workers was smashed by the authorities and many leaders were arrested before the monarchy itself fell a victim to the same war.

THE REVOLUTIONARY ERA

After three winters of bitter fighting, bloody losses, and patent mismanagement of the war, widespread discontent and hatred of the regime found a focus. In February 1917, cold and hungry women of the capital (renamed Petrograd) rioted, beginning an uprising that led to the collapse of the Romanov dynasty within a week. With the men at the front and the women left behind as workers, breadwinners, and heads of households, the women of the lower classes perceived food shortages and related deprivations as a menace to their very existence and to their roles as women.[11] They struck, demonstrated, rioted, and appealed to the class solidarity of garrison troops to persuade the troops not to fire upon them. When the tsar abdicated, the revolutionary parties linked up with the masses of women. A band of energetic Bolshevik women organizers—including Kollontai—created a network of agitation that was effective in spite of tactical squabbles and the enormous problems of communication in the midst of a major revolt. This network produced mass female demonstrations on behalf of Bolshevik issues, organized women in factories, and enlisted others in political, paramedical, and paramilitary work. Bolshevik leadership and dynamism in this arena proved vastly superior to that of the other radical parties, and Bolshevik hostility to the now-revived feminist movement was active and unambiguous. Out of this year of struggle and organization in many cities emerged the symbolically important "presence" of women in the October Revolution as well as the foundations of a postrevolutionary women's movement.

The Bolsheviks took power on October 25 (November 7 in the modern calendar), 1917, and established a Soviet socialist regime; in 1918 they moved the capital to Moscow, issued a constitution that was the framework for the world's first socialist state, and made peace with Germany. The first years of the new regime were marked by ruthless political struggle on all sides, a bloody and cruel civil war, intervention in that war by foreign troops on behalf of the anti-Bolshevik forces, and a deepening of the extraordinary economic hardship set off by war and revolution and made inevitable by the very backwardness of the country.

How, in this time of dreadful calamity, did the Bolshevik regime perceive the issue—historically always seen as marginal by all governments—of the emancipation of women? What did they do about it? The answers are very complicated; any assessment of their response depends upon how one views revolution in general and the Bolshevik Revolution in particular, and upon one's expectations from an insurgent, culture-changing government that sets out to remake the face of one of the largest countries in the world.[12]

The men and women in the Bolshevik party displayed the contradictions inherent in all forceful agents of social and cultural change: practicality combined with vision, the imperatives of survival combined with the dream of transformation. The party's leader, V. I. Lenin, as both a Marxist and a Russian revolutionary, committed himself and his party to the educational, economic, legal, and political liberation of women; to the interchangeability of gender roles in a future under communism; and to special protection for woman as childbearer and nurturing mother. In addition, Lenin possessed an almost compulsive hatred of the domestic enslavement of women to mindless household work which he called "barbarously unproductive, petty, nerve-wracking, stultifying and crushing drudgery."[13] Lenin's male and female colleagues shared his opinions on these major issues and framed their laws and policies accordingly. Most important, they endorsed the creation of a special women's organization to oversee the realization of these programs in Soviet society. Women did not play a major role in the upper reaches of the party hierarchy; and indeed hostility toward the expenditure of time on women's issues persisted in the party at various levels. This was an inheritance of the twenty years of underground life of party struggle, of the military mentality of Bolshevism that hardened during the Civil War, and of the upsurge within the party of people holding "traditional" patriarchal views of the female sex. In spite of these obvious weaknesses, it is astonishing what the Bolshevik regime proclaimed and actually carried out in the early years of Soviet power.

In a series of decrees, codes, electoral laws, and land reforms, the Bolsheviks proclaimed an across-the-board equality of the sexes—the first regime in history ever to do so. All institutions of learning were opened to women and girls. Women attained equal status in marriage—including the right to change or retain their own names—divorce, family, and inheritance and equal rights in litigation and the ownership of property. By separating church and state, the Bolsheviks legally invalidated all canonical and theological restrictions on the role of women in modern life—a sweeping and drastic measure in a land wrapped in the constraining meshes of traditional faiths, particularly Russian Orthodoxy and Islam. In 1920 the Bolsheviks legalized abortion. On the other hand, prostitution (legally licensed under the old regime) was made illegal. Taken together, these measures offered a structure for equality between the sexes unprecedented in history. The Bolsheviks offered a process as well: the organizations that helped overthrow the old order would help to erect the new one; art, culture, symbol, and mythic vision would reinforce the values of sexual equality.

The organizational form of women's liberation in the first decade of the Bolshevik (now renamed Communist) regime was the Women's Department of the Communist Party (1919–1930), known by its Russian abbreviation Zhenotdel. Founded as an arm of the party rather than as an independent feminist organization, Zhenotdel—led by Inessa Armand and Alexandra Kollontai in the early years—worked to transform the new revolutionary laws into reality through education, mobilization, and social work. Understaffed and hampered by a small budget, Zhenotdel went into the factory neighborhoods, the villages, and the remote provinces of the new Soviet state to bring the message of the Revolution to the female population. Instructors and trainees from among workers and peasant women addressed the practical concerns of women. In the towns they monitored factory conditions and fought against female unemployment and prostitution. In the countryside they opened literacy classes and explained the new laws. In the Muslim regions they opposed humiliating customs and attitudes. Everywhere they counselled women about divorce and women's rights—and tied all such lessons to political instruction about the values and aims of the regime. Activated by Zhenotdel, women virtually untouched by political culture entered into the local administrative process. Most crucial of all, the activists of Zhenotdel learned the rudiments of organizing and modernizing and taught themselves the meaning of social revolution.[14]

Bolshevism contained vision as well as social policy. In societies wracked by poverty and dislocation, social vision—utopian or otherwise—plays a key role in capturing the sentiment of people, particularly the literate and the already engaged. Speculation about the future of sexual relations often helped to reinforce the process of working for improving such relations in the present. The most active and articulate Bolshevik woman activist, Kollontai, gave special attention to a program of communist sexual relations and communal "family" life. In regard to the first, Kollontai vigorously defended woman's need for independence and a separate income. This in turn would give her the dignity and strength needed for an equal and open love–sex relationship and would enhance the pleasure and quality of sexual intercourse. As to the second, she believed in a "marriage" unfettered by economic dependence or responsibility for children. The latter were to be cared for in communal facilities to which parents had easy access. Kollontai believed in parenthood—her ideal in fact for all humans—and in regular contact between parents and children. The material life of the children, however, was to be the responsibility of the local "collective" of work or residence. Housekeeping was to be no more than an "industrial" task like any other, handled by specialists—never the domain of a wife (or husband) alone.[15]

Some of the more daring aspects of Kollontai's sexual theories fell victim to misinterpretation in the 1920s. Hers was an overall vision of equality in life, work, and love that matched the utopian visions of the science fiction writers and revolutionary town planners and architects who were the major futuristic thinkers in this decade of experiment. In the 1920s about 200 science fiction titles appeared, many of them outlining a future world of perfection characterized by social justice and ultramodern technology. Such utopian pictures almost invariably revealed a unified, urbanized globe bathed in peace, harmony, and affluent communist civilization inhabited by a near-androgynous population with genderless names and unisex costumes. Sexual tensions no longer tormented the human race, women worked as equals to men in a machine-run economy of universal participation and communist distribution, and healthy children thrived in colonies.

Architects and town planners of the 1920s and early 1930s designed living spaces as "social condensers"—communal buildings that would shape the collective consciousness of their inhabitants. Although the projects varied in scope, size, and density, almost all of the architectural planning of that period provided for private rooms for single persons and couples, easy divorce by changing rooms, communal care for children, communal cooking and dining, and an environment of male-female cooperation in household tasks. Some of these communal homes actually were built; others remained in the blueprint stage. As a whole, visionary architecture and town planning of that period attested to the central importance of woman's new role as an independent and equal member of society.

The ultimate experiments in sexual equality—the rural and urban communes of the 1920s—put communalism (the complete and equal sharing of lives, partly inspired by Chernyshevsky) into practice wherever space could be found. Thousands in the countryside and hundreds in the cities joined to share goods, money, books, land, and property of every sort. Members of these collectives rotated work, apportioned income equally, and pooled all resources. Sexual equality worked better in the workers' and student communes of the cities than in the countryside, where the sexual division of labor often prevailed: women took over the big communal kitchens while men labored together in the fields. In the town communes, students and workers made sexual equality a mandatory condition. In these "living utopias," males learned how to cook and iron and wash floors under the guidance of women so that all could take their turns at housework on a strictly rotational basis. In some of the more rigorous communes, love and friendship were declared indivisible—cliques and romantic pairing were outlawed as violations of the collective principle. Tensions and flaring tempers beset many of these communes all through the 1920s; but they persisted as "laboratories of revolution" where communism could be practiced and lived day to day.[16]

This part of the picture of women's liberation—the idealistic foreground—deserves emphasis because it is so often overlooked in assessments of the Revolution. Endemic misery and material poverty hampered these experiments, and cynicism and indifference made mockeries of the dreams, but the experiments and dreams persisted. Life for women—and men—was very difficult in the early years after the Revolution. The rural world presented a vast terrain of disease and superstition, suspicious peasants, archaic tools, and ancient agronomical technique. Towns were filled with unemployed women, deserted and abandoned children, criminals and organized gangs, and conspicuously wealthy businessmen. These last comprised a class created by the introduction of Lenin's New Economic Policy in 1921, which allowed a mixed economy, a limited arena of capitalism and hired labor with enclaves of privileged specialists, government leaders, and foreigners. Women were hit very hard by all of this. About 70 percent of the initial job cutbacks that occurred periodically during this period affected women. Between 70,000 and 100,000 women in *de facto* marriages with men possessed none of the financial security or legal protection that might have been vouchsafed them with registered marriage.[17]

Equality of the sexes did not become the norm in Soviet life—even in the relatively free and pluralist 1920s. Peasant "lords" held sway in their wooden cabins. In the factory towns, women were fired or laid off before men. Male preeminence continued to hold sway in all walks of life—including the party and the state. Few women reached high political positions, none the top. Old ways, rooted in thousands of years of tradition, died hard in spite of laws, campaigns, organizing efforts, and attempts to create new images and myths. The Zhenotdel was in fact weaker at the end of the decade than when it was formed. The sexual revolution launched by the Bolsheviks got out of hand; males abused the new ethos of sexual equality by deromanticizing love and exploiting women for easy sex in the name of a "proletarian morality." Moral conservatives among the Bolsheviks in the mid-1920s began a backlash against the new sexual culture (and against excesses that they unfairly laid at the door of Kollontai's teaching); and the voices of peasant and working class women rose in opposition to the "immoral" divorce laws during the marriage debates from 1925 to 1926.

The revolutionary process did not end in 1928—in fact that year marked the launching of a new stage in the process of social change. But it was the end of an era—variously known as the revolutionary decade, the NEP period, the Age of Lenin, or the experimental age of Bolshevism. Many things perished with it: a relatively pluralistic social landscape, vigorous political and economic debates, and an atmosphere of frenetic and often joyous experimentation. During the period the Bolsheviks accomplished many things besides their consolidation of political power, the defense of the republic against external menace, and the winning of recognition by foreign powers. They had laid the foundations of a socialist system in a one-party state, begun the process of mobilizing the masses of underprivileged Russians, and launched a multitude of struggles against social evils—disease, prostitution, illiteracy, and cultural backwardness.

THE STALIN PERIOD

The ascendance of Stalin at the end of the 1920s and the revolution from above that his government launched changed the face of the USSR while retaining certain basic ideological and mythic features of the early Bolshevik period. The political revolution was particularly harsh, marked by Stalin's pathological attempt to eradicate all his enemies (real or imagined), a termination of all political discourse, and a cult of personality that pictured the leader as an all-knowing secular god. The economic revolution—whose achievements and weaknesses outlived Stalin's excesses and crimes—collectivized the peasantry and launched the rest of the population into a gigantic and uneven surge of massive, centrally planned industrialization. The accompanying social revolution brought the elimination of the old revolutionary elite, the rapid rise of workers into positions of management and leadership, and the transformation of Soviet cities by some nineteen million immigrants in the years from 1926 to 1939. This was more than the familiar urban in-migration that comes with industrialization. Its magnitude was so great and its force so sudden that it changed the social face of major Soviet cities, rusticating them by peasant influx. Peasant forms of motion and work, living-habits, customs, modes of speech, and social attitudes created a rural atmosphere in these towns and cities.[18]

Such a complicated and immense revolution had to produce complex and contradictory results. Among them must be recognized the unimaginable suffering inflicted upon millions—victims of famine, collectivization, terror and repression—and, for others, the overcrowding and urban dehumanization with the attendant negative impact on families. Against this must also be set the genuine industrial growth, the forging of economic and military sinew that enabled the Soviet people to survive and win the war against the Germans in the years from 1941 to 1945. The combination of upward mobility for the lower classes, the change of the cities by displaced peasants, the increasing isolation of Soviet Russia from the West, and the upsurge of xenophobia that came with it led to a cultural reorientation away from that of the 1920s—a search for *kulturnost*, or respectability, a turn to middle-brow tastes by the new elite, and a return to certain traditional values of the old regime. Among such traditional values was conservative nationalism, the exaltation of ancient military and patriotic heroes of the Russian past, and a strong revival of patriarchalism at many levels, especially in the form of dictator-worship, and the cult of Stalin. Much of the utopian experimentalism of the 1920s—egalitarianism, communes, speculation about the future—was repudiated in the 1930s even at the level of idealistic myths and dreams.[19]

The great transformation of the 1930s affected the lives of women more profoundly than any development in Russian history. With it came a dramatic, revolutionary rise in women's upward mobility, their professionalization, and their entry into all sectors of the urban economy. Special campaigns promoted women and sent them to technical and medical schools. Since precise quotas required that a certain percentage of women be admitted, this technique actually pushed a previously underprivileged segment of the population forward—a policy now called "affirmative action." In the 1930s the regime laid the foundations of the occupational structure of women's employment in the Soviet Union. In practice as well as theory this represented a huge advance for the Soviet female population into a world once designated as male—the world of the laboratory, construction site, technical college, planning office, and other arenas of a society dynamically engaged in rapid construction and economic development. Between 1926 and 1939 the reported percentage of literate females rose from 42.7 percent to 81.6 percent. The proportion of women at institutions of higher education rose from 31 percent in 1926 to 58 percent in 1940. Moreover, as Krupskaya forcefully noted, these were educations, not in lacemaking or embroidery, but in agronomy, animal husbandry, sanitation, and technology.[20]

In the realm of family life, the industrial revolution of the Stalin period resulted in more traditional and authoritarian definitions of women's productive and reproductive roles. To promote family stability, protect women from male irresponsibility, and increase the population, the regime tightened the divorce laws and outlawed abortion. Although the authorities expected practically all women to engage in productive work outside the home, they exalted motherhood as a patriotic function. A sugary image of the Soviet mother bedecked with maternity-heroine medals and beaming over a large and healthy family replaced the earlier revolutionary image of the female warrior. Individual family housekeeping units survived the dreams of a communal life and women were again given the principal responsibility for childcare and domestic work (including the "esthetic" job of adorning the home). Wives of high political leaders, business executives, managers, and engineers, however, were not required to work. To justify their existence, they busied themselves by organizing a "movement" concerned with the interior decoration of offices and the beautification of the grounds and premises of their husbands' factories and enterprises. In the meantime, the vast majority of Soviet women held full-time jobs and then performed what was called their "second shift" of shopping, cooking, housekeeping, and childcare.

Stalin's economic and social revolution thus possessed a dynamism that propelled people up the social scale and opened up vistas for education and opportunity—especially in science and technology. At the same time, it exalted power, authority, and inequality. Stalinism brought no return to tsarism but rather a revolutionary mix of upheaval, social advancement, and the resurgence of some traditional values. The redefinition of women's roles in the 1930s that held women to be equally liable for production and solely responsible for reproduction and family management must be understood in this context.

Women's experience in the war against Germany vividly illustrates this new set of roles. Aside from the millions pulled into war production and civil defence, about one million women actually served in the war, 800,000 of them in the uniformed armed service as soldiers and officers in combat, in auxiliary roles (supply and medical), as antiaircraft gunners, snipers, tankers, pilots and bombardiers; others were behind-the-lines partisans and underground saboteurs. Thousands died or suffered wounds in battlefield fighting; hundreds fell before the execution squads of the German occupiers. Zoya Kosmodemyanskaya—tortured and hanged by the Germans for partisan activity—became a national martyr, symbolizing the struggle of Soviet women against the invader. The fact that the vast majority of women held low or middle ranks, staff jobs, and subordinate positions (as in civilian life) does not diminish the epic quality of this experience.[21]

Writers of the late Stalin period spoke of "the solution of the woman question"[22] in Soviet Russia. In reality, women's role was frozen into a position defined by the regime. After the tragedy and grandeur of military service, Soviet women were sent back to the civilian sector (as in the United States) to resume their heavy double burdens, in the economy and in the home—a home that was frequently bereft of a male breadwinner. The postwar years were among the most difficult that Soviet women have ever had to endure. The hideous bloodletting of the 1930s and World War II had left millions of women lonely, prematurely old, overworked, bitterly saddened, and largely ignored.

THE POST–STALIN PERIOD

The death of Stalin in 1953 unlocked many doors in the Soviet system, not the least being the prison gates that had surrounded the inmates in the forced labor camps of the Stalin era. His successor, Nikita Khrushchev (in power from 1953 to 1964) released millions of prisoners and delivered his famous "destalinization" speech which furthered the process of cold-war thaw and domestic reform. Specific reforms of women's rights and status began in the Khrushchev period and have continued since his fall from power. After considerable debate, abortion was legalized in 1955. Laws enacted in 1965 and 1968, made divorce simpler and much easier to obtain. Abandoning the restrictions on marriage and divorce of the previous era, the regime quietly introduced in the early 1960s a national system of civil rituals designed to solemnify and sacralize certain rites of passage— including matrimony.[23] Maternity protection now entitles the expectant mother to 56 days of maternity leave before the birth and 56 days after the birth.[24] Coeducation, partly abolished in 1943, was restored after Stalin's death. Just as important, the educational system continues to prepare huge numbers of women for professional, scientific, technical, and higher educational degrees, which allows many of them to achieve careers in professions.

Genuine policy debates and political actions related to interest groups— including women—can and do occur. The notion of Developed Socialism, promulgated under Leonid Brezhnev (in power from 1964 to 1982) as an intermediate road to full communism, opened a wide-ranging discussion of welfare and public facilities for all Soviet citizens. The press and public organizations—local soviets and party groups—have taken up specific lobbying issues such as kindergarten care, flextime, maternity protection, and the availability of health facilities that impinge closely upon women's daily lives. Academic disciplines—sociology, for example—that had been outlawed in the Stalin years have reappeared. The mountain of statistical data about women's lives and the mass of monographs, reform projects, press articles, and fiction, taken together, amount to a steady public campaign to improve the lot of women within the parameters of the political and economic system.[25] The continuing growth in the number of civic-minded and politically active educated women has sharpened the perception of remaining inadequacies in the system vis-à-vis women's equality.

What are these? They fall into two fundamental categories: inequality in the workplace and inequality in the home. In the workplace, a kind of vertical segregation works against women. They rarely reach top positions of earning power and authority in factory, enterprise, office, or laboratory. Even in occupations and professions that are largely feminized—such as medicine—leadership, directorship, and management are most often in the hands of men. Saddled by home responsibilities and faced by persistent attitudes of male preeminence, women find it difficult to rise to the peak of their professions. Horizontal segregation, on the other hand, channels women into low-paying jobs and professions—such as medicine—and reserves the higher-paying ones for males. Although a policy of equal pay for equal work has existed since the beginning of the Soviet regime, the dual segregation phenomenon turns women into economically second-class citizens. The exclusion of women from the highest ranks of political power is closely related to what happens in the economic arena; both types of segregation arise from deeply ingrained male attitudes that achieved full prominence in the 1930s.

Inequality in the home, which results in the "double shift" for women, has evoked the most bitterness from women critics. Women and girls, married and unmarried, are almost universally expected to take primary responsibility for childcare and do most or all of the housework—work that is especially difficult in a land that still suffers from a shortage of labor-saving home appliances and from a retail system that makes shopping a tedious and time-consuming chore. Official rhetoric defines the woman's role as threefold: to contribute to the productive process by working outside the home; to take on the prime responsibility of household management; and also to participate in what is called "public-spirited" or volunteer work on behalf of society (party, Communist Youth League, trade union, or similar activities). The tension inherent in this three-way system of demands is clear—and it helps augment the high divorce rate, the family conflicts, and the relatively low rate of professional advancement of women.[26]

All of these problems—heightened by increasing alcoholism and the continued insufficiencies in housing and transport—have been richly documented in the Soviet press over the past generation. Detailed reports provided by foreign journalists and scholars and by underground feminist writers reveal vividly how deeply these problems are felt by many Soviet women. The new feminist movement in Soviet Russia is a direct response to these problems—and others. In 1979, a tiny group of dissident women of Leningrad published a collection of grievances, Almanac, which has appeared in many editions aboard but never legally in the USSR.[27] A forthright and eclectic mélange of lament, description, and protest—far beyond anything uttered in the press—it marked the birth of a new women's movement in Russia.

Like all such movements in Russian history, and like most contemporary Soviet dissident movements, the feminist movement divided almost instantaneously into clearcut factions. The secular wing, represented by Tatyana Mamonova, who was expelled and has since settled abroad, offers a classic protest against the injustice of the regime in general and against its treatment of women in particular. About the other faction, much less is known. It is a Christian group that produces a journal named after the Blessed Mother (*Mariya*, or "Mary"). In a country whose government has actively fought against religion in general and Russian Orthodoxy in particular since its very inception, it is not surprising that some feminists should express their grievances and their aspirations in a religious idiom. Some of the most important dissident voices in the Soviet Union in the last twenty years have been those of committed Christians who posit a return to the values of Holy Russia as the true alternative to Communist rule.

The philosophical character of the schism makes it strikingly different from most of the divisions among western feminists and from the division between "bourgeois feminists" and "proletarian women's movement" of the Russian past. Harrassed by expulsion orders and arrests, divided internally, ignored by many western feminists and western leftists as well, and faced with the prospects of stony silence on the part of the female masses inside their country, these Soviet feminists stand in a precarious and lonely position—as their grandmothers and greatgrandmothers had done over a century previously when they launched the first women's movement in Russia.

CONCLUSION

There is no simple way to sum up what the Russian Revolution has meant to women. No one can leave the study of a major social revolution without a feeling of both exhilaration and anguish: exhilaration about the dramatic forces unleashed, the heroism manifested, and the achievements registered; anguish and pain about the price that so many people had to pay for these achievements. The Bolshevik Revolution has been seen as a social disaster, a liberating force, a chronicle of heartless violence, and a builder of the nation. The Soviet Union is today viewed as a scourge to humanity, an uplifting inspiration to millions of people across the globe, a totalitarian menace, and a bastion of justice. It may take generations before these colliding images converge into a sober and detached historical perspective. In the meantime Soviet women and we who study them may look back into the revolutionary movement of the nineteenth century and at the Revolution itself and see either a tragic episode or a glorious epic. The wisest may even see both.

NOTES

1. N. G. Chernyshevsky, *Chto delat?* (1863; Moscow, 1963), p. 67.
2. Barbara Engel, *Mothers and Daughters* (Cambridge: Cambridge University Press, 1983) p. 125.
3. Linda Edmondson, *Feminism in Russia, 1900–1917* (London: Heinemann, 1984), p. x.
4. David Ransel, "Abandonment and Fosterage of Unwanted Children: the Women of the Foundling System," in David Ransel, ed., *The Family in Imperial Russia* (Urbana: University of Illinois Press, 1978), p. 195; Richard Stites, "Prostitute and Society in Pre-Revolutionary Russia," *Jahrbücher für Geschichte Osteuropas*, 31 (1983) 348–64.
5. Rose Glickman, *Russian Factory Women* (Berkeley: University of California Press, 1984), p. 276.
6. Jay Bergman, *Vera Zasulich* (Stanford, Calif.: Stanford University Press, 1983).
7. See N. K. Krupskaya, *Memories of Lenin* (London, 1930).
8. According to Amy Knight's figures cited in Stites, *The Women's Liberation Movement in Russia* (Princeton, N.J.: Princeton University Press, 1978), p. 271.
9. The best studies of Kollontai are Barbara Clements, *Bolshevik Feminist* (Bloomington: Indiana University Press, 1979) and Beatrice Farnsworth, *Aleksandra Kollontai* (Stanford, Calif.: Stanford University Press, 1980).
10. Edmondson, *Feminism in Russia*.
11. See Temma Kaplan's essay in this volume.
12. On the culture-changing aspects of the Revolution, see *Bolshevik Culture: Experiment and Order in the Russian Revolution*, ed. A. Gleason, *et al.* (Bloomington: Indiana University Press, 1985).
13. V. I. Lenin, *On the Emancipation of Women* (Moscow: n.d.), pp. 61–62.
14. On the social function of propaganda, see Peter Kenez, *The Birth of the Propaganda State: Soviet Methods of Mass Mobilization 1917–1929* (Cambridge: Cambridge University Press, 1986).
15. Alexandra Kollontai, *Selected Writings*, ed. Alix Holt (New York: Norton, 1982).
16. Stites, "Utopias of Time, Space, and Life in the Russian Revolution," *Revue des études slaves*, 56/1 (1984) 141–54.
17. Wendy Goldman, " 'Free Union' and Working Women: Marriage and Material Life in Russia, 1917–1928," American Historical Association paper, December 1985; quoted with permission.
18. See Moshe Lewin, "Society, State, and Ideology during the First Five-Year Plan" in S. Fitzpatrick, ed., *Cultural Revolution in Russia, 1928–1931* (Bloomington: Indiana University Press, 1978) 41–77.
19. Nicholas Timasheff, *The Great Retreat: the Growth and Decline of Communism in Russia* (New York: Dutton, 1946).
20. Gail Lapidus, *Women in Soviet Society* (Berkeley: University of California Press, 1978) 95–122, 136–7, 149.
21. Ann Griesse and Stites, "Russia: Revolution and War," in N. Goldman, ed., *Female Soldiers* (Westport, Conn.: Greenwood Press, 1982) 61–84.
22. Vera Bilshai, *Reshenie zhenskogo voprosa* (Moscow, 1946).
23. Christel Lane, *The Rites of Rulers* (Cambridge: Cambridge University Press, 1981).

24. Details and deficiencies on health and maternity care in Barbara Holland and Teresa McKevitt, "Maternity Care in the Soviet Union," in Holland, ed. *Soviet Sisterhood* (Bloomington: Indiana University Press, 1985), pp. 145–78.
25. Mary Buckley, "Soviet Interpretations of the Woman Question" in Holland, ed., *Soviet Sisterhood*, pp. 24–53.
26. In addition to the works cited above and below, see C. Hansson and K. Lidén, *Moscow Women* (New York: Pantheon, 1983).
27. Tatyana Mamonova, ed., *Women and Russia* (Boston: Beacon, 1984), a translation of *Almanakh* (Almanac).

SUGGESTIONS FOR FURTHER READING

For a general overview of the period from 1860 to 1930, with an emphasis on the revolutionaries, see Richard Stites, *The Women's Liberation Movement in Russia* (Princeton: Princeton University Press, 1978). Of the many popular accounts of women radicals in the nineteenth century, the liveliest is Vera Broido, *Apostles into Terrorists* (New York: Viking, 1977). For serious historical interpretation one must turn to Barbara Engel, *Mothers and Daughters* (Cambridge: Cambridge University Press, 1983), a broad study of women of the nineteenth century intelligentsia. With Clifford Rosenthal, Engel has also edited *Five Sisters: Women against the Tsar* (New York: Knopf, 1974), a vivid collection of memoirs. On the tension between professional and radical careers for women, see J. Meijer, *Knowledge and Revolution* (Assen: Van Gorcum, 1955), a study of the Russian radical community in Zurich. A mandatory work for understanding Russian radical sensibility in the 19th century is N. G. Chernyshevsky, *What Is To Be Done?* (New York: Vintage, 1961). Works on individual women revolutionaries available in English are: Vera Figner, *Memoirs of a Revolutionist* (New York: International Publishers, 1927); Jay Bergman, *Vera Zasulich* (Stanford: Stanford University Press, 1983); Catherine Breshkovsky, *Little Grandmother of the Russian Revolution* (Boston, 1930) and *idem., Hidden Springs of the Russian Revolution* (Stanford: Stanford University Press, 1931).

For the generation directly preceding the Revolution (ca. 1890–1917), the radical women have received much more attention than the feminists—for whom the standard work is Linda Edmondson, *Feminism in Russia, 1900–1917* (London: Heinemann, 1984). For Kollontai, see: Barbara Clements, *Bolshevik Feminist* (Bloomington: Indiana University Press, 1979), Beatrice Farnsworth, *Alexandra Kollontai* (Stanford: Stanford University Press, 1980)—excellent biographies that complement one another—and Kollontai, *Selected Writings* (New York: Norton, 1982), with a valuable essay by Alix Holt. There is a biography of Krupskaya by Robert McNeal, *Bride of the Revolution: Krupskaya and Lenin* (Ann Arbor: University of Michigan Press, 1972) and a partial autobiography: Krupskaya, *Memories of Lenin* (London: Lawrence, 1930) and many other editions. An illuminating memoir by a Menshevik woman is Eva Broido, *Memoirs of a Revolutionary* (London: Oxford University Press, 1967). The tragic fate of a Socialist Revolutionary female terrorist is examined in Isaac Steinberg, *Spiridonova* (London: Methuen, 1935). Women of the lower classes have received less attention from historians. The major exception is Rose Glickman, *Russian Factory Women* (Berkeley: University of

California Press, 1984), a perceptive study of proletarian women in the workplace, the family, and politics. Some good material on peasant women's lives can be found in the fine collection edited by David Ransel, *The Family in Imperial Russia* (Urbana: University of Illinois Press, 1978).

The best study of women in the Soviet period is Gail Lapidus, *Women in Soviet Society* (Berkeley: University of California Press, 1978). A number of pathbreaking articles on the subject can be found in *Women in Russia*, ed. D. Atkinson, A. Dallin, and G. Lapidus (Stanford: Stanford University Press, 1977). On specialized topics, see Norton Dodge, *Women in the Soviet Economy* (Baltimore: Johns Hopkins University Press, 1966); Xenia Gasiorowska, *Women in Soviet Fiction* (Madison: University of Wisconsin Press, 1968); Rudolph Schlesinger, ed., *The Family in the U.S.S.R.* (London, 1949); Kent Geiger, *The Family in Soviet Russia* (Cambridge: Harvard University Press, 1968). Still very useful are the rich, vivid, and optimistic treatments of women in the Revolution and the early Soviet years written by sympathetic women: Fanina Halle, *Women in Soviet Russia* (New York: Viking, 1933); and Ella Winter, *Red Virtue* (New York, 1935). A convenient collection of Lenin's views on women is V. I. Lenin, *The Emancipation of Women* (New York: International Publishers, 1972). The darker side of women's role and status in the Soviet Union is shown in Gregory Massell, *The Surrogate Proletariat* (Princeton: Princeton University Press, 1974), an intriguing study of Bolshevik policy toward Muslim women; and one of many camp recollections by a victim of Stalin: Evgenia Ginzburg, *Into the Whirlwind* (Harmondsworth: Penguin, 1968).

For opposing views of how Soviet women live in the present age, see William Mandel, *Soviet Women* (New York: Anchor, 1975), a very glowing account of Soviet life and women's role in it; and Tatyana Mamonova, ed., *Women and Russia* (Boston: Beacon, 1984), a dismal, first hand underground report on realities of everyday existence written by Soviet women. Carola Hansson and Karen Lidén, in *Moscow Women* (New York: Pantheon, 1983), offer thirteen interviews with Soviet women from all walks of life. Barbara Holland, ed., *Soviet Sisterhood* (Bloomington: Indiana University Press, 1985) is the best and fairest assessment to date of the lot of Soviet women.

Reality and the dream. In the 1920s and 1930s, the ideal of glamor, stressing women's sexuality, contradicted and masked women's increasingly routine work lives. This polarization, along with changes in the family as an institution, created a new identity crisis among women. *Above:* The Sylvester Jazz Band, 1927. (Ullstein Bilderdienst) *Below:* Factory interior, *c.* 1938. (Topham/The Image Works)

chapter 18

Something Old, Something New: Women Between the Two World Wars

Renate Bridenthal

The twentieth century prided itself on gains in women's rights. Suffrage was attained in many countries, and World War I brought women into new fields of work, some of which remained accessible to them after the war. However, as has been demonstrated so often in this volume, legislation and political events had less influence than slow-moving but powerful economic and social forces, and these were not always beneficial to women. Renate Bridenthal indicates that profit maximization led to merger and new technology in agriculture and industry, displacing the smaller enterprises in which women could play a leading role. Rationalization and mechanization created new unskilled jobs and mushrooming bureaucracies while commercial distribution created low-level office and sales jobs. All of these recruited women for their docility and because they would accept lower wages than men. This new female labor force was younger than before and more stereotypically feminine. Appearance and pleasing demeanor were important new attributes in these jobs, which depended so heavily on extensive social contact. Thus, women experienced contradictions. They had greater economic independence, but it depended on age and behavior. New sexual attitudes allowed them greater freedom but also commercially exploited female sexuality in the media. In their family role, women experienced a similar contradiction. Birth control spared them from a constant cycle of childbearing, but their energies were redirected by more professional notions of parenting. Finally, women gained more equality in companionate marriage, but this itself was a mere remnant of the premodern productive and politically important family. Modernization appears here as a problematic advance, welcomed by some and feared by others.

Women's efforts at peace keeping may have seemed like never-ending tasks, but their contributions once war broke out were clear and simple. As national populations drew together in 1914 to fight in a common cause, a temporary truce was declared in the war between the sexes. Most of the women's organizations, such as the International Council of Women and its national affiliates, turned dutifully into "ladies' auxiliaries." They organized home front activities, trained and counseled housewives, coordinated job placement for women, organized policewomen and patrols, did relief work, helped evacuate people from threatened areas, and set up kindergartens and orphanages. For the sake of the greater cause, they countenanced the shelving of the woman suffrage issue and the suspension of protective legislation. Middle-class women took up white-collar jobs, working-class women moved into better-paid industrial jobs, farm girls swarmed into factories, and peasant women took charge of farms. It all seemed natural, under the circumstances and for the duration of the war.

Yet, the move of womanpower from some sectors of the economy to others simply accelerated a trend well under way before the war. Postwar attempts to halt and reverse it failed, though they did manage to create hardship and ill will. In many other ways, too, women seemed after the war to have suddenly acquired equality. They won the vote in Germany, Sweden, Russia, the successor states of the Austro-Hungarian empire, the Baltic countries of Latvia, Lithuania, and Estonia, and in Great Britain. France and Italy held back, their clerical and socialist parties fearing each others' potential gains. Sexual liberty seemed to be in the air as young women crowded the popular dance halls and movie theaters. Many people saw this use of leisure as the first step down the ladder of vice. And women would not disappear from factories, stores, and offices; indeed, they seemed more visible every day. Champions of women's equality cheered each apparent advance; opponents dreaded what they perceived as the decline of western civilization. Both were wrong. Women had a far more complicated experience. Their situation revealed some of the growing contradictions of modern capitalist Europe; they were personally torn between an old form of life and a new.

The trend, for working women of the advanced industrial European nations in the twentieth century, was to move with growing rapidity into a conflict relationship between their jobs and family activities. Increasingly, as business and government took over the family's historical functions of production and socialization, it became a unit of consumption and an emotional fortress. For women, this meant that their traditional domain shrank. Yet they recaptured that domain in part by becoming wage earners in the very institutions that eroded family functions. In the factories they made products for the home under male supervisors and for male employers; in education and social services they carried out the ameliorative policies of male statesmen. Independent incomes gave women the bargaining power needed for greater participation in decision making in the family. As wage earners, they won some freedom from their husbands' authority, where family law allowed. As sexual beings, they won recognition of the right to fulfillment. However, a layer of institutionalization intervened between women and their work, depersonalizing it and legitimizing male authority even more than before. And their total life options were limited by discriminatory hiring and pay.

Women both gained and lost. But that in itself does not tell the whole story. Women did not simply face new tensions with the double burden of home and work, exacerbated by the spatial division of the two. Rather, the tensions were dynamic and demanded a new synthesis, although they also carried the dangers of a reaction. The reaction expressed a yearning for restoration of a lost world; it often seemed easier to fall into stereotypical behavior considered feminine than to explore uncharted areas of work and sexual demeanor.

In this chapter, we will examine the elements of this creative tension as they emerged out of World War I. Mainly, we will analyze changes in the structure of work and how these affected women. Then, we will look at changes in family patterns and sexual behavior and note some correlations.

To begin with the economic factors, we note that postwar reconversion was in many ways an unsettling experience. Veterans, women, and youth competed for available jobs after factories had tooled down from arms manufacture. Thousands of women lost their jobs in the metal and chemical industries, in construction and engineering, in civil service and transport. They were even dismissed from waiting on tables. Some remained where women had always worked: at lower levels of skill and pay. Soon the employment pattern of women in the major western European countries stabilized at one-fourth to one-third of the total working population. It shrank, in most cases, from prewar levels of employment among women, as Table 18-1 shows.[1]

What was going on? Briefly, and excluding marginal errors due to census procedures, male employment expanded even more than female employment and women were changing their occupations rather than first entering the work force, a process that continued throughout the interwar period. The major shift was from agriculture into the industrial and service sectors. In the course of this transition, many women dropped out of employment altogether.

THE AGRICULTURAL SECTOR

In the European experience, the larger agriculture figures in an economy, the greater the percentage of women active in the economy, though not necessarily in paid employment. In the postwar period, rural exodus reached such

TABLE 18–1

COUNTRY	PERCENTAGE OF ECONOMICALLY ACTIVE WOMEN OUT OF TOTAL FEMALE POPULATION			PERCENTAGE OF ECONOMICALLY ACTIVE WOMEN OUT OF TOTAL ECONOMICALLY ACTIVE POPULATION		
	Prewar	1920s	1930s	Prewar	1920s	1930s
Belgium	28.6 (1910)	21.3 (1920)	24.1 (1930)	30.9	25.0	26.3
Denmark	27.2 (1911)	24.1 (1921)	26.9 (1930)	31.3	29.7	30.5
France	38.7 (1911)	42.3 (1921)	34.2 (1936)	36.9	39.6	36.1
Germany	26.4 (1907)	35.6 (1925)	34.2 (1933)	30.7	35.9	35.5
Great Britain	25.7 (1911)	25.5 (1921)	26.9 (1931)	29.5	29.5	29.8
Ireland	19.5 (1911)	23.5 (1926)	24.3 (1936)	23.7	26.3	26.2
Italy	29.1 (1911)	27.2 (1921)	24.8 (1936)	31.3	28.7	28.7
Netherlands	18.3 (1909)	18.3 (1920)	19.2 (1930)	23.9	23.2	24.1
Norway	23.0 (1910)	21.9 (1920)	22.0 (1930)	30.1	27.8	27.1
Sweden	21.7 (1910)	25.8 (1920)	28.7 (1930)	27.8	29.8	31.0
Switzerland	31.7 (1910)	31.4 (1920)	29.0 (1930)	33.9	33.9	31.5

SOURCE: Based on P. Bairoch, *La population active et sa structure* (Institut de Sociologie de l'Université Libre de Bruxelles, 1968), pp. 27–34.

striking proportions that it became a matter of national concern to many states. In some cases, women seemed to be hastening away from the farm even more rapidly than men. In Germany, for example, where the war had left women in the majority of the agricultural labor force, about 320,000 of them had fled the countryside by 1933, compared to 99,000 men. In France, roughly 1,040,000 women dropped out of agricultural work between 1921 and 1936, compared to 848,000 men. In Italy, from 1921 to 1936, 326,000 women left the agricultural sector, compared to 228,000 men. By 1935, the rural exodus had become primarily a feminine phenomenon. The drop in the percentage of women in agriculture was dramatic: in Italy it fell from 59 to 45 percent of economically active women from 1921 to 1936; in France, from 46 to 40 percent from 1921 to 1936; in Germany, from 43 to 38 percent from 1925 to 1939.[2]

Of course, there were reasons unique to each country. In Germany, a democratic socialist government improved labor conditions for the industrial working class, which lured relatively disadvantaged rural labor into the cities. In France, modernization lagged altogether and a particularly inefficient method of agriculture and pattern of landholding spurred members of the rural population to leave. In Italy, the countryside was partly "deproletarianized" as agricultural workers became owners or tenants by seizing landed estates or by settling newly cleared lands. Others fled virtual serfdom for the towns. In most economies of Europe, agriculture was the least attractive sector, and women would not stay on the farm after so many veterans who had "seen Paree" failed to return.

The rural housewife had to work harder than ever before, as her hired help sought out industrial jobs. Her daughter, disinclined to follow her example, left also, especially since the prior male rural exodus had reduced her choice of marriage partners. Countrywomen had few alternatives: where agriculture modernized, it offered few careers to women. Indeed, the countrywoman's source of independent income from her chickens, dairy, and garden produce slowly gave way to male-dominated big business. Here women filled only lower-ranking positions because they lacked expertise in the new technology and were denied entry into agricultural schools to acquire it and because men purportedly would not accept supervision from them. For the female hired help, the disadvantages of the country far outweighed those of the city. Women agricultural laborers still earned only about 50 percent of the male wage. Why stay, when in industry they could earn 60 to 70 percent of the male wage and have a wider selection of husbands besides?

There were alternatives to leaving, however. Both the propertied and the employed women tried to improve their positions by organizing, though their interests conflicted with each other. In 1929, the International Council of Women sponsored a conference of national organizations of propertied rural women in London. The organization's Scottish president, the Marchioness of Aberdeen and Temair, presided in stout majesty, her very person breathing the ideals of ladies from the landed property-owning class. She noted that the precursor of the Women's Rural Institutes in her own country had been the Onward and Upward Association, whose purpose was to create common interests between mistresses and their servants in rural districts. Officially, the international organization claimed to be nonpolitical. In fact, however, the goal of consensus between classes was enunciated by most national representatives, who included a sprinkling of aristocracy—a countess from Germany, another from France, and a princess from Rumania— and the wives of many well-to-do estate owners from the major countries of Europe and their imperial possessions abroad.

Most of them represented organizations formed before the war, though they began to flourish only afterward. Belgium's women farmers' circles, begun in 1906, aimed to keep people on the land and educate them. For similar purposes, the English Women's Institutes enjoyed support from the Ministry of Agriculture, while several of the French groups were affiliated with religious organizations. The German Association of Agricultural Housewives, dating back to 1898, focused on what came to be called home economics.

The war had given these landed countrywomen a sense of their own importance and strength, since the reduction in trade had forced most nations to rely on internal resources. Now they anxiously held their ground, literally and figuratively. From the time of their first meeting to World War II, they tried to defend their interests. Their efforts included raising the standards of homemaking and agriculture to higher professional levels, standardizing produce and controlling and improving its marketing, stemming the drift into towns, and influencing legislation that affected them. The last revealed such "unwomanly" positions as that of the German countess who opposed child labor legislation by arguing that goose herding was not very strenuous. Her idealized version overlooked the reality of exploited children deprived of play and education. But few of the countrywomen sounded so sinister. For the most part, the Rural Women's Organization acted as an information exchange and as a social nexus to overcome rural isolation. The Canadian representative said her organization preserved the sanity of women on the prairies, and the Norwegian one recounted an incident in which two old women rowed in an open boat for three hours each way to attend a housewives' get-together.

By 1933, the international association had grown to 1,000,000, of which about 800,000 were North American. By that time, however, apparently despairing of having much effect on large-scale agriculture, it had become merely quaint. Toward the end, it looked nostalgically at local costumes and customs. Its last book—a collection of national recipes—showed how far it had abdicated economic and political effectiveness.[3]

The hired female help these landed proprietors so desperately tried to keep on the land had quite different problems. Their only voice was a feeble one in the International Landworkers' Federation, which for the most part represented men. In the 1920s, with employers and governments fearing socialism and famine, the threat of landworkers' strikes could compel the extension of some industrial labor legislation to agriculture. Generally, this meant some regulation of hours, wages, and conditions of work. For women, the most basic protective measures, like maternity leave, were granted. However, equal pay for equal work was not even discussed at the international congress. Not even the women there stressed it. At the first meeting in Amsterdam in 1920, Argentina Altobelli, a firebrand from Italy, presented resolutions condemning war and urging the socialization of the land and the rejection of nonsocialist unions by the federation. By 1924, however, the

Italian landworkers' organization had been dismantled by the fascist government and Altobelli disappeared from the records. The agricultural and industrial depression of the 1930s finally destroyed the federation itself.[4]

The landworkers' federation was too weak to do much for female agricultural workers, and the Women's Bureau of the International Labor Office in Geneva did not do much more. In 1921, it adopted a recommendation that maternity benefits guaranteed to women in industry under the convention of 1919 be extended to women in agriculture. By 1939, sixteen nations had ratified a draft convention to that effect. The main motive, however, was not the political pressure exercised by women but fears of a falling birthrate. Even so, a formal convention was not passed until 1952, because governments and agricultural interests recoiled at the financial burden.[5]

In summary, women had little incentive to stay on the land and demonstrated little sisterhood across class lines. Daughters of propertied families moved into middle-sized cities and either took respectable jobs in public administration or social service or married and became full-time bourgeois wives and mothers. Daughters of agricultural laborers sought work in factories or shops, where at least they could hope for higher wages and better regulation of work conditions. About half of them also married and at least temporarily dropped out of the economically active population. Rural exodus, a by-product of industrialization, narrowed the horizons of many women to their homes and to their roles as consumers, wives, and mothers.

Some women, however, continued as producers. Let us follow them as they joined their sisters on the assembly line.

THE INDUSTRIAL SECTOR

The ranks of industrial labor were swelled not only by country girls but also by former domestic servants. During the war and after, hundreds of thousands of women left private service. A combination of new work opportunities and declining middle-class wealth accounted for this phenomenon. Yet, the percentage of women's employment in industry as a percentage of women's total employment remained remarkably stable. From another perspective, the proportion of women in the total manufacturing workforce actually fell. Table 18–2 tells the story.[6]

What this means is that economies industrialized and deployed their working populations differently from before, absorbing reduced proportions of women into industry. Yet, male workers complained continuously that women were taking away jobs. What was the trouble about?

The answer lies in an analysis of the changes within industrial work itself, for modernization meant not only more jobs but quite different jobs. An overview shows that the branches of manufacturing traditionally occupied by women declined more rapidly than the new areas that employed them expanded. For example, textile and clothing manufacture dropped off faster than the metallurgy, chemical, and electrical industries picked up. At the same time, the newest industries organized along rationalized lines, that is, by producing standardized parts on assembly lines timed for maximum productivity. The system created jobs for unskilled, patient, precise workers; such qualifications spelled "women." The women thus employed had to keep up with high-speed, often dangerous, mind-numbing work at barely subsistence wage levels, while men grew hostile at the "unfair" competition.

In Germany, where American loans primed the pump of postwar recovery, consumer industries grew after 1925. The chemical industry, supplying everything from synthetic fibers to dyes, flourished. The electronics industry turned out light bulbs and radios. The paper and carton industry, an important concomitant of consumerism and bureaucracy, burgeoned. Metallurgy, including unobtrusive rearmament, grew apace, and the manufacture of optical instruments became Germany's pride. In all of these, women, who in some cases had first entered during the war, stayed and increased their numbers. Other less visible changes took place. The textile industry, in which women traditionally predominated, began to languish from competition with synthetic materials. In the clothing industry, large-scale production sharply reduced the number of small, female-directed businesses. The same held true of the food and beverage industry. Throughout the economy, the trend toward merger and monopoly edged out small entrepreneurs, especially women. Rarely did they find the same kind of work in industrial management. Leadership in large hierarchical corporations was reserved for men.[7]

In France, a similar development occurred. The number of women employed in textiles and clothing fell, while the number of those in tanning, metalworks, motor car manufacture, and the chemical, paper, and electric

TABLE 18–2

		FRANCE		GERMANY		ITALY	
		1921	1936	1925	1939	1921	1936
%	Women in industry / Women employed	22.2	21.6	24.7	27.0	23.6	24.1
%	Women in industry / Total population in industry	31.2	27.6	22.2	21.1	27.2	25.0

apparatus industries rose. The war had brought women into armament manufacture and metallurgy, but here, as elsewhere, they were not trained for postwar skills. Rather, work was reorganized into elementary operations supervised by male foremen. The gap between men's and women's work in industry widened. As in Germany, small, independent businesswomen lost out rapidly, while white-collar employees, usually younger women in nonmanagerial capacities, grew in numbers. The number of small entrepreneurs who were female declined from about 1,243,000 to 835,000 from 1921 to 1936, while the number of female salaried workers rose from 855,000 to 1,034,000 in the same period. This meant a net increase of about 179,000 office workers for a net loss of about 408,000 independents.[8]

Both Germany and France showed considerable regional variation in their economic development, but in Italy the differences were more dramatic. Here, the south was still virtually enserfed, while the north resembled other advanced industrial nations. In Italy also, the drop in the number of women in industry accompanied the decline of some traditional industries that had employed them, such as straw manufactures and textiles, where automation displaced many workers. On the other hand, the food industry increased its employment of women, as did shoes and chemicals. Since industrialization in Italy generally lagged behind that in France and Germany, the tendency for women's work in industry to decline became clear only after World War II. Then, women lost about 60,000 jobs in "female" sectors to men, while taking about 35,000 in "male" sectors. The absorption of women into Italian industry was retarded because scarcity of capital prevented investment in the kind of machinery that would have produced changes in the mode of production.[9]

Job competition provoked conflict between the sexes on a continent-wide scale. The hostility often carried over into workers' organizations. Unions in the interwar period showed a mixed record of cooperation and competition between women workers and organized labor. Individual unions and union federations varied in their official attitudes toward women workers, and much of the rank and file only reluctantly acknowledged the legitimacy of their presence. In itself this was understandable, given the historical tendency of employers to hire women in order to undercut wages. In addition, antifeminism reinforced organized labor's inclination to give low priority to women's demands for equal pay for equal work and for protective legislation. On the other hand, women were hard to organize. Many made home and family a priority and they anticipated only temporary participation in the work force. As girls, they had been raised to be docile; hence, employers could dissuade them from joining unions. Even when they accepted their role as workers, union dues were often too steep for their low wages. At union meetings, women often found themselves patronized, if listened to at all, so potential female leadership was lost. Finally, for those who did make it into meetings, continued attendance was difficult, since most women also had household duties. As a result, female union membership was discouragingly low.

Women were most unionized in Germany. Thanks to vigorous left-wing political parties, workers' consciousness was relatively high. From here, after all, had come Marx and Engels, who predicted women's emancipation as a by-product of industrialization, and August Bebel, whose *Woman Under Socialism*, first published in 1883, had gone through fifty German editions and at least fifteen foreign-language editions by World War I. The Christian unions, which aimed to protect artisan labor from industrial incursion and to prevent socialist unions from monopolizing labor, also attracted many women.

The French labor movement was divided on the "woman question." The "free" or non-Christian unions, especially the Marxist ones, upheld the revolutionary and utopian socialist tradition, which theoretically espoused equality of the sexes. However, another wing, influenced by the nineteenth-century anarchist Pierre Joseph Proudhon, clung to the view that women belonged in the home. The Christian unions joined in this attitude, echoing Vatican pronouncements on the matter. Pope Leo XIII in 1891 issued an encyclical, *De Rerum Novarum*, which stated:

> Women, again are not suited to certain trades; for a woman is by nature fitted for home work and it is this which is best adapted at once to preserve her modesty, and to promote the good bringing up of children and the well-being of the family.

The same sentiment was repeated forty years later by Pope Pius XI in his encyclical, *Quadrigesimo Anno*. As for the Italian labor movement, it was soon swallowed up by the fascist corporate state.

Relations between women and men unionists got off to a bad start immediately after World War I. Demobilization caused severe competition for fewer jobs and brought out the worst in most people. Again and again, women union leaders protested when their male colleagues collaborated with employers in phasing them out of work rather than joining in collective defensive action. Afterward, over the span of the interwar period, discussions on women's work and women's membership in unions reflected the economic cycle. Predictably, during recession, debate intensified over women's physiological and psychological fitness. During the "normalcy" of the later 1920s, meetings tended to run out of time when women's issues arose.

Yet, the picture was not entirely bleak. At best, unions won reductions in the wage gap between men and women, maternity provisions, and protective legislation. The last raised new problems of its own: it increased the costs of female labor and hence sometimes disemployed women. Given the conditions of work, however, it constituted a sufficient advantage to be a major priority of female unionists. Also, unions, especially the socialist ones, selected women union officials and continually recruited with lectures, slide shows, social gatherings, and special newspapers. Militant women often joined in job actions and strikes, initiating some and supporting others, including sympathy strikes with male workers.

Another source of labor reform was the International Labor Organization, a specialized agency of the League of Nations. While the ILO had no enforcement powers, it did have prestige and it set minimum standards of treatment. From 1919 on, it held annual conferences at which it issued conventions and recommendations, building up an international labor code intended to equalize working conditions in member countries as far as national differences would allow.

In 1919, trade union women from Europe, America, and Asia convened the first International Congress of Working Women in Washington. To begin with, they requested the International Conference of Labor to require women representatives. Then followed proposals for labor standards: an eight-hour day or forty-four-hour week for all workers regardless of sex, weekly rest of at least one and a half days, minimum daily rest of half an hour. The minimum age for labor was to be sixteen. Maternity benefits should include free medical care and a monetary allowance sufficient for six weeks before and after childbirth. The word "sufficient" masked a controversy over the amount and its relation to the woman's wage. The congress also proposed protective legislation, such as limitations on night work and on the use of poisonous materials like lead. The women strongly demanded that protective legislation be extended to all workers regardless of sex, not only in the interests of fairness but also because special legislation for women often limited their scope of work, excluding them from certain industries. Finally, in a somewhat utopian vein, the congress asked for international conventions for equal distribution of raw materials in the world—a still elusive goal.[10]

By 1931, the number of states officially providing benefits for six weeks' leave after childbirth had risen to twenty-two from twelve in 1921, and fifteen others provided for from three to five weeks. Under the best schemes, maternity benefits generally came to only 50 to 60 percent of basic wages, which in the first place often fell below the requirements for a reasonable standard of living. Many categories of wage earners were not covered and of those that were many had difficulty retaining their jobs after pregnancy. Finally, the European nations did not extend these meager gains to the women in their colonial possessions.

By 1939, the ILO reported that protective labor legislation applicable to all workers had expanded considerably, but it also noted that new circumstances—meaning the depression—had given prominence to the problem of women's right to employment. The two observations were not unrelated. The encouragement of maternity as jobs got scarcer made sense. It reduced two anxieties at one time: that about population decline and that about women competing for work. Even the unpolitical ILO finally admitted that women did constitute a reserve of labor from which state and private employers drew freely during periods of economic growth and with which they dispensed during downturns. Thus, in Nazi Germany, the Unemployment Act of June 1, 1933, offered marriage loans of up to 1,000 Reichsmark on condition that the bride leave her job and not return until the loan was repaid. As a further incentive, the loan was reduced by 25 percent with the birth of each child. In Italy, a law of 1934 allowed women to be replaced by men even in work normally done by women. Companies set quotas for female employees in commerce, banking, and insurance. Not only in the fascist countries but in France, Belgium, the Netherlands, and Great Britain there were similar schemes and laws against double-income families, especially in civil service.[11]

Thus, the changing structure of industry shuffled many women from one branch of manufacturing to another, often giving the wrong impression that they were taking men's jobs. The Depression, a monumental crisis of capitalism that accelerated these shifts, contributed to this misperception, as male-dominated industries such as construction and machine building at first were hit harder by unemployment than female-dominated industries such as office work and the manufacture of nondurable goods. During the unstable interwar period, hostility between male and female workers peaked in times of economic crisis. In times of relative stability, women workers made important changes by organizing. Their share of manual labor remained generally stagnant, however, and much of it was marginalized and undercounted in the abysmally paid, unregulated home industries, which largely involved subcontracted sewing. A new future for women's employment lay elsewhere.

THE SERVICE SECTOR

In the growing areas of commerce and public and private administration, the influx of women was greatest. The fast-growing service sector included a wide variety of occupations essential to a modern economy: transport, communications, office and sales work, social work, and even some professions sometimes loosely labeled "services." Because it was a relatively undeveloped sector, the sexual division of labor within it had not yet been clearly defined. Furthermore, women had entered it relatively easily during the manpower shortages of World War I. The return of "normalcy" brought expanded consumer production and with it new mass distribution techniques, providing thousands of counters and cash registers for women to staff. Economic dislocation and fears of Bolshevism led to a mushrooming of ameliorative services, such as social work and nursing, considered particularly well suited for women. Technological needs for a more educated workforce and the threat of youthful unemployment increased the school population and lengthened the time it spent behind desks, providing new jobs for teachers.

Work in the service sector had certain obvious advantages: it was clean, it paid better than unskilled industrial women's work, and it carried more prestige than other kinds of employment such as domestic service. However, the overall move of women within the employment structure from agriculture to industry to service rarely affected a single individual in the course of her work life or even several generations of the same family. Class limited an individual's options.

Typically, agricultural workers moved into domestic service or factory work; second-generation industrial workers might enter new branches of industry or sales or office work. Almost an equal number of saleswomen and clerks, however, came from the lower and middle echelons of the middle class. They worked for several reasons: war casualties had produced a "surplus" of women who had to support themselves and their dependents, such as children and aging parents; large businesses and industries displaced smaller shops and artisan establishments, impoverishing some members of this group and forcing their daughters into paid employment; and economic crises eroded the real income of the salaried middle class, with the same result. Women of middle-class origin, however, groomed for leisure or possibly a career, suffered status loss. Now, standing next to girls from the lower class waiting on customers or typing and filing, they often felt like the governesses of the nineteenth century—declassed—though only temporarily, they hoped. They waited for Prince Charming in a business suit. If and when he appeared, they eagerly left work.

Everywhere, the "new" female workforce was considerably younger than the previous one, and a far smaller proportion of married women worked for wages than in the premodern economy. The vast majority of women in the service sector were under thirty. Several circumstances accounted for this. For one thing, women had little opportunity to rise through the ranks of commerce or government into more interesting and responsible positions. Discrimination kept them in dead-end jobs, bias colored recognition of their abilities, men would not accept their authority in superior positions, and they were expected to marry and drop out. Therefore, many women lost whatever confidence they possessed, underachieved sometimes, and were bored into leaving as soon as they could afford to. Employers also preferred younger women in work involving public relations for their attributes of docility, gratitude, and sexual attractiveness. When their youth faded, their employability diminished. Soon these jobs became stereotyped: the cute secretary and the flighty salesgirl became stock figures of cartoons. The governments themselves, on whom the ILO depended for execution of equitable labor legislation, became prime culprits when budgets were cut. They provided models of discriminatory behavior by reserving certain civil service posts for men, by firing married women, and by turning guidance counseling and placement into tracking.

In Germany, the percentage of women in the service sector out of all economically active women rose from 18.8 to 24.6 percent between 1925 and 1933. Their proportion of the sector as a whole during the same period rose from 29.4 to 32.7 percent. In France, between 1921 and 1936, the percentage of working women who were salaried employees rose from 27.2 to 34.3 percent, but their share of the sector remained about the same at 40 percent. In Italy, 25 percent of all employed women worked in nonagricultural and nonindustrial pursuits in 1936, compared to 18.3 percent in 1921, while for this occupational category as a whole, their share grew from 28 to 30 percent.[12]

However, women tended to lose their independent positions in the traditional parts of the economy faster than the modern parts could absorb them. For example, in France from 1921 to 1936, the number of female small proprietors dropped by 408,000 while the number of female salaried employees rose by only 179,000. Male proprietors, by contrast, increased by 156,000, and over 100,000 men became salaried employees. Germany had a similar pattern: from 1925 to 1933, women independents in such branches as clothing, food and beverages, industry and crafts, inns and taverns, fell by over 300,000, while women white-collar workers in the same period increased by about 250,000. In Italy, as we have seen, female disemployment resulted from a shrinking agricultural sphere, a relatively slowly expanding industrial sphere, and a lagging service sector. Chronic unemployment and underemployment ensured that most new jobs were filled by men.[13]

If the development of the lower levels of the service sector did not bring unalloyed improvement to women employed in it, neither did the development in higher levels, which shaded off into the professions. The most promising areas for those in the middle class who could afford the education were teaching, nursing, and social work. These were mostly civil service jobs. Here, discrimination often took the form of differential job classification.

In France, the number of women in public service and the professions, including teaching, increased from about 417,000 to 507,000 from 1921 to 1936, a fairly large gain numerically. However, their proportion of the whole expanding category increased a scant 1 percent, from 30 to 31. In Germany, the number of women teachers actually fell between 1925 to 1933, from 97,675 to 94,140, and their share in the profession fell from 32 to 30 percent. The number of nurses rose from 117,128 to 131,794 in the same period, and nursing remained a predominantly female profession. In social welfare, in contrast, although the number of women rose from 54,582 to 69,895 between 1925 and 1933, their predominance became precarious as men swarmed in: women's share fell from 82 to 67 percent of the profession. In Italy, the trend was again retarded. The number of women teachers rose between 1921 and 1931, from 128,266 to 134,985, making a proportional gain of 70 to 73 percent. However, by 1961 the trend reversed itself as the sector grew and attracted more men: women's share fell to 67 percent. The number of nurses increased from about 14,200 to 19,000 from 1921 to 1931, but nursing was only a little over half female. After World War II, those parts of the Italian service sector that expanded most rapidly had a shrinking proportion of women. It rose only where an insignificant number of them were employed at all: in banking, insurance, finance, and transportation.[14]

In short, men and women jostled each other for work in the "helping professions." These jobs represented state institutionalization of traditional family functions such as household management, education, and health care, which the family could no longer effectively fulfill in modern society. Previously, women had performed this kind of work in the family. After professionalization, these activities offered a minority of women opportunities in a modern economy, while leaving the majority alienated from these aspects of their traditional role.

Not many women had higher aspirations. The few hundreds of women whose families both cared to and could afford to send them to the university encountered different sorts of difficulties. Besides the taunts of teachers, colleagues, and public opinion, they suffered material hardships. Girls often got smaller allowances than boys, and many of them could not afford books. They could not rent rooms as easily and received worse medical care. Nor did they find much warmth in comradeship. One German woman law student wrote that in class women were laughed down whether they answered correctly or not; in discussions of family law, male students waxed enthusiastic over prereform legislation, which had subjugated wives, and once held up the lecture for ten minutes in indignation when the teacher stated that women could now become judges in commercial courts. Socially, male and female students did not know how to act toward each other. Male students recognized only two kinds of women: virginal marriage candidates and "other," usually sought in the town on evenings out. Independent women nonplused them. Female students had few role models and sometimes fell into one of two patterns. Each bore its own stigma: if they dressed attractively, they were not taken seriously, if they dressed "seriously," they were not considered attractive. A comfortable identity remained elusive even after graduation.[15]

For the successful graduates, there were further obstacles. Medical associations put quotas on female entry into the profession (a favorite among women students), antiquated legislation restricted female lawyers' range of possibilities, female engineers and chemists found jobs only in the lowest ranks of industry and science, and female university professors were as rare as diamonds. For these lucky few, the road ahead was still less smooth than for their male colleagues. Women doctors did not enjoy the full confidence of the public and had difficulty establishing a private practice. More women doctors than men ended up working in clinics, hospitals, and public health institutions. Dentists had a better time of it; for a while it even seemed as if odontology might become a feminine field. As always, in such cases, women's "special qualities" were noted: their precision, dexterity, patience, and personal sensitivity, especially with children. Women lawyers faced problems more like those of doctors. Few had their own practice and most of those dealt with family law or protective factory legislation for women. One perceptive French observer recorded the subtle bonding in exchanges of glances between male judges and lawyers on cases involving female lawyers. Similarly, male collusion kept female journalists from news scoops and interviews. Some women's ambitions in these new and open fields seem quixotic today: in aviation, for example. In France, one woman aviator held a world record for distance and another one held it for looping. A British woman, Beryl Markham, was first to fly solo across the Atlantic from east to west in 1936, nine years after Charles Lindberg had flown in the other direction. All these joined Amelia Earhart among history's curiosities. Flying did not become a woman's job.

Legal emancipation and technical breakthroughs seemed to open many new vistas. The full strength of the reins of custom had yet to be tested. These consisted not only of men's bias but also of women's own internalized feelings of inferiority and responsibility to families. Women's work lives suffered repeated interruptions. Whatever else they might be, women had to be not only good wives and mothers but also good daughters and sisters, putting family needs above their own at all times. Avoiding marriage did not always free women for single-minded pursuit of their work. The resulting discontinuity in their work lives blunted their career trajectories, especially where seniority and keeping up to date was crucial. If they did give their careers priority, they suffered caricature as cold-blooded, hard-bitten, pinched-faced old maids. The image frightened another whole generation into the waiting shelter of conformity.

THE FAMILY AND SEXUALITY

Conformity meant marriage and children. Even professional women were not exempt from the first female "duty." Statesmen and observers watched the declining birthrate with dismay bordering on panic. Demographers' calculations indicated that key European populations were not replacing themselves. England, Denmark, France, Germany, Sweden, Austria . . . all had birthrates below the acceptable minimum. Alarmists spoke of race suicide and misogynists were not the only ones to ascribe the phenomenon to women's purported new liberties. Quiet sabotage was implied in such titles as *The International Birth Strike* by Ernst Kahn and *Revolt of Women* by Hamilton Fyfe. Increasing numbers of miscarriages, in some cases exceeding live births, looked suspiciously like abortions, which were illegal. Illicit birth-control clinics and information offices spread, and Margaret Sanger took her battle for contraception to an international level.

The upper and middle classes had been limiting their families for several centuries. What caused alarm was the working-class emulation of this pattern. On the one hand, a large, dissatisfied working class with rising demands could be politically threatening. On the other hand, a large pool of labor could keep wages competitively low, and manpower was also needed for armies. Sober demographers worried about Europe becoming unable to produce enough of the "right breed" in the face of the populations multiplying in Asia, Africa, and India. Most voiced concern about their immediate neighbors; each country counted the others' populations anxiously, measuring off potential armies. Would-be guardians of public morality predicted the crumbling of all human relationships following the decline of female chastity. To them, an obvious symptom of moral decay was the disregard of the law shown by the purchase of contraceptives and procurement of abortions in the face of stiff penalties. Finally, the whole thing smacked of Bolshevism to those who, in the 1920s, looked across to the Soviet Union, where free love was institutionalized for a time.

Feminists and other proponents of birth control succeeded in winning over some conservative opinion by arguing the case for eugenics and poverty control. Neo-Malthusian Leagues had formed in Great Britain, Holland, France, and Germany in the 1870s and had held international conferences since 1900. Part of their appeal lay in the alternative they proposed to socialism, namely, to diminish the birthrate among the lower classes so that these could fit themselves to their wages rather than trying to fit their wages to their needs. This offered several advantages: it would keep the poor from demanding a redistribution of wealth, it would keep the upper and middle classes from being swamped numerically and perhaps politically, and it would "improve the quality of the race." However, no one explained who was to select "the best" or how. If birth control offered an alternative to civil war, it similarly offered an alternative to revolution and international war. It could obviate the need, so some thought, for a radical redistribution of wealth and power, nationally and globally.[16]

While public opinion slowly shifted, family size continued to shrink. There were many reasons for this. Women's employment outside the home was by far not the only one, though its rise does correlate with lower fertility. Full-time housewives, however, also reduced the number of their children. For one thing, more children survived infancy, so sheer quantity of progeny was no longer necessary for family continuity. Related to this was the hope for social mobility. Families had fewer children, who would not merely survive but rise to a higher socioeconomic level. This meant prolonged training for a skill or profession; family resources went toward grooming one or two, usually boys, rather than toward propagating many. Furthermore, urbanization itself made a difference; in the country, children helped with farm work; in the city, they became liabilities, mouths to feed for increasingly long periods of time as the age for leaving school rose. Finally, the postwar period brought new attention to the nature of the family; with the decline of other of its functions (such as production), the focus sharpened on intrafamilial relations and personality development. Fewer children with longer lives entailed stronger emotional commitment to each one and heightened concern for the quality of child care. Expert opinion sought to professionalize motherhood. Domesticity became scientized as home economics. Thus, while some forces freed women from the endless cycle of childbearing, traditionalism crept in by another door in another guise.

Family sociology began to move in the direction pioneered by Talcott Parsons, who after World War II categorized men's role in the family as "instrumental" (manipulating the environment for the benefit of the family) and the wife's role as "expressive" (facilitating emotional interactions within the family). Educators, psychiatrists, sociologists, and social workers all studied the failures of the family with a view to saving it. Most were conservative, in that they tried to halt the apparent dissolution of the family. Some researchers, drawing their empirical evidence mainly from welfare cases and broken homes, concluded from their untypical samples that lack of family cohesion was the cause rather than the effect of many social problems. They also traced school failures and a rising crime rate to the absence of working mothers from the home. True, others faulted endemic under- and subemployment and instabilities resulting from social injustice. But in general family sociologists joined the chorus of medical experts and psychologists, who advised women not to deny their purported biological and psychological nature by slighting their families. Duty underscored nature.[17]

The majority of women, of course, were ill equipped for sophisticated motherhood. Many of them were barely literate newcomers from the country. They could hardly fulfill their function as socializing agents in a rapidly changing world, especially if they lacked contact with it through work and remained in their communities. If anything, they would lose status as traditional authorities for their daughters and sons and be woeful role models for the former. Trained female educators stepped in to fill the vacuum. They worked in kindergartens, as the child development theories of the educational reformers Johann Heinrich Pestalozzi and Friedrich Wilhelm August Froebel were revived, and they continued through elementary school. Middle-class women found careers in child care and teaching, yet often became distanced from their own children. Thus, while some people began to express fears about the feminization of education, women as parents and as teachers came to be a step removed from children at both ends of the process of socialization, as the skills required for adulthood changed. A layer of male-directed institutionalization intervened between them and children.

Not only parent-child relationships but also husband-wife relationships were examined more closely. What shape those really took must remain a matter for conjecture, given the immature state of the discipline of family sociology then. However, we can extrapolate a tendency from existing studies. A pioneering work by Theodor Adorno and Max Horkheimer, *Authority and the Family*, begun at the Institute for Social Research in Frankfort on the Main, Germany, and published in Paris in 1936 after its authors fled Nazism, examined family interaction in order to find clues to political behavior. On the basis of a questionnaire, crude by today's standards, they found links between patriarchal authoritarianism and the development of personalities prone to totalitarianism. From a different, psychoanalytic perspective, Wilhelm Reich, in his *The Mass Psychology of Fascism* (1933), drew similar conclusions. German sociologists emerged from World War II on the defensive and claimed instead a growing equalization of power distribution within the family. Cross-national research now confirms that egalitarian companionate marriage tends to replace patriarchy when women work outside the home.[18]

Less remarked upon is the fact that the arena thus more equitably shared had itself become smaller. The family had been reduced in many of its historical functions: as a unit of production, as the transmitter of economically significant property such as land or small independent artisan or trade establishments, and as the main socializing agent. Production, socialization, and many supportive services were assumed by big business and big government. The family provided little besides companionship and mutual self-help when larger social institutions failed. Even these functions began to dwindle in the interwar period. Young people drifted away to their peer groups, leaving parents to relate to each other as best they could. The "generation gap" was noticed. In sum, companionate marriage, whatever its rewards, was a remnant. Women had made gains in a shrinking sphere.

But were unmarried women enlarging their sphere of personal relations outside the family? How true to life was the image of the promiscuous flapper? How new was the "new woman" of the twenties? Could she really be an easygoing and free lover, as men had been in the past?

We cannot answer these questions to our satisfaction, but the intensified debate of the interwar period points to a great preoccupation with the subject of sex. Popularizations of Freud reached people through movies and cheap literature; one of the messages: women could and did have pleasure in sexual relations. It was a complex message, which easily shaded back into an older stereotype: women *are* pleasure (for men). The film sexpot was born. But so were some new types: the bachelor girl and the lesbian, both of them potentially sexual subjects, rather than objects for others.

The bachelor girl was best described in a widely read novel of 1922, *La Garçonne*, by Victor Margueritte. The heroine, Monique Lerbier, wore her hair and skirts short; she danced, played sports, took courses at the Sorbonne, found an interesting job, drove her own car, and enjoyed recreational sex. Her straightforward manner, her direct gaze, her vigorous handshake bore witness to a change unimaginatively called masculinization. The novel enjoyed instant success. Twenty thousand copies sold in advance and it was grabbed off the shelves at the rate of ten thousand a week soon after its appearance. By 1929, one million copies had been sold. Although the author was stripped of his Legion of Honor medal for writing the book, it became popular throughout Europe, translated into a dozen languages. *La Garçonne* was not only French; an international cross-class "girl culture" appeared, partly thanks to the homogenization made possible by a global consumer capitalism radiating out from the United States.[19]

Only relatively few well-paid professional women, however, could afford Monique Lerbier's bachelor life. Such women threatened men by more than direct economic competition. Erich Kästner's popular moralist novel *Fabian* (1931) — a kind of latter-day *Candide* — has a counter-heroine, Cornelia, whose ambition leads her from law school to movie stardom via the producer-director's bed. Her selfishness and sexual freedom stand in stark contrast to the tradition of self-sacrifice exemplified by Fabian's long-suffering mother. By contrast, Vicki Baum's novel, *Stud. chem. Helene Willfuer* (1928), gives a more sympathetic picture of the new woman without denigrating older values. Its heroine is a chemistry student who gets pregnant after a tender but doomed affair with a suicidal fellow-student. After running the gamut of bad choices for an illegal abortion, she ultimately decides to keep her child. She becomes famous and wealthy by discovering an elixir of youth and finally marries her adored professor, whose philandering wife has meanwhile left him. Here, too, there is a moral: sexual freedom carries serious consequences for women and should soon give way to marriage. Even so, the novel gave some meager encouragement to young women, who many years later confessed that "they read 'Helene' when they were schoolgirls, read the forbidden, dirty book secretly, in most cases in the toilet."[20] Baum, a hugely successful author and screenwriter, was herself painfully self-deprecating. She thought it quite proper that her husband, an orchestra conductor, did not read her books or notice her fame, and she even professed delight at her ten-year-old son's "thoroughly masculine" evaluation of her books as "stupid and boring."[21] It was not yet easy for a woman to be the center of her own life, sexually or otherwise.

For lesbian as well as for heterosexual women, expanding choices also meant a simultaneous narrowing of options. Freud's elucidation of the unconscious mind ended an age of innocence in which women's loving friendships had been above reproach. The notion of a free-roaming libido sexualized all relationships. Yet legitimacy remained elusive. Despite a small flourishing of lesbian bars in Berlin and despite the happy insularity of lesbian artistic and literary communities in Paris, like Natalie Barney's, homosexual women remained outcasts or, more commonly "in the closet." Gertrude Stein lived openly with her lover, Alice B. Toklas, but still made only veiled references to their relationship in her poetry. This ambivalence reflects the continuing unease of the interwar period, one of transition between moral and medical interpretations of nonconforming sexual behavior. While criminal persecution relaxed and the breaking of sexual taboos became marginally fashionable, pleas for a wider compassion depended on a medical view of homosexuality as deviant, if no longer morally degenerate. Thus, Radclyffe Hall, in her famous novel, *The Well of Loneliness* (1928), the first to portray a lesbian heroine, depicted her as a freak of nature but otherwise sane and upright. Virginia Woolf, on the other hand, celebrated her sometime affair with Vita Sackville-West in her playful historical novel *Orlando*, whose central character undergoes a sex change that greatly enlivens her/his relationships during the transition.

For the majority, however, the fear of being considered homosexual reinforced pressures toward companionate marriage, in which husband and wife were urged to see one another as best friends as well as passionate lovers. Where before there had been economic advantage and obligation to ensure stability, a new ideal raised expectations that often crashed in disappointment and divorce.

Indeed, the new freedom in matters of sex and love was new mainly for the downwardly mobile part of the middle class, whose property had been eroded by postwar inflation, the Depression, and the centralization of capital. "Freed" from property, they were now free to indulge in the transient relations that had long been common in the economically more precarious working class. Thus, the anxiety expressed by contemporary middle-class observers had to do with much more than women's changing behavior. It reflected their fears of proletarianization. The working girl and the sexually loose woman became conflated into the same figure. Her sheer existence threatened the stability of bourgeois values and lifestyles and her nonreproductive sexuality, supported by improved birth control technology, suggested the need for a more controlling population policy to some.

A backlash swiftly ensued. Since sexual fulfillment could no longer be denied, it was channelled. A new prescriptive literature began to stress the importance of sex in marriage and the best ways of achieving it. Sex reformers focused on technique and once again women became objects, this time for men's virtuosity. A new frankness emerged and advice columnists in mass magazines began to address the sexual anxieties of married couples. The standard reference work was Theodore Hendrik van de Velde's *Ideal Marriage* (1927). It put forward a set of sexual standards for mutual orgasm, predicated on an experienced husband and a virginal wife. Since the author also opposed nonmarital sex, the source of the husband's experience remained unclear. In any case, sex no longer had to be repressed, it was coopted. It could be celebrated, but not freely or "abnormally." Sex had to serve the stability of the nuclear family.[22]

For all the talk of a "new woman," the interwar period kept much that was old. Not quite as restrictive as in the past or as permissive as in the future, it provided a tenuous bridge between them. Uncertainty about gender roles created anxiety, which in turn led to reaction. When women became more visible in the labor force, putting the sexual division of labor into question and blurring gender lines in the popular mind, experts mobilized to set things right again. The brief flirtation with androgyny symbolized by the boyish flapper soon ended with a firm recommitment to gender difference. With the Depression, the well-rounded female figure reappeared in the mass media. A new mother and wife role stressed domestic virtues based on heightened consumerism, a boon for expanding capitalist markets. Home economics claimed the status of a science and dignified the housewife as an expert, although the working woman still had to juggle job and homemaking. On the eve of World War II, the image was clear: a woman was a woman again, her gender carefully reconstructed for modern times.

CONCLUSION

Must we conclude, then, that between the two world wars, women's emancipation, so highly touted, was a mirage? Or may we look for glimmers of progress and future promise? The answer is a qualified yes to both.

More women than ever before worked for wages outside the home because capital accumulation entailed the absorption of smaller enterprises like family-run farms and businesses. If women themselves were owners, they suffered a loss of power and independence similar to that of the men of their class, but the next generation fared worse. Daughters, usually forced to work for wages due to the decline of family fortunes, landed rather lower in the new hierarchy of jobs than sons. Where agriculture, industry, and service modernized, women got the least skilled, worst paid jobs with little hope of advancement. When rationalization broke down highly skilled old crafts into ignominious tasks on an impersonal assembly line staffed by women, men feared them as wage-depressors. Nevertheless, women became more visible now even to each other—except for those still in home industries—and so were able to organize to improve their work conditions. Some professions proved more accommodating: women entered teaching, nursing, and social work in large numbers, although more lucrative careers in medicine and law remained elusive.

The process of removing production from the home, begun in the Industrial Revolution, was virtually completed in the twentieth century, finally eroding old forms of family cohesion. Children, less of an economic asset and more of a liability, were less affordable. The birth rate fell in proportions that alarmed nationalist observers. However, a new form of family cohesion emerged: emotional companionship. Women were now expected to be pals and playmates for their husbands, psychologists for their children, and home scientists for the sake of hygiene and efficiency. At the same time, public institutions took over some of those functions and dispensed expert advice, challenging women's authority in those roles. If women had paid jobs in addition, the double burden of home and work became more onerous for being in two places instead of one as in the past.

In the area of sexuality, women made the clearest gains, though even these held some ambiguity. Female desire was recognized, lesbian identity acknowledged, and unmarried unchaperoned women could flaunt their freedom in public places. However, women's sexuality could still be legitimated only in marriage. Anything else seemed decadent, yet another symbol of the decline of bourgeois values.

Nostalgia fostered reaction, deepened by world-wide Depression. Conservative political parties thrived on the growing reactionary mood and attacked the ideals of the women's movement. Soon another war created another generation of ladies' auxiliaries—helpmeets rather than independent actors. The traditional ideology of women's role triumphed again for a time.

NOTES

1. Paul Bairoch, *La Population active et sa structure* (Brussels: Editions de l'Institut de Sociologie, Université Libre de Bruxelles, Institut de Sociologie, Centre d'Economie Politique, 1968), pp. 27–34.
2. Henri Fuss, "Unemployment and Employment Among Women," *International Labor Review*, 31 (1935), 490; Renate Bridenthal, "Beyond *Kinder, Küche, Kirche:* Weimar Women at Work," *Central European History*, 6 (June 1973), 151–2; Françoise Guelaud-Leridon, *Le Travail des femmes en France* (Paris: Institut National D'Etudes Démographiques, Travaux et Documents, Cahier no. 42, Presses Universitaires de France, 1964), p. 25; Rosa Anna Perricone, *L'Inserimento della Donna nelle Attivitá Economiche in Italia* (Rome: Nuova Serie, Società Italiana di Economia Demografia e Statistica, 1972), p. 18.
3. Rural Women's Organization, *What the Country Women of the World are Doing*, vols. 1–5 (London: International Council of Women, 1929–1936).
4. International Landworkers' Federation, Reports of the Congresses, *Report of the First Congress*, Amsterdam, 1920; *Report of the Fourth Congress*, Geneva, 1926; *Report of the Fifth Congress*, Prague, 1928; *Report of the Sixth Congress*, Stockholm, 1931.
5. International Labor Organization, *Studies and Reports*, Series I, no. 1, Geneva, 1921, p. 11, and Series I, no. 4, Geneva, 1939, pp. 19, 33.
6. Table 18-2 represents a compilation of data from a number of sources: Germany, Statistisches Amt, *Wirtschaft und Statistik*, vol. 14 (1934), Sonderbeilage 24, p. 4; Perricone, *L'Inserimento*, pp. 18, 35; Guelaud-Leridon, *Le Travail;*

Pierfrancesco Bandettini, "The Employment of Women in Italy, 1881–1951," *Comparative Studies in Society and History*, vol. 2 (1959–1960), p. 374.

7. Bridenthal, "Beyond," pp. 159–161.

8. Jean Daric, *L'Activité professionnelle des femmes en France* (Paris: Institut National D'Etudes Démographiques, Travaux et Documents, Cahier no. 5, Presses Universitaires de France, 1947), p. 43.

9. Franco Archibugi, "Recent Trends in Women's Work in Italy," *International Labor Review*, 81 (1960), 290–295.

10. International Congress of Working Women, *Resolutions adopted by the First Congress of I.C.W.W. in Washington, U.S.A., October 28 to November 6, 1919* (Chicago: National Women's Trade Union League of America, 1919).

11. International Labor Organization, *Studies and Reports*, Series I, no. 4, Geneva, 1939, pp. 346–347, 359, 362.

12. *Wirtschaft und Statistik*; Guelaud-Leridon, *Le Travail*, pp. 14, 25; Perricone, *L'Inserimento*, p. 35.

13. Daric, *L'Activité*, p. 43; Bridenthal, "Beyond," p. 161; Nora Federici, "Evolution et caractéristiques du travail féminin en Italie," *Cahiers de l'Institut de Science Economique Appliquée*, 122, series AB2 (Paris: Institut de Science Economique Appliquée, February 1962).

14. Guelaud-Leridon, *Le Travail*, p. 25; Bridenthal, "Beyond," pp. 163–164; Perricone, *L'Inserimento*, pp. 39, 89; Archibugi, "Recent Trends," p. 296.

15. Michael H. Kater, "Krisis des Frauenstudiums in der Weimarer Republik," *Vierteljahrschrift für Sozial- und Wirtschaftsgeschichte*, 59, 2 (1972).

16. Sixth International Neo-Malthusian and Birth Control Conference, vol. 1: *International Aspects of Birth Control*, ed. Margaret Sanger (New York: The American Birth Control League, Inc., 1925), pp. 13, 132.

17. Georg Schwägler, *Soziologie der Familie, Ursprung und Entwicklung*, Heidelberger Sociologica, 9, Mohr (Siebeck), Tübingen, 1970, pp. 86–108.

18. Robert Blood and Donald Wolfe, *Husbands and Wives* (New York: Free Press 1960); William J. Goode, *World Revolution and Family Patterns* (New York: Free Press, 1970); Günther Lüschen and Eugen Lupri, *Soziologie der Familie* (Opladen: Westdeutscher Verlag, 1970); *Journal of Marriage and the Family*, vol. 31, no. 2, is a special issue about cross-cultural family research.

19. Victoria de Grazia, "Puritan Mind, Pagan Bodies: American Mass Culture in the Making of Europe's 'New Woman', 1920–1945." Paper presented at the Sixth Berkshire Conference on the History of Women, June 19, 1984. Also Atina Grossmann, " 'Girlkultur' or Thoroughly Rationalized Female: A New Woman in Weimar Germany," *Women in Culture and Politics: A Century of Change*, ed. Judith Friedlander, Blanche Wiesen Cook, Alice Kessler-Harris, and Carroll Smith-Rosenberg (Bloomington, Ind.: Bloomington University Press, 1986).

20. Vicki Baum, *It Was All Quite Different* (New York: Funk and Wagnalls, 1964), p. 260.

21. *Ibid.*, p. 249.

22. Atina Grossmann, "The New Woman and the Rationalization of Sexuality in Weimar Germany," *Powers of Desire*, ed. Ann Snitow, Christine Stansell, and Sharon Thompson, (New York: New Feminist Library, Monthly Review Press, 1983).

SUGGESTIONS FOR FURTHER READING

There is still no English work available on European women in general in the interwar period, although primary sources have now been translated in the impressive compendium edited by Susan Groag Bell and Karen M. Offen, *Women, the Family, and Freedom: The Debate in Documents*, vol. II, 1880–1950 (Stanford, Calif.: Stanford University Press, 1983).

Some national studies are valuable. For France, see Theodore Zeldin, *France 1848–1945, Vol. 1: Ambition, Love and Politics* (New York: Oxford University Press, 1973) and James F. McMillan, *Housewife or Harlot: The Place of Women in French Society 1870–1940* (New York: St. Martin's Press, 1981). For England, Jeffrey Weeks, *Sex, Politics and Society: The Regulation of Sexuality Since 1800* (London and New York: Longman, 1981) and Jane Lewis, *Women in England, 1870–1950: Sexual Divisions and Social Change* (Bloomington, Ind.: Indiana University Press, 1984) are useful. For Germany, *When Biology Became Destiny: Women in Weimar and Nazi Germany*, ed. Renate Bridenthal, Atina Grossmann, and Marion Kaplan (New York: New Feminist Library, Monthly Review Press, 1984) offers several articles on this period. Unfortunately, Italian scholarship on women still remains untranslated.

A welcome beginning on the history of lesbian women is Lillian Faderman's *Surpassing the Love of Men* (New York: William Morrow, 1981). Michel Foucault, in *The History of Sexuality*, vol. I: *An Introduction* (New York: Random House, 1978) offers a challenging hypothesis about the politicization of sex over time. Jacques Donzelot, in *The Policing of Families* (New York: Random House, 1979) theorizes about the historically changing relationship of state and family.

The ideal mother and her perfect son: the cover of a Nazi women's periodical. (With permission of Institut fuer Zeitgeschichte, Muenchen)

chapter 19

The Fascist Solution to the Woman Question in Italy and Germany[1]

Claudia Koonz

While feminists in the twentieth century continued the struggle for equality within the contexts of liberal and socialist movements, nationalist crusaders for women's rights in Italy and Germany blended their belief in separate spheres with the fascist emphasis on national glory. Threatened by secular society and fearful that women would become "masculinized," they left politics to male leaders and devoted themselves to cultivating their own "feminine" world. Since women could not compete successfully against men in their "masculine" arena, women who supported fascism worked to upgrade traditional women's roles. They accepted Nazi and Fascist leaders' public praise, material rewards, and new programs for motherhood, naively hoping to protect the family. In reality, fascist programs aimed at intervening in private life and imposing fascist values on individual decision making. Thus, fascist women officials actually participated in the breakdown of the family. Vast differences in the level of industrialization and in Mussolini's and Hitler's political careers created significant contrasts in the realization of these goals. But in both nations, women as victims and resisters, opposed fascist rule. Under conditions of extreme danger, women constituted vital links in the clandestine world of anti-fascism.

THE FORMATION OF FASCIST VALUES

British feminist Sylvia Pankhurst declared in 1936 "Fascism and the emancipation of women are inherently opposed. Fascism is the rule of force . . . essentially and in theory . . . [whereas] the women's movement could only develop as the rule of reason, justice and humanity replaced the rule of might." In addition to attacking fascism, Pankhurst charged that the Catholic Church defended Mussolini and oppressed women. Controversy erupted at once. Anne Brock Griggs, member of the British Union of Fascists, accused Pankhurst of ignoring "the magnificent work done by Mussolini for the physical and mental health, not only of mothers and children, but of all his people." Rev. W. Dempsey, S. J., who shared Pankhurst's hatred of fascism, deplored her allegations against the Catholic Church, which he praised as the "true champion" of "sound Feminism."[2] The three discussants elaborated their opinions in the context of an international debate about the woman question—the term used at the turn of the century to describe the tensions between feminists' demands for civil equality in public life and social expectations that women as mothers bear special responsibility for private, family life.

Pankhurst made equal human rights the bedrock of her position and held that men and women should share responsibility for family decision-making and support. Her opponents believed that fundamental differences in masculine and feminine nature made equality unthinkable. In their belief in polarized gender roles, however, conservatives differed sharply from fascists. Conservatives wanted to restrict women's activities to their homes and families, with the father as the breadwinner and source of authority. Fascists, rather than viewing each family primarily as a unit under the father's control, emphasized women's responsibilities to serve their communities in special "feminine" areas of public life. While conservatives believed that families, helped if necessary by charity, ought to bear responsibility for their kin, fascists approved of state support to mothers whose husbands defaulted on their obligations. In social policy and doctrine the fascist promise to create "more masculine men and more feminine women" fit easily into a racist context that pitted "Roman" and "Aryan" elites against "inferior" races.

Although other nations during the 1930s experimented with eugenic policies and tolerated blatant, public expression of anti-Semitism, only Hitler and Mussolini made their prejudices about race and gender the basis of social policy and official ideology. In a completely fascist society, individual motherhood would be reduced to biological reproduction because state-sponsored child care and educational facilities, staffed by women, would assume full responsibility for socializing "racially acceptable" children to collectivist values. Ultimately, too, both men and women would be considered only in terms of the contributions they could make to a powerful state. The nature of these sacrifices was linked inexorably to notions about masculine and feminine. Italian soldiers sang, "Death lets itself be kissed only by soldiers. Forward comrades, let's make her [death] at home. Leave the shirking to the women." German girls learned "Be Pure, Be True, Be German" while their brothers promised to "Fight Bravely, Live Honorably, Die Smiling!"

Unlike other twentieth century ideologies, fascism had no nineteenth-century tradition, and it left no respectable heritage after 1945. Although powerful symbols, such as the swastikas, jack boots, and whips, evoked by fascist propaganda haunt the fringes of erotic culture today, fascism as an intellectual and political force emerged at the close of World War I and died with the Allied victory in 1945.

However, we see remnants of fascist values today in movements to restore law and order at the cost of basic freedoms, to revive motherhood at the expense of women's rights and sexual freedom, and to thwart progressive change by segmenting society into rich and poor, male and female, white and non-white, Christian and non-Christian. The importance in modern political life of mass media was foreshadowed in the consensus-building campaigns of the Fascists and National Socialists. Mussolini and Hitler, masters of propaganda, were the first leaders to exploit newspaper, radio, and film as political tools. Adapting war-time propaganda methods, they staged lavish ceremonies, called for plebiscites, bestowed honors on worthy subjects, and launched crusades for national objectives like better wheat production, economic autarky, and higher birthrates.

In both Germany and Italy, the mobilization of women was fraught with contradiction. Nazi and fascist men prided themselves on the exclusively masculine élan of their movements and did not welcome women in their ranks. Moreover, they wanted their wives to obey them, not the state. In both nations, debates about women's clothing hinted at men's ambivalance. A woman in uniform connoted a public citizen, active and responsible to the leader. But the ideal wife, loyal primarily to her husband, selected her own fashions to please him. Ultimately, the fascist insistence on every citizen's direct responsibility to the government won out, and women in party organizations wore uniforms, or at least distinctive clothing with insignia denoting rank. Whatever their personal ambivalence about women in public life, both Mussolini and Hitler realized that women provided essential services and needed their own separate organizations to become effective. Recalling the spirit of World War I, they called on men and women (in separate ways) to relinquish rights and make sacrifices for the common good. Loyal subjects lost their liberties but won rewards for services rendered. While promising to restore women's exclusively domestic roles, fascist propaganda made women feel that their nations (as in wartime) depended upon their sacrifice, and promised them rewards as women.

The public fanfare about motherhood followed logically from the doctrine of separate spheres. If women and men fulfilled distinct functions, then they needed special and very different reward systems and women required a cadre of educated and ambitious women as leaders. These careerists resembled, in their personality traits if not in their values, the New Woman that Fascist and Nazi propaganda decried. Under the guise of traditionalism, both *il Duce* and *der Führer* launched drives to 'modernize' women without making them independent. Encouraged to participate in sports and physical fitness activities, honored in public ceremonies and lavishly praised in the media, the New Mother emerged as counterweight to the New Woman. To make motherhood seem more desirable than wage-earning in offices, factories, and professions, the Italian and German governments funded home economics institutes, supported radio programs for the modern homemaker, and awarded official honors to capable mothers. A revival of motherhood, of course, swept through Europe in the 1930s, but to a unique degree, Mussolini and Hitler made the policy of population increase and the strategy indoctrinating the young into the cornerstones of their social programs.

Similar personal backgrounds account in part for the parallels between the two dictators. Each had grown up in lower-middle-class Catholic environments with devout mothers and atheist, abusive fathers. Before 1914, both young men had drifted on the fringes of society without clear vocational goals, and both openly despised Catholicism. Mussolini wrote a novel about scandal in the church, *Claudia Particella, The Cardinal's Mistress*, and Hitler ridiculed priests as "skirts." Although each had avoided the draft before 1914, as soon as their respective nations declared war, they enthusiastically enlisted and served as regular soldiers. The war transformed them both, as did the aftermath. Although Italy emerged on the winning side, Mussolini, like many nationalists, believed the Allies had cheated his nation out of the spoils of victory. Hitler blamed German defeat not so much on the Allies as on what he saw as the inner corruption caused by a Jewish conspiracy. Mussolini and Hitler, eloquent and emotional public speakers, recruited the young and the disenchanted into paramilitary movements that revived memories of the war. In their party programs, they swore to wage war against labor unions and wealthy capitalists, to strengthen the solid middle class and peasantry, and to restore a "healthy" relationship between men and women. Members of the Black Shirts, or *Fasci di Combattimento* and the Brown Shirts, or *Sturmabteilung*, swore total dedication to *il Duce* and *der Führer*. Before seizing national power, both men warned about the threat of communist revolution. Both men came to power backed by conservative leaders who saw a dictatorship as the only way to roll back the gains of liberal politics and strong labor unions. Once in power, each relied on a combination of terror, bluff, and duplicity to destroy socialism, while offering industrialists the prospects of huge profits and depriving everyone of basic liberties.

The parallels end here. From the standpoint of foreign policy, bureaucracy, and political organization, it may be appropriate to emphasize similarities between the two fascisms, but from the perspective of women's history, the parallels give way to dramatic contrasts. Most obviously, while both men revived pagan nationalist traditions, myths about the Roman and Germanic past differed. Mussolini revived the image of the Roman matron and replaced common law with early Roman law, which vested household power entirely in the father. Hitler drew on tribal myths of a Germanic society structured around strong same-sex peer groupings. Some Nazi writers even extolled a prehistoric matriarchy and glorified Brunhilda as the ideal woman.

In their personal lives, Mussolini and Hitler exhibited quite different values as well. Before 1922, Mussolini lived with the woman by whom he had two children. In 1925 he married her in the Church and had his children baptized. Although Mussolini's long-term love relationship with Clara Petacci (his "official mistress") and his many extramarital affairs hardly conformed to Catholic doctrine, he did not openly violate Italian convention, especially as he appeared to be a devoted family man adored by his children and wife. Hitler's private life, by contrast, was not congruent with fundamental family values. Before 1933, Hitler pursued a love affair with his niece that was ended by her suicide. After becoming dictator, Hitler settled into a semisecret relationship with Eva Braun but did not marry her until the eve of their joint suicide. Mussolini epitomized the good family man with strong heterosexual urges, while Hitler, as he himself often boasted, wanted no bride except his *Vaterland.*

Crucial pragmatic considerations enhanced these personal differences. Although both Nazism and Fascism emerged out of the crucible of World War I, Mussolini became dictator in 1922, when King Victor Emmanuel appointed this upstart rabble-rouser to end the threat of left-wing revolution. The fact that the king could dismiss him at any time placed constraints on Mussolini with which Hitler did not have to contend after being appointed Chancellor. In addition, the Catholic Church wielded a great influence over Italian public opinion, while in Germany Protestants and Catholics never formed a unified response to Nazism. Mussolini boasted about revolutionizing family life and revitalizing the Roman race, but in reality his social policies conformed to the conservative patriarchal model espoused by king and church.

Like *il Duce,* Hitler won his position because the chief of state saw him as the only alternative to socialism and revolution. President Paul von Hindenburg appointed Hitler Chancellor in January 1933. After the Reichstag (the national legislature) granted him dictatorial powers and Hindenburg died, Hitler was responsible to no higher authority. The decade Hitler spent waiting for a chance at national power gave the Nazi party a very different character from the Fascist party. While Mussolini in 1922 commanded fewer than 20,000 black-shirted paramilitary troops, Hitler on the eve of his victory had the backing of 400,000 storm troopers, over a million party members, and one third (14,000,000) of the German electorate. Women comprised under 5 percent of the party membership, but they contributed nearly 50 percent of the Nazi vote during the Depression years, when the Nazi Party rose from ninth to first place among the seven major political parties.

However, even more important than these contrasts in political setting was the striking difference in the level of Italian and German industrialization. Although Mussolini's economic policies did speed industrialization, Italy remained a fundamentally agrarian and Catholic nation, glossed by Mussolini's slick, modern style. Hitler, on the other hand, piously swore to uphold traditional values, but in fact accelerated the modernization of one of the world's most powerful industrial nations.

While Mussolini and Hitler revived polarized gender stereotypes and removed women from formal political life, their conceptions of family and community differed in fundamental ways. Mussolini, the pragmatist, governed an extremely traditional nation and actually shored up the authority of both individual fathers and the Catholic church. In the Italian paradigm, the politically emasculated father was compensated with greater control over his family. Nazi social engineers deployed sophisticated welfare, health care, educational, and cultural institutions to invade every aspect of private life. Ultimately, the *Führer* would undercut the individual father as the source of authority and support.

War, of course, destroyed both societies. But even before defeat, it became clear that fascism in Germany and Italy encountered opposition from many quarters. Women felt the impact of fascism most directly when it touched their religious faith, family life, and occupational goals. An examination of women's responses to fascist policies related to demography, religion, the economy, and politics suggests both the extraordinary power of fascism to mobilize people and the limits beyond which not even massive government programs and brilliantly staged media campaigns could reshape basic values.

FASCISM AND ITALIAN WOMEN

A 1919 list of Fascist principles included the promise of equal vote and rights for women. Although some evidence suggests that a few women's units, or *fasci*, had formed before the March on Rome, support could not have been very widespread. When Amalia Besso called a Fascist Women's Congress in 1921, only fourteen women delegates attended. After Mussolini became dictator, however, most middle-class women's organizations accepted the invitation to support the new state. Although women in left wing political movements felt the escalating repression just as men did, conservative and religious associations barely noted the loss of democracy or the potential threat of Fascism to women's status. Loyal to the King who had appointed Mussolini as dictator, the women's rights movement did not criticize Fascism in theory or practice. Their acceptance becomes somewhat understandable when we remember that these women endorsed Mussolini's promise to eliminate atheism and communism. Moreover, Mussolini proceeded cautiously in his attack on democracy. For several years, nonsocialist opposition parties continued to run candidates and even to participate in Mussolini's government. Circulation figures of non-Fascist newspapers ran several times higher than those of the government newspapers. Some non-Fascists kept their military and administrative posts, the press remained somewhat free, and after 1929 the Church gave its blessings to the Fascist state.

The Status of Women

After becoming dictator in 1922, Mussolini made no statements about women's civic status. But even before an official policy on women emerged, the government press left little doubt about the position of women in the Fascist state. When, for example, a woman became the director of the La Scala opera in Milan, the government newspaper asked, "Is our revolution so poor in *men*, that a woman should be appointed to the premier theatre of Italy?" Still, hopeful signs appeared. In early summer of 1923, when the International Alliance for Women's Suffrage met in Rome, *il Duce* vaguely mentioned women's suffrage. It quickly became obvious, however, that this speech resulted from Mussolini's desire to cultivate a good image in the international press and not from any willingness to consider women's rights. The first official pronouncement on the woman question dispelled their optimism by banishing women from politics and encouraging volunteer charity work.

At the end of 1923, *il Duce* dropped his support for a proposal to enfranchise women at the local level if they were veterans' widows, literate property-owning women, or recipients of war medals. "Naturally, I do not wish to turn women into slaves. But it would be a personal affront to me if they voted. In our state women will count for nothing."[3] Besides, Mussolini asked rhetorically, if women did not vote in Switzerland, the world's oldest democracy, why should they vote in Italy? Subjects, Mussolini reminded the Italians, had obligations as members of a trade, a family, or a community. As in wartime, citizens could expect rewards for sacrifices, but not rights. *Il Duce* told an exiled German journalist,

> Women must obey. My opinion of the role of women in the state is opposed to feminism. If I were to give women the vote, people would laugh at me; in a state like ours they ought not to count. Do you know how the Anglo-Saxons will end? In the Matriarchate![4]

Mussolini appealed to the Roman tradition according to which, he said, social power and imperial grandeur had been achieved by maintaining three hierarchies—of brains, beauty, and force. Everyone knew his or her place, and sacrificed for national greatness within that framework, which was based on rewards, not rights. Mussolini's preconceptions excluded women from the realms of brains and force, but left them ample scope in the area of beauty. "If a woman does not know she is pleasing, she is nervous and unhappy," Mussolini once told Margherita Sarfatti, his admirer and probably also his mistress for over two decades. Approvingly, Sarfatti described her idol's views of womanhood, which recalled the women slaves in ancient Rome who were allowed to pour water at banquets and public celebrations.

> Tall, pure and open, with the basket well balanced on her head—like the peasant women of old—leaving her hands free to knit away and avoid wasting time while she strides along carrying bricks. From under her skirt, disheveled little heads stick out, with the last-born peeping out of the breadbasket.[5]

Mussolini's view of women as decorative objects and hard workers meant that women leaders operated under severe constraints.

Women's Organizations

The women deputized to organize women's support for Fascist aims were handicapped by men's mistrust of their autonomy. Fascist women, however, knew how to assuage men's suspicions. The Countess Casagrande, the chief of the Fascist women's organization, told *il Duce*:

> We have raised our children. But it is you who have inspired them. With your soul you have enflamed in their bodies not just a torch but a flaming fire. . . . These are your soldiers, the finest flower of the Italian springtime . . . [giving you their] constancy and sacrifice. . . . We stand at your side [for] . . . in this battle, when all is said and done, it is the woman who provides the aroma which stimulates the male vigor to battle.[6]

No doubt Mussolini felt flattered by such praise. But during the 1920s he paid little attention to women as potential supporters of Fascism.

The state created a *Fasci Femminili*, but it languished from lack of funding. By 1924, only 40,000 women had joined. Although its new leader, Elisa Majer Rizzioli, defended women's rights, her words made no impact on policy. In 1925, the Ministry of the Interior ordered the reorganization of Fascist women. Ten women could form a local group, provided each member had been recommended by at least two women Fascists in good standing and demonstrated, "leadership ability [*Fede*], morality, and true Fascist devotion." In all, 4,000 locals provided the regime with "shock troops" to fight decadence, improve education, promote the purchase of Italian-made products, and spread fascist doctrine. Despite the scope of such plans, however, the women's organization remained an auxilliary and its most important function consisted of organizing leisure-time activities for women workers, in the *Dopolvaro* program. Women Fascists' periodicals featured essays on women as authors and famous men's wives, as well as photographs and news items about women's sports. Women in this Fascist elite saw themselves as wives, but shared the special, modern glamour that came from physical fitness, literary creation, and association with the Fascist state.

Rather than recruiting a mass following among ordinary women, Fascist organizations attracted "a genteel and beneficent" bourgeois population primarily from urban settings.[7] These women from wealthy and aristocratic families had no desire for careers or even employment, but actively participated as volunteers in community activities. The goals of this small group contradicted traditional notions about women's role as religious, monogamous, subservient, and motherly. Considering themselves ladies (*signora*), as opposed to merely women (*donne*), they gave a certain glamour to the Fascist image.

To some young, educated, and progressive women, Fascism appeared to offer a new freedom. Contorted as their arguments may seem to us, these women Fascists welcomed the retreat from feminism and at the same time despised conservative notions about women's role as religious, monogamous, subservient, and motherly. One former member of a Fascist youth group, Luce d'Eramo, in 1983 reminisced about growing up as the daughter of convinced Fascists, describing how the ideal of a vigorous Fascist woman had liberated her from her passive resignation so she "could stride vigorously forward" with her husband. A new generation of young men and women among the Fascist elite enjoyed a measure of sexual and social freedom unknown among other groups. In explaining her peers' contempt for sexual prudishness, d'Eramo quoted a hit song from the period, "The Modern Bride Doesn't Come to the Altar in a White Gown," (the symbol of virginity). D'Eramo recalls her intellectual excitement as a student in a prestigious Fascist university. She passed her examination in the 'history and doctrine of Fascism' with high honors, having written a dissertation on her heroine, Rosa Luxemburg (the Communist theorist and politician murdered during the Spartacist uprising in Berlin in 1919). In a stunning example of Fascist eclecticism, or perhaps merely confusion, d'Eramo honored Luxemburg as a precursor of Fascism.[8]

Fascism offered young and progressive women an escape from family life—characterized by public activities and organized leisure programs. Since Italian women had never enjoyed even the official promise of equality, the Fascist state did not deprive them of legal status. Moreover, in distinctively modern ways, Fascist programs created a mentality and a new esprit de corps for younger, urban women that appeared to involve them in public life without giving them entry into formal politics. At least in theory, woman had an alternative both to backward-looking Catholic parochialism and to the feminist vision of an equal future. Sibella Aleramo, author of

Italy's first feminist novel, *A Woman*, declared in 1930 that Fascist victory, by ending all hope of women's access to higher education, professions, and political power, actually "liberated" women from an unpleasant man's world. Under Fascism, she claimed, women enjoyed a unique opportunity to create the "splendid richness of their race." This Fascist stalwart called on women to cultivate their self-esteem and deepen a "female solidarity" on the basis of their domestic responsibilities. "Inner," not superficial and man-made goals, she said, offered women their only hope of selfhood. As a contemporary put it, "The Italian woman is no longer the passive, ignorant creature of yesterday. She joins in the national life, work, problems and pride."[9]

For all Aleramo's rhapsodizing, the exclusion of women from politicians' attention resulted in very low budgets for women's organizing. With an annual expenditure of 179,000 lire (about $6000 in 1930) the *Fasci Femminili* ranked far behind other organizations, such as the male youth organization, which received 2,500,000 lira per year. Nevertheless, by 1929, the organization increased its membership to about 1,350,000 by absorbing all other civic women's groups. However, compared with the two million men in the Fascist party, this was a poor showing.[10]

Fascism, the Church, and the Revival of Patriarchal Power

Mussolini's campaigns for total loyalty to Fascism inevitably conflicted with Italians' allegiance to Catholicism. Ninety-eight percent of all Italians had been baptized Catholic, and about a fourth of the population (overwhelmingly women) attended church regularly. The 1929 agreements between Mussolini and Pope Pius XI affirmed the close cooperation between Fascist rule and Catholic religion; Mussolini formally granted to the Vatican control over large areas of public life, including women's organizations such as the *Unione Feminile Cattolica Italiana*, the *Unione donne Cattoliche Italiane* and the *Gioventu Feminile Cattolica Italiana*, which together claimed over a million members. The number of nuns grew dramatically under Fascism, from 71,000 in 1921 to 129,000 in 1931 and increasingly their duties integrated them into community service.[11] Starting with the encyclicals, *Arcanum* and *De Rerum Novarum*, in the late 19th century, the Vatican had vigorously denounced women's emancipation and communism as twin threats to patriarchy and property. The 1930 papal encyclical *Casti Connubi* defended the husband's absolute rights over his wife; the government gave couples copies at their weddings. In the following year the Pope issued *Quadrigesimo anno*, which ordered women to view motherhood as their major commitment in life. Mussolini and the Catholic Church had arrived at a modus vivendi.

As Mussolini strengthened the church's responsibility over social programs, he also reinforced a father's rights over his family. A "reform" in 1929 supported a husband's right to "physical correction and discipline" in the family. A runaway wife could be pursued by the police and, if caught, subjected to a two-year prison term. A woman's adultery could result in a two-year prison term (men remained virtually unhampered in this regard). Rapists faced no punishment if it could be demonstrated that the victim (no matter how young) had a poor reputation or had behaved seductively. A 1932 law decreed that if a man murdered his wife, mother, or sister because of her purported adultery, his act became a "crime of honor" and exempt from punishment. In the wake of this new ruling, the homicide rate dropped by 50 percent, which suggests that half the number of murders before the "reform" might have been considered as affairs of "honor."

To provide men with incentives to fatherhood (and perhaps, too, to compensate them for their loss of political liberty), Mussolini further increased male prerogatives at the expense of women. In certain instances paternal privilege superseded even the drive for population growth. For example, persons convicted of spreading birth control literature could receive two year jail sentences, and punishments for abortion were far worse, but an abortion performed, with or without the woman's consent, was considered an act in the *interests of family honor* (as defined by the man) and treated as a minor crime. "Family honor" might be involved, for example, if a daughter became pregnant without marrying. The penalty for abandoning a child in a case of "family honor" was reduced to virtually nothing, while abduction could result in fourteen years at hard labor. These laws formalized the assumption that children belonged to their fathers. Despite Mussolini's oath to improve women's position, a series of laws gave their fathers and husbands more authority than ever over dependents. The state that reduced men from citizens to subjects, endowed fathers with dictatorial powers over their wives and children. The Roman *patria potestas* had returned to modern Italy.

Women Workers Under Fascism

Considering the strengthening of paternal power in the home and Mussolini's views on womanhood, discrimination against women in the workforce came as no surprise. Before Fascist legislation, labor law pegged women's wages at between 65 and 70 percent of men's for the same work, but the 1927 Charter of Labor decreed that women would earn only 50 percent in all but a few select occupations. The Fascist system of workers' compensation for unemployment, illness, and accident favored men. Male workers were also given longer vacations.[12] After the Depression, policies and laws operating to women's disadvantage proliferated. In 1938, regulations limited female employment to 10 percent of the total labor force. Statistics collected in six censuses between 1881 and 1951 show a long-term *decrease* in women's share of the labor force (from 35 percent to 25 percent) with little change in the rate of decline during the interwar period. About one-third of the paid labor force was female throughout the Fascist period, in other words slightly less than in industrialized Germany and Great Britain. We know, too, that despite laws restricting women's employment, the traditional Italian life cycle remained in force. Growing numbers of young women worked in industry from their mid-teens until they married and had children. In addition, after the World War I, many Italian women worked outside the social security system on the "black" labor market and therefore remained uncounted.[13]

Women with professional aspirations had always faced barriers in Italy because of chronically high rates of white-collar unemployment. Even before the Depression, women teachers were barred from teaching courses in the humanities at the *lycée* (university preparatory high school) and were not allowed to apply for administrative jobs in education. When economic crisis brought production to a standstill, Mussolini blamed women and the machine for stealing skilled workers' jobs. While admitting that no industrialized nation could turn back the technological clock, he did call for a ban on women workers whose "work is the source of moral and political bitterness."[14] He told employers to advertise only for men workers. The fact that many of these laws and regulations had to be repeated, however, suggests they did not solve the problem. The needs of an industrializing economy in the north demanded women's cheap labor, especially in health care, white-collar jobs, and poorly paid industrial jobs. Women students more than held their own in the universities and a few women even managed to become professionals. Women's university enrollment was 4 percent of the total in 1912, but increased to 17 percent in 1935 and to 30 percent after young men were drafted. The tertiary (or service) sector absorbed increasing numbers of women—especially in transport, office work, and public administration. Economic need counted for more than *il Duce*'s pronouncements, and women remained at their jobs, despite low pay and poor prospects for advancement.

For all Mussolini's claims to have revolutionized Italian life, industrial progress under Fascism continued at the same rate as before 1922 and after 1943. Legal changes left women more subject to fathers' and husbands' wishes than before and labor legislation barred them from attaining equality in the labor market. But along with these restrictive policies, the Fascist state inaugurated several facilitative programs to benefit mothers. In 1925, the National Program for the Protection of Mothers and Infants (ONMI) was established to improve infant health and public morality; in 1929 wage earning mothers received maternity leaves; after 1933 the government provided small monthly payments for poor families with many children and legislation in 1934 provided for extensive maternity benefits for factory and office workers.

Motherhood and the Patria

Mussolini's military ambitions had a more significant impact on most Italian women than his hazy proclamations about motherhood. Planning for a foreign war, Mussolini declared that the *Patria* needed women as mothers, morale builders, consumers, and volunteers in the fight against "inner weakness." A special organization for rural women recruited 845,000 members by 1940 and a working women's association drew 1,650,000 members. The *Fasci Femminili* organized homemaker helper programs, taught courses in home economics and infant care, and raised funds. Mussolini announced on Ascension Day 1934 that he had just diagnosed a dual national threat, decadence and depopulation. But he told his subjects not to worry, "I am a clinician who never overlooks a single symptom," and declared he had discovered the cure: a new program of incentives to foster higher birth rates. Sociologists, led by Corrado Gini, warned of demographic disaster and urged emergency measures to restore the birth rate. In addition to material aid, the government began a propaganda campaign. The popular press took up the theme, telling women to bear many children because, "After the revolution there will be bread and glory for all!" Italians, who had already heard themselves summoned to fight the "battle of wheat" or the "battle against the Mafia," now heard slogans for a "battle for births" that promised state subsidies for child support, mother relief programs, and a levy on bachelors that doubled unmarried men's income tax. "Marry young," the official newspaper told Italians. "Marriage at 20 is a splendid thing."[15]

Although real wages fell slightly under Fascism, spending for social welfare increased dramatically (from about 7 percent of the total state and local receipts from taxation in 1930 to about 20 percent in 1940). About a million new mothers every year received some benefits (in the form of financial compensation for not only births but miscarriages); and family assistance programs together with marriage loans aided poor families with many children. However, agricultural women workers remained outside coverage until 1936.[16] In 1929 the legal minimum age of marriage was reduced from 15 for women and 18 for men to 14 and 16 respectively. By contrast, German law stipulated 16 and 21 while France held to 15 and 18.

Mussolini, imitating Hitler, called for higher birthrates to vindicate the lie that Italy had to conquer new territories to feed its growing population. "Expand or explode!" he shouted in dozens of speeches. Propaganda decreed that four children per marriage constituted the ideal for a happy and well-balanced family life. Starting in 1933 Italians celebrated Mother and Child Day on December 23. Every town held ceremonies honoring its most prolific mothers; and 90 mothers were singled out to meet *il Duce* and join in celebrations in Rome. In the Hall of Battles, Italy's fifty-eight most fertile couples (who had produced 1544 healthy offspring) received special honors in September 1936. Later that year, thousands of mothers gathered in Rome to see Mussolini, chanting, "Thank you, Duce, for all these babies!" When the top ace pilot landed at a women's celebration on on the beach in Rimini, 60,000 women carrying their infants chanted their welcome.

Once the Fascist government took notice of women, more comprehensive aims became apparent. In the mid-1930s, for the first time, Mussolini and his advisors seemed to grasp the importance of recruiting mothers to indoctrinate their children in the cardinal Fascist virtues, such as obedience to authority and sacrifice for the collective good. "We must make a total demographic policy and give to the propelling organ behind it a political character."[17] The entire society rests, sociologist Ferdinando Loffredo continued, on three powerful *fasci:* the individual, the state and the family. Where liberals saw the family as a school for individualism, Fascist theorists enlisted the family as preparation for collectivism, as one Fascist put it a "weapon" against "selfish and egotistic" instincts.

Birthrates, like the level of women's participation in the labor force and the rates of women's participation in Fascist programs, reflected the relative ineffectiveness of these measures. Mothers may have appreciated the public attention, but parents did not alter their choices to fit Fascist priorities. The use of birth control and abortion despite harsh laws suggests one form of women's resistance to Fascist power.[18] Infant mortality and miscarriage rates remained high, as did infanticide. In Italy, infant mortality stood at about 123 per 10,000, as compared with 155 for Soviet Russia, 64 for Germany, and 23 for France, and 70 for the United States. Birthrates leveled off at about 250 per 10,000 as compared with 343 for the Soviet Union, 189 for the USA, 190 for Germany, and 180 for France. During the pronatalist drive of the late 1930s the births per year increased somewhat (from 960,000 to 1,000,000), even though the marriage rate declined slightly.[19] Even this small rise in births resulted from the fact that Italians born in the post–World War I "baby boom" reached childbearing age in the late 1930s. The average age at marriage continued to rise, and in the cities increased to about 29 for men and 25 for women in the late 1930s.

The Effect of Propaganda

Despite the failure of Fascist propaganda to alter long-term demographic trends, women at least felt that their government noticed them. War brought women to their leaders' attention in a new way. Studies in the mid-1930s reported that women spent about 60 percent of a family's income and played a vital role in maintaining morale on the home front. Starting with the Ethiopian campaign, newspapers featured women in news photographs and graphics related to wartime ceremonies. The image of the Italian lady was used to affirm Mussolini's claim that Italians brought a higher culture to their "inferior" victims, even as Fascist soldiers slaughtered Africans who were armed only with spears. Significantly, the media did not feature women with Fascist insignia, but instead relied on patriotic appeals from royal princesses, noblewomen, and the mothers of fallen heroes. In 1935, when the League of Nations condemned Italian aggression and reinforced its censure with economic sanctions, Mussolini made women of all classes part of the "Self-defense" against "immoral" foreign hostility. Newspapers and posters throughout the fall of 1935 rallied Italians to collect scrap metal, paper and rags, as "ballots" in a "plebiscite" for Mussolini against the League.

In October 1935, *il Duce* begged women to contribute their wedding rings, the only piece of gold most of them would ever posses, to the national treasury. Recalling the Oppian Law of 195 B.C. that required Roman women to donate their precious possessions for the war effort, *il Duce* demanded sacrifice. In an elaborate ceremony in December, Mussolini "married" the million women who had donated their gold rings; they received as replacements iron wedding bands.[20] Flanked by women of the royal family, a few Fascist women leaders, and many mothers of dead soldiers, Mussolini accepted the contribution standing in front of a brazier mounted on an imitation of the classic Roman three-legged altar. The press release called the wedding ring donors the "avant garde of the feminine army," and an artist's rendering of the event featured three hands virtually in the flames.

During the late 1930s, Mussolini introduced racial concepts. Citizens henceforth were forbidden to shake hands (an intimate, "soft" gesture), but had instead to use the Roman salute. Soldiers marched in the Roman (goose) step and civil servants received uniforms. A propagandist wrote, "the two names, marvellously joined together in love and faith, are today on the lips of Italian youth. 'Mamma!' 'Duce!' " Indoctrination programs expanded. But over half of all Italians still lived in rural villages dominated by tradition and Catholicism. Women in the south, for example, barely ventured into public places without male escorts and had only the haziest notion of what "nation" meant. Thoroughly imbued with Catholicism, most of these women remained unavailable to Fascist propaganda. In addition, because Mussolini's accelerated drive for racial identity and total Fascist commitment occurred mainly in the context of war and privation, it is doubtful that they took hold deeply anywhere. These constraints, combined with Mussolini's rather conventional views about families and social hierarchy, meant that Fascist social policy resembled that of other interwar European governments more than Nazi policies.

THE NAZIS AND GERMAN WOMEN

In 1923, Hitler imitated Mussolini's March on Rome by leading an assault (the Beer Hall Putsch) on Munich. But the German president did what the Italian king had not dared to do and called up the troops. Hitler landed in jail instead of the President's palace. While Mussolini maneuvered to create his Fascist state in the 1920s, Hitler remained at the margins of power as the crackpot leader of a noisy band of followers. Hitler's failure to win power immediately after World War I meant that he spent a decade planning for Nazi society, refining his political tactics, and recruiting a grassroots following. This waiting time made his claims more total and his ambitions more comprehensive than Mussolini's ad hoc legislation. The decade Hitler spent at the fringes of political respectability also had important consequences for the party's women adherents.

Women's Place in the National Socialist Party

Unlike Italian women, German women won the vote and a constitutional guarantee of equality in the aftermath of World War I. After Hitler's attempt at a military *coup d'etat* failed in 1923, he shifted strategy from armed rebellion to legal political activity. Women could, therefore, contribute to Fascist conquest at the polls. Yet Hitler displayed little interest in winning their support, and many of his male deputies routinely insulted women. The leadership of all six major political parties in the Weimar Republic welcomed women as voters, ran women candidates, and appointed women to lobby for women's concerns. However reluctantly, even the most conservative of politicians officially supported women's equality. Only Hitler insisted on the absolute exclusion of women from any responsibility in his movement. Yet as the party's popularity escalated during the Depression, no significant gender gap appeared. Why did women voters support the only political party that at best ignored them and at worst insulted them?

Women, like men, voted for the Nazis because of the party's general goals and the élan exhibited by its leaders; but while their behavior mirrored that of their male counterparts, the process by which they rallied to the party and their experiences in it differed dramatically from men's. Paradoxically, Nazi men's misogyny provided women with an opportunity to organize their separate movement without men's intervention. Whereas leaders of other parties anxiously watched their women followers for any show of feminist activity, Nazi leaders simply did not care. This meant that Nazi women organized on the fringes of the Nazi Party, much as the Nazi Party itself militated at the margins of mainstream political life in Weimar Germany.

Party leaders, by their refusal to pay much heed to women followers, inadvertently provided Nazi women with considerable latitude which they used to shape their own ideology, build their own grassroots organizations, and set up community services for Nazi men and their families. Because women counted for so very little in the Nazi scheme of things, they enjoyed much de facto freedom. Although Hitler's male associates worked under his constant surveillance, women operated far from headquarters at the "Brown House" in Munich. While stormtroopers beat up their enemies, women established soup kitchens. As men staged mass rallies, women spoke on street corners and carried on day-to-day publicity programs. Reviving the crisis atmosphere of wartime, Nazis worked at a fever pitch. Alarmed at what they perceived as social chaos and the threat of socialist revolution, they became fanatics in their own complete subculture. Even though Nazi men did not notice them, women made a vital contribution to the Nazi appeal. Like camouflage in jungle warfare, women's presence misled observers by offsetting the brutal masculine type exalted by Hitler. Taken together, the image of powerful manhood and the image of loving womanhood offered to "true believers" the feeling their counterculture prefigured the ideal of a total Nazi society in the future.

As long as the postwar economic recovery continued through the late 1920s, German democracy survived. However, because the German economy depended so heavily upon the United States for loans and trade, the stock market crash of 1929 had a more devastating impact on Germany and Austria than on any other nation. Major banks collapsed, the stock market closed for months at a time, profits dropped, and unemployment rose from a few percent in 1929 to nearly thirty percent among men and ten percent among women in 1932. As the economic crisis deepened, debates in the Reichstag produced a deadlock between conservatives and socialists.

Voters went to the polls in five national elections from 1930 to 1932. Between 1928 and 1932 the Nazi party moved from ninth to first place in 1932. From a mere 2.6 percent share of the 1928 vote, its support jumped to just under 20 percent in 1930 and achieved a high of just over 37 percent in July 1932, most of its support coming from Protestant, rural North German regions. Although far fewer women than men had voted Nazi before 1930, women (often going to the polls for the first time) turned out in great numbers to vote Nazi as the Depression deepened. Did women surrender to Hitler's hypnotic charisma, as so many observers believed? The evidence suggests not. On the two occasions when Hitler personally ran for office, women preferred President Hindenburg to Hitler. Because so many German states barred Hitler from making public speeches and because the Nazi party had virtually no access to radio networks before 1933, relatively few voters, male or female, actually saw Hitler. Local organization, rather than Hitler's personal appeal, was the reason for Nazi popularity. The élan and zeal of Nazism led women throughout Germany not to surrender to, but to join the Nazi crusade and develop their own tactics, doctrine, and style.

Gregor Strasser, Hitler's brilliant organizer, explained the Nazi formula for success in a secret memo circulated to district leaders in 1932. Superficially, he observed, it appeared that voters threw themselves into the arms of an authoritarian party and its charismatic leader. But, he continued, in reality the opposite tendency played an even more crucial role. Behind the facade of order, he readily admitted, lay chaos. The Nazi Party, which had increased from 27,000 in 1925 to 850,000 in late 1932, could not possibly impose order on its membership. Paradoxically, Strasser suggested, the combination of a superficial discipline plus a de facto decentralization maximized Nazi appeal. All over Germany little Hitlers discovered their own political talents and galvanized friends and neighbors into zealous "cells." Strasser concluded that Hitler had evoked "an entirely new political type—a soldier-preacher," who demonstrated extraordinary energy, calling meetings and demonstrations, putting up posters, harrassing rivals, smuggling illegal propaganda, and speaking and brawling in the streets. Had Strasser thought about the female half of the Nazi vote, he might have coined another term, "the mother-preacher," who, no less than the men, conducted the day-to-day work of organizing new followers, demonstrating, public speaking, and setting up community programs. The secret of Nazi success, in other words, depended as much on populist spontaneity as on centralized authority. Calling themselves members of "The German Freedom Movement," Nazi women leaders developed their political organizations under the banner of a stridently misogynist movement.

Although many of his deputies insulted women, Hitler personally refrained from displaying contempt and purported to honor women as long as they remained in motherly roles. In adjusting to the realities of a movement that explicitly barred them from politics, women may have harkened back to the Christian traditions in which they had been raised. It was after all St. Paul and the church fathers, not Christ himself, who had openly decreed women's inferiority. Nazi women were not the first to ignore hostile men as an inevitable fact of life while plunging ahead into the task of organizing their own separate submovement.

Memoirs, letters, printed campaign literature, and monthly activity reports from the Nazi party before 1933 yield a composite portrait of the "Nazi woman" that bears little resemblance to the swooning women in Leni Riefenstahl's *Triumph of the Will*. Dozens of local and regional leaders emerged, each with her own special style and dogma. The most flamboyant of the early leaders, Elsbet Zander, presented a public image that in many ways resembled Hitler's own. Unmarried, she was in her early sixties during the 1920s. Her usual attire was a plain housedress, and she did not try to appear attractive. In front of her audience, however, she came to life, exhorting women to take pride in their conventional roles. Castigating the women's movement for "masculinizing" and perverting womanhood, she urged women to crusade for motherhood as a fulltime profession. Zander included prayers (always for Hitler and sometimes for herself) in her newsletter and offered little in the way of policy except effusive praise of the home and motherhood. A hopelessly inept administrator, she suffered bouts of moodiness which alternated with spending sprees. When news of her slovenly manner and irresponsible conduct of a rest home for Storm Troopers came to light in 1931, a minor scandal broke. However, party leaders decided her popularity made her too valuable to dismiss.[21]

At the opposite extreme, Guida Diehl appealed to educated, civic-minded women in Protestant circles. During World War I, she had founded her own New Land movement to bolster morale on the homefront. After the defeat, she mobilized her organization to fight the communist menace. Unlike Zander, Diehl did not officially join the National Socialist Party until the eve of Hitler's takeover. Instead, she worked for Nazi victory from an independent position. In her periodical, *Neuland*, and in two weighty books, Diehl developed a detailed blueprint for creating a powerful women's world in Nazi society without rebuke from the Brown House. Diehl believed that women's rights leaders had derailed the woman's cause, and she recruited from the most conservative members of the BDF (Federation of German Women's Organizations).[22] She opposed women's right to work in jobs outside the household. Recognizing that not all mothers would have husbands who could support them, Diehl proposed state subsidies to enable mothers to remain at home with their children. As compensation for losing rights in men's political sphere, women would defend their interests in a separate women's legislature elected by women only. One woman who shared Diehl's views put it well, "We want more than the three K's (*Kinder, Küche, und Kirche*, or children, kitchen, and church). We want *Krankenhaus* (hospital) and *Kultur* (culture) as well." Diehl understood that the modern woman with traditional values must "go public" to defend her traditional roles.

When Diehl, Zander, and other early women leaders spoke of their world, they often used a term common among middle-class women's rights advocates, *Lebensraum* (or living space). In Hitler's rhetoric, the word served as a pretext for German expansion into the rich agricultural lands of Central Europe in order to feed the expanding German population. When middle-class women used the term, they invoked an image of harmonious public life (a 'living-room' in German society) that lay outside the devisive and materialistic worlds of class and politics. Only women, they believed, could bring health to the nation through a female solidarity that would unite "Aryans" of all classes.

Although the confused amalgam of ideas put forth by women Nazis included some of the goals advanced by conservative women's organizations, a striking contrast emerged when it came to style. Unlike Italian Fascist women, Nazi women deplored the "lady" image, which to them connoted an idle, helpless, decorative object. One Nazi woman proudly declared, "We are not a tea and cakes gossip society!" Nazi women's belief in womanhood gave them the means of rationalizing behavior that did not at all fit conventional stereotypes of "femininity." Nazi women, while endorsing conventional women's roles, violated their own vision of peace-loving and domestic womanhood. Conservative women collected for charity and agonized about public morals; Nazi women faced down hecklers, smuggled weapons, spoke on street corners, served as couriers past police check points, and marched behind swastika banners, despite insults like "brown goose!" or "Hitler whore!" In their memoirs, they recall that harrassment (in the words of one woman) "forged a unity among us that no power on earth could have rent asunder."[23]

The crisis atmosphere, exacerbated by fire and brimstone rhetoric, kept them in a constant state of *Angst* and harkened back to the days of war, death, blockade and defeat. The belief that Germany ("mother Germany," in their words) was in desperate straits allowed them to tolerate Nazi men's violence and their idealism about a collectivist future helped them rationalize their own legal infractions.

Women's Role in the Nazi State

When President Hindenburg named Hitler chancellor in January 1933, dreams of a separate Nazi women's world came to an end as surely as economic demobilization had followed the armistice in 1918. The dynamic leaders from the "old days" of the movement had proven their worth at mobilizing voters and support networks, but the Nazi state demanded a new type of personality—a leader of women who would follow men. Within a year, virtually every "old timer" woman leader had been driven from office and a new generation of docile bureaucrats stepped into power. The Nazi state, more than any other secular government in history, confidently believed it could intrude in the lives of all citizens by controlling their thoughts and shaping their ideals. For this the state needed women as missionaries. Finally, Nazi men took notice of women. Official recognition meant the end of autonomy.

For over a year Nazi ministers experimented with several leaders and organizational forms—and even for a brief time named a man as chief of the Nazi Women's League (*Frauenschaft*). In selecting an appropriate leader they faced a quandary. An energetic woman who had demonstrated her initiative before 1933 might act too independently, but a colorless bureaucrat might not have the dynamism to lead others. Even more perplexing was a second conundrum: A woman without a husband would have the time to devote herself totally to her job, but she would project the wrong image. A wife would embody the correct values, but would owe her first allegiance not to her job but to her husband. During the spring of 1934, the perfect candidate appeared. Without any record of independent action or national reputation at all, Gertrud Scholtz-Klink (mother of four) arrived in Berlin to head up the Women's Labor Corps. Utterly docile, "racially correct," and opportunistic, she conformed to every requirement. The fact that her devoted Nazi husband had died of a heart attack during the excitment of a party rally two years earlier further enhanced her reputation. As widows had done for centuries, Scholtz-Klink pledged to replace her husband and went directly to the district leader to volunteer. After being appointed Nazi Leader of Women in 1934, she administered vast programs for eleven years without ever deciding policy. She made the Nazi choice and rendered obedience to superiors while enjoying broad administrative authority over underlings. As a woman, however, she settled for fewer rewards and less influence than her male counterparts.

Scholtz-Klink fulfilled her central charge: to integrate all non-Socialist and non-Communist women's associations into the Nazi network. This meant encouraging women to belong to both Nazi women's associations and non-Nazi organizations. Leaders of non-Nazi associations had to join her *Frauenwerk* (Women's Bureau), submit annual plans to Nazi officials, and divulge financial and membership records to state authorities. Most importantly, they had to expel their Jewish members, a provision which affected Christians with Jewish ancestors as well as members of the Jewish community.

Protestant women leaders told their two million followers to accept the Nazi state without reservation in 1933. Nearly a million organized Catholic women awaited orders from the Vatican, and when it came with the Concordat in 1933 they also cast their lot with the Nazi state. Even the women's rights movement, called by American sociologist Clifford Kirkpatrick, the "fortress of feminism," marched into the new state. Although the BDF (Federation of German Women's Associations) decided to disband, its member organizations purged Jewish women and "integrated" themselves into the Nazi framework. Jewish women departed "with great sadness," after decades of cooperation and trust in a common women's endeavor.

The women's rights movement, along with thousands of non- and even anti-Nazi women's associations which had for decades been prominent in German public life, surrendered with little protest to a dictator who had never received a majority vote in any free election. How did it happen? The BDF itself had for several years moved steadily toward conservatism, giving up its claims for rights in order to gain privileges. German middle-class women, like their Italian counterparts, applauded when the new leadership swore to protect the family, restore the economy, repress Communists and Socialists, and underwrite middle-class status. In addition, a younger generation, which found the call for equality passé, expressed more concern for women's special nature and needs. Even before Nazi victory, longtime defenders of women's emancipation confronted a backlash from men, antipathy from traditionalist women, and apathy from younger women. Marianne

Weber, a longtime feminist and the widow of a well-known sociologist, reminisced sadly, "We have been so busy fighting the men who block our way as we go forward," she said, "that we forgot to look at the wake behind us."

Within a few years Scholtz-Klink's *Frauenwerk* had eight million members, including thousands of former fighters for women's rights, as long as they had no Jewish ancestors or ties with Marxist organizations. Many women leaders felt they had little choice but to adapt to the new state. After all, wrote Gertrud Bäumer (for three decades a major figure in the women's rights movement) in June 1933, women rarely control the political boundaries of the nation in which they live, so they must fight for women's rights within whatever context they happen to find themselves, including a fascist one.[24] But these women did not quietly dissolve into the Nazi state. When Nazi policies touched issues that concerned them, civic and religious women leaders demonstrated considerable independence. True, they acquiesced without a murmur to the requirement that they make their organizations "Jew free," but they protested on behalf of their own jobs and autonomy. For example, within weeks of becoming chancellor, Hitler ordered that all women be expelled from high state jobs. Gertrud Bäumer, who had a post in the Education Ministry, received one of the first letters of termination. Overnight, women mounted a campaign to defend her, and angry telegrams flooded the administration. Despite the protest and Bäumer's claim (in her revised vita) that she had long been of the "national socialist persuasion," her expulsion held. However, her contributions to the women's rights periodical *Die Frau* continued, and in 1938 the Nazi Women's Bureau honored her birthday.[25]

Middle-class women's defense of their own right to work achieved surprising success. Laws that extended Weimar discrimination against married women's employment met with such a protest that Interior Minister Wilhelm Frick apologized in the early fall of 1933. At the next Nuremberg party rally, Scholtz-Klink herself endorsed women's participation in the labor force. Over the next several years, opportunistic women from the women's rights movement discovered that they could find employment in state programs as long as they demonstrated their pro-Nazi zeal. A government determined to shape every citizen's values depended upon skilled teachers, social workers, and administrators to carry on that offensive against privacy. Gradually, as in Italy, rigid quotas against women university students relaxed, although women never received training in the Nazi institutes designed to indoctrinate the future elite for rule. In Germany, as in Italy, long-term patterns of women's employment continued with little disruption.

Misogyny and Anti-Semitism

The major policies affecting women, however, did not arise from Scholtz-Klink's office but from racial planners and eugenics experts who, beginning in 1933, converted Hitler's prejudices about women and Jews into social policy. Even as they staged a national boycott against all Jewish businesses, expelled Jewish professionals from their jobs, and excluded Jewish children from many public schools, party leaders drafted legislation to force "racially unfit" men and women of the "Aryan race" to undergo sterilization. After January 1934, social workers everywhere in Germany received orders to refer schizophrenics, deaf and dumb people, the mentally retarded, alcoholics, and epileptics to special eugenics courts which would pass judgment on the damage they could do to the "race" if they bore children. In all, it is estimated that over 375,000 people were sterilized, and, after 1940, an additional 150,000 killed, in the euthanasia program.[26]

Besides these efforts to "prune the unfit," Nazi policy encouraged the "fit" to bear more children by outlawing all birth control and increasing the already severe punishments for abortion. They also offered material incentives to aid wives who bore children. The Marriage Loan Program (greeted as a "stroke of genius" by Catholic women leaders) offered financial aid to young couples who promised that the wife would not seek paid employment and could demonstrate "Jew-free" family trees. These substantial loans came in the form of coupons for the purchase of home furnishings; and a tax on unmarried adults funded the program. Every child born reduced the loan by 25 percent. Mothers' psychological needs, too, received ample attention in thousands of radio programs, workshops, reading circles, night school courses, and national conferences designed for the homemaker. New advanced degrees with prestigious sounding titles further honored the "expert" in women's fields. The government adapted a program begun in France and awarded motherhood medals (bronze, silver, and gold) to mothers of six or more children. Mothers of nine children (or seven sons, whichever happened first) received the right to name any national leader as godfather of their child. Until his death, Hindenburg proved more popular than Hitler. The marriage rate did increase dramatically during the early years of the program, which probably represented a recovery from an unusually low marriage rate during the Depression. In any case, an increased birthrate, the real aim of the program, was not achieved. Germans, like Italians, did not significantly alter their family plans in response to material incentives and propaganda campaigns.

The Education Ministry set to work in 1933 teaching girls to reorient their values. Directed by the fanatic and efficient Dr. Auguste Reber-Gruber, Nazi teachers inculcated anti-Semitism, "racial science," physical fitness, and home economics into a generation of girls. Reber-Gruber worked tirelessly to elevate sexual identity to the importance given to racial identity. Whenever possible, coeducational schools were resegregated, on the grounds that boys and girls possessed markedly different psychological and physical makeups. As one administrator commented, "We Nazis abhor grey. We want either black or white."

Memoirs suggest that many girls liked the new emphasis on nature, sports, and comradeship. Christa Wolf, through the character Nelly from her book *Model Childhood*, described the excitement of belonging to a group of girls who adored their leader "Mickey" and thrilled at the independence from parental authority as they hiked, sang, and studied for the *Führer*.

> "What a pleasure it was to enjoy the joviality of the leader. . . . to crowd around the leader, together with all the others, at the end of the evening, forgetting one's own shyness, to grasp her hand, to enjoy the extraordinary familiarity. . . . There was something her mother couldn't give her, something she didn't want to miss."

Nelly dreamed of becoming the kind of person her leader wanted her to be. "It meant being tough."[27] But as girls grew older, they noticed that the spirit of the Hitler youth organizations disappeared. Girls in the BDM thrilled to physical activities and a collectivist élan, but as women, they had to learn submission. Darning socks and doing the washing for the boys' Hitler Youth did not measure up to the outings with the leader. They had been taught that girls and boys were equally valuable (*gleichwertig*); now they noticed the disparities in funding, glamor, public attention, and opportunity between the worlds of men and women. Hitler made it explicit at the 1934 Nuremberg party rally. To women belonged the "smaller sphere" of communal life while men would confront the "larger sphere" of public battle. Although between 9 and 12 million women belonged to the *Frauenwerk*, that figure meant little, because membership was required of all women wage earners, and all civic organizations had to affiliate their members with the *Frauenwerk*. Few members bothered to subscribe to Nazi periodicals, and attendance at meetings was generally low. In Nazi Germany the most reliable indication of any institution's status was the percentage of party members among its employees. The *Frauenwerk* and *Frauenschaft*, along with the Labor Front, had the lowest party participation. Less than 15 percent of all participants in the Labor Service programs were young women. After the massive increase in party membership during 1933 (from 850,000 to 2,000,000), women comprised less than five percent of the party membership.[28]

One day I saw a new book by Scholtz-Klink in a feminist book store. Realizing she must be alive, I found her and asked her some of the questions I had pondered for years. Most importantly, I wanted to know whether she believed she had contributed to an evil regime. Forty years after the Nazi defeat, she answered clearly. First, the Nazis had, she believed, launched many positive programs, (e.g. to help overworked mothers and teach girls home economics) most of which had been directed by women. Second, she had cared very little about the broader implications of women's activities and recalled for me the kinds of nonideological work that women had accomplished for centuries. She had hoped merely to give women a broader frame of reference than their own homes.

Nazi Women's Disillusionment

Although Scholtz-Klink did not admit it, the task was far from easy. Nazi leaders ordered them to indoctrinate a new generation of girls. But women did not receive either the budgets or sufficient authority to accomplish the charge. Reber-Gruber complained constantly that women administrators received shabby treatment in the educational bureaucracy. She barraged her superiors with a steady stream of protests. How, she asked, could women inculcate pride into their girl students when their own male superiors routinely insulted them? After four years of Nazi rule, she lamented, girls' textbooks had not even been Nazified and women teachers depended upon books from the "decadent" Weimar era, and the "black" (Catholic) teachers she despised remained at their posts.[29]

Reber-Gruber's disillusionment reflects a more general phenomenon among German women. Although 1933 constituted a watershed for Socialists, Communists, Jews, and other "enemies" of Hitler, most women did not experience much change in their daily lives. As Nazi leaders rearmed the nation and prepared for war, however, three related changes wrought havoc in the "women's world." *Frauenwerk* publicity urged women to abandon the housewifely roles they had so recently been told to take up; eugenics programs encouraged new schemes to improve the birth rate; and, perhaps most devastating, Hitler attacked both Catholic and Protestant organizations.

The danger signs first appeared when Scholtz-Klink reversed her earlier position and declared that all members of Nazi organizations must resign from non-Nazi organizations. Christians had until then reconciled their Nazi politics with their religious faith. Then Hitler told Germans in the mid-1930s that they had to choose between "brown and black," slang for Nazi and Christian. But women's allegiance to the state rested on their belief that Nazi goals harmonized with their Christian values. Women expected protection from powerful male church hierarchies. One of the most remarkable examples of a loyal Nazi who attempted to retain some degree of autonomy was Agnes von Grone, Nazi Party member and strong-minded leader of the German Protestant Women's Federation. She nazified her organization so thoroughly that she assumed Nazi leaders would respect her independence, but even her bishop ordered her to accept Nazi interference in women's every activity. Von Grone fought for over a year against the Party and the state—and against her own "protector," the National Protestant Bishop who supported Hitler against the Protestant women he was supposed to protect.

In this contest, no ideological issues were at stake. Von Grone, insisting on her devotion to Hitler, refused to give up her autonomy. She stood no chance. Even after being dismissed, she appealed her case and ultimately faced charges of treason. For several years she waged a hopeless legal battle to defend her reputation as a loyal Nazi.[30]

Catholic women, led by several powerful figures like Gerta Krabbel and Antonie Hopmann, waged a similar effort to defend their autonomy under the protection of the Church. Perhaps because of the Concordat or because of the Catholic Bishops' more effective organization, Catholic women operated until the beginning of World War II "behind church walls" as they put it. From the outset, Catholic women's organizations had harbored a deep distrust of Nazi policies because eugenics programs offended their beliefs. Both state and church denied women's rights to make decisions about childbearing; but while the Church taught that God intended that every pregnancy be brought to term, the Nazis claimed the right to proscribe births among the "racially unfit" and promote births among the "fit." Even when their prelates abandoned them, Catholic women adhered to a strict doctrine. The total claim of religion confronted the total demands of the state.[31] While many progressive Protestants deemed eugenics socially useful, Catholic women remained intransigent. As war approached, the crisis became acute.

Most leaders, when preparing for war, take measures to ensure the broadest possible base of solidarity against a foreign foe. Not Hitler. Just when he needed mass support, he accelerated the "racial revolution" which had formed the heart of his goals from the beginning. Following the nationwide pogrom in November 1938, Himmler unveiled his *Führer's* plans for breeding a superior race, telling his SS soldiers to leave sons behind before they marched to war. Under the Nazi dispensation, unwed, "racially fit" mothers received allowances and care in special homes and deserved as much (or more) respect than married mothers. Himmler's breeding schemes had a minimal impact on the birth rate, but they alarmed millions of otherwise loyal citizens and dampened morale. Women did not react enthusiastically. "How," asked Reber-Gruber in the Education Ministry, "can teachers command the respect of their communities, if they are told to honor the local kindergarten teacher who proudly announces she is pregnant without a husband?" Even Nelly in Christa Wolf's *Model Childhood* worried. "There she sat, a thirteen-year-old girl wedged between her mother's warnings not to 'throw herself away' and the *Schwarze Korps* [magazine of the SS] request for unconditional submission for the sake of the *Führer."* Guida Diehl, who had remained quietly in the background after her dismissal in 1933, spoke out when Nazi propaganda made heroines of mothers without husbands. For decades she had called for Christian forgiveness of their "sin" as well as material aid; but praise of bastardy went too far. At about the same time as the SS breeding schemes created a public stir, news that Jews were being deported also spread. Diehl, a lifelong anti-Semite, nevertheless deplored violence against Jews and wrote to Heinrich and Margarethe Grüber, the directors of a clandestine rescue mission to help Protestants with Jewish ancestry escape from Germany. After months of debate, the Nazi Party high court pronounced her guilty of treason.[32] Unlike thousands of other convicted traitors, however, she was excused from jail because of her advanced age.

Although Scholtz-Klink remained in office, she lost all influence as the rigors of war eroded her programs and converted women into pawns of the state. Ultimately, the futility of grafting a reactionary family policy onto an industrialized economy became obvious as inconsistencies hampered the war effort. By paying high benefits to soldiers' wives and widows (and reducing these allotments if women worked), Nazi policy makers undercut women's economic motivation to seek employment. Women responded poorly to propaganda telling them to look for jobs. Many evaded employment registration; middle-class women refused to relinquish their domestic servants; and newlyweds and young mothers preferred to remain at home. Perhaps family life appeared as a welcome respite in a society saturated with propaganda and poisoned by spying. Scholtz-Klink ignored the situation and devoted her time to the country estate in Poland, which she and her new husband, SS training chief General Heissmeyer, purchased. Many of her underlings protested and complained about their loss of control over the women's sphere. Their acceptance of state funds, however, had undercut their independence, and by sending their social workers into women's homes they had broken into the very privacy that has been the hallmark of family values.

Looking back on those years, Scholtz-Klink believes that "her" women had done no wrong because she kept them so far from politics and, by implication, remote from evil. A blind spot mars her hindsight, however, for nothing in the Third Reich remained beyond politics—not even programs designed to remove women from politics. When I asked her how she felt when in 1942 so many Berliners were forced to wear yellow stars, she answered without hesitation, "It was somehow aesthetically unpleasant. There were so many you know." Inge Deutschkron, one of the very few Jewish Germans to have lived underground in Germany throughout the war, told Claude Lanzmann (in the film *Shoah*) how she felt on another day several months later. "I remember the day when they made Berlin *Judenrein* ("Jew-free"). The people hastened in the streets; no one wanted to be in the streets; you could see the streets were absolutely empty. They did not want to look, you know. . . . They herded the Jews together, from the factories, from houses, wherever they could find them."[33]

Four decades after those events, Scholtz-Klink believes that her work for the Nazi state deserves the respect of a younger generation of Germans. She forgets the wives of Nazi bosses who acquired the furniture, paintings, and other property of deported Jews. She overlooks wives like Gerda

Bormann, who urged her husband not to rest until "every single Jew" had disappeared. What of other wives, such as Auschwitz commandant Rudolf Höss's wife, who sedulously preserved domestic happiness by refusing to concern themselves with their husbands' careers?

Several months after speaking to Scholtz-Klink, I came across the autobiography of a Jewish German woman who recalls how she "sold" her household furnishings to a representative of "One Frau Kling-Scholz, or maybe I have it backward, who was the director for all women." When I spoke to Scholtz-Klink, she complained about an "ungrateful Jewish woman" whom she had helped. "After the war you'd think she could have at least written me a thank you card." Scholtz-Klink had ordered the furniture removed and afterward had paid only a tiny fraction of what she had promised. Reber-Gruber routinely requisitioned Jewish property to replace equipment damaged in air raids. Only once did she refuse to share the spoils of "Aryanization." She turned down a country villa because she thought it inappropriate to educate girls in a house once owned by a descendent of Bismarck's Jewish banker, Gerson Bleichröder. The Nazi woman, charged with preserving love and gentleness in a society polluted by deceit and fear, demonstrated her hardness. Perhaps the extreme role divisions between masculine and feminine facilitated a certain emotional role reversal that enabled tough "men" to cry at the funeral of a dead comrade and compassionate "women" to turn away when a Jewish neighbor called for mercy.

RESISTANCE

Women, as members of the inferior sex in the superior race, invariably experienced the contradictions of their position. In Italy and Germany ordinary women who generally approved of fascist government found ways to circumvent laws and programs they disliked. But that behavior, like grumbling about Fascist youths as *maccheroni* ("young ones who don't want to work") or making jokes about the "perfect Aryan" ("as blond as Hitler, slim as Goering, and as athletic as Goebbels"), was not significant opposition. Afterwards, a younger generation eager to find honor in their elders extolled such single issue objections as "everyday resistance." Agnes von Grone, having fought in the Nazi Party court for three years to regain the leadership of Protestant women, portrayed herself as a resister after the war's end. Sibella Aleremo emerged as a "grandmother" of Italian feminism in the 1970s. These women, and millions of others, had opposed some aspects of life under fascist rule; but criticism of misogyny, corruption, or intrusive bureaucrats did not preclude worshipful support for Mussolini or Hitler. Nor did support for fascism entirely extinguish decency. The narratives of escapees and survivors abound in stories about women who performed acts of kindness as a part of daily routine. Under both Nazism and Fascism, untold numbers of ordinary people kept their jobs, dissembled in public, and retained private, independent views. Many, perhaps most, of these critics had at one time shared the national enthusiasm for *il Duce* or the *Führer*. These disillusioned Germans and Italians opposed fascism, but they did not resist.

From the beginning of the fascist movement, there were those who despised the fascist vision of a "better" life and worked to prevent it. Socialists, Communists, Jehovah's Witnesses, and a tiny minority of Catholics and Protestants refused to capitulate even as their neighbors cheered fascist victories. Until recently, memoirs and histories of the resistance featured men. But no gender gap existed in the resistance. Although only about one in five people arrested for crimes against the state was female, arrest records do not provide reliable evidence. When victims of fascism pay tribute to people who risked their lives to help them, women equal or outnumber men. Several factors suggest why women resisters were less often apprehended than men. In Germany, the Gestapo waited until 1937 to execute a woman, after the execution of 23-year old Liselotte Hermann for treason (although dozens had been killed while in jail). The public outcry that ensued had a damaging effect on morale. "Why," asked one Nazi woman, "must our wonderful and all-powerful state deprive a child of its mother?"

On occasion, male arrogance led fascists to assume women were too naive to present a threat. Women resisters knew how to play to guards' prejudices. Gertrud Staewen, for example, recalled how Protestant women collected Motherhood medals and borrowed children to disguise Jewish women who crossed the Swiss border. Carola Karg, carrying pounds of illegal pamphlets under her maternity dress, worked as a peasant on the French border. Maria von Maltzan routinely arrived late at the train station and posed as slightly drunk when she wanted to smuggle her news dispatches to Paris.

In the early years of Mussolini's dictatorship, women textile, agricultural, and tobacco workers struck in opposition to state-sponsored labor organizations. Later, partisan units attacked Fascist military positions, and women fought along with the men. Lucia Canova, a lifelong Communist, dodged arrest and joined a brigade in the countryside.[34] After deportations began and orders went out to arrest all Jews, only women could dare to walk in the streets with forged Christian identity cards, because the police conducted routine strip searches and arrested all circumscised men with doubtful papers. In Germany, where no armed units existed, the work of resistance consisted of rescuing victims, maintaining underground communications networks, distributing anti-Nazi propaganda, and gathering information— essentially women's tasks. Often, too, with male leaders in jail, leadership fell to women.

After the war, when the refusal of resisters to join in the fascist enthusiasm had been vindicated, many anticipated receiving the gratitude of those who had followed. These expectations proved naive. Neighbors resented them for their rectitude. Colleagues felt guilty. Antifascists remained isolated. Three decades after the defeat of fascism, a younger generation has begun to gather oral histories and source material about those who had stood apart.

As fascism recedes into the past, our definition of resistance moves beyond the heroic vision of the daring and defiant act and broadens to include the practical work of saving lives, disseminating news, linking clandestine communities, and damaging morale. Instead of making dramatic gestures (which led inevitably to death), some resisters plotted to survive and preserve a moral tradition. To help focus this changing view of resistance, autobiographies by famous leaders have been augmented by oral history projects and memoirs of average people honored for their courage in sheltering victims. Of the half a million Germans defined as Jewish by Nazi race laws, over half left the country by 1939. Less than 20,000 lived to see the end of the war. In Italy 45,000 Italians of Jewish descent (and about 10,000 Jewish refugees) confronted rising anti-Semitism after Mussolini and Hitler joined forces on the eve of World War II. Despite the Jews' desperate situation, resistance occurred within the Jewish community as well. On occasion, young people chose heroic action, as for example, Herbert and Marianne Baum, organizers of a group of Communists with Jewish ancestors who plotted to explode a bomb at a Nazi exhibit in Berlin. The Gestapo discovered their plans and executed them. A very different form of protest was Jolana Roth's only option. Deported to Auschwitz at age 14, she worked in the barracks where victims' clothing was sorted so it could be distributed to needy "Aryans." Having spoken with Scholtz-Klink and other not-so-ex Nazis, I listened intently to Dr. Roth's account of her life. "The Kapos ordered us to remove the yellow stars," she said. "After I heard that, I always left a tiny scrap of yellow in a pocket or hem. Someone, I told myself, will start to wonder. Someone, sometime will care." For her, resistance meant sending the truth out of Auschwitz first as scraps of yellow fabric and then 45 years later by making her memories part of the historical record.

CONCLUSIONS

Sylvia Pankhurst was correct. Without a liberal political system that at least officially acknowledges equality among all citizens, feminists have no forum in which to fight for equality. But her opponents were not completely wrong. Even in fascist states, women lobbied for particular programs, organized their separate sphere, and worked for the state. Despite its overt opposition to women's equality, the fascist vision of an ideal society incorporated the notions of nineteenth-century women's rights advocates who envisioned a strong society founded on separate but equal spheres. Post-war policies further complicate the debate between Pankhurst and her opponents because welfare states have incorporated social policies advocated by both Hitler and Mussolini. Family allowances, leisure programs, publicly funded health care for women and children, advanced training in "feminine" fields, liberalized divorce laws, and the destigmatization of unmarried mothers and their children have all become features of the postwar welfare state in Europe. In fascist nations, these policies gave women a measure of independence from their fathers and husbands; but they also tied women more closely to a frankly male supremacist state in which women could never become equals. In a liberal democratic context, however, most feminists view these programs positively because they free women from economic dependence on men and erode patriarchy. As we look to a more equitable future, the fascist solution to the woman question reminds us that particular social policies will succeed in liberating women only in the context of institutions that guarantee equality to all citizens and allow women access to power.

NOTES

1. I want to express my special thanks to Victoria de Grazia for having made valuable comments on an earlier draft of this essay and to Alice Kelikian for telling me about her research and making bibliographical suggestions.
2. E. Sylvia Pankhurst, "Women under Fascism," *The Hibbert Journal* vol. 34:2 (1935–36), pp. 219–227. The replies follow in the June and July issues.
3. Mussolini, quoted by Maurice de Valefe, *Le Journal*, Paris (November 12, 1922).
4. Emil Ludwig, *Talks with Mussolini* (New York: AMS, 1982) original edition published in 1933.
5. Quoted in Maria Antonietta Macciocchi, *La Donna 'Nera': 'Consenso' Femminile e fascismo* (Milan: Feltrinelli, 1976), p. 104; and translated by Maurizio Vannicelli and Lionel Honore, S. J. The fact that Sarfatti was Jewish adds to the irony of a woman slavishly worshipping *il Duce*, but it also illustrates the lack of overt anti-Semitism in Mussolini's policies during the early years of his rule. Margherita G. Sarfatti, *The Life of Benito Mussolini* (London: Thornton Butterworth, 1925), pp. 21–57.
6. *Almanacco della donne italiana*, I (September 1923) quoted by Macciocchi, *La donna 'Nera,'* p. 37. On the complementary image of "Mussolini, Machismo, Marriage," cf. ibid., pp. 50–61 and 94–96.
7. Victoria de Grazia, *The Culture of Consent* (New York: Cambridge, 1981), pp. 38–44 and 55. The ideal of the "Italian lady," (described by Martin Clark as "graceful, tender, and self-sacrificing," *Modern Italy*, p. 163.) had emerged in the late nineteenth century and persisted under Fascism. pp. 162–163.
8. Conversation with the author. Cf. Luce d'Eramo, "Die Rhetorik der faschistischen Machtausübung oder: Opfern ist Macht," in Barbara Schäffer-Hegel, ed., *Frauen und Macht* (Berlin: Publica, 1984), pp. 75–80. D'Eramo is especially articulate on

the emotional appeal of the slogan "power through sacrifice." Cf. Maria Pascolato, *Gerarchia*, (Milan, 1937).

9. Sibella Aleramo, "Die italienische Frau," *Der Querschnitt*, vol. 10/2 (1930), p. 721. These ideas were followed up in *Giornale di Italia* (December 18, 1935), p. 284.

10. Lesley Caldwell, "Reproducers of the Nation: Women and the Family in Fascist Policy," in David Forgacs, ed., *Rethinking Italian Fascism: Capitalism, Populism and Culture* (London: Lawrence and Wishart, 1986), p. 130. *Corriere della Sera*, 1 (March, 1934). Only about 53,000 university students belonged. *Les Archives Contemporaines 1934–5*, Keesing, lists about 2,500,000 Fascist Party members without male-female breakdown. Victoria F. de Grazia, "Fasci Femminili," in *Historical Dictionary of Fascist Italy*, ed. P. V. Cannistraro," (Westport: Greenwood, 1982), pp. 202–204. Edward R. Tannenbaum, *Modern Italy: A Topical History* (New York: New York University Press, 1974), p. 156. The adult female population was 14,000,000, compared to 42,500,000 total population. *J. Fasci Femminili* (Milan: Liberia d'Italia, 1929), vol. 8. On the urban nature of the movement, cf. Tannenbaum, pp. 154–155. Party membership remained relatively low even though in 1932 earlier restrictions on new members were lifted and "every good Italian" with "a clean moral and political past" could join, Starachy, quoted in Macciocchi, *La Donna 'Nera,'* p. 93.

11. Alice Kelikian, *"Sisters of Sales," Social Welfare and the Italian State*, in press. Martin Clark, *Modern Italy* (New York: Longman, 1984), pp. 256–257.

12. *Les Femmes sous le Joug Fasciste* no. 1, Documents de la conference Mondiale des Femmes (Paris, 4–6 August, 1934). Women's virtual exclusion from government jobs prevented their sharing in the expansion of the Italian bureaucracy, from about 500,000 in the 1920s to over a million in the following decade.

13. Caldwell, "Reproducers," pp. 123–128. The number of women employed in factories increased—and about 25 percent of all women industrial workers were under eighteen. *Les Archives Contemporaine*, Keesing, 2.1.1933, p. 594. Pierfrancesco Bandettini, "The Employment of Women in Italy, 1888–1951," *Comparative Studies in Society and History* (1959), vol. II, pp. 369–374. "Women's Work in Fascist Countries," *International Trade Union Movement*, 18:8–10 (August–October, 1937).

14. Benito Mussolini, "Macchina e donna," (1934), reproduced in Susan Groag Bell and Karen Offen, *Women, the Family and Freedom* (Stanford: Stanford University Press, 1983), vol. II, pp. 369–370. Originally published in *Popolo d'Italia*, 206 (August 31, 1934).

15. Quoted in Macciocchi, *La Donna 'Nera,'* p. 78. Ferdinando Loffredo, *La politica della famiglia* (Milan: n.p., 1938), pp. 35–65, 364–565.

16. Gisela Augstin, "Die Sozialpolitik des Fascismus," *Reichs-Arbeitsblatt* (Nicht amtlicher Teil), 1937–38, vol. II, p. 340. Workers paid about 2 percent of their weekly earnings to subsidize the program after 1934. *Critica fasciste* 1.9.38. Adelheid Dehio, "Die italienische Frau in der vaterländischen Arbeit," *Die Frau* 43:8 (1936), pp. 281–282.

17. I am indebted to Maurizio Vannicelli for this translation. Ferdinando Loffredo, *La politica della famiglia*, (Milan: 1938), preface by Bottai, p. 345. On the women's organizations, cf. Augusto Turati, *Il Partito e i suoi Compiti* "Alle Donne." Macciocchi, *La Donna 'Nera.'*

18. Luisa Passerini, "Work, Ideology and Consensus under Italian Fascism," *History Workshop*, issue 8 (Autumn 1979), pp. 62–108.

19. Tannenbaum, *Modern Italy*, pp. 157–160. In 1939, Britain had 8.6 marriages per 1000, Germany 11.8, and Italy 7.3. Cf. *Almanacco* (1932), vol. XIII, p. 260. Maria Castellani, *Donne Italiano di eri e di oggi* (Florence: Bemporad, 1937); Clark, *Modern Italy*, pp. 162–164, 250–251.

20. Cf. several front-page articles in the Fascist newspaper "Vibranti radun Feminnili" (November 12, 1935), the photo at the Tomb of the Unknown Soldier, and "La Regina e tutte le donne d'Italia donaro oggi alla Patria l'annello nuziale" (Dec. 3, 1935) *Il Popolo d'Italia* 14. Macciocchi, *La donna 'Nera,'* pp. 85–87.

21. BA (Federal Archives) Koblenz, NS 22/vorläufig 349 and Sammlung Schumacher/ 320. Cf. also the personnel file on Zander in the Berlin Document Center.

22. Guida Diehl, *Christ sein heisst Kämpfer sein. Die Führung meines Lebens* (Giessen: Brunnen, 1960), pp. 127–131; and idem, *Die deutsche Frau und der Nationalsozialismus*, 5th ed., (Eisenach: Neuland, 1933), pp. 17–19, 54, 129.

23. These quotations come from the file of essays at the Hoover Institution at Stanford University that sociologist Theodor Abel collected as the basis of his book, *Why Hitler Came to Power: An Answer Based on the Original Life Stories of 600 of His Followers* (New York: Prentice-Hall, 1938). Special thanks to Agnes Peterson for calling this valuable collection to my attention.

24. Gertrud Bäumer, "Lebenslauf" and protests against her dismissal from the Ministry of Education, BA Koblenz, R 18/7108 and R36/2379. Some of her published responses were: "unsere Nationalsoziale Bewegung und der National-sozialismus," *Die Hilfe*, 39:6 (March 8, 1933), pp. 246–251, and "Umwege und Schicksal der Frauenbewegung," *Die Hilfe*, 39:9 (June 1933), pp. 385–387; "Evolution nicht Reaktion," *Die Frau*, 40:11, (August 1933), pp. 658–663 and "Spiessbürgertum in der Frauenfrage," *Die Frau.*, 41:6 (March 1934), pp. 321–322.

25. Richard Evans, *The Feminist Movement in Germany, 1848–1933* (London and Beverly Hills: Sage, 1976), pp. 28–30, 238–247; Jill Stephenson, *Women in Nazi Society* (New York: Barnes and Noble, 1975); Barbara Greven-Aschoff, *Die bürgerliche Frauenbewegung in Deutschland, 1894–1933* (Göttingen: Vandenhoeck & Ruprecht, 1981).

26. Timothy Mason, "Women in Germany," *History Workshop*, I and II (Summer and Autumn, 1976). Gisela Bock, *Zwangssterilisation im Nationalsozialismus. Untersuchungen zur Rassenpolitik und Frauenpolitik* (Berlin: Zentralinstitut für Sozialwissenschaft, Freie Universität, 1985).

27. Christa Wolf, *A Model Childhood*, trans. Ursule Molinaro and Hedwig Rappolt (New York: Farrar, Straus and Giroux, 1980), pp. 189–190.

28. Jill Stephenson, *The Nazi Organization of Women* (New York: Barnes and Noble, 1981); Michael Kater, *The Nazi Party: A Social Profile of Members and Leaders, 1919–1945* (Cambridge: Harvard University Press, 1983), pp. 148–153, and idem, "Frauen in der NS Bewegung," *Vierteljahrshefte für Zeitgeschichte*, 31:2 (April 1983), pp. 202–241.

29. Reber-Gruber's extensive correspondence may be found in the Munich Haupt-staatsarchiv, NSDAP 996–1001.

30. Evangelisches Zentralarchiv, Berlin, C3/170–174 and 183–192; Hans Jochen Kaiser, *Frauen in der Kirche* (Düsseldorf: Schwann, 1985), pp. 213–236.
31. Deutscher Caritasverband-Archiv, Freiburg Im Breisgau, CA VII/R218, 580–582.
32. Guida Diehl's personnel files and court records are in the Berlin Document Center.
33. Claude Lanzmann, *Shoah: An Oral Histoy of the Holocaust*, preface by Simone De Beauvoir (New York: Pantheon, 1985), pp. 50–51.
34. Anna Maria Bruzzone and Rachele Farina, eds., *La Resistenza taciuta: Dodici vite di partigiane piemontesi* (Milano: La Pietra, 1976), pp. 212 ff. Maria-Antonietta Macciocchi, "Les Femmes et la traverse du Fascisme," *Elements pour une Analyse du Fascisme*, published proceedings of University seminars, Paris: Universite de Paris VIII, 10–18 n.d. 154–155. Luisa Paserini, "Work Ideology and Consensus under Italian Fascism," *History Workshop*, issue 8 (Autumn 1979), pp. 100–101. "La Nuova Realta. Organo del Moviemento Femminile," clandestine call to women 1945, and *La Voce delle Donne* (Paris, 1934), mimeographed pamphlet.

SUGGESTED READINGS

Azione Cattolica Italiana, *La famiglia christina* (Milano: Vito e Pensiero, 1927).

Bajohr, Stephen, *Die Hälfte der Fabrik* (Marburg: VAG, 1979).

Bremme, Gabrielle, *Die politische Rolle der Frau in Deutschland.* (Göttingen: Van den Hoeck und Rüprecht, 1956).

Bridenthal, Renate, Atina Grossmann, and Marion Kaplan, eds., *When Biology Became Destiny: Women in Weimar and Nazi Germany* (New York: Monthly Review, 1984).

Bruzzone, Anna Maria and Rachele Farina, *La Resistenzia taciuta Dodici vite di partigiane piemontesi* (Milan: La Pietra, 1976).

Caldwell, Lesley, "Reproducers of the Nation: Women and the Family in Fascist Policy," David Forgacs, ed., *Rethinking Italian Fascism: Capitalism, Populism and Culture* (London: Lawrence and Wishart, 1986).

Cammet, John M., "Communist Women and the Fascist Experience," Jane Slaughter and Robert Kern, eds., *European Women on the Left* (Westport, Conn.: Greenwood Press, 1981).

Clark, Martin, *Modern Italy, 1871–1982* (New York: Longman, 1984).

de Grand, Alexander, "Women under Italian Fascism," *The Historical Journal*, 19:4 (1976), 947–968.

de Grazia, Victoria, *The Culture of Consent* (New York: Cambridge, 1981).

Elling, Hannah, *Frauen im Widerstand* (Frankfurt: Roederberg, 1981).

Glass, D. V., *Population Policies and Movements in Europe* (Oxford: Clarendon Press, 1940).

Frauengruppe Faschismus Forschung, *Mutterkreuz und Arbeitsbuch* (Frankfurt: Fischer, 1981).

Henry, Frances, *Victims and Neighbors: A Small Town Remembered* (Northampton: Bergen and Garvey, 1984).

Kelikian, Alice, *"Sisters of Sales," Social Welfare and the Italian State,* in press.

Kirkpatrick, Clifford, *Nazi Germany: Its Women and Family Life* (Indianapolis: Bobbs-Merrill, 1938).

Klinksiek, Dorothee, *Die Frau im NS–Staat* (Stuttgart: Deutsche Verlags-Anstalt, 1982).

Koonz, Claudia, *Mothers in the Fatherland: Women, the Family and Politics in Nazi Germany* (New York: St. Martin's Press, 1987).

Macciocchi, Maria-Antonietta, *La Donna 'Nera': Consenso femminile e fascismo* (Feltrinelli, Milan, 1976.) *Elements pour une Analyse du Fascisme* (Paris: Seminaire Paris VIII, 1974–1975). This is a slightly different version of the Italian original.

Mitchell, Brian R., *European Historical Statistics* (New York: Facts on File, 1980).

Mosse, George, *Nationalism and Sexuality: Respectability and Abnormal Sexuality in Modern Europe* (New York: Fertig, 1984).

Passerini, Luisa, *Torina operaia e fascismo* (Rome: Bari, 1984).

Ravera, Camille, *La Donne italiana dal 1 al 2 Risorgimento* (Rome: Cultura Sociale, 1951).

Sarfatti, Margherita, *The Life of Benito Mussolini* (London: Thornton Butterworth, 1925).

Stephenson, Jill, *The Nazi Organization of Women* (New York: Barnes and Noble, 1981).

Stephenson, Jill, *Women in Nazi Society,* (New York: Barnes and Noble, 1975).

Szepansky, Gerda, *Frauen leisten Widerstand* (Frankfurt: Fischer, 1983).

Thalmann, Rita, *Etre Femme dans le Troisieme Reich* (Paris: Lafont, 1981).

Tannenbaum, Edward, *Modern Italy: A Topical History* (New York: New York University Press, 1974).

Triolo, Nancy E. *"Grazie Duce per Tanti Bambini" The Modernization of Maternal and Child Health Care in Sicily.* Dissertation. University of California at Berkeley, 1986.

Turati, Augusto, *"Il Fascismo e la donna," Il Partito e i suoi Compiti* (Rome: Littoro, 1928).

Weber, Marianne, *Lebenserinnerungen* (Bremen, Storm, 1948).

Wiggershaus, Renate, *Frauen unterm Nationalsozialismus* (Wuppertal: Hammer, 1984).

British women demanding equal pay parade outside the residence of the Chancellor of the Exchequer in October 1952. (Topham/The Image Works)

chapter 20

Both Friend and Foe: Women and State Welfare

Jane Jenson

In the aftermath of World War II, as after World War I, Europeans began to reconstruct their world; but they also endeavored to refashion the social order according to ideals of social justice and greater equality. This promise, largely unrealized in the 1920s, was partially fulfilled after 1945. Whereas Koonz sees precedents for the post-war welfare state in fascism, Jane Jenson links the welfare state to the concept of "social citizenship" that emerged within post-war liberal settings. In western Europe, women gained greater political equality relative to men at the same time as all citizens benefitted from more equal access to health care, education, and employment. Using France and Britain as case studies, Jenson concludes this volume with an incisive analysis of the dilemma that feminists have faced for generations: is the state a potential force for greater equality or an instrument of patriarchal oppression? In the contemporary world, the answer depends on whether politicians define women's rights in terms of a universal concept that sees all citizens, male and female, as wage-workers, or in terms of women's obligations as wives and mothers. In France, where the former definition prevails, feminists have located the source of women's inferior status in an unjust economic system and a misogynist culture; but in England, where wives gain benefits from the welfare state in terms of their husbands' status, feminists have blamed the state for women's inequality. This essay moves the theoretical debates surveyed by Sowerwine, Offen, Freder, Stites, and Bridenthal onto new terrain because, with the emergence of the welfare state and an official commitment to women's equality, these two contending paradigms hold out concrete and different opportunities to women as citizens.

After the battles and destruction of World War II, the people of most Western European countries were determined to establish the political consensus and economic well-being that had eluded them before and during the war. The world was to be made anew. Victory, liberation from occupying forces, and in some cases escape from domestic fascism all served as moments of opportunity to recast social relations. From these societies' optimistic response to both harsh necessity and great possibility came one of the most important legacies of World War II: the welfare state.[1] State welfare, perhaps more than anything else, has profoundly affected the ways in which women live and has contributed to an unprecedented and unique kind of women-centered politics. This chapter explores the consequences of state welfare for women as well as the politics developed by women to alter some of its negative effects.

The welfare state can be understood most simply as an interconnected set of social programs designed to alleviate such consequences of economic cycles and individual life cycles as poverty, sickness, unemployment, and old age. The welfare state also usually encompasses other state programs intended to equalize opportunity—widening access to education, for example—and to redistribute income within society through taxation so that citizens with more resources take on financial responsibility for the poor.

SOCIAL CITIZENSHIP: AN UNREALIZED IDEAL

Before World War II, many states provided pensions for some of the elderly, health care for the indigent or for participants in state insurance programs, poor relief for the most poverty stricken, maternity benefits and leaves for women workers, family allowances for those with many children, and other payments to relieve financial distress. After 1945 these programs became more comprehensive and coordinated. More importantly, they were given a new rationale—the right of every citizen to certain minimum standards of life.

Despite differences in detail, the similarities among the programs of the various nations indicate that something new had been created in the aftermath of war. An important aspect of this development was an ideological commitment to the notion of "social citizenship."[2] Many programs that most touched women's lives were designed with reference to this concept of extended citizenship. The period since the eighteenth century had seen struggles first for civil rights (including the right to work and equality before the law) and then for political rights (including universal suffrage—or at

Research for this paper was partially supported by the Social Science and Humanities Research Council of Canada. For helpful suggestions on an earlier draft I am grateful to C. Blacklock, S. Evans, F. Keyman, R. Kybartas, C. McBride, and S. Whitworth.

least universal manhood suffrage). The last half of the twentieth century was a time for the extension of new social rights. The architects of state welfare in many European countries agreed by the middle of the twentieth century that all citizens who needed help had the right to that help from the state. For example, when they grew old, citizens had a right to state pensions; when they had children, they had a right to maternity benefits and family allowances that would make it possible for them to provide decent lives for their children; when they were unemployed, they had a right to lost wages in the form of unemployment insurance; when they were sick, they had a right to inexpensive and quality health care; when they could not find affordable housing on the private market, all citizens had a right to safe, sanitary and inexpensive state-subsidized homes; and so on.

Underlying the concept of social citizenship was a particular set of ideas that determined the nature of the discourse of state welfare that both guided policy makers and provided a rationale for their actions in the eyes of the public. One important idea was that state welfare should be based on universal access. For the architects of the state welfare systems, social citizenship was usually thought to derive from the seemingly universal condition of waged work. In this formulation the wage earner was the "model citizen" and everyone was assumed to approximate that condition or at least aspire to it.

Obviously, however, not all citizens were wage earners, and policy makers had to decide how to incorporate those who weren't into the state welfare system. Some cases were relatively simple. Old-age pensions could be based on the recipients' previous participation as wage earners. But the treatment of women, especially married women, within the new social programs required a more difficult decision. Should women be dealt with as individuals, eligible for benefits in their own right because they too were citizens? Or should they be considered as part of a family unit, linked to the activities and rights of a male wage earner and treated as minors by the state welfare system because they themselves did not meet the definition of the "model citizen"?

This chapter will demonstrate the fundamental importance of the decisions made in two countries—Great Britain and France—about women's access to the new rights of social citizenship. The promise of universality made by those employing the discourse of social citizenship was sometimes contradicted by the actual programs, which provided differential access depending upon marital status. Later, opposition arose and protest against the welfare state itself developed out of the contradictions between the promise of universality and the reality of women's unequal status.

In postwar Europe there had been a high level of ideological consensus. Old and bitter class and gender conflicts seemed to have been overcome by the establishment of welfare states by Social Democratic, liberal, and Christian Democratic governments and by the stress on equality in the discourse of postwar politics[3]. Thinking the old ideological combats vanquished by the new welfare state, many observers announced the "end of ideology." Many people, therefore, were surprised when protest exploded in most Western European countries in the late 1960s. Workers went on strike and took to the streets. Students occupied schools and universities, defied their professors and tried to hasten the revolution. Demonstrations against war and colonialism were frequent.

An increasingly visible component of this new upsurge of protest was the women's movement, demanding "women's liberation." In all countries of Western Europe, virtually simultaneously, small groups of women met and then quickly discovered many other women also meeting to discuss their lives. They greeted the growing social movement for women's liberation with immense optimism and enthusiasm. In Britain, feminists took as their preferred target—second only to men—the system of state welfare. Women singled out the very programs intended to provide security as a major cause of their continued subordination. In France, the women's movement also reflected the anger and frustration which women felt in the 1960s and 1970s. The French women's movement focused more on the workings of the economy and cultural practices as the major sources of women's subordination to men, than on the state itself and its social policies.

Why did the two women's movements differ? Did British feminists err in focusing their actions too exclusively against the state? Were the French too naive about the impact of state welfare systems? Or, did the differences in strategies reflect the existence of real differences in the mechanisms by which oppression was reproduced? Should feminists reject, and even fear, state welfare because it is the product of a capitalist and patriarchal state; or can the welfare state be reformed and used as part of the struggle, first to protect women from oppression by men and then to liberate them? This chapter argues that differences in the decisions about how to incorporate women into the state welfare system are in part an explanation for the differences between the two women's movements.

THE ESTABLISHMENT OF THE WELFARE STATE IN GREAT BRITAIN

Ironically, in the immediate postwar years many British feminists became complacent; they claimed the extension of state welfare and the development of the notion of social citizenship as their victory. Throughout the interwar years, feminists had demanded state programs to ease the burden of poor women and their families and many of these demands became state policy by 1945. Thus, Vera Brittain, a long-time feminist, celebrated the success in this way: "The welfare state has been both cause and consequence of the second great change by which women have moved . . . from rivalry with men to a new recognition of their unique value as women."[4] Her words reflect the view of many British feminists: At last the state had recognized the important contributions that women—as mothers, especially—made to Britain. Family allowances to mothers with more than one child won widespread approval. After decades of campaigning for such reform, feminists like Eleanor Rathbone took pride in what seemed a victory.

Rathbone based her proposal for family allowances on a critical analysis of the wage structure. Trade unions had for decades struggled so that all workers, whether they had children or not, might receive a "family wage." Rathbone criticized this principle because it failed to take into account the difference in real needs of single men and of men with dependent families of varying size. She asserted that family allowances, based on the number of children, should be paid to mothers. Rathbone identified a second problem that would be resolved by paying family allowances in this way. Dependent wives without a regular source of income would no longer be at the mercy of their husbands' decisions about how to spend the family's income. If husbands spent their wages on drink or otherwise squandered them, women and children would no longer be left destitute. Finally, Rathbone advocated family allowances as recognition of the social contribution of mothers because for her state payments were the best way to accomplish this important goal.[5]

If family allowances had been instituted in Britain in the way that Eleanor Rathbone and many other feminists had hoped, the labor market would have been fundamentally reorganized and the state's relationship to the family dramatically altered. When family allowances were actually instituted during the war as part of the plan implemented by Lord Beveridge— the major architect of the British welfare state—the scheme differed substantially from the one endorsed by Rathbone's Family Endowment Society. The payments were much smaller and went only to families with two or more children.[6] The scheme was altered in large part because of the influence of political parties and labor unions on the idea of the state welfare system.

While political parties and labor unions talked about social citizenship, during the war, state welfare was considered to be part of a system of policies designed to control the economy; family allowances and other social programs were discussed as part of the debate about wages.[7] Therefore, when state welfare was incorporated into the Labour Party's program for recasting social relations in postwar Britain, trade union opposition to Rathbone's calls for a system of family allowance that would protect women and children was influential. Social democrats and other reformers would discuss the issue of family allowances only in economic terms.

Feminists did, however, have a substantial influence on the way in which the notions of social citizenship were put into practice. Even though the reforms did not include programs supportive of women's economic independence, the state made use of the feminists' analyses of the family and women's dependency within it. Many parts of the British left believed that women should be able to avoid waged labor and should stay at home with their children. Therefore, a general agreement emerged about the advantages of keeping women out of the labor force.[8] The feminists and other reformers disagreed, however, over the extent to which women had the right to an independent source of income when they were not part of the paid labor force. Ironically, the feminist analysis of women's situation helped to bring about the establishment of a state welfare system that substantially reinforced wives' dependence on their husbands.[9]

When both Labour and Conservative parties and the trade unions thought about the family, state welfare, and social relations in general, they assumed that the maintenance of the traditional family—that is, a working man and a non–wage earning mother with several children—was a major goal. They also assumed women had special roles within the family. Thus, the British state decided that wives gained access to the system of state welfare through their husbands, rather than because of any universal claim to social citizenship, and the new programs assumed that married women were, and should continue to be, dependent on men for their support.

As Lord Beveridge wrote in 1942:

> During marriage most women will not be gainfully employed. The small minority of women who undertake paid employment or other gainful occupations after marriage require special treatment differing from that of a single woman. Since such paid work will in many cases be intermittent, it should be open to any married woman to undertake it as an exempt person, paying no contributions of her own and acquiring no claim to benefit in unemployment or sickness. If she prefers to contribute and to requalify for unemployment and disability benefits she may do so, but will receive benefits at a reduced rate.[10]

We see in this quotation the ways that presumptions about the gender division of labor structured not only society's assumptions about the place of women but also the programs themselves.

First, married women gained access to the welfare system through their husbands' payments; the *husband* was the citizen whose rights were recognized. Secondly, their dependency was further reinforced; if they did become sick or disabled—*even if they were paying contributions themselves while working*—simply because they were married, married women workers received lower benefits than men or unmarried women. Because of this, they needed their husbands' wages in order to get by. Moreover, the system could encourage a reliance on married women for part-time work; since so many part-time workers were married women, it was easy to assume that their husbands' contributions would protect them.[11] Policy-makers retained the longstanding assumption that "marriage means total and permanent economic dependence for most women . . ."[12]

Some feminists were, of course, critical of Beveridge's plans. Eleanor

Rathbone, for example, wrote: "The economic dependency of the married woman is the last stronghold of those who, consciously or unconsciously, prefer woman in subjection and that perhaps is why the stronghold is proving so hard to force."[13] Nevertheless, Rathbone's proposal for substantial family allowances paid to mothers, to give them an independent source of income, did nothing to challenge the very assumptions about women and the family which supported the traditional notions of the gender division of labor. Consequently, these notions became deeply embedded in and reproduced by the new system of state welfare. It was left to a later generation of feminists to challenge not only the role of state welfare in reproducing women's dependence on men but also the family system which both traditionalists and reformers, female and male, had assumed to be "natural."

FRENCH SOCIAL SECURITY CONTRASTED WITH BRITAIN'S

The system of state welfare established after World War II in France resembled in many ways the one instituted as a result of the Beveridge Report in Britain. Like Britain's, France's system was an effort to help citizens meet family responsibilities and to protect them from the risks of unemployment, accident, and sickness by providing lost income and relief from exceptional expenses. The program of the *Conseil National de la Résistance* (CNR) coordinated proposals for social security, covering unemployment, sickness, housing, and family allowances.[14] The CNR was made up of supporters of General de Gaulle and the major political parties, such as the Communist party, that had resisted the German occupation of France. The CNR was primarily responsible for the development of the social programs and economic arrangements of postwar France.

As in Britain, state involvement in social policy had its roots in interwar politics and everyone entered the postwar period with ideas fixed by earlier experiences. Although many of the programs appeared similar to those established in Britain, they were actually quite different, reflecting the historical position of women within France and within the family. Two related concerns shaped the development of state welfare, the needs of workers and the needs of the family. Both together explain the way in which particular notions of women came to be embedded in French social policy.

Following the Liberation, French legislators revamped the system of *Sécurité Sociale* as part of improvements in existing labor legislation. All working women and men received the same rights and access to social security regardless of marital status.[15] Payments, responsibilities, and benefits were made as equal as possible, although it was understood that working women were frequently mothers. Therefore, improved conditions for workers also included paid maternity leaves and other pre- and postnatal protection. The programs had none of the differentiation found in

Britain, where distinctions were made between single and married women. Although non–wage earning wives in France depended on their husbands' participation in the Social Security system, all women, no matter their marital status, gained equal social rights in the Social Security system as soon as they took up a paid job. Because they acquired full social citizenship, they did not suffer from the ambiguity that affected married women in Britain.

This variation in policy can best be explained by examining the ways in which the discussion of the issue of women's work differed in the two countries. In Britain, as we have seen, many feminists, trade unionists and social reformers worked with models of the labor force and the family that included the assumption that married women did not work; many also admonished that women *should not* work. By contrast, in France, where the rate of female participation in the labor force was higher than in most other industrialized countries, there had long been a recognition that a dynamic economic system depended upon women wage earners.[16] Therefore, discussions of social policy rarely assumed that all wives and mothers would leave the paid labor force.[17] Capitalists and industrialists understood that the French economy depended on women working.[18] The French left believed that only when women became wage earners would they support the struggle for socialism. Therefore, the Communist Party, in particular, tried throughout the interwar years to organize women into trade unions and political parties. Moreover, between the wars members of the autonomous feminist movement were also more likely than their British counterparts to stress the emancipatory effects of women's work. For many French feminists, women's emancipation depended upon women's economic independence, which could not come from state payments but only from their ability to earn their own wages and to take effective political action. Thus, feminists associated with the Socialist Party and the Communist Party, as well as several autonomous feminist groups, demanded better training, more access to jobs, and worked for higher rates of unionization for women.

A consequence of these differences in conception of women's social roles and of the correspondingly different strategies of the French leftist parties and feminist groups was that the postwar Constitution guaranteed all French citizens the right to work. This constitutional right helped a great deal in the campaigns against employers who tried to fire women to make way for men returning from the war. Moreover, as the Gaullists and the Left took control of the state apparatus, they passed legislation that gave women the right to equal access to civil service jobs and the right to equal pay for equal work. Therefore, the social security system that treated female workers in the same way as men was only one example of the effects of a political, cultural, and economic tradition in which women's work was seen as both necessary and desirable.

This experience stands in sharp contrast to that of Britain, where both the state and the male-dominated labor unions vehemently rejected demands for equal pay during the war. In fact, the labor unions threatened to stop wartime production if such a change were made.[19] In large part this opposition to equal pay followed from the British labor unions' strategy of claiming the right to the family wage. Male unionists feared that if women received equal pay employers would seize the opportunity to lower the wages of men and to challenge the legitimacy of the family wage. French unions, in contrast, had abandoned the family-wage strategy by the beginning of the twentieth century and instead advocated equal pay for equal work as a way of preventing employers from replacing male with female workers as a cost-cutting device. French unionists assumed many women worked and as a result attacked employers' power from a position of male and female solidarity. The "spill-over" effects of this strategic difference were important. In the postwar discussions of social security, the French labor movement did not insist on emphasizing the fundamental difference between women and men, and as a result no one in the French debate could use that notion to justify maintaining male workers' wage superiority over women.

The situation looks different, however, when the second major aspect of postwar French state welfare is examined. Much of the system was founded on family allowances, which were large payments (sometimes approaching one third of the family income) to men with dependent children. Whereas family allowances were finally relatively unimportant in the British system, where unemployment and medical assistance provided the pillars of the welfare state, family allowances were central to the French system.[20] When family allowances were instituted in Britain, they were hailed as a recognition of the *mother's* contribution to British society, but the actual programs were criticized by supporters like Eleanor Rathbone for being too small and insignificant to have the desired effect. Labor-union opposition and reformers' assumptions about family structure made payments for lost male wages—that is, unemployment insurance—the major way for society to assume some of the risks of economic and life-cycle changes. In France, by contrast, the combined influence of a strong profamily movement and an almost fanatical fear of depopulation produced the important program of *Allocations Familials* (Family Allowances). The policy had been established in the 1930s and was extended after the war with a focus on *children*. It was intended to guarantee that all French children would have similar opportunities in life.[21] Its second goal was to encourage French families to produce as many children as possible; therefore, the extra costs of large families were to be partially offset by the family allowance payments.

Because the focus was almost exclusively on the child's welfare and because both parents were assumed to be performing a duty to the nation in carrying out their family responsibilities, there was not a great deal of emphasis on women or their roles as mothers. French family allowances could never be described, as they sometimes were in Britain, as mothers' allowances. Nobody argued that their purpose was to free women and children from the financial tyranny of the father. Rather, all payments (with the exception of a small pre- and postnatal allowance) went to the father, even if the mother was herself a full participant in the Social Security system.[22] The father was still legally the head of the French family and he received the payment. Since the program's intent was to lessen the risk to families of the extra cost of having children and to encourage them to assume that risk for the good of the nation, the discussion of family allowances was not exclusively linked to consideration of the wage system or the labor market. Instead, it became a component of foreign policy, since many people assumed that France could not maintain its position in the world if its population did not grow. This fear had dominated discussion of the family policy, had produced a complete ban on access to contraceptive devices, and lay behind the postwar stress on family allowance payments.[23]

As a result a large national consensus emerged in support of family allowances. The system reflected no widely shared assumption that only non–wage earning mothers would be involved in raising children for the nation. All women—and all men—were called upon to perform that civic duty. Moreover, because concerns for population size so dominated the discourse, any efforts to impose a traditional family morality were over-whelmed by the desire to support the children of all French women—even the unmarried. Therefore, "natural families" (i.e., families in which the parents were unmarried) and single mothers were entitled to full benefits, and any man who lived regularly with the family could become the recipient of payments made for those particular children if the natural father were no longer living with the family.[24] In other words, the *children* were entitled to family allowances and the morality, salary, and living arrangements of their parents did not alter that entitlement.

Just as in Britain, French women's groups hailed social security and family allowances as a great victory not only for workers but also and more particularly for women. And the system did become important in women's lives where, again in contrast to Britain, it could be used to cushion the effects of social change. The relatively amoral system in France could quite easily accommodate the changes in life style that came with higher rates of divorce, family instability, and an increase in women's labor force participation. While family allowances contributed little directly to women's liberation from male oppression, they also made a relatively lower contribution to women's dependence on their husbands and other men than did the British system of state welfare.

In contrast, the assumption of married women's dependence continues to underpin the contemporary revamping of state welfare in Britain. For example, the Family Income Supplement, introduced in the 1970s to help families with a low wage earner, requires that "in the case of a couple it must be the man who is in full-time work".[25] In this way, state policy discourages redistribution of labor within the family to involve fathers in childcare or to give mothers a real choice about working.

In France, as the postwar world changed, and as more women entered the paid labor force, it became possible to use the family allowance system both to support women's labor force participation and to encourage it. Virtually all French policy makers agreed that women will work; rare is the speech or publication that does not contain the phrase, "the present level of female employment is irreversible." For example, Pierre Boisard, the president of the French National Family Allowance Fund (who personally regretted the rise in mothers' employment) indicated that even his own organization, that bastion of profamily ideology, was now providing analyses of the following sort:

> There is currently a pervasive move to encourage the development of the personality. Even the National Family Allowance Fund has become caught up in this. In one of its publications, *Informations sociales*, the following passage appears: "Once a woman has a child, she disappears as a social being. Feminists consider motherhood as a sort of prison from which women must be rescued at all cost."[26]

Recognizing the inevitable, French policy makers have enacted several programs to cover the child-care expenses of working mothers and expand state child-care facilities (although never rapidly enough to meet the burgeoning need). Finally, with no presumption that mothers did not or should not work, it became possible in the 1970s for policy makers concerned with both labor markets and families to develop training schemes to move single mothers and mothers with few skills into the labor force. Since a major revision of the family allowance program in 1977, all recipients of the new family subsidy automatically enroll in the state pension plan, whether they are employed or not. Thus, non–wage earning mothers as well as those who were earning wages could accumulate pension coverage. In all these cases, the family allowance program was used as a way of financing and organizing the change.[27]

This consideration of French social policy provides an example of the ways in which some programs that do not have assumptions embedded within them about women's economic dependency could be used to provide support for the reform of women's condition in a changing labor force and society. It is important to recognize, however, that the example also demonstrates that the subordination of women to men is reproduced by much more than state actions. While the French state assumed that most women, including most mothers, did and would work and designed state welfare policy accordingly, that presumption did not override or eliminate the effects of many other social structures—culture, the family, and schools, for example—which reinforce the gender division of labor and the subordination of women. Therefore, although the French state was not quite as much the foe of women as the British, it was little more than a helpful friend. The limits of state-centered reform become clear when we look at the history of the two women's movements that appeared after 1968 in both countries.

THE NEW WOMEN'S MOVEMENT: STRATEGIC DILEMMAS

The system of postwar state welfare was based on the goal of universal social citizenship; the discourse of equality required that. Reformers thought they would achieve universal social citizenship by providing for citizens' needs with state programs of welfare or social security. Nevertheless, despite their good intentions, reformers built into the actual programs forms of inequity and structures that contributed to women's subordination to men within the family. Therefore, as feminists mobilized to demand that the state begin to meet their needs as women, they attacked the false promises of these supposedly egalitarian programs. They organized to alter any program which sustained the unequal structures of the family and reinforced women's subordination within it, in doing so they changed the terms of the discussion of state welfare to stress difference more than universality.

The welfare state had three major effects, each of which helped to bring about the mobilization of the new women's movement. It contributed immensely to the feminization of the labor force, it withdrew large categories of the population in advanced capitalist societies from the labor force, and it provided a social basis for political organization that depended neither on individuals' relationships to work nor on traditional party systems.

Feminization of the Labor Force

Employment of women by the state long predated 1945. Women's involvement in welfare services had become important by the end of the nineteenth century when the nursing and social work professions expanded in response to changes in social policies.[28] Moreover, as the state took over programs of private philanthropy, women who had staffed the charity organizations found new jobs in state projects. The trend increased massively after the establishment of coordinated state welfare. Employment in education expanded, and teachers were disproportionately female. Social workers—also disproportionately female—provided social support programs to families and children. Huge clerical establishments staffed by women administered social security. State-provided health care resulted in the growth of medical establishments that needed nurses and other paramedical workers. In other words, as state employment expanded, more and more women began to work, and to work for the state.

Expanding Categories of State Dependents

At the same time that more women took up paid work, the welfare state itself permitted whole categories of the population to withdraw from the labor force and be supported by state programs. Payments for mothers with children, extended education (which kept young people in school longer), pensions for older workers, and other programs of the same kind all had the effect of making whole categories of people less dependent on labor force participation.[29] Since people in such categories had little relationship to the labor market they were unlikely to identify strongly with the employed. Rather, their identity—their sense of self—was more likely to be based on other aspects of their lives, such as their age or family status. Therefore, the probability mounted that novel forms of political mobilization would emerge.

Class politics have characterized politics in most Western European countries in the twentieth century. This type of politics rests on the claim, which leftist political parties worked hard to make convincing, that the most important fact about modern social life was the experience of work and social relations in the production process. Even center and right-wing parties were compelled to respond to this claim and to offer programs that promised to alleviate some of the inequities of capitalist social relations. The permanent, long-term removal of many categories of recipients of state welfare from the labor market made it unlikely that the people affected would respond to the appeals of class-based politics. These people had a difficult time identifying their interests in the speeches and platforms of the political parties that continued to stress the political importance of the social relations of production—of which these people were less immediately a part.

The New Women's Movement and the Fragmentation of Class Politics

By the late 1960s, as these social changes worked their effects, the new women's movement became increasingly important. A marked shift occurred, towards a new politics based on differentiated rather than universalistic identities. The fragmentation of class politics into many social movements independent of the control of traditional political parties and insistent upon the overriding importance of their own positions was hastened by the development of women's movements in all Western European countries. These movements praised pluralism and democracy and opposed too much state control over citizens' lives. They appealed to women as women, no matter what their class or social position. They emphasized the distinctiveness of women and the characteristics that made them different from men, and they claimed that politics must henceforth be organized around gender identities in place of or in addition to those of class. The women's movements began to dismantle the constituencies of traditional parties.[30] The stress on gender difference as well as the themes of democracy and hostility to the state put women's movements on a collision course with state welfare. In mobilizing around themes of difference and decentralization, the women's movements challenged postwar systems of state welfare that were universalistic programs brought by the state to the people.

Despite the commonality of themes across many societies, however, there were important cultural and national variations, particularly in the extent to which the new women's movements directly challenged state welfare programs. The difference seems to derive largely from the actual form of the social programs. In Britain, the state became the target because social programs had directly and obviously contributed to the subordination of women within the family and had been designed to locate married women in the labor market in a different way than single women or men. Where the social programs had simultaneously assumed and facilitated women's participation in the paid labor force and had stressed the traditional family's civic responsibilities, as in France, a women's movement emerged that was both less fearful of the state and also less sensitive to its potentially negative effects.

THE FRENCH WOMEN'S MOVEMENT

The new women's movement in France appeared during a time when fundamental changes were occurring in the balance of political forces. One way to follow the changes is to observe the development of a new way of talking and thinking about women and women's condition. The women's movement promoted this new approach in part by its claim to speak for *women* —not just for working women or for mothers but for all women irrespective of their productive and reproductive activities.

The stress on the importance of a female identity, based on sex more than on social roles, differentiated the new feminists from their precursors. For new feminists, any effort to define or confine women to the role of mother or to try to absorb them into a universalistic identity of worker or citizen risked contributing to women's continued subordination. The new feminists criticized the traditional family as a mechanism for reproducing women's subordination. Capitalists also came under attack for paying women less than men for the same work. Feminists also assailed the political parties and trade unions, saying that they did not sufficiently understand that the liberation of women—under capitalism or under socialism—depended on accepting the need for women's separate struggle to achieve their liberation.

French feminists' analysis grew out of their experience in the French new left which had become politically important in the mid-1960s, and had popularized a politics founded on democracy and antistatism. The new left advocated greater control by workers over their work and by citizens over their politics. In addition, it sharply criticized the centralized state that the postwar left had accepted as necessary to the construction of social citizenship. The new left's criticisms of the society led it into an inquiry into all forms of oppression. Women who had found traditional ideologies incapable of explaining their political invisibility adapted these new democratic and pluralistic ideas for their purposes. They claimed the right of women—as individuals and without any reference to their family status—to become the subject of political discourse. Women had become the central focus of politics for feminists taking such widely divergent positions as those of the separatist *Psychanalyse et Politique* group, radical feminist Christine Delphy, or the collective *Elles Voient Rouge* (Women See Red) within the Communist Party in the late 1970s.

Feminists analyzed the everyday workings of male domination and introduced issues of particular concern to women into a discussion already focused on democracy. For example, women's demands for the control of their own bodies and the elimination of the traditional family resulted in campaigns to end restrictive abortion legislation.[31] Feminists claimed that women had specific disadvantages which they had to struggle against, without men and in alliance with other women. In other words, they insisted on an autonomous women's movement, dedicated to destroying the structural and ideological institutions and forces oppressing women. The traditional Left goals of equal rights—based on the assumption that women and men, once engaged in paid labor, would have similar goals—were replaced by greater attention to *difference* and *specificity*.

Even more importantly in France, the new women's movement pointed out that culture constrained women.[32] French feminism has made an important contribution to political thought by analysing the interconnections of language, power and knowledge. For example:

> The intellectual context of French feminism has mirrored the political context in that it too has an anti-authority and anti-hierarchy focus. In philosophical terms, this means not questioning the relation of state and civil society, or the deficiencies of political parties, but attacking the authority of meaning and the systems of domination and exclusion that underpin political authority. To the ultimate set of norms and values that exists in every society, feminism opposes otherness—alterity—and multiplicity, and suggests that a plurality of modes of thought is both possible and preferable to the monolithic, monological masculinity that dominates in patriarchy.[33]

Although not all French feminists used the philosophical terms of the most intellectualized currents of the movement, the notion of *femaleness* as *difference* pervaded popular discourse. Philosophical ideas intersected with the feminism represented within political currents like the new left and the movement for *autogestion* (workers' control) as well as in some currents within the trade unions and the Communist party.[34] They all coalesced into a type of feminism that was pluralistic, antistatist, and oriented towards cultural change. This orientation, however, meant that feminists paid relatively little attention to social policies.

As a result, although the appearance of new feminist politics in France after 1968 can in part be traced to a state welfare system that encouraged the feminization of the labor force, made more problematic the development of class-based identities, and made possible a new politics of differentiated identities, the French women's movement from the outset was little concerned with the the the state.[35] Moreover, French feminists tended to ignore or at least downplay the effects of the labor market or social policies in the reproduction of oppression. Instead, the sources of women's oppression were identified in cultural and family relations. As a result of this lack of attention to the actions of the state and their effect, the impact of the state escaped analysis.

A result of this lack of attention became obvious when the economic crisis of the 1970s began to restructure the French economy. As the international economy became more interdependent and jobs migrated from countries where wages were high to those where wages were low, and from the industrial to the service sector, unemployment rose in France. At the same time, employers sought ways to cut costs and escape the burden of contributing to state social programs. For example, they often laid off full-time workers, for whom social payments had to be made, and hired part-time or temporary workers who could be paid minimum wages and who had few rights to social benefits. Women's employment rates rose, because firms more often hired them to work in these marginal jobs in manufacturing and in the service sector. Therefore, even as women's employment rate rose, so did the percentage of women in the part-time (with few or no benefits), poorly paid types of jobs.

Feminists were not prepared for the form that restructuring took, which pushed women to the margins of the labor market, in part-time and temporary work. Steadily isolated from well-paid work with good benefits, women had less and less expectation of achieving full economic citizenship. Ironically, part of the reason for the state's acceptance of women's marginal economic status can be found in the labor union movement and the state's adoption of the very concept of "difference" promoted by feminists. By the mid-1970s the French unions had been influenced by feminists both within and outside their organizations to become sensitive to women's special difficulties in the labor force. The unions developed the notion that women were not only exploited by capitalists but also subordinated to men and that this double oppression led to their marginalization.[36] This analysis helped the unions to understand the capitalists' and the state's efforts to legitimate a "dual society" of full-time, well-paid "real" workers and part-time, poorly paid marginal workers. Unions, whose strategy had always been founded on the concept of universality and equality—the belief that all workers should move together towards socialism—now insisted that all workers were not the same.

Nevertheless, although the older ideal of universality disregarded the effects of the labor market on women and ignored their special needs, the new emphasis on women's difference and the specificity of women's situation in the labor market did not take into account women's demands for full integration into the labor force and for protection from more than the effects of marginality. Moreover, the popular assumption that women might, at times, seem to prefer part-time work—because of family responsibilities and to escape the infernal rhythm of the assembly line—did not encourage unions to mount a thorough-going attack on the social structures that induced women to express the preference in the first place. This introduction into the debate of the notion of women's difference supplied a new way of rationalizing a gender-based division of labor within the family and the firm. This new analysis described that division—previously overlooked— yet it failed to evaluate adequately the structures which reproduced it, because it stressed difference among workers, rather than their equality.

The state, too, used the concept of women's difference to explain the effects of economic restructuring. When the government of the right was in power, it accepted and even promoted the development of a "dual society." When the left formed the government in 1981 steps were taken—at the urging of the unions—to protect part-time and temporary workers by giving them access to social security and collective rights within the firm. Nevertheless, while the protections were important, they also became a way for the state and unions to rationalize the continuation of the forces moving towards a more fragmented economy, because they symbolized the unions' and the state's acceptance of a segmented labor force.

The arguments and analyses of the unions, the parties, and the state could never be neutral because they rested on assumptions about the appropriate roles for women and men. The stress on the "difference" between men and women in the labor market unintentionally increased women's difficulty in attaining full economic and social equality. French feminists had not anticipated the capitalists', political parties', and unions' use of the feminists' arguments to justify the very policies that were increasing women's difficulties.

BRITAIN'S NEW WOMEN'S MOVEMENT

British feminists, in contrast to their French sisters, were much more likely to identify the state and its welfare program as a major part of the difficulties that women faced in escaping from their subordination to men. British feminists like Michèle Barrett and Mary McIntosh have made major contributions to international feminism by developing sophisticated state theory. From the outset, all the various elements of the British women's movement identified the state as a large part of the problem. For liberal feminists, the state contributed to women's oppression because it did not treat women as equal to men and it did not act to overcome the effects of centuries of socialization, which had taught girls and women to define their social roles as mothers and dependents of their husbands. Radical feminists saw the state as part of the problem because it was a "patriarchical state," reflecting the relations of gender power that dominated the whole society. To the radical feminists, women's only hope was to destroy patriarchy and in the process transform the state. Socialist feminists identified the state as part of the problem because it reflected the capitalist relations of production, within which women were valued either as a source of inexpensive, temporary labor or as the performers of "free labor" that permitted reproduction of the labor force from day to day and from one generation to the next.[37]

Each element of the movement attacked the state and its social policies. Feminists campaigned for greater state involvement in child care and for better access to jobs for women. Moreover, recognizing the effects of the system of state welfare on maintaining women's continued dependency on men, they demanded individual and separate coverage by social programs for all women, irrespective of their marital status. Writing about women and state welfare, Jennifer Dale and Peggy Foster observed:

> Feminists' distinctive contribution has been to link the issue of hardship and bureaucratic insensitivity to the wider principle that women should be treated as independent individuals throughout the income maintenance and taxation systems. Feminists have called for disaggregation of needs and benefits such that any man or woman can claim benefits in their own right and be treated separately for the purposes of taxation.[38]

By so often taking the state as its target, the British women's movement avoided the surprise that overtook the French movement when the state began to make use of the feminist idea of women's difference to justify the marginalization of women workers and the legitimation of a two-tier labor force. British feminists had always been on guard against the state and were ready, then, when the Conservative government led by Margaret Thatcher began to cut back social programs and in the name of "privatization" tried to reallocate responsibility for providing care from state services to the family and to women within the family.

There were, of course, limits to British feminists' ability to oppose the state. The major limit was one of perspective; they could see the state only as a foe to be vanquished. Working within theoretical perspectives that perceived the state as only a reflection of social relations and often seeing women more as victims or subjects than as active creators of their own lives, British feminists tended to have a pessimistic view of the state and its potential for changing women's lives.

French feminists placed a great deal of emphasis on the creative potential of women's actions and on the importance of developing identities that would allow women to act independently and differently, celebrating lives of their own creation. However, they failed to recognize the possibility that the state could, with its policies, move away from the egalitarian positions won in the postwar years towards labor and social policies that reinforced both capitalism and patriarchy. They let down their political guard and saw the victories of earlier feminists who had struggled for equal rights overturned by governments—of both the right and the left—that had become convinced that women were "different." Failure to maintain the protections afforded by already-acquired equal rights contributed to the further weakening of women's economic and social position. Just as in Britain during and after the Second World War, feminists' discourse had been used against them.

CONCLUSION

There are, then, two lessons to be learned from this review of the histories of two women's movements. The first is that women must be constantly on guard against perversions of their own analyses of women. The wartime experience of the establishment of state welfare systems demonstrates that feminists depend on allies who share fundamental goals. In France, for their own reasons, organized labor, leftist political parties, and feminists all sought equal rights for women and men. The social security system that this alliance constructed was more supportive of working women and their needs and less likely to contribute to women's economic dependence on men than was the welfare state created in Britain. In Britain, the alliance that formed around state welfare was based less on a shared desire for equality between women and men and more on a traditional, gender-based division of labor. Feminists used arguments that appealed to British trade-union men—particularly the concept of separate spheres of activity for men and women. Although some feminists thought family allowances would end women's dependence on men, the whittled-down program finally enacted did more to protect the unions' long-time strategy of demanding the family wage and the state's notion of "healthy" family life than it did to emancipate women.

In the feminism of the 1960s, the national experiences were somewhat reversed. Feminists in France promulgated a new theory of "difference", which they considered more progressive than the older equal-rights feminism that lay behind the labor law and the social security system. However, the new feminists could not anticipate that the state, capitalists, and the unions would use their own arguments to legitimize the economic restructuring of the 1970s and 1980s. Ultimately, gender came to divide the alliance of the left and feminists. Left parties and unions now defined women almost exclusively in terms of their gender; as a result, women were perceived as "different workers," with fewer needs and different concerns than men. Moreover, while the state was asked to protect these workers, it was not asked to elevate them to the status of "full-time" or "real" workers. The state had become involved in sustaining the ideology of a gendered labor force, in a way none had existed before.

The second lesson of the postwar movements is, then, that whether the state is friend or foe depends on the conditions of political conflict and the forms of struggle. Where women and their allies mobilize around programs designed with emancipatory goals, they may make some gains; and reforms may be enacted. When, however, feminists ignore the state, or when everyday politics and the balance of political forces continue to be tilted against women, then the state will reinforce and even intensify existing gender relations. Creative politics and constant vigilance provide the only chance for movement towards liberation.

NOTES

1. By "welfare state" I mean a comprehensive system of state welfare, which was instituted in several western European countries after World War II. I *do not* use the term to describe a new form of state.
2. For the origination of this concept see T.H. Marshall, "Citizenship and Social Class" in his *Sociology at the Crossroads* (London: Heineman, 1963).
3. Elizabeth Wilson, *Women and the Welfare State* (London: Tavistock, 1977), p. 60.
4. Quoted in Jennifer Dale and Peggy Foster, *Feminists and State Welfare* (London: Routledge and Kegan Paul, 1986), p. 3.
5. For details on Eleanor Rathbone's career and activities see John Macnicol, *The Movement for Family Allowances, 1918–45: A Study in Social Policy Development* (London: Heineman, 1980), Chapter 2; and Hilary Land, "The Family Wage," *Feminist Review*, 6 (1980), pp. 62ff.
6. The initial plan was to pay allowances to fathers; mothers became the recipients only after the government permitted a free vote (i.e., a nonparty vote that did not engage "confidence" in the government) in Parliament.
7. Family allowances were feared by trade unionists because they undermined the longtime strategy of seeking wages high enough to support a dependent family. In the interwar years, family allowances had been advocated by Beveridge himself as a way to reduce wages in the mining industry—overall wage cuts would be instituted and then family allowances paid to men with several dependent children. Macnicol, *Family Allowances*, pp. 33–34.
8. Land, "The Family Wage," pp. 74; and Hilary Land, "Women: Supporters or Supported?", in Diana Leonard Barker and Sheila Allen, *Sexual Divisions and Society: Process and Change* (London: Tavistock, 1976), p. 102.
9. Wilson, *Women and the Welfare State*, Chapter 4.
10. Quoted in Land, "Supporters or Supported?," p. 110.
11. For details see ibid., pp. 110–11.
12. Ibid., p. 128.

13. Quoted in ibid., pp. 129–30.
14. For details see Y. Durand, *La Politique contemporaine de sécurité sociale* (Paris: Dalloz, 1953), pp. 120–21.
15. Odile Dhavernas, *Droits des femmes, pouvoir des hommes* (Paris: Seuil, 1978), p. 191.
16. For details on women's labour force participation see J. Daric, *L'Activité professionelle des femmes en France—Etude statistique, évolution, comparisons internationales* (Paris: PUF, 1947).
17. For the policy effects of different notions of women's work in an earlier period see Jane Jenson, "Gender and Reproduction: Or, Babies and the State", *Studies in Political Economy*, 20, Summer 1986, pp. 9–46.
18. Even during the Vichy regime, when the government tried to expel married women from the labor force, capitalists made it clear to the state that this would have disastrous effects on the French economy.
19. Dale and Foster, *Feminists and State Welfare*, p. 15.
20. Durand, *La politique contemporaine*, p. 124.
21. Pierre Laroque, et al., *Succès et faiblesses de l'effort social français* (Paris: Armand Colin, 1961), pp. 30ff.
22. Dhavernas, *Droits des femmes*, pp. 206ff.
23. For details about these interconnected policies see Jane Jenson, "Struggling for Identity: The Women's Movement and the State in Western Europe", *West European Politics*, 8, (1985), pp. 7–18.
24. Dhavernas, *Droits des femmes*, pp. 207–08.
25. Quoted in Land, "Supporter or Supported?," p. 129.
26. Pierre Boisard, "Family Policy in France, 1960–80: Achievements and Prospects," *Labour and Society*, 8, (1983), pp. 419, 426.
27. Dhavernas, *Droits des femmes*, pp. 211ff.
28. For details see Yvonne Kniebiehler, *Nous les assistantes sociales: Naissance d'une profession* (Paris: Aubier, 1980); and Dale and Foster, *Feminists and State Welfare*, Chapter 2.
29. Mary McIntosh, "Feminism and Social Policy", *Critical Social Policy*, 1 (Summer 1982), p. 36.
30. For details see Sheila Rowbotham et al., *Beyond the Fragments: Feminism and the Making of Socialism* (London: Islington Community Press, 1979); Anna Coote and Beatrice Campbell, *Sweet Freedom: The Struggle for Women's Liberation* (London: Picador, 1982); Jane Jenson, "The Modern Women's Movement in Italy, France and Great Britain: Differences in Life-Cycle" in *Comparative Social Research*, 5, (1982); Naty Garcia Gaudilla, *Libération des femmes: le mlf* (Paris: PUF, 1980); Yasmine Ergas, "1968–79—Feminism and the Italian Party System", *Comparative Politics*, vol. 14, #3, (1982) pp. 28–40.
31. Claire Duchen, *Feminism in France* (London: Routledge and Kegan Paul, 1986), pp. 49–60 and Jenson, "Struggling for Identity."
32. Duchen, *Feminism*, Chapters 4 and 5.
33. Ibid., pp. 68–69.
34. Jane Jenson, "The Modern Women's Movement," pp. 346ff.; Margaret Maruani, *Le Syndicalisme a l'épreuve de féminisme* (Paris: Syros, 1980); and Danielle Leger, *Le Féminisme en France* (Paris: Sycomore, 1982).

35. The exception was the state's control over women's bodies through abortion law and the legal relations that sustained the bourgeois notion of the family.
36. Maruani, *La Syndicalisme,* passim; and Jane Jenson, "The 'Problem' of Women," in M. Kesselman (ed.), *The French Workers' Movement* (London: Allen and Unwin, 1984) passim.
37. For descriptions of the three tendencies in Britain, see Dale and Foster, *Feminists and State Welfare,* Chapter 3.
38. Ibid., p. 108.

SUGGESTIONS FOR FURTHER READING

Barrett, Michèle, *Women's Oppression Today* (London: Verso, 1980).

Barrett, Michèle and Mary McIntosh, *The Anti-Social Family* (London: Verso, 1982).

Dale, Jennifer and Peggy Foster, *Feminists and State Welfare* (London: Tavistock, 1986).

Duchen, Claire, *Feminism in France* (London: Routledge and Kegan Paul, 1986).

Jenson, Jane, "Gender and Reproduction: Or, Babies and the State," *Studies in Political Economy,* 20 (Summer 1986).

Kuhn, A. and A.M. Wolpe, *Feminism and Materialism* (London: Tavistock, 1978).

Leger, Danielle, *Le Féminisme en France* (Paris: Sycomore, 1982).

Lovenduski, Jill, *Women and European Politics: Contemporary Feminism and Social Policy* (Amherst, MA: University of Mass, 1986).

Wilson, Elizabeth, *Only Half Way to Paradise: Women in Postwar Britain, 1945–68* (London: Tavistock, 1980).

Wilson, Elizabeth, *Women and the Welfare State* (London: Tavistock, 1977).

Notes on Contributors

Harriet Applewhite, Professor of Political Science at Southern Connecticut State University, received her Ph.D. in political science from Stanford University. She has published articles on the French Revolutionary National Assembly, and has completed a manuscript on the deputies' political alignment. She edited, in collaboration with Darline Levy and Mary Johnson, *Women in Revolutionary Paris, 1789–1795*. She and Darline Levy are continuing their work on studies of gender and political culture in France, other European countries, and America in the late eighteenth century.

Marylin B. Arthur received her Ph.D. in classics from Yale University, and is currently Associate Professor of Classics and Department Chairman at Wesleyan University. She teaches in the Women's Studies and Judaic Studies Programs, as well as in the Classics Department, and she is currently completing a manuscript on myth and narrative in Hesiod's *Theogony*.

Renate Bridenthal received her Ph.D. in history from Columbia University. She is Professor of History at Brooklyn College, City University of New York, where she is also affiliated with the Women's Studies Program. She has coedited *When Biology Became Destiny: Women in Weimar and Nazi Germany*, coauthored *Household and Kin: Families in Flux*, and published articles on German women and German intellectual history. She is currently writing a book on the rural and urban housewives' associations in Germany.

Elizabeth Fox-Genovese is Director of Women's Studies and Professor of History at Emory University. She has served as general editor of *Restoring Women to History* and, with Susan Stuard, as coauthor of the volume for Western Civilization I. Her writings on eighteenth-century France include *The Origins of Physiocracy: Economic Revolution and Social Order in Eighteenth-Century France;* a translation of *The Autobiography of DuPont de Nemours;* "Introduction" and "Women and Work" in Samia Spencer, ed., *French Women and the Age of Enlightenment;* and, with Eugene D. Genovese, *Fruits of Merchant Capital: Slavery and Bourgeois Property in the Rise and Expansion of Capitalism.* She has also published various articles on women in history and women in literature.

Laura Levine Frader is Associate Professor of History at Northeastern University. She received her Ph.D. from the University of Rochester. She is currently writing a book, *Labor and Protest in Southern France: Agricultural Workers, Strikes and Politics in the Aude,* and has published articles on agricultural workers, and collective action in southern

France. Her current research interests are rural women and urban working-class women in France in the 1920s and 1930s.

Jane Jenson received a Ph.D in political science from the University of Rochester. She is Professor of Political Science at Carleton University in Ottawa, Canada and a research associate at the Center for European Studies, Harvard University. She has written and edited several books on Canadian and European politics, including *The View from Inside: A French Communist Cell in Crisis; Crisis, Challenge and Change: Party and Class in Canada;* and *Behind the Lines: Gender and the Two World Wars.* Current research projects include an examination of women's contribution to the early stages of the welfare state as well as a book on the political economy of women in postwar France.

The late **Joan Kelly-Gadol** was a scholar specializing in the Renaissance. Her earlier writings included *Leon Battista Alberti: Universal Man of the Early Renaissance.* She subsequently became concerned with women's history and with fundamental theoretical issues of feminism. The results of this later work are to be found in the posthumously published *Women, History and Theory: The Essays of Joan Kelly.* Joan Kelly was Professor of History at City College, City University of New York, and was also affiliated with the Sarah Lawrence College Program in Women's History and The Institute for Research in History. The Joan Kelly Prize in Women's History, awarded by the American Historical Association, was established in her honor.

Temma Kaplan, winner of the Berkshire Society of Women Historian's prize for her book *Anarchists of Andalusia, 1868–1903* received her Ph.D. from Harvard University. She now directs the research institute known as The Barnard Women's Center at Barnard College. The article in this volume and her forthcoming book *Red City in the Blue Period: The Political World of Picasso's Barcelona* complete work she has published in numerous articles including "Female Consciousness and Collective Action: The Case of Barcelona, 1910–1918," *Signs: Journal of Women in Culture and Society.*

Claudia Koonz, who holds her Ph.D. from Rutgers University, teaches history at the College of the Holy Cross. In several articles and a book, *Mothers in the Fatherland: Women, the Family, and Nazi Politics,* she investigates women in inter-war Germany.

Eleanor Leacock, who holds a Ph.D. in anthropology from Columbia University, is Professor of Anthropology at City College, City University of New York. Her research has included studies of schooling in New York and Zambia, the social history of native Americans, the problems of youth in contemporary Samoa, and women cross-culturally. She has authored *Teaching and Learning in City Schools* and *Myths of Male Dominance,* and has co-edited *North American Indians in Historical Perspective; Politics and History in Band Societies; Women and Colonization;* and *Women's Work, Development and the Division of Labor by Gender.*

Barbara Switalski Lesko did her undergraduate and graduate work in Egyptology at the University of Chicago's Oriental Institute, and has taught in adult education programs at the University of California, Berkeley, Mills College, and Brown University, where she is Administrative Research Assistant in the Department of Egyptology. She has lectured widely on topics of ancient Egyptian culture, authored *The Remarkable Women of Ancient Egypt*, and is coediting a four-volume *Dictionary of Late Egyptian* with her Egyptologist husband, Professor Leonard H. Lesko of Brown University.

Darline Levy received her Ph.D. in history from Harvard University, and is now an Associate Professor of History at New York University. She is the author of *The Ideas and Careers of Simon-Nicolas-Henri Linguet: A Study in Eighteenth-Century French Politics*, and of several articles and reviews on eighteenth-century France. In addition, she is the coeditor, with Harriet Applewhite and Mary Johnson, of *Women in Revolutionary Paris, 1789–1795*, and is currently collaborating with Harriet Applewhite on several projects on the theme of gender and political culture in France and elsewhere in Europe and America at the end of the eighteenth century.

Jo Ann McNamara is Professor of History at Hunter College, City University of New York, and an active participant in various organizations of feminist historians. She received her Ph.D. from Columbia University. Her most recent book is *A New Song: Celibate Women in the First Three Christian Centuries*. She is currently working on a history of Catholic nuns and has published numerous articles on early Christian and early medieval women.

E. William Monter received his Ph.D. in history from Princeton University, and is currently Professor of History at Northwestern University. Originally a specialist in the history of John Calvin's Geneva, he has also done significant work in the history of European witchcraft and is now working on the Spanish Inquisition.

Karen Offen is an independent scholar affiliated with the Center for Research on Women at Stanford University and the Institute for Historical Study in San Francisco. She is a coeditor of *Victorian Women: A Documentary Account of Women's Lives in Nineteenth-Century England, France, and the United States* and of *Women, the Family, and Freedom: The Debate in Documents, 1750–1950* (2 vols.). She is completing a book (in two volumes) on the woman question in Third Republic France, 1870–1940, and has published related articles in *Third Republic/Troisième République, Women's Studies International Forum, French Historical Studies, American Historical Review,* and *Journal of Modern History.*

Charles Sowerwine received his Ph.D. in history from the University of Wisconsin. He now teaches French and women's history at the University of

Melbourne (Australia), where he was appointed Senior Lecturer in 1980. He is the author of *Les Femmes et le socialisme: cent ans d'histoire* and *Sisters or Citizens? Women and Socialism in France since 1876*, and editor with Aude Sowerwine of *Le Mouvement ouvrier contre la guerre 1914–1918*. His article, "Workers and Women in France before 1914: The Debate over the Couriau Affair," *The Journal of Modern History*, was awarded the William Koren Prize by the Society for French Historical Studies.

Richard Stites, Associate Professor of History at Georgetown University, received his Ph.D. in History at Harvard University. He is the author of *The Women's Liberation Movement in Russia* and recently coeditor of Alexander Bogdanov, *Red Star: The First Bolshevik Utopia* and *Bolshevik Culture*. He is now completing *Revolutionary Dreams: Utopia and Experiment in the Russian Revolution*.

Margaret Strobel, Associate Professor and Director of the Women's Studies Program at the University of Illinois at Chicago, received her Ph.D. in African history from the University of California in Los Angeles. Her book *Muslim Women in Mombasa, 1890–1975*, was cowinner in 1980 of the Herskovits Prize awarded by the African Studies Association. She has completed three life histories, in Swahili and English, of women from Mombasa and a short monograph on European women and empire. Her current research covers the socialist feminist women's unions in the U.S. from the late 1960s to the 1970s, focusing on the Chicago Women's Liberation Union.

Susan Stuard is a medieval historian concerned with social and economic questions. Her interest in women may be seen in twin volumes from University of Pennsylvania Press, *Women in Medieval Society* and *Women in Medieval History and Historiography*. She is currently Visiting Associate Professor of History at Haverford College.

Suzanne Fonay Wemple is Professor of History at Barnard College, Columbia University, and she holds a Ph.D. from Columbia University. Her specialization is social and intellectual history of the early Middle Ages. She is the author of *Women in Frankish Society; Marriage and the Cloister, 500–900*, and she is coeditor of *Women in the Medieval World*. She has written numerous articles on medieval women's history and is now working on a study of female monasteries in Italy up to 1500.

Merry E. Wiesner is Assistant Professor of History at the University of Wisconsin-Milwaukee. She taught for six years at Augustana College in Rock Island, Illinois, where she established the women's studies program. She has authored *Working Women in Renaissance Germany* and articles on women and the Reformation, urban social history, women's public role in the Renaissance, and women's work. She has also compiled an extensive bibliography on women in the sixteenth century for the Center for Reformation Research bibliography series.

Index